W9-CLH-985

WITHDRAWN
No longer the property of the
Boston Public Library.
Sale of this material benefits the Library.

THE ANCIENT WORLD

A Social and Cultural History

D. BRENDAN NAGLE

THE ANCIENT WORLD

THE ANCIENT WORLD

A Social and Cultural History

D. BRENDAN NAGLE

Department of History
University of Southern California

PRENTICE-HALL, INC., *Englewood Cliffs, New Jersey 07632*

Library of Congress Cataloging in Publication Data

Nagle, D Brendan (date)
The ancient world.

Bibliography: p.
Includes index.
1. Civilization, Ancient. I. Title.
CB311.N25 1979 930 78-11960
ISBN 0-13-036400-2

© 1979 by PRENTICE-HALL, INC., Englewood Cliffs, New Jersey 07632

All rights reserved. No part of this book may be reproduced in any form or by any means without permission in writing from the publisher.

Printed in the United States of America

10 9 8 7 6 5 4 3 2 1

Cover Illustrations: Old woman, 4–3rd centuries B.C., courtesy of the J. Paul Getty Museum, Malibu. Woman, CA. 2nd century A.D., courtesy of the J. Paul Getty Museum, Malibu. Harmodius and Aristogeiton slay Hipparchus, CA. 470 B.C., courtesy of Martin von Wagner Museum, Würzberg. St. Michael in ivory, CA. 400 A.D., courtesy of the Trustees of the British Museum.

Prentice-Hall International, Inc., *London*

Prentice-Hall of Australia Pty. Limited, *Sydney*

Prentice-Hall of Canada, Ltd., *Toronto*

Prentice-Hall of India Private Limited, *New Delhi*

Prentice-Hall of Japan, Inc., *Tokyo*

Prentice-Hall of Southeast Asia Pte. Ltd., *Singapore*

Whitehall Books Limited, *Wellington, New Zealand*

For Garrett and Eliza

Contents

3

The Near East to the Persian Empire **31**

4

Religion and Culture in the Later Period **44**

TWO

The Greek World

5

The Beginnings **63**

The Archaic Age **78**

7

From the Persian Wars to the Collapse of the Great Powers **108**

Classical Athens **130**

From the Rise of Macedonia to the Decline of the Hellenistic Monarchies **182**

Society and the State in the Hellenistic Period **195**

THREE
The Roman World

Preface

Modern authors of social and cultural history can generally assume that their readers will share with them a number of fundamental presuppositions about the nature of present-day society. They can take for granted, for example, that there will be no argument with the proposition that society is something very different or even opposed to the state and its institutions. Similarly, they do not have to establish that the modern state is a complex mosaic of classes and cultures which interact in turn with a large number of public, semi-public, and private bodies such as churches, corporations, educational institutions, labor unions, branches of government, cultural organizations, and the like.

Unfortunately, a similar set of shared presuppositions does not exist for the ancient world. In a majority of cases none of the institutions mentioned above existed in antiquity and those that did functioned at such a rudimentary level that they counted for little. Even the ancient world's class system operated on quite a different set of principles to that of the modern state. Particularly in their classical formulations ancient societies were tightly knit communities in which political, cultural, and religious life closely intermingled. Society was not something set apart from the state but was, rather, closely identified with it. As a result, it is possible to write of ancient society as an independent sphere of human activity in the modern sense in only a very limited way, and what this book seeks to do, instead, is to pursue the distinctive forms society took in the ancient world and especially the unusual relationship between society and the state that characterized the social order of antiquity. Detailed descriptions of the highly integrated world of the classical period are given, placing special emphasis on its culture, social structures, moral values, and political processes. The inner workings of the Athenian democracy and the Roman Republic are discussed at length, and art, literature, and religion—especially how they functioned vis-à-vis society—receive prominent attention. At the same time, recognizing that the closely unified societies of the classical period changed radically in the course of time, special consideration is given to the much altered world of the Hellenistic period (third to second centuries B.C.) and the Roman Empire (first to fifth centuries A.D.). The last chapter describes the new society that began to make its appearance toward the end of antiquity and that laid the foundations for the modern world.

I owe special thanks to Professors Stanley M. Burstein of California State University, Los Angeles, Rory Egan of the University of Manitoba, and John K. Evans of the University of Minnesota, for reading and commenting critically on various parts of this book. I also owe a great deal to the assistance of Janet Crusius, Jerry Gluck, Pat Patterson, and Lee Reams. The editors of Prentice-Hall were constant in their patience and encouragement.

Unless otherwise indicated, the translations are my own.

THE ANCIENT WORLD

ONE

THE ANCIENT NEAR EAST

1

The Early Civilization of Mesopotamia and Egypt

So far as we can presently tell, the great leap from peasant village to true city occurred about 3000 B.C. in the land of Sumer in the southern part of Mesopotamia. Here for the first time human energies were directed to the creation of great temple complexes and large-scale irrigation and flood-control projects. Directing these operations was a talented elite who drew upon the then revolutionary information-recovery technique of writing to control the collection, storage, and redistribution of the agricultural surpluses on which this new mode of human organization depended. In time the capacity of writing evolved to the point where it was possible to record in different literary forms the religious and cultural values of the civilization. The resulting body of literature, through various intermediaries, has influenced western cultural values to the present time.

Paradoxically, this spectacular development took place in what is, from many viewpoints, a hostile environment. The climate of central and southern Mesopotamia is dry and subtropical, with temperatures reaching 120°F in the summers and an average annual rainfall of less than ten inches. Unlike the Nile in Egypt, which floods at a time suitable to the cereal crop cycle, the Tigris and the Euphrates flood between April and June, too late for the summer planting and too early for the winter planting. As a result, agriculture is possible only by means of artificial irrigation and careful crop management. In order to bring streams to the fields during the planting seasons, when river water levels are low, deep canals must be dug and maintained. Silting is a perennial problem and can be resolved only by unending labor and a high degree of community cooperation. Another difficulty is salinization, especially in the south where the low water-table encourages salt to collect and rise to the surface when the fields are not properly leached by fresh inundation. Without adequate drainage, the soil quickly becomes sterile, and difficult if not impossible to restore to productivity. The rivers themselves, with their unpredictable and often violent flood levels, are yet another threat to the cities and villages precariously located along their

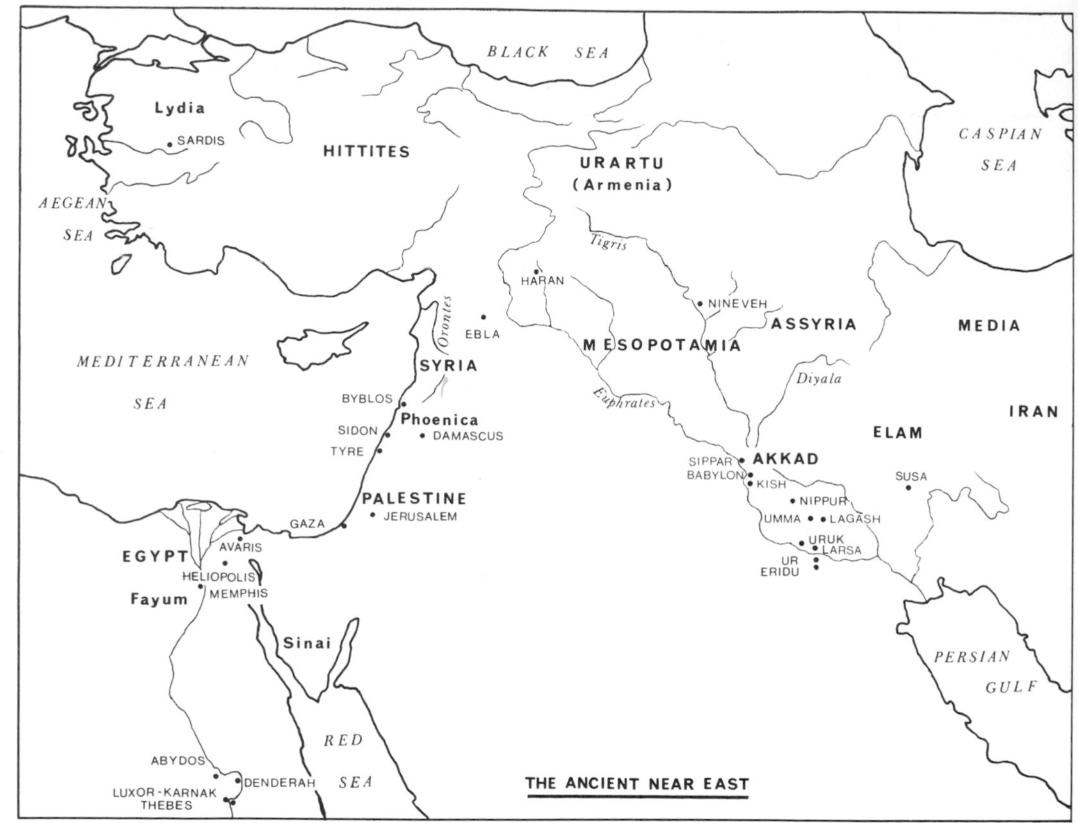

banks. Without human intervention, southern Mesopotamia hovers between swamp and desert. Yet it offers immense advantages over the surrounding regions. When properly irrigated, the land is extraordinarily fertile and in antiquity it was one of the richest food-producing areas in the world. The rivers themselves provide excellent means of transportation, and their regular burden of alluvium, although not as rich as that of the Nile, constitutes the basis for the natural fertility of the region. It was these factors, together with the organizational abilities of the Mesopotamians that sustained the brilliant civilizations that flourished there for thousands of years.

THE FOOD-PRODUCING AND URBAN REVOLUTIONS

Broadly speaking, the development of Mesopotamian civilization occurred in two stages. The first, the Food-Producing Revolution, took place between 8000 and 4000 B.C. and the second, the Urban Revolution, about 1000 years later.

Although the general outline of both developments is easily enough described, it is extremely difficult to do more than theorize about the causes of each and there is a standing temptation to rely on overly rational and functional hypotheses. For example, the mere presence in any given region of plants and animals suitable for domestication (or which were in fact later domesticated) is not in itself a sufficient explanation—even assuming we can tell *where* domestication might have first occurred or whether plant and animal species now apparently native to the area in question were indigenous to it 10,000 years ago. Nor is it possible to assume a similar kind of "natural" impulse that would have forced populations that had successfully reached the food-production stage to move on to the building of cities. We know that many societies, both ancient and modern, that went through the first process never went on to the second. Furthermore, the once widely accepted theory that hunting and fishing groups were the evolutionary and necessary predecessors of early agriculturalists is now complicated by the realization that quite involved man-plant and man-animal relations go back long before the usually accepted moment of domestication during the so-called Neolithic period. It now seems clear that there was no one center of domestication or one moment when the revolutionary techniques of agriculture were uncovered once and for all; rather, there was a long process lasting thousands of years in which widely scattered groups in different parts of Eurasia were involved. It is even possible that certain plants and animals may have been domesticated more than once by different peoples. As a result, recent investigations tend to avoid broad generalizations and instead give special emphasis to microenvironments and the complex interrelationships between their plant and animal ecologies and man. What follows is an attempt to apply this approach to the very early history of Mesopotamia.

Between approximately 8000 and 5000 B.C., a wide-spectrum system of food gathering and animal and plant husbandry had been successfully established in the regions along the coasts of Palestine and Lebanon and in the hills above the Mesopotamian plain. Here men lived on a varied diet made up of foods from a large number of plants and animals, some of which were domesticated and some of which were not. Among these were legumes and wild grasses such as barley, rye, and wheat, and animals including goats, sheep, pigs, gazelle, wild fowl, and fish.

About the middle of the sixth millennium (ca. 5500 B.C.), groups of settlers driven by growing population pressures made their way down into the plains of the Tigris and Euphrates and took up residence in the more promising of the multiple environments that the region offered. In the marshy south, fish and wild fowl contributed a major element to the diet of the settlers; in the central steppe area—the *edin* of the Sumerians—sheep, goats, and cattle did well. Having brought with them the grains they had cultivated in the northern hills and valleys, the settlers quickly found that barley could tolerate the somewhat more salty farmlands of the south and that wheat did better in the north. Both crops, however, required irrigation of some kind. Initial efforts along these lines were on a small scale, but it was early learned that the volume of grain from the irrigated patches was out of all proportion to the amount of land irrigated and significantly more than had been produced by means of the dry farming techniques the early farmers had practiced in the hills. The settlers also found that date palms, which provided an easily storable, high-calorie source of food, flourished along the canal and river banks. Thus, through transfer and adaptation of techniques and crops that had proved successful in one area to a potentially richer area, the foundation for a truly self-sustaining agricultural economy was established in southern Mesopotamia between about 5000 and 3000 B.C.

Although the foregoing hypothesis is probably a fairly accurate one, we should not forget that a good deal of it is theory and that too much emphasis may have been given to the purely practical and functional steps that seem natural to us looking back to this very ancient period. We know nothing, for example, of the other factors that normally influence behavior, such as politics, religion, war, and human creativity, not to mention the unpredictable and irrational aspects of life.

It is equally difficult to discover the causes of the next stage of development, the Urban Revolution (ca. 3000 B.C.). Archaeological sources indicate that in the fourth millennium (4000–3000 B.C.) there were many widespread, though rather uniformly distributed, agricultural settlements, generally villages and towns, in southern Mesopotamia. These communities practiced small-scale irrigation and they mixed food production with food gathering. There were in addition a number of religious centers, such as Uruk which by 3500 B.C. was a substantial ceremonial center surrounded by a large number of towns and villages. Then, around 3000 B.C., Uruk suddenly expanded. At the expense of its surrounding communities, it became a true city with a population of 40,000–50,000. This pattern of rural incorporation was repeated in many areas of Sumer so that by the middle of the millennium (ca. 2500 B.C.) there were eight centers that could be classified as true cities.

This process of urbanization was not, it seems, brought about by the need for concentrating resources for the purposes of irrigation, since irrigation certainly predates the emergence of the cities. There is thus no support—at least in Mesopotamia—for the widespread theory that great public undertakings tend to create centralized governments and massive bureaucracies. A more likely explanation is to be found in the centripetal role of the centers of common worship, where divergent groups of settlers met for purposes of ritual celebration and incidentally for the exchange of goods and ideas. Here temples arose, staffed in time by permanent priesthoods who accepted offerings from the worshippers on behalf of the gods and then redistributed them in various ways to the community. In time, these religious centers developed administrative techniques, including writing, to facilitate operation. As population pressures, the needs of defense, and the threat of famine increased, the priests found that they had come to occupy a central place in the urbanization process itself. The people gravitated toward the shrines for religious purposes, for sustenance, and for protection, and no doubt for many other reasons we can only guess at. Eventually palaces arose and their similar organizational structure allowed them to play an economic role analogous to that of the temples. In the course of time they even usurped the latter's political position, though the temple remained an essential element of Mesopotamian city-state life throughout the ancient period.

THE EARLY HISTORY OF MESOPOTAMIA: THE SUMERIAN PERIOD (3100–2000 B.C.)

When Mesopotamia emerged from the prehistoric into the historic period, about 3000 B.C., there were in the area two principal linguistic groups: the Semitic-speaking Akkadians in the north and the Sumerians in the south. In terms of language, at least, the Akkadians were related to many other inhabitants of the ancient Near East, but the origin of the Sumerians is to this day a mystery. They were not, however, the earliest occupants of the region that came to bear their name.

From its inception Mesopotamian history fluctuated between times of unification, when one or another city succeeded in dominating some or all the others, and times when the individual cities went their own anarchic ways. At an early date the city of Kish gave some kind of unity to the states of Sumer and the term *king of Kish* became synonymous with the term *king of Sumer.* Another city, Nippur, provided the religious sanction for Sumerian overlordship, and it was there, in times of extraordinary danger, that the leaders of the cities assembled to elect one of their number to the kingship. Eventually the endorsement of the priesthood of Nippur became an essential part of the legitimation process and was eagerly sought by would-be contenders for the overlordship of Sumer.

Although the unity of the cities under the leadership of one of their number represents one aspect of Mesopotamian political life, the other and more common aspect includes endless internecine battles and shifting alliances as the cities struggled over boundaries and irrigation water. We know, for example, in rather great detail the quarrels that occurred around 2500 B.C. between the city of Lagash and its neighbor Umma over a stretch of territory lying between them. First we learn that

> the ensi [leader] of Umma, at the command of his god, raided and devoured the Gu-edin, the irrigated land, the field beloved of Ningirsu . . .[1]

But the phalanx of Lagash, led by their *ensi* Eannatum, assailed the invaders and "heaped up piles of their bodies in the plain."[2] A century or so later the tables

[1]Georges Roux, *Ancient Iraq* (Harmondsworth: Penguin Books Ltd., 1966), p. 131. By permission of George Allen and Unwin Ltd.

[2]Roux, *Ancient Iraq*. By permission of George Allen and Unwin Ltd.

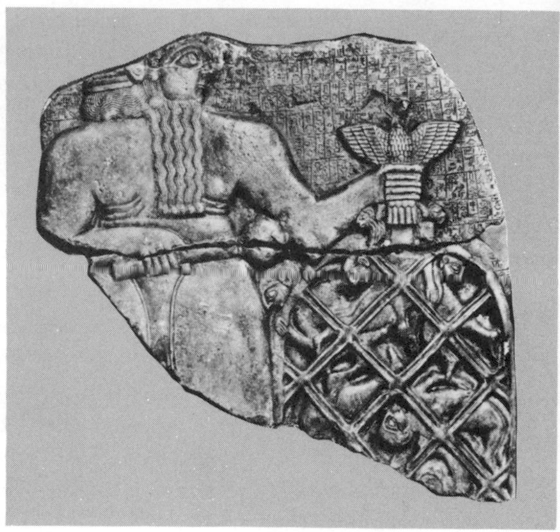

Eannatum leads the army of Lagash into battle assisted by the god Ningirsu (right), who holds a net symbolically containing the enemies of his city. Fragments from the victory stele of Eannatum in the Louvre.

were turned and Lugalzaggesi of Umma sacked Lagash. An unknown author wrote the following lament over the ruined city:

> The men of Umma have set fire to the temple Antasurra, they have carried away the silver and the precious stones. . . . They have shed blood in the temple E-engur of the goddess Nanshe . . .[3]

Despite this setback, Lagash recovered. Two centuries later its leader, Gudea, was dedicating temples, extending the city's irrigation network, and fostering long-distance trade. Yet another 200 years after that, Lagash was embroiled with another Sumerian city, Larsa, and came under its control.

Under the pressure of continuing warfare of this kind, the kingship ceased to be the ad hoc arrangement to provide essential leadership that it had once been, and a whole new ideology of the divine rights of kings evolved. At the same time a gradual redistribution of wealth and the development of private land reduced the importance of the temples and pushed the once free commoners into becoming clients of either the temple, the palace, or the nobility.

A beneficiary of this general process and one of its protagonists was Sargon of Akkad (ca. 2300–2230 B.C.). According to one romanticized version, he was of humble origins:

[3]Samuel Noah Kramer, *The Sumerians: Their History, Culture and Character* (Chicago: The University of Chicago Press, 1963), pp. 322–23. © 1963 by the University of Chicago.

My . . . mother conceived me, in secret she bore me.
She set me in a basket of rushes, with bitumen she sealed my lid.
She cast me into the river which rose not over me.
The river bore me up and carried me to Akki, the drawer of water.
Akki, the drawer of water, took me as his son and reared me.
Akki, the drawer of water, appointed me as his gardener.[4]

By degrees Sargon rose above his modest beginnings, first becoming king of Kish and then king of all Sumer. Eventually his kingdom reached from the Mediterranean to the Persian Gulf.

Despite his Akkadian background, Sargon respected Sumerian customs, and his daughter, Enheduanna, was installed as the high priestess of the moon god Nanna at Ur, a custom that was followed by his successors with their own daughters. Her finely crafted hymns in honor of Inanna, the goddess of fertility, make her the world's first known literary figure.

Sargon's empire lasted through the long and vigorous reign of his grandson, Naram-Sin, but then sank slowly into anarchy, aptly described by the words of the Sumerian King List: "Who was king? Who was not king!" Various enemies, the Amorites of the desert, the Hurrians of the north, the barbarians of the mountains, and the ever-rebellious city-states of Sumer, had a hand in its downfall. After the empire's collapse, Ebla in Syria, the "Akkad of the North," which had been sacked by Naram-Sin, recovered and held sway over northern Mesopotamia, while in the south the individual city-states once more became independent.

Between Sargon's empire and the rise of Babylon under Hammurabi 400 or so years later, there occurred the Sumerian renaissance of Ur III, as it is called (ca. 2100–2000 B.C.). Under its vigorous ruler Ur-Nammu, temples were rebuilt and Ur's great ziggurat, which still dominates the plain for miles around, was erected. Overseas trade developed and irrigation was extended. One of Ur-Nammu's greatest achievements, however, was the publication of a code of laws intended to systematize and make public the customary rules under which society was administered. This late flourishing of Sumeria under Ur-Nammu's leadership was the last effort of the Sumerians as an independent people. Continuing pressure from the Amorites and from Elam in the east gradually weakened Ur and the city was finally captured and sacked, probably by the Elamites. Ur's fame lived on, however, and its destruction was later lamented by an unknown author whose description is so vivid that for a long time he was assumed to have been a contemporary of the event:

O Father Nanna, that city into ruins was made . . .
Its walls were breached; the people groan;

[4]From "Akkadian Myths and Epics," transl. E.A. Speiser in James B. Pritchard (ed.), *Ancient Near Eastern Texts Relating to the Old Testament* (copyright © 1969 by Princeton University Press): p. 119. Reprinted by permission of Princeton University Press.

In its lofty gates, where they were wont to promenade,
dead bodies were lying about;
In its boulevards, where the feasts were celebrated, scattered they lay . . .
In its places, where the festivities of the land took place, the people lay in heaps . . .
Ur—its weak and its strong—perished through hunger . . .
O Nanna, Ur has been destroyed, its people have been dispersed.[5]

EARLY EGYPT TO THE END OF THE OLD KINGDOM (CA.3100–CA. 2100 B.C.)

Egypt had considerably more potential for unification than did its great northern neighbor, Mesopotamia. Early in its history unity was achieved and maintained—though not without occasional relapses into anarchy—under the rule of a god-king, the pharaoh. The Nile itself was a major factor in this early achievement of national unity since it provided a first-class means of transportation for movement both upstream and downstream. A steady northern wind provided power for ships sailing against the current while coming in the opposite direction they had the assistance of the flow of the river itself. Control over shipping amounted to control not only of troop movements but also of the flow of essential goods in either direction. The administration of large irrigation projects was an important factor, though only a contributing one, to the early emergence of centralized government. Egypt's protected geographical position, however, was of major importance and gave it an enviable degree of security from its enemies. To the east and the west deserts offered protection and limited the potential invasion routes to two relatively easily defended passageways, the Gaza Strip to the northeast and in the west the route from Libya through El Alamein. Although Egypt's southern border with the Sudan (Nubia) was sometimes troublesome, there was nothing to fear from equatorial Africa thanks to the vast, impenetrable swamp, known as the Sudd, in the southern part of the Sudan.

In its early form the Nile Valley must have been much more like its modern southerly reaches, with their huge stretches of marsh and papyrus jungle inhabited by teeming wildlife, than the neat open landscape of the historical period. For a vast amount of time men struggled in this inhospitable jungle environment. Then, toward the end of the prehistoric period, there were important contacts with Mesopotamia, and Egyptian artifacts of the time evidence a high level of artistic achievement. One of the major themes that appear on the finely carved cosmetic palettes and ivory knife handles of the period is fighting, so it can be assumed that a good deal of disturbance and

[5]From "Akkadian Myths and Epics," transl. E.A. Speiser in James B. Pritchard (ed.), *Ancient Near Eastern Texts Relating to the Old Testament* (copyright © 1969 by Princeton University Press): p. 459. Reprinted by permission of Princeton University Press.

conflict among the regions was common before unification. Rather suddenly, however, around 3100 B.C., Egypt was united by the conqueror Menes and we enter the historical stage of its development.

The unification of Egypt was apparently accomplished by conquest from the south, but almost immediately the new rulers moved their capital to Memphis, a point just below the apex of the Nile Delta, where northern and southern sections of Egypt meet. Of this long, early historical period (ca. 3100–2700 B.C.), only the great rectangular tombs or *mastabas* of the pharaohs and their officials survive. The high craftsmanship of the tombs and the quality of the grave furnishings indicate, however, the significant level of civilization that Egypt had attained. By the end of the period the basic pattern of Egyptian civilization had been established and Egypt was ready to enter its Golden Age, the Old Kingdom (ca. 2700–2100 B.C.).

The Old Kingdom was undoubtedly Egypt's most typical and spectacular period. During it, Egypt was the foremost civilization of the world, rivaled only by the short-lived empire of Sargon of Akkad. Unfortunately ancient Egypt's antihistorical tendencies make it practically impossible to reconstruct a connected history of the period. Were it not for the tombs of the pharaohs and their associated monuments and burials, it would be practically impossible to say anything of the Old Kingdom. Unlike the cities of Mesopotamia, Egypt's ancient urban centers have disappeared practically without trace and we are left with the pyramid complexes of the western desert as almost our sole source of information.

The pyramids were built throughout the Old Kingdom and were the normal form of burial for the pharaohs until the middle of the next millennium (ca. 1500 B.C.). The remains of about 80 pyramids are known. The majority of these lie scattered along a 70-mile stretch of the desert bordering the Nile just south of the point where the river enters the delta. To this day the pyramids, with their enormous mass and stark simplicity, bear witness to the power and majesty of the rulers who erected them. By contrast, it takes an effort of the imagination to evoke the greatness of the Mesopotamian achievement from the decaying and weathered heaps of mud brick that constitute the remains of that civilization. The largest of the pyramids, that of Cheops, is 481 feet high and is composed of 6 million tons of stone set on a base covering 13.1 acres. Its foundation is level to within 0.004 percent of true plane and its sides square to 0.09 and 0.03 percent respectively. The interior corbeled gallery leading to the burial chamber is a marvel of engineering construction and one of the most impressive feats of the pyramid builders. Such fidelity and finesse are not, however, present in all the pyramids and, especially toward the end of the Old Kingdom, there is much evidence of hasty and shoddy workmanship.

Although the pharaoh was the all-powerful ruler of Egypt and in theory directly administered the land himself, he was in reality assisted by a huge corps of well-trained officials. At the beginning of the Old Kingdom this administration was highly centralized, with the pharaoh clearly the dominant power, but

Although pillaged and stripped of its original covering of limestone, the Great Pyramid still suggests something of the power and resources of its creator, the pharaoh Cheops.

toward the end his influence declined and the provincial officials began to act as feudal lords in their own right. Part of this devolution of power was caused by the necessity of maintaining the numerous pyramids with their supporting priesthoods and lay staffs and the huge estates set aside for their sustenance. Over the years rewards to faithful and successful officials constituted another drain on the pharaoh's resources while inner power struggles, about which we know little, also took their toll. By the end of the Sixth Dynasty (ca. 2180 B.C.) the centralized authority of Egypt had virtually disappeared. All the land was in turmoil—aptly described by a later writer, the seer Ipuwer:

> The land is full of gangs,
> A man goes to plow with his shield.
> Crime is everywhere . . .
> Lo, the land turns like a potter's wheel,
> The robber owns riches, the noble is a thief.
> People flap like fish . . .
> Lo, the desert claims the land.[6]

[6]Miriam Lichtheim, *Ancient Egyptian Literature: A Book of Readings* (Copyright ©1973 by The Regents of the University of California): pp. 151–52. Reprinted by permission of the University of California Press.

2

Religion and Culture in Early Egypt and Mesopotamia

In their early, classical periods all the great civilizations of the ancient world were tightly knit, highly integrated societies. They were utterly unlike the modern state, which is to a large extent a conglomeration of public, semipublic, and private bodies such as unions, corporations, churches, schools, and governmental agencies, which may or may not work in harmony with each other. In these ancient societies power was concentrated rather than diffused. Religion was not something separate from the state; rather, it was so closely identified with the state that its priests were also its great landowners, generals, and judges. Temples were not places where the individual worshipped according to a privately held set of religious beliefs. They were institutions where rituals essential to the operation of the state were performed. Behavior was dominated by public, community-held conventions rather than by the individual conscience informed by ethical theories or beliefs. Culture and art were principally a matter of state concern and the private connoisseur and the professional practitioner were a long way off in the future.

RELIGION AND CULTURE IN EGYPT

In Egyptian belief, the sun rose daily and traveled across the sky to the western horizon where it entered the netherworld. From there, after fighting off the forces of chaos and disorder, it emerged the following morning with renewed strength, to repeat its daily passage through the sky. For the Egyptian this was no purely natural occurrence, no impersonal movement of one of the heavenly bodies operating mechanically according to the physical laws of the universe. It was rather a great religious drama in which the Egyptian was vitally involved. Similarly the Nile was thought to pass annually through a cycle of birth and death that affected everyone in Egypt. For months it lay dessicated and reduced to a muddy stream between fields burned brown by the hot sun. Then miraculously it gathered force and swelled until it overflowed its banks and spread a great revivifying mantle of water over the surrounding countryside. Gradually shrinking, it left a rich deposit of silt from which the new crops sprang. Both events—the daily passage of the sun and the annual death and rebirth of the Nile—were paradigms for the rest of Egyptian life, models of the unchanging cosmic rhythm, the eternal interchange of the elements of the universe that the Egyptians perceived at work all around them and of which they were a part.

The Pharaoh and Egypt

The marvelous, orderly world of the Egyptians was believed by them to have been brought into existence and fixed for all time in the first moment of its creation by the gods. The interworking of its various parts and the balance of its elements were described by the term *ma'at,* which can be translated as either "order," "justice," or "truth." The course of the stars, the sequence of day and night, and the passage of all things from life to death were part of this universal *ma'at* established by the gods in the beginning. The cosmos did not advance or retreat but rather repeated itself in an eternal "now." What lay outside this was exceptional, a violation or an aberration that had to be endured until the gods once more restored due order. Nothing in this world was transitory or accidental.

Although the universe was created in this fashion it was not an unfailing mechanism in which the activity of the gods or men was irrelevant. We have seen how every night the sun in its passage had to fight off the forces of evil seeking to destroy it in the underworld, and although always victorious the struggle had to be renewed each evening. When it came to maintaining the *ma'at* of Egypt the gods delegated one of their number, Horus, the son of Osiris, to be the guarantor of its balance and harmony. His function as the divine pharaoh was twofold: to ensure the continuing existence and activity of the gods on earth by means of religious acts, and to maintain the natural order (principally the flow of the Nile) and the fertility of the soil. His authority was thus neither political, social, or economic, but cosmic. It sustained all of Egypt's life, controlled disease, and repelled Egypt's enemies. By pharaoh's word the Nile rose and fell. Victories in defense of the land were won by his hand alone and his divine counsel always prevailed over the merely human advice of his courtiers. When Pepi II appropriated the names of enemies defeated by one of his predecessors 200 years earlier and Ramses III borrowed from Ramses II who in turn copied from Thutmosis III, they were not engaged in a form of self-glorification but were simply repeating a perennial Egyptian truth; namely, that the pharaoh always triumphed over Egypt's enemies.

The archetypal myth of Egypt was the succession of Osiris by his son Horus. According to the story the reigning king, Osiris, was killed by his brother Seth and his body was dismembered. Ultimately it was put together again by Osiris' wife, Isis, and he became the Lord of the Dead while his son Horus

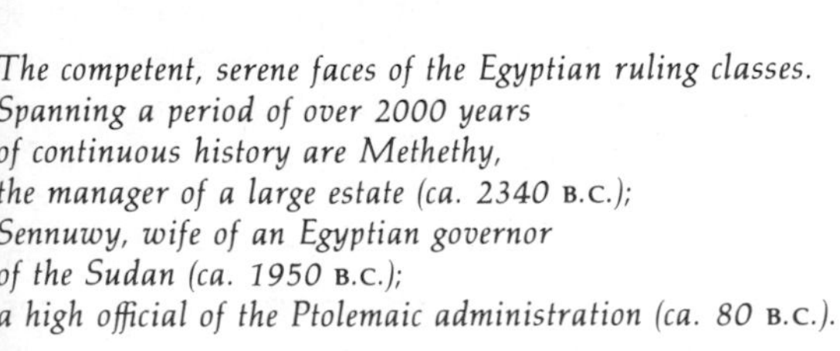

The competent, serene faces of the Egyptian ruling classes. Spanning a period of over 2000 years of continuous history are Methethy, the manager of a large estate (ca. 2340 B.C.); Sennuwy, wife of an Egyptian governor of the Sudan (ca. 1950 B.C.); a high official of the Ptolemaic administration (ca. 80 B.C.).

succeeded him as Lord of the Living. Thus pharaoh did not succeed pharaoh in lineal, human succession as one king might succeed another, but instead every living pharaoh was Horus and every dead one Osiris. Alternatively—since for Egyptians one religious viewpoint did not replace but complemented another—the king at death "went up to heaven to be united with Re, his father," or he was the Nile dying and coming to life. At the same time, in order to ensure his successful passage to the next world—whether as Re or as Osiris—it was necessary to guarantee the actual preservation of his physical remains and supply them with all the essentials for the transition to the next world. In view of the pharaoh's central importance to all aspects of Egyptian life this was not a private matter, of concern only to the king and his family, but a work of national importance on which the Egyptians felt it necessary to lavish their resources. In this way they could assist the divine pharaoh in his task of ruling the land according to the cosmic plan of the gods.

Although the authority of the pharaoh was unchallengeable, it was not, theoretically at least, despotic. The pharaoh was charged by the gods with the care of Egypt, not as his private possession for his own personal enjoyment, but in accordance with the original act of creation. He was the shepherd of his people: "the herdsman of all men . . . [who] has spent the day caring for them,"[1] according to the words of one of the pharaohs, Merikare. Appropriately, one of the earliest of the king's insignia was the shepherd's crook. Ideally he was accessible to everyone, for Egyptian law was not administered in an impersonal fashion according to written and publicly proclaimed law codes, as in Mesopotamia, but according to custom that was tempered, hopefully, by mercy and justice. The king alone was the source of all law and could adjust it according to the particular circumstances of the case. Naturally the pharaoh did not and could not administer justice to the millions of Egyptians, but his delegates did, and so far as we can tell it was taken seriously. Even the lowliest peasant could press his claim against unjust treatment by pharaonic officials:

> Rudder of heaven, beam of earth,
> Plumb-line that carries the weight!
> Rudder, drift not,
> Beam tilt not,
> Plumb line, swing not awry![2]
>
> Do justice for the Lord of Justice . . .
> For justice is for eternity:
> It enters the graveyard with its doer.
> When he is buried and earth enfolds him,
> His name does not pass from the earth;

[1]J. A. Wilson, *The Culture of Ancient Egypt* (© 1951 by The University of Chicago): p. 120.

[2]Miriam Lichtheim, *Ancient Egyptian Literature: A Book of Readings* (Copyright © 1973 by The Regents of the University of California): p. 173. Reprinted by permission of the University of California Press.

He is remembered because of his goodness,
That is the rule of god's command.[3]

—"The Eloquent Peasant"

Local Religions, Temples, and Rituals

Although the cult of the pharaoh occupied the most prominent place in the national religion, Egyptians worshipped a multitude of gods, goddesses, spirits, and sacred objects. Tolerant and conservative, they were reluctant to dispose of the old rituals and deities. Yet, although the country's size and its cultural complexity contributed to the perpetuation of the local gods, there was a constant interchange as the individual cults expanded, contracted, blended with one another, or disappeared.

Animal gods abounded. Seth, the rival and murderer of Osiris, was depicted with a doglike body, long neck, upright tail, and squared ears. Horus appeared as a falcon and also as a falcon-headed man. The vulture goddess Nekhbet was the tutelary goddess of Upper Egypt; her opposite in Lower Egypt was the cobra goddess Wedjet. Hathor had a human head but a cow's ears, horns, and body. Some gods, such as Min, Ptah, Atum, and Amon, on the other hand, never appear as animals and are always depicted in human form. There was a great mingling of divine personalities and traits as the political fortunes or just sheer popularity of individual gods rose or fell. When Menes, the unifier of Egypt, moved from Hierakonpolis to Memphis, the god of that city, Ptah, came into prominence. At a later date Re of Heliopolis not far from Memphis rose to a position of dominance. Blending with Horus he formed the god Re-Harakhte, the "Horus of the Horizon." The king, originally only identified with Horus, soon came to be identified also as the son of Re. In the Old Kingdom the cult of Osiris spread rapidly all over Egypt from its original home in the north; later the local god of Thebes, Amon, became prominent.

The cult of the gods was of such central importance to Egyptian life that it is understandable why the temples rose to prominence. Built of stone, these monuments were created to last forever; like the tombs of the pharaohs they became part of the eternal landscape of Egypt. Unfortunately, none of the temples from the Old Kingdom but those in the pyramid complexes survive. It is from the Empire period (ca. 1550–1100 B.C.) and later that the great temples of Thebes, Denderah, Abydos, and elsewhere date.

Egyptian temples of the Empire period were laid out axially with one room or courtyard leading to another, each one progressively removed from the outside world. Darkness increased room by room until finally the chapel of the

[3]Miriam Lichtheim, *Ancient Egyptian Literature: A Book of Readings* (Copyright ©1973 by The Regents of the University of California): p. 181. Reprinted by permission of the University of California Press.

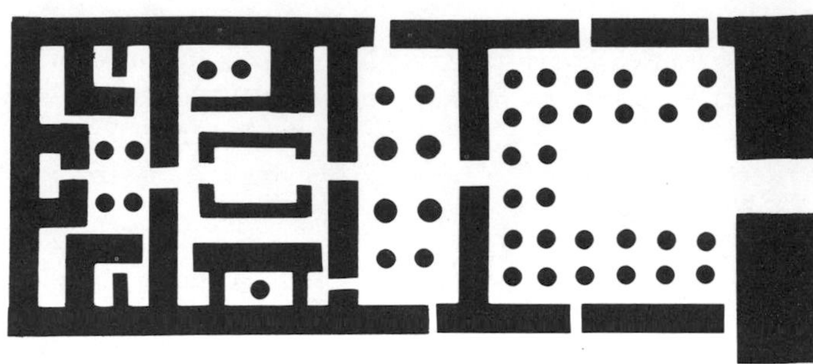

Egyptian temple

cult image was reached. Here only specially designated priests could function in the performance of the daily round of liturgical acts that guaranteed the presence of the god in the cult image. These rituals, performed in accordance with the movement of the sun across the heavens, maintained the temple in harmony with the rhythm of the cosmos. The rites began each morning with the opening of the sanctuary doors as the sun was rising. The cult statue was anointed, clothed, and fed and it was believed that at that moment the god took possession of it. Twice more, at midday and in the evening, the god was fed and entertained. At evening, as the sun set, he departed to join the sun in its nightly passage through the underworld.

The priests who performed these tasks were laymen who spent part of the year in the service of the temple and the remainder in their normal secular occupations. They were not the guardians of an orthodox revelation or a caste set aside to perform rituals or preach salvation to the unconverted. They had no ethical role to play and no one would have thought to consult them on matters of morality. Their principal function was that of assisting the pharaoh in the maintenance of the divine order of creation *(ma'at),* which was his most important function. Their job was simply to see that the temple operated properly and that the image of the deity was appropriately housed, clothed, entertained, and fed. It was a technical role requiring ritual cleanliness, not inner purity.

Aspects of the Funerary Religion

There is nothing unusual in the fact that the Egyptians showed great interest in the afterlife, but what is altogether exceptional is the amount of effort they were willing to devote to ensuring their dead a chance of survival in the next world. Although mud brick and reeds were considered sufficient for the dwellings a man used during his lifetime, his tomb was constructed of the most durable materials known to ancient man.

In Egyptian belief existence after death without some connection with the body was unthinkable. When a man died his soul, or what the Egyptians called the *ba,* fluttered around the tomb and depended on its contents for sustenance. Contracts were made and corporations formed to see that the dead were supplied with all the essentials needed to sustain them in the hereafter. Even the passerby was urged to supply the dead man's need if he were neglected by those who were supposed to care for him:

> O ye who live and exist, who love life and hate death, whoever shall pass by this tomb . . . so ye shall offer to me that which is in your hands. If nought is in your hands, ye shall speak thus with your mouth: a thousand of bread and beer, of oxen and geese, of alabaster vessels and linen, a thousand of all pure things to the revered Enyotef, son of Enyotef, son of Khuu.[4]

It is odd that although we know a great deal about the concern of the Egyptians for the afterlife and the meticulous care they gave to preparing for it, we are not altogether clear about what they thought that life was like. For some it was simply a repetition in its most earthly form of man's existence in this world but for others it was a form of reintegration in the cosmic processes. In this latter belief the souls of men became transfigured beings and joined the sun in its daily passage through the sky, or they became stars in the heavens: "Spirit to the sky, corpse into the earth!"[5] For others, again, death was an escape from the travails of life:

> Death is before me today
> Like a sick man's recovery,
> Like going outdoors after confinement.
>
> Death is before me today
> Like a well-trodden way,
> Like a man's coming home from warfare.
>
> Death is before me today
> Like the clearing of the sky,
> As when a man discovers what he ignored.
>
> Death is before me today
> Like a man's longing to see his home
> When he has spent many years in captivity.[6]

—"The Dispute Between a Man and His *Ba*"

[4]A. Gardiner, *The Attitude of the Ancient Egyptians to Death and the Dead* (Cambridge: Cambridge University Press, 1935), p. 36.

[5]H. Frankfort, *Ancient Egyptian Religion* (New York: Harper & Row, Publishers, 1961), p. 100.

[6]Miriam Lichtheim, *Ancient Egyptian Literature: A Book of Readings* (Copyright ©1973 by The Regents of the University of California): p. 168. Reprinted by permission of the University of California Press.

ART AND LITERATURE IN EGYPT

Egyptian works of art reflect many of the themes we have already encountered in the foregoing discussion of religion. Art was first and foremost sacred rather than secular in character. Tomb paintings and inscriptions served primarily religious and magical purposes and played an essential part in supplying the dead with all the essentials of life in the hereafter. They were thus neither decorative nor artistic in our sense of these words. Second, the state and its needs, especially in the Old Kingdom, overwhelmed the personal and private side of Egyptian life. All the great monuments—the pyramids of the Old Kingdom and the temples of the Empire period—reflected the power and majesty of the pharaoh and the gods, not of the individual. Nor was Egyptian art representational. It was intended to emphasize the unchangeable and the eternal, not the fleeting moment of the present. In the reliefs the pharaohs appear disproportionately large, dominating the figures of both their enemies and their own officials. Great emphasis is given to the ideal of the pharaonic order by the careful disposition of the king and his followers in clear, well-organized panels, whereas the king's enemies appear in front of him in stunned, chaotic masses. In unruffled calm the pharaoh triumphantly drives the rabble from the field or stands before prostrate bodies and discarded weapons. The message is simple: Egypt is a land cared for by a divine being whose word preserves the order of the land. Evil, on the other hand, is a challenge from the demonic outside world that will, in due course, be checked by the might of the king. According to the established canon of Egyptian art the pharaoh and his officials always appear according to a predetermined unchanging order, with eyes and shoulders depicted frontally and the head and the rest of the body in profile. With animals and the lower orders of society, on the other hand, the artists were free to use their inspiration and these appear with varying degrees of naturalism. In later periods the eternal calm of the ruling classes gave way to greater realism, but in general the canon of Egyptian art established in the Old Kingdom was to last to the end of Egyptian civilization.

As art was preeminently a matter of public rather than private expression so also was literature. Although the Egyptians developed writing as early as 3000 B.C. it always remained a clumsy vehicle of expression, best suited to terse, factual statements and to the uses of the bureaucracy. It was never a literary language in the sense of most modern tongues and its powers of expression were severely limited. Like the script of the Mesopotamians, which developed at a somewhat earlier date, that of the Egyptians could only be mastered by years of laborious study under the direction of a master scribe. Hundreds of signs and set expressions had to be memorized and one can imagine that the kind of mind that developed from such lengthy and painstaking study must have been scholarly rather than literary in inclination. There could never be the ready communication between the writer and his audience that is taken for granted by writers in modern languages thanks to the long evolution of their literary traditions and the simplicity of the alphabet, which makes it possible for anyone to master the art of communication in writing. Nevertheless, even within the limited framework of their technique the scribes created a surprising number of literary genres, including various kinds of poetry, hymns, narrative tales, and wisdom literature.

With the exception of love poetry, which developed later, the hymns and poetry of Egypt concentrated on the celebration and proclamation of the greatness of the pharaohs and the gods. In endlessly repeated refrains their mighty acts were reviewed without any attempt at developing a narrative account:

How great is the lord of his city:
    he is a canal that restrains the river's flood water!
How great is the lord of his city:
    he is a cool room that lets a man sleep until dawn!
How great is the lord of his city:
    he is a walled rampart of copper of Sinai!
How great is the lord of his city:
    he is a shelter whose hold does not fail! . . .
How great is the lord of his city:
    he is an overflowing shade, cool in summertime!
How great is the lord of his city:
    he is a warm corner, dry in wintertime![7]

The reason for this approach was not lack of inspiration but rather the very different intention of the ancient Egyptian poet, whose object was to evoke rather than analyze or narrate. His aim was to instill in his audience a sense of the fidelity, magnificence, or power of the god or pharaoh, and the endless repetition had the effect of arousing awe or confidence or mystery, whichever was desired. Unlike the modern poet, who composes almost always for a reading public, his ancient counterpart wrote for public events such as rituals honoring the pharaoh, court liturgies and dramas, burials, processions, and victory celebrations. Dull facts were elevated into religious acts and became part of the ongoing cosmic liturgy—the very antithesis of modern poetry, which dwells on subjective moods and feelings or the individual's reactions to the outside world.

Beyond satisfying the all-important religious needs of the state the principal use of writing was in the bureaucracy itself. Unfortunately, because the majority of Egyptian administrative texts were written on perishable papyrus, we are deprived of much information about this area of the government. In contrast, there is no shortage of information about Mesopotamian administrative practices because clay tablets, which have survived by the ton, were used there for these purposes. We do know, however, that the needs of the Egyptian

[7]Miriam Lichtheim, *Ancient Egyptian Literature: A Book of Readings* (Copyright ©1973 by The Regents of the University of California): pp. 199–200. Reprinted by permission of the University of California Press.

administration did lead to the creation of a huge body of specialists, the scribes, whose function was to regulate the economic and administrative life of Egypt. Understandably they took a great deal of pride in their position and it was commonplace to make comparisons between their profession and other occupations:

> Set your heart on books! . . .
> I'll make you love scribedom more than your mother,
> I'll make its beauties stand before you;
> It's the greatest of all callings,
> There's none like it in the land . . .
> I never saw a sculptor as envoy,
> Nor is a goldsmith ever sent;
> But I have seen the smith at work
> At the opening of his furnace;
> With fingers like claws of a crocodile . . .
> The carpenter who wields an adze,
> He is wearier than a field laborer . . .
> The jewel-maker bores with his chisel
> In hard stone of all kinds . . .
> The reed-cutter travels to the Delta to get arrows;
> When he has done more than his arms can do,
> Mosquitoes have slain him,
> Gnats have slaughtered him . . .
> The potter is under the soil,
> Though as yet among the living;
> He grubs in the mud more than a pig,
> In order to fire his pots.
> His clothes are stiff with clay . . .
>
> See, there's no profession without a boss,
> Except for the scribe; he is the boss.[8]

Others could claim that "the fame of writing was better than the pyramids."

The scribal system led to the development of a literature that is usually termed "wisdom" literature although the term should be understood in a practical rather than a philosophical sense. Its object was the inculcation of rules of etiquette and behavior: how to handle superiors and inferiors, how to arrange one's family life in relationship to the scribal profession. It emphasized virtues of modesty, moderation, and reserve, the importance of discretion and of listening to others:

> If thou art one to whom petition is made, be calm as thou listenest to what the petitioner has to say. Do not rebuff him before he has swept out his body or before he has said that for which he came. The

[8]Miriam Lichtheim, *Ancient Egyptian Literature: A Book of Readings* (Copyright © 1973 by The Regents of the University of California): pp. 185–86. Reprinted by permission of the University of California Press.

> petitioner likes attention to his words better than the fulfilling of that for which he came. . . . It is not [necessary] that everything about which he has petitioned should come to pass, [but] a good hearing is soothing to the heart.[9]

Most of the wisdom literature was prudential and aimed at teaching the inexperienced the arts of survival in the bureaucracy:

> Don't be proud of your knowledge,
> Consult the ignorant and the wise. . . .
> Do not malign anyone,
> Great or small . . .
> Do not boast at your neighbor's side,
> One has great respect for the silent man.[10]

Some, however, went beyond the pragmatic and emphasized moral values:

> Do not jeer at a blind man nor tease a dwarf,
> Neither interfere with the condition of a cripple;
> Do not taunt a man who is in the hand of God,
> Nor scowl at him if he errs.
> Man is clay and straw,
> And God is his potter;
> He overthrows and he builds daily . . .[11]

RELIGION AND CULTURE IN MESOPOTAMIA

If the people of Egypt had confidence in a world whose existence had been stabilized for all time in the first moment of creation, the Mesopotamians could never be sure that the once subdued forces of chaos might not at some time reassert themselves. In their violent and unpredictable environment they were compelled to face the possibility of complete annihilation or abandonment by the gods. Their creation account told of no effortless emergence of the gods from the primeval waters but of a fearsome struggle that pitted them against the demons of disorder in a battle that was long in doubt.

If the Mesopotamian view of the origin of the universe was unsettling, their belief in the way the gods cared for their creation was not any more reassuring. Whereas the Egyptians viewed the pharaoh as a god who maintained the original order of creation, in Mesopotamia a noisy and quarrelsome

[9]Wilson, *Culture of Ancient Egypt* (© 1951 by the University of Chicago), p. 93.

[10]Miriam Lichtheim, *Ancient Egyptian Literature: A Book of Readings* Copyright © 1973 by The Regents of the University of California): pp. 63–64. Reprinted by permission of the University of California Press.

[11]W. K. Simpson, ed., *The Literature of Ancient Egypt* (New Haven and London: Yale University Press, 1973), p. 262.

assembly of deities was entrusted with this task. None was so powerful that he automatically enjoyed a permanent place of preeminence. Each was entrusted with the protection of one of the cities of Sumer and was imagined to represent its interests at the general parliament of the gods. There cosmic and earthly issues were debated riotously with speeches, motions, proposals, and votes. Heads of the pantheon were voted in and out of office with much display of emotion. Thus, when Nanna, the god of Ur, was dethroned from the overlordship of Sumer, his wife Ningal pleaded passionately for the city:

> When I was grieving for that day of storm,
> that day of storm destined for me, laid upon me heavy with tears . . .
> I could not flee before that night's fatality.
> Dread of the storm's floodlike destruction weighed on me,
> and of a sudden on my couch at night,
> upon my couch at night no dreams were granted me.
> And of a sudden on my couch oblivion,
> upon my couch oblivion was not granted.
> Because [this] bitter weeping had been destined for my land,
> and I could not, even if I scoured the earth—a cow seeking her calf—
> have brought my people back. . . .
> I dragged my feet and I stretched out my arms.
> In truth, I shed my tears in front of Anu.
> In truth, myself I mourned in front of Enlil:
> "May not my city be destroyed?" I said indeed to them . . .
> But Anu never bent towards those words,
> and Enlil never with an, "It is pleasing, let it be,"
> did soothe my heart.[12]

In such a world nothing was stable, nothing fixed. The political fortunes of different cities waxed and waned and even the gods had to bow before the wills of their colleagues. Generation after generation of Mesopotamians was forced to adjust to the shifting fortunes of different cities and empires, a labor the Egyptian with his belief in an eternal pharaoh never had to undertake.

The individual cities of early Mesopotamia were not simply conglomerations of men engaged in largely secular and private tasks, as are modern cities, but sacred communities dedicated to the service of the different gods. All their possessions, animate and inanimate, were at the disposal of their divine masters. From the beginning men were created to be their servants for "Ea . . . toil imposed on man, and set gods free."[13] Perhaps it could be regarded as a dignified form of servitude since men were viewed as assisting the gods in the performance of their cosmic functions and dutiful service had the desired effect of attaching the individual gods more firmly to their proprietary cities.

It is not strange that men in the precarious and difficult environment of

[12]H. Frankfort and others, *Before Philosophy* (Harmondsworth: Penguin Books Ltd., 1949), pp. 212–13. Originally published as *The Intellectual Adventure of Ancient Man* (Chicago: University of Chicago Press, 1946). By permission of the University of Chicago Press.

[13]Ibid., p. 197, by permission of the University of Chicago Press.

early Mesopotamia turned with such complete dependence to those powers of nature on whose benevolence their existence depended. The torrential rains of the storm god Enlil could destroy as effectively as the floodwaters of the Tigris and the Euphrates:

> The rampant flood which no man can oppose,
> Which shakes the heavens and causes earth to tremble,
> In an appalling blanket folds mother and child,
> Beats down the canebrake's full luxuriant greenery,
> And drowns the harvest in its time of ripeness.[14]

The civilization of Mesopotamia depended on the successful manipulation of irrigation waters, and sad experience must have early taught the lessons of the trickiness of Enki, the god of the sweet waters, or of another deity of uncertain habits, Inanna, the goddess of fertility. Others were perhaps a little less unpredictable or threatening. Around Uruk, the land of herds and herdsmen, bovine gods were supreme and Nanna the moon god appeared as a young bull grazing the heavenly pastures. Dumuzi, the god who fertilized the sheep herds, was worshipped in Babylonia, farther north; in the cities where cereal production was significant the important deities were the mysterious chthonic or underworld deities such as Ninlil, the wife of Enlil.

Temples and Palaces

In early Mesopotamia the most imposing structures of the cities were the temple complexes. Their artificial mountains, the ziggurats, reached to the heavens and dominated the flat countryside for miles around. At Ur the temple complex of Nanna consisted of an enclosed space over 200 × 400 yards containing shrines, storehouses, courtyards, and the dwelling places of the temple personnel. Over this stood the ziggurat, 70 feet tall, on top of which was a small shrine. Daily the god was fed, clothed, and entertained. His family, which also possessed temples in the city, was similarly feted. Each in turn had a role to play in the economic organization of the temple, supervising, it was imagined, a whole flock of human servants who looked after the metal shops, breweries, fisheries, flocks, herds, grainfields, orchards, and arsenals—and most important, the stores of grain on which the existence of the community depended.

The most important functionaries of the temples were the scribes who, like their Egyptian counterparts, went through years of laborious study to master the many symbols of the Mesopotamian cuneiform or wedge-shaped script. The capacity for writing facilitated, though it was not essential to, the proper functioning of the state. Incoming taxes and tribute were recorded along with the yields of the temple possessions, the amount of inventory, and the disbursement of goods from storage, for it was as distribution and regulatory agencies that the

[14]Ibid., p. 139, by permission of the University of Chicago Press.

temples performed their most important economic functions in this early period. The complete acceptance of the bureaucratic system of government was one of the most characteristic aspects of the civilization and is reflected in the belief in the existence of a scribe in the afterworld who kept the records of the dead who passed over to it daily. In turn the Old Testament picked up this tradition and Psalm 139 depicts God as a careful scribe who notes men's actions even before they occur:

> Thou has searched me and known me, O Lord;
> Thou knowest when I sit down and when I stand up;
> Thou discernest my thought from afar . . .
> Whither shall I go from thy spirit?
> And whither shall I flee from thy presence?
> If I ascend to the heavens, thou art there!
> If I make Sheol my bed, thou art there also! . . .
> When I was made in secret,
> And molded in the lowest parts of the earth,
> Thine eyes saw the sum total of my days,
> And in thy book they were all written;
> They were formed, when there was not one among them.[15]

Ps. 139:1–2, 7–8, 15–16

There has been a considerable amount of debate over the question of how literally we are to interpret the Sumerian belief that the cities and their possessions belonged to the gods. It has been pointed out that although temples did own considerable amounts of land, others in the community, especially among the upper classes, also owned land, and there are plenty of records of property being bought and sold. Political actions by the free community of property owners is also attested to in the early cities and indicates that the temples, although undoubtedly the most significant institutions, were not all-inclusive. None of this, however, will have been thought by the early Mesopotamians to have contradicted their fundamental and overriding belief in the cities as the possessions of the gods.

The other essential institution of the classical Mesopotamian city-state was the palace. As population increased and the cities prospered they became less vulnerable to the old threats of natural disaster and starvation, but considerably more exposed to destruction at human hands. Their accumulated wealth could be looted, their populations enslaved, and their canal systems destroyed or put to use by others. The cities, accordingly, turned to defense, and from about 2600 B.C. great protective walls began to appear. The kingship ceased to be the casual arrangement it had previously been and became central to the defensive system of the cities. It was no longer feasible to turn only in

[15] J. M. P. Smith and others, *The Complete Bible: An American Translation* (Chicago: University of Chicago Press, 1939). Copyright 1927 by the University of Chicago Press.

emergencies to some leader, and the maintenance of the army and the city fortifications permanently fell within the purview of the palace. Soon its organizational structure came to resemble that of the temple with its great stores of weapons and food while scribes were employed to keep track of the accumulated goods. Because of the need for constant preparedness the older, more democratic government of the early period gave way to the relatively more efficient monarchy and the palace took its place alongside the temple as one of two essential institutions of Mesopotamian civilization.

In peace the kings were expected to be the upholders of justice and the protectors of the weak and poor against the rapacious and powerful. More so than in Egypt, written law played an important part in the administration of justice. From early times laws were published and kings and priests committed themselves to uphold them. As early as 2300 B.C. Urukagina of Lagash boasted how he restored the ancient ordinances and brought justice and freedom to his oppressed city:

> Formerly . . . the man in charge of the boatmen seized the boats. The head shepherd seized the donkeys. The head shepherd seized the sheep . . . [A long list of injustices follows.] From the borders of Ningirsu to the sea, there was the tax collector.[16]

However, under Urukagina all this was changed and the king

> amnestied the citizens of Lagash who had been imprisoned because of the debts which they had incurred . . . and set them free. Finally Urukagina made a covenant with Ningirsu that a man of power must not commit an injustice against an orphan or widow.[17]

Some 500 years later the prologue of Hammurabi's code grandly stated its purpose as follows:

> To cause justice to prevail in the country
> To destroy the wicked and the evil
> That the strong may not oppress the weak.[18]

MORAL VALUES AND LITERATURE IN MESOPOTAMIA

In the Sumerian period primary emphasis in Mesopotamian society was given to the virtues of obedience to the gods and subservience to the needs of the

[16]S. N. Kramer, *The Sumerians* (Chicago and London: University of Chicago Press, 1963), pp. 317–18. © 1963 by the University of Chicago.

[17]Ibid., p. 319 (slight alterations). © 1963 by the University of Chicago.

[18]G. Roux, *Ancient Iraq* (Harmondsworth: Penguin Books Ltd., 1966), p. 183. By permission of George Allen and Unwin Ltd.

community. An orderly world was not possible without firm authority and the Golden Age was described as:

> Days when one man is not insolent to another, when a son reveres his father,
> days when respect is shown in the land, when the lowly honor the great,
> when the younger brother . . . respects his older brother,
> when the older child instructs the younger child and he abides by his decisions.[19]

Although survival in a hostile environment dominated these early years, in time men began to look beyond the restrictive bonds of their communities, and at the beginning of the second millennium (ca. 2000 B.C.) the needs of the individual, his fears, guilt, and sufferings, begin to be heard for the first time. Complaints and petitions were not, however, directed to the gods on high but to the individual's own personal god who might, if sufficiently pressed, do something to help. One such complaint has survived from the period and is sometimes known as the "Sumerian Job." In this tale a just, wealthy and benevolent man is struck down in a moment with sicknesses and misfortunes of all kinds. Even so he says he will continue to praise his god and will keep lamenting until he is heard:

> My god, the day shines bright over the land, for me the day is black . . .
> Tears, lament, anguish, and depression are lodged within me,
> Suffering overwhelms me like one chosen for nothing but tears,
> Evil fate holds me in its hand, carries off my breath of life,
> Malignant sickness bathes my body. . . .
> My god, you who are my father who begot me, lift up my face . . .
> How long will you neglect me, leave me unprotected . . .
> Leave me without guidance?[20]

Although he realizes that the blame rests on himself he asks that his hidden faults may be revealed so he may seek forgiveness for them.

The epic poem is found in Mesopotamian literature but not in Egyptian—probably because of the more warlike character of the Mesopotamians and their altogether different view of the afterlife. Unlike the Egyptian vision of the underworld, which offered possibilities of transformation to a new level of existence or at least of continuing the same life as on earth, that of the Mesopotamians was of a dreary and cheerless place, ruled by a fearsome hierarchy of demons. At most it was a dismal reflection of life on earth. No one was exempt from it, not even the heroes who struggled to avoid being dragged down into it. Of these the best known was Gilgamesh, one of the early rulers of Uruk, about whom there developed a cycle of tales that ultimately came to make

[19]Frankfort and others, *Before Philosophy*, p. 217. By permission of the University of Chicago Press.
[20]Kramer, *The Sumerians*, p. 128. © 1963 by the University of Chicago.

up the *Epic of Gilgamesh,* probably the finest product of Near Eastern literature outside the Old Testament.

In one of the early versions, the hero Gilgamesh is saddened by the thought of death brought home to him by the sight of "dead bodies floating in the river's waters" of Uruk, and he determines to make a name for himself before his own death:

> I peered over the wall,
> Saw the dead bodies floating in the river's waters,
> As for me, I too will be served thus, verily it so!
> Man, the tallest, cannot reach to heaven,
> Man, the widest, cannot cover the earth.
> Brick and stamp have not yet brought forth the fated end,
> I would enter the "land," would set up my name,
> In its places where the names have been raised up, I would raise up my name,
> In its places where the names have not been raised up, I would raise up the names of the gods.[21]

He sets off in quest of adventure with his servant Enkidu and a number of volunteers, and after crossing high mountains they vanquish a great monster. However Enkidu is slain by the gods for an act of impiety and in brokenhearted grief Gilgamesh leaves the city and the kingship and wanders in the steppe clothed in animal skins:

> "My friend, my younger brother—who with me in the foothills
> hunted wild ass, and panther in the plains;
> Enkidu my friend . . .
> who with me could do all . . .
> Now—what sleep is this that seized you?
> You have grown dark and cannot hear me."
> He did not raise his eyes.
> [Gilgamesh] touched his heart, it was not beating.
> Then he covered his friend, as if he were a bride . . .
> His voice roared out—a lion . . .
> Again and again he turned towards his friend,
> tearing his hair and scattering the tufts,
> stripping and flinging down the finery off his body.[22]

In the hope of avoiding a fate similar to that of Enkidu he sets off to visit the immortal Utnapishtim who alone with his wife survived the flood. On the way he is given this piece of advice:

[21]Kramer, *The Sumerians,* p. 193. © 1963 by the University of Chicago.

[22]H. Frankfort and others, *Before Philosophy* (Harmondsworth: Penguin Books Ltd., 1949), p. 225. Originally published as *The Intellectual Adventure of Ancient Man* (Chicago: University of Chicago Press, 1946). By permission of the University of Chicago Press.

Gilgamesh, whither are you wandering?
Life, which you look for, you will never find.
For when the gods created man, they let
death be his share, and life
withheld in their own hands.
Gilgamesh, fill your belly—
day and night make merry,
let days be full of joy,
dance and make music day and night.[23]

It is finally Utnapishtim who reconciles him to his mortality, though there are other adventures before he returns home once more. This magnificent poem, which deals with such eternal human problems as sickness, old age, death, fame, and the craving for the unattainable, can be considered a fine reflection on Mesopotamia's own heroic struggle to resist decay and leave a name for itself among the peoples of the earth.

[23]Frankfort and others, *Before Philosophy*, p. 226. By permission of the University of Chicago Press.

3

The Near East to the Persian Empire

THE EARLY SECOND MILLENNIUM

The early second millennium saw waves of Semitic-speaking Amorites overrun all of Mesopotamia, Syria, and Palestine and gradually settle down to form a mosaic of endlessly battling city-states. Egypt, by contrast, enjoyed a period of tranquillity and progress (the Middle Kingdom). Under some of the most effective leaders it ever possessed, the energetic pharaohs of the Twelfth Dynasty (1991–1786 B.C.), Egypt once more gathered its strength, which had been dissipated at the end of the Old Kingdom, and launched a number of ambitious projects. Large sections of Lower Egypt in the Fayum area were brought into productivity by irrigation projects and power was once more concentrated in the hands of the central administration, though not with the absolutism that had characterized the Old Kingdom. Palestine was brought under loose control. Then, as the energies of the dynasty expended themselves, Egyptian power once more decayed. Taking advantage of her weakness, the *Hyksos* ("foreign princes") pushed into Egypt from Syria and Palestine and established themselves in the delta area (ca. 1725 B.C.). A second wave of Hyksos made their appearance in the next century. Well armed with chariots and the composite bow, they ruled all of Egypt from Avaris, their fortified capital in the north.

As Egypt lost its coherence and fell into the hands of outsiders, Mesopotamia began to rise once more. Under the leadership of Hammurabi the once unimportant city of Babylon emerged from obscurity and became the center of a great empire. Though literature and the arts were also cultivated, the most famous product of Hammurabi's Babylon was the standardized code of legal traditions and customs that the king published for the benefit of his heterogeneous kingdom. Although not by any means the first code of laws it was the first of the imperial Mesopotamian codes, aimed at providing a common legal procedure for the whole area.

The power of the Babylonian Empire did not long survive Hammurabi.

Kassite tribesmen pushed down from Iran and a raiding army of the nascent Hittite kingdom in Anatolia captured and sacked the city in about 1530 B.C. Subsequently the Kassites came to stay permanently and for two centuries Mesopotamia entered a Dark Age. To the north the Hurrians under the leadership of an Indo-European warrior aristocracy established the powerful kingdom of Mitanni in Upper Mesopotamia.

In Palestine all these events were reflected in greater or lesser degree. The arrival of the Amorites is marked by the widespread destruction of inhabited centers at the end of the third millennium. Then in the nineteenth century recovery began and increased rapidly. Cities were built and urban life developed as the seminomadic Amorites began to settle down and absorb the culture of the original Canaanite inhabitants. Later Hurrians and Indo-Europeans infiltrated Palestine or passed through the land on their way to Egypt where they ruled as the Hyksos. It was in these confused times, at some point between 2000 and 1600 B.C., that the Amorite chieftain Abraham and his family moved out of Upper Mesopotamia and along with other Amorites and Hurrians devoted themselves to a seminomadic mode of existence, tending their flocks of sheep, cattle, and goats on the fringes of the settled areas. "A wandering Aramean" was how a later writer described Abraham's grandson and although the title belongs to a later period the description is accurate. Much of the account of the activities of the patriarchs, Abraham and his descendants Isaac and Jacob, is intelligible only in the context of the customs and practices of the first half of the second millennium and in particular those of the Hurrians of Syria and northern Mesopotamia. Thus the strange actions of Abraham and Isaac, which have confused many readers of Genesis, become intelligible in the light of Hurrian practices but very difficult to explain otherwise. For example, when Abraham and Isaac refer to their wives as their sisters (Gen. 12, 20, 26) they are not lying but are following the Hurrian custom of elevating one of a number of wives to blood-kinship in order to ensure her a more secure and honorable position in the community. Similarly we can understand Laban's frantic pursuit of Jacob, because in Hurrian law possession of the household gods—which Rachel had stolen—was practically equivalent to obtaining title to the inheritance.

THE EGYPTIAN EMPIRE

In the middle of the second millennium the character of Palestine changed radically. While Mesopotamia remained sunk in its Dark Age under Kassite rule, Egypt went through another of its cyclical periods of growth and decline and in a great national revival expelled the Hyksos about 1540 B.C. Thereafter the pharaohs of the new, triumphant Eighteenth Dynasty resolved never to submit to foreign domination again, and extended their control into Palestine and Syria, inaugurating the period of the New Kingdom or the Empire (ca. 1550–1100 B.C.). Sweeping over the petty kingdoms of the Canaanite and Amorite chiefs in Palestine, the rule of Egypt reached the Euphrates and collided there with

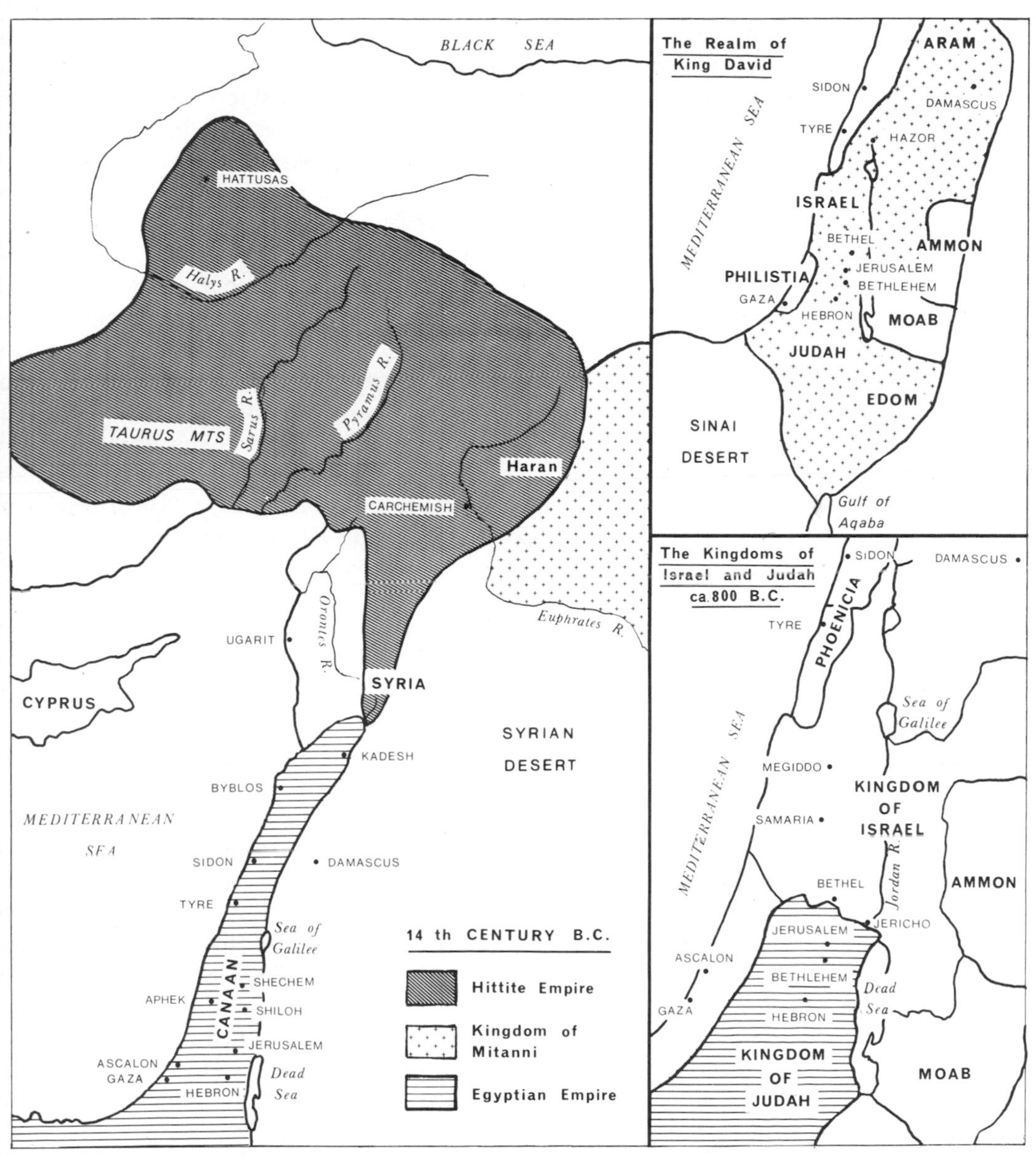

the power of the kingdom of Mitanni in Upper Mesopotamia. War lasted throughout the fifteenth century and peace was finally established under Tuthmosis IV (ca. 1412–1403 B.C.). His successors conducted few expeditions into Asia and under Amenophis IV (ca. 1364–1347 B.C.) Egyptian control of Palestine weakened considerably and we read of people identified as the Habiru invading and establishing themselves in the central areas. Their identity has been endlessly debated, from ancient times to the present, and current opinion prefers not to associate them with any particular racial or linguistic group but rather to regard them as a social category of wanderers or stateless persons who in times of disruption in the ancient Near East were able to assert themselves against the older powers. Together with runaway slaves and dissident peasants they were able to move into the settled areas and establish themselves.

The reason for Egyptian weakness at this time was the extraordinary theological revolution promoted by the eccentric pharaoh Amenophis IV. Under the pressures of imperial needs Egypt experienced a degree of social and cultural exposure to foreign cults and customs that it had never before willingly incurred. New classes of civil servants and professional soldiers arose alongside the traditional social strata of Egyptian society. The uniqueness of the Egyptian way of life and its complacent self-centeredness gave way to a new cosmopolitanism. Amenophis IV's father had inclined toward a new emphasis on solar worship but it was his son who built this into a religious doctrine and broke with the dominant cult of Egypt, that of Amon-Re and its powerful priesthood at Thebes. Moving his capital upriver to a new site called Akhetaten "the Horizon of Aten"—the modern Tel-el-Amarna—Amenophis laid the foundations for a new administration based on a renewed emphasis on the position of the pharaoh and a new religious understanding.

The meaning of the religious revolution is unclear though it seems that what the pharaoh was asserting was a form of *monolatry* (the exclusive worship of one god without, however, denying the existence or reality of others) rather than monotheism of which we have no real evidence until Second Isaiah in the Old Testament (sixth century B.C.). Whatever the theological nature of the beliefs of Akhenaten, as Amenophis called himself, Egypt was in turmoil as a result of them. The traditional forces were ranged against the new but since Akhenaten's religion was a purely personal one and in no way to be shared with the rest of humanity, let alone the Egyptian masses, it quickly succumbed to palace intrigue and outside pressures. The traditional priesthood of Amon-Re re-established itself and set out to obliterate any memory of the heretical pharaoh. His successor was the insignificant Tutankhamon (1347–1338), whose tomb—the only pharaonic tomb discovered intact to date—was found in A.D. 1922.

When Egypt emerged from the Amarna crisis, it discovered that the political situation in Asia had changed dramatically. The Hittites of Anatolia, after some centuries of decline following their lightning sack of Babylon about 1530, had recovered and had recently brought the kingdom of the Mitanni under their control. The next advance brought them south into Syria and Palestine. Meanwhile the general Haremhab (ca. 1333–1306) stamped out the remnants of Atenism in Egypt and restored the country internally. Another general, Ramses, who hailed from Avaris in the north, succeeded Haremhab and once more Egyptian power began to expand northward. Under the long-lived Ramses II (1290–1224) the armies of Egypt advanced into Syria and collided there with the Hittites. A major battle was fought at Kadesh with great slaughter on both sides and the war continued indecisively for another ten years. With both Egypt and the Hittites exhausted and Assyria threatening the Hittite eastern flank, a treaty of "good peace and brotherhood" was arranged in 1280 or thereabouts, and until the destruction of the Hittite kingdom in the mid-thirteenth century the two powers remained on good terms with each other. In the latter half of Ramses' long rule Egypt experienced peace and prosperity. Great building projects were undertaken, among them the reconstruction of the old Hyksos capital Avaris, which became Ramses' northern headquarters.

At this point the whole of the ancient Near East was once more convulsed by upheavals and invasions, which kept the area in turmoil for the next three centuries—after which a whole new world emerged. The first major catastrophe was the destruction of the Hittite Empire, which was the victim of unsettled conditions in the Aegean and Baltic regions. Then, around 1220, under Ramses' successor Merneptah (1224–1211), Egypt was assaulted by a coalition of peoples from the north known as the Sea Peoples and from the west by Libyan tribes. By dint of hard fighting Merneptah preserved Egypt but under Ramses III (1183–1152) the assaults were renewed again. Although Egypt survived it was never able to reestablish its power and sank into a long period of decay, coming successively under the rule of Libyans, Nubians, and Assyrians—and finally Persians, Greeks, and Romans. Among those repulsed by Ramses III was a group known as the Peleset or Philistines, who settled on the coasts of Palestine (to which they gave their name) at almost the same time other groups of invaders were forcing their way in from the east and the south.

THE EXODUS FROM EGYPT AND THE CONQUEST OF CANAAN

It was at some point in the chaotic events outlined in the preceding section that the second major event in the history of Israel occurred: the Exodus from Egypt. Although the biblical description of the departure of the Israelites from Egypt seems to support a massive departure of Abraham's descendants, a close study of the texts produces a much more complex picture.

It seems that at least some of the Israelites (i.e., those who later identified themselves as the descendants of Abraham's grandson Jacob, or Israel) went down to Egypt with the Hyksos in the sixteenth century and with them were expelled. The majority of the Israelites, however, along with the other inhabitants of Palestine, became subjects of Egypt under the Empire period and many must have been brought into Egypt as forced laborers, though some may have gone voluntarily. Some enjoyed a brief triumph over Egypt in Amarna times when as members of the Habiru they invaded and settled in central Palestine, only to be resubjected when the Egyptian Empire revived under Ramses II. Perhaps at this time some were brought into Egypt to work on the great building projects that were initiated in the delta region by the pharaohs of the Nineteenth Dynasty. One of these groups somehow escaped, perhaps during the rule of Ramses II, and fled into the desert of Sinai under the leadership of the Egyptianized Moses. There they met and joined forces with other tribes and,

Phoenician ivory carving found in Assyria.

inspired by the visionary genius of Moses, adopted the worship of Yahweh, perhaps a local god of the Sinai peninsula. Whether Yahweh was a god of the Sinai peninsula is not important. What is of significance is the religious insight of Moses, which radically transformed this desert deity and the people who worshipped it. Although there is no hope that we can now disentangle the exact nature of Moses' belief from later developments at the hands of other, equally gifted people, there is no point in belittling his stature as a person of authentic religious significance and the founder of the new religion. So successful was Moses in conveying his faith in the saving power of Yahweh to his followers that the religion survived transplantation to a new land and countless subsequent challenges from changing cultural, economic, and social conditions.

The land of Canaan out of which Israel was to emerge had already been fought over many times. By the time of the arrival of the group led by Moses at some date in the thirteenth century, the early Amorite invaders had mingled with the original inhabitants to such an extent that the two were indistinguishable. Together they constituted a people who shared a common culture that reached from Egypt to southern Syria. The Canaanites were in contact not only with the civilizations of Mesopotamia and Egypt but also with the Minoan and Mycenaean cultures of the Aegean area, whose pottery has been found throughout Palestine and Syria. Although the coastal and river valley regions of Canaan were thickly settled, the mountainous areas were only sparsely occupied. An agricultural people, the Canaanites worshipped the fertility gods

Baal and Astarte and the myths and ritual practices associated with them were to be in part assimilated by the invading Israelites. The most important cultural achievement of the Canaanites was, however, the invention of the alphabet, an event that made obsolete (though it did not eliminate) the laborious scripts of Mesopotamia and Egypt. At a stroke the people of Canaan made writing a relatively simple technique to master and therefore accessible to far more people than the narrow scribal castes of the ancient civilizations for whom writing constituted a secret art.

The conquest of Canaan was a slow process that took several centuries to complete. Initial toeholds were made in the mountainous areas and only gradually in the more settled regions. The newcomers, however, brought a religion whose appeal extended to those Israelites who had not gone down to Egypt or who had settled in central Palestine as Habiru as well as to others not completely assimilated by the Canaanites. At the same time non-Israelite groups such as the Kenites entered Palestine and were absorbed by one or another of the tribes who claimed descent from Abraham. By the eleventh century (1100–1000) a loose confederation of tribes sharing a common sanctuary at Shiloh had come to consider themselves members of a single kin group, worshipping the same god and descended from the same ancestor. By a process of conquest and assimilation the people of Israel had come into existence. There was as yet nothing that could strictly be called a state. The individual tribes were ruled by councils of elders. In times of great stress charismatic leaders, the "Judges" of the Old Testament, rose to lead individual tribes or groups of tribes in military ventures. Among them were such well-known figures as Deborah, Gideon, and Samson, whose successful exploits opened up new areas for settlement or repelled enemy assaults.

THE KINGDOM OF DAVID

Between 1220 and 900 B.C. the major states of the ancient Near East were in decline and only in the ninth century did one of them, Assyria, begin to recover. The result was that during this period the entire region between Mesopotamia and Egypt was left to its own devices and a host of independent principalities and kingdoms arose. Of these the most significant was the kingdom of David and Solomon and for a brief period the empire of Israel extended from Damascus to the approaches to Egypt.

The genesis of the Davidic kingdom goes back to the period of the Judges when Israel was still struggling to maintain itself against all its enemies. From the east the Ammonites pressed in, assisted by the Aramaeans of Syria while in the west the powerful Philistine coalition of city-states threatened the very existence of Israel. The Philistine states consisted of a disciplined warrior aristocracy ruling over Canaanite subjects. Although they lacked a unified government, the tyrants of the individual cities were able to cooperate effectively with one another. Armed with iron weapons and chariots they were able, in the early stages of the conflict, to confine their opponents to the mountainous areas of Palestine. At Aphek around 1050 B.C. they soundly defeated the forces of Israel, captured the Ark of the Covenant, and went on to destroy the tribal sanctuary at Shiloh. Under the pressures of Philistine encroachment as well as internal developments, the Israelites turned reluctantly from the charismatic leaders of the past to the more efficient institution of the monarchy.

The first king was Saul whose early successes gave respite from the Philistines but who in time succumbed to the pressures of his position and became mentally deranged. His successor, David, had gained experience as a guerrilla leader and as a mercenary under the Philistines and was able to unite both his own immediate supporters in the southern tribes and the tribes of the north in a successful alliance. The Philistine menace was overcome and the cities of the seacoast submitted to David. Gradually he extended his power north and east until the Israelite kingdom became the most powerful in the region between Egypt and Mesopotamia. But David did more than create an empire. He fundamentally altered the constitution of Israel by formally espousing the religion of Yahweh and identifying its cult with that of the state. The Ark of the Covenant, which had been recovered from the Philistines, was transferred with great solemnity to Jerusalem where David intended to build a temple for it. Jerusalem became the capital of the new kingdom. In place of the loose federation of tribes a central monarchy with court, scribes, and professional soldiers and administrators was created. Although Jerusalem had been a Canaanite city and David's own personal residence, it now became a national shrine.

David's son Solomon (ca. 961–922 B.C.) extended these lines of development even further. Closely allied to the Phoenician king of Tyre, Solomon set about consolidating his father's religious innovations by building a great temple at Jerusalem with the assistance of Phoenician craftsmen and artists. Friendly relations were also maintained with Egypt and other powers. The army was expanded and strengthened and the frontier cities fortified. A merchant fleet was created in the Red Sea and Solomon attempted to exploit the commercial possibilities of his kingdom's strategic location on the trade routes between Phoenicia, Syria, and Arabia. Cultural activities were also significant and the great deeds of the times of Saul and David were collected and given literary form along with the traditions of Israel's early history.

Solomon's vision far outdistanced the resources of Israel and not long after his death the empire disintegrated. The northern tribes reasserted their independence and established their capital at Samaria. Though Judah in the south remained faithful to the Davidic kings and the principle of dynastic succession, the northern state reverted to a version of the old system of charismatic leadership. For the next two centuries the two states lived side by side, alternately at peace or at war, both progressively rendered impotent by the growing power of Assyria, the first cosmopolitan empire of the ancient Near East.

FROM THE ASSYRIANS TO THE PERSIANS

By the end of the ninth century, Mesopotamia and Palestine had fully recovered from the effects of the great disturbances that occurred at the end of the second millennium and had begun to reach new heights of economic prosperity. Iron was coming into widespread use and the camel, whose carrying capacity was far greater than that of the traditional beast of burden, the ass, was making its contribution to the development of trade.

Assyria survived the period of unrest by dint of constant fighting, its hardy peasantry constituting the nucleus of its powerful army. The founder of the empire was Adadnirari II (911–891), but it was his grandson Ashurnasirpal II (883–859) whose campaigns in Syria and Phoenicia and whose construction of a magnificent palace at Nimrud (biblical Calah) signaled the emergence of a new Assyria. Although checked briefly in 853 by the combined forces of Syria, Phoenicia, and Israel and by internal problems of succession, Assyrian power revived under the tireless organizer and conqueror Tiglathpileser III (744–727). Damascus fell and Assyrian armies reached the Mediterranean seacoast. The Armenian state of Urartu was humbled and Babylon brought under strict control. In 722/721 Samaria, the capital of Israel, fell and thousands of citizens—the Ten Lost Tribes—were deported to Mesopotamia where they mingled with the native population and vanished from history. In their place foreigners were introduced and with the remnants of the Israelite population came to form the Samaritan people of later times. Judah in the south survived precariously as a vassal kingdom of Assyria.

From the time of Tiglathpileser III the annual expeditions of the Assyrians ceased to be raids for booty and the Assyrian Empire came into being, the first we know of that possessed a true imperial administration. The Assyrian Empire

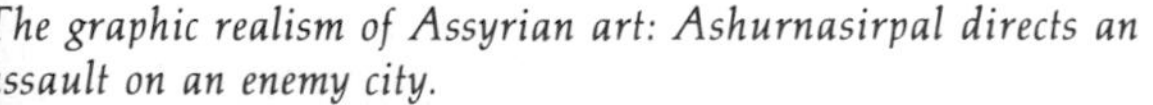

The graphic realism of Assyrian art: Ashurnasirpal directs an assault on an enemy city.

consisted of an extraordinarily heterogeneous collection of peoples and states that the Assyrians held together by means of careful organization and the systematic practice of brutality. Cities were laid waste and whole populations deported or massacred as examples to others. Frightful punishments were visited upon rebellious subjects and piles of skulls were set up as grisly reminders of the power of Ashur, the god of the Assyrians, in whose name these wars were waged. After one of his bloodthirsty campaigns Ashurnasirpal put up the following inscription:

> I built a pillar over against his city gate and I flayed all the chiefs who had revolted and covered the pillar with their skin. Some I walled up within the pillar, some I impaled upon the pillar on stakes and others I bound to stakes round [it]. . . . [#433] Many captives from among them I burned with fire, and many I took as living captives. From some I cut off their noses, their ears and their fingers, of many I put out their eyes. I made one pillar of the living and another of heads, and I bound their heads to tree trunks round about the city. [#445][1]

Despite the frightful aspects of Assyrian governmental policies, trade and industry flourished as never before. Roads were constructed and and Assyrian army provided the prerequisites for peace and order. Cities grew and the arts developed. Fine, realistic friezes of hunting and battle scenes were created to decorate the great palaces of the kings and collections of all sorts of material (literary, scientific, and other) were made. The last of the major kings, Ashurbanipal, was a polymath who received a scholarly education:

> The art of the Master Adapa I acquired: the hidden treasure of all scribal knowledge, the signs of the heaven and earth . . . I have solved the laborious problems of division and multiplication . . . I have read the artistic script of Sumer and the obscure Akkadian. [#986][2]

His great library, of which some 20,000 tablets have come down to us, include the Akkadian version of the *Epic of Gilgamesh.* History was recorded on clay and stone and the events of the different dynasties recorded year by year.

In the seventh century the Assyrians came under increasing pressure from enemies both within and without the empire. From the north Cimmerian nomads penetrated as far as Syria and Palestine and were repelled with difficulty. Rebellion after rebellion racked the inner structure of the Assyrian state. When Babylon revolted Sennacherib destroyed it, though his son and successor, Esarhaddon thought it politic to have it rebuilt. In 671 Egypt was subdued but quickly revolted and had to be beaten down again eight years later. Plagued with revolts Ashurbanipal complained of his plight:

[1]D. D. Luckenbill, *Ancient Records of Assyria and Babylonia* (Chicago: University of Chicago Press, 1926–1927), I, pp. 145, 147. Permission given by Nellie Luckenbill Scheel.

[2]Ibid., II, p. 379. Permission given by Nellie Luckenbill Scheel.

Since I have instituted offerings and the pouring of water for the ghosts of the kings who lived before me, which had been neglected . . . why is it that disease, heartache, distress, and destruction are clinging to me? Enmity in the land, strife in the house . . . disturbances, evil words are continually arrayed against me. Distress of soul and distress of body have bowed my form. I spend my days sighing and lamenting. . . . In anguish and grief, I sit lamenting day and night. I sigh: "O God, to the one who fears not, give these afflictions. Let me see thy light. How long, O God, wilt thou treat me thus?" [#984][3]

After the death of Ashurbanipal Babylon revolted and under the Aramaean or Chaldaean Nabopolassar made common cause with the Medes of Iran and the bands of Scythian nomads who had been active in the Near East for the previous half-century. In 614 Assur fell and two years later Nineveh was captured. By 610 the remnants of the Assyrian army were being stamped out in northern Mesopotamia. The prophet Nahum exulted at the news of the fall of Nineveh:

Woe to the city, bloody throughout,
Full of lies and booty! . . .
The crack of the whip, and the noise of the rumbling wheel,
And the galloping horse, and the jolting chariot;
The charging horseman, and the flashing sword,
And the glittering spear, and a multitude of slain,
And a mass of bodies, and no end to the corpses! . . .
"Behold, I am against you,"
Is the oracle of the Lord of hosts, . . .
I will treat you with contempt, and make you a horror;
So that everyone that sees you will flee from you,
Saying, "Nineveh is destroyed;
Who will mourn for her?
Whence can I seek comforters for her?" [3.1–3, 5–7][4]

With the collapse of Assyria the Near East temporarily reverted to its older, fragmented form. Most of the efforts of the Babylonians were directed to the development of their own immediate holdings in Mesopotamia and to the subjection of Syria and Palestine, not to the maintenance of a vast empire on the Assyrian model. Under its Chaldaean leaders Babylon became one of the most splendid cities in the world. Temples were rebuilt, the priesthoods enriched, and religious customs revived. The great ziggurat Etemenanki—the Temple of the Foundation of Heaven and Earth—almost 200 feet tall, dominated the city, which was surrounded by a circuit of great walls ten miles in length. The famous Hanging Gardens were constructed by Nebuchadrezzar for, it is said, the

[3]Ibid., II, pp. 337–78. Permission given by Nellie Luckenbill Scheel.

[4]J. M. P. Smith and others, *The Complete Bible: An American Translation* (Chicago: University of Chicago Press, 1939). Copyright 1927 by the University of Chicago Press.

pleasure of his Median queen, and a wide boulevard was extended through the city for religious processions.

While the Medes extended their power westward into Asia Minor and came into conflict with the kingdom of Lydia, the Babylonians advanced into Syria and Palestine. There they were opposed by the Egyptians, who had belatedly come to the aid of the Assyrians, but these forces were soon swept aside and driven back within the confines of Egypt. Judah quickly submitted to Nebuchadrezzar (ca. 602) but when the Babylonians withdrew, it rebelled again—despite the warnings of the prophet Jeremiah. In 598 the Babylonians were back and early in the following year Jerusalem surrendered. The king and the leaders of the community were deported to Babylon and the city itself was thoroughly plundered. Unrest continued under the Babylonians as it had under the Assyrians as the different parts of the empire tried to gain independence, often supported by Egyptian assurances of help. In 589 a scattered revolt, which included Judah and the city of Tyre, began. As Jeremiah predicted, the Babylonians struck swiftly and Jerusalem was soon under siege. In the summer of 587 it was captured and burned and its walls razed. More of the population were deported and the remainder, mostly the rural peasants, were left leaderless. With the elimination of the ruling house of David and the destruction of Solomon's temple the history of Israel seemed ended forever.

Nebuchadrezzar's successor was the eccentric Nabonidus (555–539), reflections of whom appear in the Old Testament book of Daniel, which was composed in the Hellenistic period. Nabonidus quickly quarreled with the priesthood of Marduk at Babylon and began interfering in the religious life of the city. An antiquarian visionary, he tried to revive ancient religious rituals and at Harran in northern Mesopotamia built a temple to the moon god to whom he was particularly devoted. Disgusted by the continuing opposition of the Babylonian clergy to his religious schemes he withdrew to a desert oasis, leaving his son Belshazzar to serve as regent.

While the power of the Chaldaean dynasty declined a new people in the north was carving out a realm for itself. In 553 one of the minor Indo-European tribes of Iran, the Persians, successfully challenged the overlordship of the Medes, and Cyrus the Achaemenian established a new ruling dynasty. The Medes acquiesced in the new arrangement and Cyrus led both peoples successfully westward, where they overthrew the kingdom of Lydia and conquered the Greek cities of the Asia Minor coastline. Next the Persians turned their attention to Mesopotamia, and conspiring with the disaffected priests of Babylon obtained control of the city peacefully in 539 B.C. The next year Cyrus issued an edict ordering the reestablishment of the temple at Jerusalem. Subsequently a number of the exiles in Babylon returned to Jerusalem and despite enormous obstacles rebuilt the temple. The project was completed in 515 B.C. but to the disappointment of those who remembered the glories of the old temple the new did not compare to it. Jerusalem had become an unimportant town in a small province of the huge Persian Empire and the principal task facing the followers of Yahweh in the years to come was the adaptation of the old traditions to the straitened circumstances of the present. Nevertheless, fortified by the great cultural legacies of the pre-exilic period and a strong sense of continuity, the community adjusted itself rapidly. Gradually the main outlines of the religion of Judaism began to make their appearance. Largely independent of the cult center in Jerusalem the new religion pursued cultural ideas implicit in the old traditions and evolved institutions, such as the synagogue, appropriate to the cosmopolitan environment in which it grew to maturity.

The Persian Empire, which by 525 B.C. included Egypt, was the largest that had yet been created in the ancient Near East. Organized into provinces under independent governors called *satraps,* the empire united all the land from Greece to Afghanistan and from the Caucasus to the Sudan. It offered peaceful conditions, stable coinage, excellent communications and a good deal of tolerance to its subjects. It continued the cosmopolitan tendencies of the Assyrian Empire, but where the latter dealt with the inherent divisiveness of the area by means of calculated acts of brutality, the Persians acted with greater mildness and encouraged local customs and forms of government. Culturally backward, the Persians made use of Aramaic as the standard language of administration and diplomacy and adapted the arts of Mesopotamia to their own needs. The Persian religion, which consisted of the worship of a large pantheon of gods and spirits, was presided over by a priestly caste called the *magi.* At some date in the sixth century the prophet Zoroaster (Zarathustra) reformed the primitive magian religion, condemning blood sacrifice, magic, and the pantheon of gods. He proposed an impressive theology that pitted the supreme god of Light and Truth, Ahura-Mazda, against the forces of evil, Ahriman, in a battle into which all men were drawn on one side or the other. According to Zoroaster men are morally responsible for their actions and in the end there will be a General Judgment that will see the good and evil separated and appropriately punished or rewarded. Although Zoroaster met a violent end, his reforms became an enduring part of the Persian religion as well as many others in the Greco-Roman period.

4

Religion and Culture in the Later Period

RELIGION AND CULTURE IN MESOPOTAMIA: 1500–500 B.C.

During the Dark Age following the collapse of Hammurabi's Babylonian empire Mesopotamia reverted to its old form of social and political organization in which the temples provided the essential authority for the continuity of civilization. With the arts and literature in full retreat the scribes and priests contented themselves with reworking the great traditions of the past. Canonical versions of ancient stories and legends were established, as well as authoritative forms for the proclamation of incantations and omens. Epics, hymns, prayers, and rituals of all kinds were standardized, among them the Akkadian creation story known as the *Enuma Elish,* and the Gilgamesh epic.

Despite this conservative tendency there was considerable change in other aspects of religious belief. At least among the upper classes, a more personalized religion emerged. Individuals appropriated ceremonies that had previously been the preserve of the community at large, and the gods were called upon to pay more attention to the plight of the individual. Along with the rise of this individualized religion there was a corresponding weakening of the old social structures and of men's faith in the dependability of the gods. There was a feeling that it was no longer sufficient to view disasters as mere happenings or accidents over which heaven had no control. Men began to protest the injustice of the gods who seemed to permit the evil to prosper and the good to suffer. These views were expressed in a number of literary works, the best known of which is the *Ludlul bel Nemequi,* "I will praise the Lord of Wisdom," a kind of Babylonian Book of Job. In this poem the writer protests that he has been abandoned by his personal gods and inflicted with all kinds of suffering:

My god has forsaken me and disappeared,
My goddess has failed me and keeps at a distance.
The benevolent angel who [walked] beside [me] has departred,

My protecting spirit has taken to flight, and is seeking someone else.
My strength is gone; my appearance has become gloomy . . . [1.43–47][1]

My flesh is flaccid, and my blood has ebbed away.
My bones have come apart, and are covered [only] with my skin.
My tissues are inflamed . . .
I take to a bed of bondage; going out is a pain;
My house has become my prison . . .
All day long the tormentor torments [me],
Nor at night does he let me relax for a minute [2.92–96, 102–103][2]

These afflictions have come upon him despite close attention to religious observances:

For myself, I gave attention to supplication and prayer:
To me prayer was discretion, sacrifice my rule.
The day for reverencing the god was a joy to my heart;
The day of the goddess's procession was profit and gain to me.
The king's prayer—that was my joy,
And the accompanying music became a delight for me.
I instructed my land to keep the god's rites,
And provoked my people to value the goddess's name. [2.23–30][3]

Why the gods acted in this mysterious fashion is beyond the sufferer's understanding. His solution to the problem is akin to one of those offered by Job: Man is too insignificant and too limited to know the will of the gods:

I wish I knew that these things [his religious observances] were pleasing to one's god!
What is proper [pleasing] to oneself is an offense to one's god,
What in one's own heart seems despicable is proper [pleasing] to one's god.
Who knows the will of the gods in heaven?
Who understands the plans of the underworld gods?
Where have mortals learnt the way of a god? [2.34–38][4]

Men's views are circumscribed by their brief lives and their constantly changing emotional states:

He who was alive yesterday is dead today.
For a minute he was dejected, suddenly he is exuberant.

[1]W. G. Lambert, trans., *Babylonian Wisdom Literature* (© Oxford University Press, 1960): by permission of Oxford University Press.

[2]Lambert, *Babylonian Wisdom Literature* (©Oxford University Press, 1960): by permission of Oxford University Press.

[3]Lambert, *Babylonian Wisdom Literature* (©Oxford University Press, 1960): by permission of Oxford University Press.

[4]Lambert, *Babylonian Wisdom Literature* (©Oxford University Press, 1960): by permission of Oxford University Press.

One moment people are singing in exaltation,
Another they groan like professional mourners . . .
When starving they become like corpses,
When replete they vie with their gods.
In prosperity they speak of scaling heaven,
Under adversity they complain of going down to hell. [2.39–47][5]

As had happened after the collapse of the central authority of Hammurabi's Babylon, the temples became refuge places and centers of social, economic, and cultural life during the period of the Aramaean invasions in the tenth and ninth centuries B.C. When Assyrian power reasserted itself and brought the temples under tight administrative and financial control they nevertheless managed to retain much of their former prominence. The Assyrian kings relied on them to a considerable extent to maintain order in the southern portions of Mesopotamia. Their successors, the Neo-Babylonian Chaldaeans, committed themselves to a full program of religious revival and the temples of Mesopotamia experienced a renaissance. Sanctuaries were rebuilt, ancient rituals restored, and much emphasis given to ceremonial display. Many of the old cities of Sumer—among them Uruk, Ur, and Sippar—once more became centers of religious importance, but it was Babylon itself that was the recipient of the greatest attention of the kings. When the Greek historian Herodotus saw it around 460 B.C. he was astonished by its size and proclaimed that "it surpassed the splendor of any city in the known world" [1.178].

At the center of Babylonian religious life was the great Esagila temple, a complex of large buildings and courtyards built to honor Marduk, the tutelary deity of Babylon. All the kings had bestowed their favors on it but most of all Nebuchadrezzar:

> Silver, gold, costly precious stones, bronze, wood from Magan, everything that is expensive, glittering abundance, the products of the mountains, the treasures of the seas . . .[6]

Here at Babylon the New Year's festival, which annually reenacted the great cosmic struggle between the forces of chaos and order, was celebrated. During the first eight days Marduk, who was believed to be dead and held captive in the underworld, was mourned and rituals enacted to secure his return to earth. Among these was the recitation of the creation epic, the *Enuma Elish,* which described in graphic detail the original struggle between Marduk and the demons of disorder. On the eighth day Marduk was declared to be alive once again and was joyously reinstalled in his temple, there to preside over the ongoing life of the city and the state.

[5]Lambert, *Babylonian Wisdom Literature* (©Oxford University Press, 1960): by permission of Oxford University Press.

[6]Georges Roux, *Ancient Iraq* (Harmondsworth: Penguin Books Ltd., 1966), p. 359. By permission of George Allen and Unwin Ltd.

The process of urbanization, which had begun millennia earlier in Sumer and at times seemed on the verge of disappearing, was by 1000 B.C. firmly established throughout the Near East. There was no longer any danger that the collapse of any particular ruling regime would threaten it with extinction. Once the disturbances of the end of the second millennium had died down, the old cities revived and new ones sprang up all around the periphery of Mesopotamia. In Syria, Damascus became a major center of trade between Babylon and the west; along the Phoenician coast a string of cities including Sidon, Byblos, and Tyre introduced the urban style of life to the Mediterranean world. In the west, on the fringe of the Aegean, Sardis, the capital of Lydia, became a prominent center; to the south Palestine was studded with small, thriving cities.

The cosmopolitan tendencies of the times were accelerated by Assyrian domination of the Near East from the ninth century onward and the normal barriers of distance, culture, language, and religion were gradually broken down by their relentless energies. Great roads were built, facilitating the movement of both armies and trade. Willingly or otherwise whole groups of people were transferred from one end of the empire to the other. The easily learned language of the Aramaeans (Aramaic) became the *lingua franca* of the whole region. The introduction of the alphabet made obsolete the old and impossibly difficult writing systems of classical Mesopotamia.

Despite their calculated acts of frightfulness in war the Assyrian kings pursued culture with an insatiable curiosity and made significant contributions to the advancement of the arts. Paintings and friezes, "the greatest and most original achievement of the Assyrians,"[7] decorated their palaces. In an unusual departure from tradition the Assyrian kings appeared humanized, in conventional scenes of daily life, rather than as the larger than life-size figures of the Egyptian pharaoh. Assyrian scribes were sent all over Mesopotamia to gather inscriptions and information about the ancient civilizations of Akkad and Sumer:

> When you receive this letter take with you these three men . . . and the learned men of the city of Barsippa, and seek out all the tablets, all those that are in their houses and all those deposited in the temple Ezida. . . . Hunt for the valuable tablets which are in your archives and which do not exist in Assyria and send them to me [Ashurbanipal].[8]

Under the Assyrians and their Neo-Babylonian successors, Mesopotamian scholars reached new heights of learning. Philological studies continued in

[7]H. Frankfort, *The Art and Architecture of the Ancient Orient* (Harmondsworth: Penguin Books Ltd., 1954), p. 84.

[8]E. Chiera, *They Wrote on Clay* (Chicago: University of Chicago Press, 1938), p. 174. Copyright by the University of Chicago Press.

the classical Sumerian and Akkadian languages and the endless memorization of vocabulary and technical terms in those tongues led to the organization of knowledge in the form of lists. Great encyclopedias of information about plants, animals, and minerals as well as geographical, medical, and astronomical observations and historical events were assembled in this fashion. Derogatorily, Mesopotamian science has been referred to as a "science of lists."

The most significant advances were made in mathematics and astronomy. The Babylonians worked on hypothetical examples, not just the practical solution of mathematical problems connected with construction, logistics, and the like. They knew how to take square and cube roots and used place-value notation. Algebraic, as well as arithmetic methods, were employed to solve problems. The Babylonians' astronomical observations, encouraged by practical religious and administrative needs, were the most accurate in the ancient world and made a vital contribution to Greek theoretical astronomical advances in the Hellenistic period.

The great days of Mesopotamia were numbered, however. Under the Persians and their successors the Greeks, Babylon became just one province in an enormous, cosmopolitan empire stretching from the Aegean to India and from the Sudan to southern Russia. Trade routes bypassed it and hordes of foreigners, bringing with them different cultures, settled in its midst. Weighted down with an increasingly irrelevant literature in an archaic script Mesopotamian culture slowly stagnated. Having lost its political independence, Mesopotamia progressively lost its cultural identity also, and was absorbed into the larger, surrounding civilization.

RELIGION AND CULTURE IN EGYPT

During the Old and Middle Kingdoms the geographic isolation and cultural precocity of Egypt allowed it to maintain an attitude of smug superiority toward the outside world. Asiatics were thought of as being "miserable," inhabiting lands cursed by quarrelsome and unsettled populations, while Egyptians lived in serenity, blessed by the gods and ruled by a god-king. This complacency was shattered, however, when the well-armed Hyksos overwhelmed the land in the sixteenth century and ruled it as a conquered province from armed camps in the north. Of necessity Egypt had to come to grips, first, with its most immediate enemies, the Hyksos, and then with the influences of the empire it created to protect itself from future invaders.

The maintenance of an empire that saw Egyptian fighting forces located deep in the Sudan and as far north as Syria brought into existence new classes of imperial bureaucrats and army officers. Opportunities for advancement and the necessity of having a standing army in distant places meant that Egyptians were placed in lasting contact with foreigners and in turn large numbers of outsiders were introduced into Egypt itself. With them came new cultural influences, and pressures to break away from the rigidities and peculiarities of Egypt's ancient social and cultural system. To the new administrators, merchants, and army officers who now came to exercise more and more power, Egyptian customs must have seemed oppressively archaic and parochial.

As commander of what had quickly become an army composed mostly of foreigners and a bureaucracy dominated by new men, the pharaoh was particularly susceptible to these alien influences. As early as the first great empire builder, Tuthmosis III, there were indications of a breakaway from tradition. In art the familiar cubistic rigidity of Egyptian portraits began to give way to a new fluidity of movement. Simplicity and economy were progressively overshadowed by overdecoration and monumentality. In religious thought there was a tendency toward blending Egyptian and foreign gods. Since most of the principal divinities of Egypt were cosmic forces anyway this could be accomplished relatively easily. Thus Re the sun god came to be identified with Shamash, and Seth with the Canaanite Baal. Although innocuous on the surface, these tendencies spelled danger for the highly integrated religious system of Egypt where the position of the pharaoh and his brother gods was unique and could not tolerate identification with the deities of other lands without suffering dilution of power. There were other threats to the delicately poised Egyptian system. The material success of the empire meant reward and enrichment for those agencies responsible for Egypt's success abroad. The army, for one, showed increasing signs of independence and the enormous wealth and prestige of the priesthood of Amon-Re also constituted a dangerous development. Still, Egyptians had always lived with contradictions and would undoubtedly have learned to cope with the new influences had they not been brought to the point of confrontation by the previously mentioned policies of the eccentric pharaoh Amenophis IV.

A religious visionary, Amenophis espoused the worship of the Aten, the sun disk, and pushed to one side the veneration of the other gods. In particular he waged a venomous crusade against the powerful Amon-Re of Thebes. Stonecutters were sent out to obliterate the hated god's name and the pharaoh changed his own title to Akhenaten, "He who is serviceable to Aten," in the belief that the elimination of Amon's name would cripple his power. At his new capital at Amarna, far from Thebes, Aten was worshipped in open, sun-filled courts, unlike the dark recesses of the temples where the image of Amon, the Hidden One, was located. It was not, however, in Egyptian religious tradition but in its art and letters that Atenism had its most lasting influence.

A dominant motif of the new movement, especially in its artistic ramifications, was the emphasis given to *ma'at,* the ancient Egyptian concept of truth. In place of the traditional stiff, eternally young pharaoh, Akhenaten was portrayed with sloping shoulders, protruding stomach, and an extraordinarily elongated head. Others in his retinue are depicted similarly and unusual prominence was given to family scenes and to the women of the pharaoh's household. The Amarna period was, in fact, one of the two or three times in Egyptian history

Unidentified royal couple from Amarna. Possibly Akhenaten's son-in-law Semenkhkara and his daughter Meritaten.

when women exercised considerable influence on the course of political events In time the exaggerated realism was tempered and a fluid naturalism remained influential in Egyptian art thereafter. Atenism had its effect on literature also introducing a new flexibility that is reflected in the joyous celebration of nature in the well-known *Hymn to Aten:*

> How efficient are your designs,
> Lord of eternity . . .
> Your rays give suck to every field:
> when you rise they live,
> and they grow for you.
> You have made the seasons
> to bring into being all you have made:
> the Winter to cool them,
> the Heat that you may be felt . . .
> Yet you are alone,
> rising in your manifestations as the Living Aten:
> appearing, glistening, being afar, coming close;
> you make millions of transformations of yourself.
> Towns, harbors, fields, roadways, waterways:
> every eye beholds you upon them,
> for you are the Aten of the daytime on the face of the earth. [9–11][9]

Language and literature were encouraged to reflect the spoken tongue and foreign words and colloquialisms were permitted to enter into official, secular documents although the classical language remained dominant in formal

[9]William Kelly Simpson, ed., *The Literature of Ancient Egypt* (New Haven and London: Yale University Press, 1973), pp. 293–94.

religious pronouncements. Thus did Akhenaten's "truth" have lasting influence on Egyptian art and culture.

At the heart of the Atenist revolution lay the interpretation of the pharaoh's position in the sacred state of Egypt. Was he a god-king who ruled the state by his word directly or was he merely the channel through which the divine guidance came? By accepting the cooperation of the priesthood of Amon and the general tendencies of the empire, Akhenaten's immediate predecessors had tacitly accepted the second position. Consciously or not they recognized the existence of a new Egypt with a number of diversified centers of power in the bureaucracy, the army, and the priesthoods. By espousing his beliefs in Aten the new pharaoh attempted, in effect, to return to the old pattern of rule by a god-king whom all Egypt worshipped. Yet, despite these clearly defined tendencies there were contradictions in Akhenaten's reforms. His new religion was entirely personal, limited to him and those immediately connected with him. It was not for the population at large. If the major gods of Egypt had always been somewhat distant and unapproachable, Aten was no exception.

At the same time, Akhenaten's emphasis on *ma'at* had led to his humanization. Instead of an austere triumphant king he now appeared as an affectionate father playing with his children or conversing with his wife. These contradictions did nothing to heal the schism within the ruling establishment, a schism caused by Akhenaten's assault on the power of Amon and his supporters, the old landed aristocracy and ruling elite of Egypt. Together, these two groups brought down the new regime and put an end to both its novelties and its anachronisms. Egypt resumed where it had left off before the explosive rise of Akhenaten, and the coalition of old and new, of the army, the bureaucracy, and the preisthood of Amon, was renewed. Egypt's empire was briefly reestablished until widespread disturbances in the Mediterranean around 1200 and thereafter led to its final dissolution and the permanent withdrawal of Egypt within its own boundaries. From this time onward Egypt turned progressively inward and looked to its past for sustenance. Artistic models of the Old Kingdom were consciously imitated and more personal styles of piety became prevalent, emphasizing resignation and acceptance. Silent submission rather than self-assertion was encouraged and the individual was urged to be circumspect in his dealings with others, as we see in the "Instructions of Amenemope":

Do not get into a quarrel with the argumentative man
  Nor incite him with words;
Proceed cautiously before an opponent,
  And give way to an adversary;
Sleep on it before speaking,
  For a storm come forth like fire in hay is
The hot-headed man in his appointed time. [5.10][10]

[10]Ibid., pp. 245–46.

On the other hand life should be enjoyed; a man could not take his possessions with him to the next world, so says the "Song of the Harper":

> Place myrrh upon your head,
> Clothe yourself in fine linen. . .
> Increase your beauty,
> And let not your mind tire.
> Follow your desire and what is good:
> Acquire your possessions on earth.
> Do not control your passion . . .
> Make holiday,
> But tire yourself not with it.
> Remember: it is not given to man to take his goods with him.
> No one goes away and then comes back.[11]

RELIGION AND CULTURE IN ISRAEL

The earliest stages of Hebrew religious history are set against a background o tribal organization and seminomadic life. Whereas the Egyptians and Meso- potamians looked back to heroic kings and divine founders, the Israelite celebrated their humble origins in the cultic refrain, "A wandering Aramaear was my father," and regarded their experiences in the desert of Sinai as a golder age of youth and innocence: "When Israel was a child," declared the prophe Hosea, "I came to love him and from Egypt I called him."[12] Nomadic ideals o brotherhood, hospitality and asylum, and the system of the vendetta profoundl influenced the development of religion, law, and culture in Israel, preventin it from evolving along the same lines as those of its highly organized neighbors Yahweh, the god the Israelites encountered in the desert, had no need of th apparatus of a state to fulfill his promises to his people or to communicate wit them.

The first great challenge experienced by the newly arrived Israelites wa one of the very survival of the religion of Moses in the seductive atmosphere o Canaan. The austere, intolerant Yahweh of the desert was utterly at odds wit the earthy, heavily sexual deities of the new land. In addition, much of th Israelites' nomadic experience was irrelevant to the needs of a settled existence They knew little of the cultivation of the soil and stood in awe of the myster that brought forth life from the earth year after year. In an environment wher the effectiveness of purely magical techniques of agriculture could not be readil disentangled from secular ones, the Israelites were strongly tempted to take ove the entire apparatus of cultivation, religious and secular together. To some exten they did so and by a gradual process they reinterpreted the Canaanite agri

[11]Ibid., p. 307.

[12]Hos. 11:1. This and all subsequent biblical quotations in this chapter are from J. M. P. Smith anc others, *The Complete Bible: An American Translation* (Chicago: University of Chicago Press 1939). Copyright 1927 by the University of Chicago Press.

cultural festivals, giving them places in the traditional history of Yahweh and adapting the Canaanite calendar to their own particular needs. Similarly the municipal codes of Palestine became models for their imitation, though the egalitarian traditions of brotherhood and the covenant with Yahweh affected all such developments.

The second great challenge came when the community of Yahweh was radically transformed by the work of the early kings. From a loosely organized coalition of tribes participating in a cultic league, Israel emerged by the middle of the tenth century as one of the most powerful states in the Near East, with borders reaching from Egypt's frontier to Syria. Imitating its neighbors, Israel employed professional soldiers and administrators. In place of the independent clans and tribes making their own decisions, it was the court at Jerusalem that imposed taxes, declared wars, and made treaties. Yet no divine sanction accompanied the selection of Jerusalem. It was "David's city," an old Canaanite stronghold he had seized by his own efforts. From exclusive dependence on Yahweh who raised up leaders at moments of national peril, as in the time of the Judges, Israel now came to depend on the chariots and soldiers of the kings. The first task facing the new kingdom was therefore to bring the institutions of the monarchy into accord with the old and the form that this adaptation took led to the development of an enduring, if controversial, tradition in Hebrew religious thought. Yahweh, who in times past made a covenant at Sinai with Moses and the Israelites, now entered into a similar relationship with David and his descendants. David was to become Yahweh's adopted son, whose task it was to shepherd and rule Yahweh's people and to wage his wars. With the bringing of the Ark of the Covenant to Jerusalem and the construction of a temple there, the task was complete: The city became a national sanctuary, a holy place, its foundation celebrated by an annual festival recording the bringing of the Ark to the city.

Although the monarchy of David entered into the national religious tradition, it always remained in tension with the earlier beliefs that emphasized unconditional dependence on Yahweh. David's military census and Solomon's aggrandizement of the state at the expense of the tribes brought about a fierce reaction which found expression in the rise of the prophets, whose origins can be traced to the charismatic leaders of the period of the conquest. At least equally important, however, was the emergence of a powerful cultural movement that gave a lasting form to the oral traditions of the past. At some time between 950 and 800 B.C. a number of gifted individuals felt impelled to reflect upon the experiences of the past and bring them into living relationship with the present. Possessing an astonishingly wide vision they tried to make an intelligible whole of the chaotic mass of legends, songs, cultic practices, prayers, sayings, proverbs, and laws that constituted the traditions of the tribes. Some of these elements had already been worked over but there was as yet no comprehensive narrative of the history of the people of Yahweh from their beginnings. It was to this task that the group of writers under David and Solomon turned and to their efforts are due the bulk of the material found in Genesis, Exodus, Numbers, Judges, and

Samuel. Their theme was a great one and with high artistry and keen psychological insight they described the faith and doubt of Abraham, the indulgence of Jacob by his father Isaac, the jealousy of Joseph's brothers, the mordant and depressed Saul, and David in all his greatness and weakness. In some instances they employed a variety of advanced literary techniques, such as the placing of speeches in the mouths of the protagonists, whereas at other times the simplicity of the original accounts were allowed to stand unadorned. To this day some of the stories in Genesis and the tale known as the Succession Document (2 Sam. 9–20; 1 Kings 1–2) which tells of David's troubles with his family and the revolt of Absalom stand as masterpieces of historical narration.

The Prophets

Although the narrative writers tackled the problems of their times from the viewpoint of a sophisticated intellectual class interested in connecting the past with the present, the prophets took a more direct approach and assaulted the evils of the day by means of sermons and symbolic actions. Unlike priests and kings whose offices were hereditary and whose tasks were prescribed for them by rules and precedents, the prophets claimed to convey messages directly from God himself. Some wrote or at least had their followers record their comments, while others, such as Elijah and Elisha, did not write, although some of their sayings and pronouncements have survived.

Amos, the first of the great writing prophets, made his appearance in the northern kingdom in the eighth century, some time before its destruction by the Assyrians. Amos spoke at a time when Israel had just defeated Damascus, but for the prophet the victory was no assurance of continued peaceful occupation of the land. It was, rather, a prelude to disaster. The people had been unfaithful to the demands of the covenant on which the possession of the land depended and had neglected the weak and the poor, while thronging to worship God by sacrifices and gifts at the various shrines throughout the kingdom:

> I hate, I spurn your feasts,
> And I take no pleasure in your festal gatherings . . .
> Take away from me the noise of your songs,
> And to the melody of your lyres I will not listen.
> But let justice roll down like waters,
> And righteousness like a perennial stream.[13]
>
> Hear this, you who trample upon the needy,
> And would bring the poor of the land to an end . . .
> Making the ephah small and the price great,
> And falsifying the scales.[14]

[13]Amos 5:21–24.

[14]Amos 8:4–5.

Hosea also preached in the northern kingdom but somewhat closer to the time of its destruction than did Amos. His message was essentially the same as that of his predecessor, although his stress was not on social negligence so much as the cult of idols and the political errors that this had led Israel to commit. His uniqueness consists in his contribution of a new terminology to describe Israel's failure. He speaks of his nation's sin as that of a wife unfaithful to her true husband (God) and who runs instead after lovers (idols). The relationship established between God and Israel during the days of the Exodus is like a marriage contract, but Israel had become unfaithful and its piety ephemeral:

> What shall I do with you, O Ephraim?
> What shall I do with you, O Judah?
> For your piety is like a morning cloud,
> Or like the dew that leaves early.[15]

However, Yahweh so loves Israel that he will take her back to himself again:

> How can I give you up, O Ephraim!
> How can I surrender you, O Israel!
> How can I treat you like Admah!
> My mind turns against me . . .
>
> I will not carry out my fierce anger;
> Nor will I again destroy Ephraim;
> For I am God and not man.[16]
>
> I will heal their backsliding;
> I will love them voluntarily.[17]

In typical prophetic fashion Hosea made his point by way of symbolic action by actually taking a prostitute as a wife and loving her despite her infidelities.

The greatest prophet of the eighth century was Isaiah (Isa. 1–40). As in Hosea the basic problem is seen as the lack of loving closeness (knowledge in the biblical sense) to God among the people. Self-satisfied and smug they pursue their own ways without attention to the terms of the covenant:

> Woe to you who join house to house,
> And add field to field,
> Till there is no more room,
> And you are left to dwell alone
> In the midst of the land![18]

He sees Assyria as the instrument of God's judgment on Israel but one that will itself be disciplined after fulfilling God's purposes. However darkly he paints

[15]Hos. 6:4.
[16]Hos. 11:8–9.
[17]Hos. 14:4.
[18]Isa. 5:8.

the picture Isaiah offers hope for the future and predicts a glorious kingdom in which a king rules who will sway the hearts of men by love rather than by force or fear.

The Prophets and Writers of the Seventh Century and Following

Although the eighth century closed with the destruction of the northern kingdom and the deportation of many of its inhabitants, the bulk of its theological traditions and its literature passed into the possession of Judah. Among these were the traditions regarding the ancient covenant renewal ceremony held at the sanctuary at Shechem. Here a particular viewpoint of the history of Israel had been given special preeminence and eventually found its way into written form. It today constitutes the core of the Book of Deuteronomy. This book in turn came to form the preface or introduction to a panoramic history of Israel from the occupation of the land to the fall of Jerusalem in 587 B.C., composed by an anonymous writer of the sixth century, usually referred to as the *Deuteronomist historian (D).*

This interpretation of Israelite history is the most thoroughgoing in the Bible and one of the most impressive intellectual feats of the ancient world. It attempts to account for the fall of both the northern and the southern kingdoms in terms of the Sinai covenant, which both of them failed to observe. Out of all the nations, God had chosen Israel to be his special possession, not because of any merit on its part but solely because he loved it:

> It was not because you were the greatest of all peoples that the Lord set his heart on you and chose you (for you were the smallest of all peoples), but it was because the Lord loved you, and would keep the oath that he swore to your fathers, that the Lord brought you out by a strong hand and rescued you from a state of slavery, from the power of Pharaoh, king of Egypt. Be assured, then, that the Lord your God is God, a trustworthy God, who to a thousand generations keeps loving faith with those that love him. . . .[19]

He could not however, be served with divided loyalty:

> Listen, O Israel; the Lord is our God, the Lord alone; so you must love the Lord your God with all your mind and all your heart and all your strength.[20]

The promise of the land was a conditioned promise to be fulfilled only if Israel was faithful to the covenant. For the Deuteronomist historian the entire period

[19]Deut. 7:7–9.

[20]Deut. 6:4–5.

The high demands of Yahweh collide with the hard realities of Near Eastern politics: King Jehu of Israel does obeisance to Shalmaneser III of Assyria.

between the occupation of the land and the fall of the kingdoms was an endless cycle of infidelity. With each failure to live up to the terms of the covenant came a dissolution of the tribes or a failure of the monarchy. Worship of idols is viewed as inherently divisive and destructive. King after king "did evil in the sight of the Lord," with the result that the purpose for which the land was given was annulled. Because kings and people were unfaithful God used the events of international history to punish his people. The failure was not God's but the people's and especially the kings', who were expected to live up to the high standards of an idealized Davidic kingship. Both the covenant at Sinai that Yahweh made with Israel as a whole and the covenant between him and the dynasty of David had been repeatedly broken. As a result, both northern and southern kingdoms were allowed to fall prey to their enemies.

The capture of Jerusalem and the dissolution of the Davidic state had a profound effect on the development of the next round of literary compositions that found their way into the Old Testament, Deutero or Second Isaiah (Isa. 40–66), and the anonymous compilation known as the Pentateuch (the first five books of the Bible). Second Isaiah has some of the most elevated and beautiful language of the Old Testament. This anonymous prophet addressed himself to the question of the restoration of Israel and what form it was to take. Although the Deuteronomist historian hinted at a solution in the form of a renewed monarchy under a king after the likeness of David, Second Isaiah rejected this and said that God has no need of temples or kingdoms but is more concerned with the spirit of men:

> Thus says the Lord.
> "The heavens are my throne,
> And the earth is my footstool;
> What manner of house, then would you build for me,
> What manner of place as my residence?
> My hand made all these things,
> And all these things are mine," is the oracle of the Lord
> "Yet to this man will I have regard—
> The one who is humble and contrite in spirit,
> And who trembles at my word.[21]

What counted was not God's material presence but his spiritual presence with men. God is fettered by neither temple nor people; his power rules the world and the course of history:

> I am the Lord, and there is no other;
> Beside me there is no God.
> I will gird you, though you knew me not,
> That men may know, from the east
> And from the west, that beside me there is none.
> I am the Lord, and there is no other—
> Who forms light and creates darkness,
> Who makes weal, and creates woe—[22]

Among those deported to Babylon at the time of the destruction of Jerusalem were the priests who had attended to the temple and conducted its rituals. This group, in particular, must have felt the impact of the end of the regular cult practices and they responded characteristically. Faced with the problem of ensuring that the generation now growing up in Babylon would not lose contact with the viewpoint, laws, and customs of the nation and be swallowed up like the deportees of the northern kingdom, the Jerusalem priests made an effort to bring all the ancient traditions together into a comprehensive whole. Their work of compiling and editing can be traced in the first four books of the Old Testament, Genesis, Exodus, Leviticus, and Numbers, and is referred to as P or the Priestly History. Convinced that the destructions of 721 and 587 B.C. came as a result of the failure of the people to know and obey the law, the

[21]Isa. 66:1–2.

[22]Isa. 45:5–7.

priests resolved that this would never happen again. Taking the accounts of the older writers, they inserted new materials concerning cult practices and rituals and added a fresh editorial viewpoint. This was the belief that the God who in the beginning had called Abraham from the midst of the sinful people of Mesopotamia and snatched his descendants from Egypt would once more repeat the miracle for them. It was they who composed or appended the story of creation to Genesis (1:1–2:3) and organized the material of the early history of men from the time of Adam to Abraham, demonstrating artistically the care of God for Israel's ancestors and in particular his power as contrasted with the nonexistent power of the deities of other nations. Their aim was to prove through history that despite appearances God always cared for his people. Thus, although Jerusalem had been destroyed by the Babylonians their gods were still as nothing compared to Yahweh. Unlike the cosmological myths of the nations where the gods struggled against the forces of chaos, Yahweh was depicted as above and beyond these battles. He stood outside the forces of nature and was neither one of them nor their sum total. For the composers of the Priestly History the work of creation was an orderly process in which God systematically and calmly brought into being the whole universe. There was no danger of the creating deity or of the world itself falling victim to the forces of chaos, as in the pagan myths. Furthermore, it was this same God who continued to care for his people even in their apparently desperate circumstances, surrounded and about to be engulfed by the materially and culturally powerful peoples of Mesopotamia.

Post-exilic Israel was radically different from the Israel that preceded it. Gone was the structure of the state, the kings, their administrators, their staffs, and their armies. Politically Israel was reduced to the role of an insignificant temple-state in the huge empire of the Persians and later of the Greeks, who succeeded the Persians. Nor were the inhabitants of this state any longer identical with the people that claimed descent from Abraham. There were large communities in Egypt and Babylon and elsewhere, and the needs of this new people of Yahweh were altogether different from those of the Israel of the past. More and more it was the observance of the Mosaic law that determined who belonged to the community and who did not. What constituted this law was therefore of foremost importance in the period after the exile and it was with the task of defining it that the handful of individuals we know of in the early post-exilic period struggled. Ezra and Nehemiah were major figures in the fifth century, and not long after 400 B.C. Chronicles was written to assure the new community that it was really the heir of all that had gone before and that there was indeed a direct connection between the old and the new temples. Wisdom literature, an ancient part of the heritage, was given greater emphasis. The Book of Job was composed in post-exilic times, as was Proverbs. The psalms were collected, along with the sayings of the prophets, and by the end of the second century B.C. all the books of the Old Testament, with the exception of Daniel and possibly Esther, were in existence. As a consequence, the post-exilic Israelites, or Jews as they began to be known, came into the possession of an extraordinarily comprehensive and well-developed body of literature, laws, history, and cultic material, which more and more defined the character of religious belief rather than the cultic community centered around the temple at Jerusalem. Translations were made into Greek and Aramaic and a class of professional interpreters of the traditions—the scribes and the rabbis—came into existence along with a new institution, the synagogue. The transition from a national community limited in time and space to a universal religion transcending both was a slow process and the greatest of the achievements of Israel after the exile.

TWO

THE GREEK WORLD

5

The Beginnings

THE GEOGRAPHICAL SETTING

The homeland of the Greeks presents no easily comprehended landscape of river, irrigated land, and desert such as we have encountered in Mesopotamia and Egypt. It is, rather, a land broken up into an infinity of sharply defined regions by intruding bays and gulfs of the sea and by steep mountain ranges. Landlocked valleys, hills and plains, peninsulas and islands set a pattern of fragmentation that was followed and even surpassed by the political divisions of the Greeks. The sea was everywhere present, and it, rather than the land, formed the center of the Greek world. As Aristophanes, the Athenian playwright, put it, "We sit like frogs around a pond," the pond being the Aegean Sea and the frogs the hundreds of Greek cities that clustered about it.

With the exception of some of the larger inland valleys Greece was not rich in agricultural land. There were no large, well-watered, easily traversed alluvial plains, which might invite exploitation by a highly organized central government. Instead, the multitude of separate enclaves in coast, mountain, and valley led to the concentration of Greek energies on the development of local communities and stimulated their individual creativity.

In the larger context of the Mediterranean and especially in regard to the older civilizations of the Near East, Greece and the Aegean formed a barbarous fringe area, narrow in scope and poor in natural resources. Yet Greece, like so many other borderland regions, benefited from its position on the rim of the civilized world. Far enough away to escape political domination by the great political powers of the Near East, it was still close enough for a rich cultural and commercial interchange to take place. The first civilization of the Aegean area, that of Minoan Crete, was stimulated by eastern contacts and, at a later date, yet another intrusion of eastern influences contributed to the emergence of the Greeks from their Dark Age and the awakening of their renowned Classical Age.

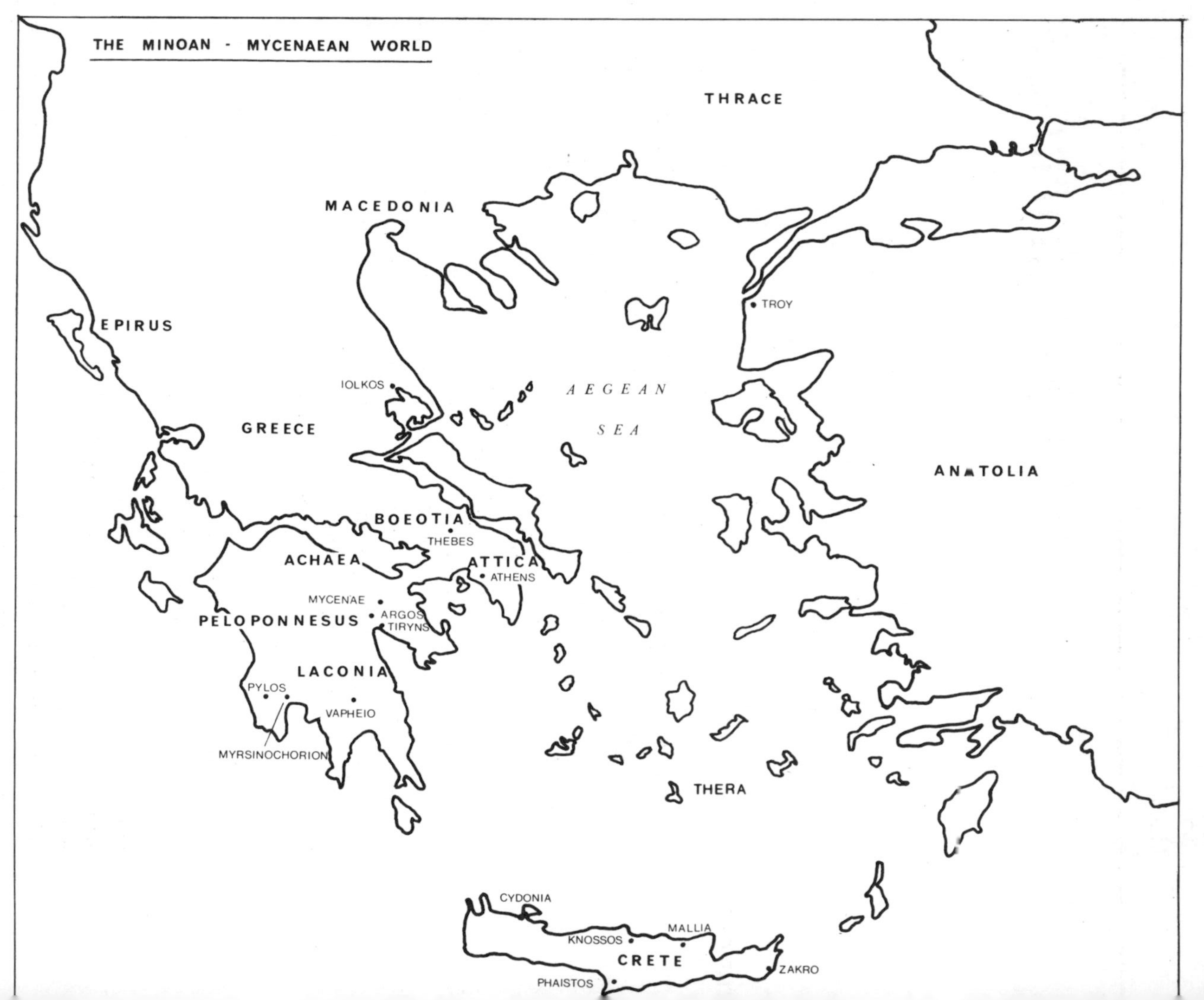
THE MINOAN - MYCENAEAN WORLD
THRACE
MACEDONIA
EPIRUS
TROY
IOLKOS
AEGEAN
SEA
GREECE
ANATOLIA
BOEOTIA
THEBES
ACHAEA
ATTICA
ATHENS
MYCENAE
ARGOS
TIRYNS
PELOPONNESUS
LACONIA
PYLOS
VAPHEIO
MYRSINOCHORION
THERA
CYDONIA
KNOSSOS
MALLIA
CRETE
ZAKRO
PHAISTOS

THE COMING OF THE GREEKS

It is difficult for us not to believe that culturally well-defined groups of people such as the Israelites and the Greeks did not arrive in their homelands en masse, complete with fully developed cultures, languages, and even physical characteristics. Yet even a little reflection on our own national experience makes us aware that except in the most isolated instances, all national or cultural groupings are the product of long evolutionary processes, lasting in some instances over periods of centuries. We do not, therefore, envision the Greeks arriving in the Aegean with preestablished cultures like so many Englishmen or Spaniards descending from their ships in the New World; rather, we see the Greeks as emerging after a long and complex period of development. The problems begin, however, when we attempt to determine when this process of evolution began and when it was completed.

The volume of evidence, both archaeological and linguistic, is enormous and the interpretation of it extremely difficult. Some scholars, in reaction to an earlier tendency to explain all cultural alterations by migrations, have pointed out that major changes in history such as the introduction of Christianity to the Roman Empire and the revival of learning in the Renaissance occurred without any suggestion of invasions or migrations from the outside. They have also stressed the great length of time it takes for languages to develop and in general have argued that we are better off seeking the origins of the Greeks at a very early rather than late date. Some even suggest the first migration of farmers from Anatolia (Asia Minor) in the late Neolithic as an appropriate time. Others are convinced that the only sufficiently well-defined place in the archaeological record for the introduction of something as significant as a new language is considerably later, about 1600 B.C., for example, when the warlike Mycenaeans first made their appearance, or around 1200 B.C., when Mycenaean civilization was violently destroyed. Most scholars take an in-between position, believing that Greek or proto-Greek was certainly spoken in the Aegean area between 2000 and 1500 B.C. and probably earlier, though not before 2500 B.C. They are confident that Greek as a developed language was in existence by at least the middle of the second millennium (1500 B.C.) and had developed into its dialectical forms some 500 years later. This allows for the arrival of the Greeks at either the end of the second phase of the Early Bronze Age (ca. 2300 B.C.) or at least toward the beginning of the Middle Bronze Age (ca. 2000–1900 B.C.). Some think that the interruption of the culture of the eastern Mediterranean around 2300 B.C. was due to the intrusion of the Indo-European-speaking peoples. These scholars associate the arrival of the Greeks with this movement; others see the arrival of the Greeks as a much more gradual process of intrusion by small bands of people over a long period. The majority opinion favors the identification of Mycenaean culture as Greek and the true, though distant, ancestor of classical Greek civilization.

MINOAN-MYCENAEAN CIVILIZATION

In the 1870s great interest in early Greek history was stimulated by the spectacular finds of the amateur archaeologist Heinrich Schliemann at the sites of ancient Troy and Mycenae. This interest was maintained by the discovery in 1900 of a massive palace complex at Knossos on Crete by Sir Arthur Evans. Hundreds of sites have since been excavated in the Aegean and the adjacent Balkan areas, and archaeologists and historians have struggled year after year to place the different finds in some kind of cultural and chronological order. The result has been the slow unfolding of one of the most brilliant of the world's forgotten cultures.

The Minoan Period

Perhaps by way of Anatolia, civilization first made its way to Crete at the beginning of the Early Bronze Age (ca. 2800 B.C.), though there had been a long period of preparation that stretched back into the middle of the Neolithic, at least 1000 years before. The arrival of high civilization in Crete was not, however, accompanied by massive migrations, and the slow process of "Minoanizing" Crete went on peacefully all through the Early Bronze Age. By about 2000 B.C. the civilization of Crete had reached significant heights of technical and artistic achievement, which found its principal expression, if we are to judge from the archaeological remains, in the construction and decoration of palace complexes. There were at least three major complexes—at Knossos, Phaistos, and Mallia—but smaller complexes were probably built in every valley and plain area of Crete; a number of these have already been found.

The palaces were complicated structures consisting of a honeycomb of residential and storage rooms designed in general relationship to a large courtyard. The palaces varied considerably in size; Knossos, for example, covered over three acres, with even more buildings lying outside the palace proper. They were well constructed. The lower courses of the walls consisted of stone and the upper generally of mud brick with timber reinforcements to help resist earthquake shocks, which were common in Crete. Illumination for the inner rooms was provided through light wells, and drainage and water supplies were good. Oil, wine, and grain were stored in huge jars, and more perishable goods, such as clothes, were kept in lead-lined stone chests. Many of the rooms and passageways were decorated with colorful frescoes depicting various aspects of Cretan life. The men appear beardless, wearing codpieces or kilts, and the women have elaborate hair designs and dresses with flounced sleeves and pinched waists. Exquisite garden scenes portray a flourishing plant and animal life. Jewelry was one of the fields in which the Minoan artists excelled; they produced marvels of delicate carvings in ivory, faience, gold and silver, precious and semiprecious stones. Vase painting, especially where marine themes were employed, represents another area where the Minoans were unchallenged masters.

Most of our understanding of Cretan society depends on the interpretation we attach to the functions of the palaces. Writing was present on Crete in pictographic form from the third millennium, but at some time after 1700 B.C. a syllabic script known as Linear A was introduced. It has not been deciphered, but its successor, Linear B, dating from the time of the arrival of the Mycenaean mainlanders (ca. 1450 B.C.), has been identified as Greek. Both were used for the purpose of recording palace transactions and keeping track of inventories of food, clothes, weapons, and the like. Most of the writing perished long ago since it was done on clay tablets, skin, and bark. Only the accidental burning of an archive which baked the tablets hard, has preserved any of them. It is from these rather limited sources that we have to make our inferences about life in the palaces. (More will be said about this in the section dealing with Mycenaean civilization since it is to this period that the translated tablets belong.) In general it is safe to infer that the palaces functioned as regulators of the various commercial, agricultural, and industrial activities that took place in the regions surrounding them. Trained scribes and administrators kept track of and controlled local life, though how closely they did so is hard to tell. The size and wealth of the palaces indicate something more than merely local exploitation of agricultural riches and there appears to have been a substantial volume of overseas trade. Minoan exports consisted of such things as wool, oil, and timber as well as finished goods, including pottery, while raw materials and luxury items were the principal imports. Located on the fringes of the barbarian and civilized worlds, Crete was in an ideal position to act as a trade intermediary. Her merchant and naval fleets must have been significant, and efficient-looking warships make their appearance in the frescoes from the nearby island of Thera.

If the temple-states of the Near East are to be taken as models for Crete we should probably expect to find a close intermingling of religious and civic life. Female deities were common. Predominant among them was the Great Mother Goddess, who is depicted in many forms, including that of a goddess grasping two snakes—the symbols of her divinity—and that of a huntress, the so-called Lady of the Beasts. Trees and pillars were worshipped (in a way reminiscent of Canaanite practice) and the sanctuaries located on the mountain tops suggest the "high places" that the Old Testament prophets attacked so vehemently.

Women—at least of the upper classes—were prominent in Minoan religious and social life. They appeared in processions and at athletic events, and they even participated in the mysterious bull-leaping ceremony. From this and some other scattered evidence it has been inferred that women had some kind of dominant political role—that Crete was a loosely defined matriarchy. There is no evidence for this highly imaginative theory. It is in fact an inference from a now long-outdated anthropological theory that assumed a linear progression from a

Minoan snake-goddess. The numbers of these statues and the prominence of women at social and religious events has contributed to the belief in the existence of a form of matriarchy in ancient Crete.

peaceful, supposedly matriarchal society dominated by female deities to a more warlike patriarchal society in which male gods were supreme. It is nevertheless remarkable that the women of Crete had such prominent social roles, especially in view of the generally depressed position of women in later Greek society.

The Collapse of Minoan Civilization

Between about 1450 and 1350 B.C. this glittering civilization came to a dramatic and sudden end. All the palaces were reduced to rubble and ashes and were never rebuilt. Unfortunately, neither the causes nor the chronology of their destruction allows us to do more than guess at what brought about their catastrophic demise.

The essential points that almost all scholars agree on are these: (1) down to about the middle of the fifteenth century B.C. Crete flourished, but thereafter, within a relatively short time, its exports overseas were eclipsed by those coming from the mainland. (2) Shortly after 1400 B.C., all the palaces lay in ruins. From the evidence provided by the discovery of Linear B at Knossos and more recently at Cydonia in the west of the island, it has been inferred that the Mycenaeans had taken over Crete; the date is usually given as around 1450 B.C. How they arrived on the island, whether peacefully or as invaders, and how much Minoan prosperity was affected by the great natural disaster of the volcanic explosion of the nearby island of Thera are the principal points of disagreement.

One theory has it that the Greeks arrived peacefully at Knossos, perhaps by way of intermarriage among ruling Mycenaean and Minoan dynasties, and from Knossos they ruled the rest of the island with little or no interference. Their principal contribution, in this view, was the adaptation of the syllabic script Linear A to Greek (Linear B) and the introduction of a style of pottery known as Late Minoan II. According to this hypothesis all the palaces, including Knossos, were destroyed at the same time around 1400, probably by mainlanders who had resolved to eliminate the competitive trading power of Crete for good. Although the theory is attractive, the identification of Late Minoan II as Mycenaean is a crucial point that has not been widely admitted. Many scholars favor giving some role in the destruction to the mighty explosion of Thera, 70 miles north of Crete, at some date early in the fifteenth century; they also depict a more warlike arrival of the Greeks. In this explanation Thera was overwhelmed by a tremendous eruption, which showered volcanic debris on the towns of the island, driving their inhabitants overseas; the volcano then exploded with colossal force, sending out clouds of gas and ashes and huge tidal waves. Somehow Knossos and Phaistos escaped severe damage and were rebuilt, but the eastern palaces, including Mallia and Zakro, were overwhelmed. The Minoan fleet would have been particularly susceptible to tidal waves. Even here there is disagreement, some scholars believing that it is more natural to explain the destruction of the eastern palaces as an act of human violence, resulting perhaps from the Greek occupation of Knossos. If in fact the main victim of Thera was the Minoan fleet, this would account for the sudden appearance of the Greeks at the surviving unfortified palaces of Crete, though the reason for the palaces' ultimate demise is still shrouded in mystery.

The Mycenaean Age (ca. 1600–ca. 1150 B.C.)

The Mycenaean Age of Greece lasted over twice as long as the Classical Age of Greek history yet we know more of some years, months, or even days of the latter age than we do of the four and a half centuries of the Mycenaean—in spite of the existence of about 5000 tablets dealing with the period in a language we can translate. Unfortunately, most of them concern a single year in the life of only one mainland palace toward the end of the thirteenth century B.C., and the rest relate to Mycenaean Knossos over two centuries earlier. None refer to what we could call traditional historical events—battles, treaties, invasions, laws, internal struggles for power and the like—and what passes for Mycenaean history is principally a reconstruction of its beginning and end, and an attempt to evoke from the archaeological evidence some idea of the kind of life associated with the different phases of Mycenaean development. If this gives the appearance of being a negligible accomplishment, it is in fact a great achievement, made possible only as a result of one of the most painstaking and intensive archaeological efforts undertaken anywhere.

The first phase of Mycenaean civilization is the Shaft Grave era, which lasted from roughly 1600 to 1500 B.C. It is known principally from the contents o the 5 shaft graves uncovered by Schliemann in 1876 (one more was discovere later in the same grave circle), and the 24 found by Greek archaeologists in 1951 1952. The former were the richer and yielded an incredible trove of golde crowns, diadems, masks, and jewelry as well as hundreds of swords, daggers spearheads, knives, axes, arrowheads, and shields. There were also gold an silver goblets, alabaster and faience vases, rings, combs, disks, silver boxes pieces of amber, and fragments of linen armor. The graves represent about century of use and were periodically opened for new burials.

Except for the graves themselves, which indicate continuous occupation o the site for a long time, there is no evidence for the palaces or dwellings that wen with them. They may be buried under later buildings or have been of such temporary character that they rapidly disappeared and were eventually replace by more permanent structures. The contents of the graves suggest a warlik society engaged in raiding and fighting but also open to foreign contact an especially susceptible to Cretan influences. Although much of the art i specifically Mycenaean with its peculiar interest in violent, narrative scenes an bizarre monsters and animals, the influence of Minoan artists and craftsmen i everywhere apparent. We should probably see early Mycenaean society as fairl typical of the warrior culture that extended over much of Bronze Age Europe but differing because of the close contact between the Mycenaean aristocrat and the high civilization of Crete, which had the effect of ameliorating thei barbarism and allowing them to develop aesthetic tastes of their own.

By the mid-fifteenth century the Mycenaeans were still burying their dea in communal fashion but were now placing them in great beehive-like *tholo* tombs under mounds of earth. We know of over 80 of these tombs, scattere from Thessaly to the Peloponnese but few have been found intact, though thos that have survived are probably a fair indication of what all of them containec Three tombs, Vaphio, Myrsinochorion, and Dendra, supply the bulk of th remains. These include the usual arsenal of weapons, though with the additio of something that had not been found before—a bronze cuirass together wit greaves and a boar-tusk helmet with metal cheek pieces. The Vaphio tom contained a hoard of beautiful gems and the often-reproduced gold drinkin cups.

The tombs themselves are indicative of the growing power and technica ability of the Mycenaeans. One of them, the Treasury of Atreus, dates fron around the end of the *tholos*-tomb period and represents the culmination o Mycenaean architectural ability. Having survived intact for over 3000 years, it i one of the architectural wonders of the world. Its vault, over 40 feet high inside was the largest in the world until the building of the Pantheon by Hadrian a Rome in the second century A.D. Closely fitting blocks of stone form a marvelou corbeled vault and the huge entryway is roofed by blocks weighing over 10(tons. Although the Treasury of Atreus is contemporary with the palace phase o Mycenaean culture, there is again no evidence for palaces and towns during th main period of the *tholos* tombs.

MYCENAEAN PALACES

At some time in the fifteenth century the assimilation of Cretan civilization was complete and around 1400 the Mycenaean world entered its third and most developed phase, the period of the palaces. Simultaneously, in foreign trade the Cretans gave way to the mainlanders as middlemen in the commerce between Europe and the east, and Mycenaean wares began to appear in Egypt, Syria, Phoenicia, and in the west in Sicily and southern Italy. The militaristic baronies of the past now became more like the palaces of Crete—administrative centers attempting, on Minoan lines, to control the commercial, industrial, and agricultural activities of the regions over which they ruled.

We know of five principal palaces: Mycenae, Tiryns, Athens, Thebes, and Pylos. There may, however, be others among the hundreds of known but unexplored sites. None of the main palaces are as large or as elaborate as their Cretan counterparts. Unlike the latter, the typical Mycenaean palace had as its center a great hall or *megaron,* whose focus was a central hearth. It was entered through a wide, columned portico from a courtyard. The same techniques of construction as were used in Crete were also employed on the mainland, though the Mycenaean palaces tended to be a lot darker than those on Crete. They were well drained and had good water supplies. The *megaron* served as a central meeting place where the king could hold court, receive reports, give banquets, and generally conduct public business. Outside the great hall were the residential quarters and storage facilities for wine, oil, grain, textiles, metals, and war materiel. There were workshops for the smiths, masons, potters, chariot builders, wheelwrights, tailors, and textile workers who were essential to the palace's functioning. All were closely supervised by a corps of administrators who were able to write, though handwriting experts have been able to determine that these were not professional scribes but palace administrators who had other functions to perform.

As economic centers the palaces were by no means negligible. One of them, Pylos, controlled the production of 400 smiths in groups of up to 26; at Mycenaean Knossos there were almost 600 textile workers. The smiths at Pylos received exact amounts of metal intended for the manufacture of specific items so that control over production remained exclusively in the hands of the central administrators. This corps of closely supervised specialists provided for the needs of the individual kingdoms as well as for the export market. Thousands of stored pots ready for use or distribution have been found at Pylos and Thebes and the tablets clearly indicate that there was large-scale production of wool on Crete and flax on the mainland, as well as of more common products such as oil, wine, fruits, spices, honey, and livestock. A network of roads, some of which can still be traced, together with their bridges and culverts, played an important role in the Mycenaean economy.

Mycenaean society had at its head a king (or *wanax)* assisted by a number of close officials, the Followers or Companions, evidently drawn from the ranks of the aristocracy. The chief landowners were designated by the title *damos* or

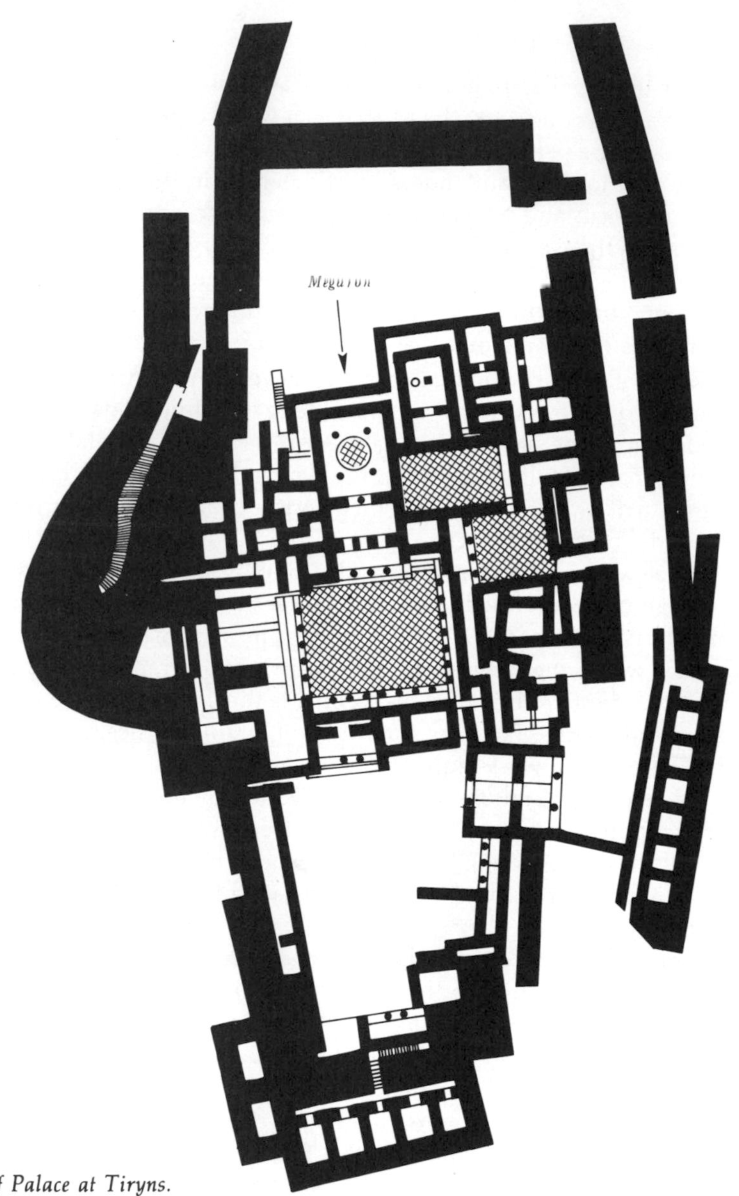

Citadel of Palace at Tiryns.

"people," and seem to have had access to public land. There is, at any rate, a famous tablet recording a legal dispute between the *damos* of Pylos and the priestess Eritha over some property claimed by both. Accurate records of landholdings were kept and there was a fairly complicated system of tenancies and subtenancies. There is plenty of evidence for slaves at the bottom of society and they seem to have played a major role in the industrial and storage activities of the palaces. It is unlikely that a free merchant class existed, since it was at least the intention of the palace to exercise complete control over all commercial activities. Religion had an integral role in the organization of palace activities and the gods were served by a variety of male and female priests and priestesses. Altars were located by the hearths of the great halls and suggest a traditional association of throne, hearth, and altar. Although the Great Mother Goddess was a major deity all over Greece as she was on Crete in the Minoan period, the male deities Zeus, Poseidon, Hermes, Apollo, and Dionysus are strongly represented in the Linear B tablets.

he End of Mycenaean Civilization

About a century or a century and a half after their founding, all the palaces, with the exception of Athens, were attacked and burned. In some instances the surrounding areas were so disastrously affected that major social and economic changes resulted. When the palace at Pylos was destroyed the site was never reoccupied and the population of the region dropped to perhaps 10 percent of what it had been previously. In Boeotia the number of occupied sites dropped from 27 to 3 and in Laconia from 30 to 7. The surviving inhabitants withdrew to more defensible places or fled to other parts of Greece, such as Achaea or Attica, or even overseas. Mycenae itself and Attica recovered, but a second round of disturbances around 1150 finished off the former. By the end of the century Greece had entered a period of economic, social, and technological backwardness. All the arts of high civilization—writing, fresco painting, seal engraving, faience making, ivory carving, even the shaping of stone for building purposes—were lost. The trade network that had united the Aegean area with the Near East collapsed and Greece slipped into a period of isolation broken by only the most limited contacts with the outside world.

The identity of the destroyers of Mycenaean civilization is one of the great mysteries of ancient history. The Greeks of later ages did indeed know something of the calamities of the late thirteenth and twelfth centuries, but not their magnitude. They believed that the sack of Troy was the beginning of a period of troubles for all of Greece, and that when the returning heroes reached their homelands they found them unsettled by intrigues, political unrest, and pressures from outside invasion. Of the wholesale decline from high civilization into barbarism, however, the Greeks knew nothing.

Modern explanations range from many differently identified groups of invaders to hypotheses of catastrophic climatic change resulting in prolonged droughts and social unrest. In all the explanations at least one factor remains

Despite its massive defensive walls, a section of which is shown here, Mycenae was violently assaulted and sacked at some date in the twelfth century B.C.

constant: The latter half of the thirteenth century and the whole of the twelfth were periods of widespread disturbances and destruction, not just in Greece proper but all over the Aegean world and the eastern Mediterranean. About 1220 Egypt was invaded by a coalition of Libyans and northern peoples and in the list of the invaders' names is the suggestive title Akaiwasha or Achaean—the principal title given by Homer to the Mycenaean Greeks at Troy. Thereafter Egypt was constantly on the defensive against outsiders. Around 1200 the empire of the Hittites in Asia Minor was overwhelmed and its capital at Boghazkoi destroyed. Along the coasts of Asia Minor, Syria, and Phoenicia, a whole string of sites including Troy (level VIIa), Tarsus, Mersin, Ugarit, and Sidon went up in flames. We have even a record of the communications between the last king of Ugarit and the king of Cyprus, in which there are complaints about threatening fleets of pirate ships. In the Balkans, "Lausitz" invaders pushed into Albania and Epirus and from there into central Macedonia, sending shock waves of other peoples in front of them. About 1190 Egypt was again invaded by northerners, among whom are named the Pelest (the Philistines) and Denyen (Danaans)—one of the other titles given by Homer to the Mycenaeans. At some point in the midst of these confusing movements of peoples the Mycenaean centers of power came under pressure. We do not know the exact chronology of the fall of the individual palaces, which quite easily could have been the handiwork of different groups of invaders arriving at different times and from different places. There is no evidence of massive migrations of peoples; rather, there are suggestions of continuing unrest and small groups of raiding parties who at times combined to take on major projects such as the invasion of Egypt (or even the destruction of Troy as described by Homer, a joint effort of a number of states). In such a world the rather fragile palace organization of the Mycenaeans, which depended on trade and widespread contacts with the east, would have difficulty in maintaining itself. Its essential imports and exports would have had little chance of getting through to their destinations and the complicated social and organizational arrangements of the palaces would have had difficulty operating under the strained and unsettled conditions of the times.

HE DARK AGE

The darkness of the period following the collapse of Mycenaean civilization was lightened by a number of technological and cultural developments. Athens—which survived and became host to numerous refugees—produced a fine new pottery in the eleventh century called *Protogeometric* and iron, which was known before the invasions, came into more general use for both weapons and agricultural implements. Masses of Greeks fleeing from the collapsing world of the Mycenaeans or mingling with the invaders emigrated to Asia Minor and the offshore islands where they laid the foundations for the rich civilization that was to develop and flourish there for the next 1500 years. Perhaps most important of all, memories of the splendid past survived in the songs of the wandering bards and these eventually culminated in the magnificent epics of Homer composed at the end of the Dark Age or at the beginning of the next age, the Archaic (ca. 750 B.C.).

Heroic poetry is common in many cultures. Such epics as the *Song of Roland* (French) and the *Cattle Raid of Cooley* (Gaelic) recount the deeds of the superhuman heroes of previous times. In a similar way the bards of the Dark Age kept alive the exploits of the long-dead warriors by borrowing from different periods of the past, whether from Mycenaean times, the period of the invasions, or the subsequent Dark Age itself. Over the centuries the traditions developed and certain plots such as the events surrounding the exploits of the Seven Against Thebes, the siege of Troy, and the Heracles legends became canonical and were elaborated in great detail. The art of the poet or rhapsode, as he was known, was demonstrated by his ability to take a well-known tale and reweave it in such a way that, while remaining true to the basic story, he captivated his audience and made them sympathetic to his interpretation of the event. Thus Odysseus wept when he heard the tale of Troy sung, and he congratulated the bard with the words:

> Demodocus, I give you the highest possible praise. Either Zeus' child, the Muse, or Apollo must have been your teacher. For it is remarkable how well you sing the tale of the Achaeans' fate and of all their

> achievements, sufferings and toils. It is almost as though you had been with them yourself or heard the story from one who was.[1]

Although deriving from the bardic tradition the poems of Homer have a complexity and sophistication found in no other heroic poetry. They contrast noticeably with, for example, the raw savagery of the Celtic epics. The Homeric tales are bloody enough, but they are suffused (especially the *Odyssey)* with an elevated and profound view of fate and the relationship of the heroes to their own individual doom.

Yet another debate rages over the identification of the society described by Homer. Is it that of Mycenaean times, and if so, what period in Mycenaean history? Homer talks knowledgeably of boar-tusk helmets and certain types of shields that he himself could not possibly have seen though they are indeed Mycenaean. At the same time he says nothing of the bureaucratic activities of the palaces that the deciphering of Linear B has revealed. Could Homeric society belong to the period of the migrations, about 1150 B.C., and is the story of the destruction of Troy perhaps a memory of that time? Or should we assign both to the more settled period of the Dark Age after 1000 B.C.?

Although due allowance must be made for Homer's ability to transcend the material that came down to him from many different periods in the past, it is still possible to trace in broad outline the type of society whose moral values his poems enshrine. It was a world of small, practically autonomous units, each one economically self-sustaining and inward-looking. Their rulers were chieftains whose principal function was the preservation of the community in the face of constant outside aggression. The chieftains alone had the economic resources to equip themselves with the requisite armor and weapons, and they alone had the leisure time to devote to their mastery. Along with the skills necessary for combat went the cult of physical strength and endurance and the virtues of bravery and high-mindedness. Homeric society was a society in which the individual noble's reputation for courage, generosity, and great feats of battle was so essential to the proper defense of the community that any suggestion of weakness on his part was an immediate threat to his position and an invitation to his neighbors to encroach on his territory. Hence the almost childlike sensitivity to insults and the instantaneous bellicosity, both verbal and physical, that characterize the behavior of the Homeric heroes. When challenged as a weakling, even the usually cool Odysseus retorts violently: "That, sir was an ugly speech, and you must be a fool to have made it."[2] Odysseus goes on to disprove the allegation by a mighty athletic feat. Later generations could not appreciate the significance of the loss of possessions or reputation to a Homeric chieftain; the historian Herodotus sardonically remarks about the abduction of Helen and the outbreak of the Trojan war:

[1]Homer, *The Odyssey,* Tr. E. V. Rieu (Penguin Classics, 1946), p. 135. Copyright © E. V. Rieu, 1946. Reprinted by permission of Penguin Books Ltd.

[2]Ibid., p. 126. Copyright © E. V. Rieu, 1946. Reprinted by permission of Penguin Books Ltd.

Long after Homer, the tradition of reciting selections from his poems became a permanent feature of one of Athens' great festivals, the Panathenaea. Here one of the competing rhapsodes recites his verses.

The Asiatics, when the Greeks ran off with their women, never troubled themselves about the matter; but the Greeks, merely for the sake of a single Spartan girl, collected a massive army, invaded Asia, and destroyed the kingdom of Priam.[3]

(The values of Homeric society are discussed further in Chapter 6, pp. 90–91).

[3]Herodotus 1.4.

The Archaic Age

OUT OF DARKNESS: HISTORICAL DEVELOPMENTS IN GREECE (800–500 B.C.)

New Perspectives

The narrow isolation into which the Aegean world had sunk after the catastrophes of the eleventh century slowly began to give way in the ninth century, when Phoenician merchants made their appearance in the west and renewed contacts that had been broken for 300 years. By the middle of the following century the Greeks had adapted the Phoenician alphabet to their own needs and were themselves trading their painted geometric pots in Syria, as the Mycenaeans had done before them. At the same time, for reasons unknown to us, the population of the Greek world began to grow rapidly. Waves of migrants issued from cities in both Asia Minor and the Greek mainland and settled hundreds of sites in the Black Sea, Adriatic, and western Mediterranean areas. Although the initial impulse to emigrate was population pressure, newly founded colonies introduced commercial motives that tended to stimulate further colonization. The peculiar experiences and individual histories of the different cities also affected patterns of colonization in a way that is today beyond recovery. Thus some cities such as Corinth, Megara, Chalcis, and Eretria on the mainland, and Miletus on the Asia Minor coast, founded dozens of colonies while others, such as Athens, sent out none.

The new contacts extended from one end of the Mediterranean to the other. At Al-Mina at the mouth of the Orontes in Syria a trading center was established. A similar center came into existence at Naucratis, near the capital of the Saite pharaohs in Egypt. In the west, Sicily and southern Italy, even parts of distant Gaul and Spain were heavily settled. The principal colony in the far west, Massilia, was to become the great city of Marseilles, and dozens of other well-known Mediterranean cities owe their founding to the Greek colonial

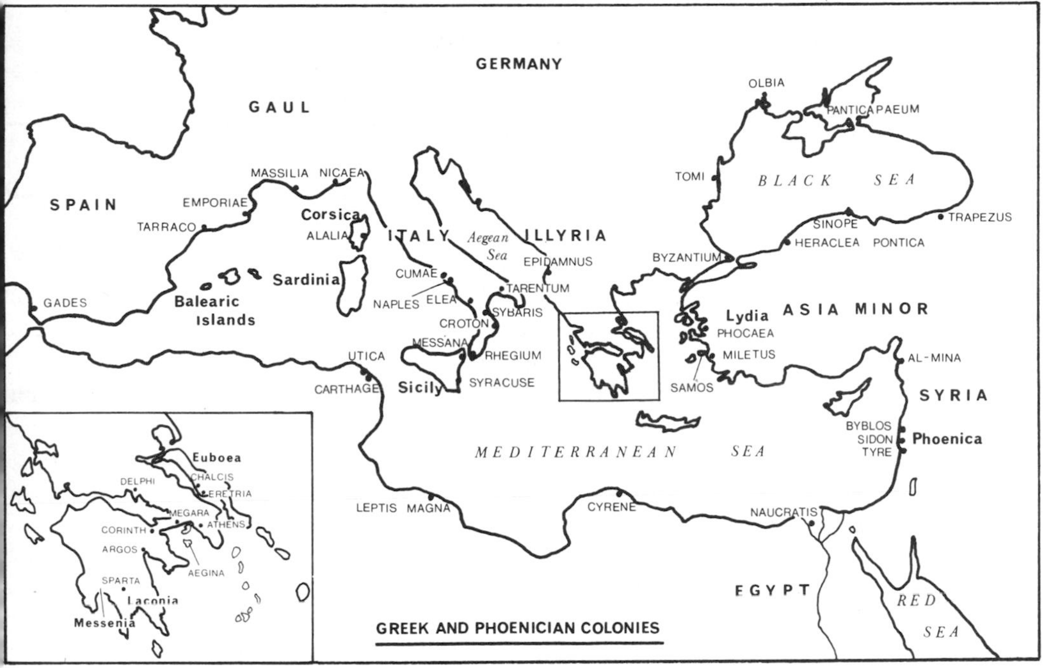

movement of the eighth and following centuries. In Africa outside of Egypt, only Cyrene in Libya was significant and the whole southwest sector of the Mediterranean became the preserve of the Phoenician traders from the coasts of Lebanon. In Asia Minor the Greeks were in close contact with the powerful state of Lydia, which in the mid-seventh century developed coinage, a revolutionary process that guaranteed the weight and purity of pieces of precious metal by stamping the imprint of the state on them.

More important to the Greeks than writing and coinage was the intellectual stimulation they received from these contacts. Emigration had the effect of compelling the Greeks to reflect on the character of their cities and the way in which they operated. Colonies required conscious formulation of laws and institutions. Cities had to be laid out, land assigned, and magistrates selected. Trade and maritime movement broke down the rigidities of the past. Producers of pottery and other goods dealt with the tastes and needs of various peoples. Traders responded to the demands of the marketplace rather than to the dictates of custom. Overseas contacts familiarized the Greeks with innumerable types of governments and customs, from the complex Egyptian and Babylonian models to those of the wild tribesmen of the Russian steppe and the Gallic wilderness. Traveling from place to place, at times living in proximity to these alien cultures, the Greeks began to reflect on the great differences between themselves and their neighbors and on the similarities among themselves. In this comparative process lay the foundations of political theory and ethnography while the more basic needs of the traders stimulated developments in such subjects as geography and navigation. Rising wealth, much of it not based on the possession of land (the old foundation of social position), made inroads into the traditional structures of society. Not just members of the aristocracy but others in the community had an alternative route to power and could escape the old equation, land equals capital equals power. This is not to suggest that a new class of wealthy merchants suddenly came into being, since much of the trading was still on a very narrow, rudimentary basis; but it does indicate that there was now a way out for many previously trapped by the rigid forms of the older societies. The landless poor might join in a colonial venture, as could members of aristocratic houses in decline, or just the footloose. The producers of pottery had new markets, and mercenary service attracted misfits from every walk of life.

The rising wealth of the Greeks provided the basis for another revolution that in turn had a profound impact on political and social developments. This is the so-called *hoplite* (heavy-infantry) revolution. Traditional fighting styles prior to the migrations and economic developments of the eighth century had given emphasis to the role of the aristocrats, who constituted a military elite and bore the brunt of the fighting on behalf of their communities. A great gap existed between the finely equipped aristocrats and their high ideals of courage and the masses of the people, whose contribution to the fighting was negligible. With the rise in wealth and the cheapening of the cost of weaponry because of the introduction of iron, the better-off nonaristocrat classes began to have an increasingly important role in military activities. More and more of them were able to equip themselves with the necessary weapons. When they fought together they soon found that their combined strength was the equal of the better armed and more skilled aristocrats. Although the traditionally equipped nobleman might outduel any number of individual opponents, he was no match for the hoplite phalanx, which was essentially the sum total of the weight of the individual infantrymen together with their armor and weapons. The phalanx, eight men deep and as wide as there were available numbers, was trained to act and maneuver in unison. If it could keep together, especially after the first shock of contact with the opposing force, it was invincible. The basic principle of hoplite warfare was not the use of the thrusting spear or the sword, the standard weapons, but the disruption of the enemy line in the initial charge. If this could be accomplished then the battle was essentially won. Hence steadiness and dependability rather than individual showmanship became the most desirable characteristics of the new kind of military man.

We have no idea how the idea of hoplite warfare came about. Perhaps the initial inspiration came from the east, where the Greeks may have seen the efficient Assyrian army in action; or they may simply have heard of it. A full hoplite panoply from the late eighth century has been found at Argos, and a vase of about the same date shows hoplites and pre-hoplite soldiers in action together. By the seventh century hoplite-style combat had become the predominant form of warfare among the Greeks. Henceforth the safety of the community depended not on the power of single individuals but on the massed strength of the phalanx. What counted was the willingness of like-minded citizens to

Ready for battle, a formidably armed hoplite takes leave of an old man, possibly his father. Heavy infantrymen such as this one constituted the principal strength of both Greek and Roman armies.

cooperate in the battle line, transcending their individual differences and subordinating their personalities to the needs and authority of the city. Numbers and community spirit became more important than individual bravado. Aristocratic display came into collision with the simpler life-style and more mundane concerns of the new hoplite classes.

All these factors—the influence of wealth, stimulation from newly established contacts with the outside world, and the development of hoplite warfare—served as potent solvents on the old social arrangements. From the beginning of the seventh century there were serious disturbances, which ultimately resulted in the formation of a new kind of society in Greece. Each city and region responded to the new forces in its own way. Many turned to tyrants—strong men with mandates for reform from at least some elements of the population—but the processes by which they came to power varied considerably. Generally the hoplites, with the assistance of out-of-power aristocrats, played a crucial role. Such was the case at Corinth in 657 B.C., when the tyrant Cypselus came to power with the backing of the hoplite army and drove out the ruling clan. In this instance the hoplites themselves did not seize power but were content to allow Cypselus, himself of aristocratic origin, to act as power-broker on their behalf. Eventually Cypselus' descendants were driven out and Corinth settled for only a modest alteration of the traditional aristocratic style of government. Almost every Greek state went through some form of upheaval and we know the names of many tyrants who came to power during this period. Unfortunately, with the exception of affairs in Sparta and Athens, not much is known of any of these revolutions. Attention inevitably focuses on the two great states that were to dominate Greece in one way or another throughout most of the remainder of Greek history. The reactions of both Sparta and Athens to the pressures of the times were in their own ways quite radical, and the solutions they arrived at were fundamentally different. But both cities did remain prototypically Greek, and they will serve as generic models of the kinds of changes that took place all over the Hellenic world in the Archaic Age.

Sparta

As population rose during the eighth century and following Sparta sought relief through the acquisition of more agricultural land and through overseas colonization. Only Tarentum in southern Italy was founded, however, and Sparta's principal efforts were directed to acquiring more territory in the Peloponnese. Expansion to the northeast was blocked after the loss of the battle of Hysiae to Argos in 669 B.C., but Sparta had more success in the west. By 600 B.C. neighboring Messenia had been absorbed, thus doubling its own landholdings and firmly establishing its economic basis of power.

The conquest of Messenia required much bitter fighting, and many fundamental social, political, and economic reforms were forced on Sparta as a result. Out of them emerged the much-admired classical constitution, which we know in considerable detail from writers of the fifth and fourth centuries. Although the Spartans themselves believed that their constitution was the work of a single individual, the lawgiver Lycurgus who lived in the tenth or the ninth century, modern opinion is not willing to concede that his purported state-building activity could have taken place much earlier than the seventh century. Even at this date Sparta's achievement was significant: The first consciously formulated constitution in Greek history and Sparta's success in bringing it about stimulated similar movements elsewhere in the Greek-speaking world.

SOCIAL AND POLITICAL ORGANIZATION

Shortly after birth each Spartan infant was examined by the elders of the brotherhood to which the father belonged and if rejected it was abandoned to die. After 6 years the child, whether boy or girl, was enrolled in a troop of his contemporaries to which he was attached until he was 18. Girls continued to live at home but boys were separated from their parents from that point on. During these years the young Spartans were led through an increasingly brutal series of courses designed to inure them to suffering and hardship and break down family relationships. Beds consisted of rushes collected by the boys themselves. They were allowed one cloak per year, and to supplement their meager diet they were encouraged to steal. Education was concentrated on music, dancing, and athletics, and a minimal amount of reading and writing. Girls received a similar athletic and musical education and shocked other Greeks by appearing at public athletic competitions. At 18 the boys began their training for war. Two years later, having passed all the tests, they were voted on for admission to one of the small (15 or so member) clubs, membership in which was the essential mark of manhood. If the vote was not unanimous the candidate was relegated to a second-class rank of citizenship and denied political rights. Those who were admitted received the title of "Equal" *(Homoios).* After this they could marry but could not set up a home for another ten years. The men continued to eat at the clubs until they were 60. Marriage was monogamous and divorce rare, but since the production of perfect physical specimens was an essential part of the system, special arrangements could be made between Spartan couples and the resulting offspring accepted without question by the community. Cuisine and conversation were kept to the simplest possible levels. Neither rhetoric nor philosophy was permitted to be taught and "laconic" brevity was considered an essential feature of all conversations. In order to free Spartans from the drudgery of work each was allotted a plot of land, which was supposed to provide him with the necessary contribution to his club. In theory all plots of land were equal, but in reality it is likely that a great deal of economic variation existed between one Equal and another. Still, the basic philosophy of breaking down family connections and restricting wealth had the effect of creating a generally homogeneous society, and this together with constant communal exercising and training allowed Sparta to build up a hoplite army second to none in Greece.

Besides the two classes of Spartan citizens just mentioned, there were two other classes, the *perioikoi* and the helots. The latter were serfs of the state, whereas the *perioikoi* consisted of those inhabitants of Laconia and Messenia who were allowed to maintain their freedom after their subjugation. Since the Spartans were barred from trade, the *perioikoi* performed most of the community's essential commercial and craft functions. The helots were the most numerous group in the population, constituting 75 percent or more of it. They were tillers of the soil, permanently attached to their particular lot, which they worked on behalf of the individual Spartan to whom it had been assigned. They also worked for themselves, however, since any surplus over and above what they were supposed to supply to their masters belonged to them. Helots could not be sold and did not constitute the private property of any individual Spartan.

Two hereditary kings provided leadership for the Spartan army in the field, and at home exercised political power through their personal prestige, their priesthoods, and their membership in the Council. The Council or Gerousia consisted of 28 men over 60, plus the two kings. It alone could put motions to the Assembly of the Spartans to which only the Equals were admitted. Five annually elected *ephors* (magistrates) conducted day-to-day business and presided over the meetings of the Assembly. The Gerousia was once thought to be the most important policymaking body in Sparta, but it has recently been demonstrated that the Assembly itself regularly made the most significant decisions. Outside Lacedaemonia, as the combined territories of Laconia and Messenia were called, Sparta exercised its power through the Peloponnesian League. This organization brought together most of the states of the Peloponnese in a protective alliance and met periodically to discuss issues of communal importance. Although there was an important provision that all members would be bound by a majority vote of the members, Sparta generally succeeded in maintaining its ascendancy within the league through its role as the most important member and by its ability to sway other states to accept its viewpoint.

Athens

Although Athens was never sacked in the disturbances accompanying the collapse of Mycenaean civilization, it probably did not maintain any control over Attica, the territory in which it was located. Only gradually was Athens able to regain power over the surrounding communities and it was not until about 650 B.C. that a unified state became established. Its authority was still weak, however, and the locally powerful families continued to wield a good deal of influence.

Up to the end of the seventh century, Athens seems to have escaped the disturbances that the new social and economic conditions produced in the other cities of Greece. Then, about 632 B.C., Cylon, son-in-law of the tyrant of neighboring Megara, attempted to seize power at Athens, but finding little popular support was forced to surrender. Although promised safe passage he was treacherously murdered by the chief magistrate, Megacles, a member of one of the old and powerful clans of Attica, the Alcmeonid. Somehow this event had an effect on the balance of power among the rival factions of Athens and the Alcmeonids were cursed and driven out, though they were to return not long afterward.

About ten years later a code of laws famous in antiquity for its severity was published by Draco, though its content, except for the homicide law, is unknown. On the basis of these occurrences—the Cylonian conspiracy and the code of Draco—we can conclude that Athens was going through the kinds of torment other Greek states had passed through earlier, with clan warfare, rising new classes, and economic disturbances. The root cause of the problems at Athens, however, has never been identified. The old explanation blamed the unrest on the pauperization of the lower classes and the rise of debt-slavery, but a more likely cause is to be found in prosperity rather than poverty. What the lower and middle classes in Athens were concerned about was the archaic social structure of the state, which kept them in economic and political bondage to the aristocracy long after they had need for protection by an aristocracy. As Aristotle put it later:

> The hardest and most hateful feature of the political situation as far as the many were concerned was their serfdom. But they also nursed

> grievances in all other respects, for they had, so to speak, no share in anything.[1]

Not only the poor and the emerging classes, but the upper classes as well were experiencing the effects of newly found prosperity. The expulsion of the Alcmeonids suggests that the ruling class itself was divided by internal feuding between in-groups and out-groups, conservative and progressive factions.

SOLON

In the midst of these troubles Solon, a man of aristocratic family whose fortune was made in trade, was elected to the chief magistracy or archonship for the year 594 and charged with the task of reforming the constitution and the laws. In essence, Solon's task was the same as that of all other lawmakers of the time: to bring peace and Good Order *(Eunomia)* to the strife-ridden society of Athens. The position taken by Solon was that only by way of law could society survive. Everyone, he proclaimed in his poetry, which was his way of communicating his ideas, must of necessity combine against the lawless and disorderly elements in society, whether at the top or at the bottom. A moralistic preacher as well as lawmaker Solon sought to convince both rich and poor that disobedience to the law was fatal to everyone and inevitably led to the establishment of tyranny, which subjected all of society to arbitrary government:

> The state [*polis*] will never be destroyed by Zeus or the will of the blessed gods . . . it is the people themselves who through their lawlessness and love of things will destroy it . . . they pay no heed to the holy foundations of Justice, who though silent knows all that happens or happened in the past and in the course of time will assuredly demand retribution. . . . As a result of lawlessness more evil things happen to the state than for any other reason, but Good Order [*Eunomia*] brings Good Behavior [*Eukosmia*] and Harmony into being and at the same time chains the evil-doers. It makes the rough smooth, checks insolence and softens injustice . . . it stops dissension and the anger of bitter strife.[2]

Solon's solutions to the problems of Athens covered a wide range of fields, ranging from legal and economic matters to the regulation of social customs and morals. Our information about Solon is undependable—as is all information about early lawmakers—and controversy surrounds most of his measures. It is generally agreed that among his principal reforms were the following: All debts—along with the system of securing loans on the person of the debtor—were abolished. Athenians already enslaved were set free, and Solon boasted

[1]Aristotle, *Constitution of Athens and Related Texts*, tr. Kurt von Fritz and Ernst Kapp (New York: Hafner Publishing Company), p. 69. © Copyright 1950, Hafner Publishing Company Inc.

[2]Solon, fragment 12.

that he had brought back many who had been sold abroad. One theory has it that those who had been obligated to give a share of their produce to the nobility as part of an old feudal type of obligation were freed from this burden and their land became their own, unencumbered property. Thus the principal grievances of the lower classes were resolved but the claim of the more radical for the division of the land was ignored. To those anxious to share in the political power of the state, hitherto reserved to the aristocrats, Solon also made concessions. In the past the Areopagus or Council of Athens had been the exclusive province of a hereditary aristocracy who entered it after serving a year's term as archon. The nine magistrates on the Council were elected by the whole Assembly of the people (generally all the freeborn men of the city). In actuality, since only nobles could hold the office, the real power of selection remained in their hands; the people merely endorsed their choice. Solon broke this monopoly by dividing the Athenians into four classes based on property: (1) those whose estates produced 500 or more measures a year *(pentakosiomedimnoi);* (2) those whose income was between 300 and 500 measures and could support and equip a cavalry charger *(hippeis);* (3) members of the hoplite class who could afford to equip themselves with the necessary infantry equipment and whose income was 200–300 measures *(zeugitae);* and finally (4) all those who fell below the last requirement *(thetes).* These classes already existed, so Solon's originality consisted not in his legal classification of them but in the use he put them to in the constitutional process of selecting magistrates. After Solon the first two classes became eligible to stand for the archonship. In a stroke the monopoly the nobility held on the political power of the state was broken. This is not to say that the Areopagus was immediately flooded by the new rich but merely that the legal barrier to their entry was removed. And as a counterweight to the Areopagus, which up to Solon's time had been all-powerful in legislative and judicial matters, Solon probably created a council of 400 members to screen legislation and other matters before they came before the Assembly. The Assembly itself was open to all four classes and could be constituted as a court of appeals for certain sentences handed down by the magistrates. So constituted, it was known as the *Heliaea.* This last step was a major move in the reform of the judiciary since now the judge who in the past could administer the law much as he saw fit, was subject to reversal by the Assembly. Solon also (probably) instituted the right of every individual to bring suit in court personally and not through someone else such as an aristocratic friend or patron who could bargain on his behalf.

What Solon's intentions were is hard to determine and Aristotle explicitly made the point in connection with him that legislators often do things without foreseeing or intending the political consequences of their actions. It is simplest to imagine Solon responding pragmatically to the needs of Athens in the late seventh and early sixth centuries, at a time when political consciousness had not yet developed to any great extent. He was less concerned with elevating the humbler classes than with restraining the greed of the well-to-do whose pursuit of wealth he judged had unbalanced Athenian society.

TYRANNY AT ATHENS

In the years following Solon's reforms and in part because of his reordering of the state, Athenian society developed rapidly. The population expanded, and noncitizens, encouraged by the city's opportunities and openness to them, flocked to Athens, contributing their talents to its economic and cultural development. During these years the island of Salamis in the bay in front of Athens was incorporated in the state and an Athenian commercial empire slowly came into being. Attic pottery reached superb heights of artistry and gradually replaced the once dominant products of Corinth.

Although there was considerable rivalry for the archonship in the years after Solon, his legislation continued to function until 561, when a relative of his, Peisistratus, seized power and set himself up as tyrant. Driven out twice in the next 15 years, he finally established himself securely in 546 and ruled Athens until his death in 528. Subsequently the tyranny continued under his son Hippias. The reason for the failure of Solon's political arrangements may have been the same as the one that brought him to the archonship in the first place, namely, the continuing economic development and rising political consciousness of the new classes in Athens. Finding that Solon's constitutional reforms needed updating the people turned to a tyrant who was able to curb the warring factions among the aristocracy by force. The Peisistratids, as the dynasty is called, emphasized the central administration of government from Athens at the expense of the local power of the nobles. Although they did not abolish the framework of Solon's constitution (the Council, courts, and elected magistracies), they made sure that only their handpicked candidates got into high office. Judges were sent in circuit to render verdicts to the people in place of the local aristocrat. Athens' first consciously nationalistic coinage was issued by the tyrants and a great building program was initiated. Water was brought to the central meeting place of Athens, the Agora, by means of aqueducts, and buildings were erected for the Council and courts. On the Acropolis, the rocky outcrop dominating the city, the temple of Athena was rebuilt and at Eleusis a new Hall of Initiation was constructed. Great emphasis was given to the Panathenaea, the quinquennial festival in honor of Athena instituted shortly before the tyranny, and Peisistratus made the recitation of selections from the *Iliad* and the *Odyssey* by rhapsodes (professional reciters) an important part of the ceremony. Another festival, established for Dionysus, consisted of music, dancing, and addresses by chorus leaders. (From these activities eventually evolved classical tragedy and comedy.) Toward the end of the tyranny the deeds of Theseus were glorified and came to represent an Athenian parallel to the feats of Heracles. A 10 percent tax levied on the produce of the land was turned back in the form of loans to struggling farmers and Attic products found a ready market, especially in the Black Sea area.

By the time the Peisistratids were driven from Athens, almost a century had elapsed since the last exercise of unrestricted aristocratic rule. For 34 years the people had experienced the working of the Solonian constitution and for

Hipparchus, the brother of Hippias, is slain by the would-be tyrannicides Harmodius and Aristogeiton. Understandably, the Athenians of the fifth century preferred to give credit for the liberation of Athens to these two heroes than to a Spartan army.

another 50 years, the firm control of the tyrants. Benefiting by peaceful internal and external conditions, Athens continued to grow. The result was that when the Alcmeonids, who had been on-again, off-again supporters of the Peisistratids made an attempt to come back to Athens in 514 B.C., and take over by force, they were not supported by the common people and were driven off. A plot to assassinate Hippias by two disgruntled aristocrats, Harmodius and Aristogeiton (for purely personal reasons, it should be added), failed, though the tyrant's brother Hipparchus was killed in the attempt. Indirectly this event did contribute to the overthrow of the tyranny insofar as Hippias thereafter became increasingly suspicious and gradually lost popular support. Nevertheless, it still took the pressure of a Spartan army to end the tyranny in 510. Immediately the traditional pattern of aristocratic in-fighting resumed at Athens.

CLEISTHENES

The main contenders were the Alcmeonid Cleisthenes and his opponent Isagoras. When the latter gained the upper hand, Cleisthenes appealed to the people. In the words of the historian Herodotus, he "made the *demos* his faction." In 508 Isagoras and his supporters were routed and Cleisthenes was able to introduce his reform platform and bring to completion the work of the previous century.

The old constitution of Athens consisted of 4 kin-based tribes broken down into 12 *phratries* or brotherhoods. The latter were administrative units that celebrated certain religious festivals, recognized newborn children, and avenged murders. All Athenians belonged to both a tribe and a phratry, but there were two other groupings, which had a different membership, the clan and the guild. The clans claimed descent from a common ancestor and one of their principal functions was the worship of this figure. Only the nobles could belong to the clans. The rest of society was divided among a number of guilds, which also had religious functions. Cleisthenes' reform began with the *deme* or precinct, the traditional territorial unit of Attica, of which there were more than 170. These he grouped into 30 divisions called *trittyes,* which were further categorized in three regional groupings: city, coastal, and inland. There were thus ten of each—ten coastal trittyes, each composed of one or more demes, and ten inland and ten city trittyes similarly constituted. These trittyes were then distributed by lot (along with their constituent demes) among ten groups called *tribes.* Each tribe had one trittys from the coastal, inland, and city districts respectively. Since demes were distributed in trittyes by population, the sizes of the tribes were all roughly equal. From these tribes were selected the Council (now raised to 500), the 10 generals, the 6000 jurors, and the magistrates.

The effect of this reform was to complete the destruction of the kin-based social pattern of the past and substitute for it a new relationship based not on blood but on geographic proximity. Demes from the different parts of Attica, representing quite different interests—various types of agricultural regions and city districts, voting groups from different backgrounds—were thrown together at random in the tribes. From these tribes in turn were selected the representatives to the Council, the courts, the magistracies, and the military commands. Regional representation, where each area selected its own representative to look after its interests in the government, was thus restricted as was local control by political bosses. In the Cleisthenic arrangement rich and poor, upper and lower classes, farmers and traders were integrated in a way modern democracies would not consider possible or probably even desirable. It is unlikely that Cleisthenes had this integration in mind when he passed his reforms and there is reason to believe that the arrangement of the trittyes may have been worked out to benefit his family and its retainers. Whatever the original intention the ultimate result was to allow Athenians to escape at one stroke the bonds of both localism and kinship. Yet because the demes were the basis of the organization the tribes and trittyes were able to function despite their artificiality. The demes became corporations in their own right with officers, assemblies, and religious and civic functions so that the connection between the local units and the state was never lost. The brotherhood or phratry system, the basis of the old aristocratic social order, was also left intact, but since deme residence was now the point of entry to all civic and much religious life, the importance of the phratries rapidly declined. The effect if not the intent of Cleisthenes' reforms was to establish legally the superiority of the community as a whole to the families, clans, and phratries, and to initiate a new interrelationship of all the units. What counted now was not family ties but domicile. On this everything else—magistracies, generalships, jury service, and so forth—now depended. With Cleisthenes the foundations of the Athenian democracy were established, though it was to take another half-century before all the ramifications of his reforms were worked out and even longer for its social impact to be felt.

SOCIETY AND THE STATE IN THE ARCHAIC AGE

Between 800 and 500 B.C. Greek society was transformed radically. The society that emerged at the end bore little resemblance, except for some important cultural and religious continuities, to that which preceded it.

At the beginning of the period most of the Aegean area was divided among independent and endlessly squabbling principalities, all of which possessed a relatively simple social structure consisting of a nobility on the top and the rest of society underneath. The individual units were economically self-contained and there was little trade or commerce beyond the passage of some essential goods such as metals and luxury items, whose exchange no Dark Age has ever interrupted. Three hundred years later the baronies and their warring aristocrats had been transformed into city-states. The nobles, instead of dominating society as they once had, were reduced to but a single, if at times still powerful, faction in the political and social structure of the state. Their value system was adapted to the needs of a far more complex society and had in turn become only one among a number of competing systems, the predominant one being that of the community itself as reconstituted in the city-state. It is this latter creation, the forging of the constitutional city-state, that is the greatest though perhaps least spectacular achievement of the Archaic Age. The reduction of the aristocracy to the service of the community, the differentiation of the rest of society into fairly clearly defined classes, and the emergence of law as the ruling force above and beyond the classes were all parts of this little-heralded process. Religion too made massive adaptations to the new shape of society, emerging at the end of the period as one of the most potent and creative forces in the community.

What usually gets attention, and deservedly so, is the emergence of new types of literature such as lyric and elegiac poetry and the much-proclaimed first glimmerings of philosophical and scientific thought. The period is studded with spectacular names from Homer to Heraclitus and on their merit alone would deserve inclusion among any of the great periods of human history.

Cultural and Religious Values

In the early period of the Archaic Age and stretching back for years before that the principal demand placed upon the aristocrat was that he should succeed in battle. There was a simple logic to this: The larger community depended almost exclusively on the local nobleman and his household to defend it from robbers marauders, and others like himself. It is the moral values of this type of society that we find reflected in the *Iliad,* from which we derive some kind of understanding of the psychological, moral, and religious values that dominated the early part of the age.

The Homeric aristocrat loved to fight, not merely because of an instinctive capacity for brawling but because combat—by definition with another aristocrat—was the ultimate test of human valor, strength, and ability. Success in this kind of combat was proof of the excellence of the victor and a vindication of his position in the community. Failure was unthinkable and unforgivable, for to the victor went the spoils, including the vanquished foe's armor, lands, cattle, and human possessions. In this kind of society ceaseless competition with one's neighbor and the probing of his strength was the normal condition of life. The successful nobleman cultivated a frame of mind suitable to such perpetual tension. There was no time for quiet reflection, none for the analysis of society or the examination of its way of operation. A man's name was all that counted and he basked in the accolades of his relatives, retainers and peers. His prowess was demonstrated in less warlike ways also, by giving splendid gifts and by competing successfully in athletic festivities. All was surface and display. It was this life-style that the bards and especially Homer raised to new heights by the imaginative interweaving of the activities of the gods in the exploits of the heroes. In the epics the human figures associate freely with the immortals, talking, fighting, threatening, and disputing with them almost as equals. The gods for their part reflect the same characteristics as the humans, especially their touchy jealousy and concern for their reputations, and it is from Homer that they receive the personalities that distinguish them from the gods of other pantheons. Both gods and men led an exultant life of competition, intrigue, and surprise. For the heroes death was the ultimate and all-important act of their lives; how they died was a vindication of their entire life-style. Death was not to come as the result of some trivial accident, or occur in a pedestrian way, but only in glorious combat at the precise moment destiny has selected for their exit. In such a world there are few complications and anxieties. All that counted for the individual was the proper frame of mind and the exertion of the utmost effort in battle. The gods themselves were as transparent as the heroes. They shared predictable human passions and the arbitrariness of fate, which cuts off some early and others late, was accepted without much reflection. Justice, other than the vindication of the rights of the hero, was unthinkable and unnecessary. It was a self-centered, childlike world. Although the heroes were tragic figures, doomed to eventual destruction, they did not brood about death or challenge the working of destiny. What concerned them was the excellence of their lives. The justice of a war was an irrelevance beside the vindication of their all-important sense of honor. Later Greeks marveled that the Homeric warriors would be willing to go to war over a stolen bride, but to the heroes of the *Iliad* it was self-evident that if a man (i.e., an aristocrat) was deprived of any of his possessions he was honor-bound to recover them—with compensation. Anything less would be an admission of failure, something unacceptable in Homeric thought.

THE SEARCH FOR NEW VALUES

As Greece emerged from the simple economy of the Dark Age and society began to diversify, the aristocracy became just one group in the community instead of its all-powerful leader. Automatically society was forced to look for new values and seek ways of bringing the old into harmony with the new. City life, with its regular commercial and business activities, had little place for the anarchic, jealous aristocrats whose only sensitivities related to their honor. The ideal of the city was justice under law and order established by rational procedure. Its protagonists were intolerant of aristocratic pastimes and attitudes. Xenophanes of Colophon pointed out the foolishness of honoring Olympic victors, as though winning a boxing or wrestling match improved the order of a city or filled its granaries. The first of the elegiac poets, the aristocrat Archilochus, made his living as a mercenary and had no illusions about war. He poked fun at heroic ideals and posturings:

> A perfect shield bedecks some Thracian now;
> I had no choice: I left it in a wood.
> Ah, well, I saved my skin, so let it go!
> A new one's just as good.[3]

> Let him go ahead.
> Ares is a democrat.
> There are no privileged people
> On a battlefield.[4]

Another elegist, Theognis, railed against the disintegration of the old aristocratic order but was forced to make a significant concession a Homeric hero would never have made—that the whole of heroic excellence *(arete)* is summed up in justice:

> Justice contains in itself all virtue;
> And all just men, Cyrnus, are noblemen. [5]

Justice was the principal need of the new age and the unraveling of its mysteries one of its great preoccupations. Some simply accepted the unpredictable flourishing of evil and the destruction of good. Theognis reflected sadly on the futility of human life:

> No one, Cyrnus, is responsible for his own ruin or his own success, for it is the gods who give both. Nor is anyone in a position to know

[3]T. F. Higham and C. M. Bowra, eds., *The Oxford Book of Greek Verse in Translation* (Oxford: Oxford University Press, 1938), no. 104, p. 184. By permission of Oxford University Press.

[4]Guy Davenport, trans., *Carmina Archilochi: The Fragments of Archilochus* (Berkeley and Los Angeles: University of California Press, 1964), no. 3, p. 3. Copyright © 1964 by The Regents of the University of California. Reprinted by permission of the University of California Press.

[5]Theognis, 147–48.

> whether an action will be for better or for worse for often a man takes good believing it to be evil or evil believing it to be good.[6]

Since the "generation of man is as a generation of leaves,"[7] Semonides of Amorgos urged men to enjoy themselves while they could. Archilochus recommended that they should adjust themselves to the back-and-forth pattern of life:

> Neither exult openly in victory nor, if you are conquered, lie down in your home and cry; but take your joy when life is joyful and in sorrow do not grieve too much; and understand the rhythm which governs human life.[8]

Gone are the heroic ideals that would have trampled such attitudes underfoot as unworthy of the great-souled man. In the old view the individual achieved his full stature as a human being only by heroically facing his end without bending to the pleasures and distractions of life.

It was in the poetry of Pindar that the dying world of the aristocrats found unsurpassed and undying expression. Although the existence of the city-state undermined the life-style of the aristocracy, and the intelligentsia pointed out the inadequacy of its ideals in the new world, it was still able to inspire defenders. Of these the most earnest was Pindar whose dedication to the preservation of the ideals of the nobility produced some of the greatest poetry ever written. His medium was the choral ode, which was intended to be sung to the Olympic victors on their return to their hometowns.

For Pindar, victory in the games constituted the most perfect achievement of mankind. Together, body and soul triumphed; in Pindar's thought there was no conflict between cultural and athletic values. On the contrary, the athletic festival was itself a cultural event of the highest significance, a religious act in which the competitors were raised to the level of the gods in whose honor the events were performed. Instead of celebrating the achievements of the heroes of the past Pindar honored those of the present in whom the heroic spirit had once more been rekindled.

The brilliant efforts of Pindar could in no way bring back to life a dying world. It could only endorse its ideals and hold them up for imitation to the newly emerging classes of the city-state. The easy, almost casual way in which the Homeric hero dispatched his enemies to Hades could find no acceptance in the new world where order was essential to the proper functioning of society. In its early days the city was weak and the control of bloodshed beyond its power; yet, if society was to survive, it somehow had to subdue the violence of its members. Similarly it could not tolerate the disproportionate growth, either in wealth or power, of any of its individual citizens. Thus in both these areas the

[6]Theognis, 133–36.

[7]Fragment 29.

[8]Fragment 72.

city-state stood in opposition to the heroic code, which encouraged its adherents to increase their power and wealth without regard for anyone; for them the shedding of blood created no remorse. Slowly the demands of the city-state, the *polis,* began to create a new religious view of the gods. Instead of taking delight in heroic deeds and the shedding of blood, the gods now took an interest in justice. In place of grabbing all he could lay his hands on, a man was now to be content with his portion in life. To step beyond this was *hybris*—insolence—which brought vengeance. A sense of guilt (though not of sin) came to replace the feelings of shame of the aristocrat. Acceptance of one's position became the new ideal and moderation and balance were put forward as standards of excellence. On all sides restraints were placed on the free, competitive world of the aristocrats as the city-state strove to turn them into god-fearing citizens.

GUILT, KNOWLEDGE, AND THE ORACLES

In the Archaic Age it was possible to contract pollution and guilt unknowingly. Pollution, however, was not sin in the way we understand it—an act conceived inwardly and committed with full knowledge and full consent of the will—but contagion, like a disease. It might even pass from generation to generation as an unexpiated curse. For some this was an obvious and even necessary aspect of the working of divine justice; assuming justice existed at all, it was clear that sometimes the wicked flourished and the good perished and that therefore retribution and justice must come in later generations. For Solon, Theognis, Hesiod, and Herodotus, inherited guilt and deferred punishment were a logical corollary to divinely administered justice. Solon considered justice an essential and inevitable aspect of the working of society. He believed that violations of justice resulted in social strife, itself a form of punishment inflicted on the community. Motive counted for nothing and forgiveness was equally unimportant. What was important was the avoidance of acts of injustice, whether these were committed knowingly or unknowingly. Men were responsible for living within the boundaries of the divine order and knowledge of whether or not an act was impious was of vital importance to the individual and the community. It was thought that inexplicable disasters—such as unexpected deaths, plagues, famines, and military reverses—were inflicted on a community because of some violation by one of its members that unwittingly implicated the rest. Hence anyone who could give reliable answers to such questions as the appropriateness of founding a colony or getting married, or who could reveal what sins had been committed and what could be done to expiate them, had extraordinary importance. The Archaic Age consequently abounded in prophets and oracles who claimed to be able to give knowledgeable answers. Of these, Apollo of Delphi, the Averter of Evil, was the most famous. In a world with neither a priesthood, church, nor bible to guide it, Apollo was an expert in the rules of the mysterious game of justice played by Zeus. To him men could turn with confidence for the answers they craved. Apollo also performed the vital ritual of purification from blood-guilt. In the Archaic Age the murderer, unlike the glorious hero of the aristocratic world, was an outcast, pursued by the implacable avengers of blood-guilt, desperately in need of sanctuary. As yet the city-state was too weak to suspend the law of the vendetta, though in time its ability to bring justice to all its citizens was to be one of its greatest accomplishments.

The message of Apollo was essentially conservative: Know yourself, that is, know your place in the cosmos and do not step above it; be wise; do nothing in excess. Such maxims appealed to some, but to others, especially those for whom the existing order was oppressive, they were stifling and artificial. For these the worship of Dionysus, which involved a cathartic purging of the soul in wild, collective frenzies, provided an escape. The devotee of the god was invited to forget himself and submerge his personality in the divine company of Dionysiac worshippers. In this way he could achieve purification from guilt, for Dionysus was the liberator whose worship enabled the individual to find a new world free of the entanglements of the old. The significance of this movement should not be underestimated and the success of the city-state in reducing this potentially explosive religion to its own uses in the form of the festivals must be rated as one of its more successful accomplishments.

Toward the end of the Archaic Age the religion of Orphism provided one of the most comprehensive solutions to the problem of guilt and evil for individual men. According to the Orphics, man was divided into two elements, the body and the soul. The soul was considered the divine spark that could not perish, and the body constituted its prison. Sin could be washed away by ritual

Scene from a fifth-century vase of a chorus being performed in honor of Dionysus at one of the Athenian festivals.

acts and the observance of certain forms of conduct including vegetarianism, silence, and certain sexual restrictions. Reincarnation guaranteed that man's real self could be separated from the weight of his sensual nature, permitting him to arrive eventually at a state of blessedness.

Not to be neglected in this brief account of the religious values of the Archaic Age are the civic religions of the newly emerging city-states. Although usually denigrated as excessively ritualistic, these religions fulfilled an enormously important need felt by the majority of men for a mechanical and reliable form of religious worship. More, however, will be said of these civic cults later in the chapter and in Chapter 8, on the working of the democracy at Athens.

THE LIBERATED SOUL

The pressures and anxieties of the Archaic Age provoked different responses in different people. Some obviously reveled in the opportunities for making money and acquiring power that the uncertainties of the times offered, though we know of these people only through the comments of their critics or from those such as Solon who sought to restrain them. Many, on the other hand, were deeply disturbed by the disintegration of the traditional patterns of life. These sought to control the forces of disorder by means of laws and constitutions, and thus once more to bring the forces of anarchy and chaos under control. Quite a different response came from a number of gifted souls who instead of turning to commerce or travel or law turned in upon themselves and made the startling discovery of the world of the emotions and the inner self. In them for the first time we catch a glimpse of the self-aware individual whose attempts to come to grips with his emotions looks strangely modern.

Archilochus we have already met. Liberated from aristocratic concerns with self-image he felt free to berate indiscriminately the high and the low, the rich and the poor:

> Now that Leophilos is governor,
> Leophilos meddles in everybody's business,
> And everybody falls down before Leophilos,
> And all you hear is Leophilos, Leophilos.[9]

He had no qualms about adjusting the aristocratic code to his own personal needs, as we saw earlier, and could make clear-cut judgments about his own wants:

> I have no desire for the gold of Gyges,
> Nor does envy have power over me;
> I am not jealous of what the gods have,
> Nor do I burn to rule.[10]

[9]Davenport, *Carmina Archilochi*, no. 213, p. 73. Copyright © 1964 by The Regents of the University of California. Reprinted by permission of the University of California Press.

[10]Fragment 15.

Just as he had no illusions about war, neither did he have any about society. Sappho of Lesbos could similarly assert her own judgment against the prevailing assumptions of society:

A company of horsemen or of infantry
Or a fleet of ships, some say,
Is the black earth's finest sight,
But to me it is what you love.[11]

The individualism of these poets is, however, still not modern, since both Archilochus and Sappho regarded the emotions as imposed from the outside, as Homer did, rather than as welling up from within the soul of the individual. Still, the lyric poets were able to go beyond Homer and they looked upon the passions as somehow connected with the laws and movements of the universe at large. Archilochus admonished his listeners to understand the rhythm that rules the world and the ebb and flow of life. Sappho, in a like frame of mind, turned to Aphrodite, whom she regarded as responsible for her suffering, and begged for deliverance with a confidence based on the goddess's past help:

God's wildering daughter deathless Aphródita,
A whittled perplexity your bright abstruse chair,
With heartbreak, lady, and breathlessness
Tame not my heart.

But come down to me, as you came before,
For if ever I cried, and you heard and came,
Come now, of all times, leaving
Your father's golden house
. . .

Come, then, loose me from cruelties.
Give my tethered heart its full desire.
Fulfill, and, come, lock your shield with mine
Throughout the siege.[12]

For Sappho love was bittersweet, an emotion that would bring her close to death:

Eros weaver of myths,
Eros sweet and bitter,
Eros bringer of pain.[13]

My tongue sticks to my dry mouth,
Thin fire spreads beneath my skin,
My eyes cannot see and my aching ears
Roar in their labyrinths.

[11]Guy Davenport, trans., *Sappho: Poems and Fragments* (Ann Arbor: University of Michigan Press, 1965), no. 25 (no pagination). Copyright © by The University of Michigan Press 1965.

[12]Davenport, *Sappho,* no. 1. Copyright © by The University of Michigan Press 1965.

[13]Davenport, *Sappho,* no. 100. Copyright © by The University of Michigan Press 1965.

Chill sweat slides down my body,
I shake, I turn greener than grass.
I am neither living nor dead and cry
From the narrow between.[14]

Philosophical and Scientific Thought

While the lyric poets explored the emotional recesses of the human heart and legislators sought to establish the mastery of law over society, the more mundane needs of society were not neglected. The expanding cities of the Aegean required the construction of defensive walls, harbors, temples, and public buildings of all kinds. The architect Eupalinus supervised the tunneling of an aqueduct almost a mile long through the mountain of Samos; although the tunnel was begun from both ends, the workmen were able to meet with only a small margin of error. Mandrocles was famous as a bridge maker, and others of his age are credited with such inventions as the water level and the lathe. Thales of Miletus founded the science of geometry by going beyond the practical problems of measurement in construction and formulating theories about measurement in general. He also knew something about astronomy and is credited, although incorrectly, with predicting the solar eclipse of 585 B.C. Anaximander, also a native of Miletus, drew a map of the world and to complement it Hecataeus gathered large quantities of historical, geographical, and ethnographic information, which he then systematically organized. His book, *The Description of the Earth,* laid the foundations of both geography and ethnography. By collating myths and legends and bringing them up to date, he became the founder of chronology.

From here the philosophers of Miletus went on to lay the foundations of philosophical and scientific thought by asking questions about the composition of the universe. For Thales, the unifying principle or basic substance of the universe was water; for Anaximander, it was air. The mystical Pythagoras of Samos generalized a theory that numerical harmony underlay the workings of the universe. This was not, however, a mathematical theory but rather a form of metaphysics based on number that ascribed qualities of excellence to certain numbers, which could be brought into harmonious accord with others. From this conception of number and harmony there emerged a view of the relationship of man to his environment and of the different parts of the universe to one another that pervaded much of subsequent Greek thought and art.

Slightly later than the foregoing and clearly in the metaphysical rather than the physical tradition of the Milesians was Heraclitus of Ephesus. A towering figure in his own age, Heraclitus established one of the essential metaphysical points of view, a landmark of philosophical speculation to the present day.

For Heraclitus the underlying substance or substrate of reality was not a single, unchanging thing like water or air, but change itself, represented by fire.

[14]Davenport, *Sappho,* no. 20. Copyright © by The University of Michigan Press 1965.

The universe was like a river in which no one could bathe twice in the same water. The only reality was Becoming, not Being. The cosmos was in constant tension and interchange but regulated by a divine law that could be apprehended by man's intelligence and to which he should conform. Just as the law strengthened the city and held it together, so knowledge of the divine law of the cosmos strengthened the individual. It was therefore essential for man to acquire knowledge of these laws so that he could live in harmony with his surroundings and so voluntarily subordinate himself to the workings of the cosmos. Heraclitus' saying that "a man's character is his destiny," was a firm rejection of the doctrine of resignation to fate or inborn luck, one of the postulates of poets such as Theognis and Semonides.

A generation later (about 450 B.C.) Parmenides of Elea established another of the great landmarks of philosophy. In opposition to Heraclitus, Parmenides asserted that the world of the senses was altogether untrustworthy and only intelligence or reason could be relied upon. All becoming or change was thought to be unreal, an apparent and delusory process; Being alone was held to be real and changeless.

Although some of the answers of the early philosophers may seem naive to us, the fact that they were formulated at all was revolutionary. That they culminated in the profound theories of Heraclitus and Parmenides is a tribute to the depth of the intellectual movement of the sixth century and to the rapidity with which it spread in Greece. In the realm of pure thought, the speculation of the philosophers represents the counterpart of the activity of the poets, lawgivers, and practical politicians in other areas in challenging the customary patterns of mythological thinking and encouraging the application of reason to human problems, both societal and individual. Perhaps they were inspired by the legislators whose implicit assumption was that events did not always occur accidentally or by the will of the gods but that there was an underlying pattern, which if discovered (or revealed) could bring peace and tranquillity to society. By asking similar kinds of questions of nature the early philosophers hoped to discover the unifying principle beneath the bewildering diversity of nature and the constant ebb and flow of change they could see taking place all around them.

Political and Social Life: Fundamental Assumptions

The creation of lyric poetry and the beginnings of scientific and philosophical speculation are the unlikely products of a society emerging from the dismal period of the Greek Dark Age. Yet what the Archaic Age brought forth in the areas of literature and culture is paralleled by equally important developments that took place in the realm of politics and society.

Modern societies establish a clear line of demarcation between society and the state. It is often assumed that if the two are not actively opposed there is at least a good deal of tension between what we call the state or the government and the society it is supposed to regulate (or serve). There is no danger that anyone in the modern world will confuse the legislative, judicial, or executive branches of government with society itself. Administrative bureaucracies, police forces, armies, and other elements of the "public" realm are clearly set off against the "private" realm, which is characterized by voluntary associations of all kinds. The polis, on the other hand, was a highly integrated type of community in which society and the state were so closely united that it was difficult to make a distinction between them. In fact, the two coincided. The state was the citizenry and the citizenry was the state. Power was not delegated to permanent institutions such as legislatures, courts, bureaucracies, or to professional classes of soldiers, lawyers, administrators, or politicians. Even in the oligarchically organized city-state the citizen had an immediate and direct role in legislation, election, and policymaking—frequently also in the judiciary. It was a fundamental principle even of these states that the personnel holding official positions should change constantly. Nor were there any of the semipublic bodies such as corporations, unions, churches, or universities that have such an indispensable role in modern societies and tend to emphasize the division between the rulers and the ruled. For the citizen of the ancient city-state, allegiances were much more simply and clearly defined than those of his modern counterpart. Families (as will be seen shortly), not individuals, were the basic units of society and these in turn fitted into larger geographic units—clans, brotherhoods, and tribes—which in turn defined and restricted the relationships of the individual to society. As a result, at least in the traditional types of polis, the individual citizen had little room to establish nonstate types of relations. There was no diffusion of loyalty—at least, the citizen had much less opportunity to indulge such tendencies. He had, for example, no choice in the matter of religion; the state gods and the gods of his family, brotherhood, and locality were his, like it or not. There were no independent cults outside the state religions to which he could turn. Similarly there were no non-state-associated cultural institutions in which he might participate: no symphony orchestras, museums, or schools to which he could turn. Culture was not something distinct from the state, the possession—as it often is in modern society—of experts or professionals. In the city-state art was public and the principal cultural events, the great festivals, were also state affairs. What was said earlier about lyric poetry needs perhaps to be corrected here. Some of it was, it is true, purely personal and individualistic in the modern sense, but most of it was composed for public occasions of one kind or another. The odes of Pindar, for example, were intended for public performance, not for publication for those who read poetry as a pastime. We have also seen how Peisistratus incorporated the recitation of Homer in the Panathenaic festival. In the fifth century the classic drama of Athens was performed at festivals. Dancing, singing, athletics, art, poetry, and drama were public events intimately connected with the life of the state. There were no poetry journals, athletic departments or independent educational institutions in the polis.

Perhaps the most marked aspect of the unity of society and the state is to be seen in the approach of the citizens to policymaking, legislation, and the judiciary. It was taken for granted that important matters in these areas were the concern of the citizenry as a whole. It is true that the definition of the "whole citizenry" was patriarchal—that is, it included only males over a certain age and under certain circumstances, and excluded women and the young—but this does not distract from the fundamental fact that the ancient polis was more open in the realm of politics and law to more people than any form of society since then. Amateurism prevailed over professionalism: in policymaking, legislation, and the judiciary the expert could be, and in fact often was, heard, but it was left up to the people to make up their own minds and then take the consequences of their actions. Power was not dissipated, therefore, as it is in the modern state among a multiplicity of institutions. It rested fully in the hands of the people, however the term was defined. Understandably it was over conditions of entry into this decision-making group that most of the internal battles in Greek cities raged. All city-states without exception restricted the franchise (as do modern states). It was merely a question of *how* restrictive the individual states might be. The general tendency was to move from greater to lesser restrictiveness and in the democracies the fullest expression of the identity of the state and society was to be found.

Since the city-state was a kind of hereditary or family-held corporation, which required for membership the possession of a certain amount of "stock"—at a minimum, citizen parentage—it was understandably difficult to obtain admission to its ranks. Foreigners might reside for generations in a particular city without being accepted into the community. Part of the reason for this was economic or at least is most easily understood from the economic viewpoint. Unlike the modern state, which tends to regard the individual's right to accumulate money as something sacrosanct, and which considers the attempts of government to regulate such activities as violations of the individual's privacy and freedom, the polis tended to regard wealth with a communitarian eye. The rich were expected to perform expensive public services or liturgies, which could range from giving banquets to erecting public buildings and maintaining warships. Money coming into the state from any source—whether as booty, tribute, or tax—was regarded as the property of the community. Citizens could thus hope to benefit by the corporate profits of the state and hence were unwilling to admit outsiders whose numbers would dilute the take of citizens by birth.

The Units and Divisions of Society

CITIZENS AND SLAVES

The citizens of a polis constituted only a percentage of the total population. The remainder consisted of foreigners, who might be visitors or permanent residents, slaves or freedmen. A great deal of diversity, however, existed among the individual city-states. There is no way of telling what percentages, on an average, of these groups might have been found in any of the city-states of Greece at any given time. Although some states can, for certain periods in their histories, be labeled slave-societies, others cannot be so labeled. Athens in the classical period could be classed as such a society, since slaves played an essential role in its economy, though not in a way analogous to the slave society of the United States, where the majority of slaves were employed in the cultivation of plantations. Only the mines, where servile labor was employed almost exclusively, offer a parallel in the ancient world. In Sparta the majority of the noncitizen population was the property of the state and was allocated proportionately to the citizenry as a work force for its sustenance. The helots, however, were not the possession of the individual citizens; they could not be sold or manumitted, and they retained a right to a portion of the crops they produced. Probably a majority of Greek city-states followed neither the Athenian nor the Spartan model, and since few reached the economic level of development attained by Athens they cannot be classed as slave societies.

Even in those states where slavery had an important role, slaves and freemen worked side by side at the same tasks. The essential difference, however, was that the free laborers worked as independent craftsmen, small farmers, or traders and almost never worked for someone else for wages. Slaves, of course, did work for others. To work for someone else on a regular basis was the mark of a slave, whereas the essential characteristic of the freeman was his economic independence, however low-level and demeaning this might be to our way of thinking. There were a number of exceptions to this general rule. In Athens freemen and slaves worked side by side on public works projects and received the same pay. The slave, however, could only keep a portion of his, whereas the freeman kept it all. In agricultural areas freemen might seasonally hire their labor out, but to work for someone permanently was unthinkable. The essential distinction between slave and free was thus, for the most part, a matter of status. A slave might be richer, better educated, and work less than the freeborn, but he was not his own master. Nor could he, of course, attend the Assembly, vote, stand for office, or in any other way except remotely, participate in the civic life of the community. Slaves were frequently rented out and because of their special skills were put in charge of important manufacturing or commercial concerns. As a result they were often better off in material things than the freeborn with whom they associated daily. The free poor, however, never regarded themselves as a working class, an oppressed proletariat, in competition with slaves for jobs. Their complaints were always directed against the rich, especially creditors, and their slogans for rebellion were almost always the division of land and the elimination of debts. Their battle with the rich was over specific rights and privileges, not the abolition of slavery, which was never challenged in antiquity but was considered a necessary social institution. Probably most ancient freeborn populations would regard modern definitions of freedom, with their lack of civic participation and their emphasis on private, professional, and material things, as anomalous to say the least, if not thoroughly servile. Not that the poor did not envy wealth. Rather, no one confused freedom with the right to work for someone else, or to pay taxes, or otherwise to perform functions they considered incompatible with the exercise of true liberty.

THE FAMILY

The constituent unit of the polis was not the autonomous individual as in the modern world, but the group—such as the family, clan, brotherhood, and tribe, generally in that ascending order. The individual was a citizen and a member of the community only insofar as he was a member of one of these groups. He received the protection of the state in this community capacity, rather than because, as in our view, he had certain inherent rights vested in him as a human being. Despite the emphasis given earlier in this chapter to the emergence of the individual, the group was never superseded as the basic unit of society in the Greek world.

In the final analysis, the ultimate unit of society was the family rather than the clan, brotherhood, or tribe, which in the earlier period had been dominant. The great achievement of the seventh and sixth centuries was that the power of the kin-groups was effectively broken and replaced by residency requirements. This one essential reform is what distinguishes the city-state from the tribal, kin-based societies to which it appears, superficially, similar.

According to Aristotle the smallest unit of society was the family or household, comprised of parents, children, and slaves. The family was, in a sense, immortal: It looked back toward a mythical first founder and forward to its own indefinite perpetuation. The individual in such a family, especially the head of the household, was responsible for the perpetuation of its economic possessions, its religious rituals, and the cult of the dead. A household without children was not a true household, and there was extreme pressure on family heads to procreate heirs in order to carry on the family. The disappearance of families meant disaster for the community at large and all sorts of emotional appeals were made in litigation on behalf of their preservation. Since the community was built up of households belonging to larger units such as brotherhoods and precincts or demes, the disappearance of households had important economic, religious, and political effects that could weaken these units. Thus fathers of households were under pressure not just from vague peer groups or ill-defined social customs but from their relatives and from the state itself. The family, which to us is a largely private group, was a much more public entity for the Greeks. All cases regarding it were considered actionable by the community at large. A private individual not related to the family could claim that he, as a member of the community, was affected by some misdemeanor within a family or by one committed by a family member and was therefore entitled to bring suit.

Religion was another element in this net of traditional obligations that circumscribed the individual Greek. Family cults were handed down from generation to generation and their maintenance was considered an essential aspect of the life of the larger community. Many of the state cults began as purely family affairs, which were democratized in the course of time and opened up to the whole community, though the family almost always continued to provide the priests and priestesses of the cult. In Athens shrines to Zeus of the Hearth were owned by the individual households, whereas the clans worshipped Apollo the Father. The city itself had temples to these gods so that both the community and the individual households were linked by a similar form of worship. Zeus was also worshipped under the formality of Zeus of the Brotherhoods. Thus, despite the formal elimination of kinship as the basis of society, religion continued to maintain the fiction of a single, kin-related community, a fiction we have already seen existing in the civic community in the artificial tribes created by Cleisthenes for Athens.

MARRIAGE, CHASTITY, AND PROPERTY

The connection between marriage and property, although weakened in modern society, is still a major aspect of all forms of marriage arrangements. In the polis where this connection was a good deal more vital and the community had a stake in the survival of the individual families, state interference in what today would be considered a private affair was common. It was generally considered disgraceful if not actually legally prohibited for a person to dispose of his ancestral property where the graves of the family's ancestors were located. At Athens a man could be prosecuted for wasting his property and if convicted was barred from making a will. Particular care was given to the status of heiresses and orphans though the motivation behind this was practical rather than humanitarian. Since the future of the city depended on the survival of the families provision had to be made for the all too common situation where a head of a household died prematurely as a result of battle or disease without leaving a legitimate male heir. In that case the property devolved upon the nearest surviving female relative. Custom and perhaps law demanded that the next of kin on the male side marry her to procreate heirs to the household and thus ensure its continuance. Obviously this kind of custom could cause all kinds of problems, for example, where the male relative was already married or the heiress was married. If she was very poor it seems to have been the custom for the next of kin to take her into his existing family but not to divorce his original wife. On the other hand it is known that divorce occurred when the heiress was rich. These complicated issues were often settled in court where it was left to the judge or jury to make a decision as to who had the right (or duty) to marry the heiress in question.

Marriages were, for the most part, arranged affairs and it was generally taken for granted that if love was to be part of the relationship it developed after the marriage. Formal betrothals before marriage were common throughout Greece and could occur at a very young age. The sister of Demosthenes was five when she was betrothed, though this may be an exception since she was an orphan. Dowries were an essential part of marriage and it was extremely difficult for a girl without a dowry to acquire a husband. The dowry belonged to the woman throughout her marriage and if divorce occurred it remained hers. Neither she, her husband, nor her guardian if she was widowed could dispose of it. The husband could use the income only as a means of supporting his wife. No special virtue attached to monogamy and the existence of the dowry made a divorcee or widow eligible to remarry. Interestingly, the children remained with the father's household. Divorce was easy for both husband and wife. When initiated by a husband all that was required was that he send his wife away. A wife needed to petition through her father or some other male citizen since she could not appear in court on her own behalf. The divorced woman could return home with her dowry and her father or guardian was obliged by law to use the dowry to provide for her. On her death it went to her children; if she had none it returned to her family.

The Greeks attached immense importance to chastity for citizen women both before and after marriage. Since the procreation of legitimate heirs was essential to the continuity of the family it was thought to be a vital requirement that the offspring of any legitimate union be unchallengeable, on the grounds of either pre- or extramarital relations. Society could not afford to see the integrity of its constituent households challenged by individuals, either inside or outside the family, who claimed that the supposed heir was not in fact the heir and thus had no right to the citizenship with its privileges or to the headship of the household. At Athens women were strictly segregated from male society, to the extent that a separate part of the house was set aside for their exclusive use. Adultery was considered a public offense—that is, an act damaging the community—and suit could be brought by any competent adult male on behalf of the state. These comments about chastity apply only to citizen women and in particular to wives of heads of households, who constituted only a small percentage of the population. Women outside these classes were considerably freer, though in common with citizen women they had no civic functions. It is interesting that only in Sparta and in Plato's ideal state, where the ties of property and the family were weak, did women have a much freer role in society.

Wives who did not have to go out to work had a tremendous number of household duties to occupy them. Slaves were common even in the less well-off households, and their work needed supervision. If there were no slaves, the wife had to do all the domestic work herself. Clothes were generally made at home, food had to be prepared, and the children cared for. The family often included elderly parents, aunts, uncles, and in-laws, which must have added considerably to the workload. The management of the home would then have occupied the greater part of a woman's day while her husband was at work or engaged in civic or military duties. Unlike modern society where functional differentiation is almost entirely independent of sex, that of the polis was not. Athletics, military training, and probably the bulk of the discussion in the Assembly concerned warfare, one of the principal occupations of Greek men. In addition, the general nature of public business tended to emphasize the role of men in preference to

Women in an elegant fountain house fill their heavy water jars. Unwittingly the scene conveys a good deal about the position of women in both the Greek household and in Greek society in general.

that of women. Judicial procedures, for example, could involve a good deal of physical compulsion. Since there was no police force and no public prosecutor's office the enforcement of judgments or the appearance of witnesses in court depended on the ability of the head of the household to keep up his connections with other family heads and obtain their help and that of friends in crucial confrontations. All this tended to favor the association of males on an equal basis and the segregation of women. This must have been reinforced by the different ages at which males and females entered marriage—30 and 14 respectively—and the educational and emotional gaps that must have existed between such husbands and wives.

When the values of aristocratic society were adapted to the needs of the city-state, admiration for male friendship was also taken over and accepted as one of the highest of human ideals. The friendship of Achilles and Patroclus, Orestes and Pylades, and Harmodius and Aristogeiton was thought to be the expression of noble ideals and was widely admired. Constant association in the gymnasium, the army, and the Assembly promoted the same kind of friendly competition and relationship among males. The symposium, from which wives were excluded, was another inheritance from the aristocratic past. At these gatherings the participants conversed, sang, and performed on the lyre, and were entertained by female courtesans or *hetaerae.* In the Agora, where a great deal of preliminary discussion was conducted before the meetings of the Assembly, the association was again predominantly male. In such a society homosexuality naturally was practiced, though perhaps not with the abandon that is sometimes assumed. Youths of school age were strictly protected by law and pederasts were excluded from public offices and could not address the Assembly. The masses generally regarded pederasty as an upper-class vice and the orators used the accusation of the practice as a means of arousing the jury against the person they were attacking.

It is important to consider, in evaluating the position of Greek women in society, the status of the women in question—whether they were citizen or noncitizen, slave or free, rich or poor—since the same generalizations do not fit all classes. Neither men nor women in the polis enjoyed a high degree of freedom in the modern sense of the term. Greek ideas of freedom emphasized the realization of an ideal that in turn implied conformity to the commonly accepted standards of one's class and position. The needs of the community circumscribed and defined the roles of both men and women and restricted the freedom of both. The head of a household had little choice of who and when he should marry, whether or not he should support his parents, give dowries to needy sisters and daughters, or even marry a female relative and divorce his wife if he was the only surviving next of kin. Law and custom demanded that he subordinate his own needs and interests to those of his family and the community at large. (Paradoxically, only individuals outside the community—slaves and foreigners, for example—enjoyed the kind of behavior that we today associate with the term *freedom.)* In return, citizen men and women enjoyed a strong and stimulating community life. There were clear functional distinctions based on economic and social realities. Women, particularly, had a high degree of security. Divorce was easy and wives were provided for through the system of dowries. When divorce occurred the children still had strong community support and were not suddenly cast off as the dependents of a woman who had both to run her household and provide the necessary income. Old age was honored and well provided for.

7

From the Persian Wars to the Collapse of the Great Powers

THE PERSIAN WARS

Located on the distant fringes of the civilized eastern Mediterranean, the Aegean world had long been immune to the political disturbances that accompanied the rise and fall of the great oriental empires. This immunity ended, however, when the Persians moved westward in 547 and overcame the Lydian kingdom of Croesus. Subsequently the Greek cities of the Asia Minor coastland were subdued and incorporated in the Persian Empire.

After chafing for a generation under the rule of despots placed over them by the Persians, the Greek cities of Ionia rebelled in 499 B.C. Democracies were established in place of the tyrannies and ambassadors were sent to the mainland for assistance. Athens sent 20 ships and Eretria also made a contribution, but Sparta, the principal military power in Greece, refused to help. At first the revolt went well. Sardis, the old Lydian capital and at that time the headquarters of the Persian province (or *satrapy*) in Asia, was attacked and burned, though the invaders failed to take the citadel. As a result of this partial success the revolt spread to Caria and Cyprus as well as to the Greek states of the Hellespont and Bosporus. For three years the war carried on indecisively, with the Persians slowly gaining the upper hand. Eventually they succeeded in bringing Miletus under siege and a great sea battle was fought off the nearby island of Lade in 494. Almost as soon as the two fleets became engaged the Samian and Lesbian contingents deserted and the remaining rebels were overwhelmed. Miletus, until then the cultural center of the Greek world, was taken and razed and its population deported or sold into slavery.

MARATHON: THE CAMPAIGN OF 490 B.C.

Accounts still remained to be settled with Athens and Eretria, the two mainland cities that had been involved in the revolt. Under the command of Datis and Artaphernes the Persian fleet sailed directly from Samos to Euboea

CLASSICAL GREECE
MACEDONIA
PELLA
METHONE
Mt Olympus
AMPHIPOLIS
PHILIPPI
Mt Pangaeus
EION
OLYNTHUS
POTIDAEA
SCIONE
Chalcidice
Thermaic Gulf
THESSALY
PHERAE
Artemisium
Thasos
Imbros
Lemnos
AEGEAN SEA
Scyros
AEGOSPOTAMI
SESTOS
Hellespont
SIGEUM
TROY
PHRYGIA
BYZANTIUM
Bosphorus
PERINTHUS
Propontis
CYZICUS
Lesbos
MITYLENE
Arginusae Is
LYDIA
SARDIS
Chios
EPHESUS
Samos
Mycale Mt
PRIENE
MILETUS
CARIA
COS
CNIDUS
Cynossema
Rhodes
Andros
Delos
Paros
Naxos
Melos
Thera
EUBOEA
ERETRIA
MARATHON
Attica
ATHENS
Boeotia
PLATAEA
MEGARA
CORINTH
EPIDAURUS
ARGOS
Methana
TROEZEN
THERMOPYLAE
Phocis
Aetolia
Acarnania
AMBRACIA
NAUPACTUS
Achaea
Elis
OLYMPIA
MANTINEA
MEGALOPOLIS
Arcadia
Messenia
SPARTA
Laconia
PYLOS
Cythera
Corcyra
Cephallenia
Zacynthos
ATHENS AND HER ALLIES
SPARTA AND HER ALLIES
NEUTRAL
CORONEA
THEBES
TANAGRA
LEUCTRA
Boeotia
PLATAEA
Corinthian Gulf
ERETRIA
DELIUM
Euboea
OENOPHYTA
DECELEA
MARATHON
ACHARNAE
Mt Pentelicus
ELEUSIS
MEGARA
ATHENS
CORINTH
MINOA
SALAMIS
PIRAEUS
Saronic Gulf
Aegina
Mt Laurium
SUNIUM

where Eretria, after a brief siege, was betrayed from within and was sacked. Embarking from Eretria the Persians next crossed the narrow Euboean channel and landed on the plain of Marathon, thereby provoking an anxious and crucial debate in the Athenian Assembly as to whether to go out to meet the Persians or to wait until they arrived before the city itself. When the decision was made to advance to Marathon a runner was dispatched to Sparta and the 9000 hoplites of Athens marched out to meet their enemies. At Marathon they were joined by 1000 Plataeans, and together the citizens of the two cities confronted the Persians.

Several days passed as the Athenian generals debated whether to attack immediately or to wait for the Spartans to arrive. The most powerful personality among the generals and the most experienced in the ways of the Persians was Miltiades, who had been involved with Darius in an expedition across the Danube. After much debate he succeeded in persuading his fellow generals not to wait any longer and to follow his proposal for handling the superior numbers of the enemy. When the two forces engaged, the Persians extended their line of battle so as to envelop the smaller Greek army. Anticipating this action, Miltiades had weakened the center and strengthened the wings so that when the two lines met the Athenian center gradually gave way but the wings routed their opponents and closed in from behind on the Persian center. Outmaneuvered, the Persians fled to their ships—losing, according to Herodotus, 6400 men to the Athenian and Plataean 192. Delayed by the celebration of a religious festival, the Spartans arrived too late for the battle but examined the battlefield and made note of the light weapons of the Persian infantry and the tactics of Miltiades.

The resounding defeat of the Persians in a set battle after the disasters of the Ionian revolt was a surprise to both Persians and Greeks, but most of all to the Athenians whose conduct of the campaign was seen by them as a vindication of their decision to adopt the democratic constitution of Cleisthenes in 508. They could reflect that it was the Assembly and not the Areopagus or Council that had made the crucial decisions of the war—first to aid the Ionians and then to fight at Marathon. Nevertheless, the significance of the battle should not be exaggerated, either as a vindication of the worth of the Athenian democracy or as

The plain of Marathon from the top of the mound that covers the remains of the Greeks who fell in combat with the Persians in 490 B.C.

a victory over the Persians. The latter had no intention of destroying Athens as they had Eretria but merely wished it to take back the exiled tyrant Hippias and acknowledge the general overlordship of Persia.

In the decade following the Persian invasion the democracy of Athens advanced to new levels of citizen participation. In the past the nine archons had been elected from candidates from the first two census classes, which guaranteed that the well-to-do would dominate the Areopagus and hold all the important magistracies. In 487, however, a modification was introduced whereby archons were no longer directly elected but were selected instead by lot from a group of candidates who were directly nominated by the demes. Once the connection between the voting public and the magistracies was broken, the archonship lost its power and the generalship, which remained directly elective, took its place in terms of political importance.

These years were also a time of intense political rivalry and fundamental decision making. The two most prominent figures in Athens were Aristides and Themistocles, who struggled with each other over issues of naval policy and political power. When a rich vein of silver was struck at the mines of Laurium, Themistocles persuaded the people to devote the income to ship construction, and by 480 Athens had a fleet of some 200 triremes. Ostracism, the process by which an individual could be exiled for ten years by a majority vote, was used for the first time in 488; its purpose was to guard against the overly ambitious or to make a clear-cut decision on conflicting policies advocated by different individuals. By exiling one person the people could endorse the policy of his opponent and ensure themselves clearly defined goals; they also removed an obstacle to attaining those goals. Initially persons connected with the Peisistratids were ostracized, but in 483/482 Aristides, Themistocles' rival, was exiled. By this act the people aligned themselves solidly behind Themistocles' policy of naval expansion and in effect chose him as their commander in chief for the anticipated second Persian invasion.

The Second Persian Invasion

Preparations for a major invasion of Greece had been under way since the repulse at Marathon, but a revolt in Egypt in 487 and the death in the following year of Darius, the Persian king, gave the Greeks a long respite. It was not until 480 that the Persians, under the leadership of Darius' weak son Xerxes, were ready to march.

On this occasion Persian aims called for a major invasion and the permanent addition of Greece to their empire. The Greeks, for their part, had to be prepared to cope with an assault by land and sea, though their most serious problems were actually to be found within their own ranks. Argos, the traditional enemy of Sparta, stood aloof, and north of the isthmus of Corinth only Athens could be depended upon. Thessaly agreed to participate, but only on the condition that the allies protect it from invasion. When this proved impracticable, the Thessalians promptly went over to the enemy.

The line of defense finally chosen was based on Thermopylae on the landward side and Artemisium at the northern tip of Euboea on the seaward. The object of this strategy was to compel Xerxes to choose between either forcing his way through the narrow, 50-foot-wide pass of Thermopylae, where Persian cavalry and superiority in numbers would be useless, or marching inland and reaching central Greece by a land route and thus losing contact with the fleet. The Greek strategy meant that it was essential for them to hold both land and sea positions since the loss of either one would lead to a flanking movement. Once the decision was made, the Greeks under the Spartans Leonidas and Eurybiades took up their positions. Leonidas had about 7000 men with him and Eurybiades 280 ships, of which 147 were Athenian commanded by Themistocles. Opposing them was an army of enormous proportions and a naval force of over 1200 Phoenician, Greek, Egyptian, and Carian warships. Fortunately for the Greeks a storm destroyed 400 of these ships before the first engagement and an additional 200 were sunk by another storm after an attempt to round Euboea and trap the Greeks at Artemisium.

Both the land and sea engagements at Thermopylae and Artemisium lasted a period of days. The Persian land forces could make no headway against the strongly positioned Greeks and at sea the Greeks held their own despite heavy losses. It was finally the land position that was turned, when on the third day the Persians, with the help of a Greek traitor, succeeded in getting behind Leonidas' army, forcing him to dismiss the bulk of his forces. Only 400 Thebans, 700 Thespians, and 300 Spartans remained with him to make a final stand. As the battle progressed the Thebans surrendered and left the Spartans and Thespians to fight on alone to the end. With the land position lost, the fleet had no choice but to retreat and all of central Greece was abandoned.

Despite the heroism displayed at Thermopylae and Artemisium the Greeks were now in the familiar position of seeing the overwhelming resources of the Persians prevail over their own. There was no hope of defending Attica so the Athenians evacuated their population to Salamis, Aegina, and Troezen, although a small contingent remained on the Acropolis, hoping to hold it against the Persians.

SALAMIS AND PLATAEA

The decision now faced by the Greeks was whether to fight at Salamis or withdraw to the isthmus of Corinth. Themistocles urged the first course and persuaded the Spartan commander to hold firm. For three weeks, hoping that the Persians would attack them in the narrow waters of the bay, the outnumbered Greeks waited, with discontent rising steadily in their ranks. Finally, recognizing that withdrawal was inevitable, Themistocles sent a trusted slave to the Persians with the message that the Greek fleet was preparing to depart and that he was ready to support Xerxes henceforth. The Persians, who were planning to attack anyway, were delighted and believed the news. They immediately sent a blocking force around Salamis to prevent escape and placed troops on an island at the mouth of the bay. There was no alternative now to fighting but the Greeks, thanks to Themistocles, were able to dictate the terms under which the battle would be fought.

At dawn the Persian ships began to move into the narrows, the Ionian Greeks on the left and the Phoenicians on the right. As they advanced the huge armada began to crowd into the confined water of the bay and the Greeks were able to maneuver against them and ram at will. By nightfall the bulk of the Persian fleet had been put out of action and the hopes of a victory in 480 were over. It was now late in September and Xerxes, having lost control of the sea and the means of supplying his huge land forces, withdrew to Asia but left a substantial contingent behind in Thessaly to continue the war.

Between September and August of the next year (479) the Greeks managed to preserve their fragile unity. After attempting to seduce Athens from the league, the Persian commander, Mardonius, ordered the razing of the city and then withdrew to Boeotia where he awaited the arrival of the allies on ground of his own choosing. The main Greek effort was now to be on land. To oppose an estimated 300,000 Persians, the Greeks by a supreme effort had assembled about a third of that number, mostly hoplites and light infantry. The commander-in-chief was the Spartan regent Pausanias while Aristides, who had fought with Themistocles at Marathon, commanded the Athenian contingent.

The problem faced by Pausanias was the same as that of the Athenians at Marathon—namely, how to engage the enemy infantry without being first cut to pieces by the superior Persian cavalry. For several weeks the Greeks waited in the foothills hoping the Persians would be tempted to attack, all the while suffering incessant cavalry raids and difficulties with supplies. When their main source of water was blocked by a Persian attack Pausanias decided to withdraw further up in the hills toward the city of Plataea. The movement was to be executed at night, but it proved to be impossible to coordinate the actions of 100,000 men. When day arrived the Athenians and Spartans were lagging behind. To all appearances the Greek army was breaking up and Mardonius ordered an immediate assault. The Persians advanced under a cloud of arrows, but the Spartans, having learned from the Athenian experience at Marathon, waited until the appropriate moment and then charged with devastating effect. When Mardonius fell the Persians broke and fled to their camp in the plain. While this battle was going on the Athenians fought a separate engagement with the Boeotians and drove them from the field. Athenians and Spartans then together assaulted the camp and annihilated their disorganized enemies. The battle of Plataea was as much a Spartan victory as Salamis had been an Athenian one, and it was the discipline and valor of the Spartan hoplite phalanx in an extremely difficult situation that turned what looked like certain disaster into victory. Probably not more than a few days later another major battle, fought at Mycale in Asia Minor, resulted in

Despite the heroic nudity of the Greek warrior in combat with the Persian bowman, it was the weight of armor and weapons and the discipline of the Spartans that won the day at Plataea.

the destruction of Persian naval power in Ionia. Although Salamis and Plataea saved mainland Greece from conquest, Ionia with its exposed hinterland—even after Mycale—was another problem. The best the Spartans could recommend to the Ionians was that they should abandon Asia altogether, but the Athenians, who had long-standing connections with this part of the world, raised objections. When the Spartans sailed home the Athenian flotilla under Xanthippus remained behind, and with the support of the Asiatic Greeks went on to clear the Persians out of Sestus, a strategic base controlling the Hellespont, Athens' lifeline to the grain-producing Black Sea region. Thus as early as 479 the divergent aims, military resources, and social structures of Sparta and Athens were revealed and the fragile unity of the Greeks began to disintegrate.

THE MILITARY SITUATION AFTER PLATAEA

The prestige of Sparta after the battle of Plataea suggested that it should remain at the head of the Greek alliance, but neither the logic of the military situation nor Sparta's own constitution would permit this.

Sparta was a hothouse society, so tightly organized that its citizens could not survive long as Spartans outside its immediate environment. This was brought home with a vengeance immediately after the war when Leotychidas, the commander of Mycale, was accused of corruption and fled into exile. More important than the inability of individual Spartans to survive outside Sparta was the inability of the Spartan army to operate for long periods of time away from home. Alone among the Greek states Sparta depended on the enserfment of masses of fellow Greeks of a homogeneous background who could be kept under control only by perpetual military surveillance. As a result, the army could never be absent from Laconia for long periods of time without inviting rebellion by the helots. In addition, although Sparta's system of government was ideally designed to satisfy the needs of a nation of soldiers and serfs, it was in every other respect slow and cumbersome, quite incapable of providing the kind of leadership needed by the volatile and anarchic Greek states of the Aegean.

The military problems, however, transcended Spartan limitations as a state. Even if its power was based on some other, less explosive social arrangement than the serfdom of the helots, Sparta still would not have been able to cope with the situation faced by the Greeks of Asia. After Plataea, defense against the Persians did not call for massive land armies but rather for both large and small fleet operations against widely scattered targets. Persian garrisons continued to maintain footholds in Europe for 15 years or more after Plataea, and major naval offensives were a possibility until Athens made peace with Persia in 448 B.C. However, the Greeks had to be prepared to handle either massive fleet concentrations of 300 or more ships at a time, as happened at the battle of the Eurymedon River (ca. 468), as well as the endless probing of Persian satraps looking for weak spots in the Greek defensive screen up and down the coast. Out-factions in the cities were always ready to call in the Persians when worsted by their enemies. The Persians for their part were still able to maintain control over large segments of Greek Asia through cooperative tyrants and oligarchies. There was thus a demand for relatively small groups of ships with a few thousand marines and hoplites, as well as for large-scale fleets for major engagements. Even the bigger states, which could support fairly substantial fleets, were easy targets for the concentrated forces of the Persians. What the Greeks needed was a well-informed, central organization that could coordinate strategy and concentrate their scattered forces to counter the enemy's great strength—centralized command and control over military resources.

There were other factors that made it difficult for a state like Sparta to provide leadership to the Greeks after the repulse of the Persians. First, the theater of war was now the eastern and northern Aegean, not mainland Greece where Sparta had traditionally operated. Then, whereas almost any city could field a hoplite phalanx, the same was not true of a fleet of triremes. Least of all was Sparta endowed with the resources necessary to sustain a navy. Ships were extremely expensive. Large crews were required to man them, and large sums of money were required for maintenance, merely to keep the fleet in existence. Hulls had to be maintained when not in use, equipment stored, and crews trained. A fleet with its dockyards, arsenals, harbors, and trained personnel such as ship architects and skilled workmen constituted a huge capital investment. The financing of crews was a major burden the naval power had to bear. The trireme, the basic fleet unit, had a complement of 200 men; a good-sized fleet of

The trireme, of which this is probably a representation, was the principal warship of Greek fleets in the fifth and fourth centuries. Propelled by oars, it was used to ram enemy ships. Because of the lack of adequate illustrations of the vessel, it is still uncertain how the rowers were seated.

about 200 ships required at least 40,000 rowers, marines, and officers (and obviously a much larger manpower pool from which to draw their numbers). Unlike hoplites, who were largely self-sustaining and who paid taxes in time of war, many of the rowers would have been propertyless. The state, therefore, that aspired to naval power had to have either a large population or a lot of money, or both. Naval warfare tended to favor (as it still does) the development of large fleets by the few states that possessed the necessary resources. It is not surprising that by midcentury only Athens, Lesbos, Chios, and Samos were making significant contributions in ships to the anti-Persian alliance, with Athens predominating.

Two final items contributed to the emergence of Athens as the leader of the alliance against the Persians. The first was the simple fact that triremes, unlike merchant ships, had a low freeboard and could not take either heavy weather or the open seas. They generally crept along the coasts, stopping every night so that the crews could eat and sleep on shore before starting off again the next morning. Movement by a fleet of triremes depended, therefore, on the possession of many stopping places (like the coaling stations in the days of coal-fired warships), and preferably well-developed, friendly harbors. Add to this the fact that Athens, unlike Sparta or most of the other Peloponnesian states, depended heavily on imported grain from the Black Sea area, and it is likely that even without the Persian threat it would have formed alliances all over the Aegean, especially the Hellespont area, to enable its fleet to protect the merchant ships bringing grain to Piraeus, the port of Athens.

The Athenian Alliance (Delian League)

Though the Greek league headed by Sparta remained intact, Athens—with the enthusiastic support of the Greeks in the east—created another alliance, the Delian League, in the winter of 478/477. Its purpose was both offensive and defensive. It aimed to preserve Greek freedom and to conduct active reprisals against the Persian Empire for the purpose of plunder to offset the expenses of the league. We are not certain about the structure of the alliance, though it was probably bicameral, with the Athenian state constituting one house and the allies the other. Whatever the arrangement, Athens, like Sparta in relation to the Peloponnesian League, was able to control the decision-making process. Though autonomy was guaranteed to each member, Athens supplied the commanders for all military operations, appointed the league treasurers, and took half of all the loot taken. The amount of contributions was determined by Aristides, who was popular among the allies and whose reputation for honesty had earned him the title of "the Just." The meeting place and treasury were at the temple of Apollo and Artemis at Delos.

The league's first actions were to drive the Persians out of Eion, their most important stronghold in northern Greece, and to coerce Naxos back into the league after an attempted secession. When a large fleet of 350 ships supported by an army was assembled in Asia about 468 by the Persians, Cimon the son of Miltiades led the league's forces against it and obtained a complete victory by land and sea at the battle of the Eurymedon. He then went on to the Hellespont where he cleared out more Persian garrisons.

Meanwhile Themistocles, despite the objections of the Spartans, supervised the rebuilding of the walls of Athens and the fortifications of Piraeus. It was his genius as well as his downfall to have an extraordinary ability to anticipate the future and then devote all his efforts to bringing others around to his views. He had been able to carry the Athenians with him in the years before the second Persian invasion, and now he espoused an anti-Spartan policy, which in the outcome was not acceptable to the Athenians. Cimon was solidly pro-Spartan, and in the public debate between the two Themistocles lost and was ostracized, probably in 472. When he continued his anti-Spartan activities at Argos, Sparta protested. Pursued by both Athenian and Spartan agents, he fled first to Epirus and then to the Persians where he was welcomed and given the district of Magnesia in Asia Minor to govern and there he died. As it turned out, Themistocles' assessment of the situation in the Greek world after Plataea was right; he correctly interpreted Sparta's resentment at being ousted from the position of leader of the Greeks as well as its growing fear of Athens. Within ten years his policies were taken up and given definitive form by Ephialtes, Pericles, and the radical democrats.

THE GREAT WAR BETWEEN ATHENS AND SPARTA (CA. 460–404 B.C.)

The "First" Peloponnesian War (460–446 B.C.)

Unlike the Spartan system of government the Athenian democracy was a constantly evolving entity. In the late 460s and 450s some radical alterations were made in the constitution. These changes were spearheaded by the aristocrats Ephialtes and Pericles, who provided the leadership, but the underlying cause was the development of the democracy itself. Unlike hoplite warfare, which was the preserve of the middle classes, naval warfare called for masses of rowers who had nothing more to offer than their muscle power and their willingness to sit for small wages in cramped spaces for long periods of time. As Athens' power shifted more and more toward naval operations, the political influence of the rowers of the fleet grew proportionately and was exercised in the Assembly with the assistance of such leaders as Pericles.

In the mid-460s the democrats began whittling away at the still significant power of the Areopagus. In 462/461 they were finally able to carry a series of laws that eliminated the last vestiges of the old aristocratic constitution and inaugurated the full democracy. The jurisdiction of the Areopagus, which originally included the right to try magistrates and supervise the administration of the laws, was now transferred to the popular courts and the Council. Only cases of religious significance (though these included homicide) were left to that venerable body. At the same time pay was introduced for the jurors. Shortly afterward (458/457) the archonship was opened to the third class, the *zeugitae,* and arrangements were made for the selection by lot of the councillors from all of the citizens, without prior election.

CIMON AND PERICLES

At the time that these reforms were taking place, Cimon, still the most powerful single individual in Athens, was in Laconia helping the Spartans put down the revolt of the helots that broke out after the disastrous earthquake in 464. Unfortunately for Cimon, the Spartans, fearing that the "adventurous and revolutionary spirit of the Athenians" would affect their own citizens and subjects, sent Cimon and his troops back to Athens ignominiously. The Athenians were enraged and with the encouragement of Ephialtes and Pericles, Cimon's opponents, formed an alliance with Sparta's enemies Argos and Thessaly. In the following year (461) Cimon was ostracized and the Athenians under new leadership committed themselves to an anti-Spartan policy, which they were to maintain until Thebes replaced Sparta as the most powerful land power in Greece almost a century later. Soon after the ostracism of Cimon, Ephialtes was murdered and his assassins were never identified, though an oligarchic plot was suspected. This left Pericles as the principal spokesman for the new policy and for the democracy at large, a position he held until his death 30 years later.

Pericles was the son of Xanthippus, the commander of the Athenian detachment at the battle of Mycale, and his mother, Agariste, was the daughter of the famous Cleisthenes, the founder of the Athenian democracy. Despite his aristocratic background Pericles was a dedicated democrat and was single-minded in his devotion to Athens. Although not a brilliantly original thinker he was a first-class orator and a capable general. His judgment was sound and under his guidance Athens flourished. Too much, however, has been made of his leadership and the myth of an Athens dominated by an Olympian Pericles is quite misleading. Athens had dozens of orators and would-be leaders in the mid-fifth century. The fact that the people of the city recognized Pericles' abilities and chose to listen to him more often than to others reflects on the soundness of their judgment as much as it does on Pericles. Ultimately the credit for the achievements of fifth-century Athens belongs to the people themselves and to their ability to make their democratic system of government work.

External events accelerated the development of a thoroughgoing anti-Spartan policy by Athens. In 459 Megara left the Spartan alliance and sought help from Athens after years of meddling by her aggressive neighbor, Corinth. This was a major coup, as possession of Megara meant control of access to Attica from the Peloponnese, a strategic factor of incalculable importance since the only serious threat to Athens came from a land invasion by the Spartans and their supporters. With Athens now involved against Corinth, Aegina joined in the fray but was defeated by Athens and in the following year incorporated in the Athenian alliance (457). The same year a Spartan army operating in Boeotia had difficulty in returning home, as the Athenians occupied the exits through the mountains as well as the coastal route. Some Athenians persuaded the Spartan commander to attack Athens and overthrow the democracy before the final stages of the fortification of the city, the Long Walls connecting it with Piraeus, were completed. A major battle resulted, and although the Spartans were victorious at the bloody battle of Tanagra, they suffered such severe losses they were forced to withdraw. A few months later another Athenian army marched into Boeotia and after a victory at Oenophyta took over control of that region. The year 457 marked the high point of Athenian success in Greece. Athens' ancient enemy Aegina, one of the last major independent naval powers in the Aegean, was eliminated and land assault by Sparta checked by Athens' control of Megara and Boeotia.

Mainland Greece was not, however, the only theater of war in these years. An inscription recording the names of 177 men from a single Athenian tribe who were killed in action in Cyprus, Egypt, Phoenicia, the Peloponnese, Aegina, and Megara in one year gives an idea of the widespread nature of Athens' military operations. The eastern involvement came about as part of Athens' ongoing policy of protecting the Greeks against Persia by weakening Persia whenever the opportunity presented itself. Thus in 460 when a fleet of ships of the alliance operating in Cyprus received an invitation from the rebel king of Egypt, Inaros, to help him, they accepted quickly. At first all went well. The Phoenician naval forces were defeated and Memphis was occupied. Then the Persians began to recover and in 455 both Egyptians and Greeks were badly defeated. The latter managed to hold out until the following year but finally surrendered. The defeat in Egypt was a major setback for the alliance and the first it had suffered since it had been formed 20 years earlier.

With the annihilation of the Egyptian expedition the Athenians transferred the treasury of the league to Athens for safety (454/453) and recalled

A mourning Athena reads a list of names of fallen soldiers.

Cimon. Two years later Athens entered into a five-year treaty with Sparta, but by 450 sufficient recovery had been made to send Cimon with 200 ships to Cyprus, where the Persians were defeated by land and sea. In the following year, however, Cimon died. With his death the impulse to continue the war against Persia evaporated. Shortly thereafter peace was negotiated with the Persians, who recognized the freedom of all the Greek cities liberated to that date, with the exception of those on Cyprus, which reverted to Persian control. The treaty is sometimes known as the peace of Callias because it was believed to have been negotiated by Callias, the brother-in-law of Cimon. With this event, the war with Persia came to a temporary halt until Sparta's failure to defeat Athens by conventional means reintroduced Persia into the Aegean a generation later.

From Alliance to Empire

With the removal of the treasury to Athens the synod of the allies ceased to meet and henceforth actions were taken unilaterally by Athens. Yet there had been indications that the alliance would or could turn into an empire from the very beginning. The treasurers of the league as well as the commanders of its joint forces had always been Athenian and the policy of Athens dominated its decision making. Secession was ruled out as a possible option of league members at an early date when first Naxos and then Thasos (465) were coerced into remaining members. The tribute of the alliance was used legitimately to subsidize the Athenian fleet, but the application of funds to rebuild the temples destroyed by the Persians raised a storm of protest, both inside and outside Athens. Probably in the early 440s Athenian weights, measures, and coinage were made obligatory throughout the alliance. By 446 Athens was claiming that all cases involving the death penalty, exile, or loss of civil rights should be subject to appeal to its courts. By midcentury the alliance of Athens and its allies had become an empire.

If the Athenian Empire is to be judged solely by the standards of autonomy and freedom as defined by the Greeks, there is no way it can be justified. Some writers have argued that the empire was beneficial to the lower classes, wherever these existed, since it protected them from their own rapacious oligarchies. There may have been no great enthusiasm for Athens but it was the lesser of evils to be subject to the Athenian people than to their own wealthy classes.[1] To this extent the Athenian Empire could be considered to have been popular among its subjects. Others prefer the opinion of a contemporary of Thucydides who expressed the view that the allies did not want to be subject to either an oligarchy or a democracy but simply "to be free with whatever kind of government they could get."[2]

During the five-year truce with Sparta the advantageous arrangements Athens had built up in Greece began to disintegrate. Argos renounced its treaty with Athens in 451 and made a Thirty-Year pact with Sparta instead. Then Pericles' proposal for a Panhellenic congress at Athens to discuss the restoration of the temples destroyed by the Persians came to nothing. In 446 Boeotia was lost at the battle of Coronea and later in the year both Euboea and Megara revolted. The former was recovered by the swift action of Pericles but Megara was lost for good. Athens was once more exposed to a land attack by Sparta. In midwinter of that year a new peace treaty that was supposed to last for 30 years was negotiated with Sparta.

For 15 years there was, in fact, peace between the two powers, but neither believed it would last. The essential cause of the conflict was Sparta's fear that Athens' spectacular rise to power and its relentless energy would affect its allies and expose Sparta itself to outside interference. Any threat to the Peloponnesian League was a threat to Sparta. A defection by Corinth or the Arcadian cities or active meddling for any length of time by Athens at Argos could not be tolerated. Several times Sparta debated coming to the aid of one or another of Athens' allies in revolt. Thasos requested help in 465 but at the time Sparta was preoccupied with its own inner problems. Then in 440 during the Samian revolt the issue was debated again but Corinthian opposition deterred intervention. Eventually it was a series of confrontations on essentially peripheral issues that involved the two states with each other in the Peloponnesian War proper.

[1]G. E. M. de Ste. Croix, *The Origins of the Peloponnesian War* (Ithaca, N.Y.: Cornell University Press, 1972), p. 4.

[2]Cited by D. W. Bradeen, "The Popularity of the Athenian Empire," *Historia* 9 (1960):268.

CORCYRA AND CORINTH

In 435 Corinth and its colony Corcyra came to blows over a colony established by the latter. A battle was fought, in which the Corcyreans came out on top. Instead of accepting the defeat Corinth began building a new fleet. Corcyra, which had traditionally avoided alliances, found itself isolated in the face of a major effort by Corinth and Corinthian allies. In desperation Corcyra turned to Athens to seek an alliance. A delegation was sent to present the thorny issue to the Athenian Assembly in 433. At issue was whether to grant an offensive alliance with Corcyra and break the Thirty-Year Treaty with Sparta, to make only a defensive alliance and provoke the ire of Corinth, or to make no alliance at all and probably see Corcyra's considerable navy fall into the hands of Corinth and the Peloponnesian League. The Athenians settled for the defensive alliance, sending only ten ships to keep an eye on the situation. However, a major battle was fought between the two contestants, and when the Corcyreans were on the verge of defeat the Athenians intervened. Just at that moment another Athenian fleet appeared on the horizon and the Corinthians, deprived of their victory, withdrew in a rage. Despite the discomfiture of Corinth the battle was a major triumph for Athens. Both Corinth and Corcyra had suffered heavily whereas Athens' fleet came through unscathed and the Thirty-Year Treaty remained intact.

The clash with Corinth made Athens reflect on one of its tributary allies in northern Greece, Potidaea, which was also a colony of Corinth and annually received magistrates from the mother city. In an attempt to anticipate Corinthian retaliation in this area, Athens ordered the Potidaeans to get rid of their system of Corinthian magistrates, pull down a section of their wall, and give hostages. Potidaea refused and obtained the support of Macedonia and Sparta, who promised to invade Attica if the city was attacked. A general revolt in the area began in 432. Corinthian and other Peloponnesian "volunteers" arrived to help Potidaea, but by the end of the summer all these forces had been beaten and the city was under siege by the Athenians.

The final spark that set off the war was the Megarian decree. Athens accused Megara, its neighbor, of cultivating and thereby violating the sacred land of Demeter and Core at Eleusis. In retaliation Athens excluded the Megarians from entering the Athenian Agora and the harbors of the empire. The purpose of this decree is disputed. One group of scholars believes that it was intended as an economic sanction against Megara and the other believes that it was a retaliation of a different kind intended merely to embarrass the trespassers. Exclusion from the Agora, which was regarded as a holy place, was an automatic penalty invoked against the ritually impure, and if Athens was looking for a way of getting back at Megara this would have been an effective means; it had the propaganda effect of branding the Megarians as violators of sacred laws and was fairly typical of the kind of religious weapons the cities of Greece used against one another. The Spartans, for example, were soon to call for the expulsion of the accursed Alcmeonids (among whom was Pericles), to which Athens quickly responded with a similar demand. Exclusion from the harbors of the empire is more difficult to explain, and this might have constituted the economic sanction that is usually seen in the decree. In any event, all three actions provoked a major debate at Sparta. Athens was given an ultimatum to withdraw the Megarian decree and give up the siege of Potidaea. To make sure the proposal was rejected, Sparta added the demand that Athens restore the autonomy of Aegina. Understandably Athens refused to accept these terms. The war came about because Sparta was ready to challenge Athens and prevent any further growth of Athens' power. "What made the war inevitable," said Thucydides in his summary of the causes of the war, "was the growth of Athenian power and the fear which this caused in Sparta."[3]

THE OUTBREAK OF WAR

The strategy proposed by Pericles for the conduct of the war was to emphasize Athens' naval strength while husbanding its limited hoplite reserves. Athens had already learned the cost of holding its land approaches through Megara and Boeotia, and Pericles argued that Athens could only survive a war with the Peloponnesians by avoiding major infantry battles and by sending out instead naval expeditions to weaken and disrupt the Spartan alliance. According to this strategy Athens had to be prepared to sacrifice rural Attica to the invaders. Athens would have to behave as an island, relying on its navy to guarantee food supplies. Accordingly, when the Peloponnesian army appeared in Attica in 431, the people and their flocks had withdrawn to Euboea or within the Long Walls. Since the Spartans were not prepared for a lengthy siege, they could only ravage the countryside and withdraw. The invasion of Attica was to become an annual occurrence, one of the recurring patterns of the war.

The following year a plague broke out in Athens. By the time it ceased in 426, perhaps one-third of the population had been wiped out. Among those who died was Pericles. Nevertheless his strategy was still generally adhered to. Athens set out to harry the enemy by creating a ring of bases on islands and headlands around the Peloponnese and using these to foment rebellion among the helots and the allies of the Spartans. From the island of Minoa, Athens was able to blockade Megara; from Cythera, Athens could intercept ships sailing to Sparta from Africa. There were major bases at Zacynthos, Cephallenia, Corcyra, Naupactus, and Acarnania, and the forts on the promontories of Pylos and Methana allowed Athens to conduct direct attacks on Messenia and the territories of Epidaurus and Troezen. It was at Pylos that one of the major successes of the war came. Here in 425 a detachment of Spartans was cut off and forced to surrender by the generals Cleon and Demosthenes. Sparta, already hard pressed, sued for peace. Hoping for larger gains and egged on by Cleon, the

[3]Thucydides, *History of the Peloponnesian War,* tr. by Rex Warner (Penguin Classics, 1954), p. 25. Copyright © Rex Warner 1954. Reprinted by permission of Penguin Books Ltd.

Athenians refused to come to terms. Operations thereafter were not so successful. A large force of Athenians was badly defeated at Delium in Boeotia, and in the north the brilliant Spartan general Brasidas was successful in provoking Athenian allies to revolt. His success in winning over the important city of Amphipolis led to the banishment of the historian Thucydides, who had the misfortune to be the commander of some Athenian forces in the area at the time. Brasidas, however, was killed shortly thereafter in an Athenian attempt to recover Amphipolis. In the same encounter Cleon also died (422 B.C.).

By this time both sides were ready to negotiate and in 421 by the terms of the peace of Nicias most of the bases captured by Athens around the Peloponnese were to be given up. Sparta in turn was to relinquish claim to the northern cities that had revolted. Unfortunately neither side lived up to the terms of the treaty. In addition Megara, Corinth, and Boeotia refused to sign the agreement; technically they were still at war with Athens. Scione, one of the cities that had revolted, was not included in the terms of the treaty and when it was taken by the Athenians all the male citizens were executed and the rest of the population enslaved. This kind of atrocity had earlier been perpetrated by the Spartans when they captured Plataea and by Athens in regard to the rebel leaders at Mytilene on Lesbos. Later the Athenians massacred or sold into slavery the population of Melos, an incident that became the basis for one of Thucydides' most famous dialogues. Atrocities were not confined to the major combatants. At Corcyra a civil war raged for several years, oligarchs pitted against democrats in a bloody conflict in which each side brought in their allies to help them. The massacre at Corcyra became for Thucydides a supreme example of how war destroys the ordinary standards of decency and brings everyone down to a common level of brutality.

THE SICILIAN DISASTER

In the first round of the war Athens fared better than Sparta. The Athenian alliance was practically intact, while Sparta's had been severely shaken. Sparta badly needed time to reassemble its forces. This Sparta succeeded in doing, despite the efforts of Alcibiades, a mercurial relative of Pericles, who had risen to power in Athens, to exploit the opposition of Argos to Sparta and use Argos as a means of breaking up the Peloponnesian League. Within five years of the peace Sparta had checked Argos and reasserted its control over its allies. Opinions were now divided at Athens between two proposed policies. Should Athens continue the war with Sparta, as argued by Alcibiades, or keep to the terms of the treaty as proposed by Nicias? Ostracism was attempted as a means of resolving the dispute but Nicias and Alcibiades avoided the decision by combining forces against a third politician, Hyperbolus, who had attacked both of them. Thus ostracism failed to resolve the issue. When an opportunity arose for Athens to exploit its alliances in Sicily, Alcibiades persuaded the Assembly to send an expedition despite Nicias' objections that Athens' true interests lay in the Aegean.

From the beginning the expedition was a disaster. Its commanders were an ill-fated trio—the unwilling Nicias, his opponent Alcibiades, and another general by the name of Lamachus. Shortly after they arrived in Sicily Alcibiades was recalled to face charges of having profaned the Mysteries of Eleusis, one of the ancient and revered religions of Attica. Although there was no proof, his profligate and irreligious way of life made him a natural suspect. Rather than face trial, he fled to Sparta. There he advised the Spartans to set up a fortified base at Decelea in Attica and support the Syracusans. Mismanaged from the beginning, the expedition finally succumbed to the poor generalship of Nicias and the unexpected strength of the Syracusans. In all, 200 ships and 50,000 men were lost by the end of the two-year campaign (415–413). Worse, the war with Sparta was resumed in 414 and in the following year Decelea was fortified. From a position of prestige and strength two years earlier Athens was suddenly fighting for its life.

THE LAST AGONY (414–404)

Cut off by land from Euboea's food supply (by Decelea) and faced by the revolt of its major allies Lesbos and Chios, Athens seemed at the end of its resources. More alarming, Sparta was now ready to accept financial help from Persia. From 412 onward the satraps of Asia Minor regularly supplied money for the maintenance of Sparta's fleet. In return, the Spartans turned over the Greeks of Asia to their enemies. Alcibiades, having lost favor at Sparta, transferred his counsels to the Persians and pretended to be in a position to sway the satraps for or against whomever he recommended. Encouraged by this belief, the Athenians entered into negotiations with the Persians and were informed by Alcibiades that if they abandoned their democratic constitution and set up an oligarchy they would draw Persian support away from the Spartans. Plans were laid accordingly for the introduction of an oligarchy. One group, led by Antiphon and Peisander, favored a narrow oligarchy but another, led by Theramenes, favored a more liberal arrangement. In 411, in its temporarily demoralized condition, the Assembly was persuaded to accept an oligarchy in which ostensibly 400 were involved but which in fact was controlled by a handful of conspirators. It immediately began negotiations with the Spartans and abolished pay for public services. A plan to introduce a similar oligarchy in Samos where the bulk of the fleet was located failed, and the democracy maintained itself under the leadership of Thrasybulus and Thrasyllus. One of the fleet's first acts was to invite Alcibiades to return and he was promptly elected to the generalship. A proposition to sail to Athens to restore the democracy was turned down but it was decided that the Four Hundred had to go. Impressed by the strength of the democracy on Samos Theramenes turned on the extreme oligarchs and the Assembly voted to replace the Four Hundred with a body of 5000 citizens.

While all this was going on at Athens, two important victories at Cynossema and Cyzicus were won by the fleet. Athens regained control of the vital grain route through the Hellespont, which it had briefly lost. Encouraged by these successes, Athens restored the full democratic constitution and prepared to carry on the war as before.

The initiative, however, now passed to the Peloponnesians and the Persians. Sparta had a piece of good fortune when the Persian king sent his son Cyrus to Asia to coordinate efforts against the Athenians and at the same time stumbled upon an able commander in the person of the general Lysander. Athens tried desperately to match the efforts of its enemies and raised money by melting down precious objects of gold and silver and pressing the allies for further contributions. Some successes were achieved and at Arginusae in 406 the Spartan fleet under Callicratidas was defeated, though the victory was overshadowed by the aftermath. Because of a storm the generals were neither able to recover the bodies of the dead nor to rescue survivors in the wrecked ships and an hysterical Assembly condemned the generals to death.

The end of the war came swiftly. Lysander, well bankrolled by Cyrus, assembled yet another fleet and surprised the Athenians, who had beached their ships at a place called Aegospotami in the Hellespont. One hundred and seventy-one ships were taken along with their crews and marine contingents. Only eight ships under the general Conon escaped. Following the now well-established practice of executing prisoners, Lysander killed the 3000 Athenians he found among the captured crews and released the rest. By the end of the year (405) Athens was blockaded by land and sea, and negotiations for peace began. Corinth and Thebes proposed that all the Athenian males be massacred and the rest of the population sold into slavery, but Sparta settled for the destruction of the Long Walls, the fortifications of Piraeus, and the abandonment of the empire. The fleet was to be given up except for 12 triremes, and Athens was compelled to become an ally of Sparta. The terms were accepted and in 404 the great war between Sparta and Athens came to an end.

THE HEGEMONY OF SPARTA AND THEBES

After its victory over Athens, Sparta was no more capable of coping with the leadership of the Greeks than it had been after the battle of Plataea 75 years earlier. Yet by 404 Sparta had arrived at the conclusion that only by maintaining an empire could its security be ensured. The internal and external obstacles to this were enormous and the burden of empire destroyed Sparta even more effectively than it did Athens.

Sparta's own losses in the war were significant. Only about 3000 Spartiates (full citizens) remained, and the numbers continued to decline as a result of constant war and social change. In the past Sparta had been able to conserve its peculiar society by rigorously isolating itself from the rest of the world. Now that Sparta had made the decision to take Athens' position as peacemaker in the Aegean, it was forced to expose its society to the unsettling influences of normal Greek life. Tribute from the empire and loot from wars poured into Sparta in violation of the traditional norms, and it began to concentrate in private hands. More and more of the Equals lost their share of land and dropped out of the ranks of first-class citizens. With so much power and influence at stake, ephors, kings, and council struggled among themselves and public policy oscillated between violent extremes. Spartan governors abroad ruled through narrow oligarchies and were almost universally hated. The experience of Athens was probably typical. There a group of 30 oligarchs led by the extremist Critias crushed the moderate opposition of Theramenes. They executed 1500 of the democratic leaders and forced 5000 others into exile. Estates were indiscriminately confiscated. It was not long before the exiles, led by Thrasybulus, the democrat who organized the fleet against the oligarchic coup of 411, attempted to return. In 403 they seized Piraeus. After Critias was killed in fighting, negotiations ensued and by the end of the year the democracy had been restored. By an act of fine statesmanship, further internal strife was avoided and amnesty was extended to all but the Thirty.

Sparta's most basic problem was its lack of resources for maintaining an empire. It possessed neither the financial superiority nor the manpower needed to control the anarchic world inherited from Athens. After the Peloponnesian War other states recovered with astonishing rapidity. Trade resumed, populations expanded and soon Sparta found itself only one of many cities with aspirations to empire. Its reputation as a champion of Greek liberties, which might have compensated to some extent for its internal weakness, was tarnished by its blatant betrayal of the Greeks in Asia to the Persians during the later years of the Peloponnesian War. More important, the same problems of naval power that had forced Athens to create an empire—the need for capital for ships and cash to pay their crews—now plagued Sparta. An adequate navy could only be maintained through significant imperial revenues or Persian subsidies, neither of which was seen as an acceptable alternative by Greek public opinion. On top of this was the altered form of infantry warfare, in which until the fourth century, Sparta had been supreme. After years of war Greece was full of men ready to serve whoever was willing or able to pay their wages. The normal citizen levy of hoplites might suddenly find itself confronted with an experienced body of mercenaries hired by its opponents. While wearing down their enemy, Sparta's opponents could husband their own manpower resources. Light infantry, having proved its ability to defeat, under proper conditions, even the renowned Spartan hoplites, now became a common feature of land warfare. Requiring special training and handling, such infantry was beyond the resources of most of the old-style city-states. Generals, too, were becoming more and more professionalized. Like the men in the ranks, they also were for hire.

THE RISE OF THEBES

In 401, with Spartan connivance, Cyrus, the Persian viceroy in Asia, raised a large force of Greek mercenaries and attempted to unseat his brother Artaxerxes II, the ruling king. He failed, and the Greek cities of Asia who had supported Cyrus called in terror upon the Spartans to defend them against Persian reprisals. The Spartans, sensing an opportunity for plunder, sent an army under the king, Agesilaus. Although the Spartans were generally successful on land, Spartan naval power was destroyed by the Persian fleet at the battle of Cnidus in 394. By a strange quirk the commander of the Persian fleet was Conon, the Athenian general who had escaped from the disaster of Aegospotami in 405 and had fled to the Persians with a handful of ships. By this battle the victory of Sparta over Athens was undone and Conon was able to go on to help in the rebuilding of the Long Walls at Athens. Meanwhile, Sparta's heavy-handedness, Persian subversion, and the natural tendency of the Greek states to combine against the most powerful had brought about the unlikely coalition of Athens, Corinth, Thebes, Argos, and Euboea against Sparta. Persia aided with lavish subsidies. As a result, Sparta was forced to withdraw its army from Asia and once more abandon the Greek cities there to the Persians. By 388/387 Sparta had had enough and sent the envoy Antalcidas to the Persian king to seek a negotiated settlement. Despite the efforts of the allies represented by Conon, the king favored Sparta and dictated a peace whose terms were left to Sparta to be enforced (the peace of Antalcidas or the King's Peace, 387). Given this breathing space, Sparta devoted its energies to eliminating the most dangerous of the alliances formed against it. Of these the special understanding between the Boeotian and Chalcidian leagues and the recent union of Corinth and Argos seemed the most dangerous. In all of these Sparta succeeded, but the garrisoning of the acropolis of Thebes in 382 in support of a narrow, pro-Spartan oligarchy led to disaster. Two years later a group of Thebans, led by Pelopidas and Epaminondas and supported by Athenian "volunteers" (since Athens was technically still at peace with Sparta), liberated Thebes. Gradually the Spartan hold on Boeotia was broken. Athens, making common cause with Thebes, reorganized its maritime empire in 377. Guaranteeing autonomy of its members, the Second Empire was initially very popular. Under the generalship of Callistratos, Chabrias, and Iphicrates, Spartan seapower was easily contained. Meanwhile Theban supremacy in central Greece began to worry Athens, and in 374 peace was sought with Sparta. It was of short duration, but alienation from Thebes was growing and in 371 a more permanent peace was negotiated (peace of Callias). Freed from the danger of Athenian intervention Sparta immediately attacked Thebes and to the astonishment of Greece, the Thebans led by Pelopidas and Epaminondas swept their enemies from the field with great slaughter at the battle of Leuctra (371). Sparta was reduced to 800 full citizens, and its power was at an end. In the winter of 370/369, and again in 368, the Thebans and their allies entered the Peloponnese and restored the independence of Messenia, thereby destroying the economic base of Spartan power. Megalopolis, the newly founded capital of the Arcadian league, hemmed in Sparta from the north, and barred access to Messenia should Sparta ever contemplate reconquering that region.

Thebes, thus, had become the predominant power in Greece and, for a brief time, maintained its hegemony. Its strength was derived from its federal constitution, which embraced practically all of Boeotia. In an unusual development the league created an assembly open to all its members, which decided common issues of policy. The individual districts elected the generals, judges and financial officers. The democratic bases of the league enabled the Thebans to draw upon a much larger reserve of manpower than was possessed by either Athens or Sparta or almost any other single city, but Thebes frittered it away after its two great leaders died in battle—Pelopidas in Thessaly in 364 and Epaminondas at the battle of Mantinea two years later. The immediate cause of Thebes' decline was a war with the minor state of Phocis (Third Sacred War, 355–336). By drawing on the resources of the temple of Delphi, which they seized, the Phocians were able to hire great numbers of mercenaries. With these they wore down the citizen levies of Thebes. At almost the same time Athens lost the power it had slowly built up in the new alliance by falling into the old temptation of attempting to convert the league into an empire. The Social War (357–355) deprived Athens of practically all its allies. Along with Sparta and Thebes, Athens joined the list of the states that had exhausted themselves in trying to build empires on too-narrow bases.

Classical Athens

CULTURE AND RELIGION IN CLASSICAL ATHENS (490–338 B.C.)

Preview and Retrospect

To an uninvolved observer the descent of the Persian expeditionary force on mainland Greece in 490 might have looked like the preliminary step to the inevitable absorption of an unimportant fringe area into the world empire of the Persians. There would have been, of course, no way to tell that in a little over a century and a half the Greeks would be on the verge of completely reversing this position, and that their former consciousness of inferiority and weakness would have given way to a sense of invincibility, not just on the battlefield, but in cultural matters also.

In this reversal of fortune Athens had a major role, first in the military sphere by leading the fight against the Persians, and then in the field of culture, for it was in Athens in this period that the culture of Greece reached rapid and full maturity in a great many areas: in sculpture, painting, architecture, philosophy, drama, history, and, above all, in political sophistication and development. Whole new disciplines and arts were created and reached levels that in some instances have never been excelled; others were launched and reached fruition at a later date.

Culturally, the period saw a great dawning of human consciousness. It began in a time when the self-contained ethics of the family and tribe were still deeply entrenched and morality was an exterior affair of what others thought or custom judged. It ended with the most modern-looking concepts of freedom and individual autonomy. The first stage in this development was the creation of a constitution and written laws restricting the arbitrary power of would-be tyrants and aristocrats and setting up standards of behavior for all. By gradual stages there next emerged an understanding that the ultimate freedom was that of the individual to his own conscience alone, a development that collided head-on with the old assumptions of the city-state and its totalitarian demands for unquestioning obedience. Under these influences the practice of justice evolved also, and considerations of status and position were put aside in favor of simple innocence or guilt before the law. Similarly, religion was humanized, passing from a vision of the gods as angry and capricious deities to one that saw them as guarantors of an orderly and just—if mysterious—world order. Philosophy and tragedy examined the foundations of morality, the role of fate, the problem of evil, and the suffering of the innocent. Art reached a stage where it was possible to portray the most exalted concepts of divine and human beauty as well as the depths of passion and emotion.

These cultural developments of the classical period generally overshadow the remarkable political and social growth of the Athenians as a people and a community. Emerging from a troubled background in the sixth century, the Athenians established a workable system of democratic government. This system for a time provided an astonishing degree of harmony among the mutually antagonistic elements in the state and enabled Athens to take the leadership of Greece against the Persians and win an empire, at the same time creating the basis for its cultural hegemony in the Greek world.

The close interrelationship between society and the state, common in all polis-type societies, reached its highest level of development in Athens. The people were collectively legislators, judges, and administrators, quite literally controlling their own destinies. How this tightly knit society stimulated and provided the essential milieu for the cultural growth that occurred in Athens in the classical period is a complex question. It cannot be treated fully here except to comment upon the close connection that existed in these years between the intellectual and artistic community and society at large. The great dramatists presented their plays as part of an essential civic function to all Athenians, not just to the knowledgeable or those who could afford the price of theater tickets. Socrates and other philosophers taught and debated in the marketplace, the Agora. Even the more strictly organized philosophical schools of Plato and Aristotle, the Academy and the Lyceum were located in the public gymnasia of the city, also important community gathering places. The great rhetoricians did not address fellow politicians and professional jurists but the masses of the Athenian people in the courts, in the assemblies, and on festival occasions. Art was public and intended for public use and entertainment, not the private adornment of the palaces of kings or the residences of the rich. The themes of the plays were not trivial, but debated different understandings of theological issues, ranging in scope from the deep religiosity of Aeschylus to the apparent blasphemy of Euripides. Although a split ultimately developed between the people and a segment of the intellectual community, segregation of society by culture was practically unknown. There was also a tendency to give the greater achievements of the classical period a permanent, or at least repetitive, character, which meant that they continued to mold subsequent generations long after the disappearance of the society that had brought them into being. A good example is the art of the period, which was enshrined in the great public buildings and the statuary of Athens. The achievements of the great tragedians were also given a quasi-permanence by means of revivals of their plays at the great public festivals. The educational system, formalized in this period in the great schools of Isocrates, Plato, and Aristotle, guaranteed that a lasting form would also be given to the ideas and philosophies developed at this time. Despite suggestions of decay, there is no reason to believe that the democracy would not have continued indefinitely had it not been overwhelmed by the Macedonians and, along with the other states of Greece, forcibly incorporated in the world empire of Alexander and his successors.

The Early Classical Period (490–450 B.C.)

In the Archaic Age men struggled with the problem of justice and order in a world of bewildering change. Cities were split by social and economic upheavals and divided by class warfare. Unlike the heroes of the Homeric poems, who feared neither the gods nor the future and had no sense of a menacing divine order, the men of the Archaic Age trembled before an arbitrary divinity that grudged them their successes and inexorably punished their self-assertion. The shedding of blood, which came so easily to the heroes of the past, became an enormously heavy burden that the men of the new age tried to discard by rationalizations and ritual.

As the Greeks strove to create constitutions and laws and bring their cities into harmony with the realities of the new world, they also began to look to the heavens for a cosmic order that was more sympathetic to their new needs. Instead of the too human Zeus of Homer, who had all the frailties and unpredictable passions of a human being, the Greeks sought a more predictable and stable guarantor of world order. This, however, was no easy task. The old myths were deeply entrenched, and it was one of the great achievements of the fifth century that the old was not cast aside but infused with a new spirit that made it meaningful and acceptable to the new age.

One of the most important consequences of the efforts to rationalize the state by means of constitutions and laws was the development of a sense of individual freedom and responsibility. The constitution of Cleisthenes had replaced tyrannical and aristocratic whim with predictable, man-made laws. It had gone further and broken up the old kinship groups and in their place substituted the new, geographically based tribal and deme structures. In the past an individual's primary relationship had been to his family, clan, and brotherhood members, but now it was directed immediately to his fellow citizens from all over Attica, whether related by blood or not. The intermediary kin groups were either swept away or weakened, and the citizen now came face to face with the state—in fact he *was* the state. At the same time the decline in the importance of kinship ties led to a weakening of the old group-style morality and in its place rose an ethical system based on personal responsibility giving special emphasis to the duties of citizens to one another.

The worth of constitutions and laws and of the new idea of individual responsibility was dramatically boosted by the Greek victories in the Persian Wars. These successes seemed to vindicate completely the concepts of discipline, order, and individual freedom against the world of the barbarians, which now began to be viewed as the epitome of the tyrannical and the unrestrained. It was the barbarians who, by attempting to step beyond their allotted place in the cosmic order, had brought down on themselves divine retribution. It was also very clear that the innocent, unfortunately, suffered along with the guilty. It was to this contradictory working of cosmic justice, which at once put down the mighty but also made the innocent suffer, that men turned their attention.

AESCHYLUS

The lifetime of Aeschylus spans almost the entire first period of the Classical Age. He fought at Marathon and possibly also at Salamis, and he survived until after the establishment of the full democracy.

His earliest surviving play, the *Persians* (472), is not a triumphal proclamation of the superiority of the Greeks but rather a thoughtful analysis of the Persian loss. The barbarians were defeated not because of the higher quality of the Greeks but because due order had been violated. They had arrogantly stepped beyond the bounds assigned to them by providence, and Zeus, the guarantor of cosmic order, had humbled them at Salamis. Other plays of Aeschylus reflect similar themes. Oedipus, who killed his father and married his mother, violated order with disastrous results for both the family of Oedipus and the state. When the Titan Prometheus tried to raise men above their appointed place in the universe, both Prometheus and mankind suffered. Yet Aeschylus did not naively believe in a universe ruled by an irrational, implacable justice that mechanically crushed the errant, whether innocent (as in the case of Oedipus) or not. Aeschylus' greatness lay in his ability to transform the old myths with their harsh morality. He was able to provide a new interpretation that made them more palatable—if not easier to live with—to the men of his generation.

He did this in two ways. In the first place, there is the essential law of suffering, which dictates that it is only by enduring what fate inflicts that men can rise to the highest levels of knowledge. Thus the chorus in *Prometheus Bound* proclaims that it has learned by watching the suffering of the protagonist and contemplating his fate. What Aeschylus is saying is that even if men cannot fully comprehend the sufferings of the individual they should still have faith that justice is being maintained. Despite appearances the divine order prevails. One should not be misled by the fate of any individual, including that of Prometheus, because even here Zeus is somehow maintaining order; and in the larger view of things, if we only possessed it, his action would be seen to be justified.

At another level Aeschylus offered a solution to one of the grimmest of the old tales, the story of Orestes. His trilogy on the subject, the *Oresteia,* was performed in 458, just three years after the democratic reforms of the court system by Ephialtes, and is usually thought to reflect his approval of the changes. It can also be seen as an example of how a story that enshrined the values of the past, in this case the tradition of the vendetta, could be updated and in the process secularized by being placed in the context of the evolving democracy of contemporary Athens.

In the traditional account Orestes is presented as trapped in the old archaic pattern of crime followed by punishment that is passed on as an inheritance from generation to generation. At the point where Aeschylus begins, the current head of the house, Agamemnon, has sacrificed his daughter to obtain the successful departure of the Greek fleet for Troy and on his return home he is slain in revenge by his wife Clytemnestra. Orestes in turn is directed to murder her by Apollo and is then pursued by the Furies, elemental spirits of the old-world order, for having shed kin blood. But Athena intervenes to resolve the contradictions of the archaic form of justice and persuades the Furies to accept the verdict of acquittal rendered to Orestes by the homicide court of Athens, the Areopagus. Thus Aeschylus was able to transform the old concept of justice by showing how the city-state, with the assistance of the gods, was capable of administering justice. Henceforth the Furies become the "Kindly Ones," maintaining order in the new spirit of humanitarian justice that is seen reflected

Urged on by his sister Electra, Orestes dispatches his mother's lover Aegisthus, while Clytemnestra gestures in futility.

in the new court system at Athens. In the *Oresteia* we have a good example of the blending of the old and the new and an instance of how the developing democracy was able to influence the old mythology and direct it into new channels.

ART IN THE EARLY CLASSICAL PERIOD

The art of the early classical period reflects many of its themes and preoccupations. It is simple and serious, rejecting the frills and complications of the preceding age. Appropriate to a time when cities struggled with tyrants, both domestic and foreign, and attempted to create constitutions and laws without offending the gods, it is severe and at times touched with a trace of melancholy. There is a new feeling of self-confidence, but not a sense of overwhelming mastery, perhaps because of the recognition that although it is possible to bring order to society men are still prone to folly that brings down divine vengeance.

The pediments of the great temple of Zeus at Olympia were created at some date fairly close to that of the performance of the *Oresteia* by Aeschylus (458). Although not Athenian they serve to illustrate in the plastic arts something of the spirit of the age that Aeschylus tried to capture in his plays.

The east pediment, which faced the sanctuary of Olympia and the starting point of the chariot races, represents the story of how the young hero Pelops won his bride from the king of Pisa. According to the legend, the king demanded as part of the price for the hand of his daughter that any successful suitor be victorious in a chariot race with him. If, on the other hand, the suitor failed, he would be killed. The catch was that the king had arms and horses provided for him by one of the gods and to date all previous suitors had met fatal ends. Pelops, however, was successful because through intrigue he was able to tamper with the king's chariot, and the king, rather than Pelops, was killed. There was an alternative story in circulation that passed over these questionable details and said instead that the arrogant king was flung from his chariot by a bolt from Zeus himself, rather than by the machinations of Pelops. The west pediment portrays one of the great traditional scenes of Greek sculpture, the battle between the Lapiths (early dwellers of Thessaly) and the Centaurs. The story depicted is that of the wedding of Perithoos (one of Zeus' sons), to which the local Centaurs had been invited. When they became drunk, however, they assaulted the women present and a wholesale battle resulted in which the Lapiths, directed by Apollo, another of Zeus' sons, slaughtered the Centaurs.

Despite the various interpretations these scenes suggested, there was one dominant theme, the maintenance of cosmic order. In the case of the legend of the east pediment there was a choice between viewing the trial of Pelops as an ambiguous affair in which the king, although arrogant, was dealt with underhandedly, and the alternate unambiguous version. If the viewer accepted the first he must have been left with a sense of uneasiness over the unresolved issues. There is tension present, both moral and religious. Nevertheless, Zeus is the central figure in the pediment, presiding over the whole affair, thus leaving it to

The serene and noble heads of Athena (from one of the metopes of the Temple of Zeus at Olympia) and Apollo (from the west pediment of the same temple) convey something of the lofty understanding of the gods possessed by the artists of the Early Classical Period.

the faith of the viewer to believe (in the Aeschylean sense) that here too, despite appearances, justice was being worked out. The other variant of the story in which Zeus himself was responsible for the destruction of the proud king, of course, offers no such problems. The west pediment is more easily interpreted. The violent, irrational Centaurs are overcome by the disciplined, unemotional Lapiths. Apollo, over whose temple at Delphi were the words "Know Thyself" (that is, know your place in the cosmic scheme of things), presides serenely over the battle. He directs the smooth-visaged Greeks to victory over their snarling grimacing enemies, who could be understood to stand for the forces of violence and the irrational, either in the individual or the eternally troubled city-states of Greece.

The simplicity and severity of the sculptural styles are also reflected in the temples of the period, which are logically proportioned, compact, and somewhat solid. Not enough of the temple of Zeus with its 2 : 1 proportionality survives to convey a good sense of the early buildings, but the so-called "Basilica" at Paestum in the south of Italy suggests something of the simplicity, balance, and measure attained by these structures.

The massive "Basilica" at Paestum. Working slightly later, the architects of the Parthenon at Athens were able to lighten the inherent heaviness of the plain Doric temple structure.

The Classical Age (450–430 B.C.)

DEMOCRACY AND THE RISE OF RHETORIC

From the time immemorial power in Athens rested in the hands of kings, tyrants, and aristocrats whose decisions were arrived at within the privacy of their palaces or assembly chambers. By the mid-fifth century, however, the locus of power was clearly established in the Assembly of the people and the popular law courts. Though in the past, privy councillors or senior aristocrats made their opinions known to their masters or to one another, it was now necessary to conduct debate in the open, before large numbers of people. Legislative, judicial, and administrative matters were entirely public affairs. Decisions had to be reached, literally, in the clear light of day.

The new decision-making process called for a great elaboration of an ancient skill, eloquence. Greeks had always loved to converse and oratory was known long before the existence of the Athenian democracy, but it was the fifth-century development of Athens that gave it its greatest impetus. There is nothing mysterious about this. The essence of oratory was—and is—persuasion. Although the terms *rhetoric* and *oratory* are often taken as synonyms for verbosity and deceit, they do not necessarily deserve these designations, which are attributable more to defects in our political system than to the nature of these subjects in themselves. The truth is that any assembly of people that has to make a decision, whether in policymaking, law, or the passing of a judicial sentence, needs to have speakers who can clearly present and if necessary reconcile opposing viewpoints. Order, especially in large assemblies, prevents presiding magistrates from taking leading roles in questioning witnesses and guiding debates. If Athenian magistrates had been able to act in this fashion in the past, the developed democracy with assemblies, and sometimes courts, of thousands made such action impossible. In judicial cases litigants had to argue their own briefs and in the legislative gatherings of the people a speaker who could clarify, analyze, and sum up matters was an essential element of the decision-making process. Vital issues such as taxes, war and peace, as well as the more prosaic aspects of day-to-day administration, were decided by the Assembly and the courts; before such decisions could be reached they had to be discussed at length. There was almost no written form of communication, no staff analysis, and no reporters, columnists, or editorial writers to digest, synthesize, and sift. As a result, set speeches in which the orators presented the ramifications of the various issues at hand and tried to make the best presentation of the views they wished to convey were unavoidable. Different speakers presented different interpretations and swayed their listeners now one way, now another. In time Athenians became connoisseurs of good speeches and enjoyed listening to them. We learn something of this from a speech Thucydides put in the mouth of Cleon:

> You have become regular speech-goers, and as for action, you merely listen to accounts of it; if something is to be done in the future you estimate the possibilities by hearing a good speech on the subject, and as for the past you rely not so much on the facts which you have seen with your own eyes as on what you have heard about them in some clever piece of verbal criticism. Any novelty in argument deceives you at once, but when the argument is tried and proved you become unwilling to follow it; you look with suspicion on what is normal and are the slaves of every paradox that comes your way.[1]

RHETORIC AND POLITICAL LEADERSHIP

For generations Athenian aristocrats had taken for granted their leadership positions within the state. In the past their special military capacity and valor—their *arete*, as it was called—had made them the most useful members of society. With the rise of the hoplites and the growth of the cities, new qualities of leadership, with greater emphasis on civilian skills, were demanded. The old combativeness of the aristocrats, so essential in the past, now needed to be restrained. It was becoming less and less acceptable to regard excellence as the exclusive prerogative of wealth and social position, and it was one of the greatest achievements of the fifth century to establish that behavior itself was a criterion

[1]Thucydides, *History of the Peloponnesian War*, tr. by Rex Warner (Penguin Classics, 1954), p. 182. Copyright © Rex Warner 1954. Reprinted by permission of Penguin Books Ltd.

of nobility and that justice, self-control, and the other moral virtues were in themselves ennobling qualities that the gods might regard with favor.

The implications of this redefinition of *arete,* or excellence, were enormous. Presumably anyone, with or without the benefits of aristocratic birth, could act moderately and justly. To achieve excellence according to the new understanding of the term was within the province of the humblest member of the Athenian democracy. With this breakthrough the way was open to the most radical definition of excellence. Paradoxically, the democracy, in breaking down the old definition and substituting in its place a universally attainable norm, also opened the way to an extreme individualism and a rejection of the very values on which the democracy itself was founded. The radical right—the Thirty for example—and the radical left—the Cynics and others who advocated withdrawal from public life—were understandable by-products of the democracy. If the aristocracy as a class was rendered obsolete by the redefinition of the traditional terminology, the recognition that such a redefinition was possible at all could lead to moral anarchy. An additional danger was the likelihood that when all were called to practice excellence, no one would, and virtue would come to be identified with middle-of-the-road timidity and support for the status quo.

Contributing to the transformation of the old values was the revolution in the ways and means of leadership. When an education in excellence could be acquired only by being born into the right family, where wealth and tradition were an age-old inheritance, the very means of becoming a leader was denied the ordinary citizen or even the citizen of wealth who lacked the necessary traditions. However, when the practical working of the democracy redefined the meaning of excellence and made it equivalent to political know-how, with primary emphasis on oral expression, then the way was open to anyone with talent becoming a leader—provided he could acquire the requisite skills. What the working of the democracy tended to do was make leadership a matter of talent and technique and this in turn created a demand for educators who could supply the necessary skills.

THE SOPHISTS

The demand for a new educational system directly geared to preparing students for a political life was supplied by professional educators known as the Sophists. It was not that the Athenian democracy gave birth to the sophistic movement as such but that, as in so many other areas, the Sophists found their greatest opportunity at Athens. They came from all over the Greek-speaking world, claiming to be able to teach the art of politics for a set fee. This fee could be quite high, but it covered several years of education. Still, it was not the fee taking itself that was the significant aspect of the sophistic movement but the revolutionary claim of being able to teach political "goodness," which common opinion until then believed rooted in family and wealth. The Sophists proved by the success of their pupils that this skill was now detachable and could be taught as could any technique, and that there was nothing mystical about it. Their aim, whatever their methods, was simply to prepare a man for a successful political career. They were not philosophers, nor had they any unifying ideology or system of educational practice. Their education was pragmatic, not speculative. They taught a man to reason dialectically, to argue back and forth all sides of a case, to discover the most effective arguments for whichever side he needed to present, and then to convert this into a persuasive speech.

The kind of truth pursued by the Sophists was relative truth, appropriate only to the case at hand. In the context of the democracy this made eminently good sense. What was needed in the day-to-day running of the city was an ability to argue the reasonableness or expeditiousness of this or that course of action, the relative "truth" of whether particular wars should be fought, alliances joined, honors conferred—the kinds of decisions we call *political* and whose ultimate truth is often ascertainable neither at the moment the decision has to be made nor years later by historians. Similarly in the courts defendants and prosecutors alike had to make the truth of their cases seem the closest approximations of reality. Sophistic techniques could be used on either side and a considerable development of the understanding of what constituted guilt and innocence, crime and appropriate punishment, resulted from the process.

MAN THE MEASURE OF ALL THINGS: THE GREAT DEBATE

Given the implications of the sophistic epistemology, it is understandable why a great debate raged around the subject of the foundations of morality and a citizen's obligations to the state. There were other factors at work that made the issue topical. As a result of travel and migration overseas, Greeks had for generations been in contact with foreign cultures, and the writings of Hecataeus and Herodotus had made at least some of them aware of the extraordinarily wide divergences of life-styles everywhere. The question arose: Is morality merely convention *(nomos)* or is there a higher sanction to be found in something else, say in nature *(physis)*? Quickly these terms, convention and nature, *nomos* and *physis*, became the poles of a great debate that went on for centuries.

Within the terms of the discussion *nomos* could be taken for the whole collection of laws and customs inherited by a city or a set of rules drawn up in rational fashion for the regulation of the state, or, finally, for an arbitrary system established by a group of men in their own self-interest. It was the second definition of *nomos* that the Greeks regarded as the great achievement of the sixth and fifth centuries. This consisted in the establishment of the rule of law against the arbitrary actions of despots or oligarchs or even the irrelevant customs of the past. With the growth of freedom, however, these laws themselves began to assume some of the irrational and tyrannical aspects previously attributed to tyrants and aristocrats. Hippias of Elis, for example, called *nomos* a "tyrant that forced men to do many things contrary to nature." Against convention was set nature, which could stand for the unwritten but unconditionally valid natural law as contrasted with the particularities of local custom, or it could mean the rights of the individual against the arbitrary rule of the state.

The figures of the first round of this debate are not nearly as well known as those of the later period, when Socrates, Plato, and Aristotle entered the discussion and pushed it to its limits. Nevertheless, as pioneers they have a special place in the history of this great topic.

It was the Sophist Protagoras who was responsible for the famous statement that man is the measure of all things, which is supposed to sum up the entirety of the classical view. What he meant was not that everything is to be regarded from the subjective view of the individual but that all human laws and practices are simply a matter of convention. It is the city-state, its constitution, and laws that decide morality. Consequently there are as many different moralities as there are cities or nations. Laws are the product of unconscious processes or the creations of the great lawmakers of the past, men endowed with special knowledge and wisdom.

The practical conclusions that Protagoras and his fellow Sophists drew from this was that what counted was not so much the constitution or the laws but the people of the city. If they could be educated—or better, for the Sophists were not interested in the masses—if their leaders could be educated, then the laws they made would be automatically good. Other Sophists reached somewhat more radical conclusions.

Phaleas of Chalcedon, for example, made a logical inference about convention when he observed that maldistribution of wealth was the cause of all strife in the cities of Greece. He presented a plan for reducing economic inequality among citizens. Democritus of Abdera, a countryman of Protagoras, spoke of the need of a sense of friendliness among co-citizens and of the importance of the rich helping the less fortunate, an unusual thought for any ancient thinker. Going beyond the bounds of the usual city-state orthodoxy, he declared "To the wise man the whole world is open; the good person has the entire world for his country,"[2] a declaration that would be taken up in the next century, and would become an article of faith of all cosmopolitan creeds to the end of the Roman Empire.

SOPHOCLES

In the midst of the rapidly changing world of the fifth century, the great tragic poet Sophocles represents a transitional figure between the old and the new. Characterized by E. R. Dodds as the "last great exponent of the archaic world-view,"[3] he stands between the closed world of the old city-state with its complete demands on the individual and the newly evolving order in which each person was expected to reason things out for himself. Sophocles was a dedicated

[2]Fragment 247.

[3]E. R. Dodds, *The Greeks and the Irrational* (Berkeley, Los Angeles, London: University of California Press, 1951), p. 49.

Athenian and profoundly involved in the affairs of the state. A friend of Cimon and a colleague on different occasions in the generalship with both Pericles and Nicias, he was appointed a special councillor to the democracy after the Sicilian disaster.

Like Herodotus, who was his friend, he did not attempt to justify the ways of the gods to men. He accepted the traditional view that if proper order was violated retribution would follow. What was of concern to him—and here his humanism makes contact with that of the Sophists—was the individual and his relationship to his destiny. Even if fate is unalterable a person is still free in how he responds to it. His reactions should not be dictated by the group or society but should be determined by the individual himself. Thus Oedipus, although he has no control over the destiny that led him to kill his father and marry his mother, is free in his response to this tragic situation. He does not allow himself to be crushed by his experiences but learns to rise above them, buoyed by his own nobility and strength of character. Similarly the confrontation of individuals with their destinies forms the center of interest of other plays. In *Ajax* the hero's decision to commit suicide is one part of the play; the second revolves around Agamemnon's refusal to allow Ajax's burial and Odysseus' opposition to this prohibition. Antigone, faced with the choice between burying her brother in accordance with the traditional laws and violating the decree of Creon, the ruler of the city, who forbade the burial, chooses the former course of action and faces her doom with heroic nobility and self-possession. In justifying her actions she appeals to the priority of the "unwritten and unchanging laws of heaven"[4] over those of men, and reproaches her sister Ismene for not helping her in her deed. In self-defense Ismene argues that even if Antigone is right they are not physically strong enough to resist the state. Antigone's retort to this is simple: "This world approves your caution—the gods my courage."[5] In defense of his decision to prohibit the burial of Antigone's brother Creon argues that obedience to the laws is vital to the survival of the state. He accuses Antigone of stubbornness and insolence. As the heroine is led off to execution she reflects on her fate and wonders why the gods have not come to her aid, but quickly reasserts her confidence in her original decision. Finally Creon, through the death of his son and wife, comes to recognize his own stubbornness and pride and the play ends with the chorus counseling wisdom and fear of the gods as the only way to happiness.

Here in this one play are to be found all the great issues of the age (the play was performed shortly before 440 B.C.). The reasonableness of the laws and the importance of maintaining their authority is put convincingly by Creon, but the chorus points out that although the city is the greatest achievement of human civilization men are still capable of blundering, and it is of course Creon's

[4]Sophocles, *Antigone,* in L. R. Lind, *Ten Greek Plays in Contemporary Translations.* Riverside Edition C19. P. 92. Copyright © 1957 by Houghton Mifflin Company.

[5]Ibid., p. 94. Copyright © 1957 by Houghton Mifflin Company.

tyrannical and ill-judged application of the laws that brings on disaster. Here Sophocles reflects the sophistic view of the relativity of laws that are human creations. But Antigone's stand on the unchanging laws of the gods puts the issue in another light, suggesting that beyond convention there really does exist a firm basis for morality. At the same time her challenge to the laws of the state creates a crisis for her and she is driven back on herself. She is alone in her decision and must seek strength in her own character since the gods do not come to her assistance. The individual who chooses to reason things out for himself according to his own inner vision, who will not simply be dictated to by custom or the opinions of men, must hold fast to the original decision and the act of faith implicit in it. It is here that Sophocles complements Aeschylus whose great contribution was his insistence on the necessity of faith in the ultimate working of divine justice. Sophocles shows how this can actually be achieved in practice and how the individual who has this faith in the justice of the gods can find the inner strength to survive the ordeals of life. The calm assurance of Sophocles' characters in the face of their fate has been justly compared to the Parthenon sculptures, which were being created the time this play was being produced (between 447 and 431 B.C.).

HERODOTUS

Herodotus, the "Father of History," also dealt with a heroic theme—the great clash between the Greeks and the Persians. In many respects Herodotus was broader in scope than his successor Thucydides and the later Greek historians who narrowly focused on Greek affairs and had little interest in the culture of the barbarians. Herodotus provides a sympathetic understanding of both the Greeks and their enemies. A native of Halicarnassus in Asia Minor, Herodotus inherited the Ionic tradition of inquiry *(historie)* into the phenomena of the physical world, and by applying the technique to human society and asking why the Greeks and the Persians came into conflict, he created the discipline of history. His answer is not a dispassionate analysis of the causes of the war but rather a colorful tale that combines cool rationalization, vivid narrative, and traditional religious viewpoints. His idea of causation is the traditional one of injury followed by retribution, so that his account of the clash between the two peoples is a long description of the chain of grievances on both sides going back to mythical days. Herodotus believed in the intervention of the gods in history to put down the ambitious and the proud, and he made no attempt to explain why the innocent should also be crushed in this process. Like Sophocles, he was not interested in accounting for the workings of providence. At the same time he gave great emphasis to the war as a struggle between freedom and despotism and highlighted the element of choice running through the deliberations of the Greek states in their decisions on whether to resist or join the invaders.

ART IN THE CLASSICAL PERIOD

Between 450 and 430 B.C., under the patronage of the Athenian state some of the greatest masterpieces of architecture and sculpture of all time were created. These were the days of the sculptor Phidias, the painter Polygnotus, and the architects Ictinus, Callicrates, and Mnesicles, whose work on the Acropolis and elsewhere in the city (in the case of Polygnotus) made Athens the embodiment of classical Greece.

The architectural forms and artistic themes were essentially the same as before. There were no daring innovations in temple design or in sculptural decoration. Greeks still struggled with Centaurs, Amazons, and Trojans and the gods contended with the giants as in so many traditional sculptural and pictorial scenes. What was new was the spirit that transformed them and the accompanying sophistication of artistic technique. The gods became more human though still retaining an essential aloofness, while men and women seemed to share in the divine character of the gods. The opposition between celestial and terrestrial realms was resolved in a miraculous sense of balance in which contending forces were present but controlled. There is nothing static or coldly formal about the great classical creations. Human emotions and divine power and energy were not eliminated or suspended but integrated with one another. Perhaps we can see in these poised works the balance of the Athenian state, which had just achieved an equilibrium of forces. For a brief moment, Athens was able to unify all the traditionally conflicting elements in the state—the rich and the poor, the

The Parthenon, the greatest architectural achievement of classical Athens.

aristocrats and middle classes, the educated and uneducated, foreigners and citizens.

The logic and solidity of the Greek temples of the early classical period have already been noted and to the casual eye the Parthenon seems but a modification of the same basic design. Nevertheless, there are important differences that work in a number of subtle ways to make it like nothing else in the history of Greek temple building.

The principle of mathematical proportionality that had been employed in the construction of the earlier temples was also used in the building of the Parthenon. Thus the same proportion is to be found in the ratio of the height of the temple to its width, the width of the cella (where the cult statue was housed) to its length, and the number of pillars in the sides and ends of the surrounding colonnade. To knowledgeable Greeks the pervasive proportionality of the temple would have had intrinsic appeal on a number of levels. One was the generally satisfying knowledge that the proportions of the temple had a rational, mathematical basis. The other, deriving from the Pythagorean belief that numbers and mathematical harmonies underlay and explained the beauty and order of the universe, would have appealed to a desire for a deeper explanation of the beauty of the building.

Had the Parthenon been constructed according to purely mathematical proportions it would in all likelihood have been rigid and lifeless, and if the ancient architect Vitruvius is right, it would also have suffered from optical distortions. Perhaps for these reasons the architects made certain adjustments or compensations in the structure. The stylobate or base was made to curve more than 4 inches higher in the center than at the sides and over 2 inches higher in the center than at the ends. This curvature was carried up into the roof structure by the columns, which were made to curve inward by almost 2½ inches. To counteract and balance this, some of the elements at the top of the entablature incline outward. The temple, in other words, was carved like a piece of sculpture to achieve satisfying human dimensions, pleasing to both the eye and the mind, blending the real and the ideal, so that whether viewed by philosopher or layman it immediately conveyed the same sense of grace, lightness, and beauty instead of the heaviness that might otherwise have been the case in such a large, geometrically shaped building.

Although the Parthenon is architecturally famous in its own right it is graced by a series of sculptural decorations that also have achieved fame. These are the sculptures of the pediments at each end, the metopes that surround the temple on the outside, and the frieze of the cella that housed the cult statue.

The metopes depict four traditional scenes in which the forces of uncontrolled emotion, disorder, and pride are pitted against the disciplined rationality and moderation of the Greeks and their gods. Greeks fight Centaurs, Amazons, and Trojans, and the gods struggle with the giants. What the viewer is presented with—or was presented with, when these carvings were intact—is a generalization into which he can read his own impressions, seeing the stories either in their original and familiar sense or as allegories depicting the ordering

The perfect balance of the classical style: Lapith and Centaur struggle with each other in one of the metopes of the Parthenon.

of the Athenian state, the subjection of its citizens to law, and the state's victories over foreigners, especially Orientals. The pediments represent themes peculiar to Athena. In the east is her birth from the head of Zeus and in the west her competition with Poseidon for the guardianship of Athens—which was won by Athena though Poseidon continued to receive special honors. Apparently accompanying Athena and Zeus in the former was Hephaestus, the god of the technical arts, who had a major temple shared with Athena in the city below. The viewer here is led to understand that the city was the recipient of the blessings of the gods from its very inception, and that these blessings included the sublime gifts of wisdom and power (symbolized by Zeus and Athena) as well as the more prosaic arts of human livelihood (Hephaestus).

The frieze around the cella represents in great detail the Panathenaic procession, the central part of Athens' greatest festival. This most important of celebrations recalled the early origins of Athens when the scattered villages of Attica were brought together in the common worship of Athena. The whole people was involved in this procession—even the metics, or resident foreigners, who were given some functions to perform. In the artistic representation of this community celebration, we have perhaps the best example of the classical spirit of idealization and exaltation of men to the company of the gods. However, the figures are not Greeks in general, nor is the procession some universal Hellenic ceremony; it is something peculiarly Athenian. Although the individuals in the sculpture are idealized, the frieze as a whole is an idealization of the Athenian state. All its members are represented—the old and the young, men and women,

The godlike youth of Athens canter majestically in the Panathenaic procession frieze from the Parthenon.

citizens and metics—all harmoniously bound together in the public worship of Athena. Here most clearly the classical spirit is most finely attuned to the inner balance and dynamism of the Athenian state itself.

The Later Classical Period (431–338 B.C.)

The last 30 years of the fifth century, during which Athens fought its bitter war with Sparta, have always been considered as years dominated by the forceful but negative views of Euripides, Thucydides, and Aristophanes, the great intellectual masters of the age. This period is seen, as a consequence, as one of disintegration and moral and social revolution, with the full impact of sophistic ideas and the disasters of the war causing a split between the intellectuals and the community, as well as between oligarchs and democrats. Indications of declining religiosity and the excesses of the democracy as exemplified in such acts as the execution of the generals after the battle of Arginusae and the massacres at Scione and Melos become, in this view, examples of moral decline.

Although there is a great deal of truth to this interpretation, the nature of the evidence also has to be taken into account. Philosophers and intellectuals pursued a life of their own that may or may not have had anything to do with the conditions of the times, whereas humorists deliberately parodied and distorted what they saw for the sake of comic impact. All our interpreters were to some extent alienated from their community. Euripides lived as a recluse and eventually fled Athens altogether, and Thucydides was an exile for 20 years. Their pronouncements need not be taken, therefore, as evidence of a massive moral breakdown, but should rather be seen as the struggles of gifted souls with the problems raised by the continuing growth of the democracy and particularly by its conduct during the long and brutal war with Sparta.

THE DEMOCRACY AND THE GROWTH OF SECULARISM

During the last years of the fifth century, the Peloponnesian War imposed excruciatingly difficult decisions on the democracy and made greater demands than ever before on the citizenry of Athens. These demands in turn had the effect of stimulating further development in the secularizing tendencies already present in the democratic processes themselves, as has already been noted in connection with the drama of Aeschylus and the role of oratory in decision making. In the period after 430, in part because of the war, the process advanced a stage farther, and it is particularly noticeable in the unmasking and secularizing of the sources of power within the state. As will be seen shortly, the use of power by Athens was the principal concern of the historian Thucydides in the *History of the Peloponnesian War,* and one of the main reasons why this work has remained a classic to the present day.

For citizens of modern democracies, despite spectacular advances in other areas, the nature and exercise of political power is shrouded in mystery. Paradoxically, in fifth century Athens, thousands of citizens were familiar with its uses and accustomed to act as free agents in assemblies and courts that exercised untrammeled power. They were responsible only to themselves and the laws. There were no tyrants and aristocrats making decisions in private and then casting around for means of communicating these decisions to the uninformed masses; no secrecy surrounded the decision-making processes of the developed democracy. There was no need to pretend to a higher knowledge and no establishment existed whose first loyalty was to maintaining itself at whatever cost. All the usual governmental pomp was set aside in favor of a depressingly common routine of daily business conducted, for the most part, under the guidance of very ordinary mortals. Subjects from the drainage of the Agora to vital matters of war and peace were debated publicly in all their hard reality. The hundreds of wrong decisions on major and minor issues were immediately laid on the shoulders of the mass of the people who, despite efforts at excusing themselves (claiming, for example, to have been absent from the Assembly on crucial days) were still ultimately responsible for all that they did. Unlike modern citizen bodies, Athenians found it extremely difficult to find scapegoats for their blunders. There was no government to blame, no independent bureaucracies, no secret policies arrived at in private and implemented clandestinely. They could vent their anger on their leaders—which they did frequently—but this was a minor matter considering how vulnerable and how easily the leaders could be dismissed and what little institutional power they exercised in any case. The only thing close to the modern sense of ignorance of government transactions and inability to do anything about them was the Athenian fear of oligarchic plots. There was a very real foundation for this fear, as even the enemies of the democracy admitted. Beyond this, the governmental process was an entirely open affair, one in which the practical relativism of the Sophists, the realism of Thucydides, and the apparent irreligion of Euripides would not have been as shockingly out of place as they may appear to us, who lack the political experience to evaluate them adequately.

THUCYDIDES

Thucydides served Athens as one of the ten generals elected in 424, but having failed against the Spartans in the north of Greece, he was exiled and returned to Athens only after the war. His account of the Peloponnesian War is considered one of the greatest histories ever written and one of the finest pieces of intellectual analysis of all time; but it is not a history in the modern sense of the term.

Thucydides' object was not just to achieve historical truth in the sense of presenting the facts accurately. He also sought to penetrate beneath the surface of individual events to discover the universal and permanent laws concealed therein, and to reveal causes that lead predictably to the same results. He pointed out, for example, that although Athens might be universally hated because it wielded almost total power throughout Greece, this was not due to anything peculiar to the nature of Athens or the Athenian people, but to the nature of power itself, which has its own laws and generates the same kind of reaction no matter who is its possessor. Similarly he noted the transvaluation of terms and the abuse of language in times of crisis:

> To fit in with the change of events, words, too, had to change their usual meanings. What used to be described as a thoughtless act of aggression was now regarded as the courage one would expect to find in a party member; to think of the future and wait was merely another way of saying one was a coward; any idea of moderation was just an attempt to disguise one's unmanly character; ability to understand a question from all sides meant that one was totally unfitted for action.[6]

War and justice, he concluded, cannot coexist; the powerful oppress the weak and all states act in their own self-interest. He sought to lay bare, in short, the

[6]Thucydides, *History,* p. 209. Copyright © Rex Warner 1954. Reprinted by permission of Penguin Books Ltd.

underlying but hidden structures of the state and the various constraints these imposed on its citizenry in the conduct of interstate relations.

Thucydides' genius lay not only in his ability to uncover the secret workings of history but to express these with compelling artistry. His most successful technique in accomplishing this was the sophistic practice of putting speeches in the mouths of different protagonists and arguing the various viewpoints of the subject under debate. Thus, in the first book of the *History* the causes of the war and motives of the contending parties are thoroughly examined by a number of speakers. In one instance a delegation of Corcyreans appeals to Athenian self-interest by pointing out the strategic location of their island on the coastal route to Sicily and the role their powerful navy would play in any confrontation with the Peloponnesians. The Corinthians attempt to persuade the Spartans of the danger from the Athenians by drawing a psychological picture of the differences between the two people:

> The Athenian is always an innovator, quick to form a resolution and quick at carrying it out. You on the other hand are good at keeping things as they are; you never originate an idea and your action tends to stop short of its aim.[7]

The Athenian viewpoint is put in the mouth of Pericles:

> I am against making any concessions to the Peloponnesians. . . . If you give in, you will immediately be confronted with some greater demand, since they will think that you only gave way on this point through fear. But if you take a firm stand you will make it clear to them that they have to treat you properly as equals.[8]

Thucydides' own view, worked out after years of thought, is expressed with the utmost succinctness:

> What made the war inevitable was the growth of Athens and the fear which this caused in Sparta.[9]

Another of Thucydides' methods is to take a single example and let it stand as a type for a whole series of similar incidents he does not want to discuss in detail, or for that matter chooses to ignore altogether. There is a detailed description of the awful social upheavals in Corcyra and then a generalization:

[7]Thucydides, *History*, p. 51. Copyright © Rex Warner 1954. Reprinted by permission of Penguin Books Ltd.

[8]Thucydides, *History*, pp. 91–92. Copyright © Rex Warner 1954. Reprinted by permission of Penguin Books Ltd.

[9]Thucydides, *History*, p. 25. Copyright © Rex Warner 1954. Reprinted by permission of Penguin Books Ltd.

> Later, of course, practically the whole Hellenic world was convulsed, with rival parties in every state—democratic leaders trying to bring in Athenians, and oligarchs trying to bring in the Spartans. . . . In the various cities these revolutions were the cause of many calamities—as happens and always will happen while human nature is what it is, though there may be different degrees of savagery, and as different circumstances arise, the general rules will admit of some variety. In times of peace and prosperity cities and individuals will alike follow higher standards, because they are not forced into a situation where they have to do what they do not want to do. But war is a stern teacher; in depriving them of the power of easily satisfying their daily wants, it brings most people's minds down to the level of their actual circumstances.[10]

Thereafter there is almost no mention of civil strife in the Greek cities. Similarly in the great Melian dialogue the right of the strong over the weak and the role of justice and fair play are debated in terms of general problems of statecraft.

The war itself was seen by Thucydides as a problem to be solved by proper analysis. Events for him were not right or wrong, good or evil. He did not view them in ethical or moral terms but rather as questions of fact: What are the causes of conflict? What courses do social revolutions take, once they begin? That men or states act from expedience or use whatever power they have at their disposal is not weighed for its good or evil consequences; Thucydides merely determined whether it is a fact or not. Men and states must act according to their natures, and Thucydides' practical aim was to unravel the nature of both and leave the answer as a guide ("as an eternal possession," in his terms) to future generations.

EURIPIDES

Since the democratic reform of the courts in 462, Athenians had become considerably more sophisticated and knowledgeable in their approach to questions of justice, and were already well on their way to establishing their reputation as the most litigious people in Greece.

As has already been mentioned, the large citizen juries that replaced the old magisterial courts required a new kind of presentation by defendants and prosecutors alike. At the same time new assumptions about what constituted guilt and how sanctions should be applied began to replace the archaic but deeply entrenched views of the past. It began to be assumed, for example, that every defendant had the right to make the best possible case for himself no matter how bad the circumstances might appear. Nor was justice any longer to be a function of social status. A case was to be resolved on the basis of the facts

[10]Thucydides, *History*, p. 208. Copyright © Rex Warner 1954. Reprinted by permission of Penguin Books Ltd.

involved, not on the wealth and family connections of the individual concerned or on his alleged services to the state—though the latter frequently was the basis for a plea for special treatment by the jurors. Despite appeals to extraneous factors, cases now began to be resolved, it would seem for the most part, on the basis of the facts at hand. What the individual did and his attitude toward the deed rather than his status came to be the basis for deciding a case.

This new understanding of the nature of justice, with its underlying assumption of personal responsibility, clashed with the old view of guilt as somehow unrelated to the subject's internal state, something objective that he contracted whether innocent (as in the case of Oedipus), or not. This left the old mythology in a vulnerable position, since it now appeared that the ways of the gods were less just than those of men. What Aeschylus and Sophocles had consigned to the realms of faith and mystery could now, with the new techniques, be resolved in favor of a more earthly explanation. By Euripides' day the crudeness of the divine order of justice contrasted sharply (at least in the eyes of the more observant) with the one evolving in Athens, where there was a growing tendency to avoid blaming a malevolent cosmic system and instead to seek for more prosaic explanations in human behavior and character. In addition the solutions of Aeschylus' and Sophocles' earlier plays, which demanded a certain greatness on the part of the protagonists, clashed with the less-than-heroic middle-class values now predominating in democratic Athens.

Euripides (ca. 485–406) faced this problem head-on and pursued the logic of the new understanding to the point where the old myths and legends frequently became practically unrecognizable. His characters complain bitterly about the injustice of the gods and man's fate. "You should be wiser than men, being gods," says the old man to the goddess Aphrodite in the *Hippolytus.* Orestes and Electra, instead of being activated by respect for religion, as they are in Aeschylus' play, act for purely personal reasons and blame the gods for their deeds. Orestes knows that his father would not expect him to avenge his death by murder yet Apollo commands the deed. "Where Apollo is stupid who is wise?" complains Electra in Euripides' play by that name. Do men know better than the gods who command such frightful deeds? Apparently they do, or should, Euripides suggests. Hercules, driven mad by the jealousy of Hera, kills his wife and children. Later, when he has regained his sanity at the end of the play, he reflects:

> I cannot believe that the gods commit unlawful acts . . . or that one god is master of another; for God, if he is truly God, needs nothing. These are the wretched imaginings of the minstrels.[11]

But this reasoning reduces the whole tale to nonsense.

Whereas Aeschylus and Sophocles were able to ascribe a positive role to human suffering, to justify it as a means to higher knowledge, Euripides observed that suffering just as easily degrades as elevates. Neither Hecuba in the

[11]Euripides, *Madness of Hercules,* 1340.

Trojan Women nor Medea in the play by that name were able to rise above their suffering. Instead both were brought down to the levels of their tormentors and became maddened, revengeful murderers themselves.

Elsewhere bourgeois views intrude to demythologize the old tales and transform their heroic character by contact with day-to-day experience. It is no surprise that domestic tragedy makes its appearance with Euripides and traditionally taboo issues such as the relations between husband and wife, parent and children are aired with an unpleasant degree of realism. In *Medea* the hero of the Argonaut saga becomes a pathetic middle-class figure, preoccupied with his station in society, ready to betray his much more heroic wife with the sophistic logic that although she saved his life and gave up her homeland for him she had been more than compensated:

> From my deliverance you have gained more than you gave as I will show. You have had the opportunity to live among Greeks instead of barbarians and to learn what justice is and what it is like to live by law [*nomos*] rather than by the arbitrary compulsion of the strong.[12]

Jason at this point has himself violated the most fundamental of all laws and is about to contract a new marriage, in defense of which the best he can say is this:

> What I most desired was that we should live well and not be in need; for well I know that a poor man has no friends. Also I hoped to raise my children as befitted my house.[13]

Euripides' pursuit of the troubled state of men's emotions led him to become, in the scholar Werner Jaeger's phrase, the world's first psychologist. His characters, confronted with the contradictions of the old myths, are left alone to struggle with their emotions. In the archaic world the passions of the mind and madness were thought to be things that came upon a person from the outside, as the word *passion* implies, but now with the gods confounded, these elements had to be accepted as part of human nature itself and not something existing in a demonic world over which men had no control. Although now unmasked and confronted they were still utterly terrifying and mysterious. If the problem of evil could no longer be shuffled off on an unseen world, it was still—or perhaps for that very reason more than ever—frighteningly real. Paradoxically, at the moment Euripides freed his characters from mythological beliefs he was forced to show that they were still the slaves of overwhelming forces. Agamemnon, although convinced of the moral rightness of freeing Hecuba, the former queen of Troy, refused to do so because of fear of the reaction of the army. Reflecting on this weakness of the king, Hecuba says: "No man is free; he is the slave of money . . . or fate, or else of the mob which rules the state."[14]

[12]Euripides, *Medea*, lines 534–38.

[13]Ibid., lines 559–62.

[14]*Hecuba*, line 864.

The democracy of Athens demanded that its citizens think about weighty matters and take positions on a variety of legal, administrative, and policy issues. The Sophists prepared men to enter public life and equipped them with the latest techniques of persuasion and dialectical analysis. In the courts, theater, Assembly, and Agora, new ideas were relentlessly discussed and argued by some of the most provocative minds in history. Fifth-century Athenians had no comfortable insulation from the intellectual life of the city, nor had their philosophers as yet built ivory-towers to flee to. The great debate over the sources and validity of moral and political obligations (see p. 140), which was now coming into public prominence, was therefore not something that concerned the intelligentsia alone but was of significance for the whole Athenian community.

For some the realization that laws were man-made conventions was a liberating experience. They were freed from what seemed to them to be meaningless rules and irritating obligations. Such was the motivation, no doubt, of the club described by the orator Lysias that made a point of having its meetings on unlucky days. For others who hoped to see the democracy founder, the new theories provided sophistic camouflage for treasonous theories. In Plato's *Gorgias* the speaker Callicles claims that the state ruined its best citizens by forcing on them an artificial inequality:

> Our way is to take the best and strongest among us from an early age and endeavour to mould their characters as men tame lions; we subject them to a course of charms and spells and try to enslave them by repetition of the dogma that men ought to be equal and that equality is fine and right. But if there arises a man sufficiently endowed by nature, he will shake off and break through and escape from all these trammels; he will tread underfoot our texts and spells and incantations and unnatural laws, and by an act of revolt reveal himself our master instead of our slave, in the full blaze of the light of natural justice.[15]

For Callicles law is a conspiracy of the weak to restrain the strong, their natural masters. The same idea is repeated in the *Republic* by the Sophist Thrasymachus who uses analogies from nature where, he claims, the larger and stronger animals devour the weaker, and the quick-witted outmaneuver the slow and stupid. He concludes with the aphorism that the "justice of men is in fact the expediency of the strongest" and that all states are rigged to suit the convenience of their rulers, whether they be the one or the many or the few. The immorality of an Alcibiades and the brutality of the oligarchs in 411 and 404 chillingly demonstrated that these were more than the philosophic or neurotic musings of alienated intellectuals.

Another way in which the new theories could be seen to have practical, if less malevolent, consequences for the city was in the impulse to withdraw from

[15]Plato, *Gorgias*, tr. Walter Hamilton (Penguin Classics, 1960), p. 79. Copyright © Walter Hamilton, 1960. Reprinted by permission of Penguin Books Ltd.

public life. Aristippus of Cyrene, a sometime associate of Socrates, said that officeholding was time-consuming and laborious and a form of slavery that the sensible man would avoid. Antisthenes, the precursor of Cynicism, tossed out the whole city-state concept and said that men should live, not according to the laws of the city, but according to the laws of virtue. His successor, Diogenes of Sinope, set himself up in the Stoa of Zeus Eleutherios ("Zeus Who Gives Freedom") in the Agora, where his life-style and his pronouncements were testimony to the new concepts of freedom and the extreme individualism that could be inferred from them.

On the opposite side, two of the most vigorous minds in history, Socrates and Plato, came to the defense of the beleaguered city-state and tried to find a new and irrefutable moral basis for it.

Socrates—insofar as it is possible to reconstruct his thought, for he left no written material—rejected the relativism of the Sophists and the belief that it is impossible to arrive at any secure basis for right and wrong. He agreed that customs differ from city to city and made a distinction between *right usage,* which might vary, and *abstract right,* which is eternal and universal. The animal world, he argued, was not a suitable term of comparison for human beings. For the basis of morality one had to pass to the suprahuman realm of Universal Right. The essential difficulty with men was their ignorance and lack of insight into the nature of good and evil. Politicians especially lacked this knowledge, and the political expertise of the Sophists, mere know-how, was totally inadequate.

PLATO

Socrates' disciple Plato (ca. 429–347 B.C.) was a member of the Athenian upper classes and a relative of Critias and Charmides, two prominent members of the Thirty who ruled Athens after the fall of the democracy. Born shortly after the beginning of the Peloponnesian War, he was a witness to the fearful events of the last years of the fifth century. The excesses of the Thirty, coupled with the execution of Socrates some years later, so disgusted him with public life that he withdrew from Athens for a time and visited Sicily and southern Italy, where his encounter with the Pythagorean sects had a profound effect on his life. He returned to Athens and around 387 opened a school beside the Academy gymnasium, in imitation of that of the Sophist Isocrates. In the 360s he made two other visits to Sicily in a vain attempt to influence Dionysius II of Syracuse. He died just nine years before Athens and the rest of Greece fell under the yoke of the Macedonians.

For Plato all existing constitutions were bad, and all laws inadequate because they were incapable of meeting the innumerable new situations created by the complex and constantly changing events of daily life. What was needed was a ruler or rulers who possessed true knowledge of what was good for the state. This was not the expedience of pragmatic politics but a transcendent understanding of the state and its nature. If men of such godlike insight could be found or trained there would be no need for laws or constitutions and the stability of the state would be permanently guaranteed.

Like Socrates, Plato held that the possession of knowledge and wisdom, not technical or practical ability, was the first and only true prerequisite for the statesman. The kind of knowledge Plato demanded was of a metaphysical and theoretical character derived from a lengthy contemplation of the ideal form of the state, which he believed could be arrived at by a process of mental training and inner recollection. The difficulty was how to produce such contemplatives, and in his masterpiece, the *Republic,* he discusses this problem.

The ideal state should be divided into three approximately hereditary groups, the Guardians, the Auxiliaries, and the rest of society—that is, the handful of guru-like rulers, their military assistants, and the rest of society. These were not economic or social classifications. The rulers were forbidden to marry, have families, or possess property as these interests could distract them from their essential purpose of guiding the state. Eugenics without reference to matrimony was to be practiced in the production of the best candidates for the top groups, and there was to be no discrimination on the basis of sex. Women would be free, if they possessed the talents, to become either Guardians or Auxiliaries. Strict control of beliefs was to be exercised throughout the state and there was to be no economic imbalance between the rich and the poor. A comprehensive education was to be provided for all, but the higher levels would be reserved for those who showed particular aptitude.

Between the *Republic* (ca. 375) and the great work of his later years, the *Laws,* Plato made his trips to Sicily to attempt to influence the tyrant of Syracuse, Dionysius II (367 and 361 B.C.). When he returned to the task of establishing the constitution of the ideal state, which he continued until his death in 347, his confidence in the ability of men to be guided directly by reason was gone and he was prepared to settle for what he called a second-best type of state. In this state men would be ruled by laws that were the creation of experts. Since these laws were to be framed after fixed and eternal models, all citizens were to be rigidly bound by them. Henceforth God, not man, was to be the measure of all things.

More than ever, in the *Laws* Plato looked outside the state for authority to bind the community together. Beyond the external acceptance of religious practices that all city-states demanded, Plato required internal adhesion to a set of orthodox beliefs. To doubt or dissent from the laws was to be not merely disobedience but sacrilege and treason because such acts were violations of divine laws and therefore offenses against the gods themselves. No dissent was possible and church and state were to be united in a perfect, theocratic union. Driven by a mixture of high personal idealism and despair over the capacities of men to reach these ideals, Plato produced a caricature of the city-state in which conditioning, not consent, was to be the essential means of holding it together. Although the Athenian democracy continued to function ably in the welter of Greek interstate politics, Plato refused to consider the possibility that the mass of men could do anything to save themselves and looked for hope beyond his own turbulent times to the serene and unchanging world of the divine.

ARISTOTLE AND ISOCRATES

Aristotle (ca. 385–322 B.C.), who also treated the question of how men should best live (or the ideal state), was much less severe in his judgment of the abilities of the masses, and a good deal more pragmatic than his mentor Plato. Following a different theory of knowledge, which looked for truth in the workings of things rather than in ideal forms in a transcendent world, he analyzed over 150 constitutions to discover the laws that kept them in existence or led to their destruction. Like Plato he did not move beyond the city-state and assumed that the "good life" could only be found within this form of human organization. From his studies Aristotle seems to have concluded that what counted was not the precise type of constitution so much as its internal balance between two opposites, narrow oligarchy and extreme democracy. He emphasized the importance of officeholders and the kinds of office they held, and in general seems to have preferred citizens who were neither too rich nor too poor—the middle classes, in other words—believing that among these could be found most readily the two essentials of a stable constitution, justice and friendship. When these were absent, there was likely to be discontent, which would soon lead to revolution. The essential stabilizing element was proportional equality, which protected the poor from oppression and the rich from expropriation as well as rewarding the able. Euripides, whose middle-class values have already been noted, also placed emphasis on the stabilizing characteristics of this group:

> For there are three divisions of the citizens:
> The rich and useless, always craving more and more;
> The ones who have not, and eke out a scanty life;
> The dangerous, who give their envy greater sway,
> Shooting its evil darts against the idle rich,
> And cheated, deceived by tongues of crooked counsellors.
> The middle one of these three parts saves every city.
> Preserving whatsoever order it sets up.[16]

Whereas Plato and Aristotle attempted to shore up the city-state by making more demands on its citizens and seeking a new basis for it in certain knowledge or workable laws, the rhetorician-educator Isocrates looked for help elsewhere. He deplored the anarchy of Greek politics, which set state against state and gave solace only to Greece's enemies, the Persians. He had no radical political solutions but made eloquent appeals to prominent fourth-century figures, such as Dionysius I of Syracuse and Philip of Macedonia, to lead a united Greece against her enemies. In opposition to Plato he defended the study of rhetoric as a legitimate means of education, arguing that moral consciousness could be developed from a study of speech:

[16]Euripides, *Suppliants*, in L. R. Lind, *Ten Greek Plays in Contemporary Translations*, p. 263. Riverside Edition C19. Copyright © 1957 by Houghton Mifflin Company.

> I believe . . . that men become better and worthier if they are determined to speak well and if they have the desire to be able to persuade their listeners.[17]

For Isocrates the essentials of rhetorical education—analysis and composition and the like—were valuable in themselves. Knowledge of the probable was attained by rhetoric and topics analyzed by the rhetorical method attained a deeper significance. It was not therefore, as Plato had claimed (in his earlier writings), a discipline without content, dedicated to deception and distortion. These high ideals were much easier to proclaim than to live up to and in the subsequent history of Greek oratory Plato's judgment on the subject was unfortunately borne out more often than not.

ART IN THE LATER CLASSICAL PERIOD

By 430 B.C. most of the civic and religious buildings destroyed by the Persian occupation of Athens in 480 had been restored or rebuilt. On the Acropolis only the tiny but elegant temple of Athena Nike and the Erechtheum sanctuary remained to be constructed. Of these, the first was finished in 425 and the second by 406 B.C. In the Agora the only new buildings added before the great construction program of Lycurgus (338–326 B.C.) were the new Bouleuterium and the South Stoa at the end of the fifth century. This means that on the eve of the Peloponnesian War Athens had almost her full complement of essential buildings, so that even without the economic stringency imposed by the war, artistic development in the city would have followed new lines anyway. There were no great new temples to be erected and it was almost three-quarters of a century after the completion of the Erechtheum that another temple was built in Athens. This, together with the overwhelming majesty and beauty of the buildings already constructed, placed a number of restrictions on the scope of future artistic endeavor in the city. It should not come as a surprise, therefore, though it is sometimes deplored and regarded as a reflection of the more general decay of Athens, that decoration comes to be almost an end in itself, or that the great themes of realism and formalism already present emerge as independent forms in sculpture and painting. There were other important contributing factors, such as the continuing secularization and humanization of the state, to which corresponded a new interest and ability in displaying and interpreting human emotions. There was the recently acquired ability to depict drapery on the human body, and there were new techniques involving perspective, shading, and composition.

One of the most notable features of the period is the emphasis on humanization and personalization. The gods come to look more and more like men and men look more like real individuals. The Olympian restraint shown by

[17]Isocrates, *Antidosis* 275.

Mother and child, symbols of Peace and Wealth, look tenderly into each others' eyes. Copy of a fourth-century statue erected in the Athenian Agora.

Phidias is removed and there is a great interest in different human emotions, ranging from anguish and pain to humor and tenderness. Eyes meet in recognition or in moments of love and affection; heroes are depicted weeping for their dead companions. In another direction altogether is the famous Aphrodite of Cnidos by Praxiteles which explored for the first time in sculpture the sensuous eroticism of the nude female figure. Having been conditioned by later imitations, we may not consider this statue particularly shocking, but to Greeks the effect of seeing it for the first time in its round temple (where it was meant to be viewed from every side) must have been electrifying. In painting the same emphasis on human emotions and realism is to be found. We know of a work by Zeuxis that showed Menelaos weeping at the tomb of Agamemnon; in another by Aristides of Thebes a child is depicted creeping toward its dying mother in a sacked town.

The style of the period tends to be decorative and ornamental. Clothes become much more complicated than before and sometimes in their extravagance, as in the parapet decorations of the temple of Athena Nike, seem almost an end in themselves. Some of this tendency toward the ornate must be due to the virtuosity of the artists, who had mastered all the old techniques and were exploring new avenues, as well as to the narrower compass of the work they were called upon to execute, but parallels have also been drawn to the lack of content and vapidity in rhetoric that drew Plato's fire at a late date.

Small bronze statuette of Aphrodite modeled after Praxiteles' original.

A Nike (Victory) adjusts her sandal and a classical artist demonstrates his virtuosity in this somewhat contrived pose.

THE STRUCTURE OF ATHENIAN SOCIETY

Everyday experiences of modern life are often poor guides for understanding the ancient world. We take for granted, for example, that despite the existence of ethnic groups within the geographical confines of many modern states, the vast majority of the population will always be citizens of these countries. It is difficult for us to imagine a situation which is the reverse of this, where the number of noncitizens exceeded the citizens, as in Sparta, or came to close to 50 percent of the population, as in Athens. One recent estimate put the total citizen population of Athens in 432 B.C. at 110,000 to 180,000 and the noncitizen population at 105,000 to 150,000.[18] It is, therefore, something of a problem to know exactly what we are talking about when we refer to "the Athenians." Although the noncitizen segment of the population was excluded from the most important functions of the state, it was still very much involved in community affairs, and it is impossible to think of classical Athens without also having in mind the large number of non-Athenians who made the city their home, whether voluntarily or otherwise.

So far as physical appearances went it was impossible to tell slave from free, metic from citizen. The cynical writer known as the Old Oligarch, while commenting on the privileged positions of slaves and aliens in Athens, explains why a slave would not step aside for a citizen on the street:

> Slaves and metics at Athens lead a singularly undisciplined life; one may not strike them there, nor will a slave step aside for you. Let me explain the reason for this situation: if it were legal for a free man to strike a slave, a metic or a freedman, an Athenian would often have been struck under the mistaken impression that he was a slave, for the clothing of the common people there is in no way superior to that of the slaves and metics, nor is their appearance.[19]

He is exaggerating, of course, for as soon as an individual opened his mouth to speak it must have been possible to tell by his accent where he came from. Xenophon, one of Socrates' students, says that there were Lydians, Phrygians, Syrians, and people (*barbarians* is the term he uses) from every country among the resident alien population. We know also of Egyptians, Phoenicians, and Carians (who had proverbially bad reputations), as well as Thracians. Athens, and especially its port town Piraeus, must have been a tremendous mix of languages, dialects, physical appearances, and ways of life. Beyond this there

[18]Victor Ehrenberg, *The Greek State,* 2nd ed. (London: Methuen & Co. Ltd.: 1969), p. 31.

[19]Old Oligarch, trans. J. M. Moore, in *Aristotle and Xenophon on Democracy and Oligarchy* (Berkeley and Los Angeles: University of California Press, 1975), p. 39. Copyright © 1975 by J. M. Moore. Reprinted by permission of the University of California Press.

was a kind of heterogeneity among the Athenians themselves despite their proud boast of an unmixed ancestry:

> Because of their control of the sea, the Athenians have mingled with peoples in different areas and discovered various gastronomic luxuries; the specialties of Sicily, Italy, Cyprus, Egypt, Lydia, Pontus, the Peloponnese or any other area have all been brought back to Athens because of their control of the sea. They hear all dialects, and pick one thing from one, another from another; the other Greeks tend to adhere to their own dialect and way of life and dress, but the Athenians have mingled elements from all Greeks and foreigners.[20]

Nevertheless, despite all appearances of heterogeneity and openness, Athenian society was no melting pot. Instead it adhered to the model of the closed, polis-type society where the main basis for differentiation between the inhabitants of any region was that of citizen and noncitizen.

Citizenship

Only citizens could own land, exercise all the rights of membership in the community, and share fully in its benefits. The franchise was exclusive and was extended only rarely to outsiders. Lysias the orator, whose father had been persuaded by Pericles to migrate from Syracuse, lost his fortune during the regime of the Thirty and solidly backed the democracy through all its tribulations, yet never received citizenship. Until 451/450 it was sufficient that one's father be an Athenian; after that date both parents had to be citizens. Residence in a deme was essential to establishing full citizenship and the deme assembly was responsible for the first examination and enrollment of candidates for the citizenship on the deme rolls. In his eighteenth year a potential citizen presented his application to the demarch (the chief magistrate of the deme) and the whole deme assembly voted to accept or reject it. If the candidate failed here he could appeal to a court in Athens, but if rejected by the court he could be sold into slavery. Successful candidates next needed the endorsement of the Council and then two years later their names were written into the list of those eligible to attend the main Assembly of Athens. So concerned were the Athenians with maintaining a strict watch on the citizenship rolls that periodic checks were made to see that no one had surreptitiously entered his name on the list or that no underage candidates had been admitted.

[20]Ibid., p. 42. Copyright © 1975 by J. M. Moore. Reprinted by permission of the University of California Press.

For a long time the ownership of land was a prerequisite for membership in the Assembly and the landless were relegated to a position of half-citizenship. Under the tyrants, land allotments were made to many of the poorer citizens, who were thus enabled to become full members of society, and by the end of the sixth century the possession of land ceased to be a requirement of full citizenship.

Since Solon's time, Athenians had been divided into various categories by census classifications, which were never abolished by law. Even under the full democracy, when access to office was practically guaranteed to everyone, a few offices, such as that of treasurer of Athena, were reserved for the very rich only. And at least in the eyes of the law, the lowest group, the *thetes,* were automatically excluded from officeholding. In practice, however, according to Aristotle, no candidate for office would ever admit belonging to this class.

Access to public office is an important way of measuring the relative openness of a society and the value of its franchise. Modern societies, although formally requiring almost no special qualifications, in practice demand party affiliation, visibility, and usually wealth within the constituency where the office is being sought. In Athens the use of sortition or random selection from a group of candidates (though *how* one became a candidate is another matter) guaranteed that a much wider spectrum of the citizenry held public office. This is in fact one of the main distinguishing characteristics of the democracy at Athens.

An interesting aspect of the evolving democracy's effect on society was its effect on the development of religion. In the past the phratry system had performed both religious and administrative functions. Registration in a phratry, for example, was sufficient to establish a claim to the citizenship. Meetings were held to honor the gods or heroes of the phratries, sacrifices were performed, and business was transacted. After Cleisthenes, however, the administrative functions were transferred to the territorial demes and the phratries continued in existence only as religious groupings. Children's names were inscribed in phratry lists at birth and this constituted good, but not full, evidence of citizenship. The families continued to administer the cults of the phratries as before, but now there was no question of excluding any citizen. Membership in a phratry did not depend upon one's relationship to a family but became one's right as a member of a deme. Thus the most fundamental religious units of the state were opened up and the private control over the cults eliminated. According to Aristotle access to the cults of the phratries and the reduction of their number was a typically democratic reform. As a result the maintenance of the state cults became an essential aspect of Athenian life, no longer merely the private responsibility of clan, family, or phratry. No one was exempt from participating, whatever he might privately think of the gods. Paradoxically, it was this fundamentally liberalized practice of religion that Socrates was thought to have offended, drawing down upon himself the ire of his fellow citizens.

Rich and Poor

Despite ease of access to office and popular control of the Assembly and the courts, the distinction between aristocrat and commoner, rich and poor was very much alive at Athens. Down to the end of the fifth century it was considered chic to proclaim one's family name, marry within the caste, and keep up family traditions and fortunes. Young aristocrats wore their hair long and competed fiercely against one another in sports, music, dancing, and horse racing. The aristocratic Alcibiades boasted to the Spartans that when Athens seemed to be at the end of its resources during one of the many crises of the Peloponnesian War he was able to enter seven chariots in the Olympic games and win first, second, and fourth prizes. "It is not useless folly," he said, "when a man by spending money benefits not only himself, but his city as well."[21] But the aristocratic life-style extended itself to less creditable occupations—to drinking parties, entertainment by female musicians, and pederasty. One anonymous critic commented that the life of the young aristocrats at Athens consisted of nothing beyond hangovers, idleness, and bathing, and that they knew nothing beyond "drinking, bad singing, gourmet cooking and Sybaritic luxuries."[22] This, of course, has to be set against the aristocratic view of the people as "ungrateful, fickle, vicious, jealous, uncultured."[23]

Distinctions of wealth were not eliminated by the democracy. The general Nicias, whose blundering led to the defeat of the Sicilian expedition, had 1000 slaves in the silver mines of Laurium, which brought him an income of 60,000 drachmae a year at a time when 130 drachmae was considered a subsistence income, and Demosthenes' father left an estate worth 84,000 drachmae. Such estates, however were not large. The gift of about 40 acres to the grandson of the famous Aristides seemed a significant amount to Demosthenes and the largest estate we know of was about 740 acres, and that must have been exceptional. The vast majority of Athenians were landowners to some degree, over 80 percent according to one calculation, but most of these were small farmers whose holdings did not exceed 25 acres. The soil of Attica was notoriously poor and encouraged thriftiness and hard work. Living within one's income came easily to such people. The small farmers were independent and conservative, as Aristophanes put it, "Marathon men, close-grained and stubborn, made of oak and maple."[24]

The Local Character of Athenian Democracy

One of the bulwarks of the Athenian democracy was the local deme organization. Attica, the geographic region in which Athens was located, had over 170 of

[21]Thucydides, *History of the Peloponnesian War* 6.16.

[22]Aristophanes, *Daitales*, Fragment 216.

[23]Ps. Plato, *Axiochus* 369b.

[24]Aristophanes, *Acharnians* 223.

these local units, each with its own assembly and elected officers, its religious ceremonies, and festivals. The assembly met locally and took care of all neighborhood administrative matters. It was here, in the transaction of village business, that the local small farmers, tradespeople, and aristocrats met and hashed out their differences and learned the process of give and take. The bulk of the population of Attica lived in villages outside the two main urban centers of Athens and Piraeus, but a major distinction should not be drawn between the urban and rural dwellers. City folk were not far removed from the land, and kept goats, pigs, and poultry themselves; they were very much aware of the weather, the crops, and rural life in general. Nor were the rustics as uncultured as might be assumed. During the rural Dionysia (see p. 179), the "hits" of the Athenian theater were performed in the local theaters. According to Plato, theater lovers followed the plays from deme to deme "as though under contract to listen to every performance."[25] The rural population had a fair amount of time on its hands. The work was seasonal and in midsummer and again in the winter after the olive harvest, they were free to do as they pleased. Given the compact nature of Attica they could attend the assemblies and the courts, especially the more important sessions, without too much difficulty. The composition of the assemblies could thus vary considerably, depending on the nature of the business at hand. At times Demosthenes seems to be addressing an assembly where the middle and upper middle classes predominate and at other times it is clearly the poor who are in the majority. Socrates, as reported by Xenophon, said that the Assembly was composed of shoemakers, fullers, carpenters, smiths, peasants, merchants, and shopkeepers—the whole spectrum of middle-and lower-middle-class Athenian society. It is likely that groups such as these, especially the urban residents, dominated the regular assemblies.

In the fifth and fourth centuries, Piraeus was the foremost port in the Mediterranean, and Athens itself was a great commercial center. Neither, however, were industrial cities producing large amounts of goods for export. The majority of workers in the nonagricultural sector of the economy were small-scale craftsmen and artisans who owned their own workshops. There they created their products, which they then carried to the Agora to sell. Large-scale production was on the whole exceptional, and the largest known workshop was in the armaments field and employed 120 slaves. The ceramics industry, one of Athens' largest, was also at the level of small-scale production. The majority of potteries consisted of the master potter, who might also be the painter, and a number of slaves who assisted him with the preparation of the clay, supervised the firing, and so forth. There were no middlemen and the potteries themselves served as shops for their goods. Nevertheless, these little industrial concerns provided sufficient income for their owners to permit them to devote themselves full time to public careers. In the late fifth century the aristocratic leadership gradually passed into the hands of the well-to-do middle classes such as the tannery

[25]*Republic* 475d.

owners Cleon, Anytus, and Timarchus; the lamp manufacturer Hyperbolus; and the knife and furniture producer Demosthenes (the father of the orator). There was no large-scale export industry that brought in a steady income, and Athens' principal source of exported wealth was the silver from the mines at Laurium, which came into peak productivity early in the fifth century. There was always a demand for Athenian silver coins, the famous "owls" of Athena that never varied in quality—an important consideration in a world where every city considered it essential to produce its own coinage.

Metics, Foreigners, and Slaves

An important segment of the Athenian community consisted of the resident noncitizens or metics. These may have been recent arrivals or they may have lived in Athens for generations without having been assimilated into the citizen body. They could not own land (without a special grant) or property, or even lend money on land as security. They could not marry Athenian citizens nor could they participate in the public life of the city. At the same time they were subject to special taxes and the liturgies (acts of public benevolence) as well as service in the army or navy in times of crisis. Still, they had a privileged position compared to other foreigners. They were properly registered in the deme rolls, and, at least down to the beginning of the fourth century, when the custom fell into abeyance, they possessed patrons who represented them in court. They could attend the public festivals and live and worship as they pleased. If wealthy they could be influential behind the scenes.

They came from all over the Mediterranean and the Greek-speaking world and brought their labor and talents to many different occupations. They were barbers, bakers, dyers, painters, as well as skilled craftsmen in the fields of textiles, leather, ceramics, and metal work. Two of the biggest workshops in Athens, both shield factories, were owned by metics. In the final stages of the construction of the Erechtheum on the Acropolis, out of 86 workmen whose status is known, 24 were citizens, 42 were metics, and the remaining 20, slaves. Contracts for construction were let to metics as well as to citizens. The merchant who sold the gold leaf for the decoration of the Parthenon had a Phoenician name. Chrysippus, the grain dealer, another foreigner, earned the gratitude of the Athenians by underwriting cheap food supplies at a time when the price had skyrocketed beyond the purchasing power of the average citizen.

Metics, as well as foreigners who did not belong strictly to this class, developed other careers in Athens besides those in trade and industry. This was especially so in the skilled professions, and artists, doctors, philosophers, and educators who wished to escape from the narrow confines of their own home states poured into Athens. Anaxagoras, the philosopher and friend of Pericles, was from Asia Minor; the Sophists Protagoras, Gorgias, Hippias, and Prodicus were from Thrace, Sicily, the Peloponnese, and the Cyclades, respectively. Aristotle was from the north of Greece; Diogenes the Cynic from Sinope in the Black Sea area; Zeno, the founder of Stoicism, from Cyprus. The famous Hippocrates of Cos practiced medicine in Athens, and Hippodamus of Miletus planned the city of Piraeus. Polygnotus of Thasos executed some famous paintings in the Stoa Poikile and the temple to Hephaestus.

Slaves were present in large numbers in Athens during classical times, but since there were no large estates in Attica requiring cultivation by chain gangs, the institution took on a different form than it possessed, for example, in Italy during the period of the Roman Republic.

Most businesses that required a regularly employed labor force, as contrasted with those needing occasional labor, such as in harvesting, made use of slaves. The mines were operated by slaves working for citizen contractors who took out leases from the state. Other slaves were employed in the metal and arms workshops, and by individual potters, building contractors and the like. Generally freemen were independently employed, the only exception to this being in the realm of public works where slave, metic, and freeman worked side-by-side for the same wages.

An important aspect of slavery in Athens was the relative degree of freedom possessed by those in bondage. Many slaves were hired out by their masters and might go from job to job as occasion demanded, or be put in charge of little workshops where they would labor in much the same fashion as free craftsmen. Many of those who worked in this way were allowed to keep part of the income from their labor, and could in time buy their freedom and continue their businesses as before. One of these freedmen was the famous Pasion, whose fortune amounted to 120,000 drachmae invested in land, a shield factory that brought in 6000 drachmae yearly, a bank that brought in 10,000 drachmae, and loans totaling 234,000 drachmae. For his services to the state—he provided 1000 shields and five triremes—he was made a citizen.

THE WORKINGS OF THE ATHENIAN DEMOCRACY

The city is not ruled
By one man only; it's a city of the free.
The people rule by class in yearly interchange;
They do not give the bulk of power to the rich:
The poor man also rules in turn with equal strength.[26]

[26]Euripides, *Suppliants*, p. 267. Copyright © 1957 by Houghton Mifflin Company.

Like all governments, that of Athens was a system of sorts, some of it rationally planned, some of it the result of accretion over the years. It had several characteristic principles of operation. All power was concentrated in the hands of the people, but since the people could not perform the myriad tasks necessary in a large state, they had to delegate this power to various magistrates and boards. These in turn were controlled by such devices as selection by lot, collegiality, rotation in office, systematic public examinations of conduct, court intervention, and removal from office. Deliberately there were no clear-cut distinctions between the branches of government. The same body of people could at one time be a legislative assembly and at another a supreme court acting in judicial fashion. Roughly, however, the main divisions corresponded to the traditional breakdown of government. They were the Assembly (legislature), the various magistracies and boards of commissioners (executive), and the court system (the judiciary).

The Assembly (Ecclesia)

> For they . . . deemed it was the way of wild beasts to be held subject to one another by force, but the duty of men to delimit justice by law, to convince by reason, and to serve these two in act by submitting to the sovereignty of law and the instruction of reason.[27]

The Assembly *(ecclesia)* of the Athenian people, when properly called into being, was the sovereign power of the state. It met four times in every 36-day period *(prytany)* of the civil year, or 40 times a year. These meetings followed a regular agenda, which included (though not all at the same time) such items as votes of confidence in the current magistrates, considerations of defense needs and food supplies, the entertainment of accusations of treason, petitions from individuals to approach the Assembly on public or private matters, foreign affairs, and religious matters. Almost all these items, however, were handled through a prepared schedule of motions that originated in the Council *(boule)* and had been published beforehand. There were, in addition, special meetings that required no particular program beyond the matter at hand. Pay was budgeted only for the regular meetings, which required five days notice together with the publication of the agenda. Emergency sessions were called by trumpeter and signal fires.

The Assembly was open to all Athenian males 18 years old and above who were not otherwise barred from attending. Normally, however, attendance would begin only after the completion of the required two years of military service. Tokens were given out, which entitled those who received them to collect the equivalent of a day's wages (1 to 1½ drachmae) for attending.

[27]*Lysias*, tr. W. R. M. Lamb (Cambridge, Mass.: Loeb Classical Library and Harvard University Press, 1930), p. 41.

Originally meetings were held in the Agora, but in classical Athens, (except in cases of ostracism), they met on the Pnyx hill, which had been carved into the shape of an outdoor auditorium with a sloping floor reaching outward in fan shape from the speaker's platform.

FUNCTIONS OF THE ASSEMBLY

The Assembly had full legislative, judicial, and executive control of the state. There was no scattering of power among the different branches and when a decision was reached it was final. There was no need for further consultation or referral to another agency, senate, or supreme court. The people in the Assembly could declare war; make peace; elect its most important officers (the generals); condemn individuals to death, exile, or fine; audit accounts; confer honors, and so on. It controlled the diplomatic life of the city, received ambassadors, designated its own envoys and instructed them, formed alliances, and debated questions of foreign policy. In military matters it determined the number of ships in the fleet, the size of the expeditions, their objectives, and their generals. It supervised the conduct of war and disciplined commanders—Thucydides the historian who failed in a campaign against the Spartans being one of those who suffered.

The main function of the Assembly—apart from its general supervision of state affairs—was the formulation of policy. As Pericles, in a speech composed by Thucydides, put it:

> We Athenians, in our own persons, take our decisions on policy or submit them to proper discussions: for we do not think that there is an incompatibility between words and deeds; the worst thing is to rush into action before the consequences have been properly debated. . . . We are capable at the same time of taking risks and of estimating them beforehand. Others are brave out of ignorance; and, when they stop to think, they begin to fear. But the man who can most truly be accounted brave is he who best knows the meaning of what is sweet in life and what is terrible, and then goes out undeterred to meet what is to come.[28]

Although many items were routine and could be quickly handled, major decisions could only be hammered out after long debate. Issues such as the decisions to put the income from the newly discovered silver veins at Laurium into warships, to fight the Persians rather than submit to them, and to resist Sparta and Macedonia were argued fiercely in the Assembly and could be settled only there. Policies regarding the allies, what to do in case of secession, and the

[28]Thucydides, *History*, p. 119. Copyright © Rex Warner 1954. Reprinted by permission of Penguin Books Ltd.

hundreds of decisions in the day-to-day handling of wars were other common issues. The consent of the people was essential, as Euripides indicates by a speech he put in the mouth of the hero-king Theseus, who, after deciding on war with Thebes, declares:

> I'll do it; I will go and liberate the dead
> Persuading Thebes with words; if not by force of spears.
> . . .
> But I desire that this be approved by all the city.
> . . .
> I'll go to the mass of citizens and win consent.[29]

Besides war and peace, there were other issues that had to be settled, such as the allocation of funds for building purposes, and the procurement of war material. If necessary, experts were brought in, as we learn from the discussants in one of Plato's dialogues:

> Now I observe that when we are met together in the Assembly, and the matter in hand relates to building, the builders are summoned as advisers; when the question is one of shipbuilding, then the shipwrights; and the like of other arts which they think capable of being taught and learned. And if some person offers to give them advice who is not supposed by them to be an expert craftsman, even though he be good-looking and rich and noble, they will not listen to him, but laugh and hoot at him. . . . This is their way of behaving about specialists in the arts. But when the question concerns an affair of state, then everybody is free to get up and give advice—carpenter, tinker, cobbler, passenger and shipowner, rich and poor, high and low.[30]

THE EXECUTIVE BRANCH

> No one, so long as he has it in him to be of service to the state, is kept in political obscurity because of poverty.[31]

It is clear that large assemblies, numbering in the thousands, could not cope with the details of routine administration. Dozens of temples and public buildings had to be maintained; ships had to be equipped and replaced, dockyards kept up, equipment procured; streets needed cleaning, taxes had to be collected, poets and choruses assigned for the festivals. Over such matters and a majority

[29]Euripides, *Suppliants*, p. 266. Copyright © 1957 by Houghton Mifflin Company.

[30]Plato, *Protagoras*. Tr. B. Jowett, revised by Martin Ostwald. (New York: The Liberal Arts Press, 1956). p. 17. Reprinted by permission of The Bobbs-Merrill Co., Inc.

[31]Thucydides, *History*, p. 117. Copyright © Rex Warner 1954. Reprinted by permission of Penguin Books Ltd.

of court cases, the people did not maintain direct control but instead delegated the responsibility to dozens of boards of commissioners and less frequently to individual magistrates. Once the Assembly reached a decision it was usually up to some other agency to see it carried out.

The general administrative principle of the democracy was to create boards of from 10 to 50 commissioners (though at times of as many as 500) to handle specific functions on behalf of the Assembly. There were two methods by which these officers were appointed; lot and election. The majority of commissioners (over 1800) were appointed by lot, whereas a little over 50 were elected.

The Council (The Boule)

> The Boule [Council] has multifarious business to deal with concerning war, revenue, legislation, the day-to-day affairs of the city and matters affecting their allies, and has to receive the tribute and look after the dockyards and shrines . . . [32]

The coordination and supervision of the majority of the boards of commissioners was the responsibility of the Council, the chief executive and administrative agency of the Athenian people.

This body consisted of 500 members, but since this was still too large a number for the handling of routine affairs, a standing committee was created comprised of one-tenth of the full membership. These were called the *prytanes,* or presidents. All 50 came from the same tribe but the order of service of the ten groups was determined by lot, so that, except toward the end of the year, it was impossible to even guess which 50 would be assigned for any of the ten periods of the year. During their term in office the *prytanes* lived and ate in the Tholos, the circular building on the edge of the Agora, close to the meeting place of the Council, the Bouleuterium. In addition to their regular pay of 5 obols a day they drew an additional 1 obol allowance. Altogether this was the equivalent of a laborer's daily wage in Athens in the fifth century and somewhat less in the fourth.

The presiding officer of the subcommittee was selected daily by lot and served for 24 hours. In the fifth century he was also chairman of the ten officers of the Council who presided at meetings of the Assembly, should one occur on the day he happened to be president. He was not reeligible for a second presidency.

The whole Council was supposed to meet every day except holidays and days of ill omen—in all, about 300 times during the year. Its agenda (the *programma)* was prepared by the *prytanes* and followed a standard order of procedure, beginning with religious matters and the reception of ambassadors

[32]Old Oligarch, in *Aristotle and Xenophon,* p. 45. Copyright © 1975 by J. M. Moore. Reprinted by permission of the University of California Press.

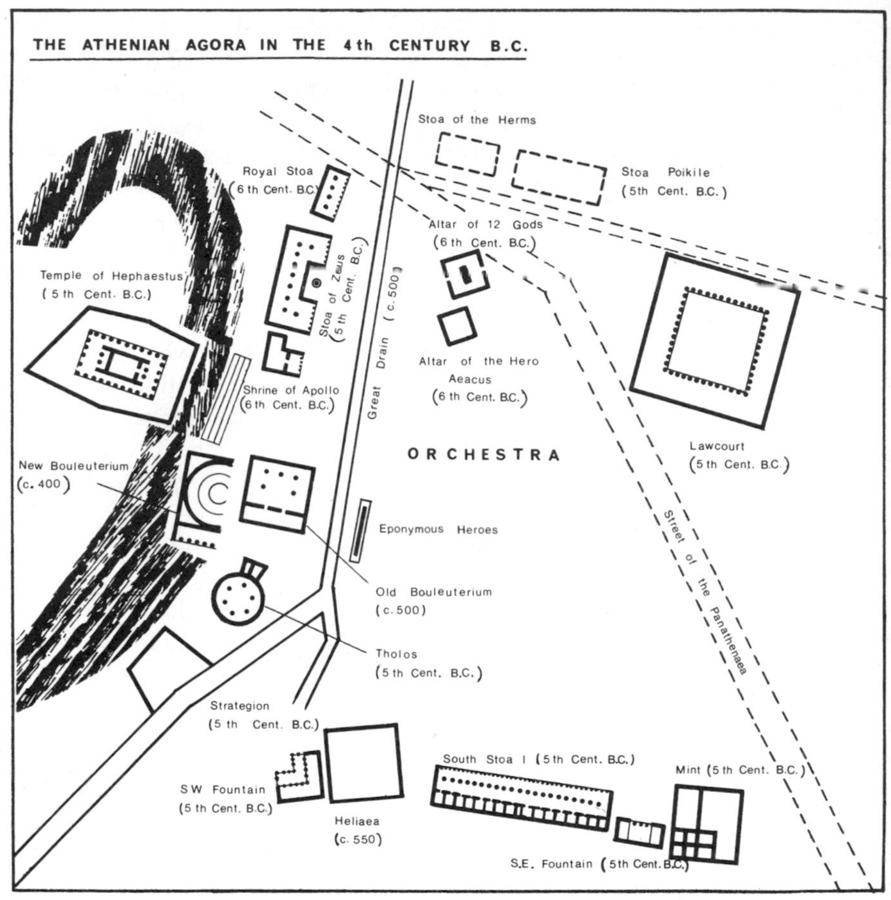

from other states. The secret ballot was used on occasion, but more often decisions were made by a show of hands as in the Assembly. It was in the Council that almost all the essential business for the Assembly was worked out ahead of time in the form of motions. Easily accessible from the teeming Agora, the councillors were very much in contact with what was going on in the city. We can imagine how, during the anxious debates on the fate of the generals after Arginusae, Socrates, who was among the presiding officers for the scheduled Assembly meeting, must have been lobbied by partisans of both sides; or how when news of Philip of Macedon's rapid advance into Greece in 338 was received by the Council, its members, who were eating their dinner in the Tholos, got up cleared the Agora, notified the generals of the situation, and prepared to debate the matter before advising the Assembly.

FUNCTIONS OF THE COUNCIL

The Council had a number of major areas of responsibility, its first being the preparation of motions to present to the Assembly. As a general rule nothing could come before the Assembly without prior examination and preparation by the Council, which therefore acted as a screening committee for the whole Assembly. It could make recommendations in the form of motions for or against a particular issue, or it could simply present the matter without offering any opinion at all. The Assembly, in turn, was free to approve, reject, or amend the proposed motions or substitute new ones.

Any individual, citizen as well as foreigner, could petition for a hearing by the Council, but it was up to this body to decide whether to quash the matter or present it to the Assembly. The Council could thus deny, or at least hinder, access to the people of Athens. There was, however, a specified time in one of the regularly scheduled *prytany* meetings (the four that occurred every 36 days) that allowed an individual to approach the Assembly directly. In most instances, however, the vote would probably be to refer the matter to the Council for an opinion and a motion.

Besides preparing the Assembly's agenda the Council also supervised a large number of boards of commissioners and had judicial functions. In the area of finances, the Council was the Assembly's chief administrative agency. When the city had an empire, the Council supervised the assessment, collection, and payment of the tribute. The principal state treasurers (the *apodectae*) came under Council control along with the board of contract supervisors *(poletae)*. Each *prytany*, all commissioners had to clear their financial accounts with a standing committee of the Council.

The Council also had primary responsibility for the maintenance of the fleet, Athens' principal military arm. This involved the supervision of those responsible for the shipyards and arsenals as well as supervision of new ship construction. Since the number of ships might reach 300—although only a percentage of these might be in active service—this was a major responsibility. Despite the fact that the operation of Athens' largest and most expensive public enterprise was spread among so many boards and individuals, it operated with efficiency. To cite one example, despite the loss of 170 ships in Sicily in 413 B.C., there were 100 ships in Samos two years later, and 180 at the last battle at Aegospotami in 405. Starting once more from scratch after the war, Athens had over 100 ships by 376 B.C.; by the middle of the century, 300 were available. The military training of the 18-year-olds (the *ephebes*) and the cavalry came under Council purview, along with many religious functions, the checking of the list of orphans and cripples who were eligible for state support, and the examination of incoming archons and councillors-elect for the coming year.

A lot of problems would, understandably, be uncovered by the Council as it functioned. Laggard trireme commanders, dishonest commissioners, supervisors who failed to maintain naval supplies or to keep the ships in good condition would be prosecuted before the courts or even before the Council itself, if the amount of the proposed fine did not exceed 500 drachmae. In its purely judicial capacity, the Council could hear accusations of treason and decide whether to refer the case to the Assembly or to an appropriate court.

The Judiciary

> The courts are also involved if someone does not refit a ship or builds on public land; in addition, every year they have to settle disputes about the provision of choruses at the Dionysia, the Thargelia, the Panathenaia. . . . Four hundred trierarchs are appointed every year, and they must judge any appeals which arise. Further, they must examine orphans, and appoint guards for prisoners. This, then, happens every year. They also have to decide cases of avoidance of military service when they arise, and any other crime which suddenly occurs, such as unusual violence or impiety.[33]

GENERAL PRINCIPLES

As in all other realms the first principle in the administration of justice was the preservation of the sovereignty of the people. Nothing was allowed to intervene between the people and those bringing suit or being sued. Athens tolerated no legal profession and had no full-time judges or attorneys, no system of criminal detection and apprehension, no public prosecutors. In the Athenian view such specialists would take power from the people and concentrate it in their own hands. In the past the Athenians had seen how much power control of the judiciary had given to tyrants and aristocrats. As expressed by Euripides:

> There's nothing more sinister for a city than tyrants,
> Where first of all there are not any laws in common;
> There one man, keeping laws unwritten, holds the rule
> Himself unto himself, and power is not equal.
> But where the laws are written down both weak and strong,
> Both rich and poor, have equal power and equal right.
> The weaker man can there talk back on even terms
> To those who are more prosperous, if they use him ill.
> The small can beat the great with justice on his side.[34]

This principle translated itself in actual practice into the conferral of minimal amounts of power on individual magistrates, the retention of ultimate control by large juries of the people, and other devices such as the right to bring suit against a presiding judge thought not to have acted impartially.

[33]Old Oligarch, in *Aristotle and Xenophon,* p. 46. Copyright © 1975 by J. M. Moore. Reprinted by permission of the University of California Press.

[34]Euripides, *Suppliants,* p. 268. Copyright © 1957 by Houghton Mifflin Company.

With no professional police to detect crime and no public prosecutor's office to lodge complaints in the name of the state, it was up to the individual injured to bring suit. This could happen in two ways. The first was where the injured party had been beaten, robbed, or otherwise directly maltreated by the accused, in which case the suit was considered private. In the second instance, if the crime could be construed to have somehow done damage to the community at large, then anyone (i.e., any male Athenian in good standing with the law) could bring suit, on the grounds that he, as a member of society, had suffered the injury along with everyone else. These suits were classified as public and it was to this category that the charges against Alcibiades and Socrates belong.

Faced with the practical problem of maintaining control over the judiciary and at the same time administering justice to the most litigious people in the world, the Athenians had recourse to the same principle that had worked so well for them in the administrative branch of government. This was the division of responsibility among a large number of magistrates or commissioners, so that none would have much power, none would have too complicated a task, so the average citizen would not be overwhelmed if he were to be selected for service. What emerged, therefore, was a system of justice that divided cases into many different, but specific categories (homicide, family matters, orphan's cases, religion, and so on). Single magistrates (occasionally groups) were responsible for each category. Their primary role was to screen cases and decide if they were serious enough to be taken further. If the answer was yes, the next step in most private cases was to send it to an arbitrator. If this proved unsatisfactory to either party, the case went to one of the large citizen juries and the original magistrate presided.

THE COURTS

The principal court of Athens was the Assembly of the Athenians themselves. Its main concern was with matters of such serious nature that all of society was thought to be threatened and needed to be consulted on what action should be taken. An individual who claimed to have evidence of such a crime (an oligarchic plot against the state, for example) could approach the Council at any time and have the item placed on the agenda (i.e., once every 36-day period). If he followed this course the case would probably be referred to the Council or to one of the standing courts for further action. Only in the most urgent cases did the people as a whole sit in judgment. The majority of other cases had to be presented to the appropriate magistrate or board for prior examination. Thus "the Forty" functioned as a small-claims court and pronounced judgments on matters involving less than 10 drachmae. If the amount was greater than this the case was referred to arbitrators. If they failed to provide satisfaction, it went to a court presided over by a member of the Forty. The most important officials were the nine archons, each of whom had his own special area of jurisdiction. In general, the bulk of the private cases came to the Forty; the six junior archons (or *thesmothetae*) handled the majority of public cases.

The courts of the people *(dicasteries)* that have been referred to must be distinguished from the individual magistrates and boards of commissioners to whom cases generally came for a preliminary examination. These courts were large, varying in size depending on the importance of the case, from 200 for private cases to 500 or larger for public cases. Pericles was tried and fined by a court of 1500 in 430 and a court of 6000 considered the case of sacrilege involving Alcibiades before the Sicilian expedition.

Jurors for the individual courts were drawn from a pool of 6000 chosen annually (the process is not known) from among the ten tribes. Jurors had to be 30 years of age or older and in good standing with the law. Originally a juror was automatically assigned to a particular court for the entire year, but late in the fifth century, due to citizen losses in the Peloponnesian War and the spectacular bribery of one entire panel by Anytus (later one of Socrates' accusers), the process of assignment was reorganized. An elaborate system of lot taking was devised. First a selection was made of the requisite number of jurors, who were then assigned to the courts in such a way that no one would know what jurors would be assigned to which cases until the day of the trial itself. The new system also guaranteed two other things: First, that whoever presented himself for jury duty would have an equal chance of being selected, and second, that all the ten tribes would be fairly represented in the drawing process.

The judicial officials and the law courts met in a number of places, most of them adjacent to the Agora. The Archon Basileus, for example, had his offices in the small Royal Stoa, which also served as a law depository. Here the laws were displayed on thin marble slabs that could easily be examined by the citizens, and copies could be made for quotation in court. Nearby was the Stoa Poikile, which was the scene of arbitrations as well as regular trials with juries of more than 500 members. The oldest of the courts, the Heliaea, was a simple walled enclosure at the southern end of the Agora, with room for 1500 jurors. Other law courts were located diagonally across from it.

PROCEDURE

In both public and private cases the basic procedure was as follows: Accompanied by one or two witnesses, the plaintiff had first to summon the defendants to appear before a certain magistrate on a given day, stating the nature of the accusation and naming the day of the appearance. At the actual confrontation before the appropriate magistrate the plaintiff made his allegation (which had to be in writing after the middle of the fourth century). If the magistrate accepted the case, fees had to be paid then and there. Generally, in private cases both parties made a deposit, and if the plaintiff did not pay up immediately there was no further action. At the conclusion of the case the losing party had to reimburse the other for his costs. The fee schedule varied, depending on the importance of the case. In actions involving less than 1000

Fragment of a cleroterion, a mechanical device created by the Athenians to help avoid stacked juries. Each juror had a ticket which was selected at random and inserted in one of the slots. Colored balls, again selected at random, were then slid down the tube, part of which can be seen at the left. Depending on the color, each row of jurors was either selected or rejected.

drachmae the fee was 3 drachmae; for cases involving under 100 drachmae, there was no fee. In public cases the accuser alone paid the fee, the amount of which is unknown. When all these preliminaries were completed the magistrate established a day for the preliminary hearing (the *anakrisis*). In the meantime the accuser's charge was published in the Agora.

At the preliminary hearing, oaths were taken on both sides, evidence presented in the form of depositions of witnesses, contracts, laws, and the like, and objections were made. The principal responsibility of the presiding magistrate was to determine whether the plaintiff really had a case, that he was the right magistrate to handle it, and that the proper form had been followed. It was generally not his job to decide the case; he merely decided whether to go on to the next step. When he was satisfied on these matters he then assigned the case either to arbitration, as was common in private cases coming before the Forty, or immediately to a court. If arbitration failed to satisfy both parties the next step was to ask the *thesmothetae* to fix a day for a trial and to assign the appropriate number of jurors.

Failure of the defendant to appear at the preliminary hearing meant that the plaintiff was granted the judgment automatically (and vice versa). Private cases could be withdrawn at this preliminary stage, but someone who had brought a public charge was fined 1000 drachmae if he failed to carry it through after the *anakrisis.* He was fined a similar amount if he failed to obtain one-fifth of the jurors' votes, the object being in this and the previous instance to reduce frivolous accusations and make people less prone to bring charges that had no substantiating evidence. Fines in public cases usually went to the state.

THE TRIAL

On the day of the trial the defendant and the plaintiff, armed with speeches (often prepared by professionals) and accompanied by friends, came to the proper court. The jurors sat on benches and the presiding officer at a platform from which he regulated the proceedings.

The litigants spoke for themselves though they could call on someone else to make a speech for them. Since paid advocacy was outlawed, pleas were generally made by people who passed themselves off as relatives or club members. Although this may seem odd to us it was considered legitimate in the context of the city-state where self-help was an essential aspect of life and where friends and relatives had to perform, in rough approximation, the duties of court bailiffs and police. Naturally the opposition tried to neutralize the effect of such speeches by questioning the motives of the speakers and their personal characters.

Litigants had a lot of work to do. They supplied both the laws and the facts. Since there was no subpoena system they also had to notify and corral witnesses with only public opinion and possibly the threat of a fine to encourage attendance—hence the importance of large numbers of relatives and friends to bring pressure on the witnesses to appear. There was no cross-examination and witnesses were brought on merely to corroborate or deny allegations. There was no expounding of the law by the presiding magistrate. Each side gave his version of the statute and it was left to the jurors to decide both matters of law and fact. Decisions were arrived at by secret ballot and had to be completed on the day assigned.

In general, decisions were regarded as final, and it was hard to reopen a case unless proof of false evidence could be procured. Harsh as this may seem, there does not seem to have been much criticism of the justice of the system. Demosthenes claimed, for example, that no one had ever demonstrated that the Areopagus (which was responsible for murder trials) had been unjust to him, and the Old Oligarch, no friend of the democracy, commented on the fewness of those who could claim that their civil rights had been violated by the democracy.

Religion, Drama, and the Festivals

Athenians were famous for the care they lavished on their public festivals, and visitors came from all over Greece to witness them. Pericles, with classical restraint, said, "We provide plenty of means for the mind to refresh itself from business. We celebrate games and sacrifices all the year round."[35] The Old Oligarch put it more bluntly. He said that the Athenians had twice as many festivals as anyone else with the result that public business suffered. In fact, the year offered Athenian citizens an opportunity to participate in as many as 50

[35]Thucydides, *History of the Peloponnesian War* 2.38.1.

festivals, one of which lasted up to nine days, and this does not include the innumerable deme festivals and private celebrations in honor of individual deities and family cults.

As in every other aspect of public life, the democracy had an impact here, generally by expanding the number of participants at every level. Boards of officials were selected in the usual fashion to organize and supervise many of the festivals. One of the principal responsibilities of the chief archon was the selection of wealthy individuals (the *choregi)* for the honor of producing the choruses and plays for the City Dionysia festival. But beyond official participation, hundreds, and at times thousands, were involved in the numerous athletic competitions, processions, dances, choruses, plays, and sacrifices that made up the festivals, as well as in the preparations—sometimes a year in length—that went into them. With the exception of the most secret aspects of the Eleusinian and other mysteries, there was little restriction on who could witness them. At some, metics paraded in glorious robes alongside citizens. These were truly community feasts and essential to the proper functioning of the state. Through them the gods were properly honored and each new generation of Athenians duly initiated into the religious and moral values of the city. All citizens were expected to attend, and so vital were the festivals considered that for at least two that we know of, and possibly more, the state funded both the expenses and the cost of the theater tickets for the participants.

From July, when the Athenian year began, festival succeeded festival. In December came a cycle of celebrations in honor of Dionysus. These are of particular interest because of the dramatic presentations that occurred during some of them. The first of these were the rural Dionysia, organized by the individual demes, which generally consisted of processions in which the *phallus* was displayed for the purpose of securing the fertility of the crops sown in the previous months. In many of the demes, however, dramatic festivals were also part of the celebrations. Plays that had been performed on previous occasions at the major Dionysiac celebrations in Athens were staged.

The City Dionysia—or Greater Dionysia—in March was the most important dramatic festival of the year, one of the festivals for which all citizens received money from the state. It began with a torchlight procession and the reenactment of the coming of Dionysus to Athens from Eleutherae, a village in the northwest of Attica. Then came several days of dramatic and musical contests whose exact order is unknown to us. There were competitions between dithyrambic choruses from the ten tribes, ten each of boys and men, with 50 members in each. The producer for each chorus was a wealthy individual nominated by his tribe and designated by the archon. This man chose both the poet and the musical instrumentalists. Prizes, such as bulls, tripods, caldrons of bronze, and amphorae of wine were distributed. These songs and dances were relatively short, to allow all 20 teams to compete, but could involve quite complicated steps and meters. At the end of each day there was a torchlight procession in honor of Dionysus.

On the following four days came the plays of which three were devoted to tragedy and one to comedy. The dramas began with a sacrifice to purify the theater, which was regarded as sacred, and libations were offered. Next the tribute of the allies and the surplus money of the state was carried across the orchestra for all to behold. Then the sons of men who had fallen in battle, who had been brought up at state expense, were paraded in full armor. They listened to a short exhortation before taking the special seats allotted to them. Prisoners were released in honor of Dionysus and the festival was also used as an occasion to confer honors on the friends of the democracy.

The last action before the plays began was the final selection of those who were to judge the plays. A number of these had already been chosen from the tribes and their names were placed in sealed urns. These were now opened and ten judges selected. At the end of the contest each wrote his preferences, in order, on a tablet and placed the tablet in an urn from which five tablets were drawn at random. The judgments were read from these. Prizes for composers, composition, production, and acting were awarded.

The order of performance had already been settled and now the plays were ready to begin. A trumpet sounded, and the 14,000–17,000 people in the audience settled down for four days of entertainment, during which nine tragedies, three satyr plays (semicomedy relief pieces), and five comedies would be performed.

THE THEATER

Music and dramatic festivals were originally held in the Agora, but at the time of Pericles they were shifted to the newly built Odeon and theater of Dionysus on the slopes of the Acropolis, near the temple of Dionysus.

The new theater consisted of a round, level dancing space (the orchestra) on which the chorus performed its dances. Above the orchestra ranged the ramp of the theater and on either side were access passages that allowed the chorus to come and go. The seats in the theater were made of wood and were not replaced with stone until much later. Behind the orchestra was the stage, a large wooden frame about 100 feet long. In front of the stage there may have been a low, raised platform (the point is disputed), connected with the orchestra by stairs, from which the actors could proclaim their pieces.

In the earliest plays there was only one actor and the chorus. Aeschylus raised the number of actors to two and Sophocles to three, and thereafter this remained the standard number. In the middle of the fifth century a prize for actors was introduced, and in time the stars of the theater came to command astronomical fees. The actors wore masks, but in classical times at least these had none of the exaggerated features—the staring eyes and high, piled hair—of later times. The masks were a necessity because the size of the theater made it difficult to see the faces of the actors, but they also permitted them to switch roles quickly. Costumes in brilliant colors matched the masks. Actors needed strong, clear voices to reach the upper rows of the theater, and they were also expected to be able to chant and sing in recitative.

The chorus usually consisted of 15 members, all carefully drilled to speak, sing, and dance as one. They were generally present during the whole play and helped to give it dramatic unity. In the days of the single actor the play consisted essentially of a dialogue between the actor and the chorus. The chorus sang its lines but what actions accompanied this and what it did during the dialogue of the actors is difficult to say. It is likely that it interpreted the action of the play by appropriate rhythmic movements. Some choruses, for whatever technical reasons, were much admired as masterpieces of craftsmanship in their own right.

Athenian audiences were made up of people from all segments of the community: Metics, foreigners, men, women, and at times even slaves were included. Plato's comment in the *Laws* in regard to different persons' criteria of pleasure is revealing. He remarks that little boys enjoy the conjurors; older boys, the comic poets; and young men, educated men and women, and the public in general, tragedy. Such audiences were highly appreciative and critical. They were easily moved, "weeping, glaring wildly . . . marvelling at what they heard."[36] They clapped, hissed, and booed to indicate their approval or disapproval, singling out for special attention the technical skills (or blunders) of chorus, actors, and playwrights. Individual lines were attacked and one line of Euripides' almost caused a riot on one occasion, forcing him to stand up and provide an explanation on the spot.

The audience sat from dawn to dusk listening to the performances, which went on without break. To fortify themselves they brought refreshments, such as wine and dried fruits (the latter also substituted as missiles to be flung at actors they disliked). However, physical violence was a capital offense, though occasionally rival *choregi* (wealthy men who financed the plays) came to blows. Once, when Alcibiades had put on a play, he was able to browbeat the judges into giving him the prize, even though the crowd favored his rival *choregus.* Politicians tried to make capital out of the staging of the plays and Nicias, who lacked eloquence, compensated for this deficiency by lavish productions that regularly won first prize.

In the theater, the Agora, the courts, and the Assembly, the Athenian people were exposed to a stimulating and demanding social, political, and intellectual environment. No one could say that the life of the average citizen was boring or that it revolved around unimportant or trivial things. He participated in all the major decisions that affected his existence and was exposed to whatever ideas were current at the time. Few nations can boast a roster of great names comparable to those that crop up at Athens in the period between the Persian wars and the opening of the Age of Alexander. None can claim a society and system of government that brought these figures and the ideas they represented into contact with the everyday lives of the man in the street.

[36]Plato, *Ion* 535e.

From the Rise of Macedonia to the Decline of the Hellenistic Monarchies

THE RISE OF MACEDONIA

For two centuries a handful of cities dominated the history of Greece. Athens, Sparta, Thebes, Corinth, and Argos were the focal points of all the major wars and of most of the social and intellectual development from at least the sixth century B.C. Then, quite suddenly, in the middle of the fourth century they were eclipsed by other states, none of which had had a significant role in the past.

For a decade after 356 the center of events in mainland Greece was the Sacred War waged by the minor state of Phocis against Boeotia, Locris, Thessaly, and Macedonia. During the same decade the Carian kingdom of King Mausolus in Asia Minor rose to importance and had a hand in the breakup of Athens' second empire. Somewhat earlier Jason of Pherae successfully united the immense potential of Thessaly behind him, but after his death the normal pattern of disunity established itself again. To the north the kingdom of Macedonia possessed the same potential as Thessaly and it was Macedonia that finally emerged as the major power of the fourth century and put an end to the Classical Age of the Greek city-states.

Macedonia was unlike the rest of Greece in many respects. It consisted of two regions: the plain around the Thermaic Gulf of Macedonia proper, and the highland region in the hinterland over which the Macedonian kings exercised only a feeble sovereignty. It had a continental climate, and unlike the rest of Greece, it was not dotted with city-states. Its tribal system was still intact and government above the tribal level consisted of an elected, though hereditary, monarchy. The kings, like many of their counterparts in similarly undeveloped societies, were at one and the same time priests, judges, generals, and treasurers. The nobles of the different tribes were bound to them by personal bonds of loyalty and were considered the kinsmen and friends of the king. The upper classes, or at least the king and his court, spoke Greek and made a point of cultivating Greek culture. Artists and poets were invited regularly to Pella, the capital, and among those who stayed there were Euripides and the painter Zeuxis. The kings were recognized as Greeks by the officials of the Olympic games, but Macedonia was not considered part of the traditional Hellenic world by the rest of the Greeks.

The potential of Macedonia was great. Its people were hardy and there was plenty of rich land and great reserves of timber and metal. It had difficulty realizing its potential because, more than any other state in Greece, it was exposed to barbarian pressures. Illyrians pressed in from the west, Paeonians from the north, and Thracians from the east. For generations the Greeks had maintained cities along the coast and in the mid-fourth century the Chalcidian League could field an army almost as large as that of Macedonia itself. On the other side of the Chalcidice, Athens had an ongoing interest in the Thracian coastal regions, and Amphipolis was always a particular concern. So preoccupied were the Macedonians with their defense problems and with holding together upland and lowland regions that it was generally safe for the Greeks to disregard them as a threat. The likelihood of Macedonia overcoming Thrace, for example, and thereby threatening the grain route to Athens through the Hellespont, or becoming a significant naval power and achieving control by that means, was not something that Athens had ever before had to contemplate.

PHILIP II

When Perdiccas III of Macedonia fell in battle against the Illyrians in 359, his brother Philip was made regent and eventually became outright king. He had spent three years at Thebes during the time of Epaminondas and Pelopidas and had an opportunity to observe the tactical innovations and reorganization of the phalanx that enabled Thebes to overcome the Spartan hoplites at Leuctra and Mantinea. Despite these lessons, the policies and strategies of Philip were peculiarly his own. He combined an extraordinary sense of timing with a Machiavellian ability to manipulate other states such that his enemies were able only slowly to divine his intentions and usually acted too late to thwart him. Although his military abilities were first-rate, Philip knew when to use force and when other tactics would be equally successful.

Heavily armed cavalry had been the traditional strength of the Macedonian army. Its nucleus was the Companion Cavalry drawn from the nobles of the different tribes and attached to the king by personal loyalty. Philip strengthened the existing hoplite forces and modified the traditional phalanx form by giving the infantrymen much longer spears or pikes and spacing them farther apart, thus giving them more mobility. Philip also made use of light cavalry and infantry. More important than the reforms themselves, however, was Philip's ability to infuse the army with a spirit of energy and enthusiasm that enabled those in it to transcend their tribal backgrounds and become a single striking-force. By dint of constant and successful compaigning Philip was able to make the Macedonian army into a force without an equal in Greece—or anywhere else.

Philip's first mission was to free Macedonia from the threat of the barbarians. One by one, he eliminated them. First the Paeonians were subdued, then the Illyrians (358). In gratitude for relief from Illyrian pressure, the king of Epirus offered his daughter Olympias to Philip in marriage. In the summer of 356 they had a son, whom they named Alexander.

While Athens was involved in the Social War, Philip took the important city of Amphipolis (357). From there he moved to establish the fortress of Philippi, which guaranteed him access to the rich gold mines of Mount Pangaeus. Producing 1000 talents a year these mines made Macedonia economically independent and provided Philip with the essential resources for financing his ambitions. His next move was to eliminate the remaining Athenian possessions in the region and in preparation for doing so he first secured the alliance of the Chalcidian League. Athens, still involved in the Social War, could only stir up the Illyrians and Thracians. It was unable to prevent the fall of Potidaea in 356. Two years later Methone, Athens' last possession, fell to Philip.

PHILIP AND DEMOSTHENES

Despite its humiliation, Athens seemed willing to accept its losses. In part this was because its main interests were in the Hellespont and the Bosporus, which were not directly threatened by Philip, and in part because of internal developments. Since 358 the *theoric* or festival fund had become an independent agency, and Eubulus, its chief administrator from 354 on, had a rule passed that all surplus revenue should go to this fund. This meant that a premium was placed on maintaining peace, since the fund was used to finance the attendance of the poor at the festivals. In times of war, the money would have to go into the war fund. Athens' naval power was not neglected, however, and with over 300 ships available it was still the most important naval power in the Aegean. It was at this time that Demosthenes, the greatest orator of the fourth century, rose to prominence. He has been variously denounced as a blind chauvinist fighting the tide of the times or hailed as a heroic patriot defending Athens' liberty against tyranny. Neither description fits the orator, who was a practical politician striving to survive in the slippery political world of democratic Athens. From at least 351, when he delivered his first Philippic (speech against Philip), Demosthenes more than any other Athenian divined the significance of the growth of Macedonian power. Aware that any single state that developed overwhelming superiority in Greece would automatically be a threat to Athens, Demosthenes consistently inveighed against Philip and tried to convince the Athenians of the potential dangers. Understandably, the Athenians, with no prior appreciation of the resources of a unified Macedonia and no precedents, were slow to act.

Having deterred the barbarians and eliminated Athenian footholds in Macedonia, Philip moved against the Chalcidian League. Although the league was no friend of Athens, Demosthenes recommended that Athens send help. However, Philip's intrigues in Euboea raised a revolt there, and Athens was able

A haggard Demosthenes, worn out by almost half a century of political struggles at Athens. His statue, of which this is a copy, was erected around 280 B.C. in the Agora of Athens.

to send only some mercenaries and a few ships. These were sent piecemeal, and could not stop Philip. In a rapid winter campaign in 348, Philip reduced the cities individually and the Chalcidian League's capital, Olynthus, fell in August. It was razed and its inhabitants were scattered. Having exhausted its revenues in its efforts to regain Euboea and help the Chalcidians, Athens was now ready for peace (the peace of Philocrates, 346 B.C.). The terms of the peace recognized the loss of Amphipolis and meant that Athens was now truly isolated though still in control of the all-important Hellespont.

Philip was at last free to achieve another ambition: a place for Macedonia in the Delphic amphictyony, or Holy League, which included such important states as Athens and Thebes. This he did by ending the ten-year-long Sacred War and displacing Phocis from its seat. Meanwhile Athens was divided between the war party headed by Demosthenes and supported by Hyperides and Lycurgus, and the peace party led by Eubulus, Phocion, and the orator Aeschines. The battle between the two factions reached its height in 343 when Demosthenes impeached Aeschines for receiving bribes in connection with the peace of Philocrates. Aeschines was acquitted, but public feeling was now running strongly against Philip. The final blow came when Philip, after securing all his other fronts, attacked Thrace and brought it under his control (342–341 B.C.). As a result, Macedonia was now in a position to close in on the essential grain route through the Bosporus and the Hellespont. Immediately Athens proposed alliances with two key cities in these areas: Byzantium and Perinthus.

When Philip attacked them, Athens' support foiled his efforts to take them. Left now with no alternative but war to removing the last obstacle to his plans to control Greece, Philip prepared for a land invasion of Attica.

A pretext of supporting the Delphic amphictyony against an offending city allowed Philip to march a large army into central Greece in the spring of 338. In desperation Athens diverted the theoric funds to the military account and appealed to its old foe, Thebes. Athens' ancient rival was itself concerned with the rising power of Macedonia and its reluctance to break its alliance with Philip was further weakened by an Athenian offer to pay two-thirds of the costs of the war. An alliance was made and at Chaeronea in the summer of 338 the forces of Macedonia and Greece met in one of the decisive battles of history. Philip strengthened his left wing, where he placed the Macedonian phalanx and the cavalry commanded by Alexander, while deliberately leaving his right wing weak. In the ensuing battle the Thebans were annihilated by the Macedonian cavalry and infantry, and the Athenians advancing on the left were enveloped or scattered and fled from the battlefield. Imposing lenient terms on Athens, Philip made peace and went on to Corinth where he convened the Greek states and compelled them to form a league to which all but Sparta adhered. The Macedonian king was to be the chief executive of the league and its military commander. A council was to represent the individual members, each of which was to remain autonomous. No state was to wage war against another, since all the Greeks were henceforth to be bound to a common peace. Theoretically, at least, this much of Isocrates' ideal had been realized. There was no tribute, but the members of the league were expected to make contributions to the federal army and to join with the Macedonians in a war of revenge against Persia for the invasion of Xerxes. In anticipation of this Philip sent an advance guard into Asia Minor in the spring of 336, but before he could follow it up he was assassinated at the wedding of his daughter. His son, Alexander, was quickly elected to succeed him.

ALEXANDER THE GREAT

At the age of 20 Alexander inherited all the glories of the Macedonian kingship and the resources so carefully nourished by his father. The army was in superb condition, and Greece appeared to be firmly under control. But Alexander also inherited the problems of the Macedonian monarchs. These were first of all dynastic, though the elimination of three rivals to the throne by Alexander quickly resolved that problem. His mother, who had been divorced by Philip not long before his death, took private revenge by murdering the infant son of Cleopatra, the woman who supplanted her, and then forcing Cleopatra to commit suicide. The other problems were handled with equal ruthlessness and speed. Those perpetual enemies of the Macedonians, the Thracians and Illyrians, were subdued in lightning campaigns (335). When false rumors of Alexander's death encouraged the Greeks to revolt, he marched south and

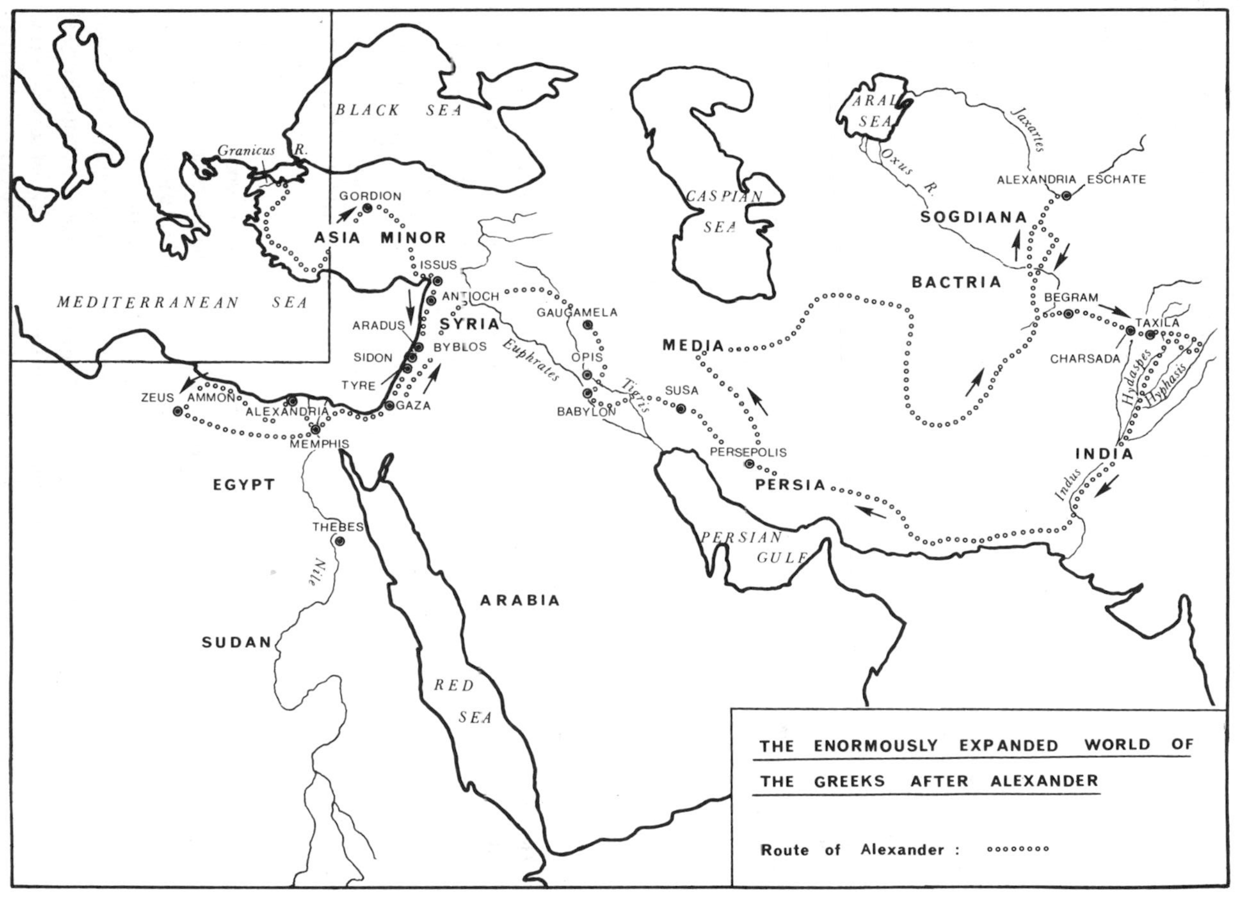
BLACK SEA
Granicus R.
GORDION
ASIA MINOR
ISSUS
MEDITERRANEAN SEA
ANTIOCH
SYRIA
ARADUS
BYBLOS
SIDON
TYRE
GAZA
ZEUS AMMON
ALEXANDRIA
MEMPHIS
EGYPT
THEBES
Nile
SUDAN
RED SEA
ARABIA
Euphrates
GAUGAMELA
OPIS
BABYLON
Tigris
SUSA
MEDIA
PERSEPOLIS
PERSIA
PERSIAN GULF
CASPIAN SEA
ARAL SEA
Oxus R.
Jaxartes
ALEXANDRIA ESCHATE
SOGDIANA
BACTRIA
BEGRAM
TAXILA
CHARSADA
Hydaspes
Hyphasis
INDIA
Indus
THE ENORMOUSLY EXPANDED WORLD OF THE GREEKS AFTER ALEXANDER
Route of Alexander : oooooooo

captured Thebes, razing it—except for the temples and the house of Pindar the poet. The population was slaughtered or sold into slavery. Shaken by the destruction of one of their legendary cities, the Greeks quickly came back to their allegiance and hurriedly voted to comply with Alexander's requests for contributions for the invasion of Persia that had been planned by Philip.

In 334 Alexander and an army of 30,000 hoplites and 5000 cavalry crossed into Asia Minor. At Troy he sacrificed to King Priam and placed wreaths on the tomb of his ancestor and model, Achilles. A shield said to have been from the Trojan wars was taken from the temple of Athena, and was always carried thereafter by his bodyguard. It was with this shield that Alexander was protected eight years later, when he was trapped in a fortress in India during one of his rasher exploits.

The Conquest of the Persian Empire

Alexander's main objective in the first portion of his campaign (334–331 B.C.) was the destruction of Persian armed forces in the west. Since his fleet was mostly Greek and therefore untrustworthy, he chose a novel method of achieving this aim: a land campaign that would have the double effect of crippling Persian land forces while eliminating the naval bases of the Persian fleet.

The first clash with the Persians took place at the river Granicus, not far from the Hellespont. Here Alexander found a large collection of Persian cavalry and Greek mercenaries waiting for him on the opposite bank. As in all his battles, he was given the initiative by the Persian commanders, whose tactics lagged far behind recent military developments in Greece. Crashing across the river, Alexander scattered the opposing cavalry and then practically annihilated the defenseless infantry, justifying his ruthlessness by an appeal to the adhesion of the League of Corinth to his Persian crusade—which technically made the mercenaries traitors to the Greek cause. From the Granicus Alexander proceeded to liberate the Greek cities of Asia Minor, which had been "freed" so many times before by different conquerors, and were to be swept over again and again before the *pax romana*, the Roman Peace, over three hundred years later brought them peace and prosperity. An attempt by the Persian fleet to raise a revolt in Greece behind him failed, and Alexander advanced in the autumn of 333 to Issus where the Persians under Darius III had gathered another large force of Greek mercenaries and Persian troops. This engagement was one of Alexander's three greatest battles, and he won it as he did the others by quickly seizing the initiative on the battlefield and making the enemy respond to his movements. Attacking as was his custom with the Companion heavy cavalry, he dispersed his opponents and then swept around to envelop the other units from the rear. Darius fled, leaving behind his mother, his wife, and his children, whom Alexander treated with courtesy though guarding them as useful political hostages. Instead of following the Great King, Darius, Alexander swung south along the Phoenician coast in pursuit of his policy of eliminating both the land and the sea power of the Persians. Sidon, Byblos, and Aradus quickly came over but Tyre resisted and for seven months a bitter siege was conducted before the city fell. Farther down the coast Alexander was again held up, this time for two months by the city of Gaza, which finally was taken after being defended to the last man. Alexander was then able to enter Egypt unopposed (late 332). At Memphis he sacrificed to the sacred bull Apis and was crowned pharaoh of Egypt by the priests. He next sailed down the Nile to the Canopic mouth where he founded Alexandria as a great business and commercial center. From Alexandria he traveled across the desert to the oasis of Siwa to worship at the shrine of Zeus Ammon. There he was greeted by the priests as the son of Ammon and received an answer from the god which he refused to reveal to anyone but which he declared pleased him. Inevitably an aura of the superhuman grew up around Alexander, aided by his own proclivity for heroic and flamboyant deeds and the tendency of all men to worship at the shrine of the successful.

Leaving Egypt in the summer of 331 B.C. Alexander advanced northward and marched through Syria to the Tigris. Blocking his route to Babylon was a huge army that Darius had gathered from all over the empire. It was weak in heavy infantry, since after Issus Darius no longer had access to the sources of Greek mercenaries in the Aegean. However, he had compensated for this by increasing the amount of cavalry and by adding scythed chariots, which were supposed to cut down the Macedonian infantry. Although Darius chose the battlefield, Alexander with his usual flair was able to take rapid control of the tactical situation. His aim was to draw the enormously long Persian line out of position and then charge into any resulting gaps. To do this he advanced obliquely to the right forcing the enemy to move with him. When a gap finally appeared between the center and the left wing, Alexander charged with his heavy cavalry and split the Persian line in two. As at Issus, Darius fled before the battle was over and was followed by large numbers of his troops. From Gaugamela, Alexander marched to Babylon, where he sacrificed to the gods and ordered the restoration of the temple of Marduk, which had been destroyed by the Persians. By December Alexander was at Susa, the ancient capital of Elam and the summer residence of the Persians. In midwinter he forced his way through the mountains into Persia proper and seized the treasures that had been accumulating at Persepolis for over two centuries. The palace of Xerxes was burned down during a drunken revel, though later apologists for Alexander claimed that it was a deliberate act intended to symbolize the end of Achaemenian rule and the wreaking of vengeance for Persian outrages in Greece. From Persepolis the army went on to Ecbatana, the Median capital, where Darius was supposed to have assembled another large army. There Alexander found that Darius had fled again and the pursuit began once more. Covering almost 40 miles a day with his men, Alexander caught up with his quarry in July, 330 B.C. On Alexander's approach Darius was stabbed by his own guard who then fled. When Alexander arrived the king was dead.

Campaigns in Central Asia (330–323 B.C.)

With the death of Darius the campaigns against Persia could be regarded as closed. Alexander was now the Great King and his troops might have assumed that he would return to more civilized regions to consolidate his conquests. Alexander, however, had different plans. To retain Mesopotamia it was essential to control the Iranian Plateau, and to hold it required in turn that the territory further north and east be occupied to prevent the entry of the marauding nomads of central Asia. That was one reason. The other was that Alexander was determined to push his conquests to the edge of the known world, which he wrongly assumed did not extend much beyond the Indus. It was precisely at this point that he first encountered opposition from his own Macedonians. After Darius' death Alexander had taken to wearing Persian dress on certain occasions involving Persian ceremonials and had begun to appoint Persians to positions of importance. Inevitably the introduction of what to the Macedonians looked like outsiders into the very personal, inner circle of command excited jealousies. Later in the year of Darius' death Philotas, son of Parmenio the commander of the Companion Cavalry was found guilty of treason and was executed. Although innocent, his father was also put to death, being in too powerful a position to be allowed to live. Two years later Alexander got into a quarrel during a drinking bout with his old friend Cleitus, who taunted him with being the son of Ammon, not Philip, and declared that he owed his victories to Philip's generals and the Macedonians, not to his own skills. In a rage Alexander grabbed a guard's spear and with it stabbed Cleitus to death. Overcome by remorse he spent the next three days without food or water in his tent until his companions persuaded him to return to his duties. A year later there was another conspiracy. When Alexander proposed that the Macedonians join the Persians in doing him obeisance the principal objections came from Callisthenes, Aristotle's nephew, who had accompanied the campaign in the capacity of a propagandist for the king. Shortly thereafter a plot was discovered among the pages whom Callisthenes tutored and the guilty were executed. Callisthenes was arrested at the same time though it is not known wheather he was involved or not. He was later executed. About this time Alexander married Roxane, the daughter of a Sogdian king; inevitably, more tensions were introduced. Further changes were brought about when Alexander ordered the training of Persians in the Macedonian style of warfare and brought Persian cavalry into his own ranks.

Despite these problems Alexander was still in complete command of the army, and the years between 330 and 327 were spent in difficult campaigns in the wild northeastern districts of the Persian Empire. With these completed Alexander prepared to embark on his last major campaign, the conquest of India. Imagining that what is now Pakistan and the Punjab constituted all of India, this was not an unreasonable plan, and it would have given him the Indus as his eastern frontier. However, opposition within the region was formidable and the last of Alexander's major battles was against Porus, one of the local kings (battle of the Hydaspes, 326). Moving through monsoon rains to what he thought was the edge of his new dominions he reached the Hyphasis (Beas) River and discovered that there was even more land to the east and another great river. At this point the troops refused to go any further and Alexander was forced to retreat. Instead of retracing his footsteps and returning to Mesopotamia by the northern route, Alexander chose to march down the Indus to the Indian Ocean and then head west along the barren coast of southern Pakistan. After desperate sufferings and tremendous losses the army, or what was left of it, finally got through to safety.

The Aims of Alexander

When Alexander arrived back in Persia he found that many of his satraps, both Greek and Persian, had behaved badly in his absence. He immediately set about reasserting his control. Fearing Alexander's vengeance, his old friend the treasurer Harpalus fled with a large sum of money and tried to find sanctuary at Athens. There some of the gold found its way into Demosthenes' pockets and he was impeached, convicted, and driven into exile. Alexander's principal aim at this point, however, was to establish some kind of a joint Macedonian–Persian aristocracy. He had already established large numbers of colonies in Asia and had associated Persians with him in high government office. Now, in a mass wedding he and 80 of the Companion Cavalry took wives from among the Persian nobility and over 10,000 of the Macedonians had their relationships with Asiatic women recognized. All these efforts at fusing the two groups did not prevent a mutiny breaking out at Opis in 324 when he discharged the veterans and prepared to send them home. The army tended to take the view that it had won Alexander's wars and now in the moment of triumph was being dismissed and replaced by the very people it had conquered. Alexander responded by discharging the whole army and retiring to his tent until his forlorn troops begged his forgiveness. With magnanimity and showmanship he welcomed them back and a great feast was celebrated at which Macedonians and Persians sat down together and drank from the same cup while Alexander prayed for concord *(homonoia)* and for a partnership in the empire between Macedonians and Persians. In the winter Alexander's closest friend Hephaistion died, leaving Alexander grief-stricken. The following year, while preparing for a great exploratory expedition to circumnavigate and conquer Arabia, Alexander contracted a fever. After lying ill for ten days he died, on June 13, 323. He was 32 years of age.

Alexander's brilliance as a general and leader of men dazzled his contemporaries and inspired countless imitators throughout subsequent history. There is no doubting his capacity to sweep up others into his own heroic vision and even today the accounts of his exploits have a magical quality that not even the most cynical can denigrate. Alexander was the living embodiment of the Homeric ideal of the speaker of words and the doer of deeds, and the mixture of courage, love of his fellow soldiers, display, generosity, ferocity, and ruthlessness were entirely appropriate in this worthy descendant of Achilles. His principal achievement, the destruction of the armed might of Persia, opened up the way for the spread of Greek influence, but Alexander himself was no empire builder. What unity and legitimacy his kingdom possessed depended entirely on his own personality and promptly disappeared after his death. His successors are often portrayed unfavorably as hardheaded pragmatists who lacked Alexander's vision of fusing east and west, Greek and barbarian, but it is a poor comparison. Alexander, unfortunately, possessed no capacity to hold his farflung empire together beyond his own flamboyant personality.

THE HELLENISTIC MONARCHIES

It is said that as Alexander lay dying his commanders asked to whom he left his kingdom, and that Alexander replied, "to the strongest." Although probably apocryphal, the tale is a good commentary on what actually happened in the years after his death. His generals at first squabbled but eventually patched up a compromise. Philip III Arrhidaeus, Alexander's feebleminded half-brother, and his son by Roxane, Alexander IV, were set up as figureheads. It was, however, an impossible solution. Young Alexander was part barbarian and therefore unacceptable to the rank and file of the army. Since neither he nor Philip III could rule without regents, inevitably the struggle for power became a battle among Alexander's generals and lieutenants.

The senior commanders were soon eliminated. Perdiccas the cavalry general and Craterus the infantry chief were both killed in 321, the former by mutinous troops and the latter in battle. Antipater, the other senior commander, survived until 319. (Unlike most of the other potential successors, he died a natural death of old age.) The blood relatives also soon disappeared. Philip Arrhidaeus was murdered in 317 by the brutal Olympias, who in turn was put to death, and Roxane and Alexander IV were done away with around 310 by Cassander, the son of Antipater.

A second line of contenders consisted of Antigonus the One-Eyed, one of Alexander's governors in Asia Minor, and his son Demetrius. Two others were Ptolemy and Seleucus, members of the Companion Cavalry. Of these Ptolemy was ultimately the most successful. In 321 he seized Egypt and consolidated his hold by sequestering the body of Alexander as it was being brought back to Macedonia for burial and by giving it a magnificent tomb in his capital, Alexandria. He immediately set out to reorganize the Egyptian economy, which had decayed under the Persians, and quickly built up a position of power for himself and his successors. This position remained intact for practically the next 300 years. Antigonus the One-Eyed came closest to reunifying the empire of Alexander, but he was defeated and killed in battle at Ipsus in Phrygia in 301 by a coalition that included Seleucus and Lysimachus, the governor of Thrace. Demetrius, after a spectacular career, drank himself to death, but his son,

Antigonus II Gonatas, was an able ruler and established himself firmly as ruler of Macedonia and Greece. His descendants maintained themselves there until the appearance of the Romans in the second century B.C. Seleucus carved out a realm for himself that consisted of the eastern satrapies to the extent that it was possible to control them, and some parts of Asia Minor. His son by his Persian wife Apama, Antiochus I, became head of the third major Hellenistic kingdom and his descendants ruled there until the first century B.C. Thus in the generation after Alexander a pattern gradually emerged that was to dominate the Greek world to the time of the Romans. The Ptolemies held Egypt, Cyprus, Palestine, and Phoenicia (until the second century), together with some toeholds in the Aegean area; the Antigonids retained Macedonia and much of Greece with the exception of the areas under the control of the Achaean and Aetolian leagues, and the Seleucids held Syria, Mesopotamia (until the second century), much of Iran (until the mid-third century), and some of Asia Minor. In the third century the kingdom of Pergamum in western Asia Minor emerged as a distant fourth among the Hellenistic monarchies, while Rhodes remained a powerful, independent state until weakened by Rome in the second century. In mainland Greece the classical cities such as Athens, Thebes, and Sparta played no significant roles.

The new monarchies depended in large measure upon their kings' energies and abilities to hold their heterogeneous possessions together. The kings were not native sovereigns ruling with local support but were rather outsiders whose power depended on their strong administrations and their large mercenary armies. All the kingdoms strove to keep their lines of communication to the Aegean open, for Greece was still the major source of manpower for both the administrative services and the armies, and the coastlands of the Levant and Egypt soon became the equivalent of the Aegean littoral in the earlier period. Whereas once the Greeks regarded themselves as frogs sitting around the Aegean pond, that pond now expanded to include all of the eastern Mediterranean.

Despite the political fragmentation and the endless wars between the Hellenistic monarchies, the leagues, the independent cities, and the native peoples, the world after Alexander was an intelligible whole. Greek culture spread from the Aegean to the Indus and from Armenia to the Sudan. The same basic political institutions, educational systems, and art forms could be found everywhere. Uniform coinage, systems of finance, laws, and language contributed to the development of commerce. Even the carnage of warfare was lessened. Since mercenaries predominated in the armed services of the kings, battles were rarely fought to the bitter end. It was usually sufficient to win the initial stages for one's opponents to give up and go over to the other side. For the first century after Alexander the economy of the Hellenistic world flourished. The great riches of the Persian Empire were released to circulate freely throughout the Greek world, and the cities attained heights of luxury and elegance that had never been achieved before. In place of a few showcase cities like Athens, there were now dozens that could boast as large or larger populations and far greater wealth. Commerce and industry developed and cities flourished in areas that had previously been only wastelands. Although few of them ever attained intellectual brilliance their contribution to overall Greek culture was immensely significant.

10

Society and the State in the Hellenistic Period

RELIGION AND CULTURE IN THE HELLENISTIC WORLD

The gods of the old homeland of Greece found it hard to move when the Greeks spread eastward in the footsteps of Alexander. From time immemorial they had been identified with particular cities and places—Athena with Athens, Apollo with Delphi, Aphrodite with Corinth. People had grown accustomed to regarding individual Olympians as their special protecting deities and to having this right recognized by others. Athena, although worshipped elsewhere, was closely identified with the city that bore her name. She had done special things for Athens and hers alone was the Parthenon and the festivals that honored her in the Athenian religious year. She had been present with the Athenians at the foundation of their city and was with them through all their trials and victories. There was no way in which this kind of association could be transplanted elsewhere. If emigrant Athenians wished to worship her they could of course do so, but there were no temples established in her honor and no recurring festivals in the cycle of the year to remind people of her. Besides, the new cities of the east were packed with emigrants from all over the Hellenic world, each with his own different tutelary deity. There was no simple, homogeneous population that believed, as Athenians had always believed, that Zeus and Apollo were their divine ancestors and Athena their protective goddess. They could only worship her until such time as temples were built to her—assuming they were to be built to her and not to some other god or goddess—in private cult associations. Such associations or corporations were entirely voluntary and personal. By contrast, in Athens the cult of the goddess Athena was an essential—if ritualistic—part of civic life, to which everyone was bound. In the new cities such worship was a matter of private devotion, the associations organized to conduct this worship became one of the standard features of the Hellenistic world and one of its most radical transformations.

In the new world the Greeks were scattered over an enormously wide landscape, altogether unlike the closely defined territories of their past. In Egypt, where the Ptolemies did not permit the building of cities outside the three major ones, the Greeks were scattered in settlements throughout the countryside and by necessity came into close contact with the natives. Although the Seleucids encouraged city building in their realms and thereby enabled the emigrants to congregate, the new establishments were frequently located close to or actually on the site of previously existing eastern villages or cities. Seleuceia-on-Tigris was founded at Opis, a native village, and its founder, Seleucus I, transferred to it a good part of the population of old Babylon. Antioch itself was established on an old native site. There was thus a close intermingling of the two populations, and like it or not the Greeks had to pay attention to the gods where they now dwelt.

There were a number of ways in which the Greeks could discharge their obligations to their host deities. They could honor them through the officially established priesthoods, for example, by paying for sacrifices and prayers to be offered in their honor. They could also identify the eastern gods with their own, as they had been doing for centuries, and worship them appropriately. Thus by syncretism the Egyptian Thoth became Hermes; the Syrian Atargatis, Aphrodite; and a whole host of storm and sky gods, Zeus. Sometimes a bridge between

The amalgamation of east and west: A classically modeled goddess representing Health stands beside a thoroughly alien-looking Asclepius, the Greek god of healing. Over his head is an inscription in Greek lettering. Significantly, however, it is in a Semitic language.

the Greek and oriental worlds was built when the priests learned Greek and attempted to communicate with their conquerors. In Babylon the priest Berossus and in Egypt another priest, Manetho, translated or paraphrased the sacred Egyptian and Babylonian texts into Greek. A line of Jewish apologists from Demetrius in the third century B.C. to Josephus in the first century A.D. attempted to explain and defend Jewish beliefs to the Greeks and, later, to the Romans.

Nevertheless there was still something missing. The eastern gods remained eastern, served by alien priesthoods. What was needed was a transformation that would take away the sense of strangeness while allowing the Greeks to believe they were honoring the gods of their new lands. Although many transformations were made—Cybele, Atargatis, Adonis, and Attis among the most popular—none was more successful than the synthetic god Serapis, his consort Isis, and his son Harpocrates.

Serapis and Isis

Serapis was the conscious fusion of the Egyptian god Osiris, a mortuary and fertility deity, and the divine bull calf Apis. This amalgamation was brought about by the first Ptolemy with the assistance of the Egyptian Manetho and Timotheus, an official interpreter of the Eleusinian mysteries. As associates Serapis was given Isis, Anubis, and Harpocrates. This combination failed to appeal to the Egyptians, who remained attached to the old forms of their gods, but it was a great success among the Greeks and eventually spread everywhere in the Greco-Roman world. Serapis was regarded as a kind and gentle god who did not punish his devotees. His image in the temple (the Serapeum), which is known through copies and literary accounts, was heavily bearded and dark in color, decorated with silver and gold and precious stones such as emeralds and sapphires. On his head was a basket for measuring grain, the symbol of his lordship of the earth. Mysterious and majestic, he exercised a special fascination for both Greeks and Romans.

The new cult operated on two levels. For the majority of worshippers Serapis was an attractive, universal god who could be worshipped and prayed to everywhere through cult associations and private shrines. But for a very special group—those with a desire or need for religious involvement—there were the mysteries of Isis, the consort of Serapis. The ceremonies and rituals of initiation connected with these mysteries were probably also devised by the same Greek-Egyptian-Macedonian trio who had successfully launched the worship of Serapis. The Greeks were already familiar with mystery religions, such as the much beloved religion of Eleusis, which conferred the hope of immortality on its initiates. Eleusis and its mysteries, however, were confined to one particular place in Greece, whereas the mysteries of Isis, like Isis herself, were universal. The new ceremonies were quite different from the old Egyptian rituals of Isis, which had publicly dramatized her mourning and search for the dead Osiris.

The compassionate Serapis responded to the needs of the Hellenistic Age for a god who could help lighten men's burdens in a fast-changing world.

There were, in fact, no initiates in the Egyptian form of worship of Isis. A more important distinction was the belief that the new mysteries conferred immortality on the initiates during their lifetime rather than making it depend, as in the Egyptian practice, on rituals performed by others after one's death.

The kind of salvation offered by the mysteries of Isis (and other mysteries for that matter) was not freedom from sin and assimilation to God as his children as in Christianity, but escape from fate or destiny and a share in the god's potency or power. As will be seen in the following section, fate loomed large in the minds of men of the period after Alexander. Escape from its inevitability through the power of a god such as Isis who was able to overcome it was avidly sought. The immortality offered by the mysteries was an immortality of the soul alone, not the body, which was assumed to decay after death—hence the reaction to Paul, who was quickly hustled out of the Areopagus when he enunciated the doctrine of the resurrection of the body before that skeptical audience. "We will hear you later," they said. Another important aspect of the mysteries was their limited extent. They were not religions proclaimed from the rooftops as was Christianity. Rather, they were esoteric associations of those who felt a special call to particular closeness to a particular deity. Initiation could, moreover, be a costly business. Under the Roman Empire, Lucius Apuleius, the author of the famous novel *The Golden Ass,* spent all his considerable fortune on Isis. It remained for Christianity to democratize the way to salvation for the masses.

If the interstate politics of the old world had been chaotic, there were always, at least, the permanent anchors of the cities themselves. Battles and wars might be won or lost but the cities went on forever. They had existed from the beginning—from mythological times—and their exclusivity had perpetuated their sense of identity. Athenians were Athenians and Corinthians Corinthians and there was no mistaking the identity of each.

This was not the case in the cities of the new world where Greeks from everywhere jostled with the natives and where the characteristic language was not Attic or Dorian or Ionic but a new kind of Greek, *koine*—the "common tongue"—which blotted out the distinctive regional variations. Without roots, the Greeks after Alexander felt particularly vulnerable to the constant wars and changing alliances between the major powers, as well as to the normal vicissitudes of life. Individuals rose and fell with dizzying rapidity. Fortunes were made and lost overnight. The old codes and conventions based on community practices had little influence on the behavior of the newly liberated emigrants, and the flamboyance and successes of Alexander and the kings who followed him seemed to reduce to impotence such old restraining notions as *hybris* and the value of moderation. The gods who had ruled in the past—whether justly or unjustly—were now as nothing compared to Fortune (Tyche) who played with men like children, loving to turn things upside down unexpectedly. Fortune was as deceitful as she was unpredictable and men swept along by the torrent of events without the sustenance of the old customs and institutions of the city-state could only pray for deliverance. Understandably they prayed to Fortune herself and made her the protective deity of a dozen new cities in the east.

There was another revolution that affected men almost as much as the opening up of the new world. This was the new astronomy, and the world view that went with it, that began to make its appearance in the fourth century and received its final form in the Hellenistic period. In the old view of things that had held throughout most of classical times, the earth was regarded as a disk or saucer surrounded by water with the sky above superimposed like a bowl. Underneath was Hades, the shadowy abode of the dead. In the heavens were the clouds as well as the planets and stars, but there was no concern with their distance from the earth since it was assumed that astral and atmospheric phenomena all occurred at the same level. The gods moved freely throughout this limited, rather cozy universe and were always close at hand. Then two of Plato's students, Eudoxus and Heracleides, revolutionized this vision. Eudoxus demonstrated that the planets obeyed regular laws and moved in circular fashion within a number of spheres. Heracleides speculated that the earth, a sphere, revolved on its own axis daily and that Mercury and Venus revolved around the sun, although all three, along with the remaining planets, revolved around the earth. These astronomical theories were quickly translated into cosmological and anthropological theories that placed the earth at the lowest level of a hierarchy of planetary bodies of progressive refinement and regarded man's soul as a spark of divine fire locked in his material body. Then after Alexander the east made two contributions that completed the picture of the new universe: the accurate Babylonian observations of the positions of the heavenly bodies and the belief in their influence on the lives of men. Out of this fusion came the baneful pseudoscience of astrology, which was to dominate both the intellectual's and the man-in-the-street's views of the universe and God for the rest of antiquity and even later.

In its strictest form astrology is atheistic, since it views the universe as a self-running mechanism that operates according to totally predictable laws without any outside intervention. Its most basic assumption is that if true knowledge of the operation of one part of the cosmos (in this instance the movements of the heavenly bodies) is known, information about the operation of the other parts, men's destiny, for example, can be inferred. Hence, if the movements of the stars and planets can be brought into coordination with important events in the life of an individual—such as his birth—it will be possible to predict his fate. In this mechanistic world there is no room for divine intervention or free will and the individual's fate is as fixed as the movements of the heavens themselves. A less strict view was that the heavenly bodies were themselves gods who might be appeased by appropriate religious action and it was this view that was most popularly accepted. In both views, the underlying assumptions about the nature of the universe as enshrined in astrology were considered incontestable and had a profound effect on Hellenistic man's religions and philosophic outlook. Once the basic tenet of astrological inevitability is admitted, one automatically conjures up its concomitant—an overwhelming desire for a means of escape. Thus the religious mood of the Hellenistic and Roman period was dominated by a longing for salvation from either the vagaries of Fortune, or the inevitability of Fate, or the weight of the material body, which weighed the spirit down. Some sought salvation by pursuing the path of mystical knowledge blazed by Plato, believing that by rising mentally it was possible to escape enthrallment to Fate (see the following section). Knowledge was freedom and union with the divine meant escape from the weakness of the material aspects of human existence. Others were given assurance by the mystery religions, and for still others the ethical philosophies of the Hellenistic Age provided a guide. None of these attempts at coming to grips with the pressures and anxieties of the times were exclusive and the lines between religion, philosophy, science, and ethics were blurred, though it was not until the Roman Empire that the distinctions disappeared completely.

Monotheism and Mysticism

Plato's profound dissatisfaction with what he regarded as the imperfections and instability of governments and laws led him to abandon the material world and seek permanence in the realm of the divine, which alone was real and unchanging. It was not just the ever-changing world of city-state politics that Plato dismissed as unreal but everything in the sensible world. According to his definition, things apprehended by the senses are mutable and finite and therefore unknowable by the mind; only the essences of things are unchanging and therefore the proper objects of knowledge. Even essences shared only partially in the highest three categories of Being: the One, the Good, and the Beautiful. The most elevated and humanly satisfying task that anyone could engage in was therefore the pursuit of these categories and beyond them their highest embodiment, the Unknown and Undefinable God. This elevated knowledge of the divine, whose possession would make men happy, was to be attained in part by rational contemplation and detachment from the world of the sensible, and in part through mystical infusion:

> This knowledge is not something that can be put into words like other sciences: you spend much time together, you live together in the pursuit of this thing; and then suddenly, like a flame kindled from a leaping fire, it comes into the soul and nourishes itself.[1]

This essentially private concern with the divine was light-years removed from the external religiosity of the old polis, whose gods were satisfied with lip service and the performance of sacrifices, games, and processions in their honor, yet it was characteristic of the new age. Plato's thought in this area, as in so many others, blazed the way for the religions and philosophies of the Hellenistic and Roman worlds in which the institutions of the city-state were incapable of providing for the religious needs of the uprooted.

It was particularly in the area of the new astronomy that Plato's contribution was significant. The calculations of his students Eudoxus and Heracleides had shown that the planetary bodies moved majestically according to predictable and regular laws. From this Plato inferred the existence of an unseen Intelligence—a World Soul—behind the visible universe, regulating marvelously all its parts. He further reasoned that the World Soul found its counterpart in the soul of man, which struggled to bring order to the chaotic material world of the body and bring it into harmony with the universe. Wisdom, therefore, was the ordering of man in accordance with the divine system of the universe. Thus in one leap Plato succeeded in reconciling religion and the new astronomy and setting up an ethics of personal salvation in place of the now outmoded collectivist model of the past. For a significant intellectual minority the contemplation of the universe and its harmonious working was from this time forward a source of inner security and consolation, which gave to the best of paganism a quality that could stand comparison with the equally high vision of Christian mysticism and had much in common with it. It also provided an important interiorization of religion, which the ritualistic civic cults so spectacularly lacked. In a general way the emphasis on the attainment of knowledge of the divine began to be viewed as a way of escaping from Fate. The person who

[1]Plato, *7th Letter* 341a.

possessed such knowledge was regarded as being free, at least in his soul, the higher portion of his being, though still weighed down by his body. Freedom in this sense meant progressive liberation from enslavement to the body and its imperious demands. The following quote from Numenius, the precursor of Neoplatonism in the Roman Empire, suggests the high levels attained by pagan mysticism:

> It is possible for us to understand corporeal things. We recognize them by their resemblance to other things of the same kind and by the signs which they offer to our senses. But there is no way of understanding the Good, neither by any sign offered to our senses, nor by any sensible object bearing a resemblance to it. This is what one must do. It is as if one were standing on a high point of vantage and looking out into the far distance at one of those tiny barks in which men go fishing. It is isolated and alone, lost in the desert of the waters, cradled in the hollow of the waves. But if one looks very hard, one will see it—for an instant. So it is with the Good. One must go far away from sensible things and converse alone with the Good alone, in a place where there is neither human creature, nor any other living thing, nor any corporeal thing great or small, but only an ineffable, inexpressible, incredibly wonderful solitude. There it is that the Good dwells in all its splendor. He himself is there, in tranquillity, in joyous mood, he the Calm, the Sovereign Guide; there he smiles, borne on the chariot of Essence.[2]

There were, of course, other factors besides Plato's religious philosophy contributing to the development of a belief in a single divinity whose visible manifestations were the orderly universe. The prevalent monarchical structure of government turned men's thoughts to the concept of a powerful, benevolent ruler of the universe something akin to the ideal the philosophers urged on the Hellenistic kings for imitation. Syncretism made its contribution too by eliminating the differences between the gods and identifying them with one another. Polytheism, of course, was never rejected, but more and more emphasis was given to the power of the gods rather than to their individual personalities, so that the distinction between them blurred and what was venerated was not so much this or that deity as the degree of divine power they were thought to possess. Writing at the time of the Roman Empire, Plutarch put it this way:

> There are not different gods among different peoples, barbarians or Greeks, peoples of the south or of the north; but just as the sun, the moon, the sky, the earth and the sea belong to all men, yet are given different names by different people, so too the one Reason which orders this world and the one Providence which governs it . . . have different honors and titles assigned by custom to them by different peoples.[3]

[2]André-Jean Festugière, trans., *Personal Religion Among the Greeks* (Berkeley and Los Angeles: University of California Press, 1960), p. 138. Copyright © 1954 by The Regents of the University of California. Reprinted by permission of the University of California Press.

[3]*Concerning Isis and Osiris*, 67.

In the classical polis the lack of ethical content in the civic religions had not been a problem until quite late in their development. The practically creedless cult of the gods was complemented by a powerful system of conventional usage and practice that governed day-to-day life. Custom was the basis of morality and governed every aspect of the individual's life. The trouble with this arrangement was that one depended and shored up the other, and once the citizen left his community he was on his own, without the customs or the religious practices of the city-state to sustain him. The potential for moral chaos and psychological disruption in such a situation is extremely high.

The situation was not as bad as it might appear, however. The citizens of some states where convention was most highly developed, such as Sparta, were susceptible to moral vertigo when they stepped outside the effective influence of the community; but those of other states, such as Athens, had long traditions of personal autonomy and individuality, and since the later fifth century there had been much speculation about alternative ethical systems. I have already discussed Plato's withdrawal from involvement in city-state life to an inner world, but there were others, such as Antisthenes and Aristippus, who anticipated the general tendency of the Hellenistic world by advocating what amounted to a totally private type of morality, independent of the conventions of the state and at times directly opposed to them. Hence the appeal of the new philosophies to the rootless Greeks of the east. Their aim was to give men adrift in this unstable world a sense of permanence and independence. They were supposed to render him self-sufficient and if possible invulnerable to the whims of Fortune—free of the powers of the planets as manifested in the unpredictable events of daily life.

CYNICISM

The Cynics taught that the principal source of men's trouble in life was their excessive attachment to society, its conventions, and its material trappings. Such possessions or attachments as a wife, children, native country, or material goods of any kind made a person extremely vulnerable to the caprices of Fortune, which could in a moment sweep all these things into oblivion. Therefore, to be truly free a person should liberate himself from these things. Teles, like his predecessor Aristippus, argued that the obligations of citizenship constituted a form of slavery and—contrary to commonly held opinion—suggested that exile from one's homeland constituted no great loss. Many people, such as women and slaves, he observed, are excluded from political life as a matter of course, yet this does not prevent them from being content with what they have. As for food and clothes, a man can live on vegetables and water, which are free, and in winter double his cloak if he needs warmer clothes. He claimed that it was not the poor who were burdened down with responsibilities but the rich, who had to worry about their properties and possessions. The most famous Cynic of all, Diogenes, trained himself to suffer the hardship of the elements by rolling in the snow in winter and exposing himself to the sun in summer. Regarded as a saint by his followers (and mad by Plato) he was the subject of many apocryphal tales. On one occasion he was supposed to have been hauled before Philip of Macedonia and accused of being a spy, and to have replied to the charge by saying that he had indeed come to spy, but only on the king's insatiable greed. When asked by Alexander what service he could do him, Diogenes replied, "Stand out of my sun." Some such as Cercidas of Megalopolis turned in despair from politics to Cynicism:

> Give to us the rivers of silver now uselessly thrown away . . . give to the poor feeding from a common bowl the money wasted on vanities; or is the eye of Justice blind, the law thwarted? How can men accept as gods those who neither hear nor see such evils? . . . who can find justice when Zeus, our parent, treats some men as their father, but others as their step-father?[4]

A commonplace among Cynics was the image of the individual as an actor on the stage performing according to the direction of Fortune. Fortune, said Teles, is like a playwright who designs a number of parts—the shipwrecked man, the exile, the beggar, the king. What a good man has to do is simply play well any part assigned to him. Fortune may indeed destroy a person like a storm sinking a ship at sea, but at least the individual will go down like a man:

> That's a fine saying of the captain: "Alright Poseidon, you may sink her, but she's on course"; so might a good man say to Fortune, "but it's a man you're sinking, not a coward."[5]

EPICUREANISM

The Epicureans also aimed to make men free, but they looked beyond the conventions of social life that were the main targets of the Cynics. They believed that if a man could avoid disturbances he would be free, and since the principal sources of upset in a person's life are fear and desire, these are the main things to be eliminated. Neither the fear of death, the gods, or pain nor the desire for unnecessary things should concern us. As one of the epitaphs put it:

> There is nothing to fear in God nor anything to feel in death. Evil can be endured, good achieved.

The object of life is pleasure, but pleasure for the Epicureans was more the avoidance of pain than hedonistic self-indulgence. The reason for this is simple: Pleasure, when excessive, can be as disturbing as pain and should therefore be taken only in moderation. Only those pleasures that are simple and attainable

[4]Meliamb 2.5–6, 15–23, 40–43.

[5]2nd ed. O. Hense, p. 62.

regularly without elaborate measures deserve pursuit. Too much effort in any direction is likely to bring disequilibrium. Thus a person should avoid the noise and bustle of political life along with its honors and responsibilities. "Live out of the public eye," was the advice of Epicurus. Choose the plainest food. If you regularly eat only dry bread a piece of cheese will give extraordinary satisfaction. "Thank blessed nature that she has made essential things easy to come by and things attained with difficulty unnecessary," was another of his sayings. Above all we should restrain desire: "If you wish to make [a man] rich do not add to his money but subtract from his desires."[6] And "a person who has the least need of riches enjoys them most."[7]

The answer to fear is knowledge, but not the pursuit of knowledge for its own sake, which is nothing but vanity. We only need to know as much as will secure us from being afraid of any natural phenomenon or the divine beings who rule the universe. Nothing exists except atoms and the void through which they fall. The cosmos and everything in it are material. Natural phenomena such as thunder and lightning have a physical explanation and should not be ascribed to the anger of the gods. The gods do indeed exist but they have no concern or interest in human beings or in the world, which operates on purely mechanical principles without outside intervention.

Epicurus stressed friendship as an important aspect of the happy life as well as good memories, and his garden at Athens was a tranquil oasis for a contented band of his followers, both men and women. In the Roman period his most distinguished disciple was Lucretius, who in his great poem, *On the Nature of the Universe*, strove to spread the good news of the deliverance of men from the fears of the irrational. He extended Epicurus' idea of friendship to include all mankind instead of just a small group of followers who sought consolation in one another's company. For Lucretius, friendship was the distinguishing mark of civilized people, something not possessed by savages. Human beings are not instinctively brutal to one another. Even in the beginning of the human race

> Venus subdued brute strength. Children by their wheedling easily broke down their parents' stubborn temper. Then neighbours began to form mutual alliances, wishing neither to do nor to suffer violence among themselves. They appealed on behalf of their children and womenfolk, pointing out with gestures and inarticulate cries that it is right for everyone to pity the weak.[8]

STOICISM

Like Plato, the Stoics accepted the new astronomy, which noted and explained the regular movements of the heavens by natural causes. Because the

[6]Seneca, *Letters* 21.7.

[7]Seneca, *Letters* 14.17.

[8]Lucretius, *On the Nature of the Universe.* Tr. R. E. Latham (Penguin Classics, 1951), p. 202. Copyright © R. E. Latham, 1951. Reprinted by permission of Penguin Books Ltd.

universe was orderly, they concluded that it must be the product of a wise design. They argued that, despite appearances to the contrary, providence, fate, or destiny—however it is termed—leads all things to their appointed ends. If we had a wider vision of things than the purely personal one we usually have we would see that this was so. As Cleanthes put it:

> Most glorious of immortals, Zeus all powerful,
> Author of Nature, named by many names, all hail.
> Thy law rules all; and the voice of the world may cry to thee,
> All things confess thee . . .
> Save what in foolishness is wrought by evil men:
> But into harmony thou canst turn such discords
> And make of chaos order; for hate with thee is love,
> And thus by thee all things of good and evil are joined
> To make thy eternal world.[9]

The soul is a divine spark in man that strives to bring order to the body and bring it into harmony with the universe. It is therefore of the essence of wisdom to conform to the order of the cosmos as it is apprehended by reason and, as the Stoics said, "live according to nature." By an extension of this thought they concluded that there were not many ways of life according to which an individual could model himself, but one. As Zeno, the founder of Stoicism, put it:

> All men should regard themselves as members of one city and people, having one life and order as a herd feeding together on a common pasture.[10]

Most things in the universe follow the divine order, either by instinct as in the case of the lesser creatures, or by necessity, as in the case of the stars, which are of the same substance as God himself and therefore cannot resist his will. Man, however, has free will and is capable of rejecting or accepting God's plan for him—or at least he has the illusion of freedom because failure to follow the divine blueprint can only lead to profound personal unhappiness and the rejection of his own true nature. A man should therefore cheerfully and willingly embrace God's plan as manifested to him by reason, not resisting or struggling against it. This ideal is expressed by Cleanthes:

> Lead me o God and thou my Destiny
> To that one place which you will have me fill
> I follow gladly. Should I strive with Thee,—
> A recreant, I needs must follow still.[11]

[9]T. F. Higham and C. M. Bowra, eds., *The Oxford Book of Greek Verse in Translation* (Oxford: Oxford University Press, 1938), no. 483, pp. 533–34. By permission of Oxford University Press.

[10]Fragment I 262.

[11]Higham and Bowra, *Oxford Book of Greek Verse*, no. 484, p. 535. By permission of Oxford University Press.

This is not a version of Christian ethics though at times Stoicism and Christianity seem close to each other. The Stoics believed that each individual had his fixed place in the universe and his duty lay in performing whatever functions attached to it and not striving for change. The good Stoic was to accept everything that came his way without rebellion or complaint, thus preserving his inner calm and tranquillity. Virtue was to be practiced for its own sake, no matter what the outcome. The individual was to leave self behind and be content with doing right, whether or not he actually achieved his goals. The result of this pursuit of virtue was to make a person like God, free and independent and above the fluctuations of earthly life.

Although the Stoics rejected the narrow confines of the city-state and believed in the universal brotherhood of men, this did not mean that they thought these ideals could be realized in practice. According to Chrysippus, men were like seats in a theater; some were simply better than others and there was nothing that could be done about it. Equality was to be achieved in the souls of men since other conditions, such as wealth or poverty, health or sickness, were of no importance. A slave, they said unconvincingly, could be as free in his soul as the freeborn.

KOHELETH

One of the best examples of the popular philosophies of the Hellenistic Age is not to be found in Greek literature at all but in the work of Koheleth, the author of the book of Ecclesiastes in the Old Testament (mid-third century B.C.). Writing in his old age, this representative of the Hellenized Jewish upper classes reflects on the course of his life and compares it to the lives of other men:

> Vanity of vanities, all is vanity!
> What does a man gain from all his toil
> At which he toils beneath the Sun?
> One generation goes, and another comes,
> While the earth endures forever.
> The sun rises and the sun sets,
> And hastens to the place where he rose . . .
> All rivers run to the sea,
> But the sea is never full . . .
> All things are wearisome;
> One cannot recount them;
> The eye is not satisfied with seeing,
> Nor is the ear filled with hearing.
> Whatsoever has been done is that which will be done;
> And there is nothing new under the sun.[12]

The rich and the poor, wise and foolish, ethical and unethical are all

[12]Eccles. 1:3–9 in J. M. P. Smith and others, *The Complete Bible: An American Translation* (Chicago: The University of Chicago Press, 1939). Copyright 1927 by The University of Chicago Press.

swallowed up in death. The same fate overtakes all. God's ways are incomprehensible and there is no way to reconcile—rationally, at least--the justice of God and the events of daily life. Koheleth frequently uses the term *chance,* which is used only a few times elsewhere in the Old Testament:

> [T]he race is not to the swift, nor the battle to the strong; nor is there bread for the wise, nor riches for the intelligent, nor favor for scholars; but time and chance happen to all of them.[13]

Death is the destiny of all creatures and everything has been laid down by a God who is as distant and unapproachable as the Unknown God of Plato. All that a man can do is resign himself to his position and enjoy whatever good things life happens to bring to him.

> [T]here is nothing good for men but to be glad and to enjoy themselves while they live. Indeed, if any man eats and drinks and enjoys himself in all his work, it is a gift from God.[14]

Ethics is a matter of expediency since no one knows what really constitutes the "good" life. A person should neither be overly righteous nor overly wise and should keep a careful guard on his thoughts and utterances. Although rooted in the Old Testament tradition of wisdom literature, Koheleth was heavily influenced by Hellenistic thought and his cool rationalism and distinctive personality were novelties in Old Testament literature. The work was composed in the mid-third century B.C. during the time of the Ptolemaic occupation of Palestine.

The Sciences

The Golden Age of Greek science came in the centuries that followed the conquests of Alexander the Great. Long years of philosophical and mathematical research culminated in the work of Aristotle, who established the principle that conclusions should be drawn only from a mass of material gathered by empirical methods. This basic principle of research was applied by Aristotle to biology, where he did his finest scientific work; some of his observations were not surpassed until modern times. Using the same technique of empirical examination he analyzed the plots of hundreds of plays to establish a theory of tragedy and gathered over 150 constitutions to try to determine what elements in them contributed to the preservation or destruction of the city-state type of society. Although Plato emphasized mathematics and made it an essential part of his curriculum, his quest for ideal forms underlying the physical universe had a baneful influence on future scientific development by encouraging researchers

[13]Eccles. 9:11. Copyright 1927 by The University of Chicago Press.

[14]Eccles. 3:12–13. Copyright 1927 by The University of Chicago Press.

to look for metaphysical forms, rather than following Aristotle's principle of scientific induction from field observations. Nevertheless, for about two centuries after Alexander, there was an outpouring of scientific studies of such quality that the world was not to see them excelled until the modern scientific renaissance.

One of the reasons for this development was the cultural involvement of the Hellenistic kings in higher education. The Ptolemies established a major research center at Alexandria, and libraries were founded at Alexandria, Pergamum, Antioch, Rhodes, Smyrna, and probably elsewhere. Athens, although eclipsed by Alexandria in the sciences and in literature, remained the world's center of philosophical and rhetorical studies.

The Museum at Alexandria was the center of the scientific movement and attracted researchers from all over the Greek-speaking world. Sponsored and financed by the Ptolemies, it was not, as the term signifies in our usage, an institution dedicated to collecting items from the past. Rather, it was a place where creative investigation in a number of important fields in the sciences and literature occurred. Despite the tendency toward pedantry, especially in later times when funds were cut back, the Museum's scholars did not deserve the description of them given by Timon of Phlius:

> In the thronging land of Egypt
> There are many that are feeding,
> Many scribblers on papyrus,
> Ever ceaselessly contending,
> In the bird-coop of the Muses.[15]

ASTRONOMY AND MATHEMATICS

Reflecting the metaphysical and theoretical predisposition of the researchers the most spectacular achievements of the Museum were in the fields of astronomy and mathematics, but there also were significant advances in medicine and mechanics. The predominantly laboratory sciences, physics and chemistry, however, developed hardly at all.

Since the discoveries of Plato's student Eudoxus in the fourth century, the predominant view of the universe was that Mercury and Venus revolved around the sun and that the sun, moon, and the other planets revolved around the earth in concentric spheres. Aristarchos of Samos (ca. 310–230 B.C.), one of the most brilliant scholars of the Museum, went further and advanced the hypothesis that all the planets revolved around the sun, which was fixed, and that the stars, which were also fixed, existed at enormous distances from the earth. Aristarchos also endorsed Heracleides of Pontus' theory that the earth revolved daily on its axis. Unfortunately there was no way of making the observed phenomena of the

[15] J. E. Sandys, trans., *A History of Classical Scholarship*, 2nd ed., Vol. 1 (Cambridge, Cambridge University Press, 1906), p. 103.

movement of the planets and stars agree with this system. Two essentials were missing: stellar parallax and the apparent increase and decrease in the size of the stars as the earth moved toward or away from them. Although the supposition of the enormous universe would account for the absence of these phenomena, no one was willing to accept such a hypothesis. Besides, there were workable alternatives that "saved the phenomena"—the apparent movement of the planets—and so Aristarchos' heliocentric theory never caught on.

Hipparchus of Nicaea (ca. 190–126), another Alexandrian scholar, calculated that the length of a mean lunar month was 29 days, 12 hours, 44 minutes, and 3⅓ seconds, less than 1 second off. He also discovered the precession of the equinoxes.

The greatest advances of the Hellenistic sciences were in mathematics, particularly in geometry, which had a special appeal to the metaphysically minded scholar-scientists of the period. The first of the great mathematicians was Euclid (ca. 300 B.C.), whose book on the fundamentals of geometry became a standard text for the next 2000 years and it was not until the nineteenth century that mathematicians managed to create what has come to be known as non-Euclidean geometry. Archimedes (ca. 287–212 B.C.), famous for his protracted defense of Syracuse against the Romans and his discovery of the principle of specific gravity while taking a bath, also calculated the value of π and invented the integral calculus. His practical inventions included the compound pulley and the endless screw, which was used to drain mines in Spain and irrigate fields in

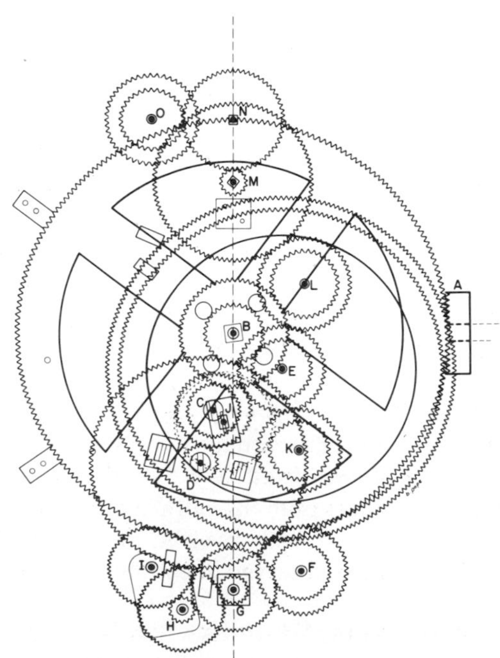

Diagram of the gears of the Antikythera mechanism. The drive-shaft that operated the small computer was connected to gear A. The differential turntable is centered at E.

Egypt. Apollonius of Perga, a somewhat younger contemporary of Archimedes, is the third of the great mathematicians. His treatise on conic sections was an exhaustive monograph on the subject and influenced mathematicians down to Newton.

A number of figures besides Archimedes dabbled in practical mechanics. Ctesibius (ca. 260 B.C.) dealt with ballistic formulae and invented a catapult that worked on compressed air. Hero of Alexandria (first century B.C.) discovered the principle of virtual work as a result of his experimentation with levers and pulleys. He also invented an early form of the theodolite, the dioptra, a portable water level for use in surveying, and a simple steam engine.

The most spectacular demonstration of Hellenistic knowledge and engineering ability is to be found in the complicated instrument known as the *Antikythera mechanism*. Discovered in the remains of an ancient shipwreck near Crete in 1900, it was not fully analyzed and described until the investigations of Derek De Solla Price in 1972/1973. The device is a calendrical sun and moon computer that coordinates lunar and solar months with the positions of the planets, the zodiacal path of the sun, and the rising and setting of the most noticeable stars. It is equipped with a number of tables and concentric dials, the latter being operated by a series of gears that include a sophisticated differential assembly. An outside crank provides the power necessary to activate the device. Price speculates that the mechanism might have been held in the hand of a statue and used as a kind of exhibition piece.

MEDICINE

Along with mathematics and astronomy, medicine made great strides in the Hellenistic period and was not excelled until the time of Harvey. Alexandria was the setting for most of these developments and here the two greatest researchers Herophilus of Chalcedon and Erasistratus of Ceos did their work. The former was an anatomist whose discoveries included the sensory nerves and their connection with the spinal cord, the duodenum, and the distinction between the cerebrum and the cerebellum. He believed that the brain was the center of the nervous system as well as the seat of intelligence and that the arteries carried blood. Erasistratus recognized that the heart was a motor that supplied the blood to the various parts of the body; unfortunately he fell back on the theory that the arteries carried air. His most important discovery was the distinction between the sensory and motor nerves, which Herophilus had missed. He was more interested in physiology than anatomy and discussed the role of diet and the process of nourishment in the body's tissues.

Theoretical research made little advance after Herophilus and Erasistratus and clinical studies came to dominate, under Philinus, Herophilus' successor at the Museum. Proven therapeutic practice rather than theoretical anatomy or physiology dominated his school, whose best-known member, Heracleides of Tarentum, concentrated on pharmacology and toxicology as well as dietetics and medical history. Asclepiades of Prusa took an almost diametrically opposed approach to Heracleides' and cured diseases by a regimen of dieting, exercise, massage, and cold baths. He placed no reliance on drugs and argued that health could be recovered by "restoration of the symmetry of the atoms" of which the body was composed. Under Augustus the encyclopedist Celsus composed a treatise summarizing the advances made in medicine since the time of Hippocrates.

From the beginning, scientific medicine struggled with magic and religion and the cures of Asclepius at Epidaurus or Serapis at Alexandria were as popular as those of the professional doctors of the age. It is usually claimed that toward the end of the Hellenistic period medicine, along with the other sciences, retreated before the rising tide of irrationality that placed greater faith in philosophy, religion, and the pseudosciences than in reason and the Greek scientific traditions. A more likely explanation is to be found in the fundamental bias of the Greek scientific enterprise against experiment and technological application as well as the much higher place given to rhetoric in higher education. Without a fundamental shift in societal values, Greek science went about as far as it could. But despite its deficiencies, it gave western science a permanent mathematical basis that ultimately led to the development of modern science.

Literature, Learning, and the Theater

The people who sat in the theaters and odea[16] to hear the plays and musical productions of the classical period were an altogether different kind of audience from their successors in the Hellenistic period. The former belonged to tightly knit communities where art, poetry, and the theater were integral parts of the religious and civic life of the cities. It was the community, not the individual, that was the patron of the arts, setting the standards and letting the contracts for architectural and theatrical productions. In the Hellenistic period all of this was reversed. The kings were the principal patrons of fine arts, and although the cities were also important patrons there were major differences from the past.

The first is connected with the loss of independence by the cities. This meant that the old emphasis on the importance of the civic religion and the performance of the festivals declined dramatically. The nexus of power and citizenship was broken and now only the kings exercised political power. What counted in the new circumstances was not community solidarity aided by the gods but opportune alignment with the appropriate royal power in the shifting political alliances of the times. As the Athenians proclaimed in their hymn to the Macedonian king Demetrius, it was the kings who saved, not the faraway gods who seemed unconcerned with men's problems.

[16]Roofed halls where musical competitions and verse renditions took place.

The second difference was the growth of a reading public, which existed on a scale unheard of before. Every city worthy of the name possessed a library, as did the gymnasia, which now became important cultural and educational centers. Private libraries were common too and literary educations could be acquired with ease. To an increasingly affluent middle class these things became commonplace and the old ideal of education through community participation was replaced by an education based on the study of books. Imperceptibly, culture came to consist of a process of initiation into literary knowledge rather than broad political, religious, and military participation in the life of the community. This is sometimes deplored, but it was inevitable in a world that had suddenly expanded from a few thousand square miles to millions, and where hundreds of cities were built in a matter of a few generations. New arrangements for cultural continuity had to be made. The old style of education, which depended on tradition built up by hundreds of years of occupation of the same site, simply did not work in the new environment.

One practice of the Hellenistic and Roman periods will illustrate this point. Alexandrian poetry is often termed erudite and allusive. It loves to show knowledge of obscure mythologies and has a special interest in etiology—the process, for example, by which the Scythians are accounted for by being made the descendants of Heracles' son Scythes; or the Galatians, by establishing the nymph Galataea as their ancestor. Two of the great Alexandrians, Apollonius and Callimachus, are unpalatable to modern taste because so much of their poetry consists in far-ranging and obscure mythological and etiological discussions, which to present-day readers seem dull and pedantic. What must be considered is the awful sense of isolation from Greek history, culture, and tradition that the inhabitants of the new world felt, and the desperate need they experienced to relate the new foundations to the old world. It was to fill this need that the poets of the Hellenistic Age composed their (to us) unappealing poems. By creating a web of stories they integrated the new cities with the old and provided them with a legitimate sense of belonging far beyond the foundation charter of the city from the king. Poets such as Apollonius were invited to write foundation poems for the new cities, but local poets and antiquarians could fill the bill as well. More curious from the modern standpoint was the acceptance of these tales as historical. It was considered legitimate to take a place name and work it into a tale involving some like-sounding hero or god. What mattered was the process—the method of making contact with the legitimate legend—not the tendentiousness of the final account, which apparently did not bother the Greeks at all. The final result of all this mythologizing was that all the peoples of the Mediterranean world and even of the land masses beyond were brought together in a great pseudohistory that was the historical equivalent of the newly expanded geographical understanding of the known world. It remained intact until, under the Christians, the classical version of prehistory was replaced by the Hebrew account of the origin of the nations in Genesis.

LITERATURE IN THE NEW WORLD

The conditions of the age after Alexander encouraged the widespread dissemination of literature and art and the participation of the most distant areas of the Greek world in its production. Bion of Borysthenes in the Ukraine developed the famous Cynic diatribe and Menippus of Gadara, a city just south of Lake Galilee on the east bank of the Jordan, was the originator of a much admired form of satire, which found imitators in Varro and Seneca among the Romans and Lucian among the Greeks. Also from Gadara were the fine epigrammatists Meleager and Philodemus, the former the real creator of the Greek Anthology, a collection of short epigrams attributed to various poets going back as far as the sixth century B.C. From Sidon and Askelon on the Phoenician and Palestinian coasts came a whole line of poets, philosophers and historians—Antipater, Boethus, Antiochus, Apollonius, Artemidorus, and many more. Others came from Armenia, Persia, Babylonia, and even farther east. The centers for the production of fine art were similarly dispersed. Alexandria was the center of cameo cutting, one of the most brilliant arts of the Hellenistic period. Some of the finest coins ever produced came from the Greek kingdom of Bactria (eastern Iran and Afghanistan). Pergamum in Asia Minor, where Greek confronted barbarian Celt, produced an unusual and new school of monumental sculpture.

The new humanism that was pioneered in Athens in the late fifth and fourth centuries continued to develop, and encouraged interest in the individual and his real-life situation. Following the widespread adoption of the Athenian dramatic festival, a huge new audience was created for fifth-century classical tragedies, epic poetry (both old and new), dithyrambs (choral odes in honor of Dionysus), music, dancing, and rhetorical exhibitions. Comedy took up new themes, some borrowed from tragedy, and made farcical and romantic love its focal point. Poetry also concentrated on the individual, emphasizing the small rather than the large aspects of life. The idyll, or "little picture," and the epigram were the most successful and original literary products of the period, which also saw the creation of the genres of biography and the romantic and the pornographic novel. History tried to make the past come alive by borrowing techniques from the theater, and the mime or playlet depicting a small but realistic slice of daily life was highly popular. Art continued the fourth-century tendency away from the ideal and emphasized the portrayal of the individual, but there was no canonical form and every style of art from the restrained classical to the flamboyant baroque was practiced.

COMEDY AND MIME

The comic playwrights of the fifth-century Athens satirized the politics and political figures of their day and devoted little attention to plot development or the characters of the individuals involved. By contrast the comedy of the century after Alexander (known as New Comedy) was almost devoid of political satire. Instead, it concentrated its attention on social manners, particularly in family situations, and on moral questions such as greed and penury, love and guilt, servility and pride. Of the plays of the 70 or so known writers in this field, only those of Menander survive in sufficient quantity for us to make a fair estimate of this kind of theater.

Menander (ca. 342–ca. 292) was a contemporary of Epicurus, with whom he served as an ephebe, and a student of Theophrastus, Aristotle's successor in the Lyceum. His plays, like almost all those of New Comedy, follow a standard plot. A young man loves a girl, whom he cannot marry, for one reason or another—she is a noncitizen or too poor or a slave for whom the owner demands an impossible price. Somehow the difficulties are overcome, either because it is discovered that the girl in question is really the daughter of a well-to-do citizen who had exposed her at birth, or because the money is forthcoming (through the machinations of a clever slave perhaps), and the play ends happily. Menander's plays have a comfortable sense of optimism about them. The evil characters are not overwhelmingly evil—nor are the good saints. The largest obstacles in life seem to be things like family disapproval or shortage of money. Gone are the heroic characters of Sophocles or the tortured figures of Euripides, struggling with giant problems of fate, suffering, and human responsibility. In their place we have prosaic and realistic human relationships, men preoccupied with the pursuit of money, soldiers who think that human relations can be bought or created to order, greedy prostitutes, and self-indulgent, superficial young men. Balanced, just, human relationships are Menander's ideals; his sins are passion, anger, and the pursuit of unnecessary things such as too much money or a reputation. Moderation in all things will produce a sense of equanimity and balance. His best characters—there are no heroes—show a capacity for self-examination but not great deeds. One of these is Charisios (Charming), who, in the *Arbitrants*, has set aside his wife Pamphile (Lovely) for having a (supposedly) illegitimate child, but when he overhears her tell her father that she will not cast him off he faces up to the fact that he has been guilty of exactly the same kind of thing himself (the scene is reported by a slave):

> Charisios
> Turned pale, then red—I really shouldn't give him away.
> He was calling aloud, "Darling, what noble words you speak!"
> Then he beat his head with clenched fists; and after a while
> He began again: "What a wonderful wife I've got," says he;
> "And what a wonderful, miserable mess I've made of things!"
> At last, when he'd heard everything he came indoors;
> And there he was in his room, groaning, tearing his hair,
> Raving incessantly, "Yes, I'm a criminal," he'd say
> Again and again. "After myself doing what I did
> And being myself the father of a bastard child
> I was such a brute and savage that I neither felt
> Nor offered her, one shred of forgiveness—although she
> Had suffered the very wrong that I was guilty of."

He loads himself with reproaches, rages at himself
With bloodshot eyes . . .[17]

The failings of the bourgeoisie and their interpersonal relations are the subject of New Comedy. No attempt is made to focus on the real villains of the age—the tyrannical sovereigns, brutal generals and soldiers, arrogant rich, and indifferent middle classes. What Menander and his fellow comic poets did was take the advice of the philosophers and withdraw to a world of small ethical problems while ignoring—except for passing remarks—the larger issues of society that have escaped their control and now rest in the hands of the kings, their courts, bureaucracies, and mercenary armies. The break with the past is complete. In place of a community struggling with its problems and seeing them reflected on the stage in philosophical plays, we have individuals on a very restricted and limited scale trying to cope with their own private, psychological problems and interpersonal relations.

Tragedy continued to be written and both old and new compositions made their appearance from one end of the Mediterranean to the other. There was a strong tendency, however, to emphasize the classical tragedies of the fifth century at the expense of the later playwrights, with the result that we know practically nothing of the work of these later writers. A poem of about 1500 lines by the tragedian Lycophron survives, and its erudite, allusive style is disliked for the same reasons that much Hellenistic poetry is condemned by modern critics. For that very reason it must have appealed to at least the bookish segment of Hellenistic audiences.

It should not be thought that popular tastes were neglected. If anything the contrary is true: The theater was taken over, certainly by the Roman period, by popularizing tendencies. For one thing, the physical arrangement of the theater changed and costuming and a high stage pushed the action back into a separate world, making the Hellenistic and Roman theaters much more like ours than like their classical predecessors. The actor came to dominate the plays and greater emphasis was given by the Romans to music, so that during the Roman Empire music-hall variety-type shows and the operetta had practically usurped the stage from the traditional plays. A major contributing factor to this development was the rise in popularity in the Hellenistic period of the mime or playlet. Either sung or spoken, mimes were written to appeal to the lower tastes of the masses. Their stock themes were adultery and seduction and they often burlesqued the traditional tales of the tragic and comic theaters. Amusing and fast moving they had an enormous appeal. Originally staged as sideshows to the main performances, they rapidly made their way onto the official programs where they remained as a sad comment on the fragmented condition of Hellenistic society.

[17]Menander, *Plays and Fragments*, tr. by Philip Vellacott (Penguin Classics, 2nd edition, 1973), pp. 132–33. Copyright © Philip Vellacott, 1967, 1973. Reprinted by permission of Penguin Books Ltd.

LOVE POETRY

Love as a topic of poetry was highly popular in the Hellenistic Age and supplied inspiration for some well-polished and original work. Apollonius of Rhodes, whose interest in etiology has already been discussed, scored a noticeable success with his fine psychological portrayal of Medea in his otherwise flawed epic on the voyage of the Argonauts. Love epigrams were another new genre in the field and one of the most successful forms of poetry to appear in this period. They grew out of the practice of composing short pieces for epitaphs and dedications as well as from the traditions of the symposium, or drinking party. The last was an old Greek form of social entertainment and consisted of songs, recitations of poetry, and literary discussion by the guests, alternating with variety turns by dancers and flute-girls. The following are two examples of the love epigram by the Palestinian Meleager, but hundreds of others are to be found in the *Greek Anthology*:

> Thou sleepest, Zenophila, tender flower. Would I were Sleep, though wingless, to creep under thy lashes, so that not even he who lulls the eyes of Zeus might visit thee, but I might have thee all to myself.[18]
>
> * * *
>
> O briny wave of Love, and sleepless gales of Jealousy, and wintry sea of song and wine, whither am I borne? This way and that shifts the abandoned rudder of my judgement. Shall we ever set eyes again on tender Scylla?[19]

HISTORY

Some historians responded to the new tastes of the reading public by borrowing dramatic techniques from the theater to make their subject more lively and readable. Duris of Samos wrote a history of the period from the battle of Leuctra to about 280 and Phylarchus of Athens picked up there and continued down to 220 B.C. Duris' portrayal of Demetrius Poliorcetes as a hero destroyed by self-indulgence and pride and Phylarchus' descriptions of the attempted reforms of the Spartan king Cleomenes III are among the most vivid in ancient history. More traditional histories were, however, also composed. Ptolemy I wrote an account of Alexander's conquests from official documents, and two other officers of Alexander, Nearchus and Aristobulus, also contributed sober accounts. All three versions are reflected in the surviving history of Alexander by Arrian written in the Roman Empire period. Another fine historian was Hieronymus of Cardia who wrote on the wars of the successors of Alexander and

[18] *The Greek Anthology*, tr. W. R. Paton (Loeb Classical Library and Harvard University Press, Cambridge, Mass., 1916), I, no. 174, p. 211.

[19] Ibid., no. 190, p. 223.

who survives in fragmentary quotations in works of other writers, including Plutarch. The majority of Hellenistic history writing, of which there was a great deal, tended to follow the lines of Duris or had propagandist aims. Most of it has perished.

Polybius in the second century (ca. 198–ca. 118) was the only other great historian of the Hellenistic period. Although written in a dry and uninteresting fashion and with distinct biases against Macedonia and Aetolia, his history of the rise of Rome to dominance in the Mediterranean between 220 and 167 is a great one. He attempts to bring all of history into focus by concentrating on this crucial event of his times. He had a full understanding of both sides, having been first a member of the ruling party of the Achaean League and then a close friend of the Roman general Scipio Aemilianus. He had a passionate desire to uncover the truth and made a point of familiarizing himself with Mediterranean geography, but in practice his prejudices against democracy, his admiration for oligarchy, and his belief that Fortune gave Rome a special role in history tended to vitiate his own principles.

An interesting response to the spread of Hellenism was the attempt by some of the native peoples to assert their own histories and cultural values. In the third century two priests, Berossus in Babylon and Manetho in Egypt, wrote histories of their respective lands in Greek. Later in the same century Fabius Pictor was the first Roman to write an account of his city's history for Greek consumption. A string of Jewish historians and apologists from Demetrius (ca. 220 B.C.) to Josephus (first century A.D.) strove to make their culture and past palatable to Greek and Roman tastes, only to be ignored and instead see crude anti-Semitic fables embraced by the reading and nonreading public alike. To be fair to the Greeks, their attitude toward the historical records of other native peoples (and that included the Romans) were equally cavalier. To them the accounts of Romans, Assyrians, Egyptians, Persians, and Jews seemed fabulous and unbelievable. The Greeks were convinced that they alone possessed the true account of prehistory, and unless others could make reference to it, they were automatically dismissed or altered to suit the accepted version. Greek ancestors could be found, if necessary, for any nations they came into contact with and in this way could be worked into the Greek scheme of early history. Although the Romans accepted the version that they were the descendants of Trojan refugee Aeneas they rejected other tales that would have made Odysseus, Heracles, or Evander the Arcadian their ancestors. It was not until Christianity that the Near East had its revenge, and then the Greek version of national origins was overwhelmed in favor of the Hebrew account in the book of Genesis.

UTOPIAN LITERATURE

The imagination of the Greeks was greatly stimulated by the enormous expansion of their world after Alexander. Travelers' tales such as those of Antiphanes of Berge, who claimed that there was a country where it was so cold in the fall that a man's words froze in the air and it was not possible to hear what he said until the spring, were common. Romances and novels in which travel and distant places were involved circulated widely. The Alexander Romance, a combination of Greek and Near Eastern sources, began circulating in the Hellenistic period and eventually spread all over Europe and Asia in innumerable versions.

Accounts of utopias were also highly popular. Euhemerus, a client of the Macedonian king Cassander, wrote a story about a utopia that popularized his theory that the gods were originally earthly rulers who were later deified. Euhemerus' utopia was located, he claimed, a few days' voyage off the coast of Arabia. Its inhabitants all possessed the franchise; there was no slavery and practically no private property. Everyone was to receive sustenance according to his needs, but those with higher responsibilities received more than the others. Cassander allowed his eccentric brother Alexarchos to found a city called Uranopolis—"the Heavenly City"—on the Mount Athos peninsula in the north of Greece, but unfortunately we know next to nothing of it except for a few coins and scattered literary references.

Iambulus, another utopianist writing about the mid-third century, described an island in the Indian Ocean that he claimed to have visited. It was one of seven called the Islands of the Sun and its inhabitants called themselves the children of the sun. Borrowing from Euhemerus, Iambulus depicts these children of the sun as living in a blissful community without war or inner strife. There was no slavery or private property and wives and children were held in common. Crops grew without attention throughout the year. There was no disease and population was controlled by voluntary euthanasia. Everyone took turns in performing the essential work of the community and leisure time was given to mutual enjoyment and the worship of the divinity. Megasthenes, the ambassador whom Seleucus sent to India, claimed that there was no slavery in that land. Onesicritus, who was in Alexander's entourage, circulated the tale that the inhabitants of one area of the Indus Valley lived to the age of 130 (Iambulus' children of the sun committed suicide at 150), ate together community style, used no money, and admitted suits for only two crimes, homicide and battery. Medicine alone was studied among the sciences, the rest being considered dangerous. The Scythians of the northland were supposed to live similar idyllic existences. Their main sustenance was milk and honey and they practiced a simple, austere life, showing no desire for wealth or their neighbor's property. The noble savage image was a handy weapon for the moralistic writers of the times to scourge the self-indulgent and oversophisticated classes of the Hellenistic and Roman world.

Education

The new world created fresh demands in the fields of communications and education. In old Greece the cities were still able to fulfill their educational functions without much change from the past. Conservative tradition was enshrined in the community's way of life and provided the essential moral framework for both old and young. The city with its festivals, courts, assemblies, and general method of doing public business inculcated each new generation with the ways of the past. Except in the realms of higher education the cities had no need of any artificial educational system independent of the community itself. Reading, writing, and calculation were taught as purely mechanical skills in private schools for a few, but there was nothing beyond that unless the *ephebeia*, the military youth-training program, happened to have been established in the city. Moral education of course, took place in the larger environment of home and city.

In the new lands, none of these assumptions about education held true. Greek cities of the east were little islands in an alien sea whose inhabitants were themselves natives of a dozen different Greek cities or regions. There was thus no preexisting set of customs or norms that would obviate the necessity for putting together a consciously designed—and therefore artificial—educational system to provide for the perpetuation of Greek culture, at least among the upper classes. The focus of this new institution was almost invariably the gymnasium, and its director, the *gymnasiarch*, became one of the most important persons in the new cities.

EDUCATION AND THE GYMNASIA

The early gymnasia had been informal affairs, located in the suburbs where the necessary space was easily obtainable. A good water supply for the baths was considered important and trees for shade were also desirable. Athens' three old gymnasia were combinations of religious shrines, parks, athletic fields, and lecture halls. Later more were built, one even in the Agora itself. In the Hellenistic period this tendency to bring the gymnasia within the walls of the city was given reinforcement as their importance as educational centers grew. In Egypt, where Greek settlements were scattered throughout the countryside and cities were few, the gymnasium became the real center of Greek political, social, and cultural life. Similarly, when native peoples such as the upper-class Jews of Jerusalem wished to acquire Greek culture they imported the institution of the gymnasium. As a result of this formal development the gymnasium came to be quite an elaborate affair, carefully planned and laid out as an integrated architectural unit. The essential elements consisted of a running track, an area for discus and javelin throwing, a wrestling place (the *palaestra*), and buildings to provide space for baths, changing rooms, lecture halls, libraries, and supplies. Depending on the space available these could be arranged at will. Delphi and Pergamum, on the sides of hills, distributed the different buildings and tracks on different terraces, but the more ordinary arrangement was to set aside a large area and surround it with a wall or colonnade and place the various rooms and halls along the different sides. Statues were common decorations and the walls were often covered with paintings and lists of pupils and athletic victors, as well as graffiti. To this day the ephebe's hall at Priene in Asia Minor shows the graffiti of its occupants.

The traditional object of Greek education had always been the maintenance of a balance between intellectual and physical education, though there was a general tendency to move more heavily in one direction than the other. Thus the gymnasia of the classical period had emphasized sports whereas in the Hellenistic period and later in the Roman period athletics gave way to scholastics. The changeover was due to a number of factors, foremost of which was the aristocratic aspect of the physical education program in the early period, which gave emphasis to competition. The rise of professional sports tended to lessen the importance of amateur athletics, but the most important factor was the new role the gymnasia played in the Hellenistic city. Here was the center where Greek ideas and ideals were kept alive. With the loss of independence the city's agora and meeting places declined in importance and the new focus of social and cultural life became the gymnasium. Education was a detached and independent process, no more an integral part of the life of the city. Its standards, too, had to derive from elsewhere, since the city itself was no longer the norm and measure of things. These derived in part from the general Greek environment—for example, the common festivals that brought Greeks together from all over the world. Even in only partially Hellenized areas they had an important function. In Palestine the five-year games held at Tyre brought Greeks—either true Greeks or Hellenized natives—together from all over the region. On one occasion the contingent from Jerusalem brought 330 drachmae with it, but remaining true to their beliefs they dedicated the money to ship building in Tyre rather than the sacrifices of the city god, Melkart-Heracles.

THE CURRICULUM

More important than the festivals, however, was the study of the classics, the great literary works thought to enshrine the most characteristically Greek views and attitudes. Preeminent among these were the works of Homer and the three tragedians Aeschylus, Sophocles, and Euripides, the greatest emphasis being given to Euripides. Hesiod, Pindar, Alcman, Alcaeus, and Sappho were also studied, and of the more recent works Menander's comedies, the *Argonautica* of Apollodorus, and the poems of the epigrammatists were popular. Prose was less studied. Of the historians, Herodotus, Xenophon, and especially Thucydides were standard fare, and among the orators Demosthenes was considered supreme. In secondary schools—for those roughly from 14 to 18 years of age—these texts were studied minutely by the most mechanical means. Painstaking lists of unusual words were prepared and supplemented by endless recitations and memorizations. Students learned to recognize the identifying marks of classical literature and tried to model their own writing accordingly. There was no interest whatsoever in original or creative writing. The object was to reproduce as closely as possible the style, syntax, and diction of the models. Beyond that the purpose of studying the classics was the inculcation of moral values and the discovery of the wisdom contained in them. Needless to say this produced all sorts of problems where the shocking behavior of the models was frequently not at all in accord with the middle-class values of the Hellenistic and Roman periods. The result was allegorical interpretations of the questionable actions of the heroes and gods, just as biblical commentators were forced into similar positions by the peculiar deeds of some of the patriarchs in Genesis. The main problem in the study of both classical and scriptural texts was the total absence on the part of Hellenistic readers of a sense of the atmosphere in which the works were originally composed and the assumption of or the desire to find an unchanging set of values in the texts. Some did appreciate the historical relativity of the compositions, but the majority of the commentators found easier solutions in imaginative explanations, such as Plutarch's claim that Homer's description of Paris and Helen retiring to bed at the end of Book III of the *Iliad* was really intended to cast discredit on evildoers.

SOCIAL EFFECTS

The same classical texts were studied in the same kind of institutions everywhere and had the effect of providing a broad cultural unity wherever the gymnasium was established. It was here that the models evolved in Athens of a detachable educational system came into their own and provided the Greeks with a solution to the perplexing problem of maintaining their identity in a sea of alien and powerful cultures. It had more important effects, however. The system of education broke down the old exclusivity of the Greek cities, which had made the assimilation of outsiders so difficult. Now all that was necessary for a person to become a Greek was a knowledge of the language and a gymnasium education. For the lower classes, who could not afford the latter, this meant little, but for those who had the resources and wished this kind of an education, either for themselves or for their children, the door was at least ajar. This last proviso is included because theoretically the gymnasium was supposed to be open only to native Greeks, though in practice non-Greeks were able to slip onto the gymnasium lists and merge with the Greek upper classes.

HIGHER EDUCATION

Not many possessed an education beyond what the local gymnasium offered and those who wished to pursue higher studies generally had to travel to one of the larger cities that had chairs of rhetoric and philosophy, the mainstay of the university curriculum in the ancient world. Of these two subjects rhetoric almost always tended to predominate. The reasons for this were to a large extent practical.

Despite the curtailing of the Greek city's autonomy, affairs within the city were conducted much as they had been in the past. The generally democratic type of constitution prevailed everywhere after Alexander until toward the beginning of the Roman period, and with it came the same kinds of public-speaking requirements as in the past. Councils, assemblies, courts, and judicial commissions all demanded formal presentations by those appearing before them. The same was true of external relations between the cities, and we constantly read of delegations being sent by this or that group among the contending city factions to argue their cases before the kings, and later the emperors. But even in more provincial settings than the courts of kings the rhetoricians had their part to play. For example, in the New Testament tale of Paul's arrest for inciting a riot in Jerusalem, we read of his accusers coming down to Caesarea and bringing with them a rhetorician by the name of Tertullus to conduct the prosecution before the Roman magistrate (Acts 24 : 1). There was simply no way of avoiding oratory; the Greeks reveled in it. Their tastes in this are, of course, far different than ours, but then so was their day-to-day political background. The fact that almost nothing of the vast mass of rhetorical output in the Hellenistic period survives says nothing against the continuing importance of the technique of persuasion in political and administrative matters. Although the great deliberative oratory of the past declined along with the freedom of the cities, and the set speech (or *epideictic oratory*) is what we know most about, it still remained true that the person with oratorical ability was the individual who could contribute most to the welfare of his city. He could do this internally through his ability to reason with people and persuade them of the wisdom of various courses of action and externally in his capacity to negotiate successfully with the other cities and powers that constituted the political world of the Greeks after Alexander. To illustrate the former we may turn again to the New Testament, which with its emphasis on the day-to-day activities of the Hellenistic cities is one of the best sources of information on the practical role of rhetoric in their administration. The central figure is once more Paul who was this time stirring up trouble in Ephesus where the local artisans had received the impression that Paul's preaching would deprive them of their livelihood. A riot had broken out and for a while it looked as though it was going to get out of hand. At this point one of the city magistrates, the town clerk or recorder, stood up and quelled the riot with the following piece of reasoned persuasion:

> "Men of Ephesus, who in the world does not know that the city of Ephesus is the guardian of the temple of the great Artemis, and of the stone that fell down from the sky? So as these facts are undeniable, you must be calm, and not do anything reckless. For you have brought these men here, though they have not been guilty of disloyalty nor uttered any blasphemy against our goddess. If Demetrius and his fellow-craftsmen have a charge to bring against anyone, there are the courts and the governors; let them take legal action. But if you require anything beyond that, it must be settled before the regular assembly. For we are in danger of being charged [by the Romans] with rioting in connection with today's events, though there is really nothing about this commotion that we will not be able to explain." With these words he dismissed the assembly.[20]

[20]Acts 19:35 in J. M. P. Smith and others, *The Complete Bible: An American Translation.* Copyright 1927 by The University of Chicago Press.

The result of this ongoing practical necessity for rhetorical ability, coupled with its traditional importance in Greek education, was that the study of the subject became the crown and object of almost all higher education, though with gestures to the study of philosophy. It was claimed, as Isocrates had argued in his debate against Plato, that the effort of learning how to speak properly had a corresponding moral effect by teaching the learner how to think and live properly. It was eloquence that distinguished the educated from the uneducated and the Greek from the barbarian. In a world where cities and citizenship meant less and less, the ideal of the cultured individual became a social category that distinguished the membership in the various classes. This was reflected in a number of ways. Gravestones proclaimed the cultural attainments of the dead they commemorated. Plato's comment that Greek culture was "the most precious endowment ever granted to mortal man" was taken seriously by the upper classes of the Hellenistic world and those who aspired to advancement—whatever their actual cultural attainments might amount to in practice. A common belief, which as we have seen went back at least to Plato, was that intellectual pursuits and studies cleansed the mind and prepared it for union with God. It was considered a liberating force from the bonds of the body and its passions. Demetrius Poliorcetes is supposed to have offered to indemnify the philosopher Stilpo for his losses in the siege of Megara, but he was rebuffed by Stilpo, who commented that he had in fact lost nothing of value that belonged to him, since he still possessed the two essentials of culture, his eloquence and his knowledge.

Art and Architecture in the Hellenistic World

The patrons of art in the Hellenistic world were as varied as Hellenistic society itself. The kings as founders of cities—and especially as the founders of capital cities—were the principal patrons, but individuals among the upper and middle classes, as well as the cities themselves, were also important purchasers of art. Corresponding to the extraordinary variety and taste of its patrons, Hellenistic art ranged from the monumental 400-foot frieze at Pergamum to tiny, exquisite gems that were the special feature of Hellenistic jewelers. Everything from the most flamboyant and vulgar baroque to the elegantly restrained classical was available—for a price. Copies of archaic and classical statues in every grade and quality, size and material could be obtained through art dealers in all the major cities. Thus the polis selecting art works and contracting for buildings for its own community needs was replaced by the individual shopping to fill his needs. Kings used art of all kinds (and quality) for propaganda purposes, but private persons also made purchases, either for their own homes or collections or in their capacities as benefactors of their cities. A class of amateur art connoisseur arose, and in art as well as literature there developed a split between the *cognoscenti* and the masses for whom it was assumed that only the obvious and gross were appropriate.

Among the artists themselves the times also brought changes. The hugely expanded demand for copies and decorations of all kinds added the dimension of trade to high art. The widely dispersed character of the cities of the Hellenistic world made it necessary for artists to travel a great deal and mix with other artists from all over the world in large, joint projects. Indicative of the broadening character of the new society is the fact that we know of the existence of a woman artist by the name of Helena who produced a painting of Alexander's battle with the Persians at Issus.

THE NEW CITIES

The cities, and especially the capitals, were the showplaces of the Hellenistic kings. Although fortresses of the rulers, they were far from merely armed camps. Unlike the Roman colonies on the Rhine and Danube frontier, where military demands were preeminent, the Hellenistic cities had much more ambitious objectives. They were the visible and permanent symbols of all that the kings and the ruling elite stood for, and it was as founders of cities that the Hellenistic kings made their most original contributions to history.

The first step in the construction of a new city was the hiring of a competent architect who could create a plan to suit the site and at the same time satisfy the military, administrative, and cultural aims of the city's founder. As in so many other things, the way toward achieving this had long been prepared by a tradition of city planning going back to at least the sixth century B.C. Hippodamus, the founder of the art of town planning, was active in the fifth century, and some superb examples of his method can be found in two cities laid out in the following century, Priene and Miletus in Asia Minor. Here careful planning organically related all the essential parts of the city—the agoras, temples, gymnasia, theaters, residential quarters, docks, and so forth—to their sites. In the case of Priene, the location was a difficult hillside, whereas for Miletus the site was a promontory jutting into the sea with accommodations for several harbors. Pergamum, the capital of the Attalids, presented formidable problems to the planners. It had a superb but difficult location on a steep hillside and the eventual solution was to divide the city into a number of levels. Alexandria, the capital of the Ptolemaic Empire, was located on a strip of land between the sea and a lake at one of the mouths of the Nile. By connecting an island that lay about three-quarters of a mile offshore with the mainland the Ptolemies created two fine harbors. One of these was connected to the lake by means of a canal where there was yet a third harbor designed to serve traffic coming down the Nile. On the island was one of the Seven Wonders of the World, the 360-foot Pharos lighthouse, whose light was visible for about 30 miles. The city itself was laid out in the classic grid pattern with special areas marked off for the palace of the Ptolemies, the temple of Serapis, the tomb of Alexander, the Museum, the library, the gymnasium, the stadium, and the racecourse. Underground cisterns, supplied from the river, provided fresh water. Although the capitals were the most spectacular examples of Hippodamian planning, cities of similar types

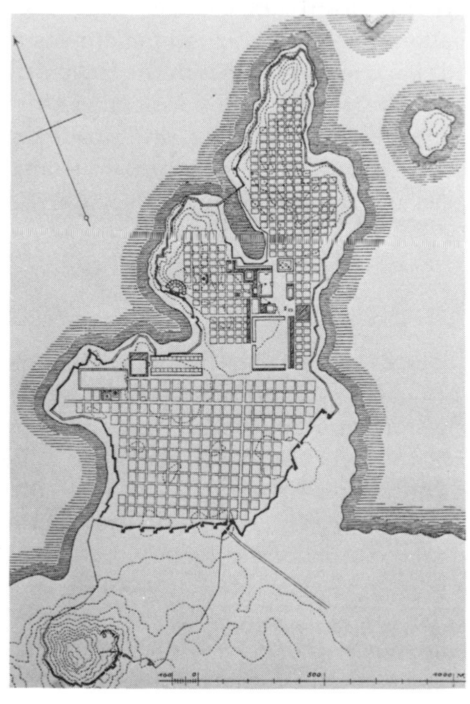

Plan of Miletus.

were built from one end of the Hellenistic world to the other. As late as the second century the work was still going on, even in far-flung Afghanistan and Pakistan, where the well-designed grids of Begram, Charsada, and Taxila testify to the persistence of the Hellenic ideal.

Once the initial stages of layout and construction had been accomplished, the next step was to decorate the city fittingly. For this task the workshops of Rhodes, Athens, Alexandria, and elsewhere could be called upon; or artists and craftsmen (now distinct) imported to do the work on the spot, or some combination of these two arranged. Since so many of the new cities were the creations of the kings it is understandable that their presence should have been strongly felt. The cities bore their names and their coinage circulated their likenesses, but there was also royal sculpture to remind the citizens of their masters.

HELLENISTIC SCULPTURE

In the fourth century there had been a steady movement in sculpture toward realistic portraiture. This tendency found its counterpart in biography in the field of literature. The historian Xenophon wrote the life stories of the Spartan Agesilaus and the Persian Cyrus, and in the Hellenistic period biography emerged as a fully developed literary genre in its own right. In the same period portraiture became a distinct field in sculpture and both biography and

A Roman copy of Lysippus' portrait of Alexander: a blend of humanity, idealism, and ruthlessness.

portraiture found ideal subject matter in the flamboyant lives of the Hellenistic kings, queens, and generals. The best sculptors were able to balance realism and psychological insight and convey a sense of the superhuman burden the kings carried as well as their special share in the divine potency. One of the early Alexandrian epigrammists commented that Lysippus' likeness of Alexander had a ferocity that might be understood as excusing the cowardice of the Persians as cattle might be excused for fleeing before a lion. This statue is perhaps one of the Roman copies we possess and it does indeed manage to portray something of the humanity of Alexander as well as his latent ruthlessness.

The kings communicated with their subjects by less obvious means also. In Alexandria the cult of Serapis—the deity who cared for his worshippers—could hardly fail to suggest the rule of the Ptolemies who also aspired to the same image of benevolent concern. The kings of Pergamum consciously intended the Altar of Zeus on the hill at the summit of the city to be another Parthenon. Its approach was designed to resemble Mnesicles' Propylaea at Athens, which concealed the view of the Parthenon until the moment when the visitor emerged from between the last pillars and suddenly beheld the Parthenon above him in three-quarters view. Like the Parthenon the Altar of Zeus had a frieze but its didactic purpose was much more evident. Instead of having to strain to see through the column shafts as he did at Athens the viewer of the Pergamene frieze could look at the sculptures almost at eye level. If there was doubt as to their meaning, the viewer could consult the inscription that

The great range of Hellenistic sculpture is suggested by these two extremes: the complicated, contorted figures of Laocoon and his sons, and the simple statuette of a contented, overweight, old woman.

accompanied each figure. The frieze, consisting of almost 400 feet of contorted, muscular giants and gods locked in fierce combat, conveyed the same message as that of the Parthenon—the victory of the gods over the forces of chaos and of the Greeks over the barbarians. Thus the Attalids, by their victories over the Celts, claimed to play the same role as the defenders of Greek civilization against barbarism that Athens claimed for itself in the wars against the Persians. It was a stunning piece of sculpture, vigorous and energetic, but utterly unlike the calm, restrained works of Phidias at Athens. Yet it was a true reflection of the power, turmoil, and freedom of the age.

Hellenistic writers largely gave up the heroic and bloodthirsty themes of early literature for more intimate and personal topics such as love and the ordinary events of everyday life. The same is true of art where love in every facet from the tender and ingenuous to the explicit and vulgar was explored in detail. Every physical and psychological aspect of man was investigated and individuals of all walks and stages of life—not just the youthful gods and godlike aristocracy—were considered fit subjects for the artists. Slaves and peasants, old men and women, the deformed and crippled, children at play and asleep, drunken gods and men were depicted in an incredible variety of poses and materials. For the first time smiling statues made their appearance, but the virtuoso artists of the period could depict any mood they or their patrons wished to convey. Sagging skin and protruding veins were depicted as readily as smooth flesh and muscles. Another fashion that was popular was veristic portraiture, which depicted with illusionistic exactitude vignettes of real life. Rural scenes with nymphs, peasants, and satyrs dancing in Arcadian simplicity were the counterpart of the bucolic poems of literature.

During the Classical Age there was no real distinction between the educated or intellectual class and the rest of society. Everyone attended the plays, recitations, and choruses of the poets and dramatists. During the Hellenistic Age, however, a new phenomenon made its appearance—the person who read in private, who possessed a library and tended to associate with like-minded people. At the professional level there were the scholars of Alexandria and the other centers of learning and the philosophers and rhetoricians who wandered the world making their services available to those seeking an education. To this class symbolical and classicizing art appealed greatly. Lysippus produced a statue called *Opportunity*, whose face was covered with hair because opportunity is hard to recognize, but whose head was bald to symbolize the difficulty of grasping it. The statue had wings on its feet and a razor in its hand to illustrate the speed and abruptness with which opportunity presents itself and must be seized. The friezes of Pergamum were an encyclopedia of learned mythology as well as symbolic representation. Classicism, the reproduction of forms canonized in the fifth century, made its appearance before the Hellenistic Age in the tomb of Mausolus in Caria, and ever after conscious appeals were made to this definitive period in Greek art. Over 800 years later we find Roman aristocrats using classical forms in the ivory plaques they exchanged among themselves.

The eternal appeal of the classical style: Compare these harmoniously arranged struggling figures from the tomb of Mausolus with the similarly balanced Lapith and Centaur in the Parthenon metope (see page 146).

Just as mimes and epigrams captured a small aspect of Hellenistic life and were among the most successful of the literary genres created in that period, so in the world of fine art some of the best achievements were in the minor arts. One of these was the art of cameo cutting from agate, sardonyx, amethyst, and other precious and semiprecious stones. This was an extremely difficult technique but one that was highly popular with both Greeks and Romans.

The homes of the newly affluent middle classes as well as the new cities themselves created a great demand for copies of the ancient masters and for other forms of decoration such as paintings, mosaics, moldings, and the like. Copies of all kinds were mass-produced. Unfortunately almost no paintings of the Hellenistic period proper survive, though some idea can be formed from those that can be seen on the walls and in the floor mosaics of the towns and villas destroyed around the Bay of Naples in A.D. 79. So much of classical and Hellenistic art survives only in copies that it is difficult to form an estimate of how good the originals actually were. Not a single original piece by the masters, such as Phidias, Praxiteles, Polyclitus, or Lysippus, can be identified with certainty.

PEOPLES AND CONSTITUTIONS

The Greek of the classical period was, typically, a citizen of a small city-state, used to moving in a world of small communities in which states like Athens or Sparta seemed like giants though still of essentially the same recognizable political type as his own native polis. In the Hellenistic world there was no such constitutional catholicity but instead a multiplicity of political forms. The most prevalent type of government was monarchy, but even here there was a major difference between the huge kingdoms of the Ptolemies and Seleucids and their heavily eastern trappings and the more conservative monarchy of the Macedonians. In between both types stood the smaller kingdom of Pergamum. In mainland Greece the old city-states still longed—and occasionally fought—for independence, though they generally remained firmly under the control of the Macedonian monarchy. Federal leagues were a new development. These combinations of city-states and rural cantons in the remoter districts of Greece had begun in the fourth century but emerged as significant powers in the third, able to fend off all the attempts of the kings to bring them under control. From the viewpoint of the old polis constitution, these were its lineal and most successful descendants. Although large in comparison to the classical ideal they preserved the essential polis quality of autonomy. Unlike the monarchies, which lived on uneasy terms with the Greek cities in their midst, the leagues were true fusions of cities and the only genuinely progressive political innovation of the period.

Monarchies, leagues, and city-states do not exhaust the list of constitutional possibilities that the Hellenistic world embraced. There were large temple-states in Asia Minor and Syria run by powerful, dynastic priesthoods. These states maintained a considerable measure of independence down to the

Roman period. The Judean temple-state in Palestine became completely independent in the mid-second century and remained so until the appearance of the Romans 100 years later. Little feudal principalities under their native aristocracies dotted the Seleucid regions, and everywhere newly founded capitals, military colonies, and cities multiplied the political forms under which the inhabitant of the Hellenistic world might live.

The peoples of this world were as diverse as the political forms it embraced. In place of the homogeneous inhabitants of the Aegean world in the classical period were the incredibly fragmented and much larger populations of the old Persian Empire, each with its own individual history and inner complexities. Egypt was predominantly a land of peasants—some 7 million of them—among whom were scattered an unknown number of Greek and Macedonian colonists and settlers. The center of Greek power was Alexandria, at its height a city of perhaps a million in population if we count all souls, both native and Greek. In the Seleucid Empire the diversity was infinitely greater. Iranian nomads wandered freely throughout the huge desert-like regions east of the old Persian capital of Persepolis. Babylonia and Syria comprised some of the most advanced and sophisticated societies in the ancient world. The Seleucid Empire's population has been estimated at 30 million, over which presided another unknown number of Greeks and Macedonians in cities scattered thousands of miles apart. Alexandria Eschate on the Jaxartes (*Syr-Dar'ya*)—"Farthest Alexandria"—was closer to modern Calcutta on the lower Ganges than it was to its own capital, Antioch, 2200 miles to the east. Yet somehow the Greeks managed to leave their imprint on these utterly diverse regions. Even while Koheleth was writing his masterpiece in Jerusalem under Greek influence, Hellenistic cities in Afghanistan were having an impact on the very different culture surrounding them. These cities, comprising part of the Greek kingdom of Bactria, were no mere frontier fortresses but well-laid-out affairs, with streets designed in formal grid pattern and decorated with the usual sculptures and inscriptions. They produced some of the finest coinage ever minted in the ancient world. It has been recently suggested that these cities, even in their later decayed states, stimulated the Kushan nomads who passed through them on their way to India, and they in turn affected the development of the famous sculptures of Gandhara in northern India.[21]

Hellenistic Social Structures

In terms of social structures, the most characteristic feature of the Hellenistic Age was the separation of the state and society, so unlike the earlier period of the polis when the two had been practically identical. In classical times there had been practically no government—no permanent legislative or judicial organs, no

[21]Mortimer Wheeler, *Flames over Persepolis.* (New York: Reynal & Co. in association with William Morrow and Co. Inc., 1968), p. 162–67.

bureaucracies or permanent executives—as distinguished from the people. In the new world the government with its kings, courts, and administrative hierarchies was emphatically not identical with the people but instead something apart from them; the state went out of its way to emphasize its different and independent sovereignty. Thus the sociopolitical basis of the old city-state, the nexus between citizenship and power, was dissolved. With it disappeared the overriding importance of the franchise. To be an Athenian or Spartan or a Theban had once meant everything—a share in the state's power, the loot of its wars, or the profits of its empire. Now, since the cities except in local matters were powerless, the citizenship as such—as long as one were still Greek, of course—no longer mattered. In the face of the might of the kings none of the old city-states could protect their citizens abroad or even at home, nor did any of the Hellenistic states possess anything like an imperial citizenship, which might have effectively offered some kind of protection against arbitrary treatment by the authorities. There was no formal, legal distinction between Greeks and non-Greeks as there was between Romans and non-Romans during the Roman Republic and Empire—a distinction so useful to a figure like Paul in his many confrontations with local as well as imperial authorities. Instead, all the inhabitants of a Hellenistic kingdom were the subjects of the monarch, who at least legally had unrestricted power over them.

Paradoxically it was the breaking of the citizenship-power connection that opened the way for the rapid spread of Hellenism. As long as the old formula of the classical city-state prevailed it was inevitable that strict control be kept over the granting of the franchise, since any expansion of the citizen body would mean a proportionate loss in power and financial recompense. As a consequence, Greek culture, which was intimately bound up with the polis and its festivals, competitions, and forms of government, was also a restricted affair, limited to those who by reason of their birth could participate in these things. Once, however, the overriding political importance of citizenship declined, there was no longer any reason to be so restrictive in admitting citizens. In the Hellenistic period, even in old Greece, we see all sorts of political exchanges of the franchise between cities, something that would have been unthinkable in the fifth or fourth centuries. Intellectually it had long been recognized that being a Greek was more a cultural than a racial matter, and that a lot of "barbarians" were in fact closer to being true Greeks than were many of the Greeks themselves. But, practically speaking, access to the benefits of Hellenic culture remained restricted until the kings took political power into their own hands. Then what counted was not so much the ability to prove one's descent from Greek parents; it was wealth, talent, and culture, one or preferably all three of these.

In classical Athens the government and to a lesser extent the armed services were so designed that, with some significant exceptions, practically anyone could be anything. Outside the elective offices talent as such was not particularly rewarded or sought out and amateurism was the general rule. By contrast, in the new states the professional was supreme and it mattered little where he came from as long as he was Greek or at least professed to be Greek. At the festivals professional entertainers, actors, musicians, and athletes replaced the amateurs of the past and made their rounds from city to city. Physicians, technicians, engineers, generals, and scholars were in great demand and moved as the opportunities presented themselves. For instance, the mathematician Apollonius of Perga was able to do most of his pioneering work on conics at Alexandria under the patronage of the Ptolemies, and then transfer to Pergamum where he dedicated a revised edition of his masterwork to his new sponsor, King Attalus. Above all, the new kingdoms needed bureaucrats—accountants, managers, and scribes—to organize and operate their administrative systems, and mercenaries to supply the backbone of their fighting forces. In such a world the old restrictive idea of citizenship, where participation in government, religion, and the army depended on the possession of the franchise, was simply obsolete.

With the clear division between state and society and the reduced importance of the citizenship, it now became more important than ever before to belong to the well-to-do classes. The distinction between the rich and poor had always been the main dividing line between the classes of the old polis, but even outside of Athens the existence of the assembly had guaranteed some power to the lower classes. Now, although all the new cities were formally democracies and possessed assemblies, the "better" classes were firmly in control. The bourgeoisie constituted the new elite, and in a sense they became the only new citizenry of the supposedly cosmopolitan Hellenistic world. The lower classes

Seated on an elaborate chair a languid lady of the Hellenistic upper classes attends to her toilette. Isolated from any meaningful role in public life, the Hellenistic well-to-do lavished their attention on their private affairs.

were progressively disenfranchised and sank in importance until in the Roman period the law took cognizance of the fact and frankly categorized the inhabitants of the Roman Empire into two groups, the *honestiores* and *humiliores*, with a different system of justice for each.

The Monarchs

The predominant political structure of the Hellenistic world was the altogether un-Greek absolute monarchy. This form of government was, however, natural to the Macedonians and to the world Alexander conquered, and the Greeks had no choice but to accommodate themselves to it. This happened with surprising quickness despite the long-standing antipathy of the Greeks to a strong executive and their tendency to characterize the subjects of kings as slaves. Athenians, for example, could chant to Demetrius of Macedon:

> The other gods are either far away or cannot hear or do not exist or do not care for us. You we can see, not in wood or stone, but face to face . . . to you we pray.[22]

They even gave him the Parthenon as his residence. This unexpected servility is not exactly what it seems. Athenians by the end of the fourth century had a thoroughly secularized view of the state and religion, though this does not mean that they were irreligious. Rather, their concept of the divinity had changed. Along with many other Greeks they were more inclined to worship manifestations or epiphanies of divine power than the more personal gods of the past. The kings of the Hellenistic world were particularly likely to be the focal point of divine emanations and were honored as benefactors and saviors who could be depended upon to protect their people from their enemies. Thus Athens was "saved" from Cassander by Demetrius, Rhodes from Demetrius by Ptolemy, and the Asiatic Greeks from the Celts by Antiochus. In addition, the theories of Euhemerus, that the gods had originally been powerful kings later deified, was widespread. All of this prepared the way for the divinization of the monarchs. Beginning in Egypt where divine pharoahs had long ruled, the kings were declared to be gods and their official cults were extended everywhere throughout their kingdoms. An important element in these cults distinguished them from the strictly oriental version of king-worship. This was the element of personal achievement by the rulers—in the form of great victories or deeds done on a heroic level or benefits conferred on humanity—which in Greek eyes justified the claim to a share in the godhead. The arrival of the Romans, despite their republican traditions, hardly changed the situation. Rome was now the new power—the new, unexpected manifestation of the working of Tyche or Fortune and therefore deserving of honor befitting the choice of mysterious destiny.

[22]Athenaeus, *Deipnosophists* ("Connoisseurs in Dining"), 6.63.253.

When finally the Romans produced a king in the person of the emperor, he too was worshipped in the traditional fashion.

The Kings and Their Subjects

The kings were surrounded by a court aristocracy of which the two highest levels were known as the Kinsmen and the Friends, but the rule of the kings was absolute and unrestrained by any constitutional conventions. Officials could be removed without formality and the king's will in the form of edicts and decrees had the force of law. He and his court were the state and the kingdom he ruled was in no sense a community of people—a republic, commonwealth or city-state—where individuals had the rights of citizens. The people were simply the subjects of the king and life and death lay in his hands. In practice, however, his absolutism was tempered by a number of factors. He could not administer his huge realms without a bureaucracy and weak or indolent kings were automatically its prisoners. Nor could he rule without the support of the Greeks dwelling in the country, in either the cities, colonies, or rural districts. Apart from the mercenary army and the bureaucracy, these were the king's main support though they could not be trusted to the extent of providing troops or administrative services. For those the king preferred to collect taxes directly and then raise mercenaries and pay his officials with the proceeds. The recalcitrance of the mass of natives in the countryside was proverbial. In Egypt strikes and revolts forced the Ptolemies to make concessions and take more Egyptians into the government itself and in the Seleucid Empire the Parthians and East Greeks quickly won and maintained their independence at the expense of the central state. More so than the Ptolemies the Seleucid rulers had to contend with a naturally difficult geographical region, enormous distances, numerous Greek cities, and native aristocracies and temple-states. Egypt, on the other hand, benefited by its traditional geographical isolation and its long history of internal unification under a powerful monarchy. Even there the Ptolemies faced enemies, in the native priesthoods and the stubborn peasant masses who never ceased to regard them as alien conquerors. Even Alexandria, the capital, with its heterogeneous and unruly population, presented great difficulties to the rulers as it later did to the infinitely more powerful Roman emperors. Divine rulers faced altogether intractable human problems. Still, the bureaucracy created by the Ptolemies was an efficient machine, the like of which the Mediterranean had never seen before. Although a centralized administration had existed previously, the new rulers refined and improved its operation, so that life down to the most minute details was regulated and supervised. Monopolies in essential goods, such as salt, beer, oil, and cloth, were maintained; rents were bid upon so that the highest prices could be obtained. Irrigation was maintained by forced labor; the huge sums of money extracted were poured into the administration, the armies of mercenaries, and the fleets the Ptolemies deemed necessary to maintaining their kingdom and their militaristic ventures overseas.

Cities

With the exception of Egypt the essential means of preserving the self-identity of the Greek ruling class was the city and to a lesser extent the military colony. In Egypt, where outside Alexandria and two other lesser cities there was no urbanization, the Greeks were scattered throughout the countryside in corporations (*politeumata*), which found their focal points in the local gymnasia.

The polis was selected by Alexander as the main means of maintaining control over the vast regions of the newly conquered Persian Empire. Traditionally he is credited with founding 70 cities and in this work he was followed by his successors. Seleucus I, for example, founded 16 Antiochs, 9 Seleuceias, 6 Laodicaeas, 3 Apameas, and 1 Stratoniceia—named after his father, himself, his mother, and his wives, respectively. Military colonies often became cities, but retained the distinction of not owning their territory outright and being subject to military levies.

Generally the cities had democratic constitutions and at least formally almost all that has been said of the Athenian system of government can be applied to the Greek cities of the Hellenistic period. They had their assemblies, councils, and elected officials and the principle of collegial or group magistracies was maintained as well as rotation in office. Generally the rotation was an annual affair but in some places the magistracies changed twice a year, as at Rhodes and Cnidus. There was, with few exceptions, no attempt to limit the franchise to a narrow oligarchy, although citizenship continued to be confined to Greeks who could prove Greek descent on both sides. The maintenance of the franchise was a policy of all Greek cities down to the Christian era, though in practice many non-Greeks were able to acquire it through grants or marriage arrangements as well as by more surreptitious means.

The Cities and Their Classes

From the social point of view the main distinctions in the cities were between the well-to-do and the poor and as time went on the democratic form of the city came to mean less and less. The council tended to be made up of persons from the middle and well-to-do classes and since revenue for the city's needs was always a problem, the custom arose for magistrates upon entering office to take responsibility for many public services previously funded from general revenues. By the second century B.C. democracy was in practice dead and the Roman process of assimilation of the council to the Senate, whose membership depended among other things on property qualifications and was for life, was almost a predictable development.

Economically the cities were not great producers of wealth though they did supply necessary services that are more difficult to categorize. Their food supply was almost always derived from their own territory and industry was limited to the production of essential goods for local consumption. Imports consisted of luxury goods for the well-to-do, food in times of scarcity, and essential materials such as metal, stone, and timber. Wealth was mostly a matter of landholding, though fortunes were also made in trade and in some of the professions, where rhetoricians, doctors, athletes, and architects often did well. The nonproductive character of the cities should not be exaggerated, however, since there is no way of estimating how much their contributions in the fields of education, health, entertainment, and overall civility were also factors in maintaining the level of productivity in the areas where they were located. One of the most striking aspects of Hellenistic civilization is the extraordinary generosity of the well-off classes, who competed with each other in their benefactions. Again there is no way of calculating how much the wealthy contributed to their communities in this fashion, though at a guess it must compare favorably with what modern governments manage to squeeze out of the wealthy by means of taxation. If the cities by their very existence encouraged the lavish spending by the wealthy on such community functions as festivals, the maintenance and erection of public buildings, the food and water supply, then by this very fact they probably justified their existence. The alternative, which occurred in the late Roman Empire, was for the rich to withdraw to their villas in the country where their wealth was spent on essentially private functions and the masses were reduced to a form of serfdom.

In old Greece, intercity relations changed considerably though the cities themselves remained much as they had always been internally. Arbitration became a common means of settling local conflicts. The right of asylum was jealously guarded as one of the last vestiges of city-state independence and the kings tried to win popularity by conferring this right on particular cities and shrines. Some cities agreed to liberate one another's citizens if the citizens were purchased as slaves. The exchange of citizenship between cities such as was effected by Athens and Priene and Athens and Rhodes became common throughout the Aegean area. As in the past, festivals were a means of bridging the gulf between cities and many new ones were created in the Hellenistic period. The settling of internal disputes by means of judicial commissions from other cities was widely employed. These judges first attempted to settle disputes themselves and only after they failed to do so did the local juries take over. The process eventually led to the buildup of a body of common law and legal practice that effectively transcended the narrow boundaries of the individual city-states.

Leagues

One of the most remarkable developments of the age was the emergence in Greece proper of federal leagues with true representative government.

The ground for these leagues had been prepared long before they finally emerged as significant powers in the third century B.C. One of their predecessors was the religious association known as the *amphictyony,* which consisted of a number of states joined in a league for the purposes of worship at a common shrine. Among the best known were the amphictyonies of Delphi and Delos. The object of these leagues, which included all the major powers of Greece, was the maintenance of the cults and temples and to some extent the inculcation of certain rules among its members. During the festivals there was to be a truce and the shrine itself was to be regarded as an asylum. The oath sworn by the Delphic amphictyons included the following terms:

> Not to destroy any Polis of the Amphictyonies, or starve it out, or cut off its running water, either in war or in peace; if anyone transgresses these rules, to take the field against him and call up (?) the Poleis, and if anyone plunders the property of the god or is privy to such robbery or has any designs against the sanctuary, to take vengeance for it with hand and foot and voice and all one's power.[23]

Although these associations brought the separate states together in religious worship, they had no ability to break down the independence of the states and offer a basis for intercity citizenship. Similarly such organizations as the imperial leagues of Sparta and Athens created no more than a superficial unity and each state jealously guarded its own citizenship. It was thus not in the more advanced parts of Greece that true federal leagues with universal citizenship first came into existence but in the more remote regions where the tribal and cantonal structure of society still existed and the city-state was not the predominating constitutional form.

The Aetolian federal state in western central Greece evolved in the fourth century from a loose tribal organization. It consisted of a council made up by proportionate representation of delegates from the constituent villages and cities, and a primary assembly open to all citizens, which met twice a year. The Achaean League in the north of the Peloponnese also emerged as a significant power in the fourth century, and at one time no fewer than 60 cities and villages belonged to it. As in the Aetolian League there was a primary assembly that met irregularly to deal with specific, major issues such as war, peace, and alliances. Voting was by cities, who probably had their number of votes determined by their population. There was also a council whose role and composition is not clearly understood. In general the leagues recognized the right of their citizens to exercise their political rights throughout the federal territory, to move at will, to own property, and to marry whomever they chose. Internal affairs were left to the individual states, but foreign relations and military matters were the concern of the federal government, by way of either the full assembly or the council. Military service was regarded as service to the individual cities. Taxes were paid to both the federal government and the home states.

One of the great achievements of the leagues was their success in resisting the kings and adventurers of the Hellenistic Age, to whom the old classical cities like Athens fell easy prey. They preserved something of the old autonomy of the city-state with the advantages of federal government, but they never got an

[23]V. Ehrenberg, *The Greek State*, 2nd ed. (London: Methuen & Co. Ltd. 1969), p. 110.

opportunity to show what they might have accomplished in fields other than the political and military. Wedged between the rising power of Rome and the kingdoms of the east they were absorbed before any significant cultural development occurred, though Polybius, the great second-century historian, was from Megalopolis, a member of the Achaean League. Significantly, his career as a historian began only after his political career in the league had been cut short by the intervention of the Romans.

THREE

THE ROMAN WORLD

11

Early Rome

THE WESTERN MEDITERRANEAN AND EARLY ITALY

In ancient and modern times the western Mediterranean has been the focal point of the countries surrounding it. High mountain ranges and plateaus cut off the coastal areas from the interior and prevent easy communications with the land masses behind them. Long narrow coastal plains in Africa and Spain lead up to high, arid mountains and plateaus. In Africa, the Atlas range and beyond it the vast waste of the Sahara constitute even today the southern boundary of the Mediterranean region and a major barrier to communications between this area and equatorial Africa. The rich agricultural plains of Italy—Tuscany, Lazio, and Campania—face the sea, and are backed by the steeply rising peaks of the Apennines. The Cévennes and the Alps direct the inhabitants of the south of France away from continental Europe and toward the sea. Great rivers—the Ebro in Spain, the Rhone in France, and the Tiber in Italy—flow into the Mediterranean, drawing the peoples of the uplands toward the coasts where the great cities, almost all of them founded in ancient times, are located. Conveniently placed islands—the Balearics, Sardinia, Corsica, and Sicily—aid communications and in antiquity supplied handy stopping places for the coastally inclined maritime traffic. Distances are short in this world. In one of the more dramatic scenes from the period of the Roman Republic, Cato the Elder (second century B.C.), who was arguing in the Senate for the destruction of Carthage, opened the folds of his toga and let fall a bunch of ripe figs that had been picked outside Carthage just three days before—lending emphasis to his point that a vigorous neighbor like Carthage, even though in Africa, was much too close for comfort.

Greek and Phoenician Migrations

The western Mediterranean was one of the richest mineral and agricultural areas of the ancient world. In Roman times southeastern Spain, the Ebro Valley, southern France, Italy from the Arno River to Salerno, and the hinterland of

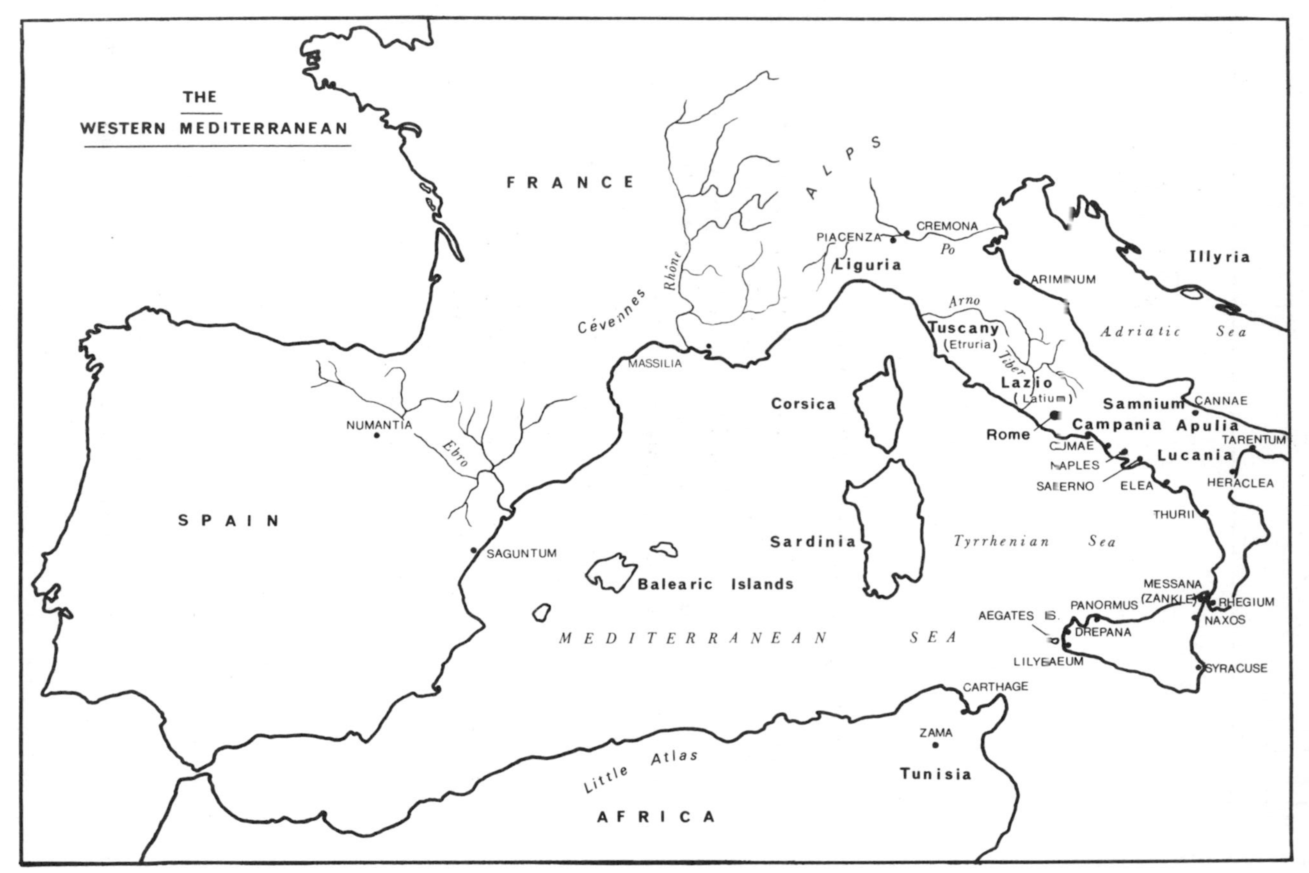
THE
WESTERN MEDITERRANEAN
FRANCE
ALPS
Cévennes
Rhône
CREMONA
PIACENZA
Po
Liguria
Illyria
ARIMINUM
Arno
Tuscany
(Etruria)
Tiber
Adriatic Sea
MASSILIA
Lazio
(Latium)
Corsica
Samnium
CANNAE
Rome
Campania
Apulia
TARENTUM
CUMAE
NAPLES
Lucania
SALERNO
ELEA
HERACLEA
THURII
NUMANTIA
Ebro
SPAIN
SAGUNTUM
Sardinia
Tyrrhenian Sea
Balearic Islands
MESSANA
(ZANKLE)
PANORMUS
RHEGIUM
AEGATES IS.
NAXOS
DREPANA
MEDITERRANEAN SEA
LILYBAEUM
SYRACUSE
CARTHAGE
ZAMA
Tunisia
Little Atlas
AFRICA

Carthage were covered with vineyards and olive groves. The export trade was a brisk one. Even today the grid pattern of the Roman field system can be seen stretching for mile after mile in the countryside of modern Tunisia. Grain from Sicily, Africa, and Sardinia fed Rome for centuries and permitted Italian farmers to concentrate on wine and oil production as well as on other cash crops.

It was the metals of the west, however, that first attracted the attention of the eastern civilizations. The Phoenicians were the first to stumble across the mineral wealth of Spain. In time its great potential was realized, and it became the Mediterranean world's principal source of silver, copper and tin. Somewhat later the iron resources of Etruria began to be tapped. Then, from the middle of the eighth century (ca. 750 B.C.) a flood of Greeks began moving across the Northern rim of the western Mediterranean, paralleling Phoenician traders who were moving primarily along the coast of Africa toward the Atlantic.

The first Greeks to settle in the west were the Chalcidians and Eretrians of Euboea who established Cumae, Naxos, Zancle, and Rhegium as colonies at strategic locations on the coasts of southern Italy and Sicily. Their object was to set themselves up as intermediaries in the trade between east and west, exchanging the manufactured goods of the east for the raw materials, especially metals, of the west. This arrangement rapidly became a model for others to imitate and set off a land-rush in which Greek cities competed bitterly with one another and with the Phoenicians and the natives of the western Mediterranean for control of strategic coastal positions. Between the eighth and fifth centuries hundreds of coastal sites were occupied by Greeks and Phoenicians, preference being giving usually to islands just off the coast or peninsulas and bays with good harbors.

At the same time that migrants from the east were settling the coastlands, the Celts were expanding from their central homeland in southern Germany into France and from there into Spain (ca. 700 B.C.). They always remained a continental power, however, outside the mainstream of interest of the Greeks, Phoenicians, and Romans.

Italy: Geography and History

Italy is divided into a number of clearly identifiable geographic regions by the switching back and forth of the Apennines, the great central mountain range. These mountains begin at the point where the Alps reach the Mediterranean coast at the Riviera, then cut all the way across Italy to the Adriatic Sea at a point below Ariminum (modern Rimini). There they begin to turn in a southeasterly direction and recross the peninsula, until they touch the Tyrrhenian coast in Lucania. From there they continue on south through the toe of Italy, reappearing in Sicily, and again in Africa as the Atlas chain.

This zigzagging of the Apennines creates three great natural lowland regions. The first two, the Po Valley in the north and Apulia in the south, open onto the Adriatic. In the west, the third, which contains the districts of Etruria

Unaffected by classical Greek ideas of form, this small bronze statuette from Sardinia breathes the independent and alien spirit of the western Mediterranean.

(Tuscany), Latium (Lazio), and Campania, opens onto the Mediterranean proper. Between Apulia and Campania the mountains flatten out to form a large plateau, known to the Romans as Samnium, which dominates the plain areas on either side.

In ancient times the richest agricultural land and almost all the mineral wealth of Italy was to be found in the western lowland region. In addition, the natural lines of communication lay in this area rather than in the mountainous central highlands or on the narrow Adriatic coastal plain. Rome, therefore, with its central location astride these routes, could prevent movement north or south or from the Mediterranean into the interior. Long before there were any roads leading to Rome, all the lines of communication converged on the site where a number of hills overlooked a ford on the lower reaches of the Tiber.

This position in the middle of Italy meant that Rome was vulnerable to attack from many sides. But Rome had an advantage in its central lines of communication. As long as it could keep its enemies from coordinating their attacks—or if it could hold one enemy off while coping with the others—Rome could use its communication lines to deploy its forces quickly from one frontier to another. Diplomacy, therefore, was an important element in Rome's dealings with its neighbors, and the principle of divide and conquer was a matter of survival for the early Romans.

The roads the Romans built provide a graphic illustration of their conquests as well as of the dictates of Italian geography. Early expansion was toward the southeast, and the first two all-weather roads, the Via Latina and the Via Appia, one following an inland route and the other a coastal route, were designed to provide permanent communications with Latium and Campania. The Via Appia was later extended through Samnium to connect with Apulia and its seaports, which in turn led to Greece and the eastern Mediterranean. In the north the Via Flaminia, built in 220 B.C., crossed the peninsula diagonally and connected with Ariminum, the entry point to the Po Valley. Finally, the Via Cassia passed through central Etruria and then, dividing near Florence, sent branches into the Po Valley and down to the coast to connect with the route leading to France and Spain.

The Peoples of Italy

The Italy of Rome's early years was a complicated mosaic of peoples, cultures, and languages. Celts began to infiltrate across the Alps in the early fifth century, and then came in massive numbers around 400 B.C., settling first in the Po Valley and then extending themselves southward along the Adriatic coast. The Greeks had been in Italy and Sicily since the eighth century. Their main concentrations were in the south along the instep of the boot, in the area known as Magna Graecia, but they also had important settlements on the Adriatic and the Tyrrhenian coasts. The Phoenicians were influential in Etruria, where they found allies to support them against common enemies, the Greeks of Italy, Sicily, and Marseilles. With the exception of the late-arriving Celts, however, these peoples never ventured deep into the hinterland and the interior of Italy remained in the hands of two groups of earlier arrivals. The first group was made up of Indo-European-speaking peoples, of whom the most important were the Venetians of the Po Valley, the Oscans and Umbrians of the central highlands and east coast, and the Latins of the west. The second group did not speak Indo-European languages and included one of the most important of the peoples of Italy, the Etruscans. Others of lesser note were the Messapians of Apulia and the Ligurians of the northwest. Thus Italy of the early Roman phase was a babel of languages and dialects and of cultures in various stages of development from the primitive to the most sophisticated.

Of all these peoples, the Oscans were the most widespread and numerous, whereas the Latins were confined to the small area between the Tiber and Campania, hemmed in by enemies on all sides. The Oscans, however, were a tribal people who only slowly made the transition to an urban form of life, and then only partially. Culturally, politically, and socially they were backward compared to the Etruscans, Greeks, and Latins, but because of their numbers, military aptitude, and strategic location in the high country overlooking the rich plains they gave the urban-based peoples some bad moments before they were finally defeated. In the late fourth century the Oscans were at their height, having destroyed all but Naples and Elea along the Tyrrhenian coast and having severely contained the Greek colonies further south.

Among the peoples of Italy it was the Etruscans (and with their help the Romans) who made the most remarkable responses to the new influences coming out of the east.[1] Around 700 B.C. the inhabitants of the rich area between the Arno and the Tiber created a flourishing city-state civilization that was recognized throughout the Mediterranean for its opulence, and at times for its peculiar customs. To the Greeks they were the *Tyrsenoi* (hence Tyrrhenian), and to the Romans *Etrusci* or *Tusci* (hence Etruscans and Tuscany).

The Etruscan cities formed a loose federation, which met annually to discuss joint action and to celebrate religious festivals in the Greek fashion. Traditionally the number of cities in the federation was 12, but from the archaeological remains we know of the existence of others, many of whose ancient names are still unknown. Occasionally cooperating, the cities of Etruria also fought bitterly among themselves. Down to the fifth century B.C. they were ruled by kings in whom were combined the functions of priest, general, judge, and political leader. After that date an annually elected official (the *zilath*, or, in Latin, *praetor*) presided, assisted by a college of magistrates. There were no senates and no assemblies of the people. Society was divided between aristocrats and a large servile lower class that was further divided into a number of grades, but there was no free middle class. Aristocratic women enjoyed what seemed to the Greeks an astonishing amount of freedom, which the Greeks accounted for by accusing the Etruscans of materialism and loose morals.

Economically, the wealth of Etruria lay in its great deposits of iron, copper, tin, and zinc, and in its fertile agricultural areas. Etruscan decorative bronzes and jewelry were unsurpassed and its farmers achieved high levels of excellence, inventing, among other things, the cuniculus or tunnel method of draining river valley bottoms. This technique had the desirable effect of eliminating meandering streams and marshes, thus prohibiting erosion and expanding cultivatable land.

Although in the Roman period the Etruscans were confined within the geographical boundaries of Etruria, at an earlier date they possessed an empire that included Campania and some of the Po Valley. This empire, together with Etruria's own resources, allowed Etruscan aristocrats to enjoy an unprecedented prosperity—and to supply, via their graves, the museums of the modern world with some of the greatest art works of antiquity.

Etruria was at its height between 650 and 450 B.C., but repeated collisions with Greeks, Latins, Oscans, and Celts shattered its military power and the Etruscans entered into a period of eclipse, as did their allies, the Carthaginians.

[1]Like so many other ancient peoples, the Etruscans had the misfortune of having their history written for them by their conquerors, and although the Romans admitted their admiration of the Etruscans in a number of areas, they suppressed or ignored much evidence. Only after centuries of archaeological research has any independent witness been established at all.

Literature was not a well-developed aspect of Etruscan culture. Chronicles or simple histories of the individual cities existed and there is mention of an author of tragedies, but we know of no poetry, either epic or lyric. On the other hand, there was a body of seers and diviners, the *haruspices* (singular, *haruspex*), who, in the early period at least, passed on their learning by word of mouth and played a cultural role somewhat analogous to that of the druids in Celtic society. Etruscan religion like the religions of the Near East (but unlike those of Greece and Rome), was believed to have been revealed, and had a strong element of the ecstatic that both attracted and repelled the Romans. Officially the haruspices were held at a distance by the Romans and consulted only in times of extreme emergency. The Romans preferred the sober (and controllable) consultation of the Sibylline books to the prophets of Etruria.

The examination of the entrails of animals, particularly the liver, was one of the principal branches of the *disciplina Etrusca*—the Etruscan art of divination. It was assumed that the liver reflected the state of the world at the moment the sacrifice was made and was capable of revealing the will of the gods as well as the future to those who could read the signs. In the ancient Near East the art of examining livers had been reduced to a standardized technique and model terracotta livers were created to assist in the process of interpretation. In northern Italy, near Piacenza, a similar model liver in bronze was found in 1877. It was divided into 16 compartments with 24 inner divisions to which the names of various gods had been assigned. According to Cicero, the divisions on the left side of the liver of a sacrificial victim were unfavorable, those on the right were favorable. Markings and unusual shapes and colorations could then be given a positive or negative interpretation by the priest and the results passed on to the inquirer.

For the interpretation of thunder or lightning the heavens were similarly divided by the haruspex, who took a position facing south, divided the heavens into 16 portions, favorable and unfavorable, and then watched to see where lightning flashes began and ended, or from what direction thunder was heard. All aspects of life were governed in this fashion and rules were provided for the establishment of an orderly society by the pronouncements of the haruspices. The founders of cities, for example, and the builders of temples, public buildings, and private homes were guided by specific aspects of the discipline. In these cases the same principle of orientation applied and the land, which was first pointed out by some sign from the gods (such as the vultures seen by Romulus and Remus at the founding of Rome), was laid out according to a cosmic model. The purpose of this was to create a sacred space clearly distinguishable from the surrounding undifferentiated profane space, which was peopled by demons. Cities had a magic circle inscribed about them by means of a plough (such as the *pomerium* around Rome). This circle designated the enclosed area as holy and protected against evil influences by its resident deities. Contact with this space ensured the inhabitants a continuous source of power deriving from its sacred character.

From the Etruscans the Romans borrowed the technique of ascertaining the will of heaven, but not the personnel that went with it, the haruspices. Instead, the taking of the *auspices* (signs), as it was termed, was reserved to the elected magistrates, assisted if necessary by the college of *augurs*, which consisted of distinguished political figures, usually former magistrates, not professional priests. Julius Caesar, for example, was both an augur and a *pontifex*, or priest. The auspices had to be taken before any major decision was arrived at and there was a special spot on the Capitoline hill, the *auguraculum*, which was reserved for this purpose. All this was taken so seriously that, in the first century B.C., when a Roman noble built a house that blocked the view of the magistrate looking for signs in the sky from the *auguraculum*, the house had to be torn down.

From the Etruscans the Romans also learned the science of boundaries (*limitatio*), which they employed in setting up their colonies and dividing the territory of the surrounding countryside, an act that was both practical and religious. The results of these acts of land division can still be seen in many areas of the Mediterranean world today, especially in north Africa and the north of Italy where thousands of square miles are broken up into neat, rectilinear grids that pass over natural obstacles without interruption.

Architecturally the Etruscan temple differed from the Greek, which was free-standing and could be walked around. Instead, the Etruscans placed their temple on a high platform at the rear of a sacred enclosure. It had long, overhanging eaves and a high gable and the worshipper's attention was immediately focused on it when he entered the sacred place. This principle of placing a temple axially at the far end of an enclosure became a standard Roman architectural device and is to be found throughout the Roman world. In this arrangement the individual is subordinated to the order and symmetry of the buildings and to the gods of the state who inhabit them. Unlike the classical Greek arrangement of temples and buildings where man is the accepted measure of things, the Romans early came to place him in an orderly arrangement, symbolizing their belief that all men had preordained places in the scheme of life, places fixed by the gods and interpreted by the state.

The temple of Venus Genetrix dominates the Forum of Caesar (dedicated in 46 B.C.). The practice of placing temples at the end of long enclosures was borrowed from the Etruscans by the Romans and eventually became a standard architectural feature of cities throughout the Empire.

Unlike the Greeks, the Etruscans did not use stone, except for their tombs and tomb decorations, until the Hellenistic period. Their temples were of wood, surmounted by terra-cotta decorations, some of which have survived and are true masterpieces. Elaborately carved sarcophagi, the lid of which portrayed the deceased either lying prone or raised on an elbow, were popular. Whole cities of the dead were laid out in grid fashion after the style for cities of the living, and tombs were elaborately cut in the rock or piled over with mounds of earth. From these have come thousands of Greek vases from the archaic and classical periods, as well as Etruscan art productions. The tombs themselves are engineering achievements and have preserved their treasures in the damp earth of Italy almost as well as the tombs of Egypt guarded theirs.

Another medium in which the Etruscans excelled was decorative bronze work, which the Greeks admired greatly and imported in quantities. Surviving cups, lamp stands, candlesticks, tripods, incense burners, mirrors, and toilet boxes are among the finest examples of Etruscan art. Etruscan jewelry was superb and in their miniature techniques, the use of granulation and filigree, and the art of engraving, they were unsurpassed.

Although the Etruscans are sometimes credited with the invention or at least the introduction of the true arch, it was the Romans who first saw and developed its possibilities. Those arches we see in Etruscan tombs have a religious rather than an architectural significance. They are the gates to the underworld and have nothing to do with Roman arched bridges, aqueducts, or basilicas, which were introduced in the Hellenistic period.

ETRUSCAN ORIGINS

One of the great unresolved mysteries of the classical period is the origin of the Etruscans, and neither modern debate nor archaeology seems any closer to resolving the problem.

The culture that immediately preceded that of the Etruscans is known as Villanovan, an Italian version of the great Urnfield culture found north of the Alps that lasted from about the twelfth to the seventh century B.C. Urnfield culture, so called from the practice of burying the cremated remains of the dead in urns placed side by side by the hundreds, was one of settled agricultural communities of some size, producing cereals and using the traction plough in place of the hoe or digging stick. Initially employing bronze, Urnfield culture gradually switched to iron, the time of the change varying from place to place. Archaeologically, Villanovan sites show a well-developed society based on agriculture, and the surprise is that in Etruria they develop quickly and without interruption in the seventh century into the full-fledged, much admired Etruscan culture known to history. Every known Etruscan city is preceded by a Villanovan settlement, a fact that has led to the debate about whether the Etruscans are transformed Villanovans (a *nativist* theory) or whether the new culture needs to be explained by the arrival of immigrants from somewhere else, usually the east (the *invasionist* hypothesis).

In antiquity a historian of early Rome, Dionysius of Halicarnassus, advocated the first position, whereas Herodotus maintained that the Etruscans were transplanted Lydians from Asia Minor. There are undeniable affinities between Etruscan arts and practices and those of the east. *Tholos* tombs similar to those found at Mycenae and on Crete have been found in Etruria, and the practice of divination by means of the entrails of animals has parallels in Mesopotamia. Many artistic motifs are found in both areas. There is even an inscription in what appears to be Etruscan on the Aegean island of Lemnos which could, logically, have been the site of one of the stages of Etruscan western migration. Nevertheless, the possibility of the unbroken, peaceful evolution of Villanovan into Etruscan sites cannot be ignored, and the particularly rich development of the Etruscan cities after the seventh century can probably be best explained in terms of the exploitation by the natives of Etruria of the great metal deposits that happened to be in that part of the Villanovan world. Etruscan culture cannot have been transplanted as a whole from one part of the Mediterranean to another.

Neither the invasionist hypothesis nor the nativist hypothesis is fully convincing, and what needs emphasis is the fact that Etruscan civilization developed in Italy and in its fullness appears nowhere else. Whatever foreign elements made their contributions to the original Villanovans, the resulting culture was the response of a local community to local social and economic conditions, thereby effecting the transformation of both the natives and the external elements— whatever they may have been—at the same time.

The Latins and Early Rome

The powerful Villanovan culture that was the immediate predecessor of Etruscan civilization did not take over completely in Italy, and in Latium, just south of Etruria, some of the older forms of Apennine culture existed side by side with the new practices, along with contributions from southern Italy. The beginning of the Iron Age in Latium (eighth century) does, however, show a considerable increase in population, which may well have included newcomers, bearers of Villanovan culture. At any rate, a combination of the old and new forms produced in Latium the culture that was to be characteristic of the area down to the period of Etruscan occupation around 600 B.C. There is, therefore, nothing that can be identified specifically as "Roman" in the prehistoric period. The city that was to dominate Italy was no more than one of a number of villages occupying the many hills of Latium and struggling to maintain themselves against their aggressive neighbors, who periodically descended on them to raid or make temporary or permanent settlements. The Romans later recalled the arrival of the hillsmen from the Sabine country and the Etruscans from across the Tiber and the many other wandering groups within Latium itself who settled down to form a composite city on the hills overlooking the Tiber.

These hills were much steeper then than they are now and offered a refuge from raiding bands, floods, and wild animals. The archaeological picture from the tenth to the seventh centuries shows little villages crowding the tops of the hills, with their cemeteries on the hillsides or at the valley bottoms. In this loose, almost anarchic setting it is easy to imagine migrating clans, individual drifters, and families cast loose from other cities and regions settling on unoccupied lands and working out communal relations with similar groups of earlier settlers. In later times it was recalled that eight of the hills constituted a religious federation (deceptively called the Septimontium), and that their boundaries were marked by three bridges, which could be opened or closed at will, across the Forum stream. The god Janus was the protector of these bridges. When he finally received a dwelling place, the opening of the gates of his temple signified that the bridges were up and could not be crossed (war). Likewise, the closing of the gates meant peace—the bridges were down and the stream could be crossed.

Two of the most important hills, the Capitoline and the Quirinal, were omitted from the original Septimontium federation. This is in agreement with the tradition that they were occupied not by Latins but by Oscan-speaking Sabines who had their own traditions and religious practices and that almost from the beginning Rome was a twin city—a *geminata urbs,* in the words of the historian Livy.

ROMAN HISTORICAL TRADITIONS

The Romans, unlike the Greeks, had no recollections of Mycenaean greatness to associate with their origins and no Homer to transform their folktales into poetic legends and myths. The reverse was the case and the Romans frequently chose to emphasize the rusticity, simplicity, and heterogeneity of their beginnings.

Although the Romans were literate from the sixth century, it was a long time before they felt a need to organize the chaotic mass of legendary materials, folktales, archaic rituals and calendars, treaties, law codes, and family histories that constituted the source of their early history. So late were they in setting about this task that no generally acceptable date for Rome's founding was available until the first century, 400 years after the founding of the Republic and almost 600 years after the founding of the city.

The impulse to give a coherent explanation of their origins came in several stages. As the power of the Romans expanded they found themselves compelled to give some kind of intelligible account of themselves to their new neighbors and subjects, so that by about the mid-third century B.C. an established version of their beginnings began to emerge, though even at this elementary stage the Romans needed the assistance of the Greeks.

The problem was to fit the strictly local Latin and Roman traditions into the wider Greek view of things. For centuries the Greeks had plied the Mediterranean from one end to the other and had already worked out synchronous chronologies for the prehistories of most of the peoples they came in contact with, linking them with their own prehistory and such helpful, but vague

Coin issued by Julius Caesar around 47/46 B.C. showing Aeneas escaping from Troy carrying his father and a statue of Athena (the famous Palladium). Founding legends were taken very seriously by all ancient peoples and Caesar was able to put to good use the claim that his family, the gens Julia, *was descended from Aeneas and the goddess Venus.*

wanderers as Heracles, Jason, Odysseus, and Evander. The local peoples who knew no more than their own traditions, and even these not very well, were in no position to make such complicated linkups. They lacked the information and even the interest, but for the Greeks it was a passionate necessity to make sense and order out of the anarchic stories of the Mediterranean peoples. (See p. 213.)

A number of possible founders had already been put forward by the Greeks, including such figures as Odysseus. However, since a Greek founder was not favored by the Romans, they settled on another possibility, the Trojan hero Aeneas, and laboriously worked him into the chronology of Romulus, who may have featured in the native legend. Six additional kings were given schematic reigns to fill in the gap between Romulus and the traditional date of the founding of the Republic (509 B.C.): Numa Pompilius, Tullus Hostilius, Ancus Marcius, Tarquinius Priscus, Servius Tullius, and Tarquinius Superbus. The historical reality behind these kings is impossible to recover at this point. All we can say is that they probably represent early leaders of the developing community, of whom some were Sabine (Numa and Ancus), some Latin (Romulus and Tullus) and some Etruscan (the two Tarquins and possibly Serviu Tullius, despite his Latin-sounding name).

Combining the archaeological evidence with the traditions of the literar sources, we have the following four-stage process of development at Rome Stage 1, lasting from approximately 900 to 800 B.C., finds echoes in th mythology of the arrival of the Trojan hero Aeneas. Stage 2 covers the period o the foundation of the city, approximately 800–750 B.C., which corresponds to th legendary story of Romulus. At this time the Palatine and Forum areas of Rom show signs of habitation. The third stage (750–600 B.C.) includes the expansio of the Palatine and Forum areas and the development of the other hills—the cit of the legendary kings Ancus Marcius and Tarquinius Priscus. Finally, in the las decades of the seventh century and the early part of the sixth (ca. 625–575 B.C we have the archaic city under Etruscan influence. At this time all the village had coalesced to form a single entity, the city of Servius Tullius and Tarquiniu Superbus.

SOCIETY AND THE STATE IN EARLY ROME

Early Rome and the Kings

The Rome of prehistory, insofar as we can reconstruct it from archaeology and the social organization of the early Republic, was a loose federation of villages whose dominant units were the clans (*gentes*). These in turn were composed of families (*familiae*) who had associated with them groups of retainers known as clients (*clientes*) who were bound by special, nonlegal ties of faith (*fides*) to their patrons. Not all families, however, belonged to the clans. The head of the household had despotic powers over all those in it and was responsible for the perpetuation of the worship of the spirits of the ancestors and the care of their graves. The families, not the clans, were recognized as the basic units of society in the first law code of the Romans, and throughout the Republic they were the dominant elements in Roman society—conservative, persistent, cooperative, competitive.

The villages had their own internal organizations, the *curiae*, "collections of men," which existed to provide a forum for the discussion of community affairs, and to celebrate banquets and religious festivals in honor of their particular gods. Each *curia* was presided over by its president, the *curio*, who had the assistance of two attendants, a *lictor* and a *flamen*. Although largely dominated by the clans and their heads (the *patres*), membership in the curiae was open to the whole community.

Outside the organization of the clans was another group known as the *plebs*, but just who the plebs of early Rome were or where they came from is hard to say. Negatively we can say that the plebs were not the same as the "people" of Rome, since technically the term *populus* ("people") was applied to the Romans in a military sense to describe the armed people of the city. The best we can do is say that the plebeians were simply those outside the clan system. Again negatively speaking, we can say that originally no derogatory connotation attached to the term *plebeian* and plebeian names are to be found among the early kings and magistrates of Rome. Even some of the hills have plebeian names. The plebs simply existed alongside the clans and their retainers and were equally a part of the community. The classic battle between patricians and plebeians is of a later date, when some of the heads of the clans, as their individual power increased, claimed a special place for themselves in Roman society and called themselves the *patres* ("fathers") of the city, from which the adjective *patrician* (or "descendants of *patres*") derives.

As the villages grew and population increased, the need for some overall unifying organization began to be felt. This was initially supplied by the kingship and by the creation of three tribes from which the army was recruited and of which the curiae, ten per tribe, became subdivisions. Each curia was expected to supply 100 men, so the total size of the army was 3000 foot soldiers. There were also 300 cavalrymen who were recruited from the tribes directly. The infantry commanders, three in number, were known as military tribunes (*tribuni militum*).

Politically, the *curiae*, when gathered together, constituted a popular assembly known as the *comitia curiata* (Curiate Assembly), but it had no formal legislative, judicial, or electoral power. What it could do was register approval by shouting, as the Spartans did in their assembly. One of its most important acts was to indicate its approval of the new king, but there was no election involved and even the process of nomination took place elsewhere, in the Senate.

The Senate, whose origins are as difficult to determine as those of the curiae, tribes, or plebs, was apparently composed of the more influential among the heads of the families in the individual villages, whether patrician or plebeian,[2] and existed outside and above the other village organizations. As such it had no formal or constitutional position and its function was primarily consultative. On the other hand it had informal political power and was conceded an important role in the nomination of the king. When the ruling monarch died the auspices were said to return to the Senate, which meant that the Senate had the job of finding an individual acceptable to the gods as a replacement, and then inaugurating him with all due attention to the religious rituals with the assistance of the Curiate Assembly.

Eventually the king became the supreme judge, high priest, political leader, and general of the federal community, but in the beginning his role must have been primarily religious and magical, and his pronouncements in areas such as law would have received their authority from his priestly character, as was the case in so many primitive communities. In other words, the king's power rested principally on his right to consult the gods or take the auspices, a right that came directly from Jupiter when the king was properly inaugurated, rather than from any power conferred on him either by the Senate or the assembled people.

Etruscan Influence

When Etruscan power expanded in the early sixth century to include Rome, the power of the Roman kings was greatly strengthened and the villages became a true city organized on a systematic, rational basis. Attempts were made by the kings to check the growing power of the heads of the great families (the patricians) by the addition of new senators (the *patres conscripti*). A great building program was undertaken to consolidate popular support, and the greatest temple in Italy was erected to Jupiter on the Capitoline hill. A rampart was built around the city and the Forum area was drained and paved. Greek pottery flowed into Rome and the city's population expanded rapidly as it came to participate in the general prosperity of the Etruscan Empire, which was then at its height. For the first time the Romans, or at least some of them, became literate, and entered the general civilized world of Greek and Near East populations, with all that that implied for the ordering of the city, and the revamping of religious, political, and military institutions.

[2]It is to be emphasized again that these terms are used without the connotation they later acquired.

One of the most important lessons that the Etruscans taught the Romans was how to fight in the new Greek hoplite fashion, and this in turn led to the abolition of the old basis of the army, the feudal levy of the clans. In its place a property qualification became the sole criterion for military service. According to tradition it was the second to last king, Servius Tullius, who made this fundamental change, though this was not the complicated system that later Romans thought he established, but a simple division of the community into propertied and nonpropertied classes—in Roman terms, the *classis* and the *infra classem*. In addition, the old method of recruitment from the original three tribes was abolished in favor of purely geographical tribes. This meant that the control exercised by the clans over the tribes through the curiae was broken, and residence rather than birth became the new basis for recruitment. The original number of the tribes established by Servius Tullius is not known, but eventually there were 35 (4 urban and 31 rural).

The Republic

THE PATRICIAN STATE

The revolutionary changes brought about by the Etruscans get scant credit from the Romans, and by the late Republic it was an established convention to portray the kings as a series of progressively deteriorating monarchs, of whom the last, the Etruscan Tarquin the Proud (Tarquinius Superbus), was the worst.

In the Roman tradition, Tarquin is the stock tyrant of Greek moralistic writing: arrogant, brutal, and corrupt. He and his sister-in-law (his wife-to-be) conspire to kill first their respective spouses and then the ruling king—his paramour's father! The reign, begun with the shedding of so much blood, progresses from one outrage to another until finally a Roman nobleman by the name of Brutus ("the stupid") had the courage to organize a revolt and drive out the oppressors. With surprising smoothness and perfect unanimity two consuls were chosen to replace the deposed king, and so without bloodshed Roman freedom was won and all classes celebrated the event joyfully. The historian Livy makes the point, however, that this was a conditioned freedom. The anarchic Romans needed the discipline of the kings and were saved from the catastrophe of pure democracy and complete freedom by the reliable hand of the Senate and the annual election of dependable nobles. Understandably the theme of the expulsion of the Tarquins and the liberation of the Roman people became one of the heroic sagas of Roman history, providing endless material for dramatists, propagandists, and moralists.

The Romans, unfortunately, had no historian to deflate this grandiose interpretation of the fall of the tyrants as did Thucydides with a similar tale enjoyed by the Athenians, and were it not for the chance survival of some fragmentary outside sources we would have nothing to go on for the founding of the Republic but the self-serving version of the Roman aristocrats. These sources, however, enable us to see the expulsion of the kings in the wider

A coin of M. Junius Brutus issued around 54 B.C. proclaims "Liberty" on one side and "Brutus" on the other. Just as Caesar made much of his family connections with Aeneas, Brutus made propaganda of the fact that his ancestor had been responsible for winning freedom for Rome from the tyranny of the Tarquins.

background of a shifting series of alliances and leagues among Etruscan and Latin cities. It becomes clear that the Tarquins were expelled not by an internal uprising but in an encounter involving the Etruscan city of Clusium (under its king, Lars Porsenna) on the one hand, and Rome (under the Tarquins), the Latins, and the Greek city of Cumae on the other. It was under the protectorate of Porsenna, who expelled Tarquin from Rome, that the Republic came into existence. All the talk of liberty and deliverance from oppression was a later elaboration—just as the Athenian version of the liberators Harmodius and Aristogeiton sought to conceal the fact that it was a Spartan army and not Athenian patriots that liberated Athens. The exaggerated account of the reign of Tarquin and the emphasis on the smooth transition from the kings to the Republic was intended to play down the revolutionary implications of the dethronement of a legitimate king by force of arms. Aristocrats of the late Republic looked back and wondered if the early history of the city might not encourage other potential revolutionaries bent on proclaiming liberty for themselves against alleged oppressors. It was a tradition that could not be suppressed and the term *libertas* ("liberty") has an interesting history of its own in the propaganda of the warring political factions of the late Republic. Still, although the traditions of later periods may have distorted the account of the founding of the Republic, the event itself was a turning point in Roman history.

The new state embodied a fundamental opposition to the old and expressed this in the term *Republic* (*res publica*), which was set in opposition to the *kingdom* (*res privata* or *res propria*) of the Etruscan kings, who were depicted as regarding the state as their own private possession. The source of power was the people properly assembled (*iure sociati*), and the magistrates of the Republic were never above the state but part of it. When the Republic collapsed 500 years later, the early emperors were careful to hide the fact that the state had once more become the private realm (*res privata*) of a king, and fostered the belief in the continuation of the Republic.

Characteristic of the new state was a clear understanding of the need to separate religious from military and political authority. To carry on the religious duties of the kings the Romans created the King of Sacrifices (the *rex sacrorum*) who, like the kings, was solemnly inaugurated for life. Unlike them, he had no political, military, or judicial roles. He was the head of the priestly hierarchy but that was to be the end of his career. Apparently, he was not chosen by election, and the other functions of the king in political, judicial, and military matters passed to annually elected magistrates.

In the confusing days after the departure of the Tarquins the only force that could be depended on for stability was the army controlled by the aristocracy. More and more, in its legislative, judicial, and elective capacities, the army became the ruling body of the city. The first officers of the state seem to have been a group of magistrates called *praetors*, ruling in collegial Etruscan fashion, presided over by a *praetor maximus*. Later, two of the group were given preeminence and as *praetores majores* exercised power jointly. In this fashion what was later known as the consulate was gradually elaborated. It is unlikely that the Romans, as was once thought, invented on the spot the consulship as it existed in later times—a collegial office of two magistrates, elected annually, with equal powers. Instead, the stress of events, and particularly the demands of warfare, probably dictated the selection of two individuals from among the magistrates to provide leadership. In the course of the following half-century the constitutional aspects of the complicated working of two individuals, each holding supreme power but working closely together, was worked out. We do know that it was not until about 450 B.C. that the term *consul* began to be used, probably indicating a new awareness of the implications of the dual office.

The emergence of the new state was further signalized by the creation of a new civic center in the Forum, which had been a shapeless, indeterminate marketplace. First the king's house (the *regia*) was transferred there from the Palatine hill and became the place where the King of Sacrifices performed his functions. It was now no longer the inaccessible private dwelling of a king but the public residence of a magistrate, located in a public place. It was established in calculated relationship to the shrine of Vesta, goddess of the hearth, and the house of her ministers, the Vestal Virgins, also now transferred to the Forum, where the hearth of the new community was to be found. The king and the Vestals were conceived as continuing the offices and cults without which the state could not continue, but in a setting adjusted to the needs of the new community. In the old the king embodied the priestly, military, judicial, and political powers of the state, and these functions were viewed as inseparable and

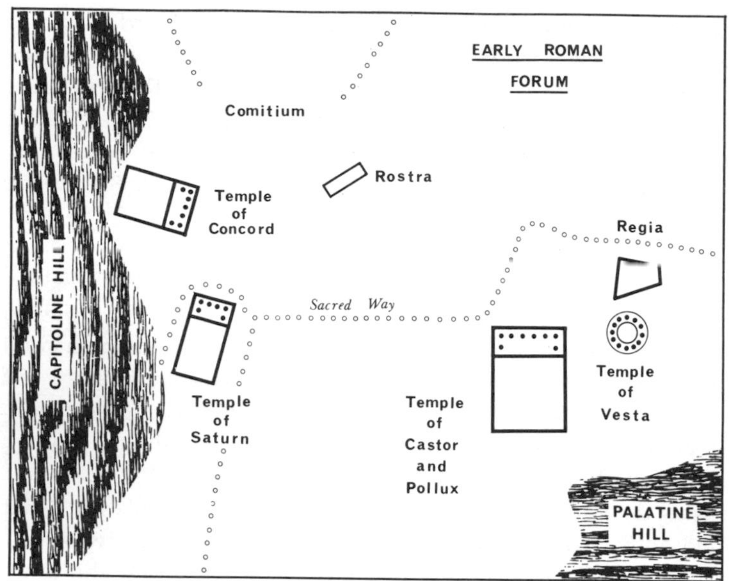

vital to its functioning. The new Republic preserved the functions but redistributed them in such a fashion as to bring about a thorough reorganization of the state without departing from its underlying religious concepts.

At the other end of the Forum from the regia and the shrine of Vesta, the *comitium*, or meeting place of the people, was created. Now the Forum had two poles, the one political and secular, the other religious, giving visible evidence of the existence of a new state based on a new set of presuppositions, the most fundamental of which was that the business of the community was no longer the private affair of an individual, but belonged to all the people—Rome was to be a Republic, not a monarchy.

The expulsion of the kings is one of the great turning points in Roman history. It is often neglected, but is comparable in its significance to the religious revival and realignment of the Republic in the time of Augustus or the adoption of Christianity by Constantine. The new state found expression in the beginnings of a new constitution, not fully elaborated but clearly different from that which preceded it, and in a religious reform. Both were materially expressed in the shape and form of the new Forum, which was to survive as an influential reminder of the change down to the end of the Roman Empire almost 1000 years later.

THE PLEBEIAN STATE

The new state, despite the achievement of selective borrowings from the past, was lacking in cohesiveness. By definition the revolution was a victory for the patrician clans, who took over when the Tarquins were unseated, but it was not necessarily a victory for the rest of society. The patricians through their clients and their special relations with one another dominated the Senate and the army and through them the state. The remainder of society—those outside the clan system or those not admitted to service in the hoplite army (the *infra classem*)—were excluded from political power. Because they were initially unorganized, they were unable to dispute the control of the patricians, which was complete for the period 500–450 B.C. and still predominant for a century afterward.

One of the principal problems faced by the dominant patricians was the tendency for powerful clans to carve out private realms for themselves at the expense of the community as a whole. The consequence was the weakening of the army, which depended upon a much wider base for support, and such exploits as the grandiose, single-handed attempt of the Fabian clan to do battle with the powerful neighboring Etruscan city of Veii were a blow to the effectiveness of the new state. There were other weaknesses, for within the army and the Senate were nonpatricians who were anxious to find a means of strengthening their position against the powerful patricians.

Pressures also came from outside Rome. Since the end of the sixth century, the Oscans had been pushing down from their crowded highland homes into the plains of Latium, and this time there was no organized Etruscan power to hold them back. In 474 B.C. the naval might of Etruria had been destroyed by the Greeks of Sicily. Before the end of the century, the Etruscans were to be driven out of Campania, their richest province. All of Etruria suffered the consequences and Rome along with it. After a promising beginning in the early years of the fifth century, the Roman building program came to an end. Imports from Greece soon stopped and Rome was faced with economic stagnation, increasing indebtedness among the lower classes, and general social unrest.

Although the patricians naturally gravitated toward their counterparts in the Etruscan cities, the Romans outside the patrician system were able to turn to a more sympathetic audience, the Greek cities of the south of Italy and the Greek traders who had an enclave on the Aventine hill in Rome itself. Coincidentally the fifth century was a time of constitution writing in Italy, and the town of Thurii received its laws from the hands of the great Protagoras during this period. Athenian influence in general was high in the west. Greek craftsmen and artists decorated the temple of Ceres, which was erected in 493, and were probably also involved in the spate of temple building at Rome that occurred around this time, including the temples of Jupiter Capitolinus (ca. 509), Saturn (497), Mercury (495), and Castor (484). It is against the background of these influences and the external problems faced by Rome that the development of the plebeian state is to be viewed.

THE PLEBEIAN REVOLUTION

When the pressures of the fifth century began to build at Rome, the declining manpower reserves of the patrician-controlled army forced the aristocrats to look for help to the people outside the system, the *infra classem*—whom for the sake of convenience we will call the *plebeians*, although the term did not have this precise significance then and was only later applied to the whole movement that brought the plebeian state into being.

Neither segment of society could function without the other, but the state was so set up and controlled by the patricians that there was little left for the plebeians. In the impasse a series of events opened the way toward a solution, much along the lines by which the consulate must also have evolved. Between 494 and 449 B.C. the plebeians hit upon a novel means of wringing concessions from the patricians. This was the process of secession, by which at crucial times when the aristocrats most needed help, the entire plebeian segment of society removed itself a short distance outside the city and continued to negotiate until the particular problem was resolved. In time the plebeians developed a sense of identity and began to view themselves as constituting a quasi-independent political community within the Roman state. From this consciousness derived the second major assembly of Rome, the Council of the Plebs (*concilium plebis*)—a parallel and alternate assembly to the patrician-controlled centuriate assembly. Unfortunately, we have no information on the details of this development, but the outcome was that the plebeians acquired a high degree of internal cohesion and began to elect their own officers, whom they called tribunes.[3] Eventually they established their own temple to their gods Ceres, Liber, and Libera and installed custodians called *aediles*. As the power of the plebeians grew and the volume of administration increased, archives were set up in the temple and the aediles were given responsibility for policing the city and supervising the markets near the harbor of Rome (the Forum Boarium on the Tiber). The tribunes and aediles were protected by a "sacred law" (*lex sacer*), which declared that anyone who violated their persons would be *sacer* ("sacred") or delivered to the gods for vengeance, and anyone could murder the offender without fear of retribution, divine or human. Initially two in number to oppose the two consuls, the tribunes grew to constitute a college of ten. Their purpose was to extend protection (*auxilium*) and if necessary intervene with their veto (*intercessio*) on behalf of plebeians threatened by the misconduct of the patrician magistrates or the assemblies they controlled. All this was done in the face of either stiff opposition from the patricians or their grudging consent. Initially organized as a way of introducing coherence to their deliberations, the plebeians were to see their creation become a standard part of the state machinery and their de facto acts acquire the force of law.

What we are witnessing in this development is on the one hand a commonsense kind of thing and on the other something quite revolutionary. Providing some kind of police system and supervising weights and measures in the marketplace was an act of self-help by the plebeians, something one might

[3]At a later stage of constitutional evolution the use of the *concilium plebis* for elections and legislation became common. When convened by a consul or praetor rather than a tribune, the Council was known as the Tribal Assembly (*comitia tributa*).

be led to expect considering the odd, heterogeneous beginnings of the city—what the state would not provide, the people themselves could. Similarly, the tribunes were initially seen as bargainers for the people, who would do their best to see that their followers did not suffer any violence, and only later did they become magistrates in their own right. In time all this became regularized by routine and the patricians were either too weak to interfere or sufficiently enlightened to take what they could get without a fight. Besides, there were those in the Senate among the nonpatricians who must have welcomed these developments, as well as perhaps a few of the more foresighted members of the patriciate itself. Whatever the process, the result was a constitutional innovation, a peacefully coexisting state within a state. This kind of successful sleight of hand, in which new structures were added without changing the old became a general characteristic of Roman statecraft and a useful way of making concessions when politics made more clear-cut reforms impossible.

The First Law Code

Under plebeian pressure constitutional development continued throughout the fifth century. The most significant sign of this development was the publication in midcentury of the first code of Roman law. This was done in a period of extreme stress by a group of ten extraordinary magistrates (the *decemvirs*) who took the place of the usual two to accomplish the task. Until this time Rome was governed by an unwritten code of customary law (the *mos maiorum* or customs of the ancestors), known only to, and administered by, the patricians. Now the laws were written down and made public so that all Romans could know what their rights were and how they could go about achieving them.

The code of laws, known as the Twelve Tables, created by the decemvirs has come down to us in fragmentary fashion. It was considered by the Romans to be the source of all law, private and public, governing such matters as the rights and duties of families, forms of marriage, inheritance, the definition of some crimes and the punishments attached to them, the right of appeal, and so on. It was learned by heart by generations of children and played a role analogous to the Magna Charta or the Bill of Rights. Some of its contents seemed archaic and even barbarous to later Romans (debtors could be killed or sold, arsonists were to be burned alive), but the general principle of establishing a single code that applied to all by a uniform process, and that was universally known, was a step of major importance. It represented a continuation of the conscious molding of institutions to serve the needs of the people rather than the tacit assumption that law was divine and outside the control of mortal men, requiring a sacred priesthood to administer it. This came to be reflected even in the use of language, where *ius*, the term for the secular concept of law, came to be applied to one body of law and *fas*, which was reserved for sacred law, was applied to another.

In other respects the Twelve Tables show efforts being expended to bridge the gap between the conflicting elements of the state. The ostentatious display of luxury in funerals, a practice the patricians shared with the Etruscan nobles, was restricted. Various crimes were mentioned and assigned specific penalties—another step toward curbing the arbitrary actions of aristocratic judges. Laws regulating debt were responses to the needs of the depressed small farmers. The extraordinary law prohibiting marriage between plebeians and patricians was not a return to an obsolete practice, but an innovation that, while attempting to preserve the patricians as a class, tacitly accepted marriage among all the other members of society, that is, among the vast majority of the population, since the patricians must not have been very numerous even at this time.

The Army and the Centuriate Assembly

The first indication of the success of the plebeian state and the effectiveness of the Twelve Tables in drawing patricians and plebeians together is to be seen in the reorganization of the army and of its political arm, the Centuriate Assembly (the *comitia centuriata*). In recognition of the growing manpower pool, the size of the army doubled, going from 3000 to 6000 men. The number of commanders correspondingly increased, the two consuls giving way in 438 to first three, then four, and finally six military tribunes endowed with consular power. To this command plebeians were admitted, until by 400 B.C. they were in the majority of those elected. The military tribunate lasted until 367 B.C. when the consulate was restored.

The political aspect of the army kept pace with its military reorganization and its expanding role in the community. The simple division of the state into property owners (the single class or *classis* of Servius Tullius) and those who were not property owners (the *infra classem*, those "beneath the class") was now developed considerably. The original class was subdivided into five classes—or, alternatively, four new ones were added to it. The expanded Centuriate Assembly consisted of the following groups:

	Assigned Votes
Cavalry	18
Class 1	80
Class 2	20
Class 3	20
Class 4	20
Class 5	30
Noncombatants	5
	193

In 443 B.C. a new office, that of the censor, was established to oversee the process by which individuals were assigned to the different classes. There was no suggestion of democracy in this new organization, since the number of unit votes, or *centuries*, was proportionate to wealth, not numbers, and the wealthy classes were assigned a sufficient number of votes so that any issue never

required more than the 18 centuries of cavalry (*equites*) and the 80 centuries of the first class. The vast majority of people were thus without influence in this assembly and the Romans were quite explicit about the de facto inequality of men. They recognized it in their political as well as their social and economic lives and deliberately assigned more influence to the wealthy. Votes, they said, should be weighed, not counted. The plebeians, although they struggled with the patricians for power, disputed not its basis but the way it was distributed. The expansion of the army gave the plebeians, for the time being at least, some of the power they wanted. Henceforth the army acting as the Centuriate Assembly became the principal legislative, electoral, and judicial body of the state, though for a long time legislative and electoral decisions required the ratification of the Senate (*patrum auctoritas*). The plebeians, for their part, continued to insist that the deliberations of their assembly, the *concilium plebis*, had the force of law.

The Patrician-Plebeian State

The beginnings of patrician-plebeian concord in the fifth century—which saw the publication of Rome's first law code and the emergence of the plebeian state—were interrupted savagely by the sack of Rome by the Gauls in 390 B.C. The resulting misery and economic dislocation unsettled the community and the struggle began all over again at a new level of intensity.

The main problems were those of land distribution, debt, and access to political office—a trio of problems that plagued all ancient societies. There was rarely anything unique about the problems themselves and the only variable factor was the different ways in which they were handled from one society to another. Sparta and Athens, for example, took a radical approach, whereas that of Rome was much slower and more conservative. As an expanding state, Rome was able to avoid facing these issues for some time. It was not until the Licinian-Sextian laws of 367 B.C. that the right of plebeian access to public land (i.e., land won by the state in war) was established. These laws also attempted to cover the problem of debt by decreeing that interest already paid should be deducted from the principal and the whole paid off in three years. Various attempts were made to cope with high interest rates and debt in the following years, but it was not until 326 (or 313) B.C. that the *lex Poetelia*, described by Livy as a new beginning of liberty, prohibited imprisonment for debt.

A vital issue settled in 367 was that of the admission of nonpatricians to the consulship. The problem here was not a law against the admission of these people, because no such law existed and plebeians had been elected to the consulship in the first half of the fifth century. What was involved was the breaking of what had become a de facto custom, which required a law for its reversal. Gradually, nonpatricians began to make their way into the highest offices and a new nobility, the patrician-plebeian nobility, emerged. Among the old families who were willing to cooperate with the rising plebeians were the Fabii, Aemilii, Sulpicii, and Servilii, who found compatible partners in the

Licinii, Sextii, and Plautii—names that were to appear regularly in the lists of Republican magistrates for the next three and a half centuries.

What was achieved in these years was the establishment of the principle that Rome was no longer to be ruled exclusively by individuals belonging to a hereditary caste. Whoever could battle his way upward, finding acceptance with both patricians and plebeians, could occupy Rome's highest offices. At a much later date Livy summed this up in his description of the thoughts that ran through the mind of Tanaquil, the ambitious wife of the Tarquin who became Rome's fifth king. She argued with herself that her husband was getting nowhere in their native Tarquinii. The people there despised him because his father had been a foreigner, a Greek, but if he would only go to Rome things would be different:

> Rome was a young and rising community; there would be opportunities for an active and courageous man in a place where all advancement came swiftly and depended upon ability [*ex virtute nobilitas*]. After all, King Tatius had been a foreigner—a Sabine; Numa had been called to the throne from his native Cures; Ancus had had a Sabine mother and no ancestor of noble blood with the single exception of Numa.[4]

Although obviously anachronistic and never of more than the most limited application, there was still a lot of truth in this summation, and with varying degrees of openness from century to century, Rome adhered to this principle throughout its history.

Plebeian access to other magistracies followed. The same year that the Licinian-Sextian laws were passed (367 B.C.), the number of commissioners who regulated various religious functions was increased from two to ten, of whom five were to be plebeians (the *decemviri sacris faciundis*). The *curule aedileship*, which was set up in 367 to share the administration of the city with the plebeian aediles, was soon open to plebeians also, and the important new office of praetor (established in 366), which took over the consul's civil jurisdiction for the city, was opened to them in 336 B.C. Other offices to which the plebeians succeeded in gaining admission were the dictatorship (a temporary emergency appointment) in 356 and the censorship in 351. It was not, however, until 300 that they achieved access to the important priesthoods of the pontiffs and augurs by the *lex Ogulnia*. In that year the number of pontiffs was raised from five to nine, and the number of augurs from four to nine, the additions in both cases being plebeians. Also in 300 B.C., at the end of a lengthy period of development and elaboration, the right of appeal to the people in capital cases and cases involving scourging was established by the *lex Valeria*.

Additional steps toward breaking down the exclusivity of the patricians came with the publication in 304 B.C., by the aedile Cn. Flavius, of a handbook of legal phrases and procedures (*legis actiones*), and the posting in the Forum of a

[4]Livy, *The Early History of Rome*. Tr. Aubrey de Sélincourt (Penguin Classics, 1960), p. 56. Copyright © The Estate of Aubrey de Sélincourt, 1960. Reprinted by permission of Penguin Books Ltd.

calendar that showed days on which public business could be transacted. These measures complemented and continued the reforms introduced by the publication of the Twelve Tables, since it was not only the law that was made public but also many of the secrets by which it was manipulated.

Part of the curtailment of the patricians and the increase in importance of the plebeians is reflected in the activity of the first great Roman statesman we can actually identify by name, Appius Claudius. As censor in 312 B.C. he allowed freedmen to enroll in the tribe of their choice and admitted sons of freedmen to the Senate. The first measure was probably directed toward resolving a problem occurring in newly incorporated territory that continued to be inhabited by its native population, some of whom would have been slaves. It was logical to allow these individuals, upon manumission and the acquisition of the Roman citizenship, to enroll in their own local tribes, instead of compelling them to register in the four urban tribes where their influence was greatly curtailed. This measure, which would have gone a long way toward breaking the control of local landlords, was reversed in 304 B.C., but was revived several times thereafter in the succeeding centuries. What to do with former slaves was an issue not easily resolved by the Republic.

The final step in the long history of the patrician-plebeian state came in 287 B.C., when the Tribal Assembly became the principal lawmaking body of the state and its decrees—or *plebiscites,* as they were called—acquired the force of law without needing the endorsement of the Senate. This law, the *lex Hortensia,* came as a result of over a century and a half of struggle. The final stage was arrived at only after several concessions, which suggests that the ultimate recognition granted in 287 had actually been won in part as early as the time of the decemvirate (451–450 B.C.). After 287 the decisions of the Tribal Assembly and the Centuriate Assembly were equal and bound all citizens, whether rich or poor, freeborn or freedmen. Henceforth the Tribal Assembly rather than the Centuriate Assembly became the principal legislative body of the state. At approximately the same time it acquired the right to ratify treaties with foreign powers and became a court of appeal for those who had been fined.

12

The Building of an Empire

THE GROWTH OF ROME IN ITALY

While the Greeks were repulsing the might of the east in the epic battles of the Persian Wars and forcefully checking the Carthaginians and Etruscans in Sicily and Italy, the Romans and their allies the Latins were having difficulty with the elementary but chronic problem of hillspeople migrating into the rich plains of Latium.

Early in the fifth century the Oscan-speaking Volsci had pushed all the way to the coast and as far north into Latium as Velitrae, only 20 miles from Rome. For most of the century, therefore, Rome's external concerns were with the movement of these peoples and the management of its sometimes difficult relations with the other members of the Latin federation to which it belonged. By about 400 B.C., however, the Volsci had been contained and Rome was off on a new venture: the elimination of the powerful nearby city of Veii.

In the following century local issues gave way to national ones as Rome and the Latins became involved in the strugggle for control of Italy among Etruscans, Celts, Samnites, and Greeks; from the struggle Rome, the least likely winner in the beginning, eventually emerged as victor. Thus, a little over two centuries of obscure wars and obscure diplomacy (ca. 500–290) brought Rome from the lowly position of a member in an unimportant league, to a position of dominance over the whole of Italy, having defeated, exterminated, incorporated, or made friends with a dozen or more formidable enemies.

Rome and the Latins

The ties that bound the villages and towns of Latium together—their common cult centers and language and their belief in a common origin—were much more strongly felt than similar ties among the Greeks. The cities of the latter had generally grown up in something close to isolation from one another in the small

plains, the landlocked harbors, and the islands of Greece, whereas the Latins were forced to live side by side in the wide-open plain of Latium. Their neighbors on all sides were foreigners with alien cultures and languages, and their ability to defend themselves lay in common effort rather than reliance on individual strength or the possession of inaccessible strongholds. The seven hills of Rome, in fact, offered little protection, and even as an individual city's territory and power expanded it became by that very fact more vulnerable to attack by outsiders.

As members of the loosely organized Latin League the cities of Latium from time immemorial had shared certain reciprocal rights: the rights *(iura)* of marriage, commerce, and probably also migration. Citizens of Latin cities could make contracts with Roman citizens and depend on Roman courts for their enforcement, and a Roman could have courts in Latin cities protect his rights. These rights were particularly important in the matter of marriage because citizenship was closely associated with parentage and the transmission of property depended on the recognition of citizenship. In Athens after Pericles, for example, both parents had to be Athenian to guarantee their children citizenship. In Latium, by contrast, citizens of different states could freely intermarry with full testamentary and paternity rights. It is also generally assumed that Latins could migrate and settle in one another's cities, acquiring in the process the citizenship of the new state without forfeiting the right to return to their places of origin. This early conditioning in openness was fundamental to Rome's ability to expand outward, progressively incorporating first its Latin neighbors, then the peoples of Italy, and eventually the whole Mediterranean world. The early stages of these developments are worth pursuing in some detail because it was then that Rome stumbled on some of the most fundamental techniques of the unique form of imperialism it was to use time and again in later stages of its Mediterranean expansion.

Early Roman historians, intent on making Rome great from its earliest days, depicted it as the supreme power in the Latin League from the time of the kings. However, even with Etruscan hegemony of the city and control of the land route between Etruria and Etruscan holdings in Campania, there is no need to assume that Rome dominated all the Latin cities. Rome remained in the league even under the Etruscans, and it was only after their expulsion with the help of Clusium and the subsequent battles with the league after the founding of the Republic that Rome found itself at odds with its old allies. As it turned out, the Latin cities were in no position to impose special conditions on Rome's return to the league, as they needed Rome's support against the most recent and significant descent of the hillspeople into Latium, in which all the territory from the interior mountains to the sea at Terracina and Antium fell under the control of the Oscan-speaking Volsci. The Romans in turn needed the shield of Latin cities to the south in order to concentrate on the Etruscans in the north, so both sides were bound by mutual interest to keep the other as strong as possible. Accordingly, the Latins and Romans renegotiated the terms of their relationship in what is known as the Cassian Treaty *(foedus Cassianum)* in 493 B.C. At a later date the Romans were to attempt to claim that the treaty explicitly conceded them supremacy in the league.

The wars of the Latins and Romans against the Oscans are told with much embellishment by Livy and feature such legendary figures as the traitor Coriolanus, who led the Volsci to the gates of Rome (491 B.C.), and the hero Cincinnatus, who was called from his plough to defeat another Oscan tribe, the Aequi, at Mount Algidus in 458 B.C. But even Livy cannot conceal the un-epic character of these conflicts. By the end of the century the threat had come to an end and Rome was able to divert its attention to an old feud with the nearby Etruscan city of Veii. At issue was control of the salt-pans at the Tiber mouth, and also of the route by which the salt was conveyed inland, the Via Salaria. Initially the Romans wrestled with Veii for possession of Fidenae, the only other crossing of the Tiber in its lower reaches, and then they attacked Veii itself. After a long siege the city fell to M. Furius Camillus in 396 B.C. According to legend, when Camillus saw the great quantity of loot from the captured city, he prayed that Rome's good luck would not provoke the envy of men or the gods, but he stumbled inauspiciously as he was pronouncing the words, and only six years later Rome fell to a band of marauding Celtic warriors.

The Sack of Rome

By 600 B.C. Celtic culture had spread throughout most of central Europe and France (the so-called Hallstatt phase, ca. 700–500 B.C.). Another major period of Celtic expansion (the La Tène phase) began about the middle of the fifth century and around 400 B.C. armed bands of Celts poured across the Alps into the Po Valley and routed the Etruscans living there. At the same time the Greek city of Syracuse, under its energetic leader Dionysius, was pressing from the south and was at war with the Etruscan city of Caere, which was friendly to Rome. In the midst of these events, the appearance of the Celts in the rear of the Etruscans gave an unexpected boost to the Greeks. According to one version the Celts even sought them out to propose joint action. In this context the rout of the Romans by the Gauls (the name given the Celts by the Romans) at the battle of the Allia in 390 B.C. and the subsequent destruction of Rome may not be as haphazard as they appear from the Roman sources, which ignore events elsewhere in Italy and make Rome the focus of the Celtic invasion.

Psychologically the effect of the sack of Rome by the Celts must have been devastating. Undoubtedly the Romans at this time reflected on the relentless pressures of the Oscan highlanders during the preceding century and on the often demonstrated undependability of the Latin League, and resolved to free themselves from these dangers in the future. Prompted by these motives they initiated a period of expansion that ultimately provided them with safe frontiers, far from Rome and even far outside Italy itself.

The End of the Latin League

The immediate effect of the sack of Rome on Rome's external relations was its loss of control of the Latin League, which went its own, independent way until 358 B.C., when the Cassian Treaty was once more enforced. During this time Rome found allies elsewhere—in Etruria, among the cities of Campania, and with the Samnites of central Italy—among peoples who viewed Roman imperialism as a lesser threat than the marauding bands of Gauls. The Etruscans, in particular, were losing ground throughout Italy. Their naval power was destroyed by the Sicilian Greeks off Cumae in 474 B.C., and by 400 they had lost Campania—their richest possession—to invading Oscans. By midcentury they were driven out of the Po Valley by the Gauls, who remained a constant threat on their northern and northeastern frontiers. By contrast the Samnites were just entering the period of their greatest power.

The alliance with the Samnites in 354 B.C. came at an opportune moment for Rome. For years the Latins had anxiously watched Rome grow beyond what seemed to them its proper place in a league of equal city-states, and in an attempt to alter the changing relationship before it was too late the Latins revolted in 340 and were joined by the cities of Campania. Both were quickly overwhelmed by the Romans with the assistance of their new allies, the Samnites, and in 338 the war came to an end. What ensued is one of the epoch-making events in Roman history, for instead of the confiscations and expropriations to which defeated enemies were usually subjected, the Romans treated their old allies in quite a different manner. To appreciate this it is necessary to review the stages by which Rome arrived at what was to become, after 338, a standard feature of Roman statecraft throughout its subsequent history.

MUNICIPIA

Since the sixth century, the nearby Latin city of Gabii enjoyed an unusual relationship with Rome, ratified by a treaty which according to first-century antiquarian Dionysius of Halicarnassus, could still be seen in his time in the temple of Dius Fidius in Rome. By the terms of the treaty citizens of Rome were full citizens of Gabii, and more important, those of Gabii were full Roman citizens, to the extent that as early as 422 B.C. a citizen of Gabii by the name of Antistius may have been elected a tribune of the plebeians at Rome. Local government was left intact at Gabii.

Before 340 B.C. another Latin town, Tusculum, was incorporated in a similar fashion, and L. Fulvius Curvus, the consul of 322 B.C., was the first of a long series of citizens from there to appear in the Roman list of magistrates. Finally, Caere, a neighboring Etruscan city, which had extended asylum to Roman exiles and to the Vestal Virgins (who had carried with them Rome's sacred objects for safekeeping) during the Gallic invasion, was granted the right of public hospitality. This right guaranteed Caeritans in Rome all the rights of Roman citizens without any of the obligations such as taxes or military or public service. All these were apparently ad hoc arrangements, which the Romans, because of their special knowledge of the internal situation of the cities concerned, could assume in advance would work. In the case of the Latin cities (Gabii and Tusculum), the barriers were less significant, and the Romans could extend full citizenship rights; with the Etruscans of Caere there was a more guarded conferral of rights. Caeritans did not have to serve in the army; but they could not run for office either.

These precedents provided Rome with practical alternatives when it was casting around after the war for substitutes to the Latin League, which had by now outlived its usefulness. The first step was to dissolve the league. Then, four of its former members were selected for complete incorporation in the Roman state, with grants of full citizenship *(civitas optimo iure)* but without the abolition of local government or laws. Henceforth, the inhabitants of these cities, like the inhabitants of Gabii, enjoyed dual citizenship and were subjected to both taxes and military service while exercising the privilege of full participation in the Roman political process. Next, the precedent of Caere was extended to a string of Oscan towns in Latium and Campania. These were partially incorporated within the Roman commonwealth and their inhabitants were granted Roman citizenship, but they did not have the power to vote in the assemblies *(civitas sine suffragio*—citizenship without the vote.) Technically these newly incorporated cities were known as *municipia.*

COLONIES

Two other governing techniques came into use at this time and became, with the two just outlined, standard Roman methods of coping with the problem of newly acquired territory and non-Roman or non-Latin populations. First, nine Latin cities were left as independent states forming a ring of border fortresses around the newly extended Roman territories. Citizens of these states kept their Latin citizenship as in the past and had reciprocal relations of commerce and marriage *(commercium* and *conubium)* with Rome, but not with one another. In addition, the Romans continued a practice long in use by the Latin League: the founding of colonies in newly acquired inland areas that required fairly large numbers of settlers for security. The league had regularly done this in the past as a joint action whereby on recently conquered land a completely new city-state was established, made up of citizens from all the members of the league, including Rome. This practice was continued and extended so that colonies were eventually placed in key locations throughout Italy, to become the foundation of Roman power in the peninsula. The attractiveness of the Latin colonies was the fairly sizable grants of land that went with them, though at least for Romans there was a drawback: Their citizenship was changed (or reduced) from Roman to Latin, and they could no longer serve in the legions or participate in political life in Rome. They could regain the citizenship, however, by leaving the colony and settling permanently once more in Roman territory.

The second technique was a modification of the first. This consisted in establishing small groups of Roman citizens (usually about 300 families) in coastal areas that needed a resident garrison. These small colonies, which were known as Roman colonies to distinguish them from the larger Latin colonies, were ultimately established at many points on both the Adriatic and Tyrrhenian coasts and became models for the establishment of Roman colonies overseas. Citizens who joined these colonies did not lose their Roman franchise and were freed from service in the legions, though this was no great concession since they were on permanent garrison duty anyway. The grants of land were small and local government was elementary, again in contrast to the fully organized city life of the Latin colonies. Inhabitants remained subject to the control of the magistrates in Rome.

These techniques, in which towns were granted full Roman citizenship *(civitas optimo iure)* or partial citizenship *(civitas sine suffragio)*, or by which Romans and Latins were established in colonies in new territories, were consciously employed as a means of settling the complaints of the Latins that they were being treated unequally, while at the same time preserving the city-state structure of both Romans and Latins. The colonies were also useful safety valves for surplus population in the home states. It was an achievement in federal organization that allowed for a maximum degree of flexibility and adjustment to local differences, without endangering the solidity of the state as a whole. The direction of military and foreign affairs was the responsibility of the federal government at Rome, and was open in varying degrees to those desiring to share in it from outside the city. Local government, on the other hand, was left intact except for the functions mentioned, and was exclusively in the hands of the elected magistrates of the individual city-states.

From Rome's viewpoint the solution of 338 B.C. was enormously advantageous. Directly or indirectly, by whole or partial grants of citizenship, Rome added over 200,000 new citizens to its population (a 42 percent increase) and over 300 square kilometers to its territory (a 37 percent increase.[1]) All of Latium and Campania, two of the richest and most developed areas of Italy, now constituted the basis of Roman political and economic power. With these resources Rome was able to control successfully the ever-present threat of the central highlanders who had never previously been handled by anyone, and eventually fight Carthage to a standstill for control of the Mediterranean.

The Samnite Wars

The most powerful single state in the Italian peninsula in the second half of the fourth century was the Samnite federation. Strategically located on a saddle of mountain land overlooking two of the major plains of Italy, Campania and Apulia, Samnium was in a position to dominate all of central and southern Italy. By the mid-fourth century it was well on the way to doing so. Previous Oscan incursions from the highlands had swept the Greeks and Etruscans out of Campania (with the exception of Naples), but when Rome incorporated the Campanians in its commonwealth in 338 B.C. the Samnites were confronted for the first time by an organized block of people reaching from south of Naples to Etruria. In addition, Rome had interests in Apulia, into which the Samnites were infiltrating, where the cities of Arpi and Luceria had requested Roman help. The great conflict was thus a struggle between the urbanized, agricultural populations of the plains and the pastoral highland peoples. For almost a generation the wars dragged on—bloody, confused, unending.

The main struggle took place in two phases: between 326 and 304 and between 298 and 290. Strategically, Rome's problem was to avoid being caught between the Samnites to the south and its other enemies, the Gauls and Etruscans, to the north. Very conscious of the possibility of a double envelopment that would necessitate fighting on two fronts, Rome went to great lengths to secure peace on its northern frontier while contending with the Samnites on the south. Almost to the end Rome was successful in this task, and when the Gauls and Etruscans finally did join in the fighting it was too late to make any difference.

The initial phase of the war saw Rome attempting direct assaults on the Samnite mountain stronghold from Campania, and failing miserably. The battle of the Caudine Forks in 321 B.C., which resulted in a whole army being forced to surrender, was in the opinion of the Romans their worst defeat in history. Subsequently, the connecting links with Campania, the Via Latina and the Via Appia, were cut, and several colonial outposts overwhelmed. With the failure of this strategy, Rome turned to another and this time found a way to take Samnium from the rear.

The new approach involved a series of diplomatic and military moves

[1]Figures from Arnold J. Toynbee, *Hannibal's Legacy*, vol. 1 (London, New York, Toronto: Oxford University Press, 1965), p. 134.

across the peninsula to the Adriatic, so that Roman armies could march down the coast into Apulia to the rear of the Samnites, where they established a colony at Luceria in 315 B.C. Other colonies were planted as fortresses on the other side of Samnium (Alba Fucens and Carseoli), and so instead of Rome being enveloped it was the enemy that was surrounded. The last major battle was fought in Sentinum in 295, where the Romans confronted and defeated a coalition of Samnites, Gauls, and Etruscans; five years later peace was made between all the contending parties.

Rome immediately set about consolidating its hold by founding new colonies and extending the road system. The solid band of territory across the peninsula Rome now held provided internal lines of communication, and allowed troops to be moved quickly from one front to another. Rome was now the dominant power in Italy. It could isolate potential enemies in the north and south and concentrate its forces against one while holding off the others. Apart from these military, strategic, and diplomatic advantages, Rome was seen throughout most of the Samnite Wars as the defender of the urban—agricultural populations against the infiltrating mountaineers. It was this threat, in fact, that had first involved Rome with the Campanians, and the process was shortly to be repeated with the Greek cities in the south.

Tarentum and Pyrrhus

Rome's appearance in Apulia put it into competition with the Greeks of Tarentum and the protectorate they attempted to maintain over the other Greek cities of the south. Granted the usual feuding both within Greek cities between upper and lower classes, and among Greek cities themselves, it was inevitable that some party supply the impetus or at least the pretext for Rome to intervene directly and displace Tarentum's protectorate with its own.

In 282 B.C. the aristocrats of Thurii appealed not to Tarentum but to Rome for help against the Oscans of Lucania, and Rome responded by supplying a garrison of Roman troops. About the same time four other Greek cities were similarly garrisoned. Tarentum retaliated by sinking part of a Roman flotilla that entered its waters and appealing for help to one of the great military adventurers of the post-Alexander world, Pyrrhus of Epirus. Hopeful of duplicating Alexander's eastern conquests in the west, Pyrrhus arrived with an expeditionary force in 280 B.C. and announced, by way of justification, that as a descendant of Achilles he was waging a second Trojan War on behalf of the Greeks against the (Trojan) Romans. In two battles in 280 and 279 at Heraclea and Asculum, he defeated Roman armies but not without serious losses to his own troops. Attempts at negotiation failed and the Romans, encouraged by their allies the Carthaginians, rejected proposals for a confederacy of southern Italy of which Tarentum would be the head. Never one to remain for long at any task, Pyrrhus left to help the Sicilians clear the island of Carthaginians. When this expedition failed he returned to Italy, where in his third battle with the Romans, near

Beneventum in 275 B.C., he was defeated and forced to withdraw from Italy. Three years later Pyrrhus removed his garrison from Tarentum and the city fell to the Romans.

With the fall of Tarentum Rome's conquest of the peninsula, except for the barbarous north, was complete. There was no power left to challenge Rome, and its general defense of the urban populations against traditional enemies of the Greeks of Italy—the Oscans and the Gauls—won Rome esteem in the eyes of Greeks throughout the world. Pyrrhus was one of the most colorful characters of the period and his military abilities were not taken lightly by either Greeks or Macedonians. Roman success against his elephants, cavalry, and infantry was evaluated accordingly. A delegation from Ptolemy Philadelphus arrived in 273 B.C. bearing gifts, and Greek historians such as Duris and Timaeus took note of the new power rising in the West. Timaeus picked Rome as the defender of Greek liberties against that other traditional enemy of the Greeks, Carthage, and made a synchronism between Rome's and Carthage's founding dates to lend dramatic emphasis to his point.

THE PUNIC WARS

Carthage, like Rome, had grown considerably since both cities made their first treaty (see below) in 509 B.C. By the time of their clash in the third century Carthage had come to dominate all the Phoenician cities in Africa, and possessed a maritime empire reaching from Ptolemaic Egypt to the Atlantic. It was renowned for its wealth and the stability of its constitution, which Aristotle so admired that he included it in his collection of constitutions as the only non-Greek example.

Carthage's wealth depended not only on its mercantile activities but also on its rich agricultural hinterland, from which food supplies were exported to the urbanized Greek east. The city was ruled by a wealthy oligarchy; the masses of the people, exempt from military service and cared for by rich patrons, lacked the political consciousness of the Greeks and Romans and were known for their submissiveness. Military and civilian powers were separated, not for any theoretical reasons, but because commerce was the predominant way of life at Carthage. Generals were elected and held office for as long as was necessary for them to accomplish their missions. Failure was treated with great harshness and unsuccessful commanders were frequently crucified.

Among the legacies the Etruscans left Rome was the alliance with Carthage, based on a lack of competing interests and shared enemies. Initially the differences were marked. Rome's wealth, such as it was, lay in agriculture. Its military power consisted of heavy infantry, and its immediate concerns were with Italy. Carthage's interests, on the other hand, were maritime and commercial, and its military power lay in its navy. In the course of time the situation changed, and the success of each power in enlarging its respective sphere of influence inevitably brought them into confrontation. With the advantage of hindsight, Livy was to comment that Rome's involvement with Campania led to the war with Pyrrhus and that in turn led to the wars with Carthage. It was not a calculated collision; both powers edged their way into the conflict and there was no careful weighing of national interests and realizable war aims.

The First Punic War (264–241 B.C.)

The occasion for the conflict arose, as might be expected, in southern Italy and Sicily where Roman and Carthaginian interests were beginning to overlap. In the past an internal squabble in a Sicilian city might have meant little to Rome, but with its involvement in southern Italy its sensitivity to such events expanded proportionately.

Campanian mercenaries in the service of Syracuse had revolted and seized the city of Messana. In 264 B.C. they were hard pressed by Hiero of Syracuse and different factions within the city appealed to the Romans and Carthaginians for help. The Carthaginians were closest and got there first, putting a garrison in the citadel.

At Rome the request for aid caused a major debate. Some saw the Carthaginian seizure of Messana as a prelude to an attempt to end the old balance of power between Greeks and Carthaginians in Sicily by a complete victory for the Carthaginians. The fact that Messana was only a few miles from Italy and lay deep in traditional Greek territory, coupled with the fact that the Carthaginians already occupied Corsica and Sardinia, would convert the entire Tyrrhenian Sea into a Carthaginian lake. Others had a personal interest in the Campanian mercenaries who were in control of Messana, and in southern Italy in general. Campania had been part of the Roman commonwealth for three-quarters of a century and Campanian senators, the Atilii and Ogulnii, for example, were powerful in Rome at this time. It might have been argued that the Romans had more in common with the Greeks of Sicily than with the Carthaginians, their erstwhile allies. In the impasse, the decision was passed to the people, who, according to biased aristocratic sources, were swayed by greed in favor of war against Carthage.

The Romans entered this conflict with a number of unresolved problems, the first of which was the question of realistic war aims. Should they restore the balance of power in Sicily? This would be a minimum achievement. Should they drive the Carthaginians out of Sicily altogether or even, at the outside, attempt an assault on Carthage itself? Since there had never been a need to debate these matters there was no clear thought on how the war should be waged and events dominated the early years of the conflict. After initial victories on land in Sicily the Romans, following in the footsteps of Pyrrhus, began to push the Carthaginians back into the west of the island, only to discover that this could never be more than temporarily successful as long as the Carthaginians held on to their main ports, Lilybaeum, Drepana, and Panormus (Palermo). It was then that the necessity of a navy became apparent, though at this stage the implications of such a commitment had not been thought through. With surprising lack of hesitation the Romans brought a fleet into being (260 B.C.) and even circumvented the superior seamanship of the Carthaginians by transforming battles at sea into land battles by the invention of a device called the *corvus*, a gangplank that also acted as a grappling iron locking two ships together, allowing Roman marines to make quick work of their opponents. With the creation of the fleet and the achievement of tactical superiority over the Carthaginians, the slow process of siege and blockade began. Ultimately this approach was to bring victory, but not before the Romans attempted some shortcuts that threatened the whole concept of naval power.

In 256 B.C. Rome sent an expedition against Carthage itself in the hope of concluding the war quickly. It failed, and Roman naval power was decimated by storms and mishandling, so that by 249 B.C. Rome was back where it started. For the following eight years the war languished until by one supreme effort a new fleet was created and the blockade resumed. The Romans won a naval battle off the Aegates Islands and Carthage, exhausted and unable to supply its forces in Sicily, including those of its most successful commander, Hamilcar Barca, agreed to negotiate (241 B.C.). The settlement resulted in the loss of Sicily, the payment of an indemnity, and various other clauses, which the Romans used as a pretext shortly afterward to seize Corsica and Sardinia.

The first war with Carthage, called the First Punic War, revealed the strengths and weaknesses of both sides. Rome suffered from incredibly inept generalship, because of its system of annual rotation in office and the resulting lack of consistent strategy. Rome's tenacity, manpower reserves, and willingness to seek victory, however, contrasted with Carthage's half-measures and its dependence on mercenaries. Roman luck made a difference too, and its ally, Hiero of Syracuse, more than once helped out in bad times.

Between the two rounds of wars (264–241 and 218–202 B.C.), the Romans

Reconstruction of a Carthaginian warship of the time of the first Punic War found sunk off the coast of Sicily. The wreck, along with the remains of a sister ship, was found in 1971–1973. Both had been recently constructed and the hold of the one illustrated contained a cache of cannabis sativa. *The discoverers of the ships speculate that it was used to help the rowers endure the agony of their long hours at the oars.*

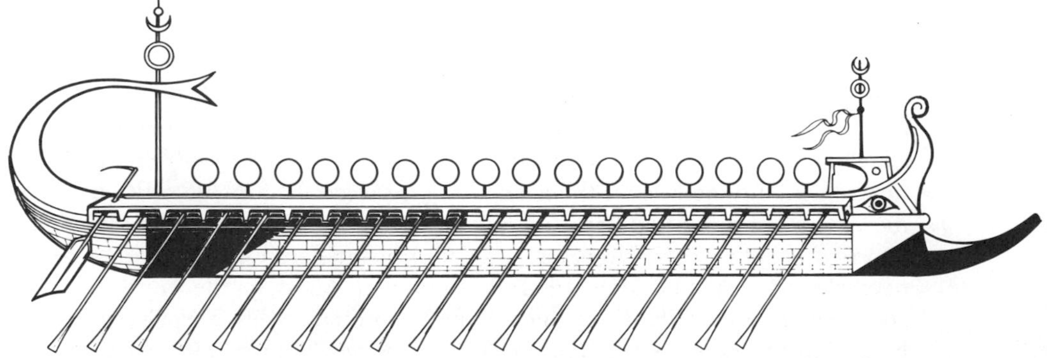

and the Carthaginians became deeply involved in their own affairs. In the Adriatic, Rome put down the pirates of Illyria who were terrorizing the Greek coastlands, and replaced Macedonia, supreme since Philip and Alexander, as the power to be reckoned with in this area. Shortly afterward, the Gauls, who had been quiet all during the war with the Carthaginians, began a major rebellion and advanced on Rome. Terrified, the Romans resorted to human sacrifice and the consultation of the Sibylline books, but finally succeeded in defeating the Gauls at Telamon in 225 B.C. This victory gave the Romans the opportunity to finish off the Gallic threat, and a series of campaigns was launched against the Gauls' homeland in the Po Valley. Colonies were established at Cremona and Placentia (Piacenza), but before the task was completed the second war with Carthage broke out. Twenty years elapsed before the Romans renewed their efforts in the north. The Carthaginians were also engaged in expansion, and under the energetic Hamilcar Barca began the resubjugation of Spain and the exploitation of its physical and human resources. Hamilcar, his son-in-law Hasdrubal, and his son Hannibal established close relations with the Spanish natives, and the last two, following Carthaginian custom, intermarried with Spanish royal houses. The Barcid dynasty in Spain grew in power and the attention of the Romans was frequently drawn there by Rome's ally Massilia (Marseilles).

The War with Hannibal (218–202 B.C.)

The pretext for the outbreak of the war was found in an attack by Hannibal on Saguntum over which the Romans claimed some kind of protectorate, although the city lay well within the Carthaginian sphere of influence. An ultimatum was rejected by Carthage and as soon as Hannibal heard the news, he marched his army out of Spain, through France and across the Alps into Italy.

The strategy employed in the Second Punic War was largely dictated by the results of the first. The Carthaginians, recognizing that Rome could only be defeated on land, conceded control of the seas to Rome; the Romans for their part planned to continue where they had left off in 241 B.C., using Sicily as a base to invade Africa, while blockading a Carthaginian invasion from Spain. Hannibal upset this plan by slipping past the Roman forces into Italy, thereby forcing the cancellation of the war in Africa. His strategy was based first on the assumption of Hellenistic warfare that a thoroughly professional general leading professional troops could defeat an amateur citizen levy, and second on the presumption that as a result of defeats in the field the Roman confederation, like all other leagues, would disintegrate. In the first instance Hannibal proved to be correct, though the element of his own genius was a factor that outweighed the others and made textbook cases out of his battles, confronting the Romans with a threat they had never faced before.

From 218 onward Hannibal remained unbeaten and one great Roman defeat followed another, of which Cannae in 216 B.C. was the greatest. But then the weight of history began to tell as Hannibal came up against the Roman conquests of the past century that divided Italy into two halves, giving the Romans internal lines of communication and preserving intact the heartland of Roman influence. Hannibal was kept in the south, the Gauls were fended off in the north, and although individual cities might revolt as did Capua and Tarentum, Hannibal could not prevent their recapture. Nor could he capture Rome itself. His army was not large enough and it lacked siege equipment. Roman colonies continued to perform the function they were assigned to perform, as self-sustaining fortresses in enemy country, and Roman roads allowed the legions to be shifted from front to front with rapidity. With its fleet, Rome could bring in supplies and deny them to Hannibal. Still, these advantages would not have beaten Carthage had it not been for victory in other theaters of the war and the emergence of a Roman military genius, P. Cornelius Scipio.

Scipio's first successes came in Spain, where he drove out the Carthaginians (210–205 B.C.) and established his reputation as a mystic and a general of the caliber of Hannibal. Given the opportunity to invade Africa he forced the withdrawal of Hannibal from Italy and then defeated him in a pitched battle at Zama in 202 when for the first time the Romans achieved cavalry superiority in the field. Carthage surrendered all overseas possessions and all but ten warships, and agreed to pay a huge indemnity and not to wage war in Africa without Rome's consent. Rome won because it was able to compel Carthage to fight on Roman terms, even though the genius of Hannibal averted defeat for years. Rome's control of the seas forced Hannibal to march overland to Italy, prevented Philip V of Macedonia, an ally of Hannibal from 215 B.C. onward, from effectively aiding him, and allowed the final assault on Africa to take place with ease from Sicily. The Romans could bring supplies into Italy from all over the Mediterranean while denying the Carthaginians the same facility. In Scipio they finally found a leader who raised their citizen soldiers to new levels of technical ability, introduced new weapons and sophisticated new tactics, experimented with mobile tactical units (cohorts), and passed on a legacy of brilliant generalship.

SOCIETY AND THE STATE IN THE MIDDLE REPUBLIC

Modern democracies pride themselves on the fact that, legally at least, citizenship in their states is a very simple matter. An individual is or is not a full citizen. There are no intermediate or secondary classifications. If a person is a full citizen, except in certain instances, he has all the rights and privileges enjoyed by his fellows and can claim equal treatment under the law. How this works in practice, and especially how this relates to the exercise of political power, is a different matter, but in essence this is how the system is supposed to work. In Roman society, on the other hand, the inequality of everyday life—economic, social, and even cultural—was built into the formal structure of society itself.

In the Republic members of the Roman state could be full citizens or citizens without the right to vote or Latins with a variety of privileges coming close to but still falling short of full Roman citizenship. One could be freeborn, a slave, or a freedman, but there were no categories of serf or helot located midway between slave and free.

In a society structured on these lines economic location in the system was not necessarily of the first importance but rather, whether one was a citizen or a foreigner, slave or free, Latin or ally. These were more crucial to an individual's status than whether he had money, an education, or ability. There were, in fact, many able, educated slaves and freedmen who were formally at least and in the eyes of the law, less favored than freeborn citizens who lacked these advantages.

Patria Potestas

Besides these classifications, which extended to individuals in any way connected with the state, the full citizen might be subsumed under other categories. Was he, for example, the head of a family and therefore legally independent *(sui juris)* or was he to some extent still in someone else's control? The power of the father *(patria potestas)* in a Roman family was unique, quite unlike that of any other Mediterranean society. He literally had the power of life and death over his sons, though in practice custom placed restrictions on its exercise. He could decide who his children should marry and, more interesting, whether they should stay married or get divorced. He owned all the family property so that even his grown sons and grandsons could not own anything until he died. Yet he had no control over the public life of his sons who might hold higher office than he ever attained. His responsibilities were heavy, for he ruled the household and owned its property not so much for his own private gratification as for the benefit of the family, which was regarded as an immortal entity, with its own religious rituals and protective deities. The father, the *pater familias,* was the religious head of the household as well as the property owner and ruler. He was responsible for the continuity of the family, its name, its burial places, and the cult of the ancestral spirits. Except for debts of the estate, which he could repudiate, the responsibilities could not be turned down by the heir. A woman, even more than a man, came under the strict control of the family. If she married according to the *manus* form of matrimony she ceased to be part of her own immediate family and passed over completely into her husband's. She worshipped the guardian spirits of his family and his ancestors became hers. Whatever property she brought with her became his and if he died she came under the guardianship of one of his male relatives. If the other, non-*manus* form of marriage was followed, the woman remained within her own family and under the power of her *pater familias.* In this instance any property she brought with her by way of a dowry remained hers, and in the case of a divorce or the death of her husband the property automatically reverted to her family. The guardian in this instance would be one of her own kin. Women, unlike men, never escaped guardianship and at least theoretically could never control or dispose of property without the guardian's approval.

Clients and Patrons

Given the importance the Romans attached to the family and the power of the head of the household, it is not surprising that paternalism prevailed throughout the state and greatly influenced political and social relations.

From ancient times certain families and individuals considered themselves the clients *(clientes)* of other families and regarded the heads of these houses as their patrons *(patroni)*, with whom they had special ties of a nonlegal, fiduciary kind. Freedmen automatically became the clients of those who manumitted them and in a less precise way great noble households acquired patronship relations with non-Roman communities, cities, and even states, such as those the Sempronii possessed with Spain or the Fabii possessed with the south of France. A complicated network of mutual duties and obligations expressed by the Latin term *fides*, or faith, bound clients and patrons together, and although not expressed in the terms of formal law possessed great moral weight.

Patrons had comprehensive obligations toward their clients and were expected to supply such things as legal advice and representation and, where necessary, political protection. Clients responded appropriately, aiding their patrons in whatever way they could, usually and most conspicuously by their political support and their votes. Neither patron nor client could give evidence against the other in court.

Fides

Of all qualities that Romans liked to think were most characteristically Roman, *fides*, which translates as "faith" but which had broader connotations of credibility and dependability, was the most favored. It had broader applicability than merely to the relationship of client and patron and permeated all Roman social relations. It existed between a man and his friends *(amici)*, between upper and lower classes, even between Rome itself and its various allies and friends. The very word was connected with the term for treaty, *foedus*, from which our own word *federal* comes, and with belief. *Fides* was one of the abstract deities, such as Concord and Piety, which the Romans so liked to venerate, and had a temple in the city going back to the most ancient times. It was not a legal but a moral and social concept. It could not be enforced in the courts, and like so much else in the Republic it depended on custom and the opinion of the community for its enforcement. Understandably, it was an essential aspect of any noble's dealings with either his clients or his equals and Roman self-identity, both individual and national, was closely connected with this concept. Foreign nations or their leaders were criticized for their lack of it, and to impugn a person's *fides* at Rome was a very serious business. The strength of the Republic was seen as flowing from the commitment of the different groups of society to this ideal rather than from any formal, legal, or constitutional structure. Obligations and duties *(officia)* were not spelled out in elaborate, ironclad contracts, but rather were left to the interpretative moral sensibilities of the parties involved and depended on the changing conditions of day-to-day life.

The Roman Concept of Order (Ordo)

Beyond these legal and moral classifications, which distinguished full citizens from half-citizens, free from slave, and client from patron, there was another series of categories based on the concept of honor, which further separated Romans and divided them from one another.

In modern industrial societies power is spread throughout a great variety of economic, political, cultural, and religious institutions, and much of the leadership also derives from these sources. Nevertheless, specialization is such that service in one type of institution tends to disqualify a person from at least simultaneous service in another. It is difficult to envision a society where the reverse might be the case—where, for example, a business or labor leader would at the same time be a general, judge, practical politician, and a priest.

There were no powerful autonomous institutions such as corporations, unions, churches, or universities in Rome, and leadership in almost all aspects of public life was in the hands of the same small, wealthy group of individuals. These men, great landowners for the most part, were also Rome's priests, judges, generals, and statesmen. Julius Caesar, one of the city's best-known politicians and generals and a man of questionable morals, was also head of the state religion *(pontifex maximus)*, as was Scipio Nasica, the political opponent and the assassin of Tiberius Gracchus, one of the tribunes of the people in 133 B.C. In general, the holding of the various priesthoods was considered an important adjunct to a successful career in politics.

Distinctions in Roman society were not based on professional skills or even the amount of money an individual possessed, but on whether he had the capacity in a broad sense for public service. To this end, the Romans arranged their society and its politics. Talents and skills that we regard highly, such as the professional skills of scientists, doctors, and artists, were relegated to the private realm and were never considered qualifications for service to the state. Instead the Romans looked for individuals who would be able to lead their armies in war and who would be looked up to in peacetime as sources of wise legislation, jurisdiction, and religious guidance.

With such an emphasis it is easy to see why honor and dignity *(honor, dignitas)* were the two most important, interrelated values in Roman life and why the esteem—not necessarily popularity—the community held for an individual was so important. This might be viewed as demonstrating that Rome was a backward, primitive society, still in the process of emerging from its heroic age. In fact, however, the way Rome set about bestowing honor on individuals was

Late first century B.C. *statue of a Roman patrician displaying the portrait busts of his ancestors. Roman nobles interested in a political career exploited to the fullest the conservative public's respect for the deeds of the heroes of the past.*

not a simple method of handing out awards to the bravest or the most nobly born, but an intricate, orderly procedure that had the effect of tying the social and political realms closely to each other, something few societies have been able to accomplish or to maintain for very long.

A key concept in this process is that of order (the Latin *ordo,* which has passed directly into most modern western languages), which for the Romans constituted the foundation of public life. It was a concept that survived the fall of both the Roman Republic and the Roman Empire.

Orders were groupings of individuals in society according to estimated worth. Each order possessed a certain rank or dignity, which gave a person belonging to it precedence and privileges over a person of a lower order. By the late Republic the word *order* was applied to all sorts of different groupings, such as skilled craftsmen, freedmen, and scribes, but it is only the rights and privileges of the two most important orders, the senatorial and equestrian, that properly reflect the meaning of the term. The reason is that the lower orders, such as those of the scribes and carpenters, had little to distinguish them formally one from the other, whereas the privileges of the senators and knights (*equites*, hence, equestrian) clearly did differentiate those who held these titles from the rest of society. The distinctions were more than nominal. They were juridical, political, and financial, for members of these orders had privileges and rights—such as the capacity to serve as jurors, bid for state contracts, and stand for higher office—which were denied the rest of society. Yet it must be stressed that these orders did not constitute a kind of hereditary, feudal aristocracy.

The Equestrian Order

Entry into the highest order, the Senate, was preceded by membership in the equestrian order, which in a sense contained the Senate. Senators, for example, voted in the equestrian centuries of the Centuriate Assembly, but eventually the juridical position of each order became clearly defined. By the end of the second century B.C. the two were quite distinct in terms of the rights and special privileges that each possessed. A senator, for example, could not bid for a state contract, whereas a knight could. Socially speaking, however, the two were always very closely related and there was constant interchange between them.

Admission to the equestrian order was not a question of wealth, although there was a fixed base amount of 400,000 sesterces. More important, recognition by the censor, whose role in classifying people in Roman society was moral as well as financial, was required. In principle, at least, the censor was supposed to look for those kinds of accomplishments that would qualify a man for inclusion in the first level of the aristocracy and even potentially in the Senate itself. A man, for example, had to be virtuous in the Roman sense. He had to have proved himself dependable on the battlefield, in the courts, as a legislator, as a patron who cared for his clients. Negatively, certain statuses, such as being a former slave, or having known moral failings, automatically removed a person from consideration. In the computation of a man's worth the skills of private enterprise and success in making money had to be related to the larger community in positive, public ways by means of benefits *(beneficia)* conferred on it. The mere possession of wealth (or culture for that matter), no matter what the degree, would not automatically qualify a man for entry into the equestrian or senatorial orders as long as the individual remained committed to a private way of life. Once in, of course, it was a different matter, and in time these criteria were less rigidly applied. Nevertheless, public service was at all times considered to be a prerequisite for entry into the ranks of the aristocracy.

Practically speaking, commendation or recommendation by a member of the aristocracy, preferably by a powerful senator, was an essential part of the process of advancement, and this in turn depended on the needs of particular individuals and families for new talent, which frequently could only be supplied by reaching down to the lower ranks. The process is not terribly well known because "new men," as they were called, were reluctant to document their rise in society where old family names meant so much. Although the military tribuneship, which was of equestrian rank, was an elective office, it is not known whether nonequestrians were elected to it and so automatically acquired this rank or whether the Romans preferred to elect individuals who were equestrian to begin with—probably the latter, considering the conservative character of the voters and the tight control the aristocracy exercised over the electoral processes.

The Senate

The authority of the Senate in the Roman constitutional setup is difficult to define because it had no official function beyond that of advising the elected magistrates. The formal powers of lawmaking, declaring war, and making peace rested with the people in the assemblies. In the course of time, especially during the Punic Wars, the informal power of the Senate, known as its authority *(auctoritas),* grew spectacularly. For all practical purposes the Senate took over control of the state. In particular, foreign policy and the conduct of war were considered the Senate's special prerogative, but there was no change in its statutory position, and *legally* there was nothing to stop consuls, praetors, or tribunes from calling the assemblies of the people to enact legislation, pass judgment, or vote independently of the Senate. Nevertheless, the power of the Senate was enormous. At its root lay the fact that, in the Republic, social and political structures coincided. In the Rome of that period political, military, social, moral, and economic eminence were all interrelated, and although there were wealthy, cultured people outside the Senate they had little power and their social position was proportionately low. The power of the Senate was such that all commands in war and all provincial governorships went to its members, and even when the people agitated for a role in these decisions—as they sometimes did—the choice still lay between senators, not between senators and non-senators.

The Senate was recruited from among the ranks of the equestian order, for membership in it was not something hereditary that could be passed on from father to son. Sons of senators were, however, automatically members of the equestrian order, and it was not uncommon for senatorial fathers to have sons who chose to remain equestrians (as was the case of the grandfather of Augustus, according to the biographer Suetonius); or the reverse, for an equestrian father to have a senatorial son. The two orders were, then, closely related, with some family members—whether brothers, cousins, uncles, nephews; or grandsons—being senators whereas others were knights. It was possible for generations to slip by without a particular family branch producing a senator. A family might drop out to recoup its finances or simply because of lack of interest and ambition among its members in a particular generation. A special inner group among the senators was that of the nobles *(nobiles),* whose ancestors had held the consulship. A census qualification for senators was set at a base figure of 800,000 sesterces.

THE CURSUS HONORUM

Entry into the senatorial order differed from entry into the equestrian order in that it involved an election by the people to an office. That office in turn had certain prerequisites, so in a sense the same principle of commendation operated here as in the case of entry into the equestrian order; voters were not invited to make selection at random from individuals who presented themselves for election. As noted above, a candidate had first to achieve equestrian rank and then to have served or at least have been available for ten military campaigns. It was only after meeting these qualifications that he could stand for the quaestorship, the first office in the senatorial career (the *cursus honorum).*

The quaestorship was an administrative office, either military or civilian, depending on whether the successful candidate was attached to a military unit as an officer in a general's staff or went off to a province as a governor's aide. Entry into the Senate came with this office by the first century B.C. although earlier the patrician or curule aedileship had been necessary. Someone at this level, however, would have very little influence and would remain a "back-bencher" unless elected to higher office.

The next required office in the senatorial *cursus* was that of the praetorship, which was essential for candidacy for the consulship. However, the intermediary step of tribune of the plebeians or aedile was advisable in order to continue the slow buildup of an individual's reputation with the various segments of the voting population. Visibility was an essential factor in advancement as were the ties of faith, clientship, and friendship *(fides, clientela, amicitia),* the informal political system that underlay the formal system and made it work.

The aedileship was another administrative office to which minor jurisdiction was attached. Aediles were responsible for the care and maintenance of the public buildings of the city, the streets, water and grain supply, and the supervision of the marketplaces, traffic, and religious celebrations. There were only four aediles, so a fair amount of business must have come their way, along with numerous opportunities for making contacts and doing favors, *beneficia* as they were called, for individuals or for the clients of individuals they hoped to receive support from later on when running for the next office. In the late Republic their responsibility for the games at religious festivals gave the aediles a special opportunity to curry favor with the public by making their own private contributions to spectacular celebrations that the allotted funds would not support. As aedile Caesar went heavily into debt to put on a series of magnificent games. They won him wide popularity, but eventually necessitated that he get a good province to rule as governor so he could pay off his creditors.

Tribunes, whose responsibilities and powers have already been discussed, also had good opportunities for making contacts with the people of the city on a day-to-day basis and winning the kind of recognition that might serve them in good stead later on. At least in the classical period of the Republic, down, say, to the mid-second century B.C., this did not mean currying popularity but performing useful functions for those who counted in Roman society, and involved actions such as vetoing measures obnoxious to various members of the nobility or proposing and supporting laws these individuals wished to see passed. All this demanded a fair amount of political sensitivity to the consequences of one's actions, and tribunes always had to keep in mind who they might offend or please by a particular action. Such a system, obviously, did not encourage the swift passage of run-of-the-mill legislation, let alone new or innovative proposals.

As praetor, one rung from the top, the successful candidate could end up as one of Rome's two chief judicial officers or as a governor of a province with military and civilian jurisdiction. In the first capacity the praetor's principal role was that of deciding how the laws should be administered in particular cases. He did not require technical knowledge of the law, which was available from unofficial specialists, the *jurisconsults.* What he did need, however, was the ability to take cases and decide whether they deserved a hearing. Then, in consultation with the parties involved, he selected the judge and the conditions under which the case would be tried. This role of the praetor and of the jurisconsults, together with the publication of the rules under which an individual praetor would adjudicate during his year in office, provided the foundation for the great edifice of Roman law which was to be systematized in the imperial period (first century A.D. onward).

After the praetorship came the consulship, the highest position in the state. Although the consuls were primarily military men, they were also the chief civil officers of the state with the right and the duty to call the Senate or the assemblies of the people together to legislate, elect, or pass judgment. Like all Roman offices the consulship was collegial in character, which meant that each consul had to take into account the veto power of his partner. There was also the built-in restriction that a consul's *imperium* or power ended precisely on December 31 (or on April 30, before 153 B.C.) and he once more became a private citizen. The process of prorogation or extending the office as a promagistracy was the only normal way of avoiding a quick return to civilian life. This typically Roman artifice of bending principle to practicality was one that the great generals of the first century B.C. used to build up enormous personal power and prestige, and which became one of the pillars of the new regime established by Augustus.

Elections

Candidates needed a thorough knowledge of the election machinery itself since different strategies were needed depending on which office was being sought. Elections for the lower offices of quaestor, tribune, and aedile, for example, were conducted in the Tribal Assembly and required one kind of approach; those for the higher offices of praetor and consul were held in the Centuriate Assembly and required another strategy. Candidates had to know which groups of voters to approach in each assembly and how to go about doing this most effectively.

In the Centuriate Assembly there were a total of 193 voting units, of which, after the reforms of the third century, 70 were assigned to the highest of the five property classes and 18 to the equestrians (including senators). Since together the two groups constituted almost a majority, and because their lead tended to be followed by the rest of the classes, it was essential for a consular or praetorian candidate to do well with these two groups of voters. The numbers were not large—for it will be remembered that the Romans weighted their votes, giving more to the rich than to the poor—so the problems were not precisely the same as in modern elections where sheer numbers do count. (Even today targeting particular groups is important, though not nearly as vital as it was for the Romans.) One of these groups was the aristocracy of the municipalities and colonies of Italy who had the leisure time and the resources to make the special journey to Rome for the elections. It was taken for granted that the masses, although they possessed the vote, would not or could not come. Influential members of the municipal upper classes would somehow have to be canvassed, either by reminding them of favors *(beneficia)* conferred in the past, or by persuading the candidate's friends to make special recommendations on his behalf. At Rome, family and marriage connections, friendships and alliances would have to be revived. It was at this point that the candidate's own clients as well as those of his connections could prove decisive. Planning for this kind of a campaign began years in advance and the election, when it finally occurred, was a true test of a candidate's support among the upper classes of the community, but not of his popularity with the masses of the voters. These were effectively disenfranchised, either by distances or by the way the Centuriate Assembly was set up.

A candidate also needed to know the organization of the tribal districts, whether his election was to be held in the Centuriate or the Tribal Assembly. Since the reforms of the third century, the voting units of the first two classes had been keyed to the tribal system. In the past, members of these classes were assigned at random to their centuries or voting units, but in the new system all members of individual tribes who belonged to the same classes would be enrolled in the same two centuries. Thus a canvass could begin with the assumption that if the key votes could be swayed in a given tribe, two centuries in the first and two in the second class would be secured and so on for the remaining tribes.

The tribes were not conveniently unified geographic units but instead had segments scattered all over Italy. Cicero's tribe, for example, had five divisions, one at Arpinum (his hometown), another near Rome, and the others in Umbria, in Samnite territory, and in the far south. Hence it would not do to carry just one segment of a tribe in one geographic area; this principle applied to all 35 tribes. A majority of 18, of course, sufficed in the Tribal Assembly, and a clever campaign manager could reduce the work of canvassing considerably by targeting key areas and key people. Rural residences, for example, could help if placed in the right districts, and games and banquets when given at strategic moments close to elections might help carry a tribe. There were many laws against election malpractices *(leges de ambitu)*, but there were always loopholes and it was extremely difficult to prove charges of bribery. "If you can prove there was bribery," Cicero keeps saying in one of his defense speeches, "I will join the prosecution."[2]

Even assuming a good preparatory canvass had been conducted there were innumerable hazards to face in the election process itself. Presiding magistrates had great power. They could, for example, refuse to recognize the candidacy of individuals they considered unacceptable. In legislative assemblies they could choose who was to vote first in each of the tribes and could fill up below-par voting units by shifting voters from others. If the vote seemed to be going the wrong way they could claim they had seen or heard bad omens and adjourn the meeting until such time as adjustments could be made to bring about a more favorable vote.

After 139 B.C., when the secret ballot was introduced for elections, the more obvious kind of pressure that could be brought to bear on voters was removed, but the brazen or unscrupulous candidate could still try stuffing ballot boxes or handing out premarked ballots. In truly desperate situations the election process itself could be tampered with by removing ballot boxes or the planks across which the voters walked to cast their ballots or by creating such disturbances that the voting would have to be given up. Since the tendency of later voters to follow the lead of those who had cast their ballots before them was well known, there was another possibility for fraud if the process of selecting the first voting units could be manipulated. This was difficult since the selection was made by lot, but the presiding magistrate could simply ignore the real outcome of the lots, as Caesar was supposed to have done on one occasion, and instead call out the units he wanted, or alternatively the lots themselves might be tampered with.

[2]Cicero, *Pro Murena,* 32.

Coin showing Roman voter crossing the raised bridge to the ballot-box and stooping to receive a tablet on which to indicate his preference. Ahead of him another voter is about to deposit his tablet in the basket.

Legislative and Judicial Assemblies

Most legislation after 287 B.C. was enacted in the Tribal Assembly, which could be called by a tribune, in which case it was called the Plebeian Assembly *(concilium plebis)* from which patricians were excluded, or by a consul or praetor, in which case it was the Tribal Assembly *(comitia tributa)* and open to everyone. The latter could only vote on measures approved by the Senate, but the Plebeian Assembly did not require senatorial approval either before or after the vote. The exclusion of the patricians could not, in practice, have had much effect on the outcome since their numbers were never great. After 131 B.C. balloting in legislative assemblies was secret, and control of the Plebeian Assembly, which had democratic possibilities, was achieved by means of the tribunician veto, since usually one of the ten tribunes could be found to block a measure the Senate found objectionable. This control, however, could be broken—as Tiberius Gracchus found when he successfully removed an obstructing tribune from office by means of the popular vote—which, at least momentarily, he was able to control. In the first century, violence, either real or threatened, became another and more effective alternative.

Since the approval of a majority of the tribes carried the measure voted on, legislators had to aim at reaching majorities in 18 out of the 35 tribes. Routinely this involved bringing in voters from the countryside who were under strict control, since the client system worked more effectively in the rural areas than in the city, and the rural tribes outnumbered the urban by almost eight to one. There was a flaw in this tactic, however, as once again the revolutionary Tiberius Gracchus was able to demonstrate. A sufficiently popular measure could flood the rural tribes with poorer voters and upset the client system at least temporarily, and then anything could happen. Freedmen were another kind of problem since they were supposed to possess special ties to their patrons, and over the years efforts were made to place them in the rural tribes where they could be more easily manipulated. Generally, however, such efforts were frustrated, and freedmen remained confined to the four urban tribes.

Both the Centuriate Assembly and the Tribal Assembly could be called upon to act as courts in serious matters. In practice, however, the Centuriate Assembly was rarely used because of its awkward voting procedure, and after the establishment of standing courts in the second and first centuries the Tribal Assembly began to be used less frequently. After 137 B.C., voting in judicial assemblies was by secret ballot.

The Senate and the Provinces

Before the third century B.C. the scope of a senatorial commander's opportunities was limited by the relatively small scale of Rome's military involvements and the restricted responsibilities that this implied. All the wars were fought in

Italy and the campaigning seasons were short even if the wars themselves were long. The Senate, consequently, had little difficulty monitoring what was going on. In peacetime, a commander's opportunities were even more limited. With the Punic Wars, however, came longer campaigns, more distant theaters of war, and greater responsibilities. Even when the wars were over, there were still major opportunities; for now there were permanent, overseas provinces to be ruled. First there was just Sicily and Sardinia, but then in the second century Spain, Africa, Macedonia, Asia, and southern Gaul were added, and in the first century came Gaul proper and a whole series of eastern provinces. It was as though Rome was put on a permanent wartime footing so far as career opportunities were concerned.

The government of permanent provinces was something new in Roman history. In the past the Senate was responsible for the city of Rome itself and such territory in Italy that did not belong to the self-governing municipalities and colonies or to the allies. "Provinces," or broad areas of responsibility, had been regularly assigned in the past to military commanders, and the term was even used to describe the responsibilities of the praetors. One praetor, for example, had the *provincia urbana* and the other the *provincia peregrina*—i.e., one was in charge of the administration of law for Roman citizens and the other was in charge of the law as it pertained to foreigners. Now the term was applied to whole countries for whose administration Rome had decided to take on permanent responsibility. Since Rome had no prior experience in this kind of administration and did not believe in professional civil servants even for its own government, it was forced to rely on the only other kind of experience it had in foreign affairs—military campaigns. Governors, either consuls or praetors, were therefore sent out every year with *imperium* (supreme power) to govern the provinces, just as Rome's military commanders, who were also consuls and praetors, were given *imperium* to conduct war on behalf of Rome against its enemies.

In the beginning, it seems, consuls simply appointed deputies to act on their behalf in Sicily and Sardinia, but from 227 B.C., when the number of praetors was raised to 4, the governorship became a regular position to be held in the senatorial career *(cursus honorum).* The number of praetors rose to 6 in 197 B.C., then to 8 at the time of Sulla, and finally to 16 under Caesar. When conditions were particularly disturbed, consuls were sent out as governors. The usual term of office was one year, though this could be extended, in which case the governor, whether he was a praetor or a consul, was generally called a proconsul. From the time of Gaius Gracchus (123 B.C.), consular provinces were selected before the elections to the consulship, but the decision as to which consuls or praetors went to which provinces was usually decided by lot at the beginning of the year.

The first task facing a newly appointed governor was to collect his staff which, considering the responsibilities, was extremely small. His adjutant was a quaestor, 25 to 30 years old, assigned to him by lot from the group selected for that year. The quaestor's job was chiefly financial, but he could be delegated to do almost anything by his superior, from holding court to commanding troops. The governor could also take a number of legates or aides with him—three if he was a consul—who were also generally senators, some of them of high rank. Cicero took his brother Quintus, who was of praetorian rank, with him when he was assigned to Cilicia. In a more warlike situation Lucius Scipio had his brother Publius, the victor over Hannibal, on his staff as a legate when he was assigned the province of Greece in 190 B.C. with permission to carry the war against the Seleucid king Antiochus III into Asia. In addition, a number of friends and relatives might be invited to come along for the experience. Tiberius Gracchus, the revolutionary tribune of 133 B.C., was, at an earlier date, the companion of his brother-in-law Scipio Aemilianus, the commander of the Roman army then besieging Carthage. The professional staff was minute. It consisted of the governor's private secretary *(accensus)*, a few scribes (who were literally the only professional civil servants Rome possessed), a doctor, a haruspex, and some others such as his lictors, who carried the rods and axes *(fasces)* which were the symbols of his office.

ADMINISTRATIVE RESPONSIBILITIES

The administration of the provinces placed great demands on the officials Rome selected in this haphazard fashion, and not just on their integrity. Although the governor had absolute power over his subjects, the problems he had to face were huge. Conditions varied widely from region to region. Sicily had 65 cities and Asia was probably richer than Italy itself, but the west was still backward and tribal and had no urban life worth talking about. Governors had little to go on. They came and went in rapid succession, taking with them their staffs, so that there was no opportunity to build up a permanent local administration that would help the incoming governor adjust to local conditions. His starting point was the provincial charter *(lex provinciae)*, which was drawn up at the time the province was founded and constituted the basic law of the province. It established, for example, such things as the statuses of the various cities and of their inhabitants, always a thorny problem, but it left much to the discretion of the governor. Information might be picked up from previous governors, but politics could easily interfere. On the other hand, there were always plenty of individuals in Rome who had special, personal interests in the provinces and who were not slow in letting a new governor know how they felt he should act where their affairs might be involved.

The system put great strains on governors in other ways. The Roman political process had an important military aspect to it and its highest office was a generalship. Names were obviously made more easily on the battlefield than in the law courts, as Cicero, who had no military ability, knew well. There was therefore a temptation to use provincial wars as stepping-stones to the next office or to the next command. Governors could expand wars, or if it looked like their replacements might be in a position to steal their laurels, they could rush to finish the fighting before the replacements arrived. Julius Caesar's designated

Roman soldiers and administrators engaged in some undetermined task, possibly taking a census, laying out a colony, or even drafting troops. This scene from the so-called "Altar of Domitius Ahenobarbus" (ca. 100 B.C.) is one of the few illustrations of soldiers of the Republican period.

province was Cisalpine and Transalpine Gaul, but by the end of his proconsulship he had added all of Gaul proper and had made separate assaults on Germany and Britain. In the west, especially, where the population was largely tribal and unsettled, there was a standing temptation to seek a quick victory in the short time allowed by a governor's term of office.

Civil administration posed another set of problems and often strained the morality of the governors to the breaking point. There was some expense money but no salary and if a governor was scrupulously honest, the holding of such an office could be an expensive business. Verres, the corrupt governor of Sicily whom Cicero prosecuted, cynically remarked that it was necessary for a governor to acquire three fortunes when in the provinces: one to pay off the debts incurred in running for public office in the first place; one to bribe the jurors if he was unlucky enough to be brought to trial; and one to live on for the rest of his days.

Provincial administration was complicated by a number of factors. It was important to get along well with the local oligarchies who were Rome's principal supporters in the provinces and who might, additionally, have powerful friends in Rome, but this could easily compromise the evenhanded administration of justice. The most difficult problems were in the richer provinces, where the Romans inherited a complicated system of taxation from their predecessors, the Hellenistic kings, who had hordes of bureaucrats to handle their fiscal problems.

Since the Romans chose to remain above such matters but not to forgo the income, they had recourse to private enterprise as they so frequently did in matters lying beyond the interest or competence of the Senate. Private—actually only semiprivate—companies *(societates)* were allowed to bid for the taxes of the provinces. The company that won would then send out its agents *(publicani)* to make the collections, which had to cover expenses as well as provide a worthwhile profit. These companies were systematically organized and drew their directors *(magistri)* and shareholders *(socii)* from among the equestrian class. They were enormously influential both in Rome and in the provinces. A governor with ambitions to advance had to be cautious how he acted on complaints brought against their representatives in the provinces. It took a great deal of courage and integrity to fight the system. One who did was the consul Rutilius Rufus, who took on the companies while governor in Asia in the first century B.C. and on his return was tried, condemned, and forced into exile by the equestrian-controlled courts. This was a notorious case, however, and the average governor would probably have been content if he succeeded in avoiding serious problems during his tenure in office.

CORRUPTION AND EFFORTS AT REFORM

There is no guarantee that a permanent administrative service created by the Senate would have done spectacularly better, since it would presumably still be reporting to the Senate. If there was to be any reform it would have had to have begun with the Senate itself and with the whole political process in Rome. Even under the Empire, when abuses of the kind common in the Republic were supposed to have been brought under control, we still hear of extortion and other crimes in the provinces. There were, however, some means of redress during the Republic, combining formal and informal features in typical Roman fashion. Some senatorial families, such as the Gracchi in Spain and the Fabii in southern France, had special interests in particular provinces, and appeal could be made to them. Much, of course, depended on the political battles that were taking place in Rome at the time the complaint was made and who was on whose side. The formal method was to bring an accusation, the commonest one being extortion, and introduce an action for the recovery of the goods extorted *(res repetundae)*. After 149 B.C. there was a permanent court to handle these accusations, but it was difficult to get a judgment. If the senators were the jurors, as they were down to 123 B.C. and then again after Sulla, they would be slow to condemn a fellow club member, and equestrians who manned the court at other times were often only concerned with the attitude of the accused to the tax companies which they ran or in which they held stock. There was, of course, no public prosecutor's office, so the action had to be initiated by the wronged provincials themselves and might be hindered by the current governor who could intimidate witnesses and otherwise harass the parties involved. Then at Rome a senator had to be found who would introduce the case. If the provincials were lucky enough to win the case they acquired Roman citizenship for themselves (if they wanted it) and double the amount they had lost. The defendant was generally expelled from the Senate and exiled.

Although the full effects of Rome's method of governing its provinces did not become apparent until well into the first century—and then the concern was mainly for the damage being done to Rome itself—a little can be said now about the defects that were present in the system from the beginning.

Collegiality, which was of the essence of the political process at Rome, was not in force in the provinces. The governor alone was responsible for what went on there, restrained only by his term of office, his estimate of the local political situation, and the few informal sanctions that might be brought to bear on him. He might do little or nothing except in the most routine fashion, or, depending on his inclination and the type of province he ruled, he might be benevolent or cruel, just or unjust. He could keep his hands clean as Cicero did during his term of office in Cilicia, attempt reform as Rutilius did in Asia, or regard the province as so much real estate to be exploited as was the case with Verres in Sicily. Rome's heavy reliance on custom to govern social relations was misplaced in the provinces. At home a magistrate was restrained by centuries of experience and hundreds of unwritten practices that did not exist in the provinces. It was to take a political revolution to create a system that could control the governors and even then the complaints continued to come in.

An Estimate of Roman Society

What can be said in favor of a system that blatantly favored the rich over the poor, the wellborn over the lowly? Can anything be said to justify such elitist principles over the egalitarian tendencies of most modern societies?

One kind of defense—the easiest—is to point out the inconsistencies and weaknesses of modern societies, where despite egalitarian sentiments the rich and powerful still exercise special influence in the elective, legislative, and judicial processes. The Romans would claim that this kind of system leads to concealment, cynicism, and irresponsibility and that at least in Rome it was perfectly clear who was powerful—and more important, who was responsible. In a crisis situation the Roman people could simply exercise their prerogative by making their own choice, either of a general, a piece of legislation, or a judicial condemnation. Outside of crisis situations, it was easy for the public to keep track of what was going on. The Senate consisted of only about 300 members, of whom 20 to 30 were key figures, all of them well known. The elective system exposed the individual to some degree of public scrutiny and the seniority system was so slow that there was always a choice between trying an older man who was well known or reaching down to the lower ranks to pick someone with talent in a time of crisis—a Fabius against a Scipio or a Marius—though of course this often happened only in a desperate situation, when enough of the old guard had been killed or shown, as they often were, to be totally inept.

And then, Romans could claim they achieved a fine blend of formal ranking by wealth as well as by public esteem—a blend of economic muscle and aristocratic excellence. Entry into the Senate or for that matter the equestrian order was not automatic and demanded some proof of public confidence in a candidate's ability and character. Theoretically wealth was not an end in itself but a means of providing services to the community. Public offices had no salaries and legal services were required by law to be free. Romans could point to the inability of most modern democracies to integrate the wealthy classes into the state as a particularly grievous failing. They could justly claim that modern individual philanthropy by the rich is too haphazard and arbitrary to compensate for their overall lack of involvement in the formal public life of the community. Socialist and communist states would be considered to have failed also. The mere elimination of a class, Romans would argue, does not eliminate human craving for distinction but merely drives it underground where it is more difficult to control.

Needless to say this kind of a debate could not have taken place at all in the context of the Republic. Language and the presuppositions underlying our use of words would have made it impossible. The concepts of the inherent rights of the individual, merit, and egalitarianism are too distinctively modern and alien to the Roman mentality to have permitted a meaningful discussion, and even if properly understood would have been rejected as self-contradictory and unrealizable. It would take yet another revolution, the advent of Christianity, to dethrone the old classical assumptions and replace them with a new set of values.

13

The Transformation of the Republic, Part One

FROM HANNIBAL TO THE GRACCHI: RETROSPECT AND PREVIEW

In 200 B.C., despite the great increase in territory and power that came with victory over Carthage, a majority of Romans still lived in the same narrow stretch of land in central Italy that constituted the Roman heartland before the wars. Except for a few scattered colonies, the rest of Italy was, as in the past, in the hands of a variety of non-Roman cultural, linguistic, and racial groups. Overseas, Sicily, Sardinia, and Corsica were provinces, but Roman presence there was minimal.

THE OLD ASSUMPTIONS

The unwillingness of Romans to expand and their geographical confinement to central Italy were in turn, reflections of their psychological assumptions about the nature of the state and how society should be structured. Old ideas about city-state life, which reached back to Rome's beginnings, took for granted that citizens should live within a day's walking distance of the capital. When Roman citizens were settled by state action in colonies outside Roman territory they were, at least prior to the second century, automatically reduced to the second-rate condition of Latin citizens. Even within Roman territory, individualistic farmsteading was not encouraged; normally, Romans were expected to settle in organized groups complete with preexisting charter, laws, and political structure. In the eyes of the ruling oligarchy, if not of the masses, the city-state had definite territorial limits beyond which it could not expand without ceasing to be a state in which public office was exchanged among a small number of families in a relatively free give-and-take process. After 241 B.C. the number of tribal units, which until then had been increasing as more territory was added, was fixed at 35 and in the future individual tribes were simply expanded to cope with new additions of territory. Only by keeping expansion under strict control was it possible for the old system to function.

Paradoxically, Hannibal's invasion had left the old system not only intact, but stronger and narrower than ever at precisely the time when new conditions were crying out for an entirely new system. The war with Hannibal made a gift of governmental control to the Senate, which still was not a constitutionally established organ of government but nevertheless exercised an even tighter control than in the past. Success, by confirming the Romans in their old ways, was the wrong formula for new times. A small coterie of some 20 families passed the highest office of state from hand to hand among themselves. By midcentury only four new families had been admitted to the consulship.

There was no change in the proposition that land, farmed by aristocrat and peasant alike, was the basis of the Roman economic system. Commercial, financial, and industrial interests were accommodated only reluctantly. Taxes were raised for current needs, surpluses—when they occurred—were returned to the people as a whole. Budget planning was unthinkable, as were paid professional administrators (except at the lowest levels), politicians, and lawyers. The nobility gave their services freely to the state in these capacities, being forbidden by law as well as ancient custom to receive remuneration for such efforts. All state contracts were let out to private companies, and in general an absolute minimum of resources was earmarked for formal government. To manage the Roman Empire in 200 B.C. there were 10 senior and 18 junior magistrates, all of them elected annually (quinquennially in the case of the censors), of whom exactly half were concerned entirely with affairs occurring within the city of Rome itself.

The army was similarly unprofessional and consisted of annual levies of amateur, peasant soldiers who were expected to supply their own weapons, food, and clothing, commanded by amateur officers who served a year and then returned to private life. Only reluctantly did the state begin to supply arms, food, and clothing and even then it made deductions for them from the soldiers' meager allowance. Service in the army was seen as a duty and privilege of full citizens only, and those lacking the requisite amount of property, which constituted their "stock" in the corporate state, were excluded from this privilege.

Rome's cultural life in 200 B.C. was as simple as its economic and administrative arrangements. Coarse native mime and farce, family histories, translations of Greek plays, and a few attempts at epic poetry in Latin by outsiders satisfied the minimum demands of Romans for literature and drama. Unlike in the more developed Greek east, the reading public was minute. Architecturally the city of Rome did not compare with even provincial Greek cities, let alone such metropolises as Athens or Alexandria, and visiting Macedonians from the court of King Philip V poked fun at the capital city of the western world. In social terms Rome was still archaic by Greek standards; family and kin ties prevailed over the more individualized pattern of ethics and legal relationships characteristic of societies in the Hellenistic east.

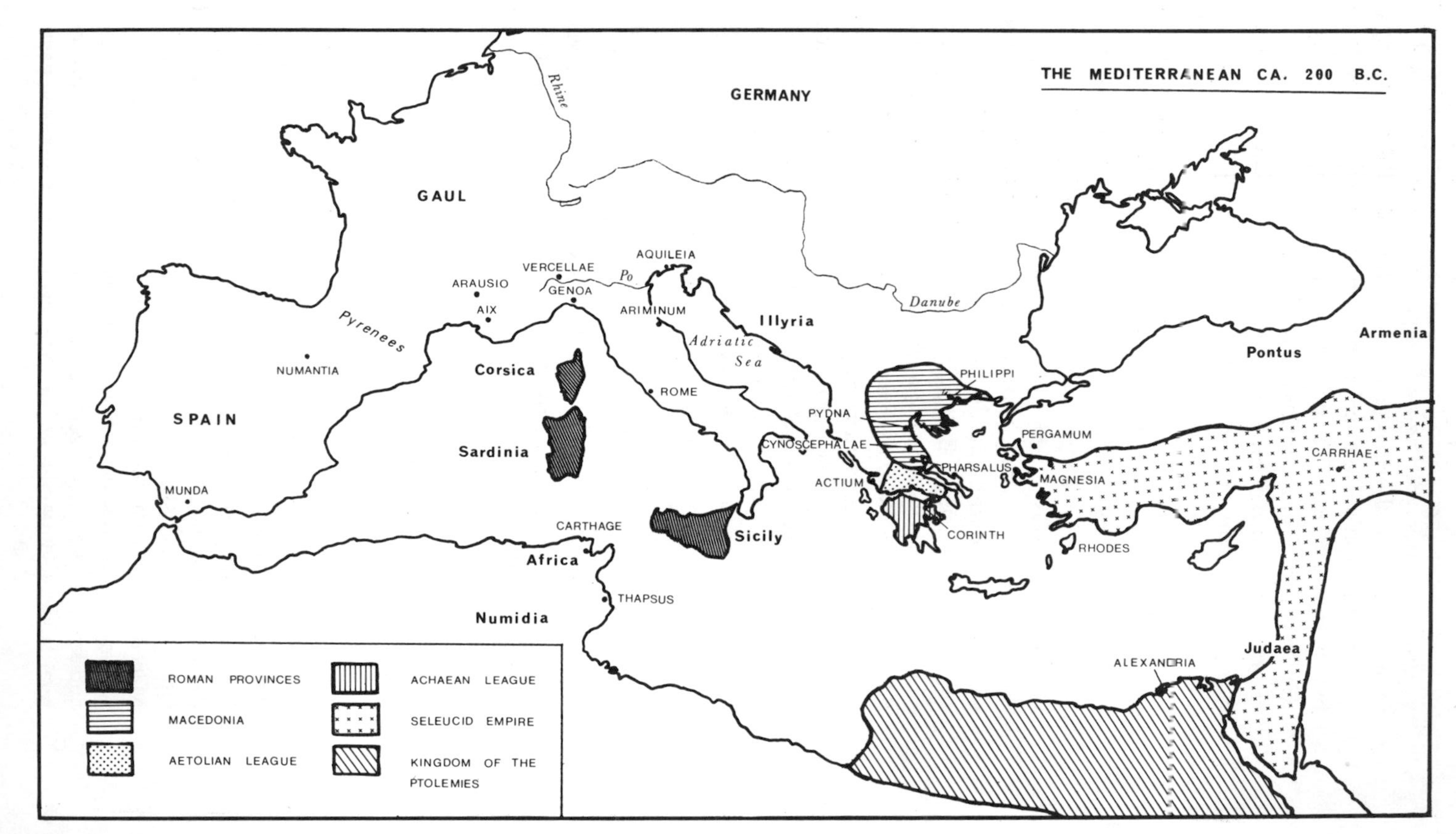
THE MEDITERRANEAN CA. 200 B.C.
GERMANY
GAUL
Rhine
Danube
AQUILEIA
VERCELLAE
Po
ARAUSIO
GENOA
AIX
ARIMINUM
Illyria
Pyrenees
Adriatic Sea
Corsica
NUMANTIA
ROME
SPAIN
Sardinia
MUNDA
PHILIPPI
PYDNA
CYNOSCEPHALAE
PHARSALUS
ACTIUM
CORINTH
PERGAMUM
MAGNESIA
RHODES
CARRHAE
Pontus
Armenia
CARTHAGE
Sicily
Africa
THAPSUS
Numidia
Judaea
ALEXANDRIA
ROMAN PROVINCES
MACEDONIA
AETOLIAN LEAGUE
ACHAEAN LEAGUE
SELEUCID EMPIRE
KINGDOM OF THE PTOLEMIES

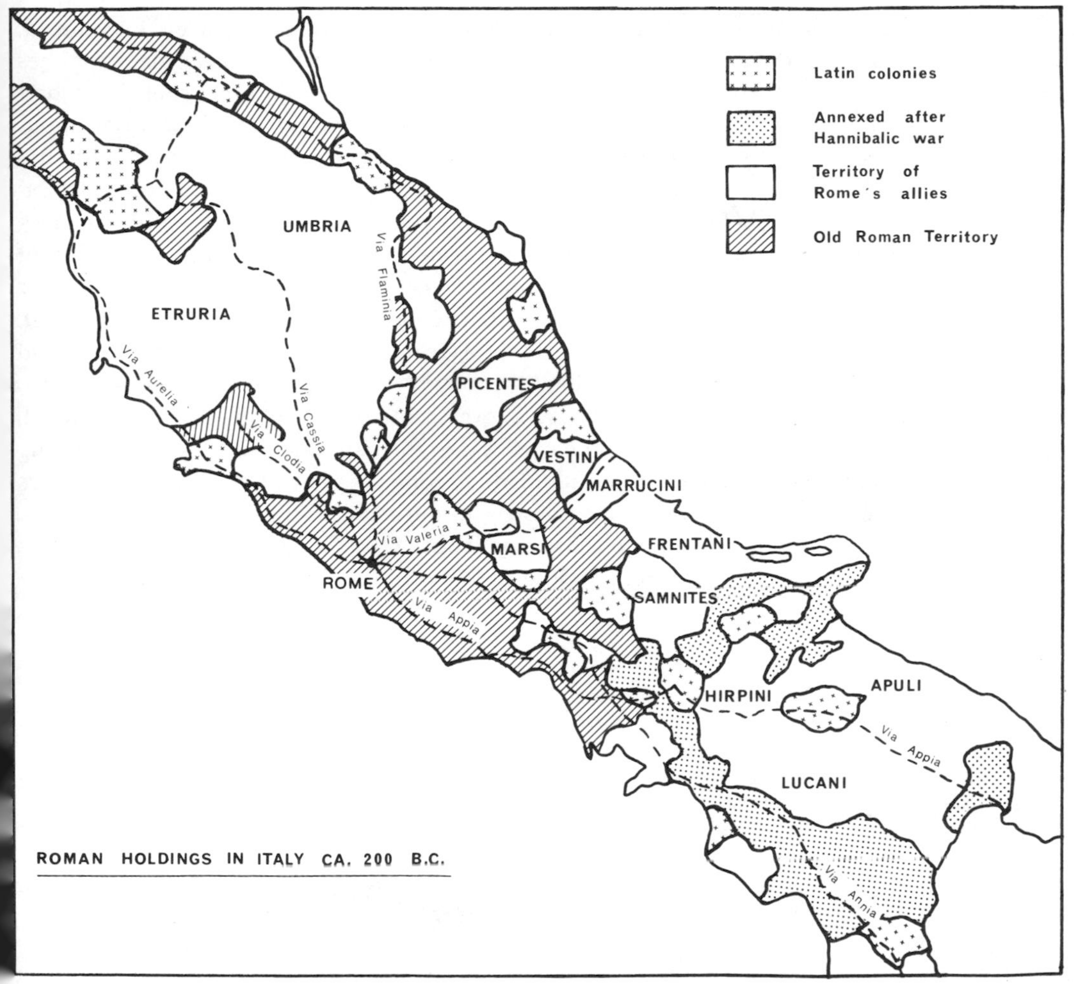

THE TRANSFORMATION

Yet, within a little more than a century all of this was to change. The whole of Italy south of the Po was to possess the franchise and Romans were to be found everywhere throughout the Mediterranean. By the end of the second century new provinces in Spain, Macedonia, Africa, Asia, and part of Gaul were added, and Roman power was everywhere supreme. Vast amounts of money in the form of loot, tribute, and indemnities flowed into Rome. Although most of this money stayed at the top, some trickled down to the masses in various forms such as improved services and communications, a share in war booty for soldiers, and most important, the elimination in 167 B.C. of the *tributum*, the principal tax to which Romans were liable. The peasant subsistence farmer, the backbone of the army, began to give way to the long-term volunteer whose loyalty was more likely to be to his commander—or to the person who could pay his wages—than to the state. New types of cash-crop farming were introduced, taking different forms in different parts of Italy. In the south giant ranches *(latifundia)* were devoted to the raising of huge herds of cattle and sheep, watched over by slave shepherds. Elsewhere, wherever market conditions warranted them, intensively exploited farms sprang up, primarily concerned with the production of wine and oil. By the first century B.C. all Italy, according to the scholar Varro, was a great orchard, and the poets praised the incredible richness of the Italian countryside. Specialized farms concentrating on the production of poultry, fish, vegetables, flowers, and all sorts of exotic products supplied the needs of affluent city populations. Subsistence farmers retreated to the remoter, less accessible areas of Italy. Forests were cleared, marshes drained, and new land constantly came into production.

During the second century a great network of roads was constructed, linking the farthest parts of the country. In the city of Rome a gigantic building program financed by the profits of its empire was launched. Masses of slaves were put to work wherever possible—on the land, in the cities, in the mines—supplementing but not replacing free labor. New classes became prominent as others declined. A complex middle class began to emerge. Large numbers of ex-

If Greeks and Macedonians saw little of cultural note in the Rome of the second century B.C., a major transformation was, in fact, already under way as the Roman upper classes acquired a taste for Greek art and commissioned a whole range of subjects, including these fine gems. The fact that so few portraits of individual Romans survive from this period makes these tiny images particularly valuable.

slaves formed a freedman class, which merged in the course of time with the old Roman stock without changing it perceptibly. New men in the Senate and freedmen attempted to be more Roman than the Romans themselves, with interesting results. Upper-class women—given independence by the long absences of their fathers, husbands, and brothers in overseas wars—emerged as important social and cultural figures in their own right.

Following the flood of money to Rome came a flood of talent from the east. Philosophers, artists, litterateurs, architects, doctors, professors, sculptors, skilled masons, jewelers—whole professional classes—came to fill the needs acquired by the well-to-do classes of Roman society. As Rome attempted to adjust to these enormous changes, the old, simple consensus dissolved. The city-state, with all its presuppositions and assumptions about society and the styles of life appropriate to a city-state, finally disintegrated under the seductive influence of success and prosperity. Roman historians of the first century point to various dates in the previous century as the time when the disruption began. For Sallust it was the destruction of Carthage in 146 B.C., whereas for Livy it was the return of the booty-laden army of Manlius Vulso in 187:

> [T]he beginnings of foreign luxury were introduced into the City by the army from Asia. They for the first time imported into Rome couches of bronze, valuable robes for coverlets, tapestries and other products of the loom, and what at that time was considered luxurious furniture—tables with one pedestal and sideboards. Then female players of the lute and the harp and other festal delights of entertainments were made adjuncts to banquets; the banquets themselves, moreover, began to be planned with both greater care and greater expense. At that time the cook, to the ancient Romans the most worthless of slaves . . . began to have value, and what had been merely a necessary service came to be regarded as an art.[1]

Even second-century historians were aware of the change. Polybius thought 168 B.C., when Rome achieved universal domination after the battle of Pydna, was the date when the old system began to dissolve, whereas L. Calpurnius Piso selected 154 B.C. By Sallust's time in the first century the revolution was well under way:

> In these degenerate days, however, one cannot find a man who does not seek to rival his ancestors in wealth and extravagance, instead of in uprightness and industry. Even newcomers to politics, who formerly relied on merit to outstrip the nobility now use underhand intrigue and open violence.[2]

[1]*Livy*, tr. E. T. Sage (Loeb Classical Library and Harvard University Press, Cambridge, Mass., 1955), 39.6, pp. 235–36.

[2]Sallust, *The Jugurthine War and the Conspiracy of Cataline*, tr. S. A. Handford (Penguin Classics, 1965), p. 37. Copyright © S. A. Handford 1965. Reprinted by permission of Penguin Books Ltd.

What was to replace the old order was not, however, to be revealed for another generation. But now we must go back to review in detail the stages of the evolution that began after the Punic Wars and resulted in the transformation of the Republic into a veiled dictatorship benignly ruling a predominantly middle-class society.

TERRITORIAL EXPANSION

Italy and Spain

The most obvious result of the Punic Wars was in the extension of Rome's commitments overseas and in Italy. Prior to this time Rome's principal concern was for her immediate possessions in central Italy. But with the defeat of Hannibal, the Romans found themselves deeply involved in northern and southern Italy, Spain, southern Gaul, Illyria (modern Yugoslavia and Albania), and north Africa, and through these areas with the eastern Mediterranean.

Much of northern and southern Italy had gone over to Hannibal during the wars and as punishment Rome confiscated gigantic amounts of land from its former allies, more than doubling its own landholdings in the process and producing an entirely new political map of Italy. Pieces of Roman territory, designated as public land, stretched from one end of Italy to the other, still occupied in many instances by their original owners. The connecting of these scattered parcels (usually the best land possessed by the original owners) by roads, and their settlement, occupation, and development by Romans was to be one of the greatest projects undertaken in the second century, offering fantastic opportunities for self-enrichment to many, especially to those belonging to the upper classes. Though the south required little pacification after the departure of Hannibal, the Ligurian and Celtic tribes of the north were conquered only after a series of lengthy campaigns lasting from 200 to 180 B.C. Even then the job was not complete, as the tribes of the Alps remained unsubdued until the time of Augustus. Romanization took place concurrently with pacification, and large colonies and major connecting roads were created.

Spain, too, fell to Rome as part of the spoils of the Punic Wars. For strategic and economic reasons it was necessary to bring Spain fully under Roman control, for it was from Spain with its manpower and mineral resources that Carthage had launched its nearly fatal attack on Rome in 218 B.C., and Rome was determined that nothing like that should happen again. Accordingly, in 197 B.C. Spain was divided into two provinces and the slow process of bringing this gigantic landmass under control began. Spain was inhabited by tribal, nonurbanized peoples, and the Romans used the same techniques of diplomacy and war they used so successfully in subduing Italy. As in all Roman undertakings abroad at this time, the object was not the direct annexation of territory. It was, rather, the elimination of groups that might possibly pose a threat to Rome's interests in the area, and the establishment of relations on a client–patron basis. Since these interests were never clearly defined and the client-patron relationship was moral rather than legal, misunderstandings and ambiguities inevitably resulted.

Between 197 and 133 B.C. Rome conducted a series of campaigns resulting in the subjection and eventual Romanization of almost the entire Iberian peninsula. Later in the century the province of Transalpine Gaul was added, guaranteeing direct access to Spain from Italy. The campaigns for the conquest of Spain were characterized not by the significance of the battles fought or the numbers involved, but by the consistency with which the legions were beaten by the skillful guerrilla tactics of the Spanish, and, on the Roman side, by broken treaties, laxness of military discipline, atrocities, and ruined reputations. In particular, the disastrous experience of one Roman officer, Tiberius Gracchus, who was serving in an army that was forced to surrender under ignominious circumstances, was to have enormous consequences. Not until 133 B.C., when the Celt-Iberian town of Numantia was destroyed by Scipio Aemilianus, who earlier had reduced Carthage to rubble, could Rome's hold on Spain be called secure. As late as the time of Augustus, recalcitrant tribes in northwestern Spain were still disturbing the *pax Romana.* It is no coincidence that some of the dates assigned by Roman historians for the decline of the Republic coincide with Rome's disastrous experiences in the Iberian peninsula.

Macedonia and the East

Before the war with Hannibal Roman suppression of piracy in the Adriatic had brought it into immediate contact with Macedonia and the usual process of making friends and allies, by which Rome established its influence, began.

Following Philip's stab in the back after the battle of Cannae, when the Macedonians allied themselves with Hannibal, Rome became more involved in the area east of the Adriatic, establishing its first formal alliance with a Greek state, the Aetolian League. With its hands freed after the defeat of Hannibal, Rome now gave its attention to the Greek sphere, as it was doing simultaneously to the other legacies of the Punic Wars in northern Italy and Iberia. Encouraged by new allies in Greece, and by Rhodes and Pergamum across the Aegean, Rome challenged Philip to withdraw from Greece. When Philip refused Rome launched a war against him. At Cynoscephalae in 197 B.C. the famed Macedonian phalanx met the Roman legions in battle for the first time and went down to defeat. Rome's object, as in Spain and elsewhere, was not the direct acquisition of territory or the complete destruction of Macedonia as a center of power, but only its weakening and curtailment within suitable limits. This was achieved by balancing Macedonia against Aetolia and winning over the Greek states by granting them their freedom. Unfortunately the term *freedom* had a Greek and a Roman connotation and it was to take more wars and the breaking up of

Macedonia before the ambiguities of the term were removed and the Roman meaning was fully understood and accepted in the Greek world.

Typically, the first of these wars was provoked by Rome's first Greek ally, the Aetolian League. This militarily powerful but culturally backward league had hoped in typical Greek fashion to fill the power vacuum left by Macedonia, but was disappointed not only in this but even in its territorial ambitions with regard to the annexation of a few adjoining Thessalian towns. Typically, also, the war involved Rome with the king of Syria, the Seleucid Antiochus III, whose possessions in Asia Minor Rome now came into contact with. The evacuation of Greece in 196 had won Rome much good will, so that when Antiochus, in response to the urging of the Aetolians, landed in Greece in 192 to "liberate the Greeks" he received a cool reception. In due course he was bundled out of Greece by the Romans, who quickly returned. Subsequently he was completely defeated in a set battle at Magnesia-on-Sipylus in Asia Minor (190 B.C.). The Romans imposed an armaments reduction and an enormous indemnity, which eventually led to the destruction of Seleucid power in the east. Rome's staunch allies in Asia, Rhodes and Pergamum, were heavily rewarded and a new balance of power established in the eastern Mediterranean (the peace of Apamea, 188 B.C.). Egypt, weak at this time, had no intention of challenging Rome, especially after seeing its two old rivals, Macedonia and Syria, go down to defeat so easily.

Rome's handling of Greece, a combination of cynical manipulation and reliance on its traditional client–patron approach, continued to lead to more misunderstandings and blunders on the part of its allies and enemies alike. In taking on alliances with Greek states and cities Rome inevitably became involved in the complicated political and social entanglements that had frustrated every effort of philosopher, statesman, and general for the preceding 500 years. Rome was constantly besieged by Greek individuals, factions, and governments attempting to manipulate it in their own self-interest against other Greeks. At one time the Senate was confronted by no less than four sets of Spartan envoys, each of whom claimed to speak for their country as legitimate spokesman. Such a situation put the Greeks at the mercy of the Romans, but it also dragged the Romans into the demoralizing world of Greek diplomacy where they quickly learned (or perfected) the arts of casuistry, equivocation, and mischief-making.

A complaint by an ally, or perhaps a suspicious move by one of the powers being watched by Rome, led, time and again, to increased suspicions and investigations by commissions that in turn often provoked confrontations. Such a combination of circumstances led, after Philip's death, to a final confrontation in Macedonia between his son Perseus and the Romans. The consolidation of Macedonia's economic and manpower resources and a marriage alliance with the Seleucids, together with the personally urged allegations of Eumenes, king of Pergamum, led to another war and the final overthrow of the Macedonian kingdom at the battle of Pydna in 168 B.C. In the aftermath Macedonia was divided into four impotent, autonomous republics. With the loss of its kings, one of the world's great nations passed into obscurity and oblivion. At the same time the Romans dissolved the Greek Boeotian League (whose democratic organization found little sympathy at Rome, where democracy was identified with instability). Rome also weakened Rhodes, an erstwhile ally, which had mistakenly offered to mediate between Rome and Perseus when the former seemed to be having difficulty bringing the Macedonians to a decisive confrontation on the battlefield. Pergamum was also involved in mediation attempts and likewise suffered eclipse as Rome's foremost ally in Asia Minor. Once again Rome refused to take on the responsibility of formal supervision of the conquered areas, though it did assume a direct financial interest by continuing to collect, at a reduced rate, the taxes the Macedonian kings had levied in the past. After clearing out the unreliable anti-Roman elements throughout the Greek cities, the Roman legions returned once more to Italy, laden with immense booty.

This was not, however, the last involvement of Rome in the tangle of Greek politics. Rome had done in Greece what it did in Italy and the western Mediterranean—namely, it eliminated one power block after another and slowly inculcated the rules under which politics were to be exercised. Allies were frequently slower to learn the rules than enemies—as the examples of Aetolia, Rhodes, and Pergamum already demonstrated. Now the Achaean League, another old ally of Rome, miscalculated just how much freedom it was allowed to settle affairs in its own area, the Peloponnese, where it maintained a permanent dispute with Sparta. This time the issue was resolved by the dissolution of the league and the barbaric sack and destruction of the ancient city of Corinth as an object lesson to the rest of Greece (146 B.C.). Greece as a whole now came under the general supervision of the Roman governor of Macedonia, which had been made into a province two years previously after yet another revolt. The same year (146 B.C.) saw the sack and destruction of another great city, Carthage, Rome's old rival for power in the west, after a three year siege. The same combination of Roman suspicions and the complaints of allies that had so often brought on confrontations in Greece had the same effect in Africa, where the basic economic strength of Carthage and the constant stream of complaints from the Numidians finally brought Rome to a decision it had avoided in the past: the destruction of the city. Yet another province, that of Africa, was added and came under the direct surveillance of a Roman governor.

In pulling together the loose ends after the Punic Wars, Rome emerged in 146 B.C. as the dominant power not just in the west but in the whole Mediterranean. Under formal supervision were the overseas provinces of Sicily, Sardinia-Corsica, Macedonia, Africa, the two Spains, and shortly afterward Asia Minor and southern Gaul. Cowed and enmeshed in the Roman system of client-patron relations were the important states of Syria, Egypt, Pergamum, and Rhodes, and dozens of petty states and cities. The social structure that served so well within Rome and had enabled it to build unobtrusive power in Italy was now extended to the whole Mediterranean and was in time to constitute the basis for the unification of the whole region in the Roman Empire. At precisely this moment the new policeman of the world fell victim to internal disorder, corruption, and revolution, brought on, paradoxically, by its efforts to bring the Mediterranean world into line with its own sociopolitical assumptions and goals.

ECONOMIC AND CULTURAL CHANGES IN THE SECOND CENTURY

The wars of the second century brought a gigantic flow of booty to Rome from the ransacked cities of Greece, north Africa, and Spain. Indemnities from Carthage and Syria, taxes from Asia Minor, and the products of the fabulous mines of Spain and Macedonia swelled Rome's income to enormous proportions. So much money flowed into Rome that 25 years worth of surtaxes collected during the Hannibalic War were returned to the people in 187 B.C., and the main tax, the *tributum*, a capital levy, ceased to be collected after 167.

With little impulse on the part of the Romans to build up capital, the money poured into public building programs and items of conspicuous consumption. Throughout Italy in the second century a great network of trunk roads was constructed, linking one end of the country with the other and tying previously existing colonies directly to the city of Rome. In the north the Po Valley was dissected by the Via Aemilia and the Via Postumia which linked Genoa on the west to Aquileia and Ariminum on the Adriatic. Another consular road, the Via Aurelia–Aemilia ran from Rome along the coast to Genoa. Other major roads were constructed in the mountainous regions of central Italy and two great highways, the Via Appia and the Via Annia gave access to the south. In addition to the trunk roads, secondary roads sprang up to serve local needs and connect bypassed towns with the main routes. New colonies were established in strategic locations, and on occasion individual grants *(viritim)* of public land were made to attract migrant peasants from the overcrowded parts of central Italy. The slow process of clearing the forests and draining the swamps of the Po Valley was begun, making this immensely fertile region available for cultivation.

Although road construction was not undertaken with economic objectives in view, it had the effect of opening up previously inaccessible and unprofitable Roman landholdings to Roman farmers, both large and small. Archaeological surveys show that land use intensified during the second century in many parts of Italy, as the primeval forest was cut down and land came under cultivation for the first time. Northeast of Rome was a large area in which specialized farms produced vegetables, poultry, fish, and all sorts of luxury items (snails, boars stags, thrushes, for example) for the Roman market. Served by three great trunk roads, the Via Flaminia, the Via Cassia, and the Via Clodia, this was a natural area for intensive farming. Similar "truck-farming" regions were probably associated with cities throughout the peninsula. Elsewhere in Italy great groves of olive trees and vineyards were planted to supply the needs of an affluent population and to provide exports for growing markets overseas, especially in the west. In the provinces, too, roads were constructed, as for example the Via Egnatia, which traversed Macedonia, and the Via Herculea in Spain.

The impact of the wealth of the Mediterranean was soon seen in other ways. Rome went on a building spree that continued, on and off, for 500 years leaving the huge monuments of brick and concrete so much admired by visitors to Rome over the centuries. Two new aqueducts, the Aqua Marcia and the Aqua Tepula, were constructed and the older aqueducts repaired with the result that the water supply of Rome was more than doubled. The censors of 184 B.C., Cato and Flaccus, spent hugh sums of money improving the drainage and sewage systems of the city. Over the years additional sums were poured into new bridges (the Mulvian and Aemilian), basilicas (Sempronian, Aemilian, and Opimian), a dozen or more temples, and half a dozen shrines, in addition to warehouses, porticoes, granaries, sidewalks, shopping areas, arches, and statues. The first marble buildings were constructed in the second century and a gilded ceiling was seen for the first time in Rome in the Capitolium. Elsewhere in Italy similar building projects embellished municipal towns with baths, forums, basilicas, and temples, some funded by the central treasury, others by local notables or municipal councils. L. Mummius, who sacked Corinth, adorned the towns of Italy and the provinces with the booty, as his surviving inscriptions proclaim. Huge private fortunes were accumulated and villas and town houses, in the past marked by simplicity of style and construction, were now built with all the luxurious embellishments that eastern architects and artists could devise. Eventually these villas evolved into the landscape-type mansions of the first century, with their grounds laid out in imitation of natural scenery. Towers, bridges, pavilions, statues, trees, and artificial islands and streams adorned the grounds, and there were aviaries, fish ponds, baths, and every known amenity.

Cultural Changes

In the second century, in addition to the other problems brought on by its military successes, Rome had to face and cope with the allurements of Greek culture. It would not be an exaggeration to say that Romans were culturally illiterate in the fields of poetry, drama, and history before the second century, though some efforts were being made in the direction of the first two at this time, chiefly by outsiders. Latin, however, was still not suited for prose writing and was only slowly being made amenable to poetry and drama. Yet it was at precisely this time that Rome had the greatest need to communicate with the rest of the world and explain its institutions and politics to the educated classes of the Mediterranean, whether Greek, Italian, or barbarian. Public opinion was important in the Greek-speaking world and it was highly necessary for the Romans to respond to questions being raised throughout the Mediterranean about where Rome sprang from; what enabled it to conquer Pyrrhus, the Gauls and the Carthaginians (the last two both ancient enemies of the Greeks); and what justification, if any, it had for possessing an empire.

The first answers were supplied by Greeks writing about Rome from a distance, such as Timaeus of Tauromenium (in Sicily) who lived in Athens in the early third century. Not until the end of the Punic Wars were Romans themselves able to give an account of their institutions and history. Writing in Greek, Fabius Pictor wrote a history of Rome that emphasized its strength, moderation, tenaciousness, and good faith, as well as the wisdom of its Senate and its strict moral code. With Cato the Elder, in the first half of the second century, Latin history-writing came into existence for the first time, representing a new level of self-confidence on the part of the Romans, who now rose to the challenge of Greek letters by composing a literature of their own in their own language. This was an achievement matched by no other people with whom the Greeks came into contact. For Cato, in fact, the Greeks no longer counted; Romans and Italians had nothing of which to be ashamed. On the contrary, they had incorporated what was best in the Greek world while preserving the best of their own rich heritage—a pardonable exaggeration with which a lot of second-century Greeks must have agreed. From this time on numerous histories in Latin by members of the senatorial class provided the growing reading public of Rome and Italy with suitably patriotic, moralizing histories, frequently laced with polemical tracts from the internal political battles of the century. There were few qualms about adapting history to the political needs of the Roman upper classes and history was seen as a means of glorifying one's achievements and the achievements of one's family as well as propagandizing for further advancement.

Although the Romans had mastered the inhabitants of the Mediterranean by the middle of the second century, at that time they considered the development of a philosophy of empire unnecessary. To them all Roman wars were defensive actions conducted in accordance with strict religious rules (known as the fetial laws) that prohibited wars of aggression. However, by midcentury, when Rome's actions were beginning to look less and less justifiable, the necessity of a philosophy to justify its actions became obvious. It was supplied by the Greek philosopher Panaetius of Rhodes, who combined the Stoic ideal of moral duty and the old Roman concept of good faith *(fides),* and argued that the empire was justified only if the Romans used their strength fairly and conscientiously for the good of the people they ruled. It was to this high duty that Rome was called by destiny and for which it was particularly well equipped. Rome had become great through its pious observance of its duties to the gods, who in turn had repaid piety with prosperity. Rome's actions were patently contradicting this theory, yet because what men believe their true motives to be are often deciding factors in shaping their conduct, Panaetius' justification of empire eventually became a model for generations of Romans who dedicated themselves to the good of the people they ruled. "It was largely to them," comments F. W. Walbank, "that the Roman empire owed its greatness, and pondering on what they did one is made aware in a salutary way of the limitations of political realism."[3]

In Cato's younger days Roman poetry and drama were rudimentary, with Livius Andronicus and Naevius providing translations of Greek poems and plays, but the first half of the second century saw the full flowering of Latin in the works of Ennius, Pacuvius, Plautus, Terence, and others. Epic poems glorifying Rome's past and its destiny were produced and Ennius' aphorisms, whic

[3]F. W. Walbank, *Journal of Roman Studies* 55 (1965): 16.

reflected the nobles' vision of Rome, became commonplaces quoted throughout subsequent Roman history. Plays celebrating historical events of the Roman past were written but never became popular. On the other hand, comedies, especially those of Plautus, were always popular, though the setting and the stock figures were Greek, for fear of offending conservative Roman tastes. There was no place for Aristophanic humor in a Rome where the aristocracy took its role as a governing class seriously and unquestioningly. Mime and farce, which were native to Italy, were the popular fare of the lower classes and eventually displaced the plays of Roman comedy altogether.

Although Greek grammarians were present in Rome in 167 B.C., they were expelled six years later. When three famous Greek philosophers—Carneades, the head of the Academy; the Stoic Diogenes; and Critolaus the Peripatetic—came to Rome to plead a case on behalf of Athens, they electrified the youth of the city with their lectures. Nothing like Carneades' lecture on justice and its application to the problem of empire, delivered on two successive days—on the second of which the speaker refuted all the theories he had put up on the previous day—had been heard before. Cato urged that the philosophers be given a quick answer to their plea so they could return to their schools in Athens as soon as possible while the "youth of Rome could listen, as in the past, to their laws and magistrates."[4] Even Scipio Aemilianus, the patron and friend of the Greek historian Polybius, attacked the corrupting influence of Greek ideas, and especially the disastrous effect of wealth on the Roman ruling class. Scipio Nasica prevented the building of a permanent theater in 154 B.C., because he feared it would lead to the speedy corruption of the Romans, and such a theater was not built for a century. A permanent amphitheater for the games, which were becoming increasingly popular, was not built until the end of the first century, presumably on the grounds that one of the best ways of controlling this form of amusement was to keep the audience from becoming too comfortable.

Religion, too, showed the effects of the upheavals brought about by the acquisition of an empire. Traditionally, Roman religion had been an integral part of state affairs. There was, of course, a "private" religion or devotion practiced within families and by individuals, but the state was involved with religion as part of its proper function. Political figures held religious offices as a matter of course and the maintenance of the peace of the gods (the *pax deorum*) was as much a part of the functioning of the state as fighting wars or hearing legal cases—the other two primary functions of Roman magistrates who inherited the triple roles of priest, judge, and general from the Etruscan kings. However, after the expansion of Rome the old system was manifestly inadequate and the very localized character of the religion made it impossible to export. Religious functions were to be performed in Rome, and various figures who, in addition to being consuls or praetors, were also priests, were hindered in the performance of their duties and in some instances could not leave Italy at all. As Rome grew and the bonds of clientship *(clientela)* dissolved, the confinement of religion to the

[4]Plutarch, *Life of Marcus Cato,* 22.5.

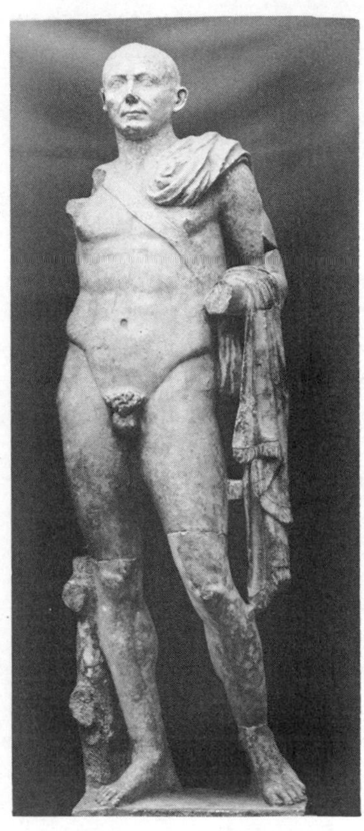

The new directions: Roman general portrayed in the Hellenistic style. First century B.C.

higher officials of state and to state functions created a vacuum. Eastern religions moved in to fill the void. The worship of the Great Mother *(Magna Mater, Mater Deorum,* or Cybele) was introduced officially in 205 B.C., and unofficially the worship of Dionysus crept into Italy and was savagely repressed as being dangerous to Rome both politically and morally. The two religions remained, however, as the forerunners of many others, including the one that was ultimately to triumph, Christianity.

New Classes Emerge

Not all the wealth that flowed to Rome was in the form of cash or movable property. Huge numbers of slaves accompanied the returning conquerors and were put to work in various segments of the economy—in agriculture, industry, the mines, and various categories of domestic slavery. No one knows the numbers but the impact was sufficient to jolt the entire economic structure of Italy out of its traditional ways and to introduce an entirely new factor into Roman society. Since Roman masters had a propensity for manumission and slaves when manumitted by Romans acquired the franchise (unlike their Greek counterparts), the existence of a large servile population guaranteed a constant stream of new blood into the free Roman population from the second century onward. The freedman class was generally made up of former domestic or urban slaves engaged in skilled and professional activities; these were, in comparison to the average freeborn Roman, well-to-do. They therefore tended to enter the middle rather than the lower classes.

An even more significant development of the second century was the increased importance of the equestrian class, the *equites.* This general term was applied to wealthy individuals outside the Senate who possessed a high census rating as well as other qualifications (see Chapter 12). Since senators were barred from contracting, banking, and trade, and manufacturing was looked down on, the equestrian class was able to exercise almost a monopoly in these increasingly important areas. One group of equestrians (called *publicani* or publicans because they served the public sector), were organized in small companies and contracted with the state for the lease of mines, the construction of roads and public buildings, the manufacture of arms, the supply of food and clothing for the

Despite their properly Roman dress and pose, the couple are in fact ex-slaves as the accompanying inscription (not shown) indicates. Late first century B.C.

armies, and so on. Since the second century was a particularly lucrative period for building contracts and arms supply, the influence of the publicans increased proportionately, although it was some time before an attempt was made to translate this newfound power into direct political influence in opposition to that of the Senate. Another group, also belonging to the equestrian order, was engaged in trade, banking, and manufacturing. Since so much capital had come to Rome, loans were readily available and Rome soon became the financial capital of the Mediterranean. Although senators could not engage directly in these activities, their surplus capital was let out on loans, and both senators and equestrians invested heavily in land in many parts of Italy, especially in the south. The differences between senators and equestrians should not be exaggerated as they both belonged to the same ruling class and shared common financial and economic interests. Nevertheless, the more actively involved groups of equestrians, along with the large new servile and freedman classes, had no traditionally established place in Roman society. Much of the turmoil and unrest of the second and first centuries involved the slow process by which these new groups carved out niches for themselves in the conservative Roman social structure. The changes did not come about easily.

The lower classes, which with the traditional patrician class formed the basis for the society of the old Roman Republic, changed enormously in the course of the second century. In the past members of these classes were almost exclusively rural and fitted into the social fabric of the state quite readily as clients of the nobility. As clients they could be either tenants on the great estates of the nobles, or free, independent proprietor farmers. Either way, the social structure was geared to a very stable economy and the unchanging although complex relationship of client to patron. In addition to the clients there were others among the lower classes who from time immemorial had remained outside the clientage system but had never, at least in the country districts, constituted an important political force.

All this began to change rapidly under the new conditions of the second century. First there were the enormous losses of the Punic Wars and subsequent wars of conquest in Spain, Greece, and north Africa. Peasants who in the early Republic could readily take time from their work to repel raiders or engage in summer campaigns in Italy now found themselves frequently assigned to quasi-permanent armies in the provinces overseas. It could be years before they returned home, and their farms inevitably suffered. Throughout the first half of the second century a considerable body of men, estimated at close to 50,000, were annually in arms. But this was not the only force that transformed the peasant subsistence farmer of Italy.

With growing markets in Italy and the introduction of new cash-crop farming techniques, the peasant found himself with yet another alternative to his previous economic mode of existence. He could, with the capital acquired in the form of war booty, transform his holding into a profitable enterprise based on slave labor, granted the right conditions of access to transportation and a good market. Probably not many peasants achieved this transformation, and intensively exploited farms were more likely to represent investments of overcapitalized senators and members of the equestrian class. With much new land coming into production in various parts of Italy, especially in the north, there were new possibilities and new incentives to move, further weakening the old social system, which was based on long-term occupation of the same farmstead and the hereditary client–patron relationship. Withdrawal from this relationship, either by emigration or by its transformation had not occurred on such a scale before. In addition, uprooted peasants and veterans flowed to Rome and to the towns of Italy, there to find partial employment in the great houses of the nobles and the huge building programs and service industries that were growing, thus creating a true urban proletariat for the first time in Roman history.

THE GRACCHAN REVOLUTION

Even before the major outbreak of violence that took place in 133 B.C., there were numerous manifestations of unrest. Recruitment for wars in both Greece and Spain was a constant cause of discontent. There was a mutiny in the army in Greece in 198 and insubordination there eight years later; in 189 B.C. Manlius Vulso was forced to relax discipline and to bribe his troops in order to get them to fight. Aemilius Paullus, the victor over the Macedonians at Pydna, had great difficulty initially with his undisciplined troops, and they later complained loudly of the small amount of loot they received and even attempted to prevent his triumph. The Spanish war, particularly, caused major outbursts. Recruitment was difficult from the beginning and discontent chronic. Draft riots broke out in 151 and 138 B.C. and the tribunes, upon being appealed to by prospective recruits, imprisoned the consuls who were conducting the enlistment. Raw recruits were frequently sent out when veterans refused to serve.

Attempts were made to cope with these indications of dissatisfaction and new laws, the *leges Porciae,* so improved conditions of military service and guaranteed the personal rights of Roman citizens that by 150 B.C., at least, the infliction of the death penalty on citizens had fallen into general disuse. Secret ballots were introduced after midcentury for elections, trials, and legislation, indicating concessions to popular demands. The latent power of the tribunate was slowly awakened, and in an increasing number of instances tribunes were willing to use their awesome power on behalf of groups or individuals who felt the state was not rendering them justice. Some nobles were not above appealing directly to the people and using tribunes on their own behalf. Scipio Aemilianus, the destroyer of Carthage, was twice elected consul and assigned provinces with the assistance of the people in flagrant defiance of custom and law. His close friend G. Laelius proposed an agrarian law that excited fierce opposition in the Senate and had to be withdrawn. Laws against corrupt electioneering practices *(leges de ambitu)* were enacted in 181 and 159 B.C., and by the end of the century there was a standing court responsible for the examination of such cases. This again indicates the rising power of independent voters, free of the patron–client system. Attempts were made by conflicting interests to control the power of the tribunes by manipulating the state religion *(leges Aelia et Fufia)* and—at about the same time—to break the hold of the nobles on the priesthoods by the introduction of a law that would require the vacancies in the priestly colleges to be filled by popular election rather than by the traditional careful process of co-option, which allowed the nobles to control these important offices closely.

All of this points to the gradual breakdown of the old predictable social bonds that united the nobles in a common front and bound the masses of the people to the upper classes by ties of patronage. With Rome's lower classes expanding, as dispossessed small farmers and veterans migrated to the city and mixed with increasingly heterogeneous classes of slaves and freedmen, the social relations of the past based on concepts of the extended family gave way to new relationships based on common economic or political interests, or mere propinquity. Votes, which in the past belonged to a patron by ancient customs, began to be thought of as free and could be sought by anyone caring to solicit them. Laws against corrupt electioneering were unavailing, and expensive spectacles or significant military achievements became alternative ways to high office, though it was not until the next century that the most flagrant abuses were found in this area. The upper classes, the senators and the equestrians, were gradually seduced from their rigorous ideals of public service by the increasingly attractive alternatives of the private realm, which offered the comforts of luxurious villas, expensive clothes and foods, and the satisfaction of their intellectual, aesthetic, and sensual appetites, which they were neither permitted nor could afford to indulge in previously. Taxes introduced by Cato on slaves with special skills or talents, ornaments, women's clothes, and other items failed to check incipient luxury, and similar taxes on statues and other *objets d'art* had no success.

The railings of Cato and other moralists against the setting up of public statues (including statues to women), and their general allegations of moral corruption, point to a major reordering of values in the second century. There was a fine dividing line between the acquisition of glory *(gloria)* in the service of the state and outright self-inflation. The values that made Rome great in war and adversity led in peace to monstrous examples of egomania and self-indulgence.

Tiberius Gracchus

The enormous social, cultural, and economic changes of the second century were channeled into an old constitutional framework designed for a city and territory a fraction of the size of the empire at that time. The political machinery of the Republic was called upon to perform tasks it was never designed for. In 133 B.C., when it was presented with major legislation that flew in the face of over half a century of development, it completely failed. The result was a division in the ruling class following roughly the lines of division that had begun to appear in Roman society at large.

The agents of this change were not outsiders to the ruling elite who emerged directly from the new forces at work in Roman society as one might expect, but descendants of two of the most prominent families in the aristocracy, the Cornelii and Sempronii. On their mother's side Tiberius and Gaius Gracchus were the descendants of Scipio Africanus, and by marriage they were connected with the most distinguished families in Rome. Their brother-in-law was Scipio Aemilianus, who in 133 B.C. was commanding the Roman forces besieging Numantia in Spain. Tiberius was married to a daughter of Appius Claudius, who had been both consul and censor and now enjoyed the title of *princeps senatus,* the foremost man in the Senate; Gaius' father-in-law, Licinius Crassus, was soon to be *pontifex maximus* (chief priest) and consul. Conveniently, Crassus' own brother was consul in 133 B.C., the very year that the elder Gracchan brother, Tiberius, entered into the office of tribune of the plebs with a radical plan to transform the foundation of the Roman state.

In the view of Gracchus and his supporters, many of Rome's problems were due to the steady disappearance of the peasant farmer, who was being pushed off the land by the rich landowners. This in turn was making it difficult to obtain adequate numbers of the right kind of recruits for the legions. Although this analysis was partially correct, it failed to do justice to the exceedingly complex problems of the second century or even to the reasons for the inadequate number of troops. By midcentury there was indeed a decline in the number of peasant farmers available for legionary service. But there was also an increasing reluctance on the part of many to serve in the new kinds of wars being fought, wars not so much for the defense of Rome but for the protection or acquisition of an overseas empire. Besides, there were new economic opportunities in Italy that made soldiering a less-than-attractive alternative.

Whatever the explanation for the decline in numbers on the draft rolls, the conclusion was still the same: There were too few recruits for the army. It was to solve this problem as well as to build up their faction's power that the Gracchans proposed their measure. The idea was to tap the huge resources of public land over which the state had sovereignty, and put it to use by granting inalienable plots to individual farmers who, with their descendants, would be forever liable to legionary service while also politically obligated to the Gracchans for the original land grant. There would be much less opportunity for these new farm owners to escape the draft, either by administrative malfunction or deliberate avoidance. So, at a stroke, the regular supply of troops would be guaranteed or at least augmented. It was estimated, presumably, that the bait of land would outweigh the general reluctance of the peasantry to serve in the legions at all.

There were two difficulties with this program. The first was that the public land concerned was already parceled out in inextricable confusion between legal renters and leaseholders who considered themselves de facto owners, and illegal squatters, both Roman and non-Roman, including in some instances the original possessors who had never vacated their confiscated land. Tiberius and his supporters first had to clear these people off the land and somehow equitably settle a large number of complicated suits before initiating their own settlement program. Since many of the leaseholders as well as the squatters with doubtful title were well-to-do, this proposal was calculated to stir up a storm of protest, which in fact it did, and continued to do long after Tiberius' death. The second problem, unanticipated at least in its size, was the large number of rural dwellers at the other end of the scale who were suddenly offered either outright grants of land, an increase in their property holdings, or the confirmation of title to perhaps some of the land on which they were already squatting. There were, naturally, more of these than of the first group of well-to-do possessors, and when the law came up for the vote Rome witnessed the extraordinary sight of masses of country people pouring into the city to support the law. With excellent markets now available for farm products, the ownership of land or the extension of one's possessions was an irresistible attraction, which for the moment overcame the problems of time and distance normally deterring rural voters from traveling to Rome. The Gracchans now found themselves, willy-nilly, at the head of an unplanned democratic movement. When other members of the aristocratic coalition backed off Tiberius went ahead with the law, which first required the unprecedented and ticklish removal from office of an opposing tribune.

With the passage of the law and the election of a commission (consisting of Tiberius, his brother, and his father-in-law!) to administer it, the rural mob withdrew from Rome and political life began to return to normal. There arose the inevitable threat of prosecution of Tiberius for illegality when his term of office was up on December 9, 133. To forestall this Tiberius attempted to have himself reelected to the tribunate. Not having the rural voters at his command as he had earlier in the year, he turned to other groups that the upheavals of the second century had also brought to the surface. To the equestrian class and better-off nonsenatorial classes he offered the bait of favorable legislation of various kinds, later developed by his brother Gaius. These new supporters were unable or perhaps not as willing as the rural crowds might have been to defend him against a determined assault by his opponents, who physically broke up the assembly on the day of the election, and in the confusion killed him and many of his followers.

The Gracchan measure was not a forward-looking piece of legislation, but one conceived to solve an immediate problem, the shortage of the right kind of recruits for the legions that defended and enlarged Rome's new empire. The measure showed an ignorance on the part of the ruling classes as well as lack of ability (or willingness, perhaps) to come to grips with the enormous changes taking place in Italy in the second century. This was particularly evident in the lack of concern on the part of Tiberius and his supporters for the allies who were deeply affected by the agrarian law and who a generation later were to bring about the needed reforms only after fighting a bloody war of secession. The Gracchans looked to the past for the solution while their opponents were content to drift with the times, trying neither to restore the past nor change the government sufficiently to cope with the new realities—at least as long as the symbols of power remained within their grasp. Efforts at solution were piecemeal and individualistic, and the oligarchy moved toward impotence, being capable on occasion of repressing movements for change (whether good or bad), but unable to initiate significant change constructively.

Gaius Gracchus

Ten years after Tiberius' death his brother Gaius, who in the intervening years had performed his required military service as well as acting as commissioner for the discharge of his brother's agrarian law, entered the same office of tribune of the plebs as Tiberius had in 133, but with a new strategy and a new plan of action. This time an appeal was made immediately to several of the newly emerging groups, though not to the rural crowds who had proved so difficult to handle in 133. The publicans were offered the contracts for the taxes of Asia, which dwarfed all others in size, as well as large contracts for the construction of roads, granaries, and public buildings. In addition, the equestrian class, to which the publicans belonged, were to be given control of the extortion court *(quaestio de repetundis),* which tried cases of senatorial misconduct in provincial administration and which up until then had been in the hands of the senators themselves. This new arrangement would ensure the publicans a high degree of political freedom from senatorial interference in their collection of the taxes of Asia. Promises of large amounts of land in Africa for well-to-do groups in Italy, grain at a fixed price for the urban crowds, some laws governing military service and personal rights, Roman citizenship for the Latins and Latin citizenship for the Italian allies were the baits offered to the final elements of the Gracchan coalition. This extraordinary combination of interests enabled Gaius to wield power for two consecutive years and enact most of the promised legislation, but in time the inevitable negative forces with which the Roman constitution abounded, in particular the tribunician veto, gradually dissolved the alliance. In 121 B.C. Gaius found himself out of office and without power. During an attempt by his opponents to abrogate one of his laws he was killed along with many of his supporters, including the ex-consul Fulvius Flaccus, and his body was thrown into the Tiber.

The end of Gaius was another illustration of the Senate's inability to rule and the power of the new forces within the Republic. Gaius' coalition of equestrians, well-to-do groups, and the urban crowds enabled him to control the Tribal Assembly for a period of time, but it did not constitute the basis for a permanent government. At the same time, the very existence of this coalition of forces showed the paralysis of the old senatorial oligarchy and the ineffectiveness of its ruling techniques. Granted that in the end the Gracchan coalition disintegrated and the old system reasserted itself, nevertheless it was to be only a matter of time before new leaders would experiment with the newly emerging forces. The Gracchans also demonstrated the power of the new groups emerging in Roman society, especially the rural voters, the equestrian class, and the urban crowds, and they also pointed out the discontent of the Italian allies. By emphasizing the power of the equestrian class they suggested that there was a basis of power other than landed wealth, and by inviting the rural voters, the Italians, and the urban crowds to involve themselves in the legal and political processes, they helped stimulate the political consciousness of these groups and encouraged them to hope for more than they had ever received in the past. It was to these groups more and more that politicians were to turn. Eventually the revolution, culminating in the rise of Augustus, was to guarantee them a place in the structure of Roman society that the old aristocracy was unable to concede them voluntarily.

14

The Transformation of the Republic, Part Two

FROM THE GRACCHI TO AUGUSTUS

The century after the Gracchi was one of slow adjustment to the great issues they raised. One by one, without following any particular program or plan, each issue was resolved in turn. The problem of recruitment for the legions was settled by Marius in 107 B.C. when he eliminated property qualifications for service in the legions. Conscription was henceforth reserved for emergency situations. The Italian allies fought for and won the citizenship in a bloody war between 91 and 89 B.C. The Senate was expanded to twice its original size by Sulla and most of the new members were drawn from the equestrians, thus hastening the unification of the senatorial and equestrian orders in the government of Augustus.

The most intractable problem was the question of who was to rule, and by what means. The old understanding about this had been undergoing change for years, but no new agreement had yet been worked out.

At issue was the question of the composition of the ruling oligarchy. In the past, by tacit agreement, a handful of families had passed the chief offices of state among themselves, and the Senate, by exercising discipline over its own membership, had been able to maintain control of the political power of the state. Toward the end of the second century, however, this discipline weakened and political power began to fragment. Though the old coterie of nobles was still regularly able to place its candidates in high office, it was unable to dominate the Senate and the political process as it had in the past. When a new ruling oligarchy emerged almost a century later most of the old families were gone and their replacements came from a much wider social and geographic background. Numerically, too, the ruling class was larger than in the past. Nevertheless, the social viewpoints of the newcomers did not essentially differ from those of their predecessors. What had changed was the locus of political power and the source of senatorial discipline, both of which now lay outside the Senate in the hands of the new political head of the state, the emperor.

The Rise of Marius

The external enemies that Rome faced in the generation after the Gracchi were not major powers on the order of Carthage or the Hellenistic states of an earlier period. There were, rather, tribal peoples, and the wars of the period followed the pattern of the guerrilla campaigns that Rome had fought in Spain. They were long, protracted, and unconventional, the kind that easily brought out the ineptness and weakness of the senatorial system of command.

In 116 B.C. Rome became involved in the disputed succession to the throne of the client-kingdom of Numidia. By 111 B.C. Roman troops were fully engaged and for a number of years thereafter the war dragged on dismally, Roman commanders appearing in unfavorable contrast to their wily opponent, the Numidian king Jugurtha. Exasperated by repeated failure and the slow pace of the war, the people turned to Gaius Marius, a "new man" of equestrian background, who promised them a quick end to the war. With great popular acclaim he was elected to the consulship for 107 B.C.

The problem faced by Marius in the African war was a basic one of guerrilla warfare: He had to have considerably more troops than the enemy, but, with another war in progress elsewhere and permanent manpower shortages, it seemed unlikely that he would be any more successful than his predecessors. However, by the simple but bold expedient of enrolling the propertyless in the legions, Marius resolved the manpower shortage problem. By 105 B.C. the war was over, just in time to allow him to return to Italy to bring another war, this time against the German tribes, to a successful conclusion.

Toward the end of the second century two large German tribes, the Cimbri and the Teutons, were driven from their homeland in Denmark by the flooding of the sea, and they began a slow march southward. Repulsed in the Danube area, they moved toward Italy and made their first contact with the Romans in 113 B.C. Thereafter they continued their wanderings, colliding with other Roman armies, which they easily overcame. A major defeat for the Romans at Arausio (Orange) in southern France in 105 B.C. brought on the possibility of an invasion of Italy. Once more the people turned to Marius and elected him consul for the next five years, flatly disregarding the law that prohibited such successive tenures of office. Immediately Marius set about a thoroughgoing reorganization and retraining of the legions, grouping the original 30 maniples in units of ten each, called *cohorts,* each with about 500 men. The cohorts were further subdivided into six centuries. The corporate identity and the continuity of the legions were fostered by giving each one its own "eagle" or standard.

Meanwhile the German tribes had once more postponed their invasion of Italy. When they did return Marius defeated them separately, the Cimbri at Aix in southern France in 102 B.C., and the Teutons the following year near Vercellae in northern Italy.

Marius, Saturninus, and the Veterans

After the German menace had been removed, the old system of senatorial rule began to reassert itself and Marius' power declined, but not before he engaged in yet another experiment.

Under the old draft system it was assumed that discharged soldiers would return to their farms and resume life where they had left off; but what was to be done with Marius' propertyless veterans, who were now an officially acknowledged part of the army? Somehow they had to be cared for, and the easiest solution seemed to be to make them land assignments. For this purpose Marius aligned himself with the ambitious tribune L. Appuleius Saturninus, and pushed for the enactment of a land law. Passage did not come easily and in the impasse Marius brought his veterans into the legislative assembly and secured the passage of the measure by force, thus writing yet another chapter in Roman history (100 B.C.). Although Tiberius Gracchus had used the rural voters and the city mob to pass his measures, and his brother had tried to forge an alliance of the equestrians and the city people, it was not until Marius that the final step of combining tribunes, military commanders, and veterans was taken. It was too effective a combination to be ignored in the future. Marius, however, was no revolutionary and a little later, when Saturninus resorted to violence in furthering his own ambitions, Marius abandoned him and Saturninus was killed in a riot.

The Social War

The issue of citizenship for the Italian allies appears to have gone underground in the years after Gaius Gracchus, but in 91 it resurfaced violently. In the intervening years there had been no letup in the exploitation by Romans of public land all over Italy, and in general the Italians felt that they were getting less than their share of the spoils of conquest. They served in the army and fought Rome's wars but were losing out in the changed conditions of the second and first centuries. When the bestowal of citizenship was raised by the tribune M. Livius Drusus in 91 B.C. but defeated by Roman shortsightedness, the Italians rose in revolt and set up an independent state, which they called Italia, with its capital at Corfinium in central Italy.

The so-called Social War was bitterly contested and not fully stamped out until as late as 80 B.C., but the main issues were resolved by grants of citizenship in 90 and 89 to cities that had not revolted and to individuals who gave up the revolt and surrendered. At last, all of Italy south of the Po was united under a single constitution and a single political system. Even then, however, the

Social War propaganda of the allies: A soldier, with a bull representing Italy beside him, tramples a Roman standard. On other coin issues of the allies the bull is shown goring the Roman wolf.

oligarchy at Rome tried to avoid the political implications of the extension of the citizenship by preventing distribution of the new citizens throughout the tribes for a number of years.

Sulla

War continued to offer opportunities to the able and ambitious among the nobility, and the dominant figures of the next half-century—Sulla, Pompey, Crassus, and Caesar—all rose to prominence through their generalship and their ability to convert success on the battlefield into political power in Rome.

L. Cornelius Sulla had served under Marius in the war against Jugurtha and had recently distinguished himself again in the Social War. Now another opportunity presented itself. In the east the kingdom of Pontus had expanded under a series of energetic rulers and had come into conflict with Roman client-kings in the area. This escalated into a major conflict when the king of Pontus, Mithridates VI, invaded the Roman province of Asia in 88 B.C. and massacred, it is said, 80,000 resident Romans and Italians.

The command of the war against Mithridates went to Sulla but was challenged by Marius, who in collusion with the tribune P. Sulpicius Rufus had himself designated commander. Just as Marius had once gone to the then-revolutionary extent of using his veterans to force the passage of a land law, Sulla now simply marched his troops on Rome, drove out Marius, killed Sulpicius, and invalidated his laws. After enacting some new provisions, he left for the east.

Advancing from Asia, Mithridates' forces had crossed into Greece, but were driven out by Sulla after a series of set battles. By 85 B.C. Mithridates was ready to negotiate, and terms were worked out by which he agreed to vacate the province of Asia and pay an indemnity. Two years later Sulla was back in Italy ready to reestablish his political power, which had collapsed in the interim. With his veteran army and the assistance of a number of young nobles who rallied to him, including M. Licinius Crassus and Cn. Pompeius (Pompey), Sulla routed his opponents and initiated a reign of terror, showing himself once again an apt pupil of the violent politicians who had preceded him. In order to raise money and eliminate his political opponents, he hit upon a novel method of murder, the proscription list, which gave the names of his enemies together with the prices he was willing to pay for their deaths. About 200 senators and over 1600 equestrians perished in these proscriptions, and from the proceeds of their estates Sulla was able to pay his troops and then settle down without fear of opposition to the reform of the constitution.

As dictator from 82 to 79 B.C., he pushed through a series of reforms intended to introduce a measure of order to the chaos of recent political life at Rome. He curtailed the power of the tribunate, increased the number of quaestors and praetors, and established a rigid schedule according to which the different magistracies were to be held. He attempted to control provincial governors whose power, like that of the tribunes in Rome, had grown and was increasingly attractive to ambitious individuals, by ruling that they should not start wars on their own or march their troops across the boundaries of their provinces.

His most important and lasting change was his reform of the Senate, whose numbers had been halved by his own massacres and the battles with the supporters of Marius. To the surviving 150 or so members he added about 400 new members, mostly from the equestrian order. Henceforth the composition of the Senate was radically altered. As a class it was now considerably broadened, and if the old families still continued to dominate the high offices it was not in the coherent fashion of the past, and new men began to make their appearance in the lower magistracies. It is against the background of this much enlarged Senate that the events from Sulla to Caesar must be viewed. The details of the wars that fill this period are not nearly as important as the rapid development of events within the Roman political system itself.

Pompey

After Sulla's death in 78 B.C., wars continued to offer new opportunities to ambitious generals and the Senate demonstrated again and again its inability to control them. It was now too unwieldy and its membership too diffuse to exercise the kind of tight, coherent action necessary to restrain the power of the newly emerging dynasts Pompey, Crassus, and Caesar.

Pompey, one of Sulla's generals, was the first to demonstrate this weakness. When confronted with a series of revolts in Italy and Spain, he maneuvered the Senate into giving him a series of special high commands (propraetorian and proconsular) even though he was still not a member of that body. Crassus, another of Sulla's generals, enhanced his reputation by putting down the great slave revolt of Spartacus in 71 B.C., and together with Pompey he was able to procure his election to the consulship for 70 B.C. Promptly both men saw to the restoration of the tribunate and set about removing what was left of Sulla's reforms.

Three years later a law was proposed to give Pompey a special command with unlimited power *(imperium)* against the pirates whose depredations had grown ever since Rome had curtailed the independent maritime power of Rhodes. The command was so large and so unusual that it provoked a storm of protest in the Senate, where only Julius Caesar, who had been elected to the quaestorship just two years earlier, spoke on its behalf. The bill (the *lex Gabinia)* was finally passed in scenes of great disorder by the popular assembly and Pompey entered his command. By means of excellent organization of his resources he cleared up the pirate menace in three months and was soon settling the remnants of their forces peacefully on vacant land in Cilicia.

In 66 B.C. another opportunity presented itself. The war with Mithridates had been revived, but after initial successes under L. Licinius Lucullus, it was not going well. It was now proposed that Pompey finish it off. Under the terms of the *lex Manilia,* supported again by Caesar and by a new man, Cicero, Pompey was given command of the provinces of Cilicia, Bithynia, and Pontus, and of the war against Mithridates. Between 66 and 62 B.C. Pompey swept through the east, first defeating Mithridates and driving him to flight, then continuing into Armenia and from there back to Syria and into Palestine where he settled a dispute over the throne of Judaea. Single-handedly he redrew the map of the eastern Mediterranean, founding cities and making provinces and treaties with client-kings. In the process, he increased Rome's annual income by 70 percent.

Pompey, Crassus, and Caesar

In Italy, meanwhile, Cicero reached the pinnacle of his career when as consul in 63 B.C. he suppressed a revolt of a group of disgruntled nobles led by L. Sergius Catilina. Crassus, in anticipation of Pompey's return, continued to build up his political strength and sponsored the promising career of Julius Caesar. Others also claimed Crassus' support, such as P. Clodius, whose alleged affair with Caesar's wife led to her divorce and Caesar's famous comment about the necessity of his wife being above suspicion.

The return of Pompey gave new impetus to Caesar's advance. Rebuffed by the Senate in his attempt to have his eastern settlements approved and land appropriated for his veterans, Pompey turned first to a tribune for help and failing there to Caesar, one of the consular candidates for 59 B.C. Crassus also backed Caesar, and with the combined support of Crassus and Pompey Caesar was returned to office, where he immediately saw to the passage of the measures desired by his allies. This alliance, is sometimes, though inaccurately, referred to as the First Triumvirate. The following year Caesar went off to his province, Gaul, where he was occupied for the next seven years. By the end of this period he had annexed for the empire a gigantic new stretch of territory, reaching from the Pyrenees and the Atlantic coast to the Rhine. The resources of this territory, both in manpower and in money, constituted the foundation of what amounted to an independent kingdom.

Although Caesar's command was the most prolonged and the most spectacular, the other members of the alliance also had their military commands during this period. Crassus and Pompey were consuls again in 55 B.C. and were granted the provinces of Syria and Spain, respectively for five years. The three men thus had control over most of the military resources of the empire.

At the end of 55 Crassus went off to Syria in an attempt to refurbish his military reputation, but two years later he was killed by the Parthians at the disastrous battle of Carrhae. This event, coupled with the death in 54 B.C. of Pompey's wife, Julia (Caesar's daughter), led to the disintegration of the alliance. Rome was left with two dominant figures, one of whom was putting the ruthless, finishing touches to one of Rome's most successful and profitable imperialistic ventures. Over a two-year period communications between the two men gradually broke down, until finally Caesar's enemies maneuvered the Senate into declaring him a public enemy and prevailing upon Pompey to "save the Republic."

The Civil Wars

The civil war that followed lasted from 49 to 45 B.C. Pompey was defeated at Pharsalus in Greece in 48 and was murdered shortly afterward while seeking refuge in Egypt. There were two other major engagements, at Thapsus in Africa and Munda in Spain, and in 45 Caesar returned victoriously to Rome. There were no proscriptions and Caesar assiduously extended clemency to his defeated foes.

Like Sulla, Caesar added new members to the again depleted Senate, expanding its numbers from 600 to 900. At the same time he made it clear that the traditions of rule of the Republic were at an end. Early in 44 B.C. he had himself declared Perpetual Dictator and commented that Sulla had committed a major political blunder when he resigned the dictatorship in 79. The Ides of March soon followed.

Between 47 and 44 B.C. Caesar had initiated a huge number of programs, many of which were incomplete at the time of his death. He tackled and solved, at least temporarily, the problem of debt, reformed the calendar, established colonies for his veterans, and initiated an enormous building program at Rome. There were also many legal and constitutional enactments. But on the Ides of March in 44, while making preparations for the war against Parthia to revenge Carrhae and the death of Crassus, he was struck down by a group of senatorial assassins led by M. Junius Brutus and C. Cassius Longinus. Almost immediately a whole new round of civil wars broke out.

In an involved series of actions, Caesar's generals Antony and Lepidus and his heir Octavian established themselves as a ruling Triumvirate. After purging their enemies in a bloody proscription that included Cicero, they divided the Roman world between them. Brutus and Cassius were eliminated in battle at Philippi in 42 and thereafter the Triumvirs ruled in an uneasy alliance. Lepidus was dropped in 36 and the two remaining partners inevitably began to drift apart.

While Octavian consolidated his hold on Italy and the west, Antony, now managing Roman affairs in the east, conducted an unsuccessful campaign against the Parthians. On his return he began to depend more and more on the resources of Egypt as well as on its capable ruler, Cleopatra. Using Antony's relations with Cleopatra as a weapon, Octavian launched a successful campaign to turn popular opinion against him, the most damaging accusation being that Antony wanted to transfer the capital of the empire to Alexandria. Matters finally came to a head in 31 B.C., and Octavian formally declared war against Cleopatra—officially this was not to be another civil war but a war against a foreign enemy. At Actium in Greece Antony and Cleopatra were decisively beaten and subsequently committed suicide. The civil wars were over and Octavian, or Augustus as he is better known to us, was left alone on stage.

THE FALL OF THE ROMAN REPUBLIC

The fall of the Roman Republic is as vast and complicated a subject as the fall of the Roman Empire, although not nearly as well known. In many respects it is also a more absorbing story because the gradual transition from the free institutions of the Republic to those of the autocracy has many more contemporary parallels than the invasion of the Empire by the northern barbarians.

The collapse of the Republic resulted from the complicated interaction of a large number of factors, some acting in an immediate and direct way, others in a less obvious fashion. It is easy enough to list the suspected causes, but much more difficult to explain how they are related to one another or even to weigh their individual importance.

There can be no doubt that the changes in the wealth, sophistication, education, and values of the upper classes had an important bearing on the transition from Republic to Empire. So did the revolutions in agriculture, finance, and commerce that accompanied Rome's rise to world power. But there were other factors. The citizenship expanded enormously and the Senate was first doubled by Sulla, then increased again by Caesar. There were problems with debt, the courts, and relations between the classes, as well as with raising troops and maintaining order in Rome and the Italian countryside. There was increasing indiscipline and irresponsibility in all segments of society.

The ancients inclined toward moral explanations for the collapse, believing that the decadence, greed, and ambition of all elements of Roman society were responsible, whereas modern investigators tend to regard these factors as superficial manifestations of deeper ills, and look for the causes in political, social, and economic factors.

The main outline of events is clear enough. From the mid-second century B.C. there was an increasing tendency toward political fragmentation in the ruling classes and consequent dissipation of power. The Senate gradually lost political control of the state and never regained it. Although the fall of the Republic had important social underpinnings, it was essentially a political, not a social, revolution.

Rome's Military Commitment and Its Effects

Rome's rise to power in the Mediterranean did not involve it in a great deal of direct administration and economic exploitation, though there was some of both. What it did commit Rome to in a major way, however, was an unending military defense of its acquisitions. Rome never gave up its conquests or forgot its legacies, even though at times it may have been slow to exploit them, as in the case of Cyrene, which was not organized as a province until 20 years after it had been bequeathed to Rome by its ruler.

Rome's commitment to maintaining peace in the Mediterranean created a major problem, since it demanded standing armies, and these in turn required either large numbers of draftees who could be quickly rotated in and out of the legions or else long-term enlisted men. Since Rome was committed to fulfilling its manpower needs from the lists of the property owners, the second alternative was ruled out. On the other hand, whether because of a decline in the number of property owners or because of increasing resistance to military service, fulfilling the needs of the standing armies—let alone supplying emergency levies—by the old method was becoming more and more difficult.

In retrospect this can be seen to have had some advantages. The reluctance (or unavailability) of draftees to fight long wars at great distances from Rome put some limitations on glory-seeking generals and even on the ambitions of the Senate and the people of Rome. After Marius, however, there was no such restriction: The draft still operated but no longer restrained commanders, and the more charismatic could always attract the numbers they needed. The Senate, which had controlled the draft in the past, thus lost control of the state's manpower reserves, and power shifted to those legions where volunteers made up a majority of the troops. Not that these soldiers were conscious revolutionaries. There was no rebellion of the proletariat in the legions against the state. Rather, the landless and the poor now had a role and an option. They could choose to fight or not to fight and they could select the leader for whom they would fight. The rest lay with the commanders.

Had the Mediterranean of the period of the late Republic been a naturally peaceful area there probably would have been no fall, or at the most a gradual transformation of the Republic would have taken place. However, the constant wars from the time of Marius, coupled with the weakened condition of the Senate, gave repeated opportunities to ambitious and able commanders, and as long as the wars went on there was no one to restrain them. In peacetime it was somewhat different, but then the more successful could combine their resources—as Pompey, Crassus, and Caesar did in 60–59 B.C.—and then their will was irresistible. The power of commanders tended to increase, not decrease. Successive years as consul or proconsul meant years of continuous patronage. Marius was consul five times in a row from 104 to 100 B.C.; Sulla held *imperium* from 88 to 79 B.C.; Caesar had nine straight years in Gaul. With these commands came the power to select and appoint officers, dispense the funds assigned to the war, and divide the booty. Nor was there any need for these generals to share their glory or power with anyone, other than those with whom they chose to share it. The age of Marius, Sulla, Pompey, and Caesar was an age of individualists who were restricted only by their vision of what they wanted and how much they wanted. In a sense this was the way it had to be. The old restraints had been swept away by Rome's commitment to maintaining order in the Mediterranean, and if the old system had been found wanting, how else was a new one to be found except by experimentation?

The New Roman Society

So far emphasis has been given only to the immediate effects of Rome's military commitment, but there were at the same time other major developments, which presented yet another series of opportunities to Rome's new leaders.

The Social War ended an old problem by eliminating *de iure* discrimination against the Italian allies, and the way was now open for Rome and Italy to merge. The problem was how to fit the Italians, especially the upper classes, into the existing Roman system. If Rome had been more openhanded earlier or if the infusion of the Italians had occurred at a less chaotic time, the Senate might have been able to cope with the influx, but it needed time and now there was no time left. The old aristocracy, slowly failing over the years, was not able to deal with the large number of newcomers, and its general attitude of social superiority must have been as grating to the Italians as it had been to rising new men at any time in Rome's past. It was therefore left to the individual Roman noble to make what use he chose of the results of the Social War and the reforms of Sulla. Caesar, whose career began later than the other dynasts, had the good fortune and the political astuteness to be able to develop the Italian connection to the fullest.

The problem of the equestrians had largely been solved by Sulla's changes and the events that followed his death. After 70 B.C., for example, no more is heard of the composition of the courts, which had been a standing battle since the time of Gaius Gracchus. Even the economic distinction between the equestrians and the Senate began to disappear as it became increasingly acceptable for senators to participate as sleeping partners in the public contracts of the state. With these changes the edge was removed from the struggle between the two orders and by the end of the Republic a new equestrian-senatorial government was well in the making. Still, the oligarchs were as incapable of coping with the flood of new men from the equestrian order as they were with the Italians. It took someone like Caesar, who surrounded himself with equestrians, or his adopted son and heir, Octavian, who was of equestrian stock on his father's side, to appreciate the opportunities here. Thus, of all the dynasts, only Caesar had the luck and the ability to put together a powerful coalition of the new forces of the Italian municipalities, the equestrian class, the new senatorial houses, the people, and the common soldiers. It was this coalition that was the foundation for the new state created by Octavian.

Literature and Society

Paralleling and complementing the evolution of a new political order was a cultural revolution of equally significant proportions. In the chaotic years between the Gracchi and Augustus Rome was transformed from a provincial city-state into the sophisticated cosmopolitan capital of a world empire. Italy and Rome overflowed with Greek works of art, and philosophers, literary figures, doctors, architects, and rhetoricians from the east catered to the growing educational needs and luxurious tastes of the new ruling classes.

Yet while Rome was rising to new levels of cultural sophistication its social cohesiveness was disintegrating. In the past Romans had been tied to one another by legally weak but morally powerful bonds of kinship, patronage, friendship, and duty, but the newly emerging society was highly fragmented. Remnants of the old patriciate clung to their old privileges, whereas elements of a new imperial nobility that included such diverse groups as freedmen, equestrians, and military men strove to establish their places in society. Others sought only to avoid political entanglements and enjoy their riches in peace and quiet. Women made independent by the decline of the rigid patriarchal system acquired riches and education and moved with freedom at the highest levels of society. As each of these social groupings evolved and developed its own codes of behavior the simple consensus of the past dissolved and the easy identification of society and the state, which had been characteristic of the Republic, vanished.

It was in the context of this rapidly changing society that Roman literature came of age. In part this was due to the emergence of the kind of un-Roman, apolitical leisurely class just mentioned, but the traditional devotion of the Roman upper classes to a life of public service, despite its weakening, also had a hand in the final shaping of Latin literature.

As the ruling class of the Republic fragmented, the Senate gradually ceased to be the place where the most important decisions were made. Increasingly, public issues were aired and settled in army camps, the courts, the

Sensitively carved, these portrait gems show the familiarity of the Romans of the first century B.C. *with the wide range of Greek portrait styles. From the left: Cicero (probably), Caesar, and the young Octavian.*

assemblies, and even on the campaign trail. In such an environment the ability to communicate and persuade was paramount, and it was in the practice of public oratory that Latin prose was molded. New men such as Cicero rose on the strength of their rhetorical ability and descendants of the old nobility quickly learned that the mastery of words could speed their advance through the *cursus honorum.* The ability to write also began to be recognized as a significant political weapon. Although Cato in the second century B.C. had shown what could be done with the publication of speeches, it was not until the time of the Gracchi and the years that followed that the full potential of the written word was realized. Speeches as well as propagandizing autobiographies and biographies were published by major figures to justify and further their careers. An enlarged reading public encouraged popularizers to churn out undependable though readable histories of Rome from the time of its founding down to their own time. Simultaneously the quality of the theater, which had been high in the previous century, declined catastrophically, as low-grade farce and mime drove out legitimate tragedy and comedy. Purely personal poetry, the epigram, love elegies, and lyrics evolved and reached extraordinary heights in the emotionally charged poems of Catullus. Under Augustus this tendency to Hellenistic-style private literature was challenged momentarily and in Virgil, Horace, and Livy the public and private realms were as perfectly blended as they were ever to be in the Rome of the late Republic.

RHETORIC, HISTORY, AND PROPAGANDA

Cicero, whose career coincided with the decline of the Republic, is the best known but by no means the only example of a public figure whose great literary talents were combined with a vigorous career of public service. A new man from the Italian municipal aristocracy, he lacked most of the normally essential prerequisites for advancement in Rome, such as family connection and military ability. His awesome oratorical and literary talents, however, compensated for these deficiencies and enabled him to play an important political role throughout most of the declining years of the Republic. Initially his talents were fostered in the courts and on the campaign trail and then before assemblies and in the Senate. It was his ear for the music of Latin and his sense of its rhythms that gave the language a form and fitted it as a vehicle of thought and expression for all time. Like those of so many of the public figures of his age, his writings cover an extraordinary range of subjects and literary genres, from poetry to antiquarian topics and from chatty letters to dignified orations. More than any other body of literature, his writings bring to life the concerns, personalities, and emotional conflicts of the late Republic. For 40 years he produced an unfailing flow of speeches, philosophical works, letters, and technical tracts. No other figure of the ancient world revealed so much of his personality as Cicero. We know of his affection for his family and his unceasing concern for the Republic, but also of his vindictiveness, his duplicity, and extraordinary conceit. He was not, of course, the only master of oratory or prose. Caesar, for example, practiced a very effective but much plainer variety of oratory and his terse written reports to the Senate from Gaul, the *Commentaries*, are masterpieces of both Latin literature and political astuteness. It is to Cicero, however, that one goes to get the full flavor of the age.

The higher value placed on public over private careers had the effect of bending Roman literary production to the political needs of factions and would-be leaders. The example of Cato has already been mentioned, but it was left to G. Fannius, the one-time friend of Gaius Gracchus, to show how effectively history could be put to the uses of a clique. His account of the events of the Gracchan revolution, written from the viewpoint of the ruling oligarchy and exculpating the murderers of the Gracchi, was so effective in swamping his opponents' version that it became the accepted view of those turbulent times. Contemporary history of this kind merged with autobiography and pure propaganda in the early part of the first century B.C., when a host of public figures wrote accounts of their careers. Rutilius Rufus, an embittered ex-governor who had been exiled after a notoriously unjust trial, wrote an apologia defending his actions. Marius and Sulla produced self-congratulatory accounts of their careers and were imitated by others, including Julius Caesar and Augustus. Sulla's biased memoirs were incorporated into the equally biased work of Cornelius Sisenna, who wrote of the Social War (91–89) and the civil wars that followed. Sallust, a supporter of Caesar, picked up where Sisenna left off. Except for fragments, both works have perished, though two of Sallust's monographs, on the Jugurthine War and the conspiracy of Catiline, have survived. His venomous portrait of the times, combined with Cicero's and Catullus' images of public and private corruption, have left an indelible, if distorted, impression of the age.

Although the active politicians concentrated their literary efforts on contemporary history and propaganda tracts, the work of writing histories in the traditional annalistic or year-by-year style passed into the hands of popularizers and romanticizers such as Claudius Quadrigarius and Valerius Antias. With an eye primarily on the demands of a public more interested in entertainment than strict truth, these writers unscrupulously twisted facts and copiously invented material wherever their sources failed them. Fortunately, there was another, more serious side to the writing of history. The past had always been grist for the propaganda mills of Rome and in an age of increasing historical awareness more people became conscious of the obscurity and archaic character of many Roman customs, religious rituals, place names, and the like. Learned antiquarians turned their attention to these matters and produced crabbed commentaries on such questions as how Rome acquired its name, and the significance of the various place names and ancient festivals. The great master of this field in the first century B.C. was M. Terentius Varro, whom Caesar appointed to head Rome's first public library. From his pen came a ceaseless flow of books on Roman antiquities and such related topics as linguistics and law, although he also wrote on estate management, philosophy, and even mathematics and astronomy. Dozens of other antiquarians and encyclopedists struggled to make sense of what had once been accepted without query and to sum up their findings in multiple publications. Even the busy Cicero was stimulated to write a history of oratory, and Caesar wrote on astronomy and grammar.

In the next generation Roman historical writing reached maturity in the great account of the rise of Rome by Livy. Unlike its predecessors, which for the most part exist only as fragments contained in other writers, considerable segments of the work of Livy have survived.

Coming at the end of a long period of development, Livy had the advantage of being able to make use of the works of the earlier historians as well as the research of the antiquarians. Candidly moralistic, Livy invited the reader

> to the serious consideration of the kind of lives our ancestors lived, of who were the men, and what the means both in politics and war by which Rome's power was first acquired and subsequently expanded; I would then have him trace the process of our moral decline, to watch, first, the sinking of the foundations of morality as the old teaching was allowed to lapse, then the rapidly increasing disintegration, then the final collapse of the whole edifice, and the dark dawning of our modern day when we can neither endure our vices nor face the remedies needed to cure them. The study of history is the best medicine for a sick mind; for in history you have a record of the infinite variety of human experience plainly set out for all to see; and in that record you can find for yourself and your country both examples and warnings: fine things, to take as models, base things, rotten through and through, to avoid.[1]

[1]Livy, *The Early History of Rome,* tr. Aubrey de Sélincourt (Penguin Classics, 1960), p. 18. Copyright © by the Estate by Aubrey de Sélincourt, 1960. Reprinted by permission of Penguin Books Ltd.

Understandably his history is full of edifying examples of virtue and vice and despite great narrative ability his characters tend to become idealized, somewhat wooden types of Roman men and women. Nevertheless, Livy's scope and his capacity for sustained narrative far outdistanced the literary talents of his predecessors and his work soon replaced theirs.

POETRY AND THE IDEALS OF PUBLIC SERVICE

The poets of the late Republic were much influenced by Alexandrian assumptions about what could and could not be attempted in poetry. Long epics on mythical or historical subjects were considered impossible, whereas short, highly polished poems, full of learned allusions, were much in vogue. Epigrams, pastoral idylls, mythical sketches, and short, artificial epics were characteristic of this kind of literature. Typically C. Helvidius Cinna, one of the most important proponents of these views at Rome, worked for nine years on the production of his masterpiece, the *Zmyrna,* of which, ironically, only three lines survive. On the other hand, Catullus raised lyric poetry to heights of unaffected passion in his addresses to Lesbia. Having fallen in love with the sophisticated wife of a Roman aristocrat, he soon discovered she had no interest in the kind of complicated love he entertained for her. Spurned, he was forced to come to terms with his own contradictory feelings:

> I hate and I love. And if you ask me how,
> I do not know; I only feel it and I'm torn in two.[2]

Like Sappho 500 years before him he turned to the gods for help:

> May the pitying gods who bring
> help to the needy at the point of death
> look towards me and, if my life were clean
> tear this malign pest out from my body
> where, a paralysis, it creeps from limb to limb
> driving all former laughter from the heart.
> I do not expect—or want—my lover returned,
> nor cry to the moon for Lesbia to be chaste:
> only that the gods cure me of this disease
> and, as I once was whole, make me whole again.[3]

Unlike the Greeks, who wrote of the effects of love in women, Catullus described his own personal feelings, and where the literary language failed him he was bold enough to introduce slang and colloquial idioms. A similarly personal attitude, though in a completely different context, was brought by Lucretius to

[2] *The Poems of Catullus,* tr. by Peter Wigham (Penguin Classics, 1966), no. 85, p. 197. Copyright © Peter Wigham, 1966. Reprinted by permission of Penguin Books Ltd.

[3] *The Poems of Catullus,* p. 188. Copyright © Peter Wigham, 1966. Reprinted by permission of Penguin Books Ltd.

an unlikely subject, the materialistic philosophy of Epicurus. Filled with a missionary zeal to free men from fear of the gods and death, Lucretius set out in magnificent verse form his own interpretation of Epicurus' views. Where Catullus was fashionable, witty and sensuous, and ultimately only successful in short verse forms, Lucretius was serious and dignified and his life's work was devoted to the production of one long poem. In the next generation Tibullus and Propertius carried on the now highly fashionable tradition of concern with affairs of the heart rather than those of the state. Tibullus could proclaim, in un-Roman fashion, that although he hated war he was a "good general and soldier in the service of love" and Propertius that "the conquest of people is worth nothing in comparison to love." All these figures reflect an age in which the horizons of the ruling classes were broadening culturally while contracting politically. Shifting from preoccupation with the competitive aspects of political life, they discovered the joys of leisure, wealth, and social prominence. As the ferocity of the political arena intensified, the attractions of the private life of luxury grew more enticing. The old traditions were not entirely moribund, however, and in Virgil's great epic, the *Aeneid,* Rome found the finest expression of its ideals of public service, though transmuted by the new environment.

The *Aeneid* is set in mythological times and focuses on the wanderings of the Trojan hero Aeneas and his final settlement in Italy. Despite the mythological setting Virgil made no attempt to reproduce in his epic the zest and spontaneity of Homer's heroes. He was too modern, and the age too psychologically self-conscious, to permit this. Aeneas, accordingly, is no naive, barbaric Achilles but a man of great complexity, not always sure of what he is doing, struggling to find out from obscure signs what destiny intends for him. In an age that saw the disintegration of Rome's old moral consensus, Virgil was able to show how the dependable virtues of the past could be adjusted and made workable in the present. His hero rejects the temptation to slip into a life of voluptuous ease when he abandons Dido and her rich Carthaginian kingdom and once more resumes his apparently endless journey. He refuses to yield to weakness or to seek solutions through violence, and resists both his own angry passions and those of his friends and foes. Midway through the tale the dimensions of his quest are revealed to him in a journey through the underworld. Here Aeneas is told of his descendants, who will make Rome great and extend its "authority to the breadth of the earth and her spirit to the height of Olympus."[4] He is warned of the horrors of civil war and the section concludes with a declaration of Rome's imperial responsibility:

> But you, Roman, must remember that you have to guide the nations by your authority, for this is to be your skill, to graft tradition onto peace,

[4]Virgil, *The Aeneid.* Tr. W. F. Jackson Knight (Penguin Classics, 1956), p. 170. Copyright © The Estate of W. F. Jackson Knight, 1956. Reprinted by permission of Penguin Books Ltd.

to shew mercy to the conquered, and to wage war until the haughty are brought low.[5]

For sustained dignity, seriousness, and nobility of theme, Virgil's epic is unsurpassed. It reflects, however, the passing of an era. In the poem's concentration on the single figure of Aeneas, its scornful attitude toward the mob, and its preoccupation with order and obedience, we miss the vigorous, competitive spirit of the Republic. More than any of the other literary figures of the times Virgil captured in his work the change in values that was taking place as Augustus assumed to himself the burdens and responsibility of rule that in the Republic had been spread throughout an entire class.

Although Horace says nothing of Roman public life he talks a great deal about moral conduct and the traditional values that were assumed to have made Rome great. Virtue is praised over wealth, moderation over excess, and the simple, frugal life over the luxurious:

The man who longs for just enough is never
disturbed by the turbulent ocean, nor by
the storm wind's wild attack when Arcturus
is setting, or when Haedus is rising . . .

If, then, a troubled man is not consoled by
Phrygian marble, nor living in purple
more splendid than the stars, nor by wine
from Falernum and nard from Persia,

why should I erect a palace, with columns
that others would envy, in the latest style?
Why should I trade my Sabine valley
for the heavier burden of riches?[6]

His poems, skilled and carefully worked, demonstrated the kind of harmonious balance he would have liked to have found in society itself. Far more than in the elevated verses of Virgil, we can see in Horace the manners, customs, and figures of the times. Here is the flesh and blood of the new age, the rich, the poor, the middle classes, the city and country folk. In the following vignette we can catch a glimpse of the Rome of Horace's age as well as sense some of the poet's frustrations with its limitations:

A confident poet will often be put in a panic
And fright when the cheapseats, so stupid, so stolid, so superior

[5]Virgil, *The Aeneid*, p. 173. Copyright© The Estate of W. F. Jackson Knight, 1956. Reprinted by permission of Penguin Books Ltd.

[6]Joseph P. Clancy, trans., *The Odes and Epodes of Horace* (Chicago: University of Chicago Press, 1960), 3.1, pp. 104–5. Copyright by the University of Chicago Press.

In numbers, inferior in taste and good sense, and quite ready
To fight if the knights demur, call out for a bear
Or a prize fight in the middle of the play. Those roly-prolies!
They came here to SEE something! But so does everyone else
Who goes to the *theatre* today, including the knights.
Pleasure has switched her allegiance from the ear to the eye.
It gets more and more spectacular: the curtain stays up
Four or five hours, while the troops dash by, the cavalry,
Then the infantry (obscene, those mob scenes). Kings are dragged in,
Their hands bound behind them . . .
Chariots, carts, wagons, and boats go whooshing
Across the stage, closely followed by captured statues,
Ivory or Corinthian bronze. Democritus *laughed?*
Were he still in earth, he'd have enough reason for mirth
Just watching the people gape at their favorite new monster,
A giraffe or a nice white elephant; he'd look at the audience
Rather than the play, as a much more interesting spectacle.[7]

[7]Smith Palmer Bovie, trans., *The Satires and Epistles of Horace* (Chicago: The University of Chicago Press, 1959), *Epistles* 2.1.182–96, pp. 255–56. Copyright by The University of Chicago Press.

15

The Roman World from Augustus to Marcus Aurelius

AUGUSTUS AND THE PRINCIPATE

The problem facing Octavian when he returned to Italy after defeating Antony was to find a political and constitutional formula that would embrace the whole state—the people, Senate, equestrian order, and army alike—in a new and lasting relationship. In addition, the system of imperial governance, so haphazard and irresponsible in the past, badly needed to be overhauled and made responsive to the needs of the provincials. The formula would have to contain elements of the old and the new, but no one, not even Octavian—or Augustus as he was called after 27 B.C.—knew the proportions. Some of the components were already to be found in the faction of Caesar, but the task confronting Octavian was that of making faction and state coincide.

Army, Senate, and People

The most pressing problem was that of the army. Between 31 and 13 B.C. Augustus reduced it from 60 to 28 legions, settling in the process over 100,000 veterans in colonies in Italy, Africa, Asia, and Syria. Under Sulla resettlement had been financed by a bloody proscription; fortunately the means for accomplishing Augustus' enormous resettlement were supplied by the treasures of Egypt, which Augustus seized after the defeat of Antony.

The matter of imperial defense was resolutely faced by making the permanent legionary forces in the provinces large enough to cope with the problems of the frontiers without having to raise emergency armies, and by regularizing length of service, pay scales, and discharge benefits. Regular pay came out of the old Republican treasury and in A.D. 6 a special military treasury, funded by a sales tax and death duties, was set up to pay the 9000 or so annually discharged veterans their retirement bonuses.

The political problem of the army was not so easily solved. Somehow Augustus had to discover a legally acceptable means of keeping control of the legions or Rome would once more be plunged into the horrors of civil war.

Having held the consulship continuously from 31 B.C., Augustus suddenly renounced his powers in 27 and declared the reestablishment of the Republic. Pressed by the Senate he retained the consulship and also proconsular control of the legions. Although this had at least constitutional form it was not completely satisfactory. It halved, for example, the number of consular positions available to the nobility and saddled Augustus with many routine duties. After a serious illness and an attempted coup he resigned the consulship in 23 but was compensated by being given special proconsular power *(maius imperium)*, greater than that possessed by any other proconsul, which allowed him to intervene in the provinces wherever he thought it necessary. This proved to be a generally satisfactory solution to the problem of the control of the legions and became one of the pillars of the new constitution.

These constitutional formalities, however, did not much concern the average soldier or for that matter the people, and it was here that the dynastic principle that was to have a major role in Roman history came into prominence. As the adopted son of Caesar Augustus had inherited the devotion of Caesar's troops, and this phenomenon of loyalty to the son of the previous ruler became another one of the foundations of the Empire. After Augustus every emperor had to be either the adopted son or the real son of the previous emperor if he was to gain the support of the army and the people.

Relations between Augustus and the upper classes were considerably eased by his concern for constitutional formalities, but there were other, less formal approaches that Augustus exploited with great ingenuity and apparent genuineness.

While Caesar had little patience with the Senate and offended it unnecessarily, Augustus went out of his way to be deferential. He did not flaunt his power and maintained a simple and modest standard of living. He wore homespun togas and lived in a dwelling such that any of the nobles might have possessed. In the matter of titles, which were so important at Rome, his preference was for an informal one, *princeps* or elder statesman. In the Republic the term had been applied to those ex-consuls whose prestige and authority were such that they were able to dominate the Senate and the government, though not in any formal or legal sense. Augustus' use of the title implied that he ruled in a similar traditional way, by his authority, and not by virtue of any alteration in the constitution. Although no one could overlook the fact that Augustus' influence went far beyond his *auctoritas*, after 50 years of bloodshed the upper classes were willing to close their eyes to the reality of his power as long as they did not also have to face the external trappings of an autocracy.

In other respects, relations with the Senate were managed with tact and dignity. Its numbers were gradually reduced from 1000 to 600 and membership in it was made hereditary, although Augustus retained the right to nominate new members. The census qualification was put at 1 million sesterces but special emphasis was placed on integrity and capacity for public office.

The powers and jurisdiction of the Senate and of Augustus tended to overlap in a number of areas, and the lines of demarcation were left deliberately vague. Both made appointments to the provinces, but the Senate sent out governors to the peaceful, senatorial provinces, whereas Augustus sent his governors to the remainder, the imperial provinces where the legions were stationed. Legislative, judicial, and financial powers were also shared between the two, although there was never any doubt as to which was the dominant figure in this relationship. Nevertheless, there was plenty of work for the senators to do, especially those of praetorian and consular rank. Ex-praetors could become legionary commanders, governors of minor provinces, or proconsuls of senatorial provinces. As consuls senators could govern imperial provinces or hold one of the important commissionerships at Rome. Since Augustus exercised either direct or indirect control over most appointments to the provinces much of the maladministration that occurred under the Republic was avoided. In addition, governors were now paid regular salaries and their terms were extended from one to three to five years. The temptation to exploit their positions was thus reduced and their lengthened tenure allowed them sufficient time to acquire expertise in the exercise of their duties. By these means and by the judicious reform of the tax-collecting system, Augustus was able to establish the provinces on a sound administrative basis.

In the course of seeking suitable legal forms for his extraordinary powers, Augustus selected one constitutional form from the old patrician state and one from the plebeian. The first was proconsular *imperium*, which gave him control of the army, and the second was tribunician power, which was voted to him in 23 B.C. Together, they were to be the real foundation of the new state. The choice of tribunician power was particularly popular with the people. For centuries they had turned to their tribunes for redress against all kinds of grievances, and now they could turn to their tribune-emperor. It was also a good choice from a purely practical, constitutional viewpoint. As tribune Augustus could veto or enact legislation, intervene on behalf of individuals, hold court, or call the Senate into session, yet the office had none of the tyrannical connotations of the kingship or even, from the people's view, of the consulship. By the same willing oversight by which the Senate and the upper classes came to accept Augustus' perpetual proconsular power as the price of peace, the people were willing to acquiesce in their loss of power by accepting Augustus as their permanent tribune.

Religious and Social Reform

Augustus attempted to stem the rising tide of moral change that had developed in the late Republic by enacting a comprehensive program of social, religious, and moral reform. Since many men and women of the upper classes preferred to remain celibate and regarded the raising and education of children as burdensome, Augustus enacted penalties for childless couples while creating special benefits for those with children, though later he was compelled to reduce or even remove the penalties and increase the benefits. To cope with adultery, which was widely condoned, Augustus made it a public crime to which severe penalties were attached. Sumptuary laws were enacted to control luxury, and attempts were made to control the haphazard manumission of slaves and the number of people eligible for free grain.

The *princeps* placed special emphasis on the traditional religion and morality of Rome. His very title, Augustus, had religious connotations and could be taken to mean that his rule had been inaugurated with all due concern for the augural requirements of Roman religion, or it might have drawn attention to his authority, the word for which was also derived from the same Latin root.

The idea that prosperity and peace in the state depended on the pious fulfillment of religious duties to the gods was an ancient one in Rome and in the Republic the magistrates had taken particular responsibility for maintaining the *pax deorum,* the peace between gods and men. Augustus made a point of stressing his concern for this traditional belief by restoring temples—82 by his own account—and becoming a member of the sacred colleges of pontiffs and augurs. He revived many cults and ancient practices, and in 12 B.C. when Lepidus died, he became *pontifex maximus.* From this date he was not only the secular but also the religious head of the state.

The peace and tranquillity that Augustus' rule introduced were deeply felt by all of Italian society, not least by its literary figures and artists. Augustus had the good fortune of finding in the persons of Virgil, Horace, and Livy spokesmen for the regime who were in genuine accord with its goals.

Both Virgil and Livy were inspired by the epic rise of Rome, its sufferings, piety, and great destiny. In the hero Aeneas Virgil discovered the ideal figure of the Augustan Age: sober, tenacious, pious, a slave to duty. Livy, as has been noted, traced the history of Rome from its meager beginnings to his own day, filling it with patriotic and moral examples, and Horace elegantly expounded in his *Odes* the virtues of the Romans, their frugality, hardiness, and simplicity. Another poet, however, failed to adjust himself to the new current of morality and was banished. Instead of writing elevating moral tales Ovid produced the *Art of Love,* a salacious sexual handbook that was not taken well by the sober Augustus. Significantly, all these literary figures, as well as others such as Propertius and Cornelius Gallus, were from Italy or the provinces, not from Rome itself. Both Virgil and Livy were from the north, the former from Mantua, a city founded by the Etruscans, and the latter from Padua, a city of the Venetians. Ovid and Propertius came from central Italy and Gallus was from the south of France. Horace's father had been a slave, then a well-to-do freedman in Venusia in southern Italy, where the young poet spent his early years. Gallus and Propertius were of equestrian rank and the rest belonged to the middle classes. It was to such men that the Augustan regime appealed.

Mother Earth, the personification of the fertile land of Italy, from the Ara Pacis. Effectively conveyed, the Augustan message emphasized the return of peace and the restoration of the old order.

More directly Augustus was able to make use of the coinage of the Empire to herald his achievement in bringing peace to the world. The plastic arts, too, were made to reflect this theme. One of the best preserved monuments of the age is the Altar of Peace, a simple altar surrounded by walls decorated with friezes whose serenity and order are immediately striking and to this day convey a profound sense of the Augustan peace.

Just as the newly established Republic found expression in the development of the Forum, Augustus' refounding of Rome was also expressed in a building program in the same area. The Forum was now, at last, given definitive shape by the construction of the temple of Caesar at one end and the rebuilding of the other three sides, the Basilicas Julia and Aemilia and the Rostra (the platform from which the orators addressed the people). Caesar's own forum, just behind the Senate House, and a new one, the Forum Augusti (centered on the great temple of Mars the Avenger), were built at right angles to it, somewhat further to the northeast. Other projects of Augustus were the Altar of Peace, which has already been mentioned, the Theater of Marcellus, the temple of Apollo on the Palatine, his own mausoleum, and innumerable restorations of older buildings. An entire new monumental center was constructed in the Campus Martius by Agrippa, Augustus' son-in-law. This included a basilica, baths, a temple, gardens, porticoes, an artificial lake and canal, and a huge hall, the Saepta, intended for voting purposes. Elsewhere in the city a great variety of new buildings were erected, including theaters, libraries, temples, arches, and warehouses. The drainage system was enlarged and overhauled and the water supply practically doubled. When the people complained on one occasion of the high price of wine, Augustus recommended that they should drink the water with which he had so liberally provided them.

The styles of the building programs reflected the complicated aims of Augustus himself. They ranged from the startlingly Hellenistic Altar of Peace to the somberly conservative Italian-style basilicas, theaters and forums. Even the building materials themselves represented innovation and conservatism. Concrete, which had been somewhat sparingly used for some time, now passed into common use. Marble was introduced for the first time on a large scale and one of Augustus' boasts, according to the biographer Suetonius, was that he found Rome brick but left it marble.

The reign brought other, more tangible benefits to the Roman people. For the first time in its history the city of Rome was provided with a proper urban administration. In addition to Augustus' personal bodyguard, the Praetorian Cohorts, a police force of 3000 men (the *Cohortes Urbanae)* was created, as well as a fire fighting force of 7000 (the *Vigiles).* New aqueducts were built and the sewage system was thoroughly overhauled. A permanent board of commissioners *(Curatores Aquarum)* was appointed to maintain the supply of water. Similar commissions were created to look after flood control *(Curatores Riparum Tiberis),* and the food supply *(Cura Annonae).* Entertainment was not neglected and the first permanent amphitheater in Rome's history was erected. Only a century later the satirist Juvenal was to use the bitter epithet of "bread and the circus" to describe the imperial people of Rome.

THE EMPIRE FROM AUGUSTUS TO MARCUS AURELIUS

Augustus rose to power as the adopted son of Caesar and maintained himself as *princeps* by the careful management of the constitution and his sensitivity to the residue of republican feelings among his subjects. These were the essentials of his rule: personal and dynastic popularity with the people and the army, and acceptance by the Senate as the "best man" in the state. The trappings of a monarchy were avoided, and technically all the emperor's powers were conferred on him by the Senate and people and would cease to exist when he died. There lay the problem. How could power be passed on in an orderly way, without civil strife, after his death?

The problem nagged at Augustus and at some point he made up his mind that the stability of the state could only be maintained if power were to be transmitted to an heir who bore his name. Unfortunately Augustus had no sons, and his daughter Julia's sons, Gaius and Lucius, died while still young. That left Tiberius, his wife's son from a previous marriage, and it was this man, already in middle age, whom Augustus finally adopted and associated with himself in 4 A.D. in the ruling of the Empire. In turn, Tiberius was forced to adopt as his heir his brother's son, Germanicus, whose mother had been a daughter of Antony and Augustus' sister Octavia. Thus, when Augustus died in A.D. 14, Tiberius succeeded as the son of Caesar to the loyalty of the people and the army, having already been constitutionally invested with most of the powers of the *princeps*.

TIBERIUS AND GAIUS

Tiberius was an extremely able military commander and a good administrator, but he was dour and suspicious and from the beginning had difficulties with the Senate. He had little time for pomp and considered public entertainment a waste of time and money, and was consequently disliked by the people as well. When the opportunity came his way in A.D. 26, he gladly left the city and retired to Capri where he spent the rest of his life surrounded by scholars, jurists, and astrologers, running the Empire from a distance through his commanders of the Praetorian Guard, the Praetorian Prefects.

Under Tiberius, Germanicus restored Roman prestige on the Rhine frontier, where it had been severely damaged by the loss of three legions in an invasion of Germany in A.D. 9. In the east the client-kingdoms of Cappadocia and Commagene were made into provinces (A.D. 17), but no major wars of conquest were fought and Tiberius followed Augustus' recommendation not to extend the Roman frontiers. A good administrator, Tiberius was able to cut in half the unpopular sales tax, which had been 1 percent, and he left a large surplus in the treasury when he died.

Tiberius' problems of succession were even more complicated than those of his predecessor. The heir apparent, Germanicus, died in A.D. 19, and Tiberius' next choice, his own son Drusus, was poisoned by the sinister Praetorian Prefect Sejanus, although the emperor was not to learn of this until much later. This left his grandson Tiberius Gemellus and a somewhat older grandnephew, Gaius. Both were made joint heirs in A.D. 36. When Tiberius died the next year, Gaius, with the support of the new Praetorian Prefect Macro, was proclaimed emperor. It was a disastrous choice, since Gaius, or Caligula ("Little Boots") as he was nicknamed, proved to be mentally unbalanced. He soon murdered Gemellus and initiated treason trials for the purpose of appropriating the fortunes of rich senators whose wealth he needed to pay for his wild extravagances. When it was rumored that he intended to make his horse a consul, and that after training maneuvers for an invasion of Britain he had marched the legions to the English Channel only to order them to pick seashells, the Praetorians took matters into their own hands and murdered him. In his place they put his uncle, the aging Claudius.

CLAUDIUS AND NERO

The bookish Claudius who had studied under Livy and had written histories of the Etruscans and of the Punic Wars, was generally considered unfitted for Roman public life. Consequently, he had not even been adopted into the Julian family (the family of Julius Caesar) and was practically unknown outside the palace. In order to gain military prestige and consolidate his support with the army, he decided to make use of two new legions raised by Caligula and to annex Britain. Not a military man himself, he made good selections in his commanders and delegated Aulus Plautius with four legions to lead the invasion. Among Plautius' legionary commanders was the future emperor Vespasian who owed his position to the influence of Narcissus, one of Claudius' freedmen. Initially the invasion went well and Roman control of the south was quickly established (A.D. 43–47). The conquest of Wales and the north of Britain was a different story, and it was to be another 30 years before the rest of Britain was secure.

Claudius proved to have unsuspected administrative abilities and organized permanent departments of finance *(a rationibus)*, correspondence *(ab epistulis)* and petitions *(a libellis)* headed by freedmen who ran them efficiently but whose great power won many enemies for their master.

The emperor's fourth wife, Agrippina, schemed to have her son by a previous marriage, Nero, placed on the throne, and to speed the succession she poisoned Claudius in A.D. 54. Under the tutorship of Seneca and the Praetorian Prefect Burrus, the reign opened favorably, but soon a savage battle for power began in the palace in which eventually Seneca and Agrippina perished. Nero emerged as an irresponsible, amoral dilettante without a shred of interest in public affairs. His only concerns were music and literature, and as the reign advanced his eccentricity increased, provoking conspiracies that further contributed to the downward spiral.

Major wars were fought in the east during Nero's reign by some of the best generals Rome had produced in many years. In a series of campaigns against the Parthians, Cn. Domitius Corbulo brought Armenia within the Roman sphere of influence and gave Nero an opportunity to stage and preside at an elaborate coronation of its king in Pompey's theater in Rome, which was gilded for the occasion.

In Judaea, mishandling of provincial affairs by successive Roman procurators provoked a major revolt in A.D. 66 and required the dispatch of a full-scale expedition to put it down. The commander selected was T. Flavius Vespasianus, whose career after his successful service in Britain under Claudius, had suffered something of a setback because of his unfortunate habit of falling asleep at Nero's recitals. Perhaps more important was the fact that his patron Narcissus had opposed the marriage of Claudius and Agrippina, so for both men passage into political oblivion followed inevitably upon the accession of Nero to power. Vespasian pressed the war efficiently and had practically ended it when civil war broke out over Nero's successor.

Most of Nero's irresponsibilities had had little effect on the provinces or the armies, but in A.D. 67 he came to suspect his generals of treason and ordered Corbulo and the commanders of the Rhine legions to commit suicide. The governor of Spain, Galba, avoided a similar fate by choosing instead to revolt, and Nero precipitously committed suicide. A bloody round of civil wars now ensued in which first Galba was slain by the Praetorian Guards and then his successor Otho was killed in battle against the Rhine legions who invaded Italy in support of their candidate, Vitellius. The Danube and Syrian legions next announced for Vespasian and marched on Rome, the former getting there first, having crushed the forces of Vitellius on the way (A.D. 69). The following summer Vespasian arrived in Rome, leaving his son Titus to finish the siege of Jerusalem.

THE FLAVIANS

The Flavian dynasty that Vespasian established was from the rural bourgeoisie of Italy and was in marked contrast to the aristocratic and eccentric Julio-Claudians who had ruled to the time of Nero. The tone of the new regime was one of modesty, simplicity, and strict adherence to the old ways. However, the weakness of the Senate and the power of the armies that had set up Galba, Otho, Vitellius, and Vespasian in turn had been demonstrated for everyone to see and was a lesson not to be easily forgotten.

Vespasian struggled to restore financial stability, which had been upset by the extravagances of Nero and the destruction caused by the recent civil wars. New senators were added, especially men from the equestrian order and from the provinces. The permanent departments in Rome, such as finance and correspondence, had since Claudius, been in the hands of freedmen. These were now transferred to equestrians—the first step in the creation of a civil service outside the traditional framework of the Senate.

Vespasian was less successful in his dynastic policies. From the beginning he had made it clear that he intended that his sons Titus and Domitian would succeed him. Though the former died before any clear judgment could be reached about him, Domitian ruled long enough (81–96) to earn the hatred of the Senate and he was murdered in a palace conspiracy that included his own wife Domitia (the daughter of Corbulo, Nero's great general). Domitian was an able administrator and made excellent official appointments, but his growing paranoia converted the later years of his rule into a reign of terror. Tacitus the historian and Pliny the Younger looked back on these years as a time of humiliation and terror.

THE "FIVE GOOD EMPERORS"

Domitian's successor was an elderly senator by the name of M. Cocceius Nerva who ingratiated himself with the legions by adopting Trajan, the popular commander of the Rhine army. Trajan's family hailed from Italica (near Seville) in Spain and he was thus the first emperor of provincial origin. After a two-year reign Nerva died and his energetic successor began a series of campaigns to round out the Roman frontier. Dacia (modern Romania) was profitably added between 101 and 106 (it had gold and salt mines), and in 114 Trajan began an invasion of Armenia and Mesopotamia. After initial successes, a major revolt in his rear forced him to retreat, and he died in Cilicia in 117. It was announced that on his deathbed he had adopted his nephew by marriage, P. Aelius Hadrianus (117–138).

Hadrian promptly abandoned Trajan's eastern conquests and spent most of his reign (12 out of 21 years) traveling all over the Empire visiting the provinces, overseeing the administration, and checking the discipline of the army. He was a brilliant administrator and concerned himself with all aspects of government and the administration of justice. He established cities in Egypt, Asia Minor, and the Balkans, and he initiated the construction of the great wall in the north of England that bears his name. He was a deeply cultured man and surrounded himself with orators and artists. He had strong ideas about architecture and one of his greatest creations, the Pantheon, stands intact to the present day. He was less tolerant when it came to non-Greek cultures and his rebuilding of Jerusalem and the erection of a temple to Jupiter on the site of the old temple provoked a major revolt (132–135) which was brutally put down.

Hadrian's first chosen successor, his close friend L. Ceionius Commodus, died in A.D. 138, and he next turned to an elderly senator, T. Aurelius Antoninus (better known as Antoninus Pius, 138–161), whose family came from Nemausus (Nimes) in the south of France. Antoninus was in turn instructed to adopt as his successor his nephew M. Annius Verus (Marcus Aurelius, 161–180), and Lucius Verus, the son of Commodus. Unlike the restless Hadrian, Antoninus lived quietly in Rome, never stirring from the city during his reign, and for 23 years the Empire stagnated.

A descendant of a Spanish family, the prim Marcus Aurelius ruled for eight years in association with Lucius Verus, a man whom he regarded as worthless. When Verus died in 169 he was not replaced. A confirmed Stoic, Marcus Aurelius had plenty of opportunities to test his commitment to this philosophy, for wars and other disasters dominated his reign. In the east a series of campaigns was waged between 162 and 166 under the nominal command of Verus, whose troops brought back with them a virulent plague that ravaged the Empire. Worse was in store—the advance warning of the catastrophes of the third

Hadrian's Pantheon with its emphasis on interior space—the high vault, splendid decorations, and unusual lighting—reflected the cultural turning inward of his own times and anticipated the stately basilicas of the late empire.

century. The Goths had been on the move since shortly after A.D. 100, forcing the German tribes ahead of them to organize in federations as a means of self-defense. In 167 one of these tribal groups, the Marcomanni, broke through Rome's northern frontiers, and Aurelius spent the best part of the next 13 years in fierce campaigns against the barbarians. He was poised for another advance when he died in A.D. 180. With the reign of Marcus Aurelius the peace of the Empire was shattered and with only brief interludes civil wars and barbarian invasions filled the next century, one of the most momentous, but also one of the least known, in Roman history.

16

The Roman Peace

The size and complexity of the Roman Empire made it an extraordinarily difficult area to govern. It had neither geographical nor cultural unity. There was never a time in the past when the regions of the Empire were politically united and after the passing of Roman rule they were never to be united again. Beyond a little trade, what could possibly have tied Britain to Egypt or Belgium to Syria? They were too far apart, even as they are today, and too culturally dissimilar to have had a natural community of interests.

The government and society that Rome managed to impose on this area were flimsy and artificial, always under challenge by local forces, which tended to reassert themselves in moments of Roman weakness and tear apart the connections that had been laboriously built up.

The cement that held the Empire together for as long as it did was social, cultural, and military in character. It consisted first of Rome's ability to involve the different classes of the Empire in the processes of government and society and so well integrate them with one another that none were permanently alienated. The Romans had no systematic ideology of empire and instead substituted the slow, pragmatic application of what they did know well, their own social system with its hierarchical organization of society on the basis of wealth and public service. Patronage established connections across class lines and careers in the army and civil service allowed the able and ambitious to rise to high office. Based on this uniform social system, a homogeneous culture derived from the study of a handful of classical texts in two languages, Greek and Latin, allowed Syrians to communicate with Africans and Spaniards with Britons in a way that had never before been possible and which has not recurred since.

Ultimately everything depended on the ability of the army to maintain the peace within and without the Empire. This in turn depended on the willingness of the Empire to foot the bill for the army. It was a complicated equation in which costs could not be allowed to outweigh the benefits for a long period and when they did, as happened in the west after the fourth century, the Empire

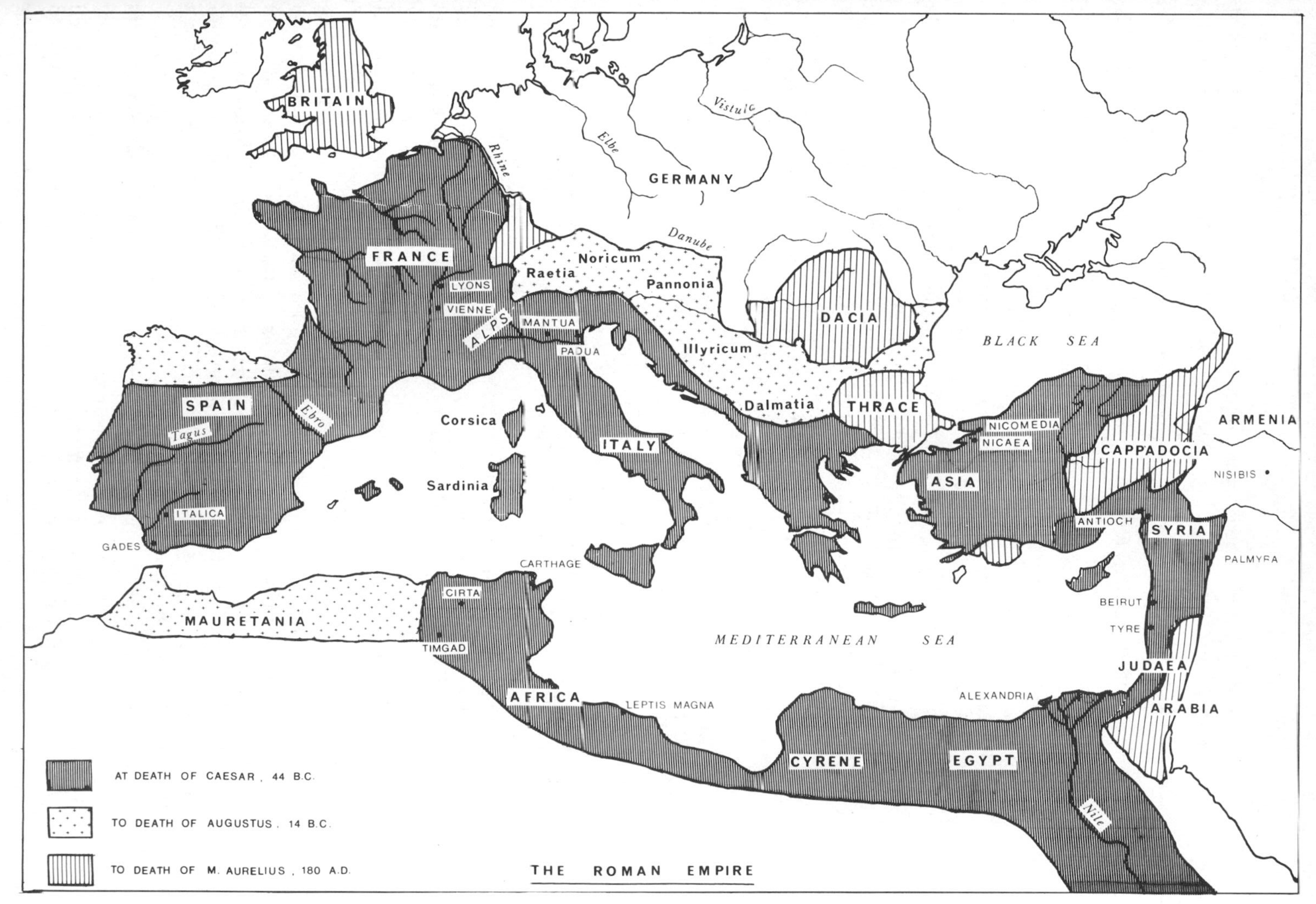

THE ROMAN EMPIRE

collapsed. In the east the equation of costs and benefits was better maintained and the Empire survived a full 1000 years after its disappearance in the west.

THE GEOGRAPHY OF THE ROMAN EMPIRE

If we include the Mediterranean Sea the geographical extent of the Roman Empire at its height was only slightly less than that of the continental United States. It stretched from the lowlands of Scotland to the Sudan, and from the Ukraine to Morocco. Great villas, towns, and fortresses lined the 1000 miles of Rhine and Danube frontier. Far into the interior of north Africa the town of Timgad was laid out in grid fashion by the veterans of Legio III Augusta and was graced with an amphitheater, baths, libraries, and portico-lined squares.

Travel had always been relatively easy in the coastal areas of the Empire and three weeks of good sailing could bring a traveler from one end of the Mediterranean to the other. Centuries of Roman effort built up a great network of roads that linked the inland regions with this central thoroughfare. Nevertheless, land transportation was always slow and expensive and the cost of hauling bulk goods prohibitive. In the late Empire a 1200-pound wagonload of wheat doubled its price over a journey of 300 miles. It was cheaper to transport grain by ship from one end of the Mediterranean to the other than to send it 75 miles overland.

Rivers such as the Rhine, Danube, Rhône, Nile, and Euphrates were vital means of communication with the interior regions. The government maintained a constant concern for the upkeep of the roads, the state-operated land transportation system *(cursus publicus)*, and the guilds of maritime shippers *(navicularii)*. The transportation system was divided into light and heavy divisions, the former providing official travelers with horses and carriages and the latter being responsible for the movement of heavy goods such as food, clothing, arms, and building materials. On the light *cursus* travelers could average about 90 miles per day. The guilds of shippers were originally independent contractors but were gradually incorporated into the state transportation system and rewarded with special exemptions from the taxes and burdensome municipal responsibilities that the middle classes in the Empire had to bear. Eventually all sorts of regulations governed the transportation system. Regulations for the number of horses, carriages, and carts that might pass a given point in a single day, together with the maximum loads, were set down—and ignored. Inspectors supervised the system, looking out for unauthorized users and out-of-date or forged passes.

Roman administrators and troops were thinly spread over the gigantic regions of the Empire, and the task of visiting and supervising them was close to overwhelming. In emergencies, such as the breaching of the frontiers by barbarians, the ability of the Empire to respond was directly related to the speed with which it could gather accurate information about the size of the horde, its composition, direction, speed of movement, and the like, and then from other theaters summon troops of appropriate armament and number to cope with the invaders, drive them out, and repair the damage to the frontier fortifications. Throughout its history, distance and time were the secret enemies of the Roman Peace. Despite the high quality of the 50,000 miles of roads, the transportation network remained that of an underdeveloped country. Burdened with a similarly weak economy and low technology, the Empire quickly used up its reserves when pressures built up beyond a certain level. Under the Roman social formula only so much could be squeezed out of the system, and to achieve anything more would have required a radical reordering of society that not even utopianists dreamed of.

CULTURAL COMPLEXITIES

The Empire was no empty landmass waiting to be filled by conquering Romans who themselves constituted a homogeneous community. The provinces won by the wars of the Republic were filled with peoples whose histories were as long and diverse as those of the Romans themselves.

Although knowledge of Latin and Greek would take a traveler comfortably from one end of the Empire to the other, the bulk of the native populations retained their native languages until almost the end of the Empire. Celtic, Germanic, Semitic, Hamitic, and Berber languages were deeply rooted in the different regions of the Empire along with the cultures they sustained. Polyglot, multiracial, and multicultural, the Empire was one of the great melting pots of all time.

The depth of civilization varied from area to area, being deepest in the eastern Mediterranean and thinnest in the west, and generally being in inverse ratio to the distance from the Mediterranean seacoast. Iron Age Celts and Germans in the west, who had only recently been introduced to written laws and literature, were united under Rome with Syrians, Mesopotamians, Jews, and Egyptians whose literacy and literature went back for thousands of years. One half of the Empire was underdeveloped and the other half was overdeveloped.

GRECO-ROMAN CULTURE

Opposing the tendency to cultural anarchy, which was the natural state of the Empire, was Greco-Roman civilization and its supporting educational system. Outside the older, developed cultures of the east it had no competitors, and by the end of the second century A.D. it provided a uniform, high culture for the upper classes everywhere and in an informal way it also percolated down to the masses.

The provincialization of Greco-Roman civilization is one of the most remarkable features of the period. The Roman satirist Juvenal complained of the number of eastern intellectual and literary figures at Rome, and in fact some of the greatest masters of Greek and Latin in this period were provincials. Lucian,

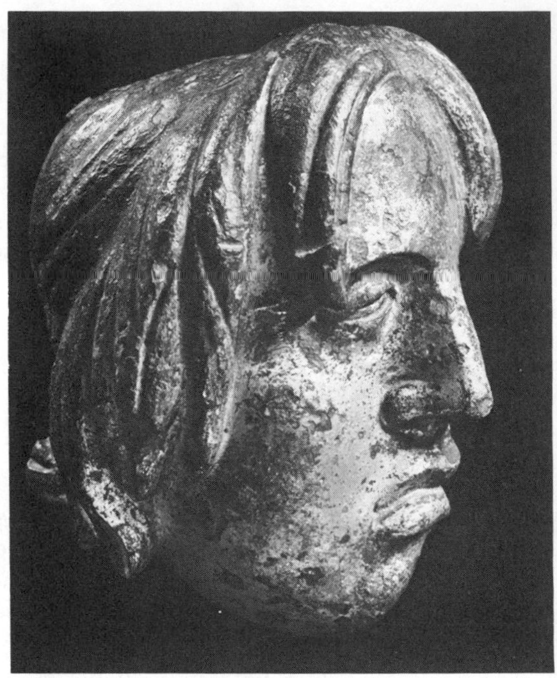

The two extremes of the Roman World: elegant aristocrat and rough peasant.

the brilliant satirist, was Syrian; the historians Arrian and Dio Cassius were from Bithynia, as was the moralist-rhetorician Dio Chrysostom; Apuleius and Tertullian were African. Although the upper classes shared the common heritage of Greek and Latin and could travel comfortably in the knowledge of finding their own type everywhere, a great educational (though not social) gap existed between them and the masses. The acquisition of an education was a long, expensive (and frequently boring) process that only the leisurely could afford.

The purpose of the educational system was not merely to teach how to read and write but how to read and write well. There was a huge difference between the practical literacy of a soldier, merchant, or ordinary town councillor and the highly literate and bookish education of the upper classes. Like wealth and titles, culture was regarded as a mark of distinction and almost as eagerly sought.

The languages studied were limited to two, Greek and Latin, and at that not the languages of current use but the Greek and Latin of the classical authors. Other languages and their literature were regarded as barbaric and were ignored. In Latin, Virgil, Terence, Sallust and Cicero were the favorite authors; and Homer, Thucydides, the Attic tragedians, and Demosthenes in Greek. These masters were accepted as authorities and students were expected to mold their styles after them. Imagination and originality were discouraged and form and style were considered more important than content. The classical texts were dissected line by line and the rules of grammar and syntax learned by memory. Technical proficiency was prized above all and generations of students went through untold suffering to master the nuances of a classical style. As an old man Saint Augustine, the great bishop of Carthage, could still recall the horrors of his early days in school and rhetorically claimed that death was preferable to what was suffered in childhood studies.

The ultimate goal of the educational system was the mastery of the spoken word. There was a close connection between civic life and the art of public speaking and since the educated regarded a public career as their normal lifetime occupation, an oratorical ability of some level was indispensable. Business that today is handled in written form or in informal conversations and meetings was then handled formally and in person. The average middle- or upper-class person could expect to have to speak at one time or another in public before magistrates seated on tribunals, before their fellow city councillors, to the people, before jurors and judges, or to soldiers, and the effective speaker was not one who could speak informally but one trained in rhetoric, the art of persuasion.

The municipalities of the Empire took a keen interest in the higher levels of education, and any city that thought anything of itself provided chairs of grammar and rhetoric. The emperors, as patrons of the arts, privately endowed chairs at Rome and at Athens but there was no philosophy of education in the modern sense of a tool for socialization purposes. Education was narrowly conceived as the prerogative of a small elite that had the time and the money to spend on it. Extending this kind of education broadly would have seemed absurd and probably impossible.

The middle classes strove for culture and advanced as far as their resources would permit them. Textbooks and summaries of all kinds existed and great collections of miscellaneous information on every conceivable subject were produced in quantity. Summaries of history, philosophy, science, and geography could be picked up from any bookseller. Even the so-called well-educated tended to the accumulation of odd bits of information—mythological, antiquarian, and historical—and their knowledge of philosophy, the sciences, and mathematics was minimal even by ancient standards.

CULTURE AND THE MASSES

Although the culture of the educated had a bookish, academic quality, Greco-Roman civilization reached out to the masses of the people, especially the city-dwellers, in a number of informal ways.

The mere fact of dwelling together in a city had the effect of extending to other classes the high culture of the upper classes. There was a much greater degree of physical proximity between the classes than there is in modern society. The cities, to begin with, were designed principally for use by pedestrians, not vehicles, and it was assumed that there would be large population densities in the downtown, forum areas where most public business was transacted. Here trials were conducted, elections held, and public announcements made. The people met again in the theaters, amphitheaters, gymnasia, and baths, and at the formal religious celebrations held periodically throughout the year. Roman imperial officials, town councillors, and magistrates could be easily identified and approached. Merchants and shopkeepers went about their daily business and life went on in a very personal, intimate manner. Gossip and rumor, functioning as the media of ancient town life, carried tales all over the city, sparing no one.

The cultured and well-to-do classes were not segregated elites whose lives had little contact with the rest of society. The very ideals of urban life demanded an interchange between the classes and the summit of a man's career was to have himself honored by his fellow citizens as patron and benefactor of his city. The rich were expected to make tangible contributions to the public life of the city in the form of serving, unremunerated, as magistrates, giving festivals, maintaining the food and water supply, erecting public buildings, and generally contributing to the essentials of a civilized life. These services were known as liturgies. The purely private enjoyment of wealth and the gratification of intellectual curiosity or aesthetic tastes were considered aberrations. Although the rich had their country villas, their primary residences were their town houses.

In an even more informal way the culture of the upper classes was passed on through the medium of classical art. New cities were laid out in grid patterns, and markets, temples, basilicas, and theaters were laid out according to carefully conceived plans. They conveyed a sense of order and dignity to the town-dwellers and to visitors from the countryside, and some cities like Timgad in the wilderness of the Algerian Atlas mountains were deliberately created as showplaces to impress the barbarians. Hundreds of cities existed in areas where today there are few. Africa had 500, for example, and there were about 300 in Asia. A great deal of cultural diffusion must have occurred even without any formal government plan. The Romans, for the most part, were concerned with the cities as administrative, not cultural, centers.

Religions of the Empire

The great cultural diversity of the Empire was also reflected in the chaotic variety of religions, cults, philosophies, and theosophies that offered themselves to the inhabitants of the Roman world. They ranged from the austere, ascetical monotheism of Judaism and Christianity and some of the philosophies to the flamboyant and bloody rituals of Cybele. There were officially sanctioned and supported state cults that functioned openly and splendidly, and small, private groups that met and worshipped in secret. Every taste and every class was accommodated.

Although scepticism prevailed among the educated and to a lesser extent

Although dully repetitious, Roman cities offered the amenities of urban life to people from one end of the Empire to the other. Left, enduring brick and concrete buildings line a street in Ostia, the port of Rome; right, Pompeii from the walls.

among the masses in the first century B.C. and the first century A.D., by the second century A.D. it was once more socially acceptable to be a believer. There was a great deal of philosophical religion. Christianity expanded, paganism revived, and prophets and oracles were sought out. Magic and the black arts flourished. Astrology was universally accepted and pagans and Christians alike believed in a world of demons, both good and evil, that mediated between heaven and earth.

There was some consciousness of the prevailing religious and moral confusion, and efforts were made both by individuals and by the government to introduce some kind of order and logic to the situation. Philosophers strove to reconcile the newly emerging belief in a single, transcendent deity with the lively mythology of the past. The emperors tried to maintain some kind of order by putting down those religions and superstitions that did not seem to fit in with their conceptions of an orderly empire. At the same time they tried to boost the old state religion.

THE CULT OF THE EMPERORS

The emperor was the high priest and head of the Roman state religion and as such was responsible for maintaining right relations between the gods and mankind. While alive he was a semidivine intermediary between men and the gods and a god himself when dead.

The cults of the spirit *(genius)* of the emperor and the gods of Rome were an essential part of public business and could no more be neglected than could the collection of taxes or the administration of justice. The cults consisted, however, of purely formal acts of ritual worship and had neither ethical nor doctrinal content. They said nothing about the nature of God, the character of human life, or life after death—questions that were of vital concern to the inhabitants of the Empire.

Despite its coldness and formality, the Romans were able to turn the cult of the emperors to practical use by tying it to the existing social order. In Rome members of the upper classes were formed into colleges *(sodales)* responsible for the cult of the divinized emperors, whereas in the cities of Italy and the provinces well-to-do freedmen were co-opted into similar organizations and given charge of the cult of the living Caesars, the emperors. At the provincial level the cult was entrusted to assemblies of the leading men of the region and the head of these assemblies was designated the Priest of Rome and Augustus. As one of the highest dignities open to a provincial it was eagerly sought out and the cult was celebrated with great pomp on the emperors' birthdays and days of accession.

MYSTERY RELIGIONS

Although the formal state cults appealed to the upper classes and the richest among the freedmen class, they lacked the stimulation and social attractiveness of the mystery religions and the little burial societies that existed everywhere to honor the spirits of the dead.

Cybele, a vegetation goddess whom the Romans adopted during the Republic, had one of the most flamboyant rituals of the mystery religions. In the course of induction into the cult the initiate had to kneel under a platform while a bull was slaughtered and its blood allowed to drip over him. The initiate then emerged from the pit to a new life, cleansed of his sins, and sat down to a sacred meal with the other members of the cult. Understandably, Christians regarded the rites of Cybele as demonic parodies of their own ceremonies.

The cult of Isis was another fertility cult that was immensely popular. Isis' fidelity to her consort Osiris and her loving relationship with her son Horus made her compellingly attractive to both men and women. Some of her imagery and titles passed over directly into Christianity and some of her statues were even accepted as those of Mary, the mother of Jesus. Her mystery cult offered initiates the hope of resurrection, and the famous novel of Apuleius, *The Golden Ass,* tells of these rites and the profound effect they had on him.

Mithraism was popular in the army and offered an attractive combination of doctrine, ritual, and ethical practice. Its adherents believed that the cosmos was in constant tension between the forces of good and evil, light and darkness, life and death. Although the soul is indeed immortal it is contaminated by its association with the body and must be liberated by an ascetical struggle in which

Mithras, who has already conquered and ascended into heaven, assists. The soul in its journey upward passes through the seven planetary spheres to which correspond the seven grades of initiation in the mystery cult. A high level of ethical behavior was expected but psychological support was supplied by the regular meetings of the Mithraic community, which took place in small, cavelike chapels and included a sacred meal.

ZEUS, SERAPIS, SOL

Serapis was a synthetic deity created by Ptolemy I in the Hellenistic period. He was a blend of Zeus, the healing god Asclepius, and the mortuary deity Osiris. His worship is found throughout the Empire, and Serapis was viewed as a kind and gentle god who did not punish men but helped them. In another form Zeus (Jupiter to the Romans) had an even more significant history that ties in with the conversion of the Empire to Christianity under Constantine. There had long been a tendency to identify Zeus with the sun and the emperors seized on this image as a means of expressing their own aims and ideals. Warm, dependable, all-seeing, always victorious, the sun's symbolism conveyed what emperors would have liked the peoples of the Empire to believe they stood for.

JUDAISM AND CHRISTIANITY

Judaism and Christianity offered yet another series of alternatives. Both were exclusive and placed emphasis on the close adhesion to strict ethical practices and dogmatic beliefs. Judaism, in addition to the attractiveness of its high moral standards and its lofty monotheism, was one of the most ancient religions of the Empire. It possessed an important collection of religious books, which propounded in organized fashion its history, laws, and philosophy. It offered a coherent account of the origin of men and their history from the earliest times. Its liturgy had the advantages of both the philosophers' lecture hall and the sense of community and brotherhood of the mystery cults.

Christianity borrowed from Judaism these traits but dropped the more extreme demands of the law such as circumcision and the laws of purification. To the Jewish belief that God was the Lord of History Christians added the assertion that history had found its culmination in the lowly person of Jesus who would return to bring the process of history to a victorious conclusion. Even more than Jews, Christians were regarded with suspicion within the Empire. They actively sought the transformation of the world they lived in, which was heresy enough, and they refused to participate in the all-important worship of the Emperor, and in civilian and military life. To Romans, who were always on the lookout for seditious organizations, the Christian practice of gathering in groups with clearly identifiable leaders who were able to communicate with one another throughout the Empire was particularly suspicious.

By the time of the Roman Peace philosophy had long since given up its metaphysical search for knowledge and devoted itself to the humbler, more practical questions of human conduct. It did not even concern itself with theories of morality, but instead sought to give concrete answers to pressing questions of daily life. What is virtue? How should wealth and power be employed? How should people cope with change and loss? How involved should a citizen be in civic life? What is human happiness?

All the great schools of philosophy of the past were ransacked to provide answers to these questions. Philosophy was converted into religion and made to reply to questions that the old philosophies and religions did not even raise. It was as though a decision had been made that what was needed was not new knowledge but practical answers to pressing moral issues. It was not theoretical information about the nature of human life that was sought but rather instructions on how to conduct one's everyday life: Art not science, salvation rather than wisdom, revealed truths in the place of reasoning and speculation. The ability of reason to give secure answers was questioned and more secure sources of authority were sought. Syncretism was in the air, and the boundaries between philosophy, science, magic, and religion became blurred to the point where all of these terms became interchangeable. Christianity could claim to be a philosophy, meaning a way of life or a way of ascending to God.

For the middle and upper classes, Seneca, Musonius, Epictetus, Plutarch, and others provided examples, sermons, and exhortations to virtue. Seneca turned Stoicism into a religion and criticized abuses of wealth and pleasure, including cultural pursuits, arguing that the true objective of philosophy was living well. He urged men on, somewhat cheerlessly, to the struggle against evil and developed such a high concept of God that some Christians later concluded that he must have been a convert.

Musonius, who was exiled by Nero, preached gentleness to wrongdoers and forgiveness of injuries and argued against the double standard for men and women. Apollonius of Tyana taught brotherly helpfulness, courage and temperance. He spoke against the luxury of the baths at Antioch and the frivolity of the Athenians. He criticized Nero as an effeminate tyrant and encouraged rebellion. Demonax successfully argued the Athenians out of giving gladiatorial contests by saying that they would first have to give up the Altar of Pity in the city before they could introduce the contests. Dio Chrysostom denounced both the sensuality of the rich and the selfishness of the mob. For him, the true community was one from which greed, intemperance, and violence were banished and everyone lived under law. He glorified the simple life of the peasants and preached moderation to the emperor Trajan. Plutarch's vast knowledge was employed in a lifetime devoted to the moral education of his contemporaries. Unlike so many of his gloomy moralist friends who viewed life with a deep pessimism, Plutarch cheerfully emphasized the power of positive thinking. People should, he said, think of the good things they have and look for the hidden hand of God in the disasters that befall them. Most of the bitterness of calamities comes from their own doing, not from events outside themselves.

The masses sought answers to the same kinds of questions that plagued the educated and received answers from hosts of prophets, preachers, oracle mongers, and magicians. The higher speculations of the moral theologians were put into handbook form or popularized by street preachers. Unwashed and rude Cynic philosophers disdained conventions and harangued the passersby, preaching renunciation of all social ties and responsibilities. Proteus Peregrinus, one of the more flamboyant of the Cynics, criticized the emperor Antoninus Pius at Rome and the powerful Herodes Atticus at Athens. Herodes, he said, merely gratified his vanity by his huge benefactions in Greece and elsewhere. Proteus committed ritual suicide in 165 and was hailed as a holy man throughout Greece. Apollonius of Tyana lived as an ascetic, performed miracles, and so impressed his contemporaries that after his death his cult spread widely.

Others were not so reputable. Alexander of Abonoteichos deliberately set out to mine the potential of the superstitious age. Selecting an out-of-the-way town with a gullible population he planted a newly hatched snake in a goose egg and then substituted a fully grown snake with a false head. Thus established he proceeded to hand out answers to sealed questions, which he claimed he never opened. The fraud was attacked by Lucian of Samosata, one of the few disbelievers in an age of credulity.

CONSTITUTIONAL AND SOCIAL COMPLEXITIES

The Cities

The complexities of race, language, and culture were further muddled by the bewildering tangle of legal and constitutional systems. The concept of unequal cities is not foreign to modern ways of thinking if we confine these to comparative size, wealth, favorable locations, and so forth. It is difficult, however, to imagine a state where individual cities had varying political and juridical statuses, arranged in descending order in which some outranked others in the number of special privileges they could claim.

At the head of the ranks of Roman cities came those that enjoyed the title of Roman colony and at the same time possessed what was called the Italian Right *(jus Italicum).* The latter privilege, in practice not very common, granted immunity from taxation and from the authority of the local Roman governor. All other cities and territories, of whatever status, paid the standard land and poll taxes, the *tributum soli* and the *tributum capitis.* Italy, as the homeland of the Romans, was immune in this period from these taxes.

Below these specially favored colonies came the other Roman colonies and below them the cities *(municipia)* of Roman and Latin citizenship. Latin municipalities were of two kinds, those whose elected magistrates received the Roman citizenship automatically on election *(Latium minus,* the Lesser Latin Right), and those where all the local senators (decurions) automatically received the citizenship *(Latium maius,* the Greater Latin Right). Everyone else in these cities was, of course, a Latin citizen and as such barred from the imperial civil service and the Roman magistracies. Practically speaking this was not a major disadvantage and Roman law was administered in both Latin and Roman municipalities.

Alongside Roman and Latin foundations were the native cities *(civitates),* villages *(vici),* and districts *(pagi),* in which the majority of the non-Roman population continued to live under its own laws and customs. These native cities were in turn broken down into those with a special status either as free *(liberae)* or federate *(foederatae)* because they had entered into special treaty relations with Rome before the conquest of the area and continued to enjoy a special relation with Rome after incorporation in the Empire.

During the Empire the Romans encouraged their subjects to build cities and settle in them, giving up their old rural haunts and inaccessible fortresses on strategic sites. These new foundations were rapidly advanced to first the Latin status and then the Roman, and in this way whole areas of the west were Romanized. The ultimate achievement was the winning of the title of Roman colony, to which great prestige was attached. Leptis Magna, the birthplace of the emperor Septimius Severus, was originally an ordinary non-Roman *civitas,* ruled by Punic magistrates. By the end of the first century it was a *municipium,* probably with Latin status, and then under Trajan it became a full Roman colony. Finally, under Septimius Severus, its native son, it received the Italian Right. By the end of the second century A.D. un-Roman sounding cities like Nisibis in Syria were made titular colonies, while Lebanese Tyre and Heliopolis were given the coveted Italian Right.

In the eastern half of the Empire, where there were relatively few Romans and citizenship was not widely extended to the native population, the pre-Roman system of local and regional government continued to operate. In the Greek areas a great network of cities existed, each with its own carefully defined and often disputed territory, ruled from within by an oligarchic elite according to its own laws, which might date to its foundation. Elsewhere non-Greek cities existed alongside later Greek foundations, as in Palestine, Lebanon, and Syria, or there were Greek cities with large numbers of non-Greeks in their populations.

This complexity was guaranteed to test the flexibility of Roman governors and administrators who in their careers might at one stage be in contentious Alexandria, which was always ready to erupt into riots between Greeks and Jews, or in peaceful Sicily where nothing ever happened, or in tribal Britain or Africa. Each region had its own particular set of problems—military, cultural, and social. It was a fine training ground for tolerance or, perhaps more frequently, benign neglect.

Citizenship

The gradations of city charters, rights, and privileges were matched or even excelled by the hierarchical organization of the population of the Empire.

First there was the complication of citizenship, since one could have Roman, Latin, or simply native *(peregrine)* status. Roman citizens were, of course, potentially capable of a full political life at Rome, but in addition they had certain rights in criminal law not possessed by anyone else. In cases in which the charge was capital they could appeal from a local court to Rome and frequently the mere status of an individual as a Roman would deter local authorities from dispensing summary justice. It was not that Roman citizens were exempt from obeying the local laws of provinces, but that being members of the ruling power their political standing was something a local magistrate needed to take into account. Saint Paul, who had the citizenship, made good use of this during his travels in the Roman world, where he frequently came into conflict with local ruling bodies. Even within the citizenship there were gradations, as some Romans belonged to immune cities and so escaped the standard forms of taxation, or were Romans but of freedman (ex-slave) status and so had other built-in restrictions, such as the inability to serve in the legions or hold public office. Then there were persons of the Latin Right, which entitled them to practically the same legal but not the same political privileges as Romans. Finally there were slaves, whose only rights were vaguely defined in the Law of Nations (the *jus gentium)* and in some specific enactments handed down by the emperors.

Most of the problems arising from citizenship were resolved in A.D. 212 when the emperor Caracalla extended Roman citizenship to almost everyone in the Empire by the *constitutio Antoniana.* This brought the vast majority of the population fully within the scope of Roman constitutional and civil law, so a uniform code could be applied everywhere. Although an egalitarian tendency can be detected in Caracalla's extension of the citizenship, there was in fact no concession to democracy. To the extent that the privileges of citizenship were thought to have been watered down by the increase in numbers, there developed another system of classification that counteracted this and ensured the preservation of the traditional system based on wealth and public esteem. This was the distinction between high-status individuals *(honestiores)* and low-status individuals *(humiliores).*

Status in the Empire: Humiliores and Honestiores

By the second century A.D. the distinction between high- and low-caste inhabitants *(honestiores* and *humiliores)* of the Empire, regardless of their citizenship, was an established fact of law. Those who could claim to belong to a high legal status could claim special treatment under the law and were subject to a much less stringent set of criminal punishments than a person classed among the *humiliores.* A provincial governor could not, for example, execute persons of high status and could only exile them after consultation with the emperor, whereas *humiliores* received summary judicial treatment and punishment. The distinction cut across citizenship bounds so that ultimately it was more advantageous to be a member, especially a powerful member, of the upper classes with high status than to be a poor citizen with low status.

Those who belonged to the *honestiores* included first of all senators and equestrians, then decurions (local senators), soldiers, veterans, and some professionals. The scramble for citizenship then became a scramble for inclusion in one of the higher classifications. Such inclusion was one of the ways the Romans could ensure themselves of a continuing interest in local administration and the army since service in either included membership in the higher caste. This is not quite so discriminatory as it seems since those who scrambled hardest also needed it the most. These were the property owners of moderate possessions whose material goods made them targets for exploitation by the tax collectors, soldiers, and imperial administrators. The lower classes—as always—had little to protect them beyond public opinion, their membership in some organization patronized by the powerful, such as the funeral societies, or direct dependence on some powerful individual. Toward the end of this period even this system of privilege failed to protect the middle-class property owners from the exactions of the tax collectors, and there was a great deal of pressure either to move up to such a high status, either equestrian or senatorial, as to be out of reach, or to quit altogether and become the client of someone powerful enough to offer adequate protection.

The Senate

Under the Republic, senators not only provided Rome with its generals, political leaders, judges, and high administrators but also controlled the city's political life. When the emperors took over the latter role from the Senate they still needed capable personnel, but because of Roman prejudice against a professional military or civil service such people did not exist outside the senatorial and equestrian classes. The dilemma of the emperors was therefore how to make use of the Senate's great ability to produce, screen, and test personnel without conceding it too much political power. So conservative was the Roman tradition that it was to take over two centuries before an independent system replaced the old method of recruitment.

The great strength of the Senate lay in its tradition of public service. By custom the Roman upper classes found their fulfillment in holding state offices and not in private business ventures or artistic or philosophical dilettantism. Even though the Senate lost its political power as a corporate, governing body, it never lost its social position. Throughout the whole period of the Empire it remained the focus of the ambitious among the upper classes everywhere, and even expanded its influence as more and more provincials entered it. Even when the Senate lost contact with the political, administrative, and military branches in the third-century crisis (see chapter 17), and ceased to be employed in high commands or as governors, the social standing and privileges of the Senate continued and ultimately outlasted even the western Empire itself.

In a status-conscious society membership in the senatorial order represented the ultimate achievement of a man's life. It was an exclusive club where the wealthiest and most illustrious inhabitants of the Roman world were to be found along with its current and future rulers. In a practical sense, too, membership in the Senate was of enormous advantage. Specific privileges included access to the highest offices, commands of armies, governorships of provinces and cities, and all the attendant opportunities for accumulating or increasing wealth and power. Down to the third century, all the emperors were drawn from the ranks of the senators. Whatever the dangers involved—and they were great when suspicious emperors occupied the throne—it was a most attractive class to belong to. In an age when public recognition meant everything, the broad purple stripe of the senatorial toga was the symbol of the highest achievement and received due recognition from the citizenry.

There were other tangible privileges. Senators traditionally claimed the right to trial by their peers and they were immune from curial obligations, that is, the burden entailed in running the cities of the Empire. In time the latter was to become one of the most attractive of the order's privileges and one not shared by the middle classes. Senators were, of course, automatically classified at the highest legal levels and benefited from their general power to fend off tax collectors, would-be claimants of a lower status, and other annoyances of life that the less privileged had to cope with.

REQUIREMENTS FOR THE SENATE

The requirements for the Senate were still largely those of the Republic: wealth and the holding of public office. Sons of senators, however, now belonged automatically to the senatorial order, though, confusingly, not necessarily to the Senate. As before there were pre-senatorial posts, such as the military tribunate, which senatorials were expected to fill, thus maintaining the important contact of the upper classes with the army. Then followed the offices of quaestor, aedile or tribune of the plebs, praetor, and finally the consulate. Posts in Rome were unpaid and required the expenditure of considerable amounts of money. The satirist Martial, for example, tells the story of a woman who promptly divorced her husband when she found out he was standing for the praetorship.

COMPOSITION

The Senate was neither a closed hereditary system nor a meritocracy. Senatorial families tended to die out and the most prominent were often targets for hostile emperors. Constant infusion of new members from the upper ranks of the equestrian class was therefore a necessity, and this class in turn drew on the one beneath it, the curial or decurion class, which made up the aristocracy of the provincial cities. In this way a healthy upward movement was maintained and over the years the composition of the Senate gradually changed. From being exclusively Roman in the early Republic, the Senate was dominated by Italians in the late Republic and under the Julio-Claudians. Then came a steady influx from the western provinces. Seneca, who acted as tutor and advisor to Nero, was Spanish, as was his brother Gallio who was governor in Achaea when Saint Paul was accused of stirring up trouble in Corinth. The emperor Vespasian was from the rural districts of Italy and his successors Trajan, Hadrian, Antoninus Pius, and Marcus Aurelius were descendants of Italian settlers in Spain and southern Gaul. Africans began to enter the Senate around A.D. 100. Lusius Quietus, who helped put down the revolt in Judaea under Hadrian, was a Moor, and in 193 another African, Septimius Severus from Leptis Magna in modern Libya, ascended the imperial throne. The eastern provinces began to make their contributions at about the same time, and in the second century new senators came from the Danube provinces and Dalmatia (Yugoslavia). By the third century, more than half the Senate was from the provinces, mostly Africa or the Greek east.

CULTURAL TRADITIONS

In addition to serving the Empire in a practical way, senators had the leisure time to devote to literature and the opportunity to acquire a good education.

Tacitus, who was the son-in-law of Agricola, one of the great governors of Britain, and a governor himself in Asia, composed a brilliant, bitter history of the first-century emperors. A friend of his, the younger Pliny, wrote a series of stylish letters that constitutes one of the principal sources for the social history of the Empire. Suetonius' *Lives of the Caesars* are full of biographical information and scandalous anecdotes, and were favorite readings among the middle classes. Many senators dabbled in poetry and all practiced rhetoric, both in the law courts and privately. Pliny tried out his *Panegyric* to Trajan on his friends in a recital lasting three days, and suffered equally at their hands. His efforts were so popular that senators at the end of the Empire in the west were still studying him and producing similar pieces of arid rhetoric. Although they did not practice the visual arts themselves, senators encouraged sculpture, painting, architecture, and the minor arts by their lavish donations to favored cities and by the building of great villas in the countryside for their own pleasure.

The Equestrians in the Empire

In the Republic the equestrian class had formed the second level of the aristocracy. Like the Senate, it consisted of two groups, those actually involved in state and public affairs and those who were content to live their lives on their estates with only minimum participation in civic life. Between the senatorial and equestrian classes there was no essential social or economic distinction. Both belonged to the leisure classes, had their capital invested in land, and shared the same conservative viewpoints.

In the Empire the same generally holds true, but with some important exceptions. Although there were still relatively few senators, 600 if we count only those who were actually in the Senate, the equestrian class had expanded enormously. Gades in Spain and Padua in Italy each had 500 equestrians on their citizen rosters. All over the Empire the propertied classes vied for membership in this class and the privileges it conferred. Outwardly these consisted of the narrow purple stripe on the toga and the right to sit in the first rows of the theater and circus, minor items perhaps, but in view of the high degree of status-consciousness in the Empire, important enough to be sought after. More significant was the special privilege of exemption from municipal burdens that equestrians shared with senators, and the right of access to the highest level of the aristocracy, the Senate.

Although many among the propertied classes were content to enjoy the privileges of membership in the equestrian order there was another, more formal aspect to it that attracted the more ambitious.

THE EQUESTRIAN CIVIL SERVICE

Obviously the Senate could not supply all the officers and administrators needed by the Empire, even allowing for Roman reluctance to create a bureaucracy. There was also the problem that many offices were not of sufficient dignity to permit a senator to hold them, but nevertheless required a certain amount of ambition, education, responsibility, and initiative. Thousands of men were needed to command the non-Roman units of the army, the auxiliaries, supervise and manage the emperor's private properties and estates, act as jurors, run the departments of the central government, and so forth. Unwilling to set up a true civil-service system and dispense with the basic idea of dignity and public service as the prime criteria for officeholding, the emperors from Vespasian on simply expanded the equestrian order and drew upon it for their manpower needs. Gradually a junior administrative service parallel to that of the Senate grew up and began to attract those interested in a career of service from all over the Empire. By the end of the second century an elaborate career *(cursus)* had been worked out with clearly defined steps and pay grades, and by the mid-third century it had successfully replaced the senior (senatorial) civil service as the administrative hierarchy of the Empire. This was not the end of the development and there will be further discussion of the equestrians in chapter 18.

REQUIREMENTS

In principle, at least, military service was an essential prerequisite for an equestrian career. Members of the local municipal aristocracy who chose this kind of a career could enter the equestrian branch of the army directly and perform their three tours of duty (the *tres militiae*) as prefect of an auxiliary unit, legionary tribune, and prefect of the auxiliary cavalry, or they could enter as centurions and follow the centurion career, sometimes preferred because it offered permanent service after the *tres militiae.* In either case, having had considerable experience, they would then enter the equestrian civil service as procurators. In this capacity they could serve in a vast number of governing and administrative posts.

At the lower levels equestrians supervised the numerous estates, mines, and possessions of the emperor. They were his tax collectors, his overseers of the mint and the public transportation system *(cursus publicus).* At higher levels they were governors of minor provinces, especially the more recently conquered, such as Austria (Raetia) or Judaea. In Rome they were in charge of the food supply *(annona),* the Fire Department *(Vigiles),* and the Praetorian Guard, the latter commanders (the Praetorian Prefects) being second only to the emperor. They were needed to head the various departments of state, such as finances, appeals, records, and communications. Overseas the most important equestrian position was that of the procuratorship of Egypt.

Alongside the military equestrian career there grew up a purely civilian one that drew upon literary figures, academicians, and lawyers. The first tended to end up in areas involving diplomacy, correspondence, and foreign languages; the legal specialists provided their services directly to emperors, governors, and procurators. As the administrative branch grew, law became more important and lawyers began to play a proportionately greater role. The legal powers of the Praetorian Prefects expanded, and when the two great jurists Papinian and Ulpian were prefects under the Severi they set about a thoroughgoing reorganization of the administration.

In general, the equestrian class made available to the emperor a pool of talent less circumscribed than the Senate and more dependable, but mostly from the same kind of desirable (in a Roman sense) social background. From the viewpoint of the propertied classes of the Empire and even for the ambitious among the lower classes, the equestrian order and an equestrian career offered social advancement, the incentive of good pay and security, and the privileges of a higher legal status.

The Decurion or Curial Class

The municipalities of the west and Roman colonies everywhere were microcosms of Rome itself. They had their senates *(curiae)* and their magistrates, which they elected annually on the Roman model, and as at Rome these were selected, at least in theory, not at random but on the basis of character, public service, and wealth.

Generally the local senates in the west consisted of 100 members, although in the east they were much larger. Each city had its own charter and laws and took care of its own administration. The local magistrates saw to the collection of

Provincial elites: Syrian man and woman with inscriptions in Syriac (a dialect of Aramaic) and Greek. Although the poses are Roman, the style—the wide-open eyes and the simplification of the facial features, for example—represent a departure from the Greco-Roman tradition and anticipate the taste of the late Empire.

the imperial taxes and were responsible for the maintenance of peace in the city and the upkeep of its public services. This involved supervising the possessions of the city, its land, mines, and properties, and from this income seeing that temples, walls, and public buildings were maintained, that the water and food supplies were guaranteed, and that essential games and festivals to the gods were performed. Since the income generally fell short of these demands the local ruling classes were expected to make up the difference out of their own pockets. In good times there was a great deal of competition among the rich to show their generosity and receive in return the shouted approval of the population in the streets and arenas and the erection of an honorary statue or inscription. Frequently such benefactors also ended up paying for the inscription or even the statue, being content, they claimed, that the population had voted the honor. Being a member of the local senate and a magistrate was thus an expensive business, but it was assumed that public accolades and recognition constituted an adequate compensation for the cash outlay. When this assumption was challenged in bad times, the Empire had a serious crisis on its hands.

The curial classes were themselves divided in ranks of dignity, as were the senatorial and equestrian classes, and they jealously maintained their gradations of honor. A standard feature of municipal life that enshrined this principle was the custom of setting up commemorative endowments by the wealthy, which made provision for the distribution of money to the townspeople on certain days, such as festivals. These distributions were made on a strictly hierarchical basis, more going proportionately to the magistrates than to the members of the senate and so on down the list to the lowest levels, the poorest receiving the least. The notion that the poor per se might be deserving was quite foreign to the mentality of the Romans.

There was a great craving for distinction of any kind and each class imitated the one above it to the degree that its financial resources permitted. If senators and equestrians established foundations and endowed them with millions or hundreds of thousands of sesterces, the other levels of society created their endowments in the thousands, hundreds or even, pathetically, the tens of sesterces. It was this desire for public recognition that accounts for the vast numbers of inscriptions that are the main source of social history in the Empire.

Freedmen and Augustales

A large segment of Roman society was held in slavery, but liberal traditions of manumission made for a large class of freedmen who either had been freed by their masters or had saved enough to secure their own manumission. Since a lot

Procession of vici magistri. *The equivalent at Rome of the* Augustales *elsewhere, the* vici magistri *were responsible for the cult of the protecting spirits of their districts* (vici) *as well as of the* genius *of the Emperor. These well-to-do freedmen took their responsibilities seriously and proudly displayed their piety and their role in the public life of the city by erecting this expensive monument. First century* A.D.

of the trade, shopkeeping, and manufacturing of the Empire lay in their hands, they were often extremely wealthy and ambitious. It was logical, therefore, for the Romans to extend to freedmen the same kind of social regimentation that existed among free persons, with the double purpose of securing the services of the ambitious and the talented and keeping down discontent.

The sensitivity of the Romans to dignity would not permit ex-slaves to participate fully in the political system but their ingenuity created a way around this by the invention of the college of *Augustales.* This corporation, which was extended to the cities of the Empire, was responsible for the upkeep of the imperial cult and consisted of the wealthiest among the freedmen. These were chosen by the local senates and came to constitute a kind of aristocracy among the ex-slaves. Although barred from office they had the right to wear purple-bordered togas, which distinguished them from the masses, both free and servile, and frequently were granted the insignia of public office, though not the office itself, a common sleight of hand by which the Romans got around impossible situations of social and political life. Like city magistrates they paid a heavy fee upon entry into their society and were then expected to contribute lavishly to the expenses of city activities. The rewards were the same as for the freeborn magistrates: public applause and recognition at the festivals and games, and the erection of honorary inscriptions and statues. Their names are associated with every known benefaction: the giving of festivals, games, and banquets; the erection of all kinds of public buildings, such as baths and arenas; and small donations such as of wood and oil for the baths. Their vulgarity as *nouveaux riches* was a well-known literary theme but nevertheless, side by side with the magistrates of the cities of the Empire, they enjoyed (or suffered) the publicity and reduction of their fortunes by the masses who knew how to extract some return for the only thing they had to offer or withhold: their applause and recognition.

The Collegia

The compulsion to organize into groups and then classify further within the groups extended to even the lowest levels of society.

From the first century, burial societies *(collegia)* were permitted by the government and rapidly spread all over the Empire. The purpose of these societies was to bury the dead and honor their memory by the erection of inscriptions and by the periodic celebrations of banquets at which all the members gathered. Each society had its own charter and bylaws, elected its officers, and had its patron deity in whose honor it gathered. Members paid an entrance fee and gathered periodically to eat a banquet or celebrate a festival of the god. The societies could own property and the better-off ones owned shrines, meeting houses, and gardens where they held their festivals. It was considered one of the civic duties of the curial classes and the *Augustales* to give gifts or endow these burial societies. Such benefactors were then honored by being elected patrons of the society—the usual Roman social trade-off. There was a practical side to this. The Roman cult of the dead was deeply ingrained and the perpetuation of it over the years was of the utmost importance. If the family should die out, the burial society would go on indefinitely honoring the memory of the deceased, especially if he were a benefactor.

The organization of these societies was modeled on that of society at large and imitated exactly the etiquette of the ruling classes. Strict precedence was observed at the gatherings, and donations from patrons were distributed in graded amounts to the membership just as in the cities when a distribution to the population at large was made. Since these societies were open to all members of society, servile or free, all classes were given the opportunity to indulge their desire to have a title, achieve some distinction and be above someone else. Even the lowliest might win the duly recognized title of tribune or quaestor of such and such a society, and to that extent participate in the larger civic life of the town.

There were other motivations. In the fluid society of the early Empire the desire to form artificial communities, especially in the cities, was very strong. Here the uprooted and the alienated could gather for mutual solace, protection, and pure conviviality. A sense of brotherhood, tempered by the hierarchical structure of the colleges, was an important aspect of life in the Empire. Roman thinking attached more importance to the group than to the individual and to have any focus or identity at all demanded membership in some larger society. From top to bottom the Roman world was grouped and categorized, each level rated on a general scale of dignity and each group further internally subdivided. Movement from one level to another was possible but slow, frequently taking generations. In the meantime a father might console himself, as we see frequently in the inscriptions, with his own achievements while hoping to see his sons rise higher. A common type of inscription is that in which parents with Greek names and freedmen status celebrate the election of a son with a different, Latin name, to aedile or quaestor of some local senate. This man's son might go on to a successful career in the equestrian civil service, perhaps emerging as a senator or governor or even emperor.

THE GOVERNMENT AND THE ARMY

The Emperor

The emperor who presided over the sprawling regions of the Roman world was no autocrat whose well-developed machinery of government enabled him to rule despotically over his docile subjects. Power came to him not from heaven but from the Senate and people of Rome, and as late as the sixth century Pope Gregory the Great could say that the difference between barbarian kings and Roman emperors was that the latter were the lords of free men. It is true, however, that the emperor was extremely powerful. He was the head of the Roman religion, the commander-in-chief of the armies, the principal lawmaker, and the ultimate court of appeal. It was only by convention that this power had to be disguised and over the years the disguise melted away. Even so, the limitations on the emperor's powers were very real and none of the emperors had anything like the resources that the modern totalitarian state can put in the hands of its rulers.

The emperor's responsibilities were overwhelming, the first being the defense of the Empire against its outside enemies. For this the army had to be maintained in constant readiness over thousands of miles of frontier. New recruits, armaments, and supplies had to be shipped to the farthest corners of the world in a regular, dependable fashion. Suitable officers from generals to centurions had to be selected, trained, and appointed—no easy task in an army of 350,000 to 400,000 men spread over provinces numbering almost 45. The military responsibilities alone would have been sufficient to have taken all the available time of an emperor, as in fact they did in times of invasion or civil war. Military responsibilities, however, were only part of the emperor's problems. He had to maintain peace within the Empire as well as without.

Relations with the Senate were never easy and remained one of the great unresolved problems of the Empire. The Senate was the common meeting-ground of the wealthiest and most influential figures in the Empire and the source of all its high administrators and military officers. Its members were the opinion makers of the Empire, with tentacles extending everywhere. Every emperor had to consider the possibility of treason in his midst, and Domitian used to complain that emperors led miserable lives because only their murders could convince people that conspiracies against them were real. At one time or another every emperor must have wondered which of his governors or 30-odd legionary commanders would be the most likely to try to unseat him. Even the much respected Marcus Aurelius was challenged by one of his most able subordinates, Avidius Cassius. Yet emperors could not govern without senatorial assistance, so some kind of working relationship had to be arrived at, and to that extent the emperor's power was restrained.

Prior to the rise of Rome, Greek cities had been racked by internal dissent and fought each other endlessly. Barbarian tribesmen had forever been at one another's throats and only the introduction of Roman rule brought peace. Although it was the proud boast of the Empire that, in the words of Epictetus, "there are no longer any wars, no battles, no brigandage, no piracy," in reality the natural state of things tended constantly to reassert itself. The mobs of Alexandria and Antioch rioted regularly and the cities, especially in the east, competed ferociously for first place in their provincial rankings. In civil wars they joined opposite sides, as Lyons and Vienne did in the war to see who would succeed Nero, and Nicomedia and Nicaea, Antioch and Laodicaea, Tyre and Beirut did in the civil war following the death of Commodus. In addition, each province had its own particular set of problems. In Bithynia in Asia at one stage it was overbuilding; in Algeria and Morocco, the raids of desert tribesmen; in

Judaea, religious unrest. The real task of the emperor was to find competent and trustworthy personnel to rule and guard such cities and regions.

Sometimes the solutions were worse than the original problems. Bad governors, rioting soldiers, and unscrupulous officials were often a greater threat to peace than the unruly urban factions and rural tribesmen themselves. One governor cavalierly dispensed justice to his subjects on a sliding scale—more for a high-ranking person than a low-ranking one—necessitated, he claimed, because of the greater risk involved. Tiberius warned his governors to shear his sheep, not flay them, but the long list of trials of governors accused of misdeeds shows that this command was often ignored. Perhaps it was some consolation to the provincials that there were any trials at all. Of the 40 known cases that came to trial from the time of Augustus to that of Trajan (27 B.C.–117 A.D.), 28 ended in conviction.

Administration

At the beginning of this period the only resources the emperor had for maintaining peace were the manpower of Italy in the army and the handful of governors and financial agents who were sent out periodically from Rome. Two hundred years later a transition had been made to an organized civil service, and the emperors were drawing heavily on the talents and ambitions of the provincials for service both in the legions and in the administrative branch of the government. But by modern standards or even the standards of the ancient Near East or China, the Empire was grossly underadministered. What little government there was tended to be informal and personal, characterized by exchanges of letters, recommendations by friends, and personal choices. For years there was no formal system of advancement that automatically produced a crop of well-trained senior administrators and army officers, and the principal work of administration, even the initial steps in collecting taxes, was left in the hands of the local city administrators. Roman official presence in the provinces outside the frontier areas, where the legions were stationed, was minimal. Over the years this early informal system gave way to a more systematic approach, but no effort was made or even contemplated to alter it radically. To do so would have necessitated a major and unthinkable reordering of the hierarchical system of Roman society itself.

Governors

Governors of the frontier provinces had the double task of ruling over the civilian population and commanding whatever armed forces happened to be there. These might consist of only a few auxiliary units, as in the case of Austria, or there might be two or three legions, as in Syria or the Rhine area. As chief administrator, judge, and general the governor needed as much political ability as military.

In the peaceful provinces the prime responsibility of the governor was that of maintaining order. He had to do this without the assistance of the legions or even of a well-developed bureaucracy. His staff was minute. At most he was allowed three or four assistants and beyond that he had to round up his own staff among his friends in Rome and the provinces and among his own servants. When Fronto, the close friend of Marcus Aurelius, was appointed governor of Asia in the mid-second century he asked friends from Cirta, his hometown in Africa, to come along, as well as some literary figures from Alexandria and a military expert from Morocco. Some other individuals from Cilicia were also invited.

The political position of the governor was crucial. With no military forces to speak of at his disposal, the peace of the province depended on his ability to maintain good relations with the ruling oligarchies of the cities. This could be complicated by collusion between these and other Roman officials already in the province, such as imperial procurators (financial agents), who reported directly to the emperor, or by personal contacts between the local aristocracy and powerful members of the Senate. Although theoretically the governor had the power of life and death over his subjects, he had to tread carefully and treat each case individually lest he stir up trouble for himself either in Rome or in the province itself.

Jurisdiction

The law of the province *(lex provinciae),* which was drafted when each province was initially set up, established the jurisdiction of the governor with regard to the various cities, towns, and districts of the province. Since these subdivisions could range from Roman colonies to simple rural districts the governor had to be prepared to receive all sorts of complicated questions involving boundary disputes, claims of change of status, privilege, and the like. All major crimes—such as murder, arson, rape, and adultery—and lawsuits involving large sums of money came to his court. Cases were heard directly by the governor who sat surrounded by the friends he had brought with him from Rome as well as local Romans invited to join this group (the *consilium).* Complicating factors were whether the defendants were Roman or not, whether from the upper or lower classes *(honestiores* or *humiliores).* In addition to the legal difficulties, there was always the lurking political question of what effect his decision might have on the general peace of the province. There was no one to tell him what to do or exactly how far his jurisdiction extended. Should he refer the case to the emperor, as Pliny did when confronted with accusations against Christians, or should he settle the matter on his own? Should he dodge hot issues or turn a blind eye to the corrupt practices he found in the province? How should he cope with provincials who were exploiting their fellows? Should he take the risk of being told by the local oligarchs that he was no friend of Caesar if he defended the poor and lowly against their highly placed oppressors? Even the most conscientious governors must have been perplexed by issues like these.

Finances

Governors were not responsible for the finances of the province except in a very general sense. The actual maintenance of roads, city walls, aqueducts, temples, and other buildings was the responsibility of the local senates, as were police surveillance and public entertainment. The city magistrates and senates were also responsible for the collection of the two main taxes, the poll tax *(tributum capitis)* and the land tax *(tributum soli)*. The first was a tax of 1 percent of capital valuation that all provincials had to pay and the second was a fixed tax on the produce of the land. In order to collect these taxes, which were then passed on to the Roman fiscal agents, the quaestors and procurators, a census of the inhabitants as well as the land in the province had to be maintained by the city councils. This census included the numbers of people, farms, acres devoted to pasturage and tilled lands, vineyards, olive groves, and even trees.

Along with receiving the taxes delivered to them by the cities and townships, the quaestors and procurators were responsible for collecting a number of other taxes. One was particularly important, the 5 percent inheritance tax, which went into the military treasury. There was also a 5 percent tax on manumissions—that is, the tax on what slaves paid their masters for manumissions—and the 2 or 2.5 percent toll tax on goods in transit (the *portorium*).

Unlike the imperial procurators, the quaestors or fiscal officers of senatorial provinces had close ties to their immediate superiors, the governors. Both were from the senatorial class and a quaestor's career was closely bound up with that of the governor. On the other hand procurators were appointed directly by the emperor and came from a different class. Almost from the beginning they acquired a reputation for arrogance and stepping beyond the boundaries of their jurisdiction. They had staffs of soldiers and civilians, and in the case of estates and mines that belonged to the emperors they acted as minor governors, settling disputes and exercising police powers. It was an intimation of what was to come, for while the power of imperial procurators grew, that of the governors and quaestors declined.

The Army

The Empire had over 6000 miles of frontier to defend, from Hadrian's Wall in Britain to the North African and Arabian deserts. Some of the frontiers were rivers, like the Rhine and Danube, along which the army had constructed an

Official view of the Roman legionary and his traditional enemy, the barbarian from beyond the frontiers. Fragment of a relief from the Forum of Trajan. Second century A.D.

elaborate chain of fortress towns, watchposts, palisades, ditches, walls, and military roads. In Syria another network of fortresses existed to defend the eastern half of the Empire against Parthia, the only major organized state with which Rome had to contend. In Africa constant vigilance was needed to keep the desert tribes from pillaging the settled areas. From year to year the army might be called upon to cope with invasions of organized infantry divisions, mounted archers, heavily armored cavalry, or guerilla infiltrators. Even assault by sea was not unthinkable.

Against these enemies Rome fielded an army of about 350,000 to 400,000 men, divided almost equally between citizen legionaries and noncitizen auxiliaries. The citizen soldiers were grouped in legions of some 5500 men each further divided into 10 cohorts and 60 centuries. Only 120 of these soldiers were cavalry. The auxiliary units, on the other hand, were much more varied, consisting of cavalry units *(alae)* of 1000 each and cohorts of 500 that could be either all infantry or part infantry and part cavalry. Serving among the auxiliaries were other, more barbarous units recruited outside the Empire called *numeri.* A Roman army could, then, consist of a legion or a number of legions with whatever number of auxiliary units and borrowed legionary cohorts as were deemed necessary for the campaign. Without changing the basic commitment to heavy infantry the Roman army was able to find flexibility by employing the special skills of the auxiliary units, which were commanded by Roman officers but fought according to their own style.

THE OFFICERS

The cement that held this heterogeneous army together was the Roman officer corps. Legions were commanded by senatorial legates who had under them six tribunes, one of them of senatorial birth; the others were of the equestrian class. (An exception to this rule of command by senators was the legion in Egypt, which was under an equestrian officer.) There were in addition 60 centurions, and assuming an equal number of auxiliaries, anything from five to ten equestrian officers commanding the noncitizen forces.

The mixture of civilian and military experience that Roman officers of senatorial and equestrian rank possessed seems strange to modern eyes, which at least in peacetime regard the two careers as separate. However, from the viewpoint of Romans of the upper and middle classes there was a self-evident connection between civilian and military life. Depending on one's status or choice of career, a young man could begin either in the army or with civilian posts and then move on to other military and civilian positions.

Sons of senators went off at about 18 to serve in the legions, and might return again as quaestors in the service of a provincial governor in their mid-twenties. Later on as legionary commanders or as governors themselves they would once more be back in the provinces, having in the meantime held civilian posts in Rome (such as the aedileship and praetorship).

Equestrian officers had even more varied careers. Usually they began as civilian magistrates in their hometowns and from there went on to become equestrian officers and serve their three tours of duty *(tres militiae)* of three or four years each. These tours rotated them through command of an auxiliary cohort, back to the legions as military tribune, and then on to the command of an auxiliary cavalry unit. They might, for example, spend a few years commanding one of the Syrian auxiliary units in Pannonia (Hungary), then more years with the noted *legio III Augusta* in Africa, and finally a few years with a cavalry unit in Britain. Technically they were still civilians and could at this point be returned to civilian life; if exceptionally able, they might move on directly to the command of a legion, with senatorial rank. More commonly, they went on at this point to a career in the equestrian (procuratorial) civil service.

Another line of advancement was through the ranks of the centurions. Simple soldiers could with luck and ability become centurions and advance through the complicated grades to the highest position, that of senior centurion for the second time *(primus pilus bis).* From this position they could enter the equestrian civil service as did the equestrian officers who went through the *tres militiae,* or they could remain in the army for the rest of their careers.

Men of equestrian rank had the option of entering the army as centurions and frequently did so. As centurions they would also pass through the various grades and emerge as candidates for civil-service posts. A fairly typical career was that of C. Velius Rufus, who began serving in Syria where he rose to be senior centurion of *legio XII Fulminata.* He saw action in Palestine during the Jewish Wars and was decorated for bravery by the emperors Vespasian and Titus. Next he went to Parthia as a member of a diplomatic mission and then served successively on the Rhine, in Africa, and on the Danube, where he was again decorated. He reached the pinnacle of his career when he was made imperial procurator for the provinces of Pannonia (Hungary), Dalmatia (Yugoslavia), and Raetia (southern Germany). Hundreds of such careers are to be found in the inscriptions, revealing how widely traveled the officer class of the Empire was. It also shows another side of Roman life not even hinted at in the literary sources, whose prime focus is Rome, the upper classes, and the emperors.

From the viewpoint of military cohesion it was the influx of these educated civilians from the towns of Italy and the provinces that provided much of the talent necessary for the proper operation of the army. The army was primarily concerned with maintaining peace, and it performed a great number of civilian functions in addition to its military duties. It was the single greatest reserve of technically trained people in the Empire—engineers, surveyors, builders, and administrators of all kinds. It was principally from this source that the emperors drew their technical staffs, their judges, their governors, and their legionary commanders. Far from being a peripheral element in the Empire, the army had a much more central role than do most modern armies. The constant movement of officers and the promotion of ordinary soldiers guaranteed a unity to the scattered legions and auxiliary units. The civilian character of the equestrian officers was an unusual feature that opened the army to whole classes of people whose careers would otherwise have terminated with the holding of a minor office in a provincial town. Men of talent could transfer their expertise to the army and find a whole new world of imperial service opened to them. The close connection between military commands and civilian administration made the army an integral part of Roman life and guaranteed that it would not become overprofessionalized. This, of course, also had its weaknesses, but at least in peaceful times it proved a brilliant solution to the problem of integration of such a diverse region as the Empire. Although not intended as such, the Roman army was the prime agent of social unity and mobility in the Mediterranean world.

RECRUITMENT AND CONDITIONS OF SERVICE

Legionaries were initially recruited in Italy and the western provinces, but by the second century A.D. the majority came from the provinces where the legions were located. Auxiliaries, too, although originally recruited in particular provinces, eventually came from wherever the individual units were stationed. The principle of obligatory military service was never dropped, and in fact when new legions were formed they were made up of levies from Italy. Throughout the Empire, providing recruits was one of the more onerous burdens the cities had to sustain.

Legionaries served for 25 years and received 300 denarii a year in three installments; deductions were made for food and clothing. Another source of income was the cash donatives made by the emperors on major occasions, such as anniversaries of their accession to power. On discharge the legionaries received either a plot of land or 3000 denarii together with the privilege of belonging to the higher legal category of *honestiores.*

Auxiliaries fared almost as well. Their basic pay was 200–300 denarii per year and on discharge they received the Roman citizenship for themselves and their children (though not for their wives). (By contrast, marriages of legionaries were not recognized until the end of the second century, a situation that caused all kinds of difficulties for their de facto wives and children.)

Pay and service conditions were considered good and a soldier could hope to accumulate some savings, learn a trade perhaps, or even advance to high rank if he had particular ability. Non-Latin speakers could pick up Latin and make contacts with upper- and middle-class Roman officers that might prove useful later on. Provincial Syrians, Africans, or Spaniards might start out uneducated and penniless in the auxiliaries, and later emerge with a rough education, the citizenship, some money, and new status. Discharged at the rate of 6000 a year the auxiliaries constituted an important addition to the Romanized population of the Empire and a continuing source of recruits for the army, since sons regularly followed their fathers into the old units.

Italians still enjoyed some advantages over the provincials. Recruitment for the Praetorian Guard took place in Italy, and with knowledge of Latin and only 16 years of service as compared to 25 for the ordinary legionaries, higher pay, and location in Rome, Praetorian troopers had an edge over their legionary competitors in the scramble for advancement within the army. The bulk of legionary centurions always remained, however, promoted legionaries, not Praetorians.

17

The Empire from Marcus Aurelius to Constantine

THE SEVERAN EMPERORS

The luck the Empire had with its rulers came to an end on the accession in A.D. 180 of Commodus, the son of Marcus Aurelius. From the time he was 15 he had been joint ruler of the Empire with his father, and immediately on Marcus' death he asserted his authority by making peace with the Germans, against whom the Romans had been fighting continuously for almost 12 years. To the dismay of the Senate he returned to Rome and promptly began spending enormous sums on extravagant spectacles in the circus while leaving the running of the government to his cronies. Dressed as the hero Hercules he performed feats of archery in the arena, which delighted the mob. In 182 an unsuccessful assassination attempt launched him on the course that Nero and Domitian had followed, but he managed to survive for another ten years before finally succumbing to a plot engineered by his mistress and the Praetorian Prefect.

His replacement, an elderly senator by the name of Pertinax, gives a good indication of the changing conditions of the second century. Although a distinguished senator and at the time of his elevation the holder of the Prefecture of the City—the highest post that a senator could hold—Pertinax was the son of a freedman from northern Italy and had served in the equestrian service before becoming a member of the Senate. A rigid disciplinarian, he was soon murdered by the Praetorian Guard, who then proceeded to the degrading auction of the Empire to whoever would pay the largest donative. The highest bidder was a senator by the name of M. Didius Julianus.

On the news of this event the frontier legions took matters into their own hands and a four-year civil war ensued. The troops in Syria proclaimed C. Pescennius Niger emperor; those in Britain, D. Clodius Albinus; and the Danube legions, their commander, L. Septimius Severus. Located closer to Rome than the others, the Danube legions got there first and disposed of Julianus. Severus then disbanded the Praetorian Guard and replaced them with veterans from his own ranks. Proclaiming Albinus his heir in order to secure his rear, he set off for the east, where he defeated Niger in 194. Antioch, which supported Niger, was sacked and lost its position as the capital of Syria. Byzantium, which had also resisted him, was razed. Turning west, he then took on Albinus and after a struggle defeated him. Lyons then suffered the fate of Antioch and Byzantium, and since a number of senators had supported Albinus, Severus turned on the Senate, executing many of its members and confiscating their estates. At the same time he announced that he was the son of Marcus Aurelius and the brother of Commodus. His sons Caracalla and Geta were declared his heirs.

Severus was a first-generation senator from the old Punic town of Leptis Magna, and according to one somewhat dubious source spoke Latin with a heavy accent. His wife, Julia Domna, was a Syrian whose family held the hereditary priesthood at Emesa. Under Severus a succession of brilliant lawyers held the position of Praetorian Prefect and began the systematic reorganization of the Empire. Severus had little use for the Senate and gave increasing importance to his advisory council, the *consilium.* From 197 to 202 he was in the east waging war against the Parthians, and six years later he went to Britain to conduct more campaigns. He died at York in A.D. 211.

Severus had left his sons as his joint heirs but Geta was soon murdered by his brother Caracalla, who, after calming the restless troops by increasing their pay, went off on a campaign against the Parthians. Revenue for the new expenditures was raised by extending the franchise to almost all the inhabitants of the Empire and then doubling the inheritance tax to which only citizens were subject.

In 217 Caracalla was murdered by the Praetorian Prefect Macrinus, another African, who now became the first equestrian to ascend the throne. Macrinus, however, had not calculated on the wiles of Julia Maesa, the sister-in-law of Severus, who announced to the troops that her grandson, Varius Avitus (Elagabalus) was the son of Caracalla. Loyal to the Severan dynasty, the legionaries killed Macrinus and proclaimed Elagabalus emperor in his place.

The new emperor turned out to be an eccentric who squandered vast amounts of state funds, and after being persuaded to adopt his cousin, Severus Alexander, as his heir, was disposed of by the Praetorian Guard at his grandmother's suggestion. Alexander was only 14 when he ascended the throne and throughout his reign he was firmly under the thumb of his mother, Julia Mammaea. The jurist Ulpian and a number of senators in the *consilium* were good influences on the young man, but his mother made the mistake of flaunting her power and the troops finally rebelled and murdered the emperor in A.D. 235.

THE THIRD-CENTURY CRISIS

With the end of the Severan dynasty the Roman world entered into a period of great peril. Within the Empire there was almost perpetual political chaos and increasing economic dislocation. Simultaneously barbarians attacked in the east and across the Danube and penetrated far into the interior of the Empire, doing enormous damage. For over half a century the pressures continued, until finally a series of great emperors succeeded in bringing Rome back from the brink of destruction and restoring peace in what amounted to a refounding of the Empire.

The peace of the Roman world depended on a balance being achieved between barbarian pressures and the ability of the legions to resist them, and between the costs of war and the resources of the state.

Augustus made the decision, which was accepted by his successors, not to expand the Empire beyond the Rhine and Danube frontiers. The legions were strung out along the great river boundaries with the object of preventing minor raiding by barbarians, not major assaults. Additions such as Britain and Dacia were made, and the client-kingdoms were dissolved and converted into regular provinces to improve the lines of defense. Gradually the frontiers developed into a complex network of roads, fortresses, outposts, ditches, walls, and palisades. All kinds of techniques were used to keep the barbarians disunited. Punitive raids were conducted, subsidies paid, and strife fomented wherever possible. On the eastern frontier peace was maintained with the Parthian Empire by means of diplomacy, backed up occasionally by displays of military power.

The weakness of the Roman position lay in the fact that by choosing a static line of defense the initiative was allowed to pass to peoples outside the Empire. As long as barbarian pressures were not too great in either the east or the west the frontier defenses sufficed, but in the face of major attacks they were bound to crumble.

For almost two centuries the German tribes had presented no major problems. Then, at the beginning of the second century, new tribes, among them the Goths and Vandals, began to move from the Baltic area southward and westward, driving the older peoples before them and forcing them to form larger groupings to resist the new pressures. The storm broke under Marcus Aurelius in 167, but the invasions of his time were only a prelude to what was to come. In A.D. 233 the Alamanni, a confederacy of German tribes, attacked across the upper Danube and from that time until the end of the century the pressures were unrelenting. The Goths concentrated in the lower Danube and Black Sea areas, and the Franks, Vandals, and Alamanni assaulted the Rhine and Danube frontiers. At the same time the old Parthian monarchy gave way to a vigorous new Persian dynasty, the Sassanids, who reorganized the state on a businesslike basis and in 231 invaded the eastern provinces in an attempt to recover the districts that had once belonged to Persia.

These years also saw a tremendous inflation in prices and the collapse of the currency system. The silver content of the coinage dropped to 1 percent by the time of Claudius II (268–270) and the price of grain went from 2 denarii per measure in A.D. 200 to 330 in A.D. 301. Surprisingly, it was the government that was hardest hit by inflation because its taxes came in the form of fixed money payments. However, since it had to feed and supply the legions it eventually was forced to fall back on requisitions in kind. At the same time developments that were already under way in the second century were rapidly advanced by the pressures of the times. The role of the army in choosing emperors was reinforced at the expense of the Senate and the emperors no longer made any pretense of being the first citizen or *princeps.* They were military men and autocrats, and the court around them began to assume an increasingly important role. More and more key personnel came from the ranks of the equestrian order until under Gallienus (253–268) senators were excluded from all military commands and most civilian positions. The number of Italians in the Senate declined and provincials, especially from Africa and the east, increased in numbers and included among them many soldiers and equestrians. The state intervened more than ever in local affairs, and the burdens of municipal administration on the town senates of the Empire increased out of all proportion to the rewards of membership. By the same token it was the relentlessness and continuity of the imperial administrative services throughout the anarchy of civil wars and invasions in the third century that kept the Empire together.

The most important social changes of these years occurred in the realm of religion. Christianity now began for the first time to find widespread acceptance among the middle classes of the Empire and to build up a respectable intellectual presentation of its tenets. At the same time its organization developed considerably, as the individual churches began to communicate more freely with one another and to meet in provincial councils to discuss their common needs and objectives.

Political Anarchy

The successor of the Severans was a soldier's soldier, a huge Thracian by the name of Maximinus. He increased his popularity with the troops by granting them pay raises and conducting successful campaigns along the northern frontiers, but his financial demands provoked a rebellion in Africa, which was supported by a surprisingly active Senate at Rome. The Africans Gordian and his son Gordian II were proclaimed emperors, and when they were slain in battle by troops loyal to Maximinus, two senators, M. Clodius Pupienus and D. Caelius Balbinus, were elevated as joint emperors and adopted Gordian's grandson as their heir. In attempting to recover Italy Maximinus was murdered by his own troops after an unsuccessful siege of Aquileia, and Pupienus and Balbinus in turn were assassinated by the Praetorian Guard, who elevated Gordian III to the throne. On campaign in the east, Gordian was slain by his mutinous troops and Philip the Arab took over in A.D. 244. It is indicative of the evolving character of the Empire that it was left to Philip to celebrate with great pomp the millennium of the founding of Rome in A.D. 247.

Philip's reign came to an end in 249 and he was succeeded by one of his generals, Decius. In order to pacify the angry gods whom he felt must have been responsible for the disasters besetting Rome, the new emperor launched the first empire-wide persecution of the Christians. Soon afterward he was killed in battle with the Goths in the lower Danube area. Decius was succeeded briefly by Trebonianus Gallus and then by the Moor Aemilianus. The next emperor was Valerian, the commander of the Rhine legions. He had good relations with the Senate and at its suggestion appointed his son Gallienus as a second Augustus or co-emperor in 253. Responsibility for the Empire was now divided for the first time, and while Gallienus remained in Gaul Valerian went to the east to repel the Persians. In 257 he launched the second empire-wide persecution of the Christians, which, however, was called off by Gallienus in 260 on the capture of his father by the Persians. In the same year the western half of the Empire, including Britain, Gaul, and Spain, was split off from the rest by the usurper Postumus, who was recognized by Gallienus, and did an effective job in defending the Rhine frontier against invaders. In the east Palmyra, under its rulers Odenathus and then his widow Zenobia, proclaimed its independence and was recognized as a client kingdom.

Gallienus' rule was beset by the greatest disasters Rome had yet suffered. Gothic fleets ravaged the Aegean, sacking Ephesus and burning the great temple

The strained faces of Romans in the age of crisis. Just as the hilosophers of the period urged their followers not to stop with the appearances of things but to penetrate to their ssences, artists from the time of M. Aurelius attempted to ortray their subjects as preoccupied with their own inner ision, transcending the changing material world around them. The Emperor Gallienus (left) and an unidentified Roman ight).

of Diana in 262/263. Then, around 267 the Heruli, a German tribe, captured and sacked the cities of Byzantium, Athens, Corinth, Argos, and Sparta. Gallienus coped as best he could and initiated a series of military reforms that placed emphasis on cavalry units (*vexillationes*). He finally succeeded in defeating the Goths in 268 at Naissus in the Balkans, but was assassinated the same year by the Illyrian generals Claudius and Aurelian.

With the defeat of the Goths and the advent of the Illyrians, Rome's fortunes began to rise again slowly. Claudius was succeeded by Aurelian in 270 and the step-by-step process of reuniting the Empire began. The Palmyrenes were overcome in 273 and in 274 Postumus' successor in the west, Tetricus, submitted. Aurelian could justly claim the title of *Restitutor Orbis,* the Restorer of the World. During his reign Dacia and the Agri Decumates, the region between the headwaters of the Rhine and the Danube, were abandoned as undefendable, and great walls were built around the city of Rome. Aurelian also attempted currency reforms, and proclaimed the sun god the universal god of the Empire. In 275 he succumbed to a conspiracy and was succeeded briefly by the aged senator Tacitus (not the historian, although he claimed descent from him). After Tacitus' peaceful death (strange in these times) another Illyrian, by the name of Probus, succeeded to the throne. Uncomfortable with his rigid discipline, the troops rebelled and killed him in 282, and the Praetorian Prefect Carus became emperor. Soon the troops proclaimed the one-time Illyrian sheepherder Diocles as emperor (284), and as Diocletian he began the work of the refounding of the Roman Empire.

DIOCLETIAN AND CONSTANTINE

Under Diocletian the Empire found peace again. His general Maximian cleared the barbarians out of the west and was rewarded by being made Augustus in 286. In 293 the imperial college was expanded to four as both Diocletian and Maximian adopted as "Caesars," or junior emperors, the generals Gaius Galerius and Flavius Constantius respectively. In order to cement the relationship Constantius put away his common-law wife Helena (the mother of Constantine) and married Theodora, Maximian's stepdaughter. The multiplication of emperors permitted a more effective defense of the Empire and Roman armies were able to beat back their enemies on all the frontiers.

THE REFORMS OF DIOCLETIAN

A born administrator, Diocletian began a thorough reorganization of the Empire. He greatly expanded the size of the army and attempted to create a stable currency. His most successful reforms were the reorganization of the requisitions in kind (which had become the principal source of income for the state in the third century) into a regular system of levies (*indictiones*), and the creation of a true budget. The administration of the Empire was now expanded and professionalized to provide the necessary taxes, manpower, and supplies for the reconstituted state.

Down to the third century the government of the Empire depended in large measure on an informal system of aristocratic government over which the emperor, with direct control of the somewhat more fully organized equestrian civil service, presided. Upper-class provincials were held responsible for the bulk of imperial administration, including the collection of most of the taxes, and were in turn supervised by upper-class Romans. The concept of the administration as a permanent collection of career officials whose loyalty was to the bureaucracy and the state and largely independent of the cities and the magistrates, generals, and emperors who came and went, was slow in developing. Even under Diocletian, when the administration had developed considerably, reliance was still placed on the local curial classes to collect the taxes although supervision of them was increased enormously.

The crisis of the third century gave impetus to the development of a true caste of administrators, so that by its end the emperor had at his disposal a thoroughly professional corps of bureaucrats at the supervisory level. The stages of the evolution are not clear, although, as has been mentioned before, senators had been excluded from all military commands and most high civilian posts by the time of the sole reign of Gallienus (after 260). It was thus left to Diocletian, as in so many other areas, to bring the process to completion by standardizing and regularizing the whole imperial administrative setup.

To a large extent the tightening up of the administration simply meant the expansion of the old system. There were approximately 50 provinces when Diocletian ascended the throne, but these were frequently inefficient administrative units. Asia, for example, had 250 cities but only one governor. Diocletian's solution was to divide the province into six smaller units, each headed by a governor with a staff of about 100. Similar adjustments were made wherever the emperor or his staff thought them to be necessary or useful, so that ultimately the number of provinces expanded to 100 and were grouped in 13 dioceses under vicars. It needs emphasis that this reorganization took place only at high levels in the administration, and there was much less proliferation at the lower echelons. It has been calculated that there were about 30,000 civil servants by the end of the fourth century, a relatively small number considering that the Empire had a population of perhaps 50 million.

The staff that looked after the provinces was also expanded and professionalized, though it remained for Constantine, Diocletian's successor, to bring the process of evolution to completion. The development began at the top with the office of the emperor and the bureaucracy (the *comitatus*) that went with it. In place of a single emperor vainly rushing from one end of the Empire to the other, there were to be two Augusti with their delegated successors, the Caesars. The attendant staff of each emperor was doubled. Under the Augusti were the Praetorian Prefects who, as the chief aides or ministers of the emperors, were responsible for all civilian and military operations in the Empire. With Constantine the Praetorian Guard was disbanded and the Prefects were relieved of their military responsibilities so that they could devote themselves full time to their civilian duties, which now consisted of supplying the army with all its material and manpower needs, supervising the provincial governors and heading the judicial system. This separation of military and civilian functions was systematically carried out throughout the system. Two generals called *magistri* took over the Praetorian Prefects' military role and were put in command of the central field armies (the *comitatenses* or *palatini*), and other generals (*duces*), numbering perhaps 20, were responsible for the frontier armies. The governors (*praesides*), relieved of military duties, devoted themselves full time to their civilian functions, principally the collection of taxes and the administration of justice.

The administrative reforms of Diocletian went hand in hand with his reorganization of the army. The ease with which barbarian invaders broke through the frontier defenses demonstrated the need for strengthening the army. Under Diocletian its numbers, which had been slowly rising, became almost double what they had been at the beginning of the third century. It is hard to believe that Diocletian would have gone ahead with his enlargement of the army if he (or his predecessors) had not already come to the conclusion that the Empire could bear the strain of increased numbers of troops and the supplies they needed. Obviously, if the army was to be expanded, there would also have to be a corresponding increase in the administrative side of the government to supply the large number of new recruits required together with the weapons, armor, uniforms, food, cavalry mounts, and pay they required. For whatever reasons—lack of time and ability, or the anarchy of the period—previous emperors in the third century had attempted to muddle through on the resources they had at hand. Diocletian's special talent, however, was administrative, and like a new Augustus he set about a thoroughgoing reorganization of the Empire in every area—military, administrative, fiscal, and economic. Like his great predecessor he was extremely successful, and in the east his work enabled the Empire to survive for another 1000 years.

CONSTANTINE

Toward the end of his reign Diocletian, urged by Galerius, initiated another great persecution of the Christians (A.D. 303). They were dismissed from the army and the civil service, churches were burned, and the scriptures confiscated. The clergy were prime targets for the persecutors and many were imprisoned and put to death.

On the retirement of Diocletian and Maximian in 305 civil war broke out again. Constantius died the following year and his son Constantine was proclaimed emperor in his place. Another contender, Maxentius, the son of Maximian, entered the contest but was defeated by Constantine at the battle of the Milvian Bridge in 312. Before the battle Constantine dreamed that he would win if he painted on his soldiers' shields the monogram of Christ, and this later evolved into the *labarum*, Constantine's personal standard, a chi rho, ☧ , mounted on a cross. Constantine's victory convinced him of the might of the Christian god and in 313 he returned the confiscated properties of the Church and extended privileges to the clergy. He at once found himself involved in the theological and disciplinary disputes of the Church and the split in the African Church between the heretical Donatists and the orthodox was drawn to his attention. After trying to settle the problem peacefully, he resorted to persecution (A.D. 317–320), but failed again. Meanwhile his relations with the co-ruler in the east, Licinius, deteriorated and war broke out between the two men. In 324 Licinius was defeated and Constantine became the sole ruler of the Empire. At this point he became aware of the great battle raging between the bishop of Alexandria and one of his priests, Arius, which had split the churches of the eastern half of the Empire. After trying personal persuasion Constantine called a council of the whole Church to meet in 325 at Nicaea and personally directed it until a moderate formula was agreed upon. The battle did not end there, however, and the controversy continued for years afterward.

In addition to problems of imperial rule Constantine was plagued by domestic difficulties. His favorite son Crispus, the offspring of his first marriage, was also favored by his mother, the pious Helena, whereas his wife Fausta promoted the fortunes and careers of her own sons by Constantine. In 326 she falsely accused Crispus of assaulting her and the emperor, without proper investigation, had his son executed. Later he became aware of his error and put Fausta to death. This tragedy clouded the emperor's later years and filled him with remorse for his crime which he attempted to expiate by lavish gifts to the Church. Fearing for his salvation he waited until close to the moment of death to be baptized.

18

The Transformed Empire

THE GEOGRAPHY OF THE LATE EMPIRE

It is not possible to study the fourth century for very long without realizing that a shift in geography has taken place. Areas that previously had been central to Roman history, such as Italy, now become backwaters, and peripheral areas become central. Before the fourth century the focus of history was the Mediterranean itself and the lands bordering it. Now there was a pronounced shift of the axis of the Roman world northward and eastward, away from the Mediterranean and toward the Atlantic and Danube. Eventually, after the Arab invasions of the seventh century, there was a further shift eastward, this time toward the Euphrates and Mesopotamia. With this last event the Mediterranean lost forever the unity that Roman rule and culture had imposed on it and also its centrality in western history.

Already in the second century barbarian pressures on the Danube and in Syria had drawn the Romans northward and eastward. Marcus Aurelius' Marcomannic campaigns kept him on the northern frontier for 12 years while his colleague Lucius Verus had earlier spent 4 years in campaigns against the Parthians. Septimius Severus was similarly drawn to the east, and throughout the third century the northern and eastern frontiers, particularly the lower Danube and Euphrates, were the constant preoccupations of the emperors. Rome itself was now considerably off the beaten path, rarely visited and of no use as a base to the emperors, whose problems lay 500–1500 miles to the north or east. New centers closer to the danger spots were essential. In the west Milan and Aquileia in Italy and Trier on the Moselle were good locations; in the Danube area Sirmium, Serdica, Thessalonica, Byzantium, and Nicomedia were tried at one time or another. In the east Antioch was the most obvious center.

Along with the transfer of the administration to the northern and eastern frontiers came a shift of wealth to these regions. All along the Danube flourishing cities came into being and new roads, bridges, dockyards, and villas

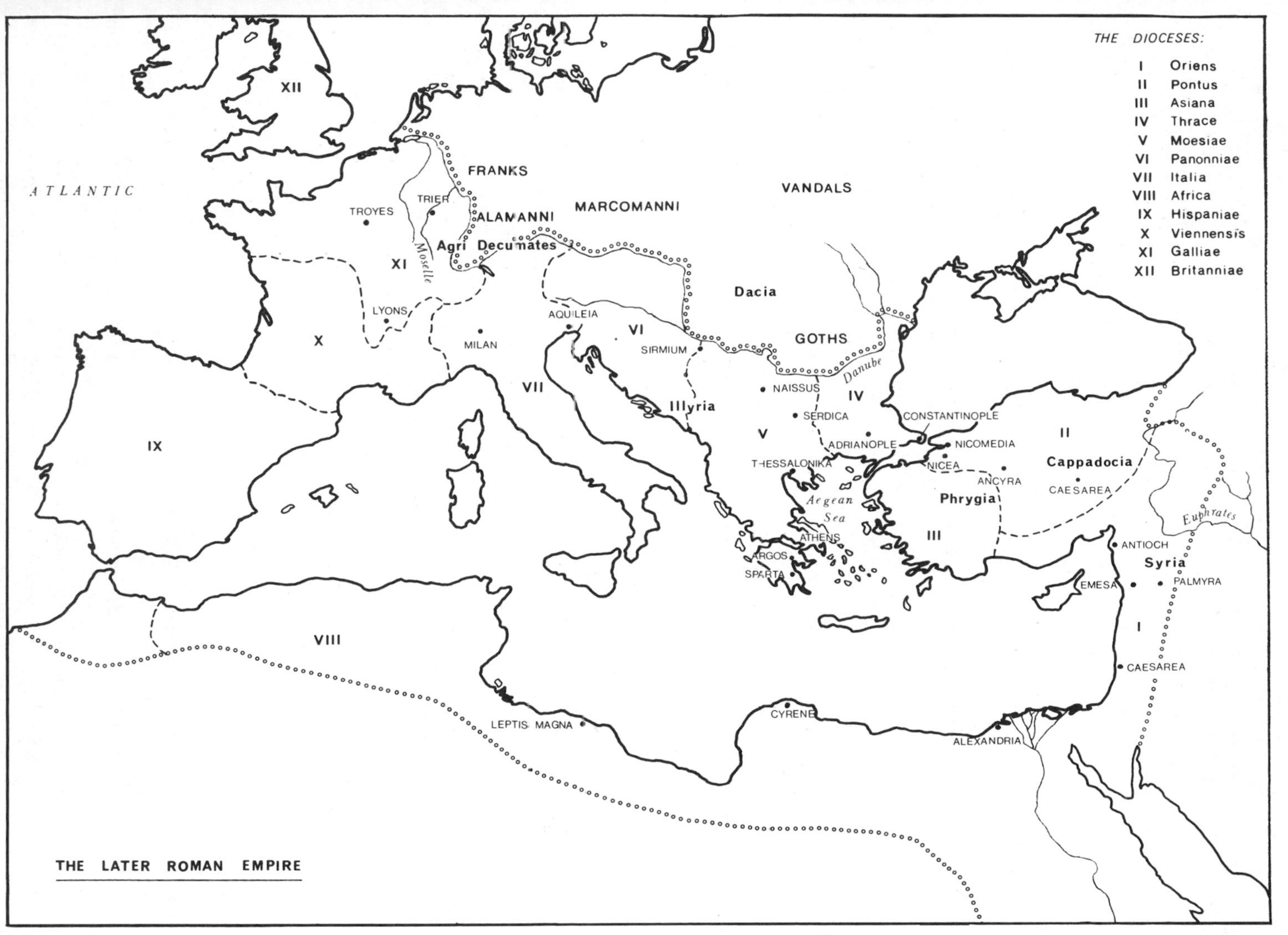

THE LATER ROMAN EMPIRE

were built. The treasury of Gaul was located at Trier on the Moselle, along with a mint and an armament factory. The emperors Constantius I and Constantine had their headquarters there, and a considerable amount of building activity resulted. Enormous baths and warehouses were constructed, as well as a great basilica, which still survives. The gates were renovated and new villas for the senior bureaucrats built in the countryside. Other emperors had their favorite sites also. Diocletian made his capital at Nicomedia in Asia Minor; Maximian erected his palace at his birthplace, Sirmium; and Galerius adorned Thessalonica with magnificent buildings. Antioch, although sacked by the Persians in the previous century, was another flourishing center, with its mints, baths, lighted streets, armament factories, and linen industry.

The logical step of establishing a major military and administrative center near both the Euphrates and Danube frontiers was taken by Constantine. After considering Sirmium, Serdica, and possibly Thessalonica, he selected Byzantium on the Bosporus. It had a superb location at the strategic and easily defended bottleneck between Europe and Asia. Supplies could be brought in by land as well as by sea and it straddled the vital east-west road that led from northern Italy down the Danube to the Bosporus, then over the Anatolian plateau by way of Nicomedia, Ancyra and Caesarea to Antioch. It was also close to the great intellectual centers of Greece, Asia Minor, and the east.

The founding of Constantinople ("the city of Constantine," as Byzantium was renamed) had profound historical repercussions. Whether Constantine intended it or not the new city provided a focus for a kingdom quite unlike the one that was developing in the western half of the Roman Empire. The language and culture of the region were Greek. Its economic resources were superior to those of the west and even its social structure offered more hope for permanence. Land was divided more evenly among the different classes and the eastern senatorial aristocracy was not dominated, as it was in the west, by an old core of great landowning nobles. There was a different understanding, too, of the role of the emperor that promoted a more stable, unified kingdom. Culturally, the east was far more deeply Hellenized than the west, and even areas that had previously not been noted for their contributions, such as Cappadocia, rural Syria, and Egypt, now began to produce some of the more significant intellectual figures of the age. In the great invasions of the fifth century, the east was able to fend for itself, whereas the more vulnerable and weaker western half of the Empire collapsed before the onslaught.

THE CULTURAL AND RELIGIOUS ENVIRONMENT

By the old standards the third century was an extremely impoverished period in Rome's history. There had been a great outpouring of encyclopedias and learned commentaries on the classical works of the past toward the end of the previous century and at the beginning of the third, but even this type of literature soon declined both in quantity and quality. The visual arts were equally affected.

Even the copying of statues died out and when there was a great revival of sculpture in the next century there was almost a complete lack of skilled craftsmen and artists trained in the classical tradition.

Despite its impoverishment in the arts and literature, the third century managed to produce two of the most important thinkers of antiquity, the Neoplatonist philosopher Plotinus and the Christian Origen. This period also saw the beginning of the dialogue between Christianity and classical culture, which was to guarantee the survival of a good portion of the classical achievement through the Dark Ages of the barbarian invasions. And although the old educational system continued sterile and traditional as ever, it received a major boost when the government in the third century turned away from the senatorial classes to the lower-ranking equestrians for its top administrators while still insisting on high standards of education. The new officials were expected to conform to the ancient norms of classical behavior, which belonged as a kind of birthright to the previous incumbents, but which had to be consciously acquired by the newcomers by a diligent study of the great masterpieces of the past from Homer to Virgil. As a result, a whole new class of men with fresh minds became enthusiastic students of the classics and brought about in the next century a renaissance the like of which was not to be seen for another 700 years. In poetry there was Claudian, Ausonius, and Rutilius Namatianus, all of them pagans. Among the Christians were Paulinus, Ambrose, and Prudentius, the last the greatest Latin poet since the time of Augustus. For the first time in two and a half centuries the field of history produced a major figure, the Antiochene Ammianus Marcellinus, writing in Latin. He was the most important historian since Tacitus, whom he excelled in some respects. In Greek, Eusebius, the bishop of Caesarea and the friend of Constantine, broke important new ground in historical methodology.

Some of the greatest minds of the period devoted themselves to theology and biblical studies, as well as to active lives in ecclesiastical politics. Such men as Basil of Caesarea, Gregory of Nazianze, and Gregory of Nyssa (all of them Cappadocians), Athanasius of Alexandria, John Chrysostom of Antioch, Jerome (from the Danube area), and Ambrose of Milan would all have made their mark in an earlier age in the secular world of letters, politics, or the army. Now they chose to serve another organization, the Church. Synesius of Cyrene moved easily from the philosopher's lecture room to ecclesiastical administration while preserving his friendship with the famous pagan woman philosopher, Hypatia of Alexandria, and when he became bishop did so on the condition that although he "spoke myths in church" he could continue to think as a philosopher in private. Augustine, from the little town of Thagaste in north Africa, pioneered the field of spiritual autobiography and expressed himself in his *Confessions* with more conscious honesty and directness than had anyone before him in antiquity. His major work, the *City of God*, became the point of transition for the Roman world from the classical to the medieval period. In it he attempted to deflate the glories of the Roman past and the hollowness of its achievements in contrast to the glorious deeds of God in history. Although, he declared, what the Romans were able to realize in their city was the best that unaided men could accomplish by themselves, it was as nothing compared to what could be realized with the assistance of grace in the Heavenly City.

Perhaps the most striking aspect of third- and fourth-century culture is the challenge it offered to the old elitist presuppositions about what constituted a genuine education and who could achieve it. There was a great deal of dilution and diffusion of classical learning as the rising classes of new men in the imperial civil service attempted to acquire the values and standards of the positions to which they aspired, which in the past had been the private possession of a snobbish, cultural elite. This kind of classical learning may not have been immediately relevant to the administrative job at hand, but the traditional association of high culture and public service could not easily be eradicated, and the Romans shied away from employing what they considered to be mere technicians in their higher civil-service posts. Specialists were available, to be sure, but they served *under* the classically educated generalists. In the east this combination of scholar and bureaucrat proved a success and provided the emperors of that region with a stable administration for the next 1000 years. In the west it was a different story, as the aristocrats withdrew from the cities to their villas in the countryside and the clergy retired to their monasteries, abandoning the army and the civil administration to their fates. By a quirk of history it was this movement into the countryside that finally extended Latin to the rural districts of the western Empire and led to the development of the Romance languages at the expense of the native tongues of Gaul and the Iberian peninsula.

The Arts

There was a new vigor in the arts and architecture, inspired by the changes that had taken place in the culture of the third and fourth centuries and men's understanding of the role of government. These new views demanded expression in the visual arts and they discovered it in the basilican form in architecture and in the new frontal style in sculpture.

For both Greeks and Romans the temple was a building whose primary purpose was to honor the god by providing a suitable dwelling place for him as well as protection for his cult statue from the elements. Primary emphasis was given to the exterior, and the interior, which was cramped and dimly lit, was of much less importance. With its sharp corners and boxy lines the Greek temple was clearly set apart from surrounding space and placed solidly on the ground. It was intended to be looked at and walked around. On the other hand, the worship needs of the new faith, which were diametrically opposed to those of the old, created a demand for fresh architectural forms. Its churches were not principally the dwelling places of a god, and what Christians were most in need of was large interior spaces where the people could gather to celebrate their rituals, preferably with unblocked views of the altar and the celebrant. Conveniently, this kind of building was readily available in the secular basilica, whose shape, coincidentally, also happened to serve the needs of the new imperial autocrats.

The rectangular basilica was an old Italian architectural form designed to serve the community's social, commercial, and legal needs. Every Italian city had its basilica or basilicas, which were located in or near the forum, the town's business area. Their purpose was to provide shelter from inclement weather for large numbers of people, and thus special emphasis was given to the interior; the outer form was of secondary importance. Barrel and cross vaults provided the essential structural elements of the building and light was supplied by clerestory windows high above the floor. The results were impressive, and in the hands of the new secular and religious authorities all the potential of this ancient architectural form was realized. New visual and spatial dimensions were opened up. In the basilica, unlike the temple, space was itself important and the classical Greek effort to limit it by sharp corners and right angles gave way to the curves of the vaults and ceilings, which conveyed the impression of distance and limitlessness. With illumination coming from high above mysterious effects of light and shade became possible. Another element was the colossal size of the basilicas of the Constantinian period. The central nave of Maxentius' basilica, for example, measured 260 × 80 feet and the ceiling, supported by three soaring cross vaults, was 115 feet above the marbled floor. A riot of colored pavements, mosaics, wall decorations, and coffered ceilings confronted the viewer no matter where he looked, yet all the elements were integrated and a focus was provided by the structure's axial lines, which drew the eye immediately to the apses at either end.

In such a building the individual was dwarfed, but at the same time swept up into the structure. Under the huge vaults all men were drawn together as one. Whereas in the classical view the individual regarded the temple from his own particular vantage point, in the basilica the individual was submerged and overwhelmed by the mass of men gathered there, his special viewpoint lost in so large a setting. As part of the mass, however, he was included, not excluded, and together with his fellows he was lifted up to the infinite, whether this was the godhead or the emperor. At Trier in Germany the Constantinian basilica survives intact, and a description of it by a modern observer will serve to give an impression of all basilicas of the period:

> Originally [its] red brick was hidden under plaster, painted around the windows (in two tiers) with yellow vine tendrils and little cupids, all on a red background. Most of the walls were pierced by pipes, and there was space under the floor, too, for the circulation of hot air. Forehall and nave were paved with a honeycomb design in black and white, while geometric patterns of many-colored marble and gilt glass covered the walls up to the second tier of windows. . . . The apse, a throne platform in its midst, was sheathed in gold and mosaics; over all, a gilt-coffered ceiling. There were no columns in the 250-foot nave to detract from the impression of enormous size; no interruption to the floods of

> light that played over the surfaces of gold, ochre, green, red, black, and white; nothing but air, it seemed, to support a vault a hundred feet above the floor. One's gaze rose involuntarily into space, floated like a mote in the stillness, rebounded from the range of colors, but came to rest inevitably at the gathering of lines in the apse. There sat or stood the emperor on ceremonial occasions for the announcement of victories, the reading of new laws, the reception of embassies. The whole building had a point. Beautiful in itself, and bringing to a focus many brilliant arts and skills, its beauty merged into the purposes of the state. It declared the power of its creator, a being who, to the awe of barbarians and peasants, could enclose so vast a space *and heat it.*[1]

The basilican plan was as perfectly adapted to the needs of the new religion as it was to those of the imperial government. In place of the emperor we should picture the bishop celebrating the Eucharist for the assembled congregation or pronouncing his homily from the high pulpit. In this setting the individual Christian was absorbed into the mass of his fellow worshippers and was united to the bishop, God's intermediary between heaven and earth. In the mystical action of the ritual he was lifted out of time and into the heavenly realm of the Eternal Banquet with God. The basilica's removal of the limits of space served the needs of the new religion particularly well. The worshipper passed through the dull outside portals and was suddenly swept up into a magnificent, heavenly world. Yet all was organized and serene. The individual had his place, but he was no longer, as in the Greek view, the measurer of things. The world, the Church, the congregation, the bishop were as clearly arranged in a hierarchical ascending framework as was the secular state. The congregation was below the bishop as the people were below the emperor, yet they were not cut off from these figures but somehow united with them. The functions of all were defined and established. In the world of the fourth century it was not so much that men's vision was turned inward as elsewhere, away from the meanness and insignificance of the world to the infinite beyond. In such a setting the individual could only discover a place for himself by relating to his fellow citizens and coreligionists in the established secular and ecclesiastical hierarchies.

The same values were expressed in the sculpture of the new age. The traditional relief style had come to an end two generations earlier and the new sculptors, emancipated from the old classical norms, went off in their own directions. Classical Greek statues were individual entities that were intended to be viewed from all sides as were Greek temples. They stood apart from the space around them and sat solidly on the ground. Similarly, classical relief panels were also intended to be seen as entities in themselves, internally balanced, organized, and proportioned, cut off from the outer world. The new sculpture, on the other hand, paid little attention to proportion or balance and had a different view of how individual pieces should relate to their surroundings. In

[1]Ramsay MacMullen, *Constantine,* p. 50. Copyright © 1969 by Ramsay MacMullen. Reprinted by permission of Dial Press.

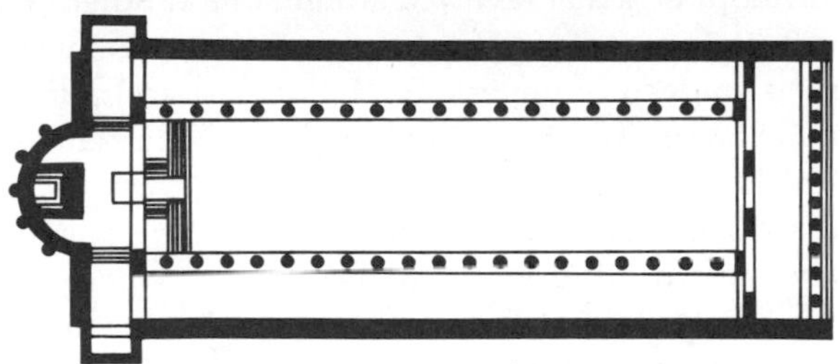

Despite considerable decorative changes over the centuries, the great basilica of St. Mary Major in Rome remains structurally unaltered since its construction around 440 A.D. Flanked by two aisles, the majestically proportioned nave suggests the grandeur of the basilican style of architecture.

relief panels the emperor (or saint or philosopher) occupied the central spot, surrounded by his attendants, who were generally depicted as squat, unimportant figures. The principal personage stared out directly at the viewer or into space, drawing the eye immediately to his central position. As in the basilica, the viewer was made to feel part of an audience, conscious that he was in the presence of someone whose vision was the source of his greatness, and which suggested that the viewer could share it only by close adherence to the visionary, whether he was emperor, bishop, saint, or philosopher. Nothing else mattered, neither human proportion, balance, nor logic.

Religion

There is a striking contrast between the religious environment of the second century with its marvelous variety of cults and beliefs and that of the fourth century, when a new and comprehensive religious unity was beginning to emerge. This newly achieved unity was, however, neither accidental nor the instantaneous creation of Constantine's selection of Christianity as the religion of the Empire. In the years prior to this event both pagans and Christians had been striving toward their own forms of unity, the former by attempting to syncretize the scattered elements of pagan religion, and the latter by coming to grips with the dominant culture of the Greek and Roman world in which they lived. In the process, the two began to move toward each other.

At times the areas of agreement between pagan and Christian seem more significant than their differences. Christians offered no radical challenges to commonly accepted Greek and Roman views of society and there was no head-on collision over such fundamental questions as the ownership and use of property—including slaves—or the hierarchical arrangement of Roman society, which set one man above another and loaded privileges on some while denying them to others. Pagans and Christians often shared common views on such different ethical issues as abortion, the exposure of infants, astrology, prostitution, the immorality of the pagan gods, and the frequently frivolous and materialistic character of urban life. They even shared much the same views of the material world around them.

Since the fourth century B.C., it had been generally held that the cosmos consisted of a series of concentric spheres that revolved around one another in a fixed hierarchy with the earth at the center. These spheres, however, were composed of matter of differing grades of fineness. At the highest and purest level were the stars; in descending order came the spheres of the sun, the planets, and the moon, and finally at the lowest and poorest level, the earth. Despite his assumption that the earth was at the bottom of the cosmic hierarchy, the average Christian or pagan did not believe that the world of matter was wholly or intrinsically evil. For the Christian there was the irrefutable endorsement of matter in the belief in the resurrection of the body at the end of the world and in the assumption of man's nature by God's son in the mystery of the Incarnation, and pagans hardly needed to demonstrate their acceptance of the material world. Alongside this mainstream view, however, there lurked a thoroughgoing suspicion of matter and the belief that the body was a weight that dragged down the soul, the purer element, whose natural tendency was to strive upward toward heavenly things. Thus the great pagan philosopher Plotinus could declare that he was ashamed to possess a body, and wondered what deterioration had reduced man to his present state, and Saint Anthony, the Christian hermit, blushed when he had to perform any of the normal bodily functions. The body, it was imagined, needed to be subdued and brought under the control of the soul by ascetical practices, which ranged from the intellectual exercises of the Neoplatonists to the fantastic mortifications imposed on themselves by the Syrian and Egyptian ascetics, such as Saint Simeon the Stylite who sat for 40 years on his pillar outside Antioch without descending.

In this world view man stood alone and alienated. The anonymous second- or third-century author of the *Letter of Diognetus* declared that although Christians are not different from the rest of men, nevertheless:

> They live in their own cities, but as if they were strangers in them; they participate in everything as citizens, yet discharge their obligations like aliens.[2]

For the emperor Marcus Aurelius life had an unreal, dreamlike character, and the battles on the Danube between Romans and barbarians in which he participated for 12 long years were like the tussles of "puppies over a bone." Yet at the same time there was a growing feeling that it was possible for the individual to realize a new self and rise to previously impossible heights of moral excellence. In the past, moral worth was thought to be the preserve of those who could, by reason of birth or wealth, achieve high military or civil office and that it was in the performance of the functions attached to these positions that an individual achieved true goodness and the fullest development of his human potential. To a lesser extent the practice and study of rhetoric and philosophy could also be a source of this excellence, and in the third century the mystical philosophy of Plotinus held out yet a higher ideal of human achievement through intellectual union with God. On the other hand, the lower classes, engaged in time-consuming menial tasks, were automatically excluded by their occupations from the possession of moral goodness. However, with the advent of Christianity and the spread of the mystery religions, even the ordinary man or woman could aspire to high levels of moral achievement without holding exalted civil or military rank or without the expense of a classical education. By a simple act of conversion or initiation an individual could begin to lead a new life of moral enlightenment. The knowledge that was acquired in this conversion or initiation was not mere information about God and the cosmos but a special kind of understanding or insight that affected the whole person, transforming mind and emotions alike. It penetrated into the individual's innermost being, converting and radically altering his life, producing a new man who was in contact with a reality greater than himself. Thus was the traditional concept of culture, and the moral excellence assumed to be attendant on its possession, transformed and democratized and extended in religious form to the masses of the Empire.

Religious Enthusiasts

There were, of course, those who felt more deeply moved by these religious currents than others and the third and fourth centuries abounded with religious enthusiasts of all kinds. Some felt they were the intermediaries of the gods and that they had been selected to convey a special message to mankind, such as that felt by the anonymous Egyptian prophet of the second or third century who proclaimed:

25.5.

> O people, men born of earth, you that have surrendered yourselves to drunkenness and sleep and ignorance of God, sober yourselves. . . . Repent you that have trodden with error and been partners with ignorance . . . take your portion of immortality.[3]

Even emperors such as Aurelian who made the sun god the preeminent deity of the Empire and Constantine who made Christianity the supreme religion and Julian who tried to turn the Empire back to paganism felt the tug of religious conviction profoundly. Frequently the visionaries were regarded as heretics, and the establishment, whether Christian or pagan, tried to suppress them. In the second century the Phrygian Montanus proclaimed that a new Jerusalem would soon be revealed and people poured out of the towns and villages to await with him the coming of Christ. A council of bishops promptly condemned him, but the movement lingered for centuries and the problem of holy men, whether prophets, martyrs, or ascetics, was a difficult one for the authorities. The riotous monks of Egypt were a well-known menace to both the ecclesiastical and the civil establishments, and in Africa Constantine attempted to suppress the rigorous Donatists who had split the Church because of the alleged indulgence of the orthodox clergy to those who had shown weakness during the Great Persecution of Diocletian.

For the average person whose visionary capacities were limited it was important to cling as closely as possible to those favored beings who seemed to have been especially chosen by God to perform great spiritual deeds and whose charisma contrasted shatteringly with the ordinariness of the usual ministers of religion. Quite spontaneously the practice of honoring the memory of the saints sprang up. Relics were treasured and circulated and the churches and monuments built to enshrine their remains quickly became places of pilgrimage. Feasts were established in their honor and grew to occupy an increasingly important place in the annual cycle of religious celebrations. A new kind of literature—hagiography or the study of the lives of the saints—developed and became one of the most common forms of popular reading for the next millennium and a half.

Faith and Reason, Christians and Pagans

Among educated pagans it was commonly accepted that the traditional gods were mediating spirits or demons but that God himself was infinitely removed from man, uncontaminated by matter and revealed only through his creations, which emanated from him in a descending series. According to Plotinus and the Neoplatonists he could, however, be reached by intellectual contemplation, since the soul had a natural tendency toward union with God and sought completeness by identifying with him. This was not, however, a matter of

[3]A.D. Nock, *Conversion* (London: Oxford University Press, 1933), p. 3. By permission of Oxford University Press.

Visionaries and authorities of the new order: a saint on his pillar ignoring the temptations of the devil (represented by the serpent), while a ladder permits the devout to approach him for consultations; another saint, probably one of the evangelists.

technique or ritual and there were no special exercises or sacraments. Union could be achieved only by intellectual asceticism and contemplation, which required long years of training and education, especially of a literary kind.[4] Understandably, this kind of rarefied Neoplatonism was accessible only to the few, but in watered-down forms it became the most popular type of religion practiced by the educated classes of the late Empire.

Christians agreed that the universe was peopled by invisible powers, the demons, and that God was indeed accessible to mankind, but whereas pagans feared the demons and struggled on their own to reach the Divine, Christians triumphantly declared that the demonic world had been overwhelmed by the intervention of God in the historical person of Jesus. All that remained was, as it were, a mopping-up operation, part of which, unfortunately, involved the dismantling of demon-ridden pagan society and the building of a new commu-

[4]See further discussion of this subject in chapter 10, pages 200–202.

nity in its place. With many pagans, Christians shared the belief in the possibility of the individual realizing a new self through revealed knowledge and achieving liberation from the spirits and demons of the world. Although the mystery religions and the theosophies of the educated claimed to be able to transmit this knowledge, they lacked a coherent theology and an organization to do this effectively. For the Christian, access to the source of power over the unseen world was easy and secure and did not depend on the maintenance of enthusiasm over long periods of time. A person was indeed converted to the new way of life, but that life was as regular and well organized as city life itself. He could turn for help to the rituals and sacraments of the church, or to the clergy, the holy men, the angels, or the saints, as well as to the local church community itself. This support was comprehensive, for it was economic and social as well as spiritual. And it was worldwide. By the fourth century a Christian could move just about anywhere in the Empire and expect to find the same organization, ritual, and beliefs. Letters of introduction from his home church eased entry into the new community, where his spiritual life could continue as before.

To pagans of the upper classes who took the trouble to observe them, the Christians of the early period seemed to be a supremely irrational group of fanatics. Marcus Aurelius and Galen the doctor were appalled at their uncritical assumptions, their lack of logic, and their stubbornness. The critic Celsus thought they were a highly dangerous sect, a people who considered themselves apart from the state and whose loyalties lay to another organization altogether. In

In art Christian and pagan often appealed to the same classical sources: a priestess of Bacchus making an offering, and St. Michael the Archangel. The images, known as diptychs, were carved in ivory and constituted the outer leaves of formal announcements of events such as weddings.

the third century, however, the gap between educated Christians and pagans was narrowed by the development of a sophisticated Christian apologetic. By the time of Constantine a bridge of understanding, if not of toleration, had been built between the two worlds by a succession of brilliant philosopher-theologians.

Clement of Alexandria (ca. 150–ca. 215) was the first to go beyond the early apologists and attempt a thoroughgoing reconciliation of faith and reason. Christians, he argued, had no reason to fear philosophy, for just as the Law was the tutor or guide of the Jews leading to Christ, so God had made philosophy the guide of the pagans. It was of divine origin and, like reason, a gift of God. Hence, he could argue, to philosophize was synonymous with being a Christian. Clement's brilliant disciple Origen also happened to be a pupil of Plotinus' master, Ammonius Sacca. For Origen the best in the pagan world had been nourished by God's providence before the appearance of Christianity, and a Christian could therefore not reject wholesale either Greek culture or the Roman Empire without refusing to accept part of God's providential plan for mankind. Christianity was, however, the true education (*paideia*) and Christ the True Philosopher who would lead men to the truth. The historical personality of Jesus was played down by these theologians and emphasis was placed instead on Jesus as the Divine Logos or Word who was God's agent in creating and ruling the cosmos, a concept that would be familiar to the Neoplatonists who believed in a whole series of beings mediating between God and man.

Both Christians and pagans placed great emphasis on prophecies and miracles, and in the eyes of Christians one of the most compelling arguments in favor of their beliefs was the fact that the coming of Christ had been foretold in the books of the Old Testament. This line of argument was considered particularly cogent in antiquity because of the great reverence people had for the written word and the veneration that was held for the wisdom of the past. Miracles were used as arguments because Christians were not debating rationalists or nonbelievers but only believers of a different kind. The argument usually went along the lines that pagan miracles were worked by demons or that those of Jesus were of a superior moral kind. Origen borrowed the method of allegorical interpretation, which had been used by generations of scholars to avoid the obvious meanings of classical texts and find new truths in them. In the absence of the tools of higher criticism it enabled both Christians and pagans to explain away the more awkward problems in their respective bodies of literature.

The most revolutionary aspect of third- and fourth-century religious development was the comprehensive attempt of Christians to reach as wide an audience as possible. By the time of Constantine Christianity was well on its way to becoming a mass religion and with its organizational structure was well equipped to handle its new role. It was no longer restricted to the small fervent cells of the past, and following Saint Paul's maxim it tried to be all things to all men. To the intellectuals and educated classes it presented the learned apologies of its philosophers from Clement of Alexandria to Augustine, couched in the language and style of argument that these classes would recognize. To the masses it presented the same message in less abstruse fashion and to all the same hope was extended of freedom from slavery to fate, the stars, the demons, and sin, as well as the possibility of overcoming human weakness and vice.

Church Rituals and Structures

The emergence of the Church as a major institution and the attempt of the government to bring it within the framework of the state are the most important developments of the third and fourth centuries. By themselves the administrative and military reforms of Diocletian and Constantine and the artistic and architectural revivals of the fourth century would have been an interesting epilogue to the end of the classical world, but it was the emergence of the institutional Church that provided the connecting link between this world and the later stages of the development of western history.

The life of the Church revolved around a series of ritual events, of which Baptism and the Eucharist were the most important, and the day-to-day contact of the average Christian with the Church was through these events rather than in any more personal or formal contacts with the clergy. The message of Christianity was deeply embedded in ritual and the incidental education that derived therefrom was probably a good deal more important than the exhortations and explanations from the pulpit.

The Christian liturgy borrowed heavily from Judaism. The calendar of feasts followed by the Church was Jewish, with the principal feasts of the year, Easter and the Descent of the Holy Spirit, occurring the same time as Passover and Pentecost. It was only after much bitter debate that the date for Easter was changed and given its present-day position in the calendar. Sunday, however, soon displaced Saturday as the most important day for Christians and each week they gathered to celebrate the resurrection of Jesus and wait for his second coming.

Baptism, a Jewish ceremony of washing, was required for initiation. Although at the beginning all that was necessary was a profession of faith, the practice of giving instructions in the essentials of the religion soon became common. A succinct expression of these essentials was found in the Symbol or Creed of the Apostles. Hence, from an early date, in addition to a moral conversion and the performance of ritual acts, converts were expected also to think correctly and to know the essential doctrinal beliefs of their religion.

The principal—and most original—act of the Christian community was the celebration of the Eucharist. This ritual consisted of two parts, the first borrowed from the synagogue service and consisting of prayers, readings, homilies, and hymns to which candidates for Baptism were admitted. The second and most mysterious part, to which only the fully initiated were admitted, was a simple meal revolving around the blessing of an offering of bread and wine and then its ritual consumption by the participants. In origin it was a common Jewish domestic ritual to which Jesus gave a special prominence at the Last Supper. It was seen by early Christians in a number of ways—as an anticipation of the messianic banquet to be enjoyed with Jesus in the Heavenly Kingdom, a repetition in symbol of the sacrifice on Calvary or as a mysterious reenactment of the Last Supper itself.

The liturgy had a dynamic of its own and made certain demands on the celebrant and congregation alike. Because its principal act, the Eucharist, consisted of a number of parts, of which the first was a series of readings and a homily or sermon, the celebrant had to be literate and possess some degree of education to be able to comment on the content of the readings and expound the essentials of Christian beliefs. The scriptures of the new religion were enshrined in its rituals, so that for the first time the masses were exposed to a literature not designed exclusively for the consumption of an educated elite. The rituals themselves were powerful educational tools so that even without any explicit inculcation on the part of the clergy (or even in the face of it) certain points were emphasized again and again and sank imperceptibly into the consciousness of the congregations. Year after year the liturgy celebrated the birth, death, and resurrection of Jesus and other events of his life. A whole history and prehistory, beginning with Adam and passing through the events of the Old Testament, was taken for granted, as were presuppositions about the movement of current history toward a grand finale, the second coming of the Lord. Local barriers were dissolved in the celebration of the liturgy and the Christian community was seen not as an isolated entity but as part of a larger body that extended everywhere in the world, embracing all peoples, whether Greek, Roman, or barbarian. Paradoxically this development occurred at the moment the secular state was beginning to disintegrate and other forms of communication were disappearing.

It was in the liturgy that the wider, organizational Church and the local communities made contact since the rituals could be performed only by a properly appointed celebrant. The bishop (or his representative) had a powerful position in the community. One element of his strength lay in the fact that he represented the outside world to his particular church since his mandate came from there, not from the people. On the other hand, he was an accepted member of the community, and whether popular or not was viewed as the means by which the grace to live a spiritual life came. He was present at all the main events in the lives of his people from birth to death, strengthening, consoling, educating. His power was not political nor even religious in the old sense. It was something quite new and around the person of the bishop a new community began to form that was unlike anything that had existed before.

Society and the Church

The Church of the fourth century was as highly structured as civil society and possessed almost as many gradations, distinctions, and honors. For the curial classes who moved in large numbers into the hierarchy of the Church, there was no loss of status and they were able to continue in their old roles as public figures in a new and more attractive environment. As civil society gradually slipped into chaos and repression, the administrative organs of the Church looked more and more attractive to the old, service-oriented aristocracies of the Empire. In addition to public positions that had honors and privileges attached to them, the Church began to have increasingly large holdings of land, buildings, and funds that needed the same kind of management that the curial classes had lavished in the past on their beloved cities. More important, the Church provided these men with a sense of community and with congregations over which they could rule without the alienation that they had experienced as civil administrators. Instead of representing a savage and distant government in its most immediate and oppressive form, squeezing taxes out of an unwilling citizenry, the ecclesiastical administrator presided over a community whose adherence to him—as well as its financial contributions—were voluntary. Constantine's endorsement of the ecclesiastical organization and his showering upon it of judicial and social privileges as well as economic benefits made it even more attractive. Henceforth

Bishop Maximianus of Ravenna and his clergy surround the Emperor Justinian, practically crowding the soldiers out of the mosaic. Although the scene probably reflects the situation at the imperial court as Maximianus would have liked it to be, the bishops of the late Empire did in fact wield immense power. Note the chi rho on the soldier's shield at left.

a flood of talented individuals from all parts of the Empire, who in the past would have ended up as governors and generals, even emperors, began to appear as bishops and patriarchs of the church. Ambrose, Athanasius, Basil, the two Gregories, John Chrysostom, and Augustine were among the most dynamic, talented, and ambitious figures of the age. They had one thing in common: They were all bishops.

At the head of each duly established church was a monarchical bishop who possessed autocratic powers over those under him. He could ordain to the priesthood and the lower orders, admit new members to the community, or expel others. He was in complete control of the finances of the church and his appointment was for life except in the off-chance that he might be deposed by a council of other bishops. Certainly the people could not depose him. Beneath this powerful figure were ranged in descending order priests, deacons, subdeacons, readers, acolytes, singers, exorcists, porters, gravediggers, hospital attendants, and many others. Rome in the mid-third century had 154 clergy, not an exceptional number compared to Carthage two centuries later, which had over 500. The emperor Justinian tried to keep the numbers at Constantinople under 500 and reduced the city's body of part-time gravediggers (who provided free burial for the city) from almost 1000 to 800. Beside the churches and their staffs there were charitable foundations, such as hospitals, orphanages, and homes for the aged, widows, and travelers, which also required supervision, staffing, and management. As early as the third century the Church in Rome was caring for 1500 poor persons and widows.

The income of the churches varied considerably, those in the rural parts being generally poorer than those in the cities. Constantine made generous gifts himself and legalized bequests to the Church so that its wealth built up quickly. In the fourth century Cyril, the bishop of Alexandria, was able to come up with 2500 pounds of gold in bribes to the imperial court, and the well-known pagan senator Agorius Praetextatus joked that if he were to be made bishop of Rome he would willingly become a Christian. By the sixth century bishops of large metropolitan churches in the east were drawing salaries equivalent to the highest paid civilian officials, such as proconsuls.

THE EMPEROR, THE ADMINISTRATION, AND THE ARMY

The Division of Power

As early as the time of Marcus Aurelius the difficulties a single emperor had in coping with the problems of imperial defense were being felt, and Avidius Cassius was delegated to handle the east while Aurelius himself faced the northern invasions. In the third century only radical regionalization enabled the Empire to survive the simultaneous attacks from the north and east. Gallienus allowed the usurper Postumus to cope with all the western provinces, and he permitted the upstart state of Palmyra under Odenathus to handle the eastern frontier, while he fought the Goths on the Danube. By the time of the accession of Diocletian (284) it was clearly impossible for any one emperor to rule unassisted an Empire that reached from Scotland to the Sudan, at least while it was under severe military pressure. The practical solution arrived at was to divide it into a number of parts. From A.D. 285, when Diocletian appointed Maximian as Caesar in the west, until 476, when the last western emperor was deposed, the united Empire was ruled by a single individual for only a matter of a few years.

Although this was the de facto solution to the problem of imperial administration, the way in which emperors and Caesars came to power was as chaotic as ever. As in the past dynastic sentiment was strong in the army and among the people, and from Constantine onward sons or relatives, and at times even children and women, were elevated on the death of a ruling emperor. Usurpers, usually generals acclaimed by their own troops, had therefore to seek the recognition of the reigning emperor (as long as one remained) or challenge him in the field. An alternative for an aspiring claimant was to remain a power behind the throne, and this was increasingly common in the fifth century when German generals rose in the service of Rome. These officers preferred this role, for in addition to being unacceptable as emperors they would probably also lose contact with their own troops, on whose loyalty they depended above all else.

The instability of the imperial office from the third century onward was a major factor in the weakening of the Empire in the west. There the tradition of autocratic rule was less firmly established and the senatorial class extremely powerful. The west was also militarily more exposed than the east, with the result that the emperors there had a much more difficult job fulfilling their role as protectors of the state, against both outside barbarians and the powerful within.

The Mystique of the Imperial Office

From the time of Augustus a religious aura surrounded the person of the emperor, and in the provinces, at least, he was worshipped as a god even during his lifetime. This all-too-natural veneration of power was given new prominence from the time of Septimius Severus onward until by the end of the third century the emperors were ruling as the earthly representatives of Jupiter himself.

Under the Severi, images of the emperor and his family decorated the altars of towns and the chapels of the legions and received the adoration (*adoratio*) of provincials and soldiers alike. Geta, one of Severus' sons, issued coins in his own image, showing him wearing the crown of the sun god and venerating his father, who was assimilated to the highest divinity. His mother, Julia Domna, appeared on coins as Cybele, the Mother of the Gods, or as the Mother of the Augusti, seated on the throne of Juno. The gods now became the assistants and companions of the emperor, and the heavenly court was modeled after the image of the imperial court on earth. New titles were added: The emperor was the Restorer of the World, the Inaugurator of the Golden Age; he was saluted as Undefeated, Eternal, Perpetual. To swear by the imperial *genius* was more significant than to swear by the gods. With Aurelian, the official title of the emperor became *Deus et Dominus,* God and Lord. Under the same emperor the sun god was adopted as the supreme deity of the Empire and a new college of pontiffs, independent of the old pontifical college, was created to serve his needs, as was a new temple at Rome. Everything to do with the emperor was sacred. His household was the *domus divina,* he dwelt in a sacred palace, his decrees and pronouncements were termed sacred, and those admitted to his presence were expected to kneel before him and venerate him as they did his images. Finally, after eight and a half centuries, the royal crown made its appearance again, and crown, scepter, orb, purple cloak, and triumphal regalia became the standard symbols of office.

Under Diocletian the evolution reached fulfillment and the emperor and his Caesar took the names of Jovius and Herculius, becoming the agents or vice-regents of Jupiter on earth (or, if their subjects preferred it, the very gods themselves—the theological niceties of the point were never precisely defined). Court ceremonial was now firmly established in its most minute detail and the emperor disappeared into the private recesses of the palace, to appear only on the rarest of occasions and then in full, unapproachable regalia. The cycle had come full around. Roman history began with the regal period, passed through the Republic and Principate, and ended with an autocracy. Appropriately, the emperor's power having become godlike, the allegiance of the people to him no longer had a secular, political basis, but was now religious. Constantine could issue coins (ca. 330) that depicted a hand stretching forth from the heavens extending to him a crown. When the Empire became Christian there was no fundamental change. In the Republic the magistrates had been priests and responsible for the maintenance of good relations between divine and earthly realms, the peace of the gods (*pax deorum*). In the Empire this duty fell to the *princeps,* and when Constantine became a Christian he still regarded it as his responsibility to maintain this relationship, though now it was the *pax Dei,* the peace of God. He also continued to hold the office of *pontifex maximus,* as did his successors down to the time of Gratian (ca. 375). Among the emperor's duties, therefore, was the care of the Church in order that God might be offered a pleasing sacrifice by men. If that involved suppressing incorrect belief, error, or indiscipline, then, so be it. The emperor was not simply entitled but *bound* to intervene in religious affairs.

Administration

In the third century the old class system of the Empire came under tremendous pressures. Until A.D. 260 the method of recruiting top administrators and army officers from the senatorial and equestrian classes continued, but with increasing numbers coming from among the latter group. Septimius Severus found it necessary to appoint equestrians to senatorial posts, giving them the title of acting governor (*procurator vice praesidis*), and more and more the emperors after him tended in the same direction, as the slow, conservative Senate with its limited membership (still around 600) and its fierce jealousies and self-centered aristocratic values proved unable to provide the kind of men the Empire desperately needed in its time of crisis. With Gallienus, senators were finally excluded from all military commands and most of the governorships and administrative posts. Not that this was the end for the Senate by any means. Especially in the west the old aristocracy continued to accumulate land, intermarry, and build up enormous fortunes. The Senate at Rome never lost its attractiveness as the oldest and most exclusive club in the Empire.

THE NEW ADMINISTRATORS

With Diocletian, who ascended the throne in A.D. 284, we enter a new era. Under his rule the army expanded to almost twice its previous size, creating a demand for masses of new officers from the rank of general on down—all from the equestrian classes. Similarly, his doubling of the number of provinces from 50 to 100 created hundreds of new equestrian positions as well as 50 new provincial governors, now called *praesides.* The result was that the equestrian order expanded greatly, and the most natural candidates for the new positions were found among the local gentry of the Empire, the decurions. In the past their main function had been to attend to the administration of the cities, collecting taxes and so forth. Some of course had already been recruited into the imperial civil service, but now many more left their local councils to take equestrian positions in the army or civilian administration. It was an attractive move, since apart from the opportunities offered by a new and wider career outside their own cities there was the higher status of equestrian rank, and freedom from the expensive burdens of city administration. There was even the possibility of returning to their native provinces with their new titles and positions as servants of the Emperor.

Qualifications for the new careerists, whether in the military or in the civilian branches (although technically all were now military and wore military uniforms), were increasingly detached from the old bases of honor, wealth, and public service that had been the dominant characteristics of the old system. Now what counted was ability and education, however the latter was acquired, whether in the leisurely aristocratic way of the past or by a more technical schooling under the tutelage of professional educators, now in great demand. The new army commanders were of a distinctly nonpatrician background, though of course this was nothing new in the third century. Diocletian was the son of a freedman from Dalmatia and his colleague Galerius had once herded cattle in Hungary. Constantine's father was a rural magnate from Naissus in Yugoslavia. Although ability and education were important for active careerists, wealth did not lose its power and successive administrations railed at the practice of well-to-do decurions buying codicils or titles to a particular office and rank without ever actually performing the duties attached to it.

The geographic and ethnic backgrounds of senators were equally diverse. There were barbarians like the Vandal Stilicho who married the niece of the great emperor Theodosius, and Bauto the Frank who was married to the daughter of another emperor, Arcadius. There were Armenians, Alans, Sarmatians, even a few Persians. Sometimes peasants rose to high rank, as was the case of Justin (the uncle of the famous Justinian) who became emperor of the eastern Empire in 518. Libanius the rhetorician sneeringly cites examples of senators who had risen from humble origins—sausage-makers and cloakroom attendants, he calls them—repeating the same kind of comments that had been made by Roman senators throughout the previous 1000 years.

Under Constantine there was another and apparently logical change. The active aristocracy of the Empire was the vastly enlarged equestrian order, but with expansion had come a cheapening of the class. Its highest rank was given out more and more easily and by A.D. 324 the lowest grade had been so debased that it was no longer given out at all. At the same time the Senate continued to exist in Rome, still enjoying immense social prestige and very limited numbers. It was also a bastion of paganism and quite determinedly hostile to the new religion and to Constantine himself. The logic of the next step was compelling: By elevating certain equestrian posts to senatorial rank and appointing senators or equestrians to them Constantine could solve three problems at the same time. He could continue the process of upgrading the equestrian class, flood the Senate with his own appointees, and win support among at least some of its members by restoring their eligibility for administrative appointments. Constantine and his successors, however, were careful in the selection of positions they opened to senators and some, such as that of general (*dux*), remained at equestrian rank until late in the fourth century.

Constantius II (A.D. 337–361) continued the policy of his predecessor and established a second Senate with 300 members at Constantinople. This grew rapidly, reaching almost 2000 by the end of the century, with a similar increase taking place at Rome. More and more offices were elevated from equestrian to senatorial rank and equestrians were appointed to them. Understandably the effects of the expansion of the equestrian order at an earlier time now began to be felt in the Senate. Decurions struggled to get promoted to the rank of senator, instead of to the equestrian order, and the wealthy, whenever they could, bought the title. The attractions were the same as before—exemptions and privileges, especially the exemption from curial services. There was also the added security from the harsh exactions of imperial governors and administrators that senatorial rank promised to its holders. The privilege of freedom from curial responsibilities was early seen as a major problem and by 436 it was restricted to those who possessed the highest senatorial rankings. With the expansion of the senatorial order and its relatively free bestowal the equestrian order gradually died out or was absorbed. By the beginning of the fifth century it had ceased to exist and in its place was the vastly expanded—and cheapened—senatorial class.

Once more it became necessary to introduce new distinctions and three grades were established—*illustres, spectabiles,* and *clarissimi*. Eventually only the *illustres* came to be considered true members of the Senate. The most important aspect of this development was that the Senate was finally converted from an aristocracy of birth to one of office because the son of an *illustris* was not automatically an *illustris* also. To become one he had to hold high office, and these now came only from the hand of the emperor.

SOCIAL CHARACTER

The Senate of the second half of the fourth century was a very mixed body. In the west there was a core of great landowners, some of whom claimed to be able to trace their ancestry back to the nobility of the Republic, but in the east the Senate was entirely new. Between A.D. 325 and 425 barbarians, lawyers, professors, soldiers, even a slave, appear in the lists of consuls.

An important feature of the senatorial aristocracy in the west was its local character. Most official appointments of senators were in their own part of the world and the influence they wielded was therefore as much their own as imperial. The degree to which taxes were collected and shipped to the central administration depended on how cooperative these local magnates chose to be. When imperial judges sat in court, the local aristocrats sat beside them. More and more the peasantry was faced with a choice between the exactions of the emperor's tax collector and the protection offered by the local magnate—along with the price to be paid for it. Men's horizons shrank and their loyalties became focused on the lord of the manor, who now began to assume a more important role than the distant emperor as lawgiver, judge, and protector. In the east, where there were few great landowning families and the bulk of the new senators were from the aristocracies of the cities, the situation was different and the Senate there constituted a true aristocracy of office and service. An important consequence of this was that in the east a large number of the new senators were Christian, since Christianity had advanced so much more there than in the west.

The new Senate at Constantinople never gained the prestige of the old Senate in the west and the power of the eastern emperor was proportionately greater. It was predominantly a Senate of service and the ideal of the scholar-bureaucrat was one that gave the eastern empire a solidity sorely lacking in the west where the two roles tended to be separated (to the considerable detriment of the state). Ultimately then, the emperors succeeded in creating a true state bureaucracy and maintaining the allegiance of the educated and well-to-do classes in one half of the empire but not in the other. In the west the emperors failed and the upper classes went their own private way.

With the expansion of the army and the administration, the middle classes of the Empire came under extreme pressure. The attractions of service in the imperial administration were more than balanced by the improved efficiency of the tax-collecting system. As decurions moved upward into the equestrian and

Ivory carving of a severe looking Roman consul (fifth century A.D.). As the power of the imperial administration in the west declined, that of the aristocracy, particularly the senatorial aristocracy, rose.

senatorial orders fewer and fewer could be found to replace them and the burdens on those that remained increased. The central administration continued to demand that essential city services be maintained and that the increased taxes be paid—all of this with reduced numbers and no increase in economic productivity. Laborers and artisans fled from the fields and workshops into the army or simply elsewhere—to other cities and towns where they thought better opportunities might await them. If there was relatively great stability in the first two centuries of the Empire, the third and fourth saw great movements of people back and forth as the emperors on the one hand encouraged them to move by creating new opportunities, and on the other tried to restrict them in order to make the new tax system work. Under Constantine the clergy acquired exempt status from curial responsibilities and a new exodus into the administration of the Church began, despite efforts by the government to restrict the number of decurions who were ordained. Periodic attempts were also made to expel those of curial origin from the Senate, but there was no way of reversing the process. Richer, luckier, perhaps more able decurions moved up into the exempt classes, and the poorer or unluckier were simply pushed down into the lower classes and were numbered among the *humiliores.* Gradually the process of simplification reduced the classes of the Empire to two: one including the newly expanded senatorial order, the clergy, and the employees of the state, all privileged and in varying degrees well off; and the other made up of the masses of the Empire, all unprivileged and extremely poor.

The division was most noticeable in the west where the senatorial order had been for centuries building up its great landholdings. Literally handfuls of great families owned most of the land of Italy and Gaul. Under these circumstances the patronage of a powerful neighbor, whether bishop or senator or military commander, was the only source to which the average citizen could turn for protection against the tax collectors or help in bad economic times. The development was not exclusively western, however. Toward the end of the fourth century Syrian villagers were in the peculiar position of paying the local military commander a fee to use his soldiers to protect them from the imperial tax collectors. A more typical situation, though, was where the local patron was a great landowner whose fee for protection was some kind of a claim or lien against the peasant's property. Over the years, either by this method or as a result of the crushing taxation, the free peasantry became tenants (*coloni*) of the landowners. Efforts were made by the emperors to fight this kind of patronage because it interfered with the flow of tax money, but some emperors were genuinely concerned with the plight of the commoners and Valentinian established the office of city defender (*defensor civitatis*), which was intended to protect the poor by offering them cheap and speedy justice.

Finances

The change in personnel was only one aspect of the transformation wrought by Diocletian and Constantine. The fiscal basis of the government was also radically altered at this time. In the past Rome, like all ancient Mediterranean states before it, collected only enough taxes to pay current bills. There were no annual budgets and no fluctuating tax rates. For political reasons the government was extremely slow to change the rate of old taxes or impose new ones. Expenses were paid directly out of current income. When a sudden crisis occurred the only way money could be raised was by the sale of state possessions or the confiscation of the estates of the wealthy. Both Trajan and Marcus Aurelius sold imperial property and the treasures of the imperial palace to raise cash, but similar expedients had been resorted to as far back as the time of the wars with Carthage. There was no issuance of war bonds or the contraction of debt to be laid on the shoulders of future generations. Nor was there any possibility of having "guns and butter" because there was no increase in productivity that would have allowed additional defense expenditures without increasing taxes. Despite the new demands of the third century, tax rates did not go up. Instead, the government resorted to confiscations, though not on a wide scale, to collections in kind, and to the process of debasement of coins, which enabled it to issue more currency for the same amount of precious metal. The Severan emperors had tremendously increased the pay of the soldiers, and larger and larger quantities of debased coins began to come into circulation. The result was that prices rose and the real income of the state, the army, and the bureaucracy declined. To compensate, the collection of taxes in kind became the principal source of income for the state, and soldiers and bureaucrats now received, in addition to payments in cash, requisitions in kind, including free uniforms, rations, and weapons. With the abandonment of fixed taxes as the principal source of income, the government was now, finally, in a position to come up with a true budget, for instead of trying to meet expenses out of a fixed income it could requisition its actual needs—so much grain, so many uniforms, and so on. Although requisitioning in kind was an accomplished fact by some point in the third century, it was again left to Diocletian to rationalize the process.

The first step was to determine the actual resources of the Empire and this was accomplished in a series of censuses held over a number of years throughout the provinces. The results were then expressed in ideal fiscal units (called *iuga* and *capita*), which allowed a uniform system of measurement to be extended to the whole Empire, and permitted the staff of the Praetorian Prefects to have a good idea of available resources. Conversion tables were worked out, establishing the ratio between actual land values, productivity, and rural population. For example, in one region, 20 Roman acres of first-class arable land or 5 acres of vineyards, or 60 acres of third-class land were calculated as one unit (*iugum*). Human beings and livestock were similarly calculated (in terms of *capita*), and then the two figures were added to give a total of the resources of the particular region. Next, the Praetorian Prefect estimated how much he needed in the way of supplies for the coming year, and knowing how much each province was worth he was able to set a rate, which at least theoretically fluctuated each year depending on the needs of the state. In fact, the rate (i.e., the percentage of available resources required in a particular year) tended to go up, and between 324 and 364 it is thought to have doubled. It was essential to keep evaluations of the resources of the different provinces up to date, and reassessments were supposed to be made every 10 to 15 years.

The burden of Diocletian's taxes fell principally on agriculture, the largest segment of the economy, and on the rural population. The collection of taxes was still the responsibility of the unfortunate curial classes of the cities, who had to be prepared to make up arrears out of their own pockets. Senators escaped these duties but were subject to a modest surtax (the *gleba* or *follis*), and merchants had to pay a five-year levy in gold or silver, which proved to be extremely burdensome. Since the efficient operation of the budget depended on the permanence of the fiscal units, Diocletian decreed that all peasants and decurions were to remain in the places in which they were registered in the census. In a similar vein, though completely without success, he enacted a decree that fixed prices for all goods, commodities, and wages.

Currency reform was achieved by Constantine, whose new taxes and dissolution of the temples made large amounts of bullion available. A new gold coin was minted, the *solidus*, appropriately named as it was the first dependable currency since the second century. It remained virtually unchanged in weight and quality for centuries afterward. Nevertheless, collection of taxes took place in kind until toward the end of the fourth century.

The emperor's subjects understandably resisted the new tax system. Corruption was rife and maneuvers of all kinds were used to avoid payments. One emperor complained of how his bureaucrats used "minute calculations of impenetrable obscurity" to cover their embezzling and then demanded receipts for past years, which most people, assuming they owed nothing, had long ago thrown away.[5] Another trick used by the tax collectors was to exploit the inefficiency of the bureaucracy, which frequently allowed arrears to accumulate and would then write them off in order to clear up the books. Crafty tax collectors gave credit to their victims at high interest rates and then waited until a general indulgence wiped out the due taxes altogether. Other administrative abuses were the failure to revise the censuses periodically, and since land use changed and population fluctuated, the census frequently failed to reflect the true situation in a given region. The worst feature of the system was its generally unprogressive character, which applied the same tax rate to rich and poor. Although senators were subject to a surtax, their land was frequently undervalued and they could postpone payments and fend off the tax collectors until inflation reduced the amount or an indulgence wiped it out altogether.

Justice

A major responsibility of the emperor was the administration of justice. During the third century the local courts had faded away and governors had become automatically the court of the first instance. Since appeals went to the emperor, the result was that with only 50 provincial governors who had other duties besides their judicial functions, and only one emperor, the courts were clogged with cases. There was the further problem of the uncertainty of the law, which did not receive its definitive form until the publication of the uniform code of Justinian in the sixth century. In the meantime, attorneys could embarrass judges by quoting from authoritative sources unknown or even inaccessible to them. The situation got so bad that in 426 Valentinian III issued a decree giving foremost authority to the five great jurists of former years, Papinian, Paulus, Ulpian, Modestinus, and Gaius. Where they differed a majority vote was to be taken with Papinian as the tie breaker.

The emperor himself was the chief legislator, and his pronouncements were the principal source of law. These consisted of judgments (*decreta*), and answers to inquiries of judges (*relationes*) and of private citizens (*rescripta*). There were also imperial edicts and constitutions that were general laws either for the whole Empire or particular provinces. The confusion created by this haphazard system was great and only slowly resolved, first by the publication of the Theodosian Code (A.D. 438), and then finally by the monumental product of Justinian in A.D. 529.

[5] A. H. M. Jones (tr.), *The Decline of the Ancient World* (London: Longmans, Green & Co., 1966), p. 175.

The doubling of the number of governors by Diocletian and the increase in the number of courts of appeal by Constantine helped considerably. City defenders (*defensores civitatis*) were established by Valentinian and had minor jurisdiction but offered cheap and quick service. Bishops were allowed to act as judges in civil cases by Constantine and their courts rapidly acquired popularity.

Justice was slow, costly, and frequently corrupt. The Justinian Code aimed at preventing lawsuits "becoming almost immortal and exceeding the term of human life" by establishing certain time limits for the passing of judgment and for decisions on appeals.[6] Distance slowed communications, courts were clogged, and governors busy at their numerous tasks. As in the case of civilian administration and legionary commands the Romans resisted professionalization down to the end. The administration of justice was regarded as merely one of the functions of a magistrate who had other duties to perform, both civilian and military, and he was allowed considerable latitude. He was expected to take into account all the aspects of a case—including its social and political dimensions—not merely its legalities. The result was that the system of justice faithfully reflected the social system, which explicitly recognized the inequality of men and accorded those higher in the system a more favorable treatment than those lower down. The case was classically put by a Greek who, after being made a prisoner of war, had elected to live among the Huns of Attila:

> The laws are not the same for all. If a rich man breaks the law he can avoid the penalty for his wrongdoing. But if it is a poor man who does not know how to pull strings, he suffers the penalty of the law—unless he departs this life before the trial, while proceedings drag on interminably and vast expenses are incurred.[7]

If there was to be a change in the legal system it would have to begin with the nature of Roman imperial society itself and there were not many advocating that.

The Army

The army of the period of the Roman Peace had been stretched out along thousands of miles of frontier. There were no reserves and expeditions could be mounted only by drawing units from the frontier garrisons. This was a self-defeating process, since any weakness in the screening forces constituted an invitation to the barbarians to break through into the Empire and make off with what they could lay their hands on before reinforcements arrived.

Already in the third century efforts were being made to build up a mobile reserve, which would be able to cope with major incursions that the frontier forces could not handle. In these forces emphasis was given to cavalry units (*vexillationes*), which were ranked with the legions. Gradually the numbers

[6]Ibid., p. 191.

[7]Ibid., p. 197.

increased and under Diocletian came to be almost double what they had been in the Principate, rising from around 350,000 to 650,000. Diocletian gave primary emphasis to the frontier forces, but under Constantine this approach was reversed and great regional reserve armies were created.

The standard divisions of the old army had been the legion, to which were attached additional auxiliary units of from 500 to 1000 men each. Since Caracalla's edict extending the franchise to the Empire, the distinction between legionaries and auxiliaries on the grounds of citizenship disappeared, but the legions themselves remained as well as the *auxilia.* Now, however, the reserve armies (*comitatenses* or *palatini*) were formed by withdrawing units, usually of 1000 men each, and adding them to the cavalry units already in existence. The original legions from which these units were taken continued in existence, but at lower manpower levels. The overall result was to create an army consisting of generally smaller, more manageable units, divided between the frontier forces (*limitanei*) and the central field armies. The majority of the troops (about 65 percent) remained on the frontiers, but their quality was not as high as the reserve forces.

The composition of the army of the late Empire differed considerably from that of the Principate. Although the tendency toward hereditary recruitment from among the descendants of army veterans and the use of barbarians had already begun long before, there was nothing like the dependence on these two sources that there was after Diocletian and Constantine. Diocletian made the military career hereditary, requiring by law that the sons of soldiers enter the profession. He also revived the draft so that in addition to supplying pay and materiel the cities of the Empire were now required to provide recruits as well. In the fourth century this was the main source of manpower, though resistance to this form of recruitment was high. The draftees had to be branded or even imprisoned at night to prevent them from escaping, and government resorted to all sorts of threats and enticements to come up with the requisite numbers. Pay and service conditions were generally good and there were special tax exemptions and other benefits. Still, the minimum height requirement had to be lowered from five feet ten inches to five feet seven inches in A.D. 367 to allow the government's net to be cast wider.

Barbarians were recruited in two ways. The first method was to enroll them in regular army units as volunteers, and apparently large numbers did volunteer, being attracted by the promotional opportunities and the regular pay. The majority were Germans from various tribes, but volunteers came from as far away as Ireland and Persia. On entry into the legions they automatically received the citizenship. The essentials of Latin were quickly learned and barbarians often rose to high rank. They gave dedicated service to Rome and there is no evidence that those who served in the regular units in this fashion were any more untrustworthy than recruits from within the Empire.

The other method of recruiting barbarians was highly dangerous. This consisted in employing whole groups of the outsiders, whether in tribes or just as individuals who put themselves under the leadership of some prominent warrior. These contingents fought alongside the regular Roman army units but were not subject to the same discipline and control. At first the numbers were relatively small, but after the battle of Adrianople (A.D. 378) they were employed in increasingly large numbers. In part this was due to the heavy losses suffered by the regular forces in the civil wars of the late fourth century and in part to the great barbarian invasions of the same period. Large tribal units such as the Visigoths, Burgundians, and Alans forced their way into Roman territory and occupied or were assigned lands, in return for which they offered their military services. Finally, the Roman army in the west consisted of practically nothing but barbarian hordes under nominal allegiance to the Roman emperor. The Roman army slowly disintegrated, the contingents in Britain, Spain, and Africa disappearing in the 450s and the last units in France in 486. Saint Severinus' biographer Eugippius described how the surviving regiments in Austria drew their last installments of pay in the 480s and were dismissed. He comments matter-of-factly:

> While the Roman empire still stood, soldiers were maintained with public pay in many of the towns for the defence of the frontier, but when that custom lapsed the military units were abolished together with the frontier.[8]

With such little fanfare did Roman rule on the Danube come to an end.

EPILOGUE: DECLINE AND FALL

The monumental reforms of Diocletian and Constantine saved the Empire from destruction and gave it over a century of relative peace and stability. Then, in the last quarter of the fourth century barbarian pressures were renewed while the imperial administration in the west began to disintegrate. By the middle of the fifth century it had practically vanished and a series of Germanic kingdoms rose to take its place in the old western provinces of the Empire.

Constantine died in 337, leaving the Empire to his three sons and two nephews. Inevitably this arrangement generated a struggle for power among the heirs, and in 353 after a series of bloody purges and civil wars the aloof and suspicious Constantius II emerged as sole ruler. Two years later he was forced by increasing imperial needs to appoint Julian, Constantine's only surviving nephew, as Caesar in Gaul. There Julian had some success against the Alamanni and when Constantius demanded that Julian lend him his Gallic troops for war against the Persians in the east, they rebelled and proclaimed Julian Augustus. Fortunately, Constantius died before civil war could break out and Julian became sole emperor (361–363).

The impulsive and rather naive Julian had for years been a secret pagan

[8]Ibid., p. 217.

and enjoyed dabbling in magic. Now he publicly proclaimed his loyalty to the ancient religion and the ideals of Hellenic civilization. Seeking to reverse the inroads of Christianity he attempted to put paganism on a similar organizational footing and demanded high moral standards of its ministers. Inevitably he became embroiled in the continuing struggles between the Arians and the orthodox in the eastern half of the Empire, and after first restoring the troublesome patriarch of Alexandria, the famous Athanasius, deposed him again. As religious turmoil increased Julian turned his attention to the frontiers. Campaigning against the Persians in 363 he was mortally wounded in battle and his successor Jovian was forced to make peace. With the death of Julian the dynasty of Constantine the Great came to an end.

After the brief reign of Jovian, the Empire was entrusted to the gruff Valentinian I (364–375), who appointed his brother Valens as Augustus of the east. Although despised by the educated classes of the Empire, Valentinian was an emperor in the soldierly tradition of Diocletian and Constantine. A stern disciplinarian and a conscientious administrator, he attempted to protect the poor from the ravages of the well-to-do and was impartial in his attitudes toward the religious disputes that continued to rage in the Empire.

A year after Valentinian's death in 375, the Visigoths, fleeing before the Huns, petitioned to be admitted into the Empire. Valens allowed them to cross the Danube and settle in vacant land, but soon the exactions of the imperial officials drove them to revolt, and in 378, at the disastrous battle of Adrianople, they overwhelmed the emperor and his army. The situation was redeemed to some extent when Gratian, Valentinian's successor in the west, appointed the able Spanish general Theodosius to succeed Valens and make a settlement with the marauding barbarians. By diplomacy and military force Theodosius brought peace to the Balkans and reorganized the eastern Roman army, incorporating in the process large numbers of barbarians and placing special emphasis on cavalry. Both Gratian and Theodosius took active parts in the battles between Christians and pagans and the Arians and the orthodox. Under the influence of Ambrose, the powerful bishop of Milan, Gratian dropped the ancient title of *pontifex maximus* and withdrew the Altar of Victory from the Senate at Rome. In the east Theodosius legislated against the Arians and in 381 convened the Second Ecumenical Council of Constantinople, which reaffirmed the traditional orthodox beliefs. Ten years later he forbade all pagan rites.

When Gratian was assassinated in 383 Theodosius defeated his usurper in battle and retained Gratian's half-brother, Valentinian II, as his colleague in the west. Later, when Valentinian also was murdered, Theodosius was forced to fight another bloody civil war from which he emerged in 394 as the last sole ruler of the united Roman world. Ironically, his reign in this capacity lasted only five months, and when he died in 395 he was succeeded by his young and ineffectual sons, Honorius and Arcadius, the former taking the west and the latter the east. Both fell under the control of advisors and generals who fought savage battles for power among themselves at precisely the time when the Empire most needed strong central control. Under the leadership of their chief Alaric, the restless

Visigoths took advantage of the weakness of the Empire to ravage Greece, desisting only when encouraged to move westward by Arcadius' principal advisor, the wily eunuch Eutropius. Initially Stilicho, the able Vandal general who commanded the western armies, was able to control the Visigoths, but in 408 he was assassinated and no one was left to stop their depredations. Rome was sacked by them in 410 and its fall sent reverberations throughout the Empire. Eventually the Visigoths left Italy and settled in southwestern Gaul as supposed subjects of the Romans.

Two years before Stilicho's murder, in the winter of 406, great numbers of barbarians successfully crossed the frozen Rhine and pushed their way through the imperial defenses and into central Gaul. From there they moved on to Spain and Africa where the Vandals established an independent kingdom for themselves, which Rome was forced to recognize. By 455 they were strong enough to raid Italy and for a second time Rome was brutally sacked.

By midcentury most of the west was in the hands of Germanic tribes. Britain had been abandoned in 407. The Franks were established in the north and central areas of Gaul and the Burgundians and Visigoths had settled along the Rhine and in the south, respectively. Still, both Romans and Germans could appreciate a common threat and in 451 they combined against the Huns of Attila and defeated them near Troyes. For 20 years thereafter a series of shadow emperors controlled by barbarian chiefs succeeded one another until the mercenary captain Odoacer swept away the illusion of Roman administrative rule in the west when he deposed the puppet emperor Romulus Augustus and sent the imperial insignia to Constantinople. In the east, because of a different set of circumstances, the Empire was able to survive the disasters that overwhelmed the west, and for the next 1000 years it successfully resisted all outside pressures.

Understandably, the great theme of the western Empire's fall has generated an enormous amount of discussion over the centuries. Barbarian pressures, declining population, the depletion of the soil, climatic changes, the rise of Christianity, the decay of the ruling classes through supposed "mongrelization," and innumerable other explanations have been proposed at one time or another. At best any specific theory can only constitute the kernel of an argument that must take into account many other factors. Hypotheses emphasizing economic causes, for example, must also show how equally well documented social, cultural, political, and military realities also fit into the theory. Similarly, explanations which would concentrate on the military or political reasons for the decline have to cope with all the other factors and so on for each explanation. Whatever "cause" is ultimately selected as the most persuasive, another equally complicated question must be faced: Why did one half of the Empire survive the upheavals that plagued the Roman world from the third century onward while the other half did not?

In keeping with the theme of this book an explanation of the fall based on social and cultural factors will be suggested here briefly. For centuries Rome resisted the formation of a true bureaucracy that would have served the emperor and the state directly, regardless of the social position of its members. Instead, the Romans clung obstinately to the archaic, quasi-familial social system of Republican times that attempted to wed state and society to each other. For several centuries this arrangement worked remarkably well and achieved prodigies of defense, administration, and acculturation. From all over the Empire the local ruling elites were drawn into the senatorial and equestrian orders while to a lesser extent the curial, freedman, and lower classes were similarly enmeshed in the Roman social structure. Under the pressures of the third century, however, this unusual socio-administrative system failed and a more formal method of extracting the necessary resources from the Empire had to be devised, one that was less closely tied to the existing social arrangements and more efficient in meeting the needs of the central government. This was the new administration devised by Diocletian and implemented by his successors. In the east, thanks to the creation of a new capital, a new senate, and the application of more despotic imperial power, the reforms were successful. In the west, in the face of a stubbornly traditional aristocracy, a more resolutely independent clergy, and a poorer, rebellious peasantry, they failed. The social coherence necessary to provide masses of willing recruits for the legions and adequate tax monies to equip the armies and maintain the bureaucratic superstructure did not survive the crisis of the third century. Instead of serving the state, the upper classes in the west co-opted the administration to their own interests. Had the west been more susceptible to absolutism and less factious, the essential resources necessary to hold off the barbarians might have been forthcoming. But the civilization of the west—at least insofar as civilization can be defined as a form of social submission to an accepted order—lacked depth. Social and administrative practices there continued to place emphasis on the more personal, paternalistic traditions of the past, and the old hierarchical layers remained intact between emperor and people. In relatively peaceful times the system worked quite well and provided the essentials necessary to the proper functioning of the Empire. In the third and fourth centuries, however, it proved unequal to the task and failed to extricate from an unwilling society those vital contributions on which the army and administration depended. In the east, where absolutism had a longer history and more willing subjects, the rulers had more immediate control of the Empire's resources, and in truncated form it survived there for another thousand years. But the price of this survival was stiflingly high. In the west society drifted in new directions, reverting in part, but not entirely, to forms it possessed before the artificial framework of the Empire was imposed upon it. Although the political, administrative, and social unity of the Empire was gone forever, a cultural unity based in part on the classical traditions of Greece and Rome and in part on the new religion of Christianity survived. From this amalgam, rather than the rigidly controlled society of the eastern empire, emerged the new dynamic civilization of western and northern Europe.

Suggested Readings

THE ANCIENT NEAR EAST

ALDRED, CYRIL, *Akhenaton, Pharaoh of Egypt: A New Study.* London: Thames and Hudson, 1968.

BRIGHT, JOHN, *A History of Israel.* Philadelphia: Westminister Press, 1959.

ČERNÝ, JAROSLAV, *Ancient Egyptian Religion.* London: Hutchinson's University Press, 1952.

DE VAUX, ROLAND, *Ancient Israel: Its Life and Institutions.* 2 vols. New York: McGraw, 1961.

DRIVER, SAMUEL R., *Introduction to the Literature of the Old Testament.* New York: Meridian Books, 1956.

EDWARDS, IORWERTH E. S., *The Pyramids of Egypt* (rev. ed.). Harmondsworth: Penguin, 1961.

FRANKFORT, HENRI, *Ancient Egyptian Religion.* New York: Columbia University Press, 1948.

——, et al., *Before Philosophy.* Harmondsworth: Penguin, 1954.

GARDINER, ALAN, *Egypt of the Pharaohs: An Introduction.* Oxford: Clarendon Press, 1961.

GLANVILLE, STEPHEN R. K., *The Legacy of Egypt.* Oxford: Clarendon Press, 1942.

HALLO, WILLIAM W. and WILLIAM KELLY SIMPSON, *The Ancient Near East: A History.* New York: Harcourt Brace Jovanovich, 1971.

HARRIS, JOHN RICHARD, ed., *The Legacy of Egypt.* Oxford: Clarendon Press, 1971.

HAYES, WILLIAM C., *The Scepter of Egypt: A Background for the Study of Egyptian Antiquities in the Metropolitan Museum of Art.* 2 vols. New York: Metropolitan Museum of Art, 1953–1959.

HIGGS, ERIC, ed., *Papers in Economic Prehistory.* Cambridge: Cambridge University Press, 1972.

JACOBSEN, THORKILD, *Toward the Image of Tammuz and Other Essays on Mesopotamian History and Culture,* ed. William L. Moran. Cambridge: Harvard University Press, 1970.

KRAMER, SAMUEL N., *The Sumerians: Their History, Culture and Character.* Chicago: University of Chicago Press, 1963.

LUCKENBILL, D. D., *Ancient Records of Assyria and Babylonia.* 2 vols. Chicago: University of Chicago Press, 1926.

MICHALOWSKI, KAZIMIERZ, *The Art of Ancient Egypt.* London: Abrams, 1969.

MOORGAT, ANTON, *The Art of Ancient Mesopotamia.* London: Phaidon, 1969.

OPPENHEIM, A. LEO, *Ancient Mesopotamia: Portrait of a Dead Civilization.* Chicago: University of Chicago Press, 1964.

PRITCHARD, JAMES B., ed., *Ancient Near Eastern Texts Relating to the Old Testament* (3rd ed.). Princeton, N. J.: Princeton University Press, 1969.

RENFREW, COLIN, *The Explanation of Cultural Change: Models in Prehistory.* London: University of Pittsburgh Press, 1973.

SAGGS, H. W., *The Greatness that Was Babylon: A Sketch of the Ancient Civilization of the Tigris-Euphrates Valley.* New York: Hawthorne, 1962.

SMITH, WILLIAM STEVENSON, *The Art and Architecture of Ancient Egypt.* Harmondsworth: Penguin, 1958.

STEINDORFF, GEORGE and KEITH C. SEELE, *When Egypt Ruled the East* (rev. ed.). Chicago: University of Chicago Press, 1957.

STRUEVER, STUART, comp., *Prehistoric Agriculture.* New York: Natural History Press, 1971.

UCKO, PETER J. and G. W. DIMBLEBY, eds. *The Domestication and Exploitation of Plants and Animals.* Chicago: Aldine, 1969.

——, ed., R. TRINGHAM, and G. W. DIMBLEBY, *Man, Settlement and Urbanism.* London: Duckworth, 1972.

WILSON, JOHN ALBERT, *The Culture of Ancient Egypt.* Chicago: University of Chicago Press, 1956.

WRIGHT, GEORGE ERNEST, ed., *The Bible and the Ancient Near East, Essays in Honor of William Foxwell Albright.* Garden City, N. J.: Doubleday, 1961.

THE GREEK WORLD

ANDREWES, A., *The Greek Tyrants.* London: Hutchinson's University Press, 1956.

BLEGEN, CARL W., *Troy and the Trojans.* New York: Praeger, 1963.

BOWRA, CECIL M., *Ancient Greek Literature.* New York: Oxford University Press, 1945.

BURN, ANDREW R., *The Lyric Age of Greece.* London: E. Arnold, 1960.

BURNET, JOHN, *Early Greek Philosophy* (4th ed.). New York: Barnes & Noble, 1968.

BURY, J. B. and RUSSELL MEIGGS, *A History of Greece to the Death of Alexander the Great* (4th rev. ed.). New York: St. Martin's Press, 1975.

CHADWICK, JOHN, *The Decipherment of Linear B* (2nd ed.). Cambridge: Cambridge University Press, 1967.

——, *The Mycenaean World.* Cambridge: Cambridge University Press, 1976.

CLAGETT, MARSHALL, *Greek Science in Antiquity.* New York: Abelard-Schuman, 1955.

CONNOR, WALTER ROBERT, *The New Politicians of Fifth-Century Athens.* Princeton, N. J.: Princeton University Press, 1971.

DE STE. CROIX, G. E. M., *The Origins of the Peloponnesian War.* Ithaca, N. Y.: Cornell University Press, 1972.

DODDS, ERIC R., *The Greeks and the Irrational* (2nd ed.). Berkeley: University of California Press, 1968.

EHRENBURG, VICTOR, *The Greek State* (2nd ed.). London: Methuen, 1969.

FESTUGIÈRE, A. J., *Personal Religion Among the Greeks.* Berkeley: University of California Press, 1960.

FINLEY, MOSES I., *Slavery in Classical Antiquity: Views and Controversies.* Cambridge: Cambridge University Press, 1960.

——, *The World of Odysseus* (rev. ed.). New York: Viking, 1965.

——, *The Ancient Economy.* Berkeley and Los Angeles: University of California Press, 1973.

FORREST, W. G., *The Emergence of Greek Democracy.* New York: McGraw, 1966.

GLOTZ, GUSTAVE, *The Greek City and Its Institutions.* New York: Knopf, 1929.

HADAS, MOSES, *Hellenistic Culture: Fusion and Diffusion.* New York: Columbia University Press, 1959.

HIGNETT, CHARLES, *History of the Athenian Constitution to the End of the Fifth Century B.C.* Oxford: Oxford University Press, 1970.

JAEGER, WERNER, *Paideia: The Ideals of Greek Culture.* 3 vols. New York: Oxford University Press, 1943–1945.

JONES, ARNOLD H. M., *Athenian Democracy.* Oxford: Blackwell, 1957.

KAGAN, DONALD, *The Outbreak of the Peloponnesian War.* Ithaca, N. Y.: Cornell University Press, 1969.

KIRK, GEOFFREY S., *The Songs of Homer.* Cambridge: Cambridge University Press, 1962.

KITTO, HUMPHREY D. F., *The Greeks.* Harmondsworth: Penguin, 1951.

LARSEN, JAKOB A. O., *Representative Government in Greek and Roman History.* Berkeley: University of California Press, 1955.

LLOYD, GEOFFREY E. R., *Early Greek Science: Thales to Aristotle.* New York: Norton, 1970.

——, *Greek Science After Aristotle.* New York: Norton, 1973.

MACKENDRICK, PAUL, *The Greek Stones Speak: The Story of Archaeology in Greek Lands.* New York: St. Martin's, 1962.

MARROU, HENRI I., *A History of Education in Antiquity.* New York: New American Library, 1964.

MEIGGS, RUSSELL, *The Athenian Empire.* Oxford: Oxford University Press, 1972.

MICHELL, HUMPHREY, *Sparta.* Cambridge: Cambridge University Press, 1964.

NEUGEBAUER, OTTO, *The Exact Sciences in Antiquity* (2nd ed.). Providence: Brown University Press, 1957.

NILSSON, MARTIN P., *History of Greek Religion* (2nd ed.). New York: Norton, 1964.

PAGE, DENYS L., *History and the Homeric Iliad* (2nd ed.). Berkeley: University of California Press, 1966.

PICKARD-CAMBRIDGE, ARTHUR W., *The Dramatic Festivals of Athens* (2nd ed.). Oxford: Oxford University Press, 1968.

POLLITT, J. J., *Art and Experience in Classical Greece.* Cambridge: Cambridge University Press, 1972.

ROSTOVTZEFF, MIKHAIL I., *Social and Economic History of the Hellenistic World.* 3 vols. Oxford: Oxford University Press, 1941.

SNELL, BRUNO, *The Discovery of the Mind: The Greek Origins of European Thought.* New York: Harper & Row, 1960.

SNODGRASS, ANTHONY M., *The Dark Age of Greece.* Chicago: Aldine, 1972.

STARR, CHESTER G., *Origins of Greek Civilization: 1100–650 B.C.* New York: Knopf, 1961.

TARN, WILLIAM W. and G. T. GRIFFITH, *Hellenistic Civilization.* (3rd ed.). London: E. Arnold, 1952.

TCHERIKOVER, AVIGDOR, *Hellenistic Civilization and the Jews.* Philadelphia: Jewish Publication Society of America, 1970.

VERMEULE, EMILY, *Greece in the Bronze Age.* Chicago: University of Chicago Press, 1972.

WEBSTER, T. B. L., *Athenian Culture and Society.* Berkeley and Los Angeles: University of California Press, 1973.

THE ROMAN WORLD

ABBOT, FRANK F. and ALLAN C. JOHNSON, *Municipal Administration in the Roman Empire.* Princeton, N. J.: Princeton University Press, 1926.

ADCOCK, FRANK E., *Roman Political Ideas and Practice.* Ann Arbor: University of Michigan Press, 1959.

BADIAN, ERNST, *Roman Imperialism in the Late Republic* (2nd ed.). Oxford: Blackwell, 1968.

——, *Publicans and Sinners: Private Enterprise in the Service of the Roman Republic.* Ithaca, N. Y.: Cornell University Press, 1972.

BOËTHIUS, AXEL and J. B. WARD-PERKINS, *Etruscan and Roman Architecture.* Harmondsworth: Penguin, 1970.

BRILLIANT, RICHARD, *Roman Art from the Republic to Constantine.* London: Praeger, 1974.

BROWN, FRANK E., *Roman Architecture.* New York: Braziller, 1966.

BROWN, PETER R., *Augustine of Hippo: A Biography.* Berkeley: University of California Press, 1967.

CARY, MAX and HOWARD H. SCULLARD, *A History of Rome* (3rd ed.). New York: St. Martin's, 1975.

CROOK, JOHN A., *Law and Life of Rome: 90 B.C.–A.D. 212.* Ithaca, N. Y.: Cornell University Press, 1967.

DILL, SAMUEL, *Roman Society from Nero to Marcus Aurelius.* New York: Meridian, 1956.

DIX, DOM GREGORY, *The Shape of the Liturgy* (2nd ed.). Westminister: Dacre, 1954.

DUCKETT, ELEANOR S., *Latin Writers of the Fifth Century.* New York: H. Hall, 1930.

DUDLEY, DONALD R. and T. P. DOREY, *Rome Against Carthage.* London: Seek and Wardburg, 1971.

DUFF, JOHN W., *Literary History of Rome: From the Origins to the Close of the Golden Age* (3rd ed.). New York: Barnes & Noble, 1960.

EARL, DONALD C., *The Moral and Political Tradition of Rome.* Ithaca, N. Y.: Cornell University Press, 1967.

FRANK, TENNEY, *Life and Literature in the Roman Republic.* Berkeley: University of California Press, 1930.

——, *An Economic Survey of Ancient Rome.* 6 vols. New York: Octagon, 1972.

GRUEN, ERICH S., *The Last Generation of the Roman Republic.* Berkeley: University of California Press, 1974.

HEURGON, JACQUES, *The Rise of Rome.* Berkeley: University of California Press, 1973.

JOLOWICZ, HERBERT F., *Historical Introduction to the Study of Roman Law* (3rd ed.). Cambridge: Cambridge University Press, 1972.

JONES, ARNOLD H. M., *The Later Roman Empire.* 3 vols. Oxford: Blackwell, 1964.

LEBRETON, JULES and JACQUES ZEILLER, *History of the Primitive Church.* 3 vols. New York: Macmillan, 1949.

LIETZMANN, HANS, *A History of the Early Church.* 4 vols. London: Lutterworth Press, 1953.

MACMULLEN, RAMSAY, *Enemies of the Roman Order: Treason, Unrest, and Alienation in the Empire.* Cambridge: Harvard University Press, 1966.

MILLAR, FERGUS, ed., *The Roman Empire and Its Neighbors.* New York: Delacorte, 1968.

MOMIGLIANO, ARNALDO, ed., *Conflict Between Paganism and Christianity in the Fourth Century.* Oxford: Clarendon Press, 1963.

MOMMSEN, THEODOR, *History of Rome.* 5 vols. Glencoe, Ill.: Free Press, 1957.

OGILVIE, ROBERT M., *The Romans and Their Gods in the Age of Augustus.* New York: Norton, 1969.

PARKER, HENRY M. D., *History of the Roman World from A.D. 138 to 337* (2nd rev. ed.). London: Methuen, 1958.

POWELL, THOMAS G. E., *The Celts.* New York: Praeger, 1958.

RICHARDSON, EMELINE, *The Etruscans: Their Art and Civilization.* Chicago: University of Chicago Press, 1964.

ROSTOVTZEFF, MIKHAIL I., *Social and Economic History of the Roman Empire* (2nd ed.). 2 vols. Oxford: Clarendon Press, 1957.

SALMON, EDWARD T., *Samnium and the Samnites.* Cambridge: Cambridge University Press, 1967.

——, *History of the Roman World from 30 B.C. to A.D. 138* (6th ed.). London: Methuen, 1968.

SCHÜRER, EMIL, *History of the Jewish People in the Time of Jesus Christ* (rev. ed.). Edinburgh: Clark, 1973.

SCULLARD, HOWARD H., *From the Gracchi to Nero: A History of Rome from 133 B.C. to A.D. 68* (3rd ed.). London: Methuen, 1970.

SMITH, RICHARD EDWIN, *The Failure of the Roman Republic.* Cambridge: Cambridge University Press, 1955.

STARR, CHESTER G., *Civilization and the Caesars.* New York: Norton, 1965.

SYME, RONALD, *The Roman Revolution.* Oxford: Oxford University Press, 1939.

TAYLOR, LILY ROSS, *Party Politics in the Age of Caesar.* Berkeley: University of California Press, 1949.

TREGGIARI, SUSAN, *Roman Freedmen During the Late Republic.* Oxford: Oxford University Press, 1969.

VOLBACH, WOLFGANG F., *Early Christian Art.* London: Thames and Hudson, 1961.

WATSON, GEORGE R., *The Roman Soldier.* Ithaca, N. Y.: Cornell University Press, 1969.

WEBSTER, GRAHAM, *The Roman Imperial Army.* New York: Funk & Wagnalls, 1970.

WHEELER, MORTIMER, *Roman Art and Architecture.* New York: Praeger, 1964.

WHITE, K. D., *Roman Farming.* Ithaca, N. Y.: Cornell University Press, 1970.

WISEMAN, TIMOTHY P., *New Men in the Roman Senate, 139 B.C.–14 A.D.* Oxford: Oxford University Press, 1971.

Maps

Illustrations

Maps and plans prepared by Thanh Xuan and the author.

Index

THE ANCIENT WORLD

A Social and Cultural History

D. BRENDAN NAGLE

Unanimous Praise!

"In general the Greek section of the work represents an accurate and informed synthesis of current scholarly opinion . . . Nagle writes a good, clear standard English . . . a sound and thoughtful introduction to the history of Greek civilization."

Another reviewer summarizes the Roman section, saying "Mr. Nagle writes in a very literate and straightforward style that should be easily comprehensible . . . the material is in general presented in a well-balanced way, with a workable compromise being established between a strictly chronological approach to the material and a topical approach to some of the basic developmental institutions of the Empire. The author seems to be up-to-date and presents the results of recent scholarly work on his subject."

Still another reviewer describes the entire book as "well written and very readable . . . accurate and the highlights selected show good judgment."

THE ANCIENT WORLD introduces the history of the Near East, Greece, and Rome by tracing the development of social attitudes and customs among its peoples. It brings history to life and, as one reviewer points out, "this is a very competent work, well conceived and well executed. It is, for once, a book that lives up to its title, emphasizing the society aspect of Roman history."

PRENTICE-HALL, INC., Englewood Cliffs, New Jersey 07632

0-13-036